25.00

NUCLEAR WAR
NUCLEAR PROLIFERATION
AND THEIR CONSEQUENCES

NUCLEAR WAR NUCLEAR PROLIFERATION AND THEIR CONSEQUENCES

Proceedings of the
Vth International Colloquium
organized by the
GROUPE DE BELLERIVE
Geneva 27–29 June 1985

Edited by
SADRUDDIN AGA KHAN

CLARENDON PRESS · OXFORD
1986

Oxford University Press, Walton Street, Oxford OX2 6DP
Oxford New York Toronto
Delhi Bombay Calcutta Madras Karachi
Petaling Jaya Singapore Hong Kong Tokyo
Nairobi Dar es Salaam Cape Town
Melbourne Auckland
and associated companies in
Beirut Berlin Ibadan Nicosia

Oxford is a trade mark of Oxford University Press

Published in the United States
by Oxford University Press, New York

British Library Cataloguing in Publication Data
Nuclear war, nuclear proliferation, and their
consequences: proceedings of the Vth
international colloquium.
1. Nuclear arms control
I. Aga Khan, Sadruddin, Prince II. Groupe
de Bellerive
327.1'74 JX1974.7
ISBN 0–19–825543–8
ISBN 0–19–825542–X Pbk

Library of Congress Cataloging in Publication Data
Nuclear war, nuclear proliferation and their consequences.
Includes index.
1. Nuclear warfare—Congresses. 2. Nuclear weapons—
Congresses. 3. Arms race—History—20th century—
Congresses. 4. Nuclear nonproliferation—Congresses.
5. Nuclear arms control—Congresses. I. Aga Khan,
Sadruddin, Prince, 1933– . II. Groupe de
Bellerive.
U263.N7784 1985 351'.0217 85–15433
ISBN 0–19–825543–8
ISBN 0–19–825542–X

Printed in Great Britain by
Biddles Ltd, Guildford and King's Lynn

PREFACE

This book contains the proceedings of a three-day conference hosted by the Groupe de Bellerive to explore and discuss the implications for humanity of nuclear war, nuclear proliferation and their consequences.

It was a particularly timely event, coming two months before the Third Nuclear Non-Proliferation Treaty Review Conference, and served to focus attention on many of the issues that were raised at the NPT Review. Seen in retrospect, the Groupe de Bellerive Colloquium and the NPT Review Conference had several important themes in common:

1. That the NPT, despite its weaknesses and possibly contentious clauses, must be maintained and strengthened. Disagreements between the Parties at the Third NPT Review Conference were put aside to agree upon a final conference resolution to protect the consensus and to maintain the momentum of the NPT as a vehicle for bringing about global nuclear disarmament. This was in contrast to the outcome of the Second Review Conference in 1980 which ended without a final conference resolution.
2. There was much greater emphasis among non-nuclear-weapon States (NNWS) upon the need for the super-Powers to fulfil their obligations under Article VI of the Treaty. As at the Groupe de Bellerive Colloquium, a Comprehensive Test Ban Treaty was seen as the best possible step towards global nuclear disarmament.
3. NNWS at the Review Conference were more aware than ever of the importance of the regional dimension to the nuclear debate. Much emphasis was placed on the need to reduce regional tensions and prevent regional insecurity from being the motor of proliferation. In addition to steps towards the approval of a South Pacific Nuclear-Free Zone, nuclear-weapon-free zones were discussed for South-East Asia, Africa, the Middle East, the Balkans, the Mediterranean and Northern Europe, while non-Parties in Latin America were encouraged to join the Tlatelolco Treaty.
4. The emphasis placed by NNWS on the active development of the peaceful uses of nuclear energy as part of the NPT, particularly as it relates to Article IV, has diminished as the attractions of nuclear energy as a source of power have waned mainly for economic and environmental reasons. This has also distinguished the Third from the Second NPT Review Conference.

It can only be hoped that these strong currents among politicians, diplomats, scientists and thinkers can, in harness with growing popular exasperation throughout the world at the madness of the arms race, influence the world's sovereign governments and particularly the super-Powers into initiating a real and long-lasting reduction and control of nuclear weapons.

In the pages that follow, what is at stake for humanity is dramatically illustrated, but so are the ways of avoiding nuclear incarceration. We must pursue these ways before it is too late.

SADRUDDIN AGA KHAN

October 1985

EDITORIAL NOTE

While every effort has been made to ensure that what follows is an accurate transcription of the papers delivered by speakers at the Colloquium, in some cases supported by prepared material from them, and of the debates held in the conference chamber, no responsibility is taken by the Groupe de Bellerive or by the editor of this book or by the Publishers either for the veracity of opinions and facts expressed by the speakers or for the faithfulness with which the papers and discussions have been transcribed.

ACKNOWLEDGEMENTS

Neither this book nor the Colloquium would have been possible without the support and co-operation of many individuals and organizations, often working tirelessly behind the scenes. The President of the Groupe de Bellerive would particularly like to thank Marc Sursock and Mark Malloch Brown for their herculean efforts in preparing the book and the Colloquium and ensuring their fluidity; Bill Miller and his colleagues for their advice; the Secretariat of the Groupe de Bellerive for its unflagging administrative support; Dorier S.A. and particularly Richard Gagnebin and Jenny Lorenzi for their prompt transcription service and organizational and technical support at the Colloquium; and Oxford University Press for the speed and thoroughness with which the proceedings have been published.

Contents

Opening Statement

PRINCE SADRUDDIN AGA KHAN

President, Groupe de Bellerive; Editor

We meet here in Geneva under two shadows and before an opportunity. A shadow is the 40th Anniversary of the atomic bomb dropped on Hiroshima on 6 August 1945. That explosion changed war forever and the way we think about it. As we listen to the discussion in the next few days, I think we may at times wonder whether the human imagination has yet taken in the full enormity of what we have done: how science has transformed war from an act which could once at least be justified as one of self-defence to one which when all the doctrines of deterrence have been pared away is an act of complete self-destruction. We are all hostages now.

There is a second shadow: again we face the onslaught of international terrorism. Once more, the thin walls that have kept the countries of the North protected from increasing instability elsewhere have been breached. Terrorism demonstrates how fragile these walls are. Everybody is the terrorist's victim. The passengers on the Air India flight, travellers at Frankfurt Airport, baggage handlers at Narita in Tokyo, hotel guests in London. Terrorism has carried its war into our lives with the simplest of weapons—the hand gun and plastic explosives. Now, as conflicts deepen and nuclear technology becomes even more accessible, we must consider how much longer the nuclear peace will last. What if those who seized the TWA flight had had the nuclear means to take their war to the United States itself?

The suitcase nuclear bomb is now feasible; indeed, a back-pack bomb is already in service. The most sophisticated defence system is no protection against such a weapon smuggled into any city in the world by any one of the means used, say, by drug smugglers in avoiding customs officers.

There is no longer a case for nuclear complacency. We cannot shelter behind super-Power nuclear deterrence: too many fingers are reaching towards the nuclear triggers. But I mentioned also an opportunity. This is the September Review Conference of the Non-Proliferation Treaty. With new weapons being deployed, it may seem to be a frail reed to hold up against the forward rush of the arms race. In its first fifteen years, the Treaty has not been crowned in glory, nor, indeed, universality. Key nuclear and near-nuclear States have stayed out. Nevertheless, in this of all cities, host to the Soviet-American arms reduction talks, I believe pessimism about the NPT Treaty is misplaced, not because of its achievements to date, although these are more than some acknowledge, but because of what it might achieve.

There are those who fear that by airing the strongly-held disagreements about how to control nuclear proliferation we can only assist to bury the Treaty.

But one can discern behind the arguments that we will hear common ground. The risk of proliferation in some ways unites us in concern, whereas the super-Power arms race seems only to divide us. This shared ground might be lost in the formal proceedings of an inter-governmental conference, but at a gathering such as this it can be built upon. The challenge for us is whether, in the cause of a common humanity, we can bind together a common strategy, not of fine words but of practical actions that might edge us towards that corner that must one day be turned if the nuclear arms race is ever to know limits, let alone an end.

We have a unique forum over the next few days. We are here as fellow citizens of one world whose inter-dependence in terms of shared vulnerability to nuclear annihilation should give all of us a say. We share a common danger because of the global consequences of a nuclear winter. This is so whatever the arguments are about exactly how much fall-out it takes to make a nuclear winter, rather than, say, just a nuclear autumn.

But the common threat grows as our governments are increasingly party to the power to trigger nuclear war. When we only shared the risk, the obstacles to halting proliferation may actually have been greater than today when we begin to share the concrete means of unleashing a nuclear war. Today's nuclear arsenal has a destructive power a million times greater than that of the bomb which destroyed Hiroshima.

We are easily mesmerized by the dizzier and dizzier heights of the super-Power arms race and overlook the outward spread of military nuclear power. The bomb has new owners; political expediency rather than technical constraints is all that has kept a number of States formally non-nuclear. There are now States which, even if they could not make a sophisticated bomb, could very quickly acquire the means to assemble one that could blow a very large hole in world peace.

The official nuclear club remains five, but any proposition that nuclear arms negotiations should only involve these five members of the club is as absurd a claim to make as it would be to say that it is these five alone that pose a nuclear threat to peace. There has been a deceptive relationship between technology and political power when it comes to nuclear weapons. In its first phase the bomb technology was exclusive so it served to guarantee the world security system that emerged in 1945. But technology never remains exclusive, and as weapons technology and nuclear materials have slipped under security barriers and across frontiers they have brought with them the potential to undermine the political power they formerly enhanced.

We are entering a second phase: a vocal constituency will call for the bomb precisely because it was the former preserve of the big Powers. If we can bring home the truth that the nuclear bomb in the hands of the weak is no less dangerous than in the hands of the strong, this conference will already have achieved a lot.

But we should seek to achieve much more than point to the threat. We do not come so much to justify, or defend official positions, but to find areas of agreement and to build on them.

I recently met with that Grand Old Man of American politics, former US Senator Jacob Javits. He described nuclear proliferation as being like drunken driving in the sense that it is not an issue of right and left, or East or West, or North or South. Everybody is against it. We have to find a way to meet this common danger that carries us forward across regional, ideological and world rivalries towards shared actions to stop the bomb.

The Groupe de Bellerive has organized this conference as the latest in a series of meetings that we have sponsored in recent years. Because of our concern with the environment we were led to the issue of nuclear energy; from there our attention was inevitably drawn to security, first in 1983 to the question of European security, and now to the wider implications of the spread of nuclear materials and know-how in an increasingly insecure world.

We provide a non-partisan forum, an opportunity for rational discussion. And if these sessions are to be more than a talking shop they must allow for the steady delineation of common ground as we share our thoughts during the next few days. What are the terms on which all would accept a strengthened non-proliferation regime? What are the securities, if I may term them that, which we are all seeking; how do we make them work and how do we weave them into a stronger fabric?

Innocent peoples' lives have been put at risk by a hijacking that has shocked the world once more. Whatever the weapon, pistol, grenade or nuclear bomb, in the hands of international terrorists it assumes an unpredictability that threatens us all. No cause is worth nuclear annihiliation, but the more desperate groups or nations become, the less ready they are to acknowledge this grim reality. We can only move back from the nuclear precipice if strengthened safeguards on the transfer of nuclear materials and know-how is matched by much more vigorous political action. It is only then that the deathly nuclear shadow of military confrontation can be dispelled.

MESSAGES DELIVERED AT THE COLLOQUIUM

Mr. Jaques Vernet

President of the Council of State of the Republic and Canton of Geneva

The Council of State of the Republic and Canton of Geneva congratulates the Groupe de Bellerive and its President, Prince Sadruddin Aga Khan, for having organized an international Colloquium on the theme you are about to consider.

The interest of this Colloquium, and it is something of a paradox, resides in the fact that none of the participants and, in particular, none of the speakers listed, has been mandated by anyone, neither governments nor political parties, pressure groups nor other bodies. You have all come to Geneva of your own accord and this should facilitate your freedom of speech. Above all, it should enable you to give a better hearing to others, which is not always possible in meetings where everyone has specific instructions. You should not fear that your words will carry less weight because you are only representing yourselves. On the contrary, it is because your statements do not embody the thinking of chancelleries that they will have more authority and your exchanges will be more fruitful.

In order to assure your credibility, the first effort each one of you will have to make—and it is undoubtedly not easy—is to base your work on respect for others, especially for those whose opinions differ from your own. Furthermore, those who wish to contribute to reducing the excessive tensions in our world necessarily have to seek their causes, but they must first of all seek the causes in themselves before trying to find them in potential enemies. One can only usefully tackle this sort of problem in a profound spirit of humility.

That being said, the objectives must be established. To try to save what is called 'the human race'—as is advocated in certain spheres—seems to me to be a statement of incommensurate pride. Man is like the dinosaur, he appeared in the world one day and he will disappear one day. Just as man himself is mortal, one does not see how—but above all why—the society he and his like constitute should be eternal. In other words, the human race, like other races, is no doubt mortal: its lifespan can be expressed in simple allotted epochs. On the other hand, to fight to preserve man's life and its quality is an act of solidarity and thus of humility. It is therefore with this in mind that I invite you to debate, given that preserving our lives calls for more concrete discussions than preserving the species; the inherent absurdity of the latter objective inevitably underlining the absurdity of the debate.

We should remember that men have always proposed miraculous solutions for maintaining peace and eliminating tension. But peace is more at risk than ever and tension is stronger than heretofore. This is no doubt precisely due to the fact that the solutions put forward have always aimed at the other party, and their advocates have tended to give lessons rather than offer contributions, giving priority to their own interests, in general for a relatively short term.

The authorities and people of this Republic, while they are happy to welcome you to a country that is propitious to the search for positive solutions for mankind, hope that your debates will take place in a spirit of mutual respect, without any preconceived ideas and without condemnation, neither *a priori* nor *a posteriori*. As Jean Guitton wrote in his *Book of Hours*, this will enable dialectic—which aims at destroying—to be replaced by dialogue, which calls for constant, almost heroic effort and consists first of all in seeing the other's point of view. It is not ideology that we urgently need, but, as you stated last Monday, Mr. President of the Groupe de Bellerive, when inaugurating the exhibition of the Treasures of Islam, a theology based on the unity of all living beings, without discrimination based on traditional dogmatism and prejudices.

A Message From Mr. Pierre Aubert, Federal Councillor and Head of the Federal Department of Foreign Affairs

Read by AMBASSADOR PAUL-ANDRE RAMSEYER
Head of the Political Secretariat

It is with regret that Mr. Pierre Aubert, Federal Councillor and Head of the Federal Department of Foreign Affairs, is unable to be here today in person at the opening of your Colloquium.

He has requested me to inform you of his deep interest in this initiative by the Groupe de Bellerive and of the importance he attaches to the convening of such a Colloquium on Swiss territory.

The theme of this Colloquium is particularly appropriate in view of the forthcoming meeting—also in Geneva—of the 124 signatory States to the Nuclear Weapons Non-Proliferation Treaty and your speakers testify to the high standing on the international scene enjoyed by the Groupe de Bellerive and its President, Prince Sadruddin Aga Khan.

Your very comprehensive programme prompts me to make a few remarks.

As you know, our country, a neutral State in the heart of Europe, attaches great importance to world peace and constantly does its best to promote it through a policy of neutrality, solidarity and availability, as exemplified for instance by its good offices.

The non-proliferation of nuclear weapons is of great concern to Switzerland and it works towards that end with conviction. Switzerland acceded to the Treaty in 1977 and follows its development closely.

In our country, we regard the Treaty as one of the pillars of the non-proliferation system. To make it a viable and effective system, based, as you know, on treatment discriminating between States which possess nuclear weapons and States which do not, two conditions must be met: first, all obligations under the Treaty have to be fully respected, and secondly, the Treaty must be made as universal as possible.

Thus, as we see it, the obligation of States not possessing nuclear weapons to remain without them implies a corresponding obligation on the so-called nuclear States to work towards halting the arms race and taking effective measures towards nuclear disarmament.

Furthermore, it is to be regretted that the Treaty has not achieved universality. But Switzerland believes that making the Treaty more attractive would make it easier to win over to its cause those States which have remained uninvolved. In itself the Treaty contains the necessary mechanisms to achieve this: it provides that the States Party should promote co-operation in the peaceful use of nuclear energy. Any restrictive measures applied unilaterally in that area could but harm the system as a whole. We also feel that non-proliferation measures can provide the best guarantees of effectiveness only if based on the broadest possible consensus.

Finally, our country regards non-proliferation as a political rather than a technical problem. Improved technical controls will never prevent any State from acting as it wishes. Renouncing nuclear weapons is therefore a matter of political will. It is that will which we must create and I am sure that your Colloquium will contribute towards this.

I wish to tell you how deeply conscious the Swiss authorities are of the concerns of the Groupe de Bellerive and also how much they appreciate the open-mindedness displayed in the programme of your Colloquium.

To conclude, allow me to join the Head of the Federal Department of Foreign Affairs in expressing the hope that the discussions at your Colloquium will have a fruitful outcome. May they contribute to a better understanding of the grave problem which proliferation of nuclear weapons constitutes for the world.

MESSAGES ADDRESSED TO THE PRESIDENT OF THE GROUPE DE BELLERIVE

Message from the Secretary-General of the United Nations

The possibility of nuclear war and nuclear proliferation requires the widest possible study and attention. I am, therefore, particularly gratified that Prince Sadruddin Aga Khan and the Groupe de Bellerive have decided to devote a Conference to these extraordinarily important subjects.

As recent scientific findings indicate, a nuclear war could well spell the end of human civilization. Among the tasks facing the world's leaders today the avoidance of such a war is clearly of the greatest urgency. That task would become enormously more difficult if more nations were to acquire nuclear weapons. Unless the nuclear arms race between the major Powers is brought to an end and the further proliferation of military nuclear capacity is deterred, the terrible possibility of mass destruction will increase yet further and fear will become the norm of human existence.

The Treaty on the Non-Proliferation of Nuclear Weapons is an essential measure against this eventuality. The Treaty has played a most constructive role in restraining the horizontal spread of nuclear weapons. Time has been provided for the understanding to grow that the possession of nuclear weapons by States not having them, far from enhancing their security, could well put it at greater risk.

On their side, the nuclear-weapon States Party to the Treaty agreed to pursue in good faith negotiations leading to nuclear disarmament. Many non-nuclear States feel strongly that the nuclear States have not done enough to meet this responsibility. This problem, which you will be examining, is bound to figure prominently in the Review Conference on the Non-Proliferation Treaty which will open in Geneva at the end of August.

All Parties to the Non-Proliferation Treaty—nuclear and non-nuclear weapon States alike—share a fundamental interest in ensuring its continued effectiveness and viability. Your discussions can make an important contribution by highlighting this interest and by identifying what the Parties to the Treaty, particularly the nuclear-weapon States, need to do to ensure that it is met.

I send you my best wishes for a most productive meeting in this regard.

H E Javier Perez de Cuellar

Message from the Holy See

On the occasion of the opening of the international Colloquium on *Nuclear War, Nuclear Proliferation and their Consequences*, Pope John Paul II has asked me to assure Your Excellency of the interest He takes in the Groupe de Bellerive's work. In view of the gravity of the dangers represented by the existence of nuclear weapons and by the possibility of their proliferation, the Holy Father expresses the hope that your assembly will make an effective contribution towards encouraging those responsible to review the causes of the present situation and to draw up a new philosophy of international relations. He hopes that a new impetus will be given to the disarmament negotiations and that progress will be made, especially with a view to decreasing the number of weapons stockpiled within the framework of the current strategy of deterrence. The Pope urges political leaders and scientists to work together to ensure that science serves mankind and peace, and to devote the maximum resources to justice on all the continents. The nomination of a representative underlines His Holiness' interest in the aims of the Colloquium and He requests Your Excellency to convey to all participants His hope that their work will achieve the desired results in favour of world peace.

His Eminence Cardinal Casaroli, *Secretary of State*

Message from the World Council of Churches

I have great pleasure in sending you cordial greetings as you meet for the Colloquium devoted to the subject of *Nuclear War, Nuclear Proliferation and their Consequences*. We are confident that this will be a significant event and that its results will have considerable influence.

You are meeting at one of the most crucial periods in human history, when the awesome choices confronting the world community will decide the destiny of humankind.

We face today some unprecedented moral issues. The subjects of your deliberations have complex technical and political dimensions on which we as a Council of Churches do not profess to have especial expertise or competence. And yet, in face of the inability to describe, to measure or even to imagine the consequences of the nuclear arms race, the decisions which need to be made are not technical in nature. They are human and ethical. The moral and ethical considerations with which we approach these issues are not exclusive to the Christian faith. Many of the world's communities share these profound concerns regarding the very survival of humanity and of all God's creation.

During the past years, the World Council of Churches has engaged in dialogue with scientists, political leaders and those involved in the peace movement. We have been challenged and inspired by the victims the arms race is producing even today. We have been encouraged by a growing awareness among large sections of our churches of the dangers inherent in the development of new generations of nuclear weapons and delivery systems.

Undergirded by our conviction that peace and justice are complementary concerns, the VIth Assembly of the WCC made the following affirmations:

—The concept of deterrence, whose credibility depends on the possible use of nuclear weapons, is to be rejected as morally unacceptable and as incapable of safeguarding peace and security in the long term.

—The production and deployment of nuclear weapons, as well as their use, constitute a crime against humanity, and there should therefore be a complete halt in the production of nuclear weapons and in weapon research and development in all nations, to be expeditiously enforced through a treaty.

—All nations should agree to and ratify a Comprehensive Test Ban Treaty as a necessary step to stopping the further development of nuclear technology.

Even as we discuss a halt to the arms race, new and disturbing developments are being conceived which could radically change the course of the arms race, projecting it far into the next century. The possibility of stationing weapons of both defensive and offensive nature in space could have an impact as serious in its consequences as was the development of nuclear weapons decades ago. We must strive together to avert this possibility.

In sending you this message, we are inspired by the prophetic vision of peace where 'justice will dwell in the wilderness and righteousness abide in the fruitful field. And the fruit of righteousness will be peace and the result of righteousness undisturbed security for ever.' Security means being able to abandon enmity in favour of growing mutual confidence.

Beyond these, we are moved by the sweeping and ennobling vision of the unity of God's creation. We are guided by the sense of responsibility that comes out of the conviction that we are heirs of a single hope and bearers of a single destiny, namely, the care and management of all God's creation. We pray for the success of your deliberations.

DR. EMILIO CASTRO, *Secretary-General*

Message from the Orthodox Patriarchate

On the occasion of your Colloquium on *Nuclear War, Nuclear Proliferation and their Consequences*, I wish to transmit a message to you, together with my best wishes for the success of your work.

The Orthodox Church is conscious of the contemporary world's concern with the burning issues of justice, freedom and peace. At its First Pre-Conciliar Pan-Orthodox Conference, held in Chambésy in 1976, it expressed its desire to collaborate with other Christians, as well as with those of other religions, to eliminate fanaticism and ensure the implementation of Christian ideals in the service of man, whatever his race or religion. It was for this reason that it included the subject of *The Contribution of Local Orthodox Churches towards the Implementation of Christian Ideals of Peace, Freedom, Brotherhood and Love among Peoples and the Elimination of Racial Discrimination* in the agenda of the Holy Grand Council.

Peace and war both spring from man's heart and, in its biblical sense, the heart is the foundation, the very kernel, of a human being; the place where a man's relations with others, with the profound meaning of life, with the values that direct his acts and with the final source of all values—God—are defined.

It is here that the basis of the Christian message resides and where the Christian's ability to make a positive contribution to building peace in the world can be found.

This is why a permanent and lasting peace, inseparably linked to justice and respect for human dignity, forms part of the Christian identity.

A person who does not spontaneously help others in their concrete sufferings can be guilty of heresy in the same way as a person denying a truth of his faith. To be quite clear: if a person stands aside from the construction of peace and justice in the world, he is also separating himself from Christ, if he is only interested in his personal peace, his own reconciliation with God, he is drawing away from Christ.

In its conciliar reflection, the Orthodox Church declared its solidarity with all movements struggling for human rights. We support all those in Africa, America, Eastern Europe and Asia who suffer and die because their specificity is not recognized. We must act together, those of all religions, so that the scandal of man destroying man is brought to an end.

Is it not the 'balance of terror' that is at present maintaining peace, even—and especially—at the risk of flagrant injustices and murderous wars? These are the safety valves for the accumulated tensions so that, at a planetary level, the world can perpetuate its guilty peace to the detriment of the weak.

The solution for a true and lasting peace is to be found in Christ's words to His disciples on the night of his Crucifixion: 'Peace I leave with you, my peace I give unto you: not as the world giveth, give I unto you. Let not your heart be troubled, neither let it be afraid.' (John 14: 27)

In obedience to the Lord's commandment, the Orthodox Church believes that it is the duty of the Christian world not only to protect man from his folly and from the means of self-destruction, but also to re-establish the plenitude of that precious possession that is peace and to give it its true worth in the life of man today.

His Eminence Metropolitan Damaskinos of Switzerland

Message from Dr. Armand Hammer, Occidental Petroleum

I regret that I am unable to be with you today, but as you convene this very important Colloquium on *Nuclear War, Nuclear Proliferation and their Consequences*, I will be in China for I am scheduled to meet with another of the world's great leaders, Vice-Chairman Deng Xiaoping of the People's Republic of China.

It is important to the entire world that leaders such as those assembled here should engage in this high-level dialogue on the most crucial issue now facing mankind—the threat of nuclear war. Your discussions, involving some of the most committed and knowledgeable leaders of our time, will represent, I am sure, the widest possible viewpoints on the issue of East–West relations and, I hope, will help to highlight the reasons why no progress is being made at the arms negotiations now taking place in Geneva.

I think it is particularly significant that your conference will hear from these knowledgeable voices from President Reagan's Administration and the United States Senate, and from the Soviet Union.

This conference is timely in that it is preceding the Non-Proliferation Treaty Review Conference scheduled in September. It is timely for me personally since, over the last two weeks, I have been fortunate to have had discussions on these same critical issues with both Secretary-General Gorbachov of the Soviet Union and President Reagan of the United States. At both of these meetings, I was able to raise the question of a summit meeting between the leaders of the two great super-Powers. I am now more convinced than ever that such a meeting must and will take place. It is only a question of where and when. As I said to both Secretary-General Gorbachov and President Reagan, I hope that the meeting will take place before the end of this year, preferably in the Soviet Union. President Reagan could win over the Russians with such a generous gesture. At a return meeting by Mr. Gorbachov next spring in the United States, he could very well win over the American people as well. Neither leader has been in the other's country.

As I said in the *New York Times* recently, what do these leaders have to lose by sitting down, getting to know one another and discussing the unresolved issues that are the causes of the stalemate in Geneva? I know that both leaders feel that something concrete must come from such a meeting, but I believe that the creation of a psychological momentum from an expression of some mutual trust could itself be one of the greatest deeds necessary for improvement in current US–USSR relations.

If, in addition, both leaders could declare to the world that neither would be the first to use nuclear or conventional weapons in an attack upon the other, this too will advance our relations and would let all of us sleep a little easier.

Finally, if these men could announce, with an earnest handshake, that they intend to hold additional meetings at regular intervals and instruct their representatives in Geneva to call them whenever they are unable to agree, I believe there would then be an electric shock of gratification throughout the world. Such a mutual announcement could cause celebrations and dancing in the streets like the declaration of a cease-fire at the end of a war. From this, in turn, would flow such a flood of approval that the process of reconciliation would be accelerated beyond any possible anticipation.

I salute you for your commitment to identifying and addressing the nuclear issues we face and I look forward to reading your report when I return from China.

DR. ARMAND HAMMER, *President*

Keynote Address

THE HON. OLOF PALME
Prime Minister of Sweden

The Threat of Proliferation

It is a great honor for me to have been invited to this Colloquium, and to have the privilege of delivering the keynote speech this morning. The program for these three days is truly impressive, and I would like first of all, to congratulate Prince Sadruddin Aga Khan on his success in assembling all these eminent persons who will enlighten us during the Colloquium.

I am confident that all the work on this project by Prince Sadruddin, and by the Groupe de Bellerive, will be worth the effort because there is no more vital issue to be discussed today in the international community—or anywhere, for that matter—than the threat of nuclear proliferation and the inherent dangers of an atomic war.

To put it very simply, we are today in a unique situation in the history of mankind. Today's weapons and today's warfare are such that we can kill not only ourselves and all others living on this planet. We can also take the lives of animals and plants, we can destroy cities and villages, we can ruin everything which has been built up through generation after generation. And above all: we can destroy the future of our whole civilization, everything that would come after us.

This is the simple truth about the potential of today's nuclear weapons. This is the threat which we, in this nuclear age, are confronted with. It has opened up awesome perspectives and terrible possibilities for us and our children.

And as if this is not bad enough, we are now faced with a threat of nuclear-weapon proliferation which increases the dangers for our peoples, our societies and our future. The number and quality of nuclear weapons are increasing, a new arms race in outer space may be initiated, and the risk of proliferation to other nations is very real. There is also a threat to results already achieved in the field of arms limitation.

I do not wish to sound overly dramatic, but I am convinced that the nuclear threat is the gravest menace to the very existence of mankind that the latter has ever faced. This is the situation as I perceive it, and this is thus the basis from which I think one has to start searching for solutions to these urgent problems. I am therefore honored to have been invited here to spark off the discussion about this threat, and about the search for a way out.

I will speak almost exclusively about nuclear weapons. That does not mean that I wish to minimize the threats posed by so-called conventional weapons. Having been involved, for instance, for some time in the Iran–Iraq war, I have been reminded very personally about the immense suffering caused by warfare today by so-called conventional means. And this is only one example. Since World War II there has been an almost uninterrupted series of wars—some 140 of them—which have been fought with conventional weapons and which have caused untold suffering and destruction. The casualties, direct and indirect, have been in their millions, often because of famines that have ensued. And the resources spent are immense: it is estimated that well over 80 per cent of total military spending is absorbed by conventional arms and armed forces.

Nuclear weapons pose a unique threat. A large-scale nuclear attack would not only destroy the enemy. There are strong indications that such an attack would also have severe climatic effects, for a nuclear exchange would throw dust and soot into the atmosphere for long enough to have disastrous effects on all life on earth. This aspect is to be taken up in detail later on, I understand, by Dr. Carl Sagan. Statements such as that by Professor Bergström will give further insight into the medical and social consequences of nuclear war.

The findings on the effects of nuclear war have convinced me that nuclear weapons are militarily useless. There is no situation in which a nuclear-weapon State, with enough probability of success, can launch a nuclear attack and count on achieving anything for itself. For a long time now, nuclear weapons have been obsolete as a tool for warfare. The only motivation for keeping them would be to try to deter the opponent from attacking. Consequently, these arms are solely political weapons. They are in a real sense useless, since their use would mean annihilation of the user.

This has not always been the case. It is sometimes useful to go back in history and see how people reflected in the past on issues which now seem very clear. In August 1945 atomic bombs were dropped over Hiroshima and Nagasaki, as Prince Sadruddin has reminded us. At that time this was seen in many quarters as a necessary way of finally ending World War II. And in the years immediately following, the atomic bomb was not seen as much more than a powerful addition to the overall strength of the United States. Later the view of nuclear weapons changed radically. When the Soviet Union developed into the second nuclear Power, nuclear weapons became the main elements in the policy of deterrence which came to be practised by both super-Powers. This also became the starting point for the development and production of a great number of new nuclear weapons systems.

Such weapons are no longer merely a question of a number of aircraft or silos on Soviet and US territories loaded with intercontinental ballistic missiles. The risk of nuclear confrontation has come much closer, not least here in Europe. This is where new intermediate-range missiles are being deployed just now, and this is where one finds thousands of small battlefield nuclear weapons along the border between East and West. 'Small' is a terrible word because each of them has a power much stronger than the Hiroshima bomb. This forward-basing has increased dramatically in the 1980s, as pointed out last week in the new yearbook from SIPRI, the Stockholm International Peace Research Institute. It not only enlarges the risk for an outbreak of nuclear war by mistake; it also increases nervousness on both sides, and thereby the risk that someone will try to 'shoot first' in a crisis situation.

The nuclear armament process has now resulted in some 50,000 nuclear weapons, in five nuclear States. Their accuracy is vastly improved, thanks in part to a wide network of satellites. Warning times are getting shorter and shorter, since the period from firing a weapon to its reaching its target has shrunk considerably. A missile from the Soviet mainland to the US Midwest takes 30 minutes; submarine-launched missiles could hit the same target in less than 15 minutes; a Pershing II takes less than ten minutes from West Germany to Moscow.

The question is: for what purpose could a nuclear-weapon State use all this sophisticated machinery?

One actual use could be to start a large-scale nuclear attack. This would most certainly destroy the enemy. But it would with almost equal certainty also destroy the attacker.

Another use could be to start a limited war, or to launch a limited nuclear response to a conventional attack. But such a project would most probably get out of hand, and escalate to a major nuclear confrontation. In that case, it would also lead to the destruction of the attacker as well as the enemy.

Lord Zuckerman has summarized today's situation very clearly in what he calls 'the nuclear realities':

> First: Nuclear war would bring terrible destruction. A full-scale nuclear attack would destroy not only the party attacked, but also the attacker and many other nations, and would most certainly pose a threat to the survival of our civilization. Second: There is no defence against nuclear weapons and, I will add, there will not be either. The people of Hiroshima could not defend themselves. The perfect symbol of this is found in the memorial museum in Hiroshima. There, on some stairs, one can see the shadow of a human being, the only thing remaining of a man or a woman who sat on those stairs when the bomb exploded. Protection against nuclear attack has not been improved much since then. There would not be enough doctors and nurses to take care of the victims even after one single attack. Third: There is no possibility of a disarming strike. The opponent will always have enough weapons left to cause massive destruction to the attacker. Even if he had only one submarine left, that one ship would have enough weapons to kill many millions of people in New York or in Moscow, in Paris or London, or in Beijing. Fourth: There is no way of ensuring that

a limited nuclear war stays limited. On the contrary, strong evidence supports the theory that limited nuclear wars will escalate.

These nuclear realities, if translated into political realities, imply that no responsible political leader could seriously conceive of using nuclear weapons.

The leaders of the Soviet Union and the United States have both declared very rightly that a nuclear war cannot be won. President Ronald Reagan has even called nuclear weapons immoral and I agree with him wholeheartedly.

Nevertheless, nuclear weapons are still very much an ingredient in military forces and in actual war-planning. This, it is said, is to deter the enemy from using his weapons. Even if it is not said in so many words, it is probably also a way of trying to gain ground politically by applying pressure by threatening with nuclear weapons. The nuclear realities have changed the role of nuclear weapons from being tools of warfare to instruments for pursuing political aims.

It is sometimes argued that in this role, nuclear weapons have served a good purpose. No war has broken out in Europe for 40 years; this is said to prove that deterrence works, and that nuclear weapons have preserved peace. That may have been true in the past, even if it is far from proven. What we do know is that the deterrence doctrine has been linked to an arms build-up of enormous proportions. We also know that deterrence only works if it is credible. This means that there must be a technical capacity to wage war as well as a political preparedness to use this capacity.

During the era of nuclear deterrence, we have seen a continuous and unbridled arms race which has produced ever more sophisticated and accurate weapons. The very fact that the *technical* preparedness and capacity to wage a nuclear war have increased is destabilizing and a threat in itself.

From the point of view of *political* preparedness, leaders in the nuclear-weapon States have to face the fact that a nuclear war would have devastating effects all over the world, including on the attacking party. The near certainty that what was intended to be defended would also be destroyed presents the leaders of those States with a serious practical, political and philosophical dilemma.

The idea of deterrence is to induce fear in the opponent. The object is to make him afraid, to be unpredictable, to make him uncertain of the next step. But to induce fear is also to encourage distrust. And in the face of fear and distrust of the opponent, it is difficult for any political system to conduct rational, reasoned and sound policies.

All this, in my experience, has contributed to making people in general more and more suspicious of nuclear deterrence, which keeps the whole of humanity as a hostage. Its stability is constantly being undermined in the never-ending arms spiral. It is like addiction to a drug—you continually need a larger and larger dose. And at the end of the road, nuclear deterrence holds out the prospect of the apocalyptic abyss.

The shortcomings of the nuclear deterrence doctrine have led to a lively international debate on alternatives to this doctrine. I welcome that debate. These shortcomings have also been recognized by at least one prominent political leader in one of the nuclear-weapon States. This is fine, and should be welcomed, even if one heartily disagrees with some of the alternatives proposed. One of these alternatives, the one perhaps most widely discussed nowadays, poses a direct threat of an enormous vertical proliferation. I am thinking of what is called the Strategic Defense Initiative.

In the independent disarmament commission, of which I have been Chairman, we had a detailed discussion four years ago—actually here in Geneva—about military technology in the 1980s, and about plans for ballistic missile defence. Now, as we have heard in the last few years, a technological breakthrough which would provide a foolproof defence is being brought forward as a real possibility. To meet the scepticism about deterrence, and to reassure one's own people, the prospect of a watertight system, which will stop every ballistic missile, is being seriously explored.

Much could be said about this—about the cost, about the possibility of actually building an absolute defence, about the worries over 'decoupling', about how SDI conforms with present arms control treaties, to name but a few of the questions raised. I will not go into any detailed discussion here about this project. What I want to say, however, is that it is absolutely clear to me than an initiative of this kind will accelerate the nuclear arms race instead of making nuclear arms obsolete, and that it will therefore be another contribution to the continued vertical proliferation of nuclear weapons. The number of warheads on each missile might be increased, as a counter measure. The offensive missiles may be modified to make them less vulnerable. The number of airborne weapons—particularly Cruise missiles—may be substantially increased. And systems for actually fighting a ballistic missile defence system may be developed. In short: the nuclear arms race would accelerate yet again. These were our conclusions in 1980 and they remain the same today.

Instead of talking about 'Star Wars' and other efforts aiming at a further militarization of space, the international community should, in my opinion, reserve this domain for peaceful, constructive purposes. One attractive idea is the launching of a satellite for the international supervision of how various arms control agreements are being really adhered to.

***

Another serious nuclear threat is that of horizontal proliferation. The risk of a nuclear catastrophe will increase dramatically if the capacity to make use of nuclear weapons were to be spread to others than the present members of the nuclear club.

One has often talked about totally irresponsible States and it is possible—to paraphrase what Prince Sadruddin said—that it is even more dangerous for nuclear weapons to fall into the hands of the weak. But in these days, when the news is filled with gruesome details of terrorist acts, one has reason to think of what it would mean if private groups, if terrorists, got hold of nuclear weapons, and Prince Sadruddin has already very eloquently pointed out the dangers of this.

Terrorists, now as in the past, show an utter contempt for human life and human values. In pursuing their goals, they are using fanatic methods which are totally inconsistent with all basic rules of a civilized society.

Many believe that it has now become quite possible for a terrorist group to acquire a nuclear device. Very small nuclear bombs are being constructed, and one could even imagine that such weapons could be smuggled into a country. This development increases the risk that we might enter an era of nuclear terrorism.

This serves as a strong reminder of the awesome responsibility which rests with all of us for fighting nuclear proliferation, also as a part of the struggle against terrorism.

The Non-Proliferation Treaty is, as was stated in the message from the Head of the Department of Foreign Affairs of Switzerland, the most important political and legal instrument we have for preventing the spread of nuclear weapons. And I do not hesitate to characterize the NPT as one of the most important international treaties signed since World War II.

It is now 15 years since the Non-Proliferation Treaty entered into effect. The Review Conference which starts in this city in exactly two months will put the Treaty to its hardest test so far.

We all know that the non-proliferation regime has its flaws. Some actual nuclear-weapon States and several potential ones are still outside the Treaty. Some States keep the option of acquiring nuclear weapons for the purpose of deterring other States in their region from acquiring such weapons themselves. Much has also been said about the discriminatory character of the NPT, the non-nuclears having done their share and the nuclear-weapon States not having fulfilled their obligations.

I will return to this question. But before doing so, I would like to add that, in spite of all its flaws, the Non-Proliferation Treaty has actually functioned in one very important way: no *new* nuclear-weapon State has, as far as we know, appeared since the Treaty was concluded. The misgivings of many people that a number of States would step over the nuclear threshold have not been borne out in these 15 years. And no less than some 130 States have become signatories to the Non-Proliferation Treaty. To sum up: the implementation of the undertakings by the non-nuclear-weapon States has by and large been adequate and satisfactory.

Unfortunately, the same cannot be said of the undertakings—in the Treaty—of the nuclear-weapon States with respect to vertical proliferation. This Treaty, solemnly signed and ratified by the United States, the Soviet Union and the United Kingdom, talks literally—in its preamble—about the cessation of the manufacture of nuclear weapons, about the liquidation of all their existing stockpiles, and about the elimination from national arsenals of nuclear weapons and the means of their delivery. Article VI of the Treaty, as you all know, spells out the undertaking in detail: 'to pursue negotiations in good faith on effective measures relating to cessation of the nuclear arms race at an early date and to nuclear disarmament, and on a Treaty on general and complete disarmament under strict and effective international control.'

This is very clear language. Still, it does not seem to have been quite understood. If the authority is to remain with the Treaty, it is above all necessary that the nuclear-weapon States, which have signed and ratified it, should also live up to the spirit and letter of their obligations. It is, in my opinion, the nuclear-weapon States themselves that have the key to progress in the work to prevent both horizontal and vertical proliferation of nuclear arms.

It is therefore a welcome development now that the super-Powers are sitting down together here in Geneva, talking bilaterally about eliminating nuclear weapons everywhere. But this is not a question for them alone. It concerns all States. Our common civilization belongs to all nations, to all peoples, to present as well as future generations. And therefore it is simply not acceptable that the future of our civilization lies in the hands of only one or two or five nuclear-weapon States.

This is the point which I would specifically like to make today. The non-nuclear-weapon States together constitute the larger part of the world. The five States with nuclear arms have together some 1,500 million inhabitants. But there are twice as many people living outside the nuclear powers. These non-nuclear countries want to maintain their independence, they want to preserve their national identity, they want to keep their right to self-determination. And last but not least: they want to survive physically.

President Alfonsin of Argentina has put it most directly: it is a question of our right to life. And therefore, we, the non-nuclears, must also have a say. We must have the right to demand that nuclear weapons are never used, that the nuclear arms race comes to a halt, and that a process of genuine disarmament is started.

I shall not hide the fact that I can understand how, in the face of the very discouraging results through the many years of disarmament talks, some nations may feel that they have as much right as the present nuclear-weapon States to arm themselves with these kinds of weapons. In fact, we had an extensive debate in my own country in the late 1950s about the advantages and disadvantages of acquiring nuclear weapons. After much deliberation, we finally came to the unanimous conclusion that a Swedish nuclear weapon would be detrimental to our own security. It would increase the risk of our neutral nation being involved at an early stage in an international armed conflict. As the then Swedish Prime Minister, Tage Erlander, said at the time about Swedish nuclear arms: 'That which should be our protection could equally well be transformed into the greatest threat to our neutrality and our peace.' Without nuclear weapons, we would stand a better chance of staying out of war. Our security—and probably also that of our neighbours—would be enhanced if we refrained from acquiring the atomic bomb. So even though we certainly had the technical capacity to build a nuclear weapon, we decided not to, and Sweden joined the NPT from the beginning.

Even if the arsenals of some of the present nuclear-weapon States are smaller than those of others, this does not exonerate them from the awesome responsibility connected with possessing these bombs. This should also be contemplated by those who may now be planning to go nuclear. They would not increase their own security by acquiring these weapons. They would only decrease the security of all of us.

What, then, can a non-nuclear nation do instead to safeguard its security and independence?

The majority of the non-nuclears are poor countries. They need to develop their economies, and they need to meet very basic and simple needs like food and shelter. They definitely need to devote their scarce resources to civilian purposes, and not to military spending.

Many of the independent States on the Earth are also very small States. There are 60 nations in the world with less than one million inhabitants. Most of them are Third World countries, and they are not only small but also economically weak. Their security dilemma is very real, vulnerable as they are. What should such a small State do to ensure its security? Should it arm itself? It could do so, but how large an army could it afford when the price of a few tanks or aircraft might be higher than its whole government expenditure for civilian purposes? Or should it put its security in the hands of a more powerful neighbour, and perhaps lose some of its independence? Or should it become an ally of one of the super-Powers? This could make it part of the East-West conflict, and bring super-Power confrontation to its region.

The security dilemma of these nations is a very real one. And whatever road they choose, they will always—as the rest of us—be potential victims of a nuclear exchange. And what can we do about that?

The allies of the major nuclear-weapon States can and do try, within their respective alliances, to influence their leading partners.

But all of us can work together to seek to build a system of collective security. Such a system—as envisaged when the United Nations was born 40 years ago—must first of all build on respect for international law. The territorial integrity of each nation must be guaranteed. But it must also be a system which recognizes and promotes common interest, and which helps to avert common threats. To this end we must strengthen the peace-keeping role of the United Nations.

The most ominous, obvious common threat is the threat of nuclear war. Therefore, while seeking a system of collective security, it is also an urgent task to join forces in order to put pressure on the leading military Powers. We must make it perfectly clear to those with the power to decide about the use of nuclear weapons—as well as those who may plan to acquire such weapons—that they are not only gambling with the survival of their own countries, they are also putting our lives in jeopardy. They must be made to realize that they have a responsibility to us, too.

Three of the nuclear-weapon States have in fact recognized this responsibility in the Non-Proliferation Treaty. They have undertaken to pursue negotiations in good faith on effective measures relating to the cessation of the nuclear arms race at an early date and to nuclear disarmament. But they have not lived up to this obligation; on the other hand, the non-nuclear-weapon States that are Parties to the Treaty have fulfilled *their* undertaking not to acquire nuclear weapons. The failure of the super-Powers to comply with their Treaty obligations may well endanger the future of the non-proliferation regime itself. The uncontrolled expansion of the nuclear arsenals, in contrast to the restraint with respect to horizontal proliferation, puts severe strain on the NPT.

The very fact that the nuclear Powers, in spite of their Treaty obligations, continue to strengthen their nuclear weapons arsenals—and do so increasingly—may also serve to legitimize these weapons as instruments of national security. And the risk is obvious that some non-nuclear-weapon States may deem it justified to try to acquire nuclear arsenals of their own, both to deter a massive strike against civilian populations, and to gain advantage in regional conflicts.

There is indeed a direct connection between the threat of proliferation and the dangers of deterrence which I was talking about earlier. The nuclear-weapon States are in effect saying that they can achieve security by building nuclear weapons, that they can gain political advantage and that they can also prevent war. People in other countries have so far been less convinced of the benefits of nuclear deterrence. But as they too consider the option of proliferation, it becomes ever more urgent to understand the addictive instability of the deterrence doctrine.

The struggle to avoid the threat of nuclear proliferation must be fought on many different levels. The most obvious step would be to conclude a comprehensive nuclear test ban. A treaty banning all nuclear weapon tests would be the single most important step to slow down the qualitative arms race. It would be a good complement to the bilateral negotiations by reducing the risk that cuts in the arsenals eventually agreed upon in the strategic talks would be nullified by the development of new nuclear systems. The work done by experts in my country in this field for a long time has convinced me that existing scientific and technical capabilities make it possible adequately to verify a comprehensive nuclear test ban.

There are many other steps which can be taken in the field of nuclear disarmament to help uphold the non-proliferation regime. A halt to the development, production and deployment of all nuclear weapons would, in my view, be helpful in promoting negotiations on nuclear weapons. This is the main proposal in the Delhi Declaration, which was signed by six Heads of State and Heads of Government who met in the Indian capital in late January this year. The question of an immediate halt to the nuclear arms race has also been discussed in the United Nations, these discussions resulting in several resolutions on a nuclear freeze, which were adopted by overwhelming majorities.

A ban on all space weapons would be another important contribution. Negative security assurances by the nuclear-weapon Powers to the non-nuclear-weapon States also belong here. The non-nuclears have every right to demand effective guarantees containing unequivocal undertakings by the nuclear-weapon States that they will not attack, or threaten to attack, them with nuclear arms.

I spoke in the beginning of my statement of the risk of the very early use of, for instance, battlefield nuclear weapons. That is why I think that the idea of a corridor in Central Europe free from such nuclear weapons is worthy of further exploration. There are several other suggestions—some of which can be taken up by the non-nuclears themselves—aimed at avoiding nuclear confrontation and proliferation. These include the establishment of nuclear-weapon-free zones, such as has been brought about through the Treaty of Tlatelolco in Latin America, and such as we are at the moment talking a great deal about among the Nordic countries here in Europe.

It is our duty, as political leaders, to use as much of our energy as we can to try to find solutions of this kind. If the work we do could be just a tiny contribution to a general public demand for a halt to nuclear proliferation, even such an effort would be something to be proud of. I am personally convinced that the repeated threats from both sides, the doctrine of nuclear deterrence and the continued arms race that has ensued, the threat of the spread of nuclear weapons to other countries, all these factors do not make people feel any more secure. I also think that those who look for an alternative to deterrence in a technological breakthrough which, ultimately, will result in an absolutely infallible system will seek in vain. I believe that this is an illusion. It is in fact a fruitless search for an illusion of safety, which will again lead to increased insecurity for us all.

Security and protection from annihilation by nuclear weapons cannot be reached by further technological innovations. The placing of greater emphasis on destructive technology cannot give any lasting security. It is only we human beings, in agreement with each other, who can provide that security, a common security. What we require is a security system which is achieved in co-operation with other nations, not at their expense. We require political, negotiated solutions, and not unilateral technological innovations. The only answer to the increasing threat of nuclear proliferation and the present danger of nuclear war is therefore to initiate a process of international disarmament in forms which do not favour either side but which ensure better security for all.

Finally, a word about leadership in world affairs. The nuclear Powers play a unique role in today's world: unique in comparison with other nations, and unique also in a historical perspective. These Powers, and particularly the two super-Powers, control larger resources than any two nations ever have before. They have at their disposal technological facilities without comparison. But above all: they can kill us all, their military might can extinguish all mankind from the face of the Earth. One can ask for what purpose this unique concentration of power is used. We can see how the super-Powers treat their small neighbours—how they brutally invade them or declare that they wish to get rid of their elected governments. One is given the impression that the internal affairs of these small countries is a decisive problem in the world today, a major threat to the security of the great Powers. Hardly anybody else sees it that way. We can see how little attention—if any—they pay to the desperate needs of the poor countries in the Third World. They are dismissed as victims of the colonization of the past, or to the magic of the market place. Above all, we can see how they continue their armaments, now reaching also into outer space, in a deadly race which if continued can only end in a catastrophe.

This accumulation of destructive machinery, as Willy Brandt pointed out in his Third World Prize lecture in April, is actually killing people without the arms being used, because it eats up the money without which people are condemned to death through starvation. The billions of dollars, Brandt said, which the world spends on military purposes this year really amount to a death sentence for millions of human beings.

What I have said now has perhaps been harsh and somewhat unfair. But I believe that there is a serious lack of leadership in the world of today. The great Powers do not provide it, they tend to aggravate the problems instead of solving them. They tend to deal with peripheral issues and their own confrontation around the globe and above it, thus avoiding the fundamental problems of disarmament and development which are the key to long-range peace and security. Smaller and medium-sized nations cannot provide this leadership. But they can at least, in all humility, point out the absurdities and raise voices of sanity, they can act together and thus take a joint responsibility for our common future.

I have already said that in matters of nuclear weapons the non-nuclears must also have a say. It is all very well that here in Geneva bilateral talks are going on, with the aim of halting and reversing the nuclear arms race. But these talks have so far produced nothing. And we who are on the outside, but who are as affected by the outcome as the negotiating parties, definitely have the right to expect more.

An active participation in the work of international organizations—especially the United Nations—is a corner-stone in a practical policy of common security. To help uphold respect for international law is another. To put more emphasis on multilateral security solutions is the best way of helping the process of co-operation for common survival.

This, again, directly connects with the theme of this Colloquium. To sustain such a process, concrete disarmament measures must be taken. In the Non-Proliferation Treaty, the Parties—including the major nuclear-weapon States—have made a contractual undertaking to negotiate in good faith on effective disarmament measures. And this is also the only possible answer to the international security dilemma.

This may seem a hopeless endeavour at times, in face of the discouraging state of international affairs. But we should remember that the opportunities are larger now than ever before. It may be easy to forget these opportunities when we face the terrible threats to our common future. But these threats have been created by man and can also be eliminated by man. And behind and beyond these threats lie the new, great opportunities. Never before have such vast resources been available for creating a liveable world for all: economic resources, technological development, our own knowledge of how people and societies work and function.

I am certain that the peoples of this world want their political leaders to work together to use these immense possibilities instead of destroying them. It can be done, if the political will is strong enough. And if the call goes out, from town meetings and demonstrations, from churches and labour unions, from congresses and colloquia like this, then we could see the start of a process to make the world free from hunger, threats and injustice. One thing is certain: this task is a common responsibility for all nations and all peoples.

I

The Nuclear Non-Proliferation Treaty and its Future

CHAIRMAN:

MR. NIALL MACDERMOT

Jurist, Secretary-General, International Commission of Jurists, Former Minister of State for Planning and Land in the United Kingdom Government

THE NPT: THE FIRST 15 YEARS AND THE CURRENT CRISIS (ARTICLE VI)

China's Position on Nuclear Non-Proliferation

HE QIAN JIADONG

Ambassador of the People's Republic of China to the Conference on Disarmament, Geneva

I am greatly honoured to have the opportunity to attend the Colloquium on Nuclear War, Nuclear Proliferation and their Consequences and to meet with so many distinguished politicians, academics and scientists from around the world. Allow me first of all to thank Prince Sadruddin Aga Khan and the Groupe de Bellerive for the kind invitation extended to me.

When we speak of nuclear non-proliferation, it must be made clear at the outset that this is to mean non-proliferation both in the horizontal sense and in the vertical sense. To approach the issue only from the angle of horizontal non-proliferation is one-sided and is not comprehensive. The whole purpose of nuclear non-proliferation stems from the consideration to avert the danger of a nuclear war and to safeguard the security of peoples. It should therefore consist of the following objectives:

1. To prevent the emergence of new nuclear-weapon States apart from the existing ones.
2. To achieve arms control and disarmament wherein the two major nuclear-weapon States should without delay halt their nuclear arms race and take the lead in drastically reducing their nuclear arsenals, leading ultimately to the complete elimination of all nuclear weapons throughout the world.
3. To encourage and promote peaceful nuclear co-operation among all States, particularly with a view to facilitating the non-nuclear-weapon States of the Third World in the development of their nuclear programmes for peaceful uses.

Of the three objectives, it goes without saying that the second is of particular importance, as it is none other than the ever-escalating nuclear arms race between the two super-Powers that is right now threatening international security and world peace.

China is not a Party to the NPT, but its stance on the question of non-proliferation is clear-cut and above-board. Pursuant to its independent foreign policy of safeguarding peace and opposing war, it stands for nuclear disarmament and disapproves of nuclear proliferation.

China has consistently worked for the complete prohibition and thorough destruction of all nuclear weapons. In 1964, it unilaterally declared that at no time and under no circumstances would it be the first to use nuclear weapons. It also pledged unconditionally never to use nuclear weapons against non-nuclear-weapon States and nuclear-weapon-free zones. It respects and supports the establishment of nuclear-weapon-free zones wherever possible on the basis of the free will of the countries concerned. In 1973, China signed the Second Additional Protocol of the Tlatelolco Treaty. With a view to promoting peaceful nuclear co-operation with other countries, China joined the IAEA in 1984 and expressed its readiness to respect its statutes. All these show that China is in favour of non-proliferation. In recent years, the Chinese Government has increasingly reiterated that China neither advocates nor encourages nuclear proliferation and that its co-operation with other countries in the nuclear field is only for peaceful purposes.

This being the case, one could well ask why then China refuses to accede to the NPT. The reason is simple. It is because China considers the Treaty a discriminatory one and as a matter of principle cannot but be critical of it.

The NPT is allegedly the outcome of a 'bargain' between the nuclear-weapon States and the non-nuclear-weapon States. For any international legal instrument, especially a contemporary one, it should embody at least a balance of responsibilities and obligations of all the parties. But this does not happen to be the case for the NPT.

In the first place, the NPT, while specifically and categorically forbidding the non-nuclear-weapon States to develop or otherwise acquire any nuclear weapons, provides only in very vague terms that the nuclear-weapon States undertake 'to pursue negotiations in good faith on effective measures relating to cessation of the nuclear arms race at an early date and to nuclear disarmament'. By comparing Article II with Article VI, one can easily see that the obligation undertaken by the non-nuclear-weapon States and that by the nuclear-weapon States are by no means equal. For the former, it entails not the slightest ambiguity, while for the latter, it is practically devoid of any binding force.

Secondly, notwithstanding the fact that the non-nuclear-weapon States Parties to the NPT have voluntarily relinquished the nuclear option, this is nonetheless not compensated by any guarantee from the nuclear-weapon States Parties to the NPT not to use nuclear weapons against them. The huge stockpile of nuclear weapons in the possession of the major nuclear Powers is a threat to all countries. It is only natural that the non-nuclear-weapon States should be protected against the use or threat of use of nuclear weapons.

But apparently the Treaty has evaded this issue. There is no mention of anything to this effect at all in the Treaty.

Thirdly, in the field of peaceful uses of nuclear energy, although it is stipulated that all States Parties to the Treaty have the inalienable right 'to develop research, production and use of nuclear energy for peaceful purposes without discrimination' and the right 'to participate in the fullest possible exchange of equipment, materials, and scientific and technological information for the peaceful uses of nuclear energy', yet, in order to exercise such rights, the non-nuclear-weapon States, apart from accepting the IAEA safeguards, are moreover required to enter into special arrangements with the supplier countries. These extra conditions have in fact hampered the non-nuclear-weapon States from enjoying what is their due.

In short, the NPT, far from being fair and equitable, is demanding much more from the non-nuclear-weapon States Parties than from the nuclear-weapon ones.

The fifteen years that have elapsed since its inception have borne full testimony to the discriminatory nature of the NPT.

In his statement to the 38th Session of the United Nations General Assembly on 4 November, 1983, Dr. Hans Blix, Director-General of the IAEA, specifically observed: 'So far, the world has been relatively successful in preventing horizontal proliferation while vertical proliferation—that is to say, the further piling-up of more nuclear warheads in nuclear-weapon States—has continued'. In other words, while the non-nuclear-weapon States have faithfully honoured their commitments not to develop or otherwise acquire any nuclear weapons, the major nuclear Powers have not only made no progress in negotiating any effective measures to halt the nuclear arms race and reduce their nuclear stockpiles, but on the contrary, have been all the time intensifying the race. In the five years following the Second Review Conference on the NPT, the world has witnessed the most massive arms build-up, both quantitatively and qualitatively. The total number of nuclear warheads has increased from 40,000 in 1980 to 50,000 today. They have not only become more accurate and faster to deliver but also more destructive and lethal. Nuclear weapons have also been deployed in countries where they were non-existent before. What is more, in their quest for military superiority, the super-Powers are even extending the arms race to outer space. Consequently, mankind is faced with an ever more serious threat of a nuclear holocaust.

For years the non-nuclear-weapon States have been pressing for effective international arrangements to assure them against the use or threat of use of nuclear weapons. The issue has been on the agenda of the Geneva Conference on Disarmament, the sole multilateral negotiating forum for disarmament since 1979. Yet negotiations have now practically come to a standstill because of divergencies between the two super-Powers, which in essence reflect their reluctance to commit themselves unconditionally not to use nuclear weapons against non-nuclear-weapon States. The non-nuclear-weapon States have time and again voiced their disappointment about and dissatisfaction with such a state of affairs.

With regard to peaceful nuclear co-operation, reference can be made again to the above-mentioned statement of Dr. Blix, in which he noted: 'trade and technology transfers in the nuclear field have always been subject to inter-government co-operation agreements, safeguards, physical protection requirements and other special arrangements. Indeed, suppliers' policies have at times given rise to friction and frustration among recipient countries, and they continue to do so'. This is a very mild description of the situation. In reality, owing to the increasingly severe restrictions imposed by the main suppliers under the pretext of preventing proliferation, international co-operation for peaceful uses of nuclear energy has been much hindered. Developing countries wish that they could be provided with more assistance for their peaceful nuclear energy programmes. But their demand has not been taken into consideration seriously. Some complain that the developing countries are still under the rule of a sort of colonial system—'nuclear colonialism' in the present instance. In a way, this is not entirely unjustified.

So, from the above, it can be seen that the NPT, instead of being conducive to averting the danger of nuclear war and safeguarding international peace and security, has in fact been exploited by the major nuclear Powers to serve their vested interests in maintaining their nuclear supremacy.

It is said that twenty years ago, there had been an anticipation that in the 1970s the nuclear-weapon States might increase to as many as 15 to 25, a situation regarded as of great danger. Now we are already in the mid-1980s, yet the number of nuclear-weapon States remains the same. This indeed is a great relief to the whole world. As was rightly pointed out by Joseph S. Nye Jr. in his article 'To Manage is Human, to Prevent is Divine': 'Since nuclear weaponry is a forty-year-old technology, what is surprising is not that it has spread, but that it has not spread further'. Of course one should not rest content with the existing situation. Efforts should be continued to stem the danger of possible proliferation. The question is how to deal properly with the issue and really achieve the desired goal.

As it is already forty years since nuclear-weapon technology was first developed, to many countries it is no longer a secret. Given the time and effort, almost any of them that wanted to go nuclear could easily build a bomb of their own, despite what restrictions other countries might impose. It would be naive to think that it is still possible to prevent proliferation through technological means. Technological control could have some effect for a time, but certainly not for ever and if it is stretched too far, it would even be counter-productive and harm the supplier countries themselves. Till recently, some circles have always been thinking in terms of technological restrictions, denials or even sanctions against States with potential nuclear-weapon capabilities. Such ideas are now sharply on the decline.

More and more people have realized that the question of non-proliferation is not a technological one, but a political one, and, in the final analysis, can only be solved by political means. While certain reasonable technological measures are necessary, emphasis should be placed on assuring the non-nuclear-weapon States from the use or threat of use of nuclear weapons, on upholding and respecting the sovereign rights and the legitimate interests of the countries concerned, on the relaxation of tensions and the strengthening of international peace and security as a whole, on strict adherence to the Charter of the United Nations and the principles of peaceful coexistence in international relations, on the establishment of a fair and reasonable new international economic order, on the resolution of regional conflicts in a peaceful way free from outside interference, and so on.

Maybe there are one or two exceptions, such as South Africa and Israel. Both of them, in their pursuit of regional domination, are frenziedly seeking nuclear-weapon capability. Actions to curb this dangerous trend have been demanded for years by the international community, in particular by African and Middle Eastern countries. They strongly demand that Africa and the Middle East be turned into nuclear-weapon-free zones. Yet some nuclear-weapon States, in sharp contrast to what they impose on the other non-nuclear-weapon States in terms of technological restrictions, have all the time been reluctant to take any effective measures against South Africa and Israel.

What has been said so far refers only to proliferation in the horizontal sense, which, if anything, is a potential danger. The much more important issue is how to prevent the further proliferation of nuclear weapons in the vertical sense.

There is no need to stress here the danger of the ever-escalating nuclear arms race between the two super-Powers. The catastrophic consequences in the event of a nuclear war have been ever more convincingly substantiated by scientific research. The cessation of the nuclear arms race, the realization of nuclear disarmament and the prevention of nuclear war are now matters of utmost concern for the peoples of the world.

It is also precisely in the hope of serving the cause of peace and in the expectation that concrete steps will be taken by the super-Powers to reduce their nuclear arsenals that most of the non-nuclear-weapon countries have joined the NPT. Unless something is done to halt and reverse vertical nuclear proliferation, any talk of non-proliferation will undoubtedly be of little significance.

China always holds that the fundamental way to the elimination of the nuclear threat and the prevention of nuclear war lies in the complete prohibition and thorough destruction of all nuclear weapons. It is gratifying to note that more and more people have come to share this view.

Of course, this is not a goal that can be achieved overnight. China realizes this and accordingly has over the years proposed as a practical step towards this goal that the two super-Powers take the lead in halting the testing, production and deployment of nuclear weapons as well as substantially reducing their existing nuclear arsenals, and that thereafter corresponding measures be taken by the other nuclear States.

The super-Powers are in possession of over 95 per cent of the total nuclear weaponry in the world and only they have the capability to fight a nuclear war. It is recognized throughout the world that they bear a special responsibility towards nuclear disarmament. Both of them have already for long acquired the 'overkill' capability. To halt their nuclear arms race and reduce their existing nuclear stockpile would affect neither the so-called 'balance of forces' nor the so-called 'equal security' which, as claimed by the two super-Powers respectively, are supposed to be the basic guiding principles for disarmament.

China is a developing country and is right now engaged in an arduous task of modernization. It ardently longs for a durable peaceful environment. It has neither the wish nor the capability to join in the arms race between the super-Powers. It is fully aware of its responsibility as a nuclear-weapon State and has no intention of shirking it. Provided that the super-Powers have taken the lead in disarming in a meaningful way, China can be counted on to take corresponding actions.

Unfortunately, to the great disappointment and frustration of the peoples of the world, the super-Powers have failed to show the necessary political will to achieve progress towards disarmament. Particularly as a result of the breaking off of the bilateral negotiations between them and the subsequent deployment of new nuclear weapons on both sides, the past year was characterized by even more increased tension and turmoil.

The world is glad to see that the bilateral talks have now resumed or restarted. While knowing full well that the positions of the two super-Powers are wide apart, China, and indeed the whole world, still hopes that this time the super-Powers will truly demonstrate their political will, undertake their special responsibilities, negotiate in good faith and come up with results really conducive to international peace and security, and to arms control and disarmament.

In order to create an atmosphere and conditions favourable to their negotiation, China has suggested that the two parties should, to begin with, stop the further deployment of intermediate-range missiles in both Europe and Asia and refrain from developing, testing and deploying outer space weapons.

Negotiations are going on also in the Conference on Disarmament. They have likewise been very unsuccessful in past years. Moreover, there is a growing tendency to ignore multilateralism and belittle the efforts of all members of the international community. The nuclear 'have-nots' cannot help demanding strongly that they should also have a say. With the resumption of the bilateral talks, it is the general hope that the CD will play a better role. The two fora are not mutually preclusive but complementary to each other.

Nuclear non-proliferation being such an important question of universal concern, it is natural that people are speculating on the future of the NPT as the Third Review Conference draws near. An objective assessment of the record of the Treaty in the past 15 years cannot but lead to the conclusion that it is indeed in a state of crisis as suggested in the subject title of this session of the Colloquium.

China shares the view that the most serious threat to the Treaty is the failure of the major nuclear-weapon States to fulfil their obligations under Article VI and to negotiate effectively for nuclear disarmament. Whether or not the super-Powers are prepared to stop their nuclear arms race and agree to disarm—this is where the future of the Treaty lies. Once they have begun the process of reversing the vertical proliferation, the likelihood of horizontal proliferation would only diminish and not grow, and countries that are considered 'problematic' would find it all the more difficult to have any rationale to go nuclear even if they wanted to do so.

The year 1985 marks the 40th anniversary of the founding of the United Nations. The UN Charter spells out clearly in its preamble that the aim of this world organization is 'to save succeeding generations from the scourge of war, which twice in our life time has brought untold sorrow to mankind'. The very first resolution adopted by the United Nations General Assembly was directed at the threat of a nuclear war. Forty years have now elapsed, but the goal is still far from being attained. The danger of war still exists. However, it is gratifying to note that in recent years the forces deterring war are also growing. China is deeply convinced that so long as the people of all countries persist in their efforts, international tension can be relaxed and world peace safeguarded.

At this very important juncture, it is of particular significance for Prince Sadruddin Aga Khan and the Groupe de Bellerive to convene this Colloquium to discuss a subject which is so vital to the destiny of mankind. I wish the Conference every success.

THE NPT: THE FIRST 15 YEARS AND THE CURRENT CRISIS (ARTICLE VI)

HE MOHAMED I. SHAKER

Ambassador, Permanent Mission of the Arab Republic of Egypt to the United Nations, New York

In a few weeks, the Third NPT Review Conference will convene in Geneva. It is quite clear from the provisions of the NPT that the objective of a review conference is to review the operation of the Treaty with a view to assuring that the purposes of the Preamble and the provisions of the Treaty are being realized (Article VIII-3).

The negotiating history of treaty provisions regarding review conferences indicates the relevance of such conferences to the achievement of measures to halt the nuclear arms race and nuclear disarmament. This had been emphasized by the nuclear-weapon States Party to the Treaty. Even the word 'Preamble' mentioned in the provisions of Article VIII-3 of the Treaty was suggested by the United Kingdom, a nuclear-weapon State Party to the Treaty. The latter explained then that 'the Preamble is . . . wider than . . . Article VI in the disarmament field and indicates in some detail what needs to be done, as well as containing an important declaration of intent to achieve at the earliest possible date the cessation of the nuclear arms race'.[1]

In the light of these facts, and because of the lack of real progress in the field of disarmament since the entry into force of the NPT in 1970, it is not surprising that disarmament issues have been and will continue to be the centre of attention at NPT review conferences. However, this attention should not, in principle, detract the Third NPT Review Conference from reviewing and assessing the implementation of the other equally important aspects of the NPT as well, and more particularly those relating to co-operation in the peaceful uses of nuclear energy. As these aspects will be dealt with by other participants at this Conference, this paper will focus on the implementation of Article VI and the corresponding provisions of the Preamble of the NPT.

In our view, any assessment of the implementation of these particular provisions of the NPT should be based on two principles among the five main principles upon which the Treaty itself had to be negotiated and concluded. These principles were the result of the efforts of a number of

[1] ENDC/PV. 358, 23 January 1968, para. 26.

non-aligned States in 1965 and were adopted by the General Assembly of the United Nations that year.[1] They are equally relevant in assessing the implementation of the NPT. The two principles in question are:

—the Treaty should embody an acceptable balance of mutual responsibilities and obligations of the nuclear and non-nuclear Powers.

—the Treaty should be a step towards the achievement of general and complete disarmament and, more particularly, nuclear disarmament.

They are two separate principles dealing with two separate sets of issues but they act and react on each other. Any assessment of the implementation of the Treaty has, therefore, to take into consideration how far a balance is being achieved between the responsibilities and obligations of the nuclear-weapon States and the non-nuclear-weapon States Party to the Treaty. Although the majority of the latter States remain unable in any case to produce nuclear weapons by their own means, their renunciation of nuclear weapons is felt to be meaningless if it is not met by concrete disarmament measures achieved by the nuclear-weapon States. It is more a question of principle than a question of security, which obviously cannot be guaranteed merely by certain limited measures. It is definitely not a question of mere rhetoric as some may feel it is. The non-nuclear-weapon States Party to the Treaty are committed to it because it is in their national interest to do so. But they would also wish to see some substantive progress on nuclear disarmament to justify their continued affiliation with the Treaty.

In the course of the two months following the signature of the NPT on 1 July 1968, the two super-Powers as well as the non-nuclear-weapon States at their Conference in Geneva in August–September 1968 proposed their respective agendas for disarmament negotiations.[2] The two agendas reflected a basic difference in approach. The super-Powers' agenda contained all sorts of measures, nuclear and non-nuclear. The non-nuclear-weapon States' agenda contained measures relating solely to the nuclear arms race and nuclear disarmament. However, with the exception of the bilateral strategic arms limitation talks, both agendas entrusted the disarmament conference in Geneva, at that time the Eighteen-Nation Committee on Disarmament, with the task of negotiating all the measures proposed.

In our view, the non-nuclear-weapon States' approach focusing on nuclear disarmament converged with the spirit and letter of Article VI of the NPT. Any measure agreed upon, if it were to have a positive impact on the NPT, should be in the field of nuclear disarmament. Future arms control and disarmament agreements must in the first place be related to the subject matter of the NPT, namely non-proliferation of nuclear weapons, and more particularly vertical non-proliferation. For example, an agreement on

[1] United Nations General Assembly Resolution 2028 (XX).

[2] ENDC/PV. 390, 15 August 1968, para. 93 and A/Conf. 35/10, 1 October 1968, Resolution C, p. 8.

chemical warfare is urgently needed but it would be irrelevant to the subject matter of the NPT. In the same category are the 1971 Biological Weapons Convention and the 1971 Agreement on the prevention of incidents on and over the high seas.

In the course of the last fifteen years since the entry into force of the NPT in 1970, the disarmament conference in Geneva, known at present as the Conference on Disarmament (CD), produced meagre results. More substantive results were achieved outside the CD and mainly by the two super-Powers. It is not our intention to dwell on these results in this paper. They are dealt with so far in a number of papers prepared for the Third Session of the Preparatory Committee for the Third NPT Review Conference which met last April.[1] Our intention is rather to briefly highlight the major results achieved and to assess their real significance with regard to the provisions of the NPT.

When the First NPT Review Conference met in 1975, SALT I Agreements had been reached and SALT II Agreements were about to be negotiated. Moreover, the Sea-Bed Treaty prohibiting nuclear weapons on the sea-bed was signed in 1971, followed by the Threshold Test Ban Agreement in 1974. Therefore, the atmosphere surrounding the First NPT Review Conference was relatively good. The atmosphere was encouraging and conducive to making further progress on disarmament issues. However, the Review Conference did not adopt its Final Declaration without great difficulties. The non-nuclear-weapon States, and more particularly those belonging to the Group of 77, were not greatly impressed by the results achieved, which in their view were marginal and cosmetic rather than real. Moreover, their various demands at the Review Conference for real nuclear disarmament with suggested timetables attached to some measures were not accepted.

SALT I Agreements acknowledged their relevance to the obligations of the Soviet Union and the United States under Article VI of the NPT. However, in terms of their quantitative aspects, the Agreements set numerical targets to be attained for certain weapons systems, and therefore there was no immediate cessation of the nuclear arms race. Moreover, in terms of their qualitative aspects, the agreements virtually transformed the arms race into a qualitatively new nuclear arms race. Modernization and replacement of weapons systems were allowed. Nevertheless, the 1972 Agreements had their positive sides such as restricting the development and deployment of certain weapons systems. They also had the virtue of creating a psychological-political climate which had allowed certain progress to be achieved in different directions. Unfortunately, SALT I Agreements and, more particularly the ABM Treaty, are being put to the test as a result of the US Strategic Defense Initiative (SDI), the so-called 'Star Wars'. Even the 1967 Outer Space Treaty is being put to the test.

[1] NPT/CONF. III/PC. III/1, 4, 5, 12 and 13.

With regard to the 1974 Threshold Test Ban Agreement, it must be noted that the Agreement was received with a great feeling of indifference on the part of United Nations member States. It implied that the super-Powers had not yet decided to give up their qualitative arms race. It remains unratified to this date. Even if its ratification were to take place today, which in itself would be a commendable step, it would hardly be hailed by the majority of non-nuclear-weapon States. The latter's real objective is a comprehensive test ban.

In the interval between the First and the Second NPT Review Conferences, in the period between 1975 and 1980, the major achievements in the field of disarmament were the 1976 PNE Agreement and the 1979 SALT II Agreements. Even these Agreements along with the 1974 Threshold Test Ban Agreement were not ratified before the 1980 NPT Review Conference and remain unratified to this date. This explains the tense atmosphere which prevailed during the 1980 Review Conference and which led to a deadlock on reaching agreement on a final declaration, in spite of the fact that a fragile consensus was reached on the issues of peaceful nuclear co-operation (Articles III, IV and V of the NPT). The Group of 77 was critical of the failure of the nuclear-weapon States to live up to their obligations under Article VI of the NPT. The Group resisted any attempt to dilute or weaken a statement on that article.

The 1976 PNE Agreement, as in the case of the Threshold Test Ban Agreement, did not generate great attention. It came out at a time when support for PNEs was waning in the United States. We were told that PNE technology was surrounded with all sorts of difficulties and therefore its potential benefits were far-fetched. If it were to be ratified today, it would be quite surprising that such a step should generate great enthusiasm. In this regard too, it must be said that a comprehensive test ban is the objective to be attained; a ban which may accommodate PNEs.

With regard to the 1979 SALT II Agreements, they too acknowledged their relevance to the obligations of the Soviet Union and the United States under Article VI of the NPT. However, in terms of their quantitative aspects, an increase in the number of nuclear delivery vehicles was permitted for one Party instead of lowering the ceiling for both Parties to a level which would have precluded such an increase. And although no increase was to take place in the number of warheads on old ICBMs, the number of warheads on each of the new ICBMs, SLBMs and ASBMs had been set very high. Moreover, in terms of their qualitative aspects, SALT II, as its predecessor SALT I, continues to transform the arms race into a qualitative renewed nuclear arms race. For example, a type of light ICBM was allowed to each Party. The Cruise missile programs had been allowed to continue unabated. In the American debate it was argued that SALT II was acceptable as long as the development of certain new weapons systems remained unhindered.

Nevertheless, SALT II Agreements are not deprived of positive aspects such as the introduction of the elements of equality and predictability in the super-Powers' rivalry.

The recent debate in the United States on whether or not to continue to abide by the provisions of the unratified SALT II Agreements left an impression of insensitivity as to the damage that might have eventually affected the NPT had the Agreements been finally scrapped. The forthcoming NPT Review Conference would have had the same fate as the Second NPT Review Conference in 1980 with unforeseen circumstances as to the fate of the NPT itself. The recent salvage of SALT II is not expected to foster progress towards concrete and substantive arms control and disarmament measures. Stronger and imaginative political will on the part of the two super-Powers is certainly needed to accomplish that.

In the aftermath of the failure of the 1980 NPT Review Conference, the early 1980s experienced a series of serious setbacks in the field of arms control and disarmament. The bilateral negotiations between the two super-Powers which began in Geneva in November 1981 on intermediate-range nuclear forces (INF) broke off on 23 November 1983 because of the deployment of Pershing-II and ground-launched Cruise missiles in the United Kingdom and the Federal Republic of Germany. Likewise, the Strategic Arms Reduction Talks (START), which began also in Geneva in June 1982 broke off on 8 December 1983. Moreover, in 1982 the US Administration decided to end negotiations with the United Kingdom and the Soviet Union on a comprehensive test ban. The main reasons given for such a decision were the verification problems of such a ban and the need to keep testing to assure the reliability of US deterrent forces. These setbacks led to the current crisis which is exacerbated by US and Soviet attempts to develop anti-satellite weapons (ASAT) and by the US Strategic Defense Initiative.

With the resumption of the arms control negotiations between the two super-Powers in Geneva in March 1985 covering strategic nuclear forces, intermediate-range nuclear forces, and space-based weapons, we may be told that these ongoing negotiations indicate the seriousness and sincerity of the two super-Powers in halting and reversing the nuclear arms race. In our view, these negotiations constitute an important step in this direction and create a favourable climate before the forthcoming NPT Review Conference. However, owing to the intricacies of the issues involved, the current negotiations are not expected to yield concrete and positive results in the near future. It took almost seven years to conclude the SALT II Agreements. This should not preclude the possibility and even the advisability of reporting some progress with regard to the ongoing negotiations before the convening of the Third NPT Review Conference. The two super-Powers should be encouraged to so do. They also ought to keep all interested and concerned parties informed about their deliberations. But are we going to let the situation boil down to such modest expectations? Is this all that we could hope for in the immediate future?

The parallel negotiations taking place at the CD in Geneva have also not produced any concrete results with regard to nuclear disarmament and it is not expected that they will yield any significant results before the convening of the Review Conference. Among all the measures discussed at the CD and at the UN General Assembly, a comprehensive test ban seems to generate a consensus as the most urgent and appropriate measure that should materialize. The political will to go ahead with a comprehensive test ban is still lacking. When the Partial Test-Ban Treaty of August 1963 was signed, it was apparent that certain tests in the three environments covered by the Treaty, i.e., the atmosphere, outer space and under water, could be carried out without being detected, but were considered, if they ever took place, to be too insignificant to have any effect on the military balance between the two super-Powers. The latter's political will in 1963 overcame the technical hurdles. Why could it not be displayed once more?

We are told that a comprehensive test ban is a long-term objective. How long is a long-term objective? Since the conclusion of the 1963 Partial Test-Ban Treaty, we have been working hard on a comprehensive test ban. The NPT itself acknowledged the prominence of that measure in its Preamble.

A comprehensive test ban is essential for the viability of NPT. It is both a vertical and a horizontal non-proliferation measure. It would have a positive influence on a number of non-nuclear-weapon States not Parties to the NPT and interested in or contemplating the creation of nuclear-weapon-free zones. For example, Brazil and Argentina, who are signatories to the 1967 Treaty of Tlatelolco but not yet full Parties to it, are urging the conclusion of a comprehensive test ban. Pakistan is sponsoring the idea of creating a nuclear-weapon-free zone in South-East Asia. The advantages of the establishment of such zones need not be stressed in this context. Suffice it to say that they will enhance and bolster the NPT regime.

As far as India is concerned, it is not far-fetched to say that if a comprehensive test ban had been reached in the 1960s or even in the early 1970s, India would have been one of the very first countries to have adhered to it. It follows that India's explosion of a nuclear device in 1974 might never have taken place unless a comprehensive test ban had allowed it under certain conditions. A comprehensive test ban which would exempt PNEs under specific procedures and regulations may induce India as well as Pakistan to adhere to it, both being long time champions of a comprehensive test ban. If this were to happen, the cause of non-proliferation would be greatly enhanced in this part of the world.

At the Third NPT Review Conference, the issue of a comprehensive test ban will figure prominently in its debates. A gesture on the part of the two super-Powers to agree to halt nuclear testing for a brief period preceding and extending beyond the Review Conference would be greatly welcomed by all parties to the Treaty, especially if such a gesture is made in conjunction with real negotiations on a CTB in the context of the CD. Such a gesture would signify in the first place that the two super-Powers can later work on and contribute to a comprehensive test ban that could last and endure. It would also signify that the two super-Powers, on the verge of a conference to which all attach great importance, have decided to pay more attention to the pleas of the non-nuclear-weapon States for real progress in halting and reversing the nuclear arms race. Such a gesture would certainly have a positive impact on the Conference and would facilitate its proceedings.

At present 128 States are Parties to the NPT. This number when compared with the state of adherence to any other arms control and disarmament agreement is the largest. This number has been increasing since the First NPT Review Conference from 96 in 1975 to 114 in 1980 and 128 in 1985. Most of the Parties have joined the NPT not because they are involved in nuclear activities that should be brought under international safeguards and not because they aspire one day to invest in nuclear power, but mainly because they believe that the Treaty is good for their security, which may be best attained through real nuclear disarmament. They see in the Treaty an ideal vehicle for disarmament. This explains their great misgivings and frustrations for lack of progress on disarmament.

The interests of the non-nuclear-weapon States Party to the NPT will be best served at the Third NPT Review Conference by a wider participation than ever before. Out of 96 Parties in 1975, 58 participated at the First Conference. Out of 114 Parties in 1980, 75 participated at the Second Conference. Now that the number of Parties has attained 128, and a great number of them (71) participated in the Third Session of the Preparatory Committee of the Conference, it is expected that about 90 Parties will participate at the Third Conference. We should not resign to such expectations. We should aim at a wider participation. If the NPT regime is to become a viable one, every Party should play a role in reviewing the operation of the Treaty. It is an opportunity which offers itself only once every five years.

The Review Conference has to be a forward-looking exercise. It is difficult to disagree with the conclusions of a recent study which indicated, *inter alia*, that the Review Conference should be an opportunity for major progress rather than a damage-limitation exercise.[1] The exercise should result in rendering the Treaty more attractive to the Parties to it as well as to countries pondering upon their adherence to it. In order to achieve this objective,

[1] *Nuclear Proliferation Toward Global Restraint*, New York: US UN Association, 1984, p. vi.

certain steps in the field of nuclear disarmament should be set in motion along with other steps.

As far as the NPT is concerned, there is no minimum to be achieved in the field of disarmament. The objective is general and complete disarmament. Even if a comprehensive test ban were to be achieved in the near future, it would not be surprising to hear at any disarmament forum, what is next? Attention would immediately focus on a number of issues which have figured for years in disarmament agendas waiting to be solved, such as a cut-off of fissionable material for weapons purposes and the non-use of nuclear weapons against non-nuclear-weapon States.

The current crisis is not insurmountable if the political will of the nuclear-weapon States overcomes the technical hurdles and if they succeed in resisting the temptations of further experimentation in new weapons systems. The nuclear-weapon States Party to the NPT should not go to the Third NPT Review Conference next September with empty hands. They should go there with some concrete and credible achievements and promise at the same time to do more. Non-nuclear-weapon States have been stretching their hands for a very long time in order to help and assist. All Parties to the NPT should work together at the Review Conference on a final declaration that would constitute a turning point in the proper implementation of Article VI of the NPT, which would bolster the non-proliferation regime.

The Non-Proliferation Treaty Fifteen Years After: Nuclear Partnership or Nuclear Apartheid?

HE Jayantha Dhanapala

Ambassador, Permanent Representative of the Democratic Socialist Republic of Sri Lanka

Mr. Chairman,

Ladies and Gentlemen,

May I begin by thanking the Groupe de Bellerive for the honour they have conferred on me in inviting me to address this Colloquium, which has attracted so many distinguished participants. I think it is important on the eve of the Third Review Conference of the NPT that we should have these opportunities for creative thinking about the Treaty rather than regard it as a political mummy to be embalmed in history. I propose this afternoon to take a retrospective view of the Treaty in all its aspects, but with special reference to Article VI.

The rationale on the part of the nuclear-weapon States Party for the conclusion of the Treaty on the Non-Proliferation of Nuclear Weapons (NPT) was best articulated in the frequently quoted statement of President Kennedy who wrote in 1963, 'I see the possibility in the 1970s of the President of the United States having to face a world in which fifteen or twenty or twenty-five nations may have these (nuclear) weapons. I regard that as the greatest possible danger and hazard'.

For the majority of the non-nuclear-weapon States Party the statement in 1950 of Albert Einstein may be said to represent their apocalyptic vision which provided the driving force in subscribing to the Treaty. Einstein stated:

> The armament race between the USA and the USSR originally supposed to be a preventive measure, assumes hysterical character. On both sides, the means to mass destruction are perfected with feverish haste behind the respective walls of secrecy. The hydrogen bomb appears on the public horizon as a probably attainable goal. Its accelerated development has been solemnly proclaimed by the President. If it is successful, radioactive poisoning of the atmosphere and hence annihilation of any life on earth has been brought within the range of technical possibilities.

Neither of these worst scenarios have materialized. And yet these twin approaches represent the inherent dichotomy in the Treaty. One approaches the Treaty primarily as a device to freeze horizontal proliferation, and other considerations therefore flow from this. The other looks on the Treaty as primarily a disarmament measure where their own publicly proclaimed nuclear abstinence is verified through full-scope safeguards in a regime intended to build international confidence and security together with the development of nuclear energy for peaceful purposes. These perceptions remain unchanged generating the stresses and strains to which the Treaty is subject.

At the Thirty-ninth United Nations General Assembly sessions the Secretary-General in an extraordinarily outspoken statement said:

> As Secretary-General of this Organization, with no allegiance except to the common interest, I feel the question may justifiably be put to the leading nuclear-weapon Powers: by what right do they decide the fate of all humanity? From Scandinavia to Latin America, from Europe and Africa to the Far East, the destiny of every man and woman is affected by their actions. No one can expect to escape from the catastrophic consequences of a nuclear war on the fragile structure of our planet. The responsibility assumed by the great Powers is now no longer to their populations alone: it is to every country and every people, to all of us.

That statement expresses the widely-shared views of many of us present here and provides us with the perspective we need as we adopt a retrospective view of the NPT.

This opportunity of looking back on the functioning of the Treaty is timely. In two months in this city we begin the Third Review Conference of the NPT. The review of the NPT at five-yearly intervals as stipulated in Article VIII would normally be an important task. The Third Review Conference has an added importance for three reasons. First, it follows upon the failure of the Second Review Conference to agree on a Final Declaration representing a consensus view on the implementation of the NPT. Secondly, it takes place at a time when the vertical proliferation of nuclear armaments is at unprecedented levels and no disarmament agreements have been reached for several years. Finally, it is the penultimate Review Conference before the expiry of the present Treaty and we must think ahead to 1995 realizing that the success or failure of the Third Review Conference will necessarily have a major impact on our policy options in 1995.

We have come three-fifths of the way in the past fifteen years. The choice before us, as I have stated in the title of my address, is a choice between genuine nuclear partnership for peace or a nuclear apartheid arrangement perpetuating the present state of tension fraught with the danger of omnicide through a horrendous nuclear war followed by the certainty of a nuclear winter. The Parties to the Treaty therefore have a grave responsibility to be present at the Review Conference and to prepare themselves for it, bearing in mind that the First Review Conference was only attended by some 60 per cent of the Parties at the time and the Second Review by 64 per cent.

The making of the NPT in 1968 and its coming into force in 1970 was part of the process of detente which drew the super-Powers to work together for a safer world. The genesis of the proposal for a NPT did not lie with the super-Powers. We have to go back to the early 1960s when in the United Nations General Assembly an Irish proposal to prevent the spread of nuclear weapons to other countries led to Resolution 1665 (XVI) which was adopted unanimously on 4 December 1961. Later, on the basis of Resolution 2028 (XX), the Geneva Eighteen-Nation Disarmament Committee and, subsequently, the United Nations General Assembly finalized a Treaty which embodied obligations cast on nuclear-weapon States and non-nuclear-weapon States.

Those who stayed out of the regime did so in protest over the Treaty's deficiencies and in particular because of the imbalance between the renunciation of nuclear weapons with the acceptance of international control over their peaceful nuclear installations by non-nuclear-weapon countries, while nuclear-weapon States merely promised to negotiate a cessation of the nuclear arms race in good faith. Significantly none of the States outside the NPT declared its intention of developing nuclear weapons as the reason for not signing the Treaty at that time. Equally significantly none of them has stated unequivocally that they would join the Treaty if the perceived imbalances are removed.

The Treaty then must be seen as a product of the convergence of super-Power interests to work for international security as perceived commonly by them at the time. It is an interesting line of speculation to ponder what the super-Powers would have done if there were no NPT. How would they, for example, have prevented horizontal proliferation which would have been a threat to their security interests? Would we have had a series of pre-emptive strikes or threats of them on the nuclear installations of incipient nuclear Powers? Whatever the practicability of this alternative course may have been, clearly the establishment of an international legal regime outlawing the possession of nuclear weapons by countries other than the five nuclear Powers did have greater international acceptance.

Notwithstanding the many criticisms made of the NPT by those outside it and within it there are undeniable merits in the Treaty. The expansion of the number of adherents alone is proof of the wider acceptance of the Treaty—although one cannot exclude the element of bilateral pressures on countries by the nuclear-weapon States Party to join the Treaty. The larger countries who significantly remained outside the NPT in 1970 continue to be unimpressed by the virtues of the Treaty. At the entry into force of the Treaty in 1970, 43 countries were Parties to the NPT. Five years later at the First Review Conference there were 96 States Party. At the Second Review Conference in 1980 there were 118 States Party. Today on the eve of the Third Review Conference we have 128 countries. This increase in membership of the NPT regime is significant. The weighted decision-making process represented by the veto power of the five Powers in the Security Council has not prevented more and more nations joining the United Nations Organization. Similarly perceptions of an imbalance in the implementation of the NPT has not deterred countries from joining the Treaty.

A close analysis of some of the articles of the Treaty is useful. The key articles are Articles I and II; Articles III, IV and V and Article VI. Articles I and II should be viewed together. Compliance with Article II is verifiable while Article I is not, especially since there is a loophole allowing nuclear trade with non-NPT countries. While these articles represent the core of the Treaty, the all important link between them and Article VI represents the political keel of the Treaty. This inter-relationship between horizontal and vertical proliferation will be examined exclusively in Main Committee I of the Third Review Conference under the new three committee structure that has been agreed upon. The First Review Conference affirmed that Articles I and II were 'faithfully observed'. At the Second Review Conference significant voices were heard stating that if reports that Israel and South Africa were developing nuclear weapons were true, certain States Party to the Treaty may be tolerating it, if not actually assisting it. The Group of 77 working paper on these articles at the Second Review Conference, while expressing its conviction that Article II had been observed, stated that Article I had only been fulfilled in appearance, with no direct transfers taking place. The Group of 77 pointed to the fact that non-nuclear-weapon States Party to the Treaty who are exporters of nuclear materials, equipment and technology should also be bound by Article I. Another loophole pointed out during the debate was that one nuclear-weapon State could help another nuclear-weapon State in the nuclear weapon field, thereby promoting vertical proliferation. The adherence of the States Party to the Treaty to the letter of Articles I and II has never been in question. However, the nuclear capability of Israel, South Africa and certain other States who may be at the threshold and the source of their expertise and equipment will continue to concern the group of non-aligned and neutral States within the NPT. Horizontal proliferation among non-nuclear-weapon States Party to the NPT has of course remained non-controversial, although the stationing of nuclear weapons on the territory of non-nuclear-weapon States is being questioned as conduct inconsistent with obligations under these Articles.

International co-operation in the use of nuclear energy for peaceful purposes is promoted and supervised by the IAEA under Articles III and IV of the NPT. Discussion on the implementation of these two Articles at the First Review Conference was non-controversial and affirmed the importance of safeguards. At the Second Review Conference the fact that the development of the peaceful uses of nuclear energy was to be in the overall context of an effective non-proliferation regime was stressed. The needs of developing countries were also highlighted and mention was made of the inadequacy of technical assistance to them. There were critical references to nuclear trade and co-operation with non-Parties where safeguards were less stringent, giving the latter privileges despite their refusal to sign the NPT. No special advantages were discernible in terms of the supply of nuclear technology and material as a result of being within the NPT regime. Eventually consensus was reached on these Articles but was not adopted because no consensus was reached on a Final Declaration. Since the Second Review Conference the establishment of the Committee on Assurances of Supply (CAS) within IAEA has been welcomed. It has however been a continuing source of concern to developing countries that the volume of assistance has remained limited. Experts have noted that the attractions of nuclear energy as a source of power have waned mainly for economic and environmental reasons. IAEA estimates the world's installed nuclear capacity at 220 Gw(e) today which is 12 per cent of the world's total electricity generation—considerably lower than projections made in the past. Despite this, NPT members would like nuclear technology to be easily and cheaply available, especially in the form of small- and medium-power reactors and for agriculture. Otherwise the so-called 'bargain' of renouncing nuclear weapons for peaceful nuclear technology would be a hollow one. In addition the security of nuclear installations under safeguards has been of serious concern after the Israeli attack on the Osirak reactor in Iraq.

The role of the IAEA, which is not an international policeman and has no sanctions to apply, has received praise and the efficacy of safeguards has not been questioned. The extension of safeguards, a greater transparency in their implementation and the full attainment of inspection goals has, however, been persistently advocated. Safeguards must be made comprehensive, more difficult to circumvent and fully applicable to nuclear trade throughout the world for greater accountability of all nuclear material and the prevention of any clandestine diversion. The IAEA's Safeguards Implementation Report for 1984 states that 39 non-nuclear-weapon States Party to the NPT have not yet complied with their obligations under Article III.4 of the Treaty regarding the conclusion of relevant safeguards agreements and out of them one State has 'significant nuclear activities'. The same report also contains a disturbing reference to an export of depleted uranium to an unnamed country which could not be adequately accounted for. While it is true that safeguards agreements are limited and are also not restricted to countries within the NPT or the Tlatelolco Treaty it remains disquieting that there is discrimination in the nature of safeguards agreements of nuclear-weapon and non-nuclear-weapon States Party to the NPT. There is a cogent case for making safeguards agreements uniform and mandatory for all States Party to the NPT.

Article VI of the Treaty has been and remains the most controversial

Article. The First Review Conference, while noting that horizontal proliferation was promoted by the cessation of the nuclear arms race, welcomed the various agreements on arms limitation and disarmament and appealed for an early and effective implementation of this Article. Protocols were proposed but were not accepted by the nuclear-weapon States. At the Second Review Conference, in the absence of an agreed Final Declaration, the President in his statement expressed disappointment in the way this Article was being honoured, noting that the arms race was in fact being intensified qualitatively and quantitatively. The non-nuclear-weapon States have stated repeatedly that the NPT was not intended to confer legitimacy on the possession of nuclear weapons by some countries or to perpetuate this monopoly. It sought rather to halt proliferation both horizontally and vertically. The years since 1980 have witnessed a deterioration in the situation and the Third Review Conference will doubtless see a sharp criticism of the nuclear-weapon States for the escalation of the arms race involving the realm of outer space as well. Armaments expenditure is running at $1,000 billion per annum; there are an estimated 50,000 nuclear warheads poised to destroy human lives and property and every year nuclear tests are conducted (43 by the USA and the USSR in 1984 alone) in order to refine these weapons of mass destruction. The admission of the non-implementation of Article VI without a corresponding commitment to halt the arms race will not satisfy the non-aligned and neutral States. Controversy therefore swirls around this Article, threatening the success of the Review Conference. The nuclear-weapon States will submit, as background documentation for the Review Conference, reports on their compliance with Article VI of the Treaty.

Security assurances to non-nuclear-weapon States have failed to satisfy those countries whose security is endangered in any nuclear war, however 'limited' it may be. Article VII raises the question as to why nuclear-weapon-free zones have to be confined to some areas and are not global in their coverage.

What then are the prospects for the Third Review Conference and for the future of the Treaty? The assiduous wooing of the non-nuclear-weapon States by the depositary States has revealed a unique convergence of views among them in upholding the NPT and a truce on mutual recrimination within the NPT context. A number of cosmetic moves will no doubt be resorted to in order to provide some basis for the claim that negotiations 'in good faith' have in fact taken place. Behind the efforts being made is a smug complacency that despite the public statements of some of the non-nuclear-weapon States they will, in the final analysis, hold back from the brink of an actual withdrawal from the NPT regime. In fact no Party to the NPT has expressed a desire to leave the regime. They have signed and ratified the Treaty in the conviction that it does make the world a safer place to live in. Their reservations about the manner in which the nuclear-weapon States and some non-nuclear-weapon States have fulfilled their obligations under the Treaty, serious as they are, do not lead to a rejection of the Treaty. No one wants to throw the baby out with the bath water. Despite this the non-aligned and neutral States wield considerable influence within the NPT regime and can use this constructively to obtain full compliance with all the provisions of the Treaty from the nuclear-weapon States Party. That means that the efforts of the non-nuclear-weapon States and, in particular, the non-aligned and neutral States, must be to make proposals in a spirit of constructive criticism in order to improve the Treaty, increasing its viability and credibility so that in 1995 there will be no controversy about extending its life for a further defined period. Their attendance in strength will enable them to obtain the working majority of voting—which is necessary by the Rules of Procedure (Rule 28)—in the face of a failure to achieve consensus.

Various proposals are already being discussed. There is no indication that they will enjoy consensus. One cynical response has been that these proposals will not induce countries outside the NPT to sign it and therefore the status quo should remain. That attitude reminds me of the story of the Prodigal Son in the Bible. The proposals must be viewed collectively since they apply to different parts of the Treaty. It would be invidious and unwise to focus on any one of them as a price demanded for the adoption by consensus of a Final Declaration at the Review Conference. For example, enhanced technical assistance to NPT developing countries alone will not satisfy these countries. Critics may consider the proposals as a mere tinkering with the system or window-dressing and not a fundamental change. Revolutionary change is only necessary when moderate reforms are not made at the appropriate time. That time is now. A comprehensive test ban as envisaged in the Preamble to the NPT is the most popular step recommended as proof that Article VI is being implemented. At the minimum, steps towards this as an earnest of 'good faith' will help, although demands for a renunciation of nuclear weapons, a freeze and agreement on 'no first use' are among the many proposals being advanced. The verifiability of a CTBT is only doubted by those who lack the political will to agree to this step and flies in the face of all scientific evidence. An agreement to protect nuclear installations under safeguard from attacks, the application of full-scope safeguards on exports to non-Parties so as to block the loophole in Article III.2, and improved technical co-operation arrangements, such as a fund for assistance to developing countries with extra-budgetary money from donors within IAEA, are other proposals. There is also a proposal to separate and place under IAEA safeguards civilian nuclear facilities and material as distinct from military facilities and material in nuclear-weapon States. An improvement of IAEA Safeguards to take into account new technologies like laser beam separation, the true internationalization of the fuel cycle, and the prevention of the transfer of plutonium from civil to military projects are also advocated.

Legally binding international security assurances for non-nuclear-weapon States are proposed. There will no doubt be more proposals that will surface. Some will be proposed at this Symposium. I would like to pay tribute to the many dedicated groups outside Governments who are working on proposals in preparation for the Third Review Conference.

There are some positive aspects in the international scene relevant to the review of the NPT which must be acknowledged. While the number of States joining the NPT regime has increased it must be noted that China has joined the IAEA and may hopefully subject itself to safeguards in some limited form in the future. China has also announced its intention to join in the work of an *Ad hoc* Committee on Nuclear Test Ban in the Conference on Disarmament if and when it is established. The USSR last year signed an agreement with the IAEA to place part of its civilian programme under IAEA safeguards. The number of nuclear-weapon countries has not increased although we continue to have grave doubts about those on the threshold. As against this the nuclear arms race continues in a more intensified form. Five nuclear-weapon Powers may be more than enough but there are still five too many. We desperately need a New International Security Order with general and complete disarmament before any other order can be viable or meaningful since our very existence hinges on it. A greatly strengthened Non-Proliferation Treaty with a truly equitable balance of duties and obligations is an important element in this.

ARTICLE III AND TECHNOLOGY AND SAFEGUARDS

The Role of the IAEA and the Existing NPT Regime

DR. HANS BLIX

Director General, International Atomic Energy Agency

Introduction

This Colloqium is focusing upon the Treaty on the Non-Proliferation of Nuclear Weapons (NPT). At the outset we should be aware however that the objective we are really seeking is to prevent the spread of nuclear weapons to further countries. Although the NPT is undoubtedly the most important treaty in this field, the same objective is served by regional arrangements such as the Tlatelolco Treaty for the Prohibition of Nuclear Weapons in Latin America. Even unilateral declarations containing commitments not to acquire nuclear weapons may be of great significance. Our starting point is the awareness that the existence of five nuclear-weapon States and the continuing escalation of the nuclear arms race has already placed humanity in jeopardy. Tangible steps towards nuclear disarmament, to begin with a Comprehensive Test Ban Treaty, would considerably improve the atmosphere in which the discussion of horizontal proliferation takes place. There is something paradoxical about nuclear-weapon States desperately urging non-nuclear-weapon States not to do what they, themselves, find it indispensable to do: namely to continue developing nuclear weapons.

Seen from the global vantage point, however, there can be little doubt that the world would become an even more dangerous place with more nuclear-weapon States. But the main reason for the success the world has had so far in slowing down the spread of nuclear weapons is that the majority of States have found it in their national interest not to go nuclear in the military sense. Several factors influence this national policy decision: alliances and availability of outside protection against nuclear attacks, security guarantees, geopolitical situations, neighbours' attitudes, or economic or supply advantages linked to a forgoing of the nuclear weapons option. These same factors have led, as we have heard, some 125 non-nuclear-weapon

States to ratify the NPT, making it the most widely adhered to arms control agreement in history.

The first and foremost barrier to non-proliferation thus remains the *political* conviction of the individual State. Commitments to non-proliferation, whether unilateral or through adherence to the NPT or other treaties, increase the international credibility of a State's declared intention not to go nuclear and constitute what you might term a *legal* barrier to proliferation.

Verification through international safeguards also serves to increase the credibility of the commitment and may be said to constitute a *third* barrier to proliferation. Non-proliferation is the only area of arms control where institutionalized international verification, including inspections *in loco*, has been established. I intend to concentrate my remarks today on the means at the disposal of the International Atomic Energy Agency (IAEA) to verify compliance with NPT commitments.

Role of the IAEA and transfer of technology

The IAEA has two main roles: to promote the peaceful uses of nuclear energy and to apply safeguards to assist in the efforts to prevent the further spread of nuclear weapons. Are these tasks compatible? Will not—it is sometimes asked—the spread of peaceful nuclear technology *inevitably* lead to acquisition of nuclear weapons capability? While some knowledge, techniques and equipment in civilian nuclear technology may be useful for weapons development as well and while preparations for manufacturing nuclear weapons may occur behind an ostensibly civil nuclear programme, it is clear that even if all civilian nuclear reactors in the world were dismantled, the ability to make nuclear weapons would remain and would be available to any State that had an adequate infrastructure and was ready to devote sufficient resources for the purpose.

Denial of technology may slow down a State trying to develop nuclear weapons, but cannot, in the long run, prevent proliferation and may in fact encourage some States to try to achieve autarchy and to opt out of international co-operation.

There is, in fact, a forum within the IAEA in which the delicate balance between non-proliferation guarantees and assurances of nuclear supplies is discussed and one could even say negotiated. That is the Committee on Assurances of Supply (CAS) which has been working since the Second NPT Review Conference in 1980 to elaborate generally accepted principles of international co-operation in the field of nuclear energy. Compared to five years ago, there is a greater measure of common understanding on this issue, not least because in most technologies and fuel cycle services there is now a buyer's market and there hardly exist any economic incentives to develop enrichment and reprocessing capacity. The main obstacle for starting and developing nuclear programmes in developing countries Party to NPT is not restricted supply, but the difficulty in raising the necessary capital. The transfer of other applications of nuclear technology, for instance in agriculture, in medicine and industry, has continued to increase and the IAEA's Technical Assistance and Co-operation Fund, is a chief means of financing such transfers. However, there remains much room for increased co-operation in this field and industrialized countries wishing better to respond to the demands of developing countries under Article IV of the NPT might simply increase the resources they channel for technical assistance through the IAEA. These resources presently stand at a modest 30 million dollars per year.

Safeguards

Article III of the NPT requires non-nuclear-weapon States Parties to accept IAEA safeguards on all their nuclear activities—what we term full-scope safeguards. So far 80 agreements have been concluded, others remain to be made, but practically all in respect of countries with no significant nuclear activities. Special technical possibilities to verify peaceful uses of nuclear energy exist because nuclear materials have unique properties and installations where such material is handled also have special characteristics. Both because of their value and their radioactivity, nuclear materials must be handled very carefully, controlled and accounted for by the operator himself. Radioactivity permits identification and measurements and, as you know, there are only two materials usable for nuclear weapons: highly-enriched uranium and plutonium.

The monitoring function performed by the IAEA is carried out by some 180 inspectors, backed up by another 70 officials at Headquarters, who visit nuclear reactors, fuel element factories, reprocessing and enrichment plants, spent fuel storages, and other installations in countries accepting the control. Nuclear materials accounting, that is to say books and inventories, indicating changes in inventions, are checked, seals are applied to verify that possible diversion routes are closed, samples are analysed, cameras continuously monitor when inspectors are absent and so on.

The safeguards system is built on several technical elements which together verify that no fissionable material is diverted.

First, information on technical characteristics of nuclear installations has to be provided to the Agency before safeguards can begin. This of course enables the Agency to identify possible routes of diversion that must be controlled.

Secondly, accounting of nuclear materials and operating records of nuclear facilities are to be maintained by nuclear plant operators; that is to say the operator must be able to show at all times where his fissionable material is.

Third, regular accounting reports of all nuclear material under safeguards are to be transmitted to the Agency. If abnormal events occur which may result in a loss of material, special reports from the operators are required.

Fourth, agency inspectors inspect the nuclear installations and material to check that the nuclear material is where it is reported to be.

Lastly, so-called containment and surveillance devices are applied; that is to say seals are applied preventing any undiscovered use of diversion routes and the same applies to the television cameras that take thousands of pictures at irregular intervals to make sure that no diversion occurs.

Safeguards have expanded greatly in scope; they cover now 98 per cent of all the nuclear activities in non-nuclear-weapon States. This whole system, covering about 900 nuclear installations in the world, at present costs some US$30 million a year to operate. It has been a long way from the first inspection of 3 tonnes of natural uranium in 1958 to today's system employing sophisticated instruments, handling around 800,000 data a year and covering some of the most advanced industrial plants. The sensitivity of the system is evidenced in the some 400, mostly minor, anomalies and discrepancies which were discovered and cleared up with national authorities in 1984.

The acceptance of safeguards is sometimes described as a limitation upon national sovereignty. In my view this is an erroneous way of regarding the system. The Agency's safeguards provide a second check on national—and in the case of EURATOM, regional—systems of accountancy and control which each State must set up for its own regulation and control of the use and movements of nuclear materials. Further—and this is the internationally essential part—it provides a kind of service similar to that of an external auditor. States wish to generate maximum confidence in the continuously peaceful nature of their nuclear activities and the IAEA safeguards system helps them to do so. Research and development of new safeguards technology is carried out both in Member States and at IAEA Headquarters and the system is constantly renewed as it expands.

The end product of our safeguards operations is a statement on the conclusions we have drawn as a result of our verification activities. While these statements are not public, the Agency each year provides to the Board of Governors—representing 35 States—a special *Safeguards Implementation Report* which reports in detail on the safeguards activities which have been carried out in the past year. The general conclusions drawn are also published in the Agency's Annual Report which is submitted to the United Nations General Assembly.

How useful have IAEA safeguards been as a barrier against the proliferation of nuclear weapons? Before answering that question one must clarify the first objective of safeguards. It has sometimes been said that the purpose of the control is to *deter* States from cheating. They might be caught in the act. However, one must be careful in using this argument. States invite safeguards verification not to deter themselves from cheating, but to create a maximum of confidence in the peaceful nature of their nuclear programmes. Verification, as a means of confidence-building is thus the first objective of safeguards and it is justified to see the system, as I said a while ago, as a service rather than as any encroachment upon sovereignty. However, in order effectively to create confidence, the system must be sensitive enough to *detect* in a timely way the diversion of any significant quantity of nuclear material from peaceful nuclear activities to other purposes should it occur. Thus the IAEA safeguards system must have the capacity to function as an alarm bell; it cannot, on the other hand, *prevent* a State from breaking its Treaty obligations if the State is intent on doing so. The *timely* warning sounded by the system, however, should give States the chance to act—singly or collectively, with diplomatic, economic or political means—to influence the State in question.

The first inherent limitation in IAEA safeguards is thus that they are not intended physically to prevent proliferation—we are not a nuclear police—but to *detect* and thereby, if needed, to *deter* proliferation. Some sanctions are foreseen within the IAEA, for instance the cutting off of nuclear assistance, but the most important sanction is referral of the case to the United Nations Security Council. The IAEA is the only UN Agency with a direct link to the UN Security Council.

A second evident limitation is that IAEA safeguards can only cover installations declared and submitted to it. They can say nothing about unsafeguarded installations in States not Parties to NPT or for which the Tlatelolco Treaty is not yet in operation. Nor can they seek out clandestine facilities, if there were any. The weakest link in the effort to prevent further horizontal proliferation, I submit, is not any weakness in existing safeguards, but the existence of nuclear facilities which some States have not been willing to submit to safeguards.

A third inherent limitation in the safeguards system is that it cannot, and was never intended to, predict future intentions and decisions of States. It is concerned with measurable and observable actions. It is for governments to assess intentions. Acting somewhat like a radar scan, safeguards confirm that a facility at any given moment is being used for a legitimate peaceful purpose or warn that it cannot make such a statement or that material has been diverted.

To sum up my answer about the effectiveness of safeguards. No, safeguards cannot *prevent* nuclear proliferation nor were they ever intended to do so. Indeed, no arms control verification system can physically ensure compliance. Safeguards *can* give assurance that nuclear material is maintained in a peaceful fuel cycle and can detect a diversion and bring it to the attention of the international community. The real proliferation problems begin where safeguards end, *not* in the majority of countries which have accepted NPT or the Tlatelolco Treaty.

IAEA safeguards have been subjected to much criticism. Constructive criticism is helpful and the system continues to evolve and to be consolidated. However, the criticism has often been unjustified or based on unreasonable expectations. Especially after the Israeli armed attack on an Iraqi nuclear installation under IAEA safeguards, there was a body of opinion that used the occasion to reinforce their view that safeguards were 'weak' or 'without teeth' or 'unable to stop diversion'. The actual situation was that safeguards had been applied in a normal fashion. Neither before nor after the attack was there anything indicating any diversion of fissionable material. There has been speculation that the Israeli attack might have been aimed at presumed Iraqi intentions rather than actions. However that may be, Israel has since, on several occasions, expressed its appreciation of the safeguards system.

Reflections on the Non-Proliferation Treaty

The NPT has three basic goals: first, to prevent the spread of nuclear weapons to further States; second, to promote the peaceful uses of nuclear energy; and third, to encourage negotiations among the nuclear-weapon States leading to a cessation of the nuclear arms race. In addition one might say, NPT manifests the dominant international view that the acquisition of nuclear weapons is not a legitimate goal. Even those countries which remain outside the Treaty have no stated policy of developing nuclear weapons, but rather insist on the peaceful nature of their nuclear activities.

There are many who would argue that the main objective of the Treaty—to prevent the proliferation of nuclear weapons—would be sufficient reason for a majority of States to join. Among Parties, there is no serious criticism of the way in which the Treaty has worked in regard to this first, basic objective. States *outside* the Treaty have voiced criticism of these Articles, on the basis of their being discriminatory in the sense that all restraints and controls are being applied to non-nuclear-weapon States and not to nuclear-weapon States. The different obligations of nuclear-weapon States and non-nuclear-weapon States were, however, freely accepted by all Parties; the Treaty was negotiated in a multilateral forum and was commended to all States by the United Nations General Assembly.

The third objective of NPT—to encourage nuclear disarmament—has certainly not been fulfilled. Others are covering this subject during this Colloquium, but I would just like to share with you an IAEA perspective on the issue. In connection with NPT, but outside the requirements of the Treaty, the three nuclear-weapon States depositaries and France have now made voluntary offers to accept IAEA safeguards on their peaceful nuclear facilities. Under these agreements safeguards are already being implemented in the United States, the United Kingdom and France; the first inspection in the Soviet Union is planned for this summer. The importance of these offers is not immediately in the field of non-proliferation. They do, however, give us the first experience of verification activities in nuclear-weapon States and may help pave the way for the verification which will be required in more far-reaching arms control and disarmament agreements, for instance a cut-off on the production of special fissionable material. Originally inspired by a desire to demonstrate that nuclear-weapon States saw no commercial or other disadvantage in accepting safeguards on peaceful nuclear installations, this acceptance by them as by the non-nuclear-weapon States, I submit, is a breakthrough in the area of verification in which arms control agreements have so often foundered.

The greatest challenge to the non-proliferation effort is the achievement of universality of acceptance. To achieve this a non-nuclear-weapon status must be made attractive to those few, but important, States that remain outside its scope, if these States are to join. Such commitment would not necessarily have to be NPT membership. It could also be done through the Tlatelolco or other future regional treaties, through mutual declarations or acceptance of full-scope safeguards. A major set-back is any military attack on a peaceful nuclear installation under safeguards. The whole idea of a non-proliferation regime is to give one's neighbours and potential adversaries assurances of the peaceful nature of installations. If any doubt were to persist in this regard, the international legal framework to investigate it should be pursued.

The world has been remarkably successful so far in preventing a spread of nuclear weapons to further countries. There is a high degree of international goodwill as regards co-operation in the peaceful uses of nuclear energy and China's taking up membership in the IAEA is indicative of the practical usefulness which that country attaches to peaceful nuclear co-operation. What remains is for the nuclear-weapon-States to take advantage of this relatively stable situation and negotiate real reductions in the world's nuclear arsenals. The risk of horizontal proliferation represents a potential threat. The some 50,000 existing nuclear warheads subject us all to an actual threat of extinction.

The Foundations for a Strengthened Non-Proliferation Regime

PROFESSOR JOSEPH ROTBLAT

Professor Emeritus of Physics, University of London

1. Vertical and horizontal proliferation

The danger of nuclear war is perceived as coming from two possible sources, commonly described as vertical and horizontal proliferation. The first refers to the growing intensity of the nuclear arms race between the super-Powers; the second to the spread of nuclear weapons among many nations. In attempts to prevent both types of proliferation a number of international treaties have been negotiated during the last few decades; some of these negotiations were successful, but attempts at others—for example, the Comprehensive Test Ban Treaty—have failed so far.

Most of the agreements were on vertical proliferation, e.g., the Partial Test Ban Treaty, ABM, SALT I, SALT II (adhered to so far although not formally ratified), but despite these treaties the arms race continued unabated, both qualitatively and quantitatively. Since the fission bomb of 1945, at least five quantum jumps can be identified: the H-bomb, ICBM, MIRV, GLCM (ground-launched Cruise missiles) and SDI (popularly called 'Star Wars'). Quantitatively, the strategic arsenals of both sides have been growing throughout the years, reaching a total of more than 20,000 warheads.

On the other hand, in regard to horizontal proliferation there has been only one treaty, the Nuclear Non-Proliferation Treaty (NPT), and this has stood firm ever since it came into force in 1970. Despite dire predictions (cf. William Epstein, *The Last Chance*, 1975) there has been no addition to the number of nuclear-weapon States since 1964. Not one of the 125 non-nuclear-weapon States Party to the Treaty has violated it. Even the 42 States that refused to join the NPT (Table 1) have not violated the main terms of the Treaty overtly, although there are persistent rumours that a few of them have acquired, or are in the process of acquiring, nuclear weapons, or nuclear weapon capabilities.

Notwithstanding the demonstrated stability of the NPT regime, there are strong fears that it may break down. Indeed, the moment of that breakdown has been pin-pointed with great precision: September 1985, at the Third NPT Review Conference. Many analysts predict that the resentment which some NPT members have nourished for a long time—and egged on by some non-NPT States apparently determined to kill the Treaty—will find open expression in notices of withdrawal, possibly followed by steps towards the acquisition of nuclear weapons.

The danger of such happening is real. Should it materialize the consequences could be disastrous; it would certainly make a dangerous situation even more perilous. Therefore, every effort must be made to prevent it. But we should aim further than such a negative purpose. Not only should member States be persuaded not to take steps that would aggravate the situation, but the opportunity of the Third Review Conference should be taken for a positive endeavour to strengthen the Treaty. We should build on the substantial and propitious changes that have occurred since 1970, to consolidate the NPT and ensure its continuance after it comes to the end of its present term in 1995.

Ten years is not a long time for international negotiations. The 1985 Review Conference should begin to concern itself with the post-1995 period; it should set itself the positive task of preparing a new formulation of the NPT which would ensure a more equitable and durable non-proliferation regime and make membership of the Treaty universal.

2. The weaknesses of the present NPT

The postulate of this paper is that the NPT is a very important international agreement that must be supported and strengthened. But this does not mean that its weaknesses should be swept under the carpet. They have to be exposed if we are to remedy them and produce a healthier Treaty.

(*a*) *Violation of the NPT by the nuclear-weapon States*

A critical evaluation of the performance of the NPT regime must begin with a severe censure of the nuclear-weapon members of the Treaty for their violation, both in letter and in spirit, of their undertakings.

Article I of the Treaty obliges nuclear-weapon States not to transfer nuclear weapons, or the control over such weapons, directly or indirectly, to other States. Yet, this is what has been practised for a long time by NATO. The most recent example is the placing by the USA of Pershing II missiles in the Federal Republic of Germany and Cruise missiles in Belgium and Italy (and exerting pressure on the Netherlands to accept such missiles). Although the details of the agreements about control over these weapons—whether the 'dual key' or some other 'joint decision' system—are not known, there is no doubt that these countries would have at least indirect control over nuclear weapons, in violation of the terms of the Treaty.

This criticism applies also to the stationing of Cruise missiles in the United Kingdom, since Article I refers to 'any recipient whatsoever'.

The Soviet Union has recently stationed some of its SS-20 launchers in Czechoslovakia and the German Democratic Republic. It is not known whether some control arrangement is involved, but the same accusation would apply, if it were.

It should also be noted that under Article II, countries which accept nuclear weapons on their territory and exercise direct or indirect control over them, are also in violation of the NPT.

Article VI is the main bone of contention between many NPT members and the nuclear-weapon States Party to the Treaty. Under this Article, these States undertook 'to pursue negotiations in good faith on effective measures relating to the cessation of the nuclear arms race . . . and to nuclear disarmament'. The history of the nuclear arms race over the past 15 years throws very serious doubt on the good faith, as well as on the capability of the super-Powers to fulfil their obligations, caught as they are in the action-reaction syndrome. Because of this, even during the 'on-periods' of negotiations on arms control, very little progress has been achieved and—as was pointed out—the very few measures agreed to were dwarfed by the qualitative and quantitative intensification of the arms race.

This failure of the nuclear-weapon States was the chief reason for the breakdown of the Second Review Conference in 1980; if so, there is real danger that the same may happen in 1985. A number of non-aligned countries are said to threaten to withdraw from the Treaty, because they can see no validity in a treaty systematically violated by its 'privileged' members. However, it is doubtful whether such threats can carry sufficient force to induce the nuclear Powers to make progress towards the reduction of nuclear arms, as long as they continue with their present policies of negotiating from a position of strength (the argument used for the need of more MX missiles and even for SDI), and—more importantly—as long as they continue to believe that the development and deployment of new offensive and defensive systems are necessary to remove the vulnerability created by the earlier systems.

Yet—quite apart from the resentment about violating an undertaking—there is a genuine and legitimate reason for the concern among the non-nuclear-weapon States, particularly from the Third World, about the lack of progress towards nuclear disarmament. They are increasingly worried about the danger of a nuclear war, which the continuing and accelerating arms race is making more probable.

In the past, many Third World countries considered a nuclear war to be an issue for the North only. As far as they were concerned it was a diversion from the real problem, the need to raise the standard of living in the poor countries. Leaders of these countries used to tell the North: 'If you want to kill each other off in a nuclear war, it is your funeral; we do not want to have anything to do with it.' This argument was never tenable, bearing in mind the interdependence of all peoples on the globe, but it is the 'nuclear winter' phenomenon that has finally put an end to this isolationist myth. It is now generally recognized that a nuclear war could affect everybody, even if all the weapons were detonated in the higher latitudes of the northern hemisphere. Indeed, the tropical zones, in which many of the Third World peoples live, might be hit hardest, because their agriculture is much more vulnerable to a reduction of temperature.

We may, therefore, expect even stronger pressure on the nuclear-weapon States to take significant steps to reduce the danger of a nuclear war.

(*b*) *The link between nuclear technology and nuclear weapons*

Articles II and IV contain a trade-off for the non-nuclear-weapon States. Under Article II they undertake not to acquire nuclear weapons, and under Article IV they receive the reward for this undertaking, i.e., help in developing nuclear technology for peaceful purposes. The allegation that this help had not been forthcoming sufficiently free and fast was one of the main bones of contention at the previous Review Conferences.

The ethics of this bargain has always been dubious: why should one be rewarded for giving up something that is bad for one in any case? That the possession of nuclear weapons is undesirable is explicitly spelled out in the Preamble to the Treaty, which states 'that the proliferation of nuclear weapons would seriously enhance the danger of nuclear war', as well as in the text, which calls for nuclear disarmament. If so, why should a State that gives it up be entitled to demand compensation? Paradoxically, the nature of the compensation is such as to make it easier for a country to do the very thing it undertakes not to do: to make nuclear weapons; because it could utilize for such purpose the help it had received in building up its nuclear know-how. It is as if a person who gives up smoking is offered a cigarette-making machine as a reward.

This is not an argument against sharing of nuclear, or any technology; it is an argument against it being used as a bargain. That Articles II and IV are a straightforward trade-off was confirmed during an important public inquiry about a reprocessing plant to be set up in the United Kingdom; the Chairman of that Inquiry—a Judge who presumably is an authority on legal interpretation—said the following in his report:

> The NPT is on its face a straightforward bargain. The essence of that bargain was that, in exchange for an undertaking from non-nuclear weapon Parties to refrain from making or acquiring nuclear weapons and to submit to safeguards when provided for peaceful purposes with material which was capable of diversion, the nuclear-weapon States would afford every assistance to non-nuclear-weapon States 'in the development of nuclear energy' . . . I also find it difficult to see how a Party, which has developed reprocessing technology or created reprocessing facilities, would be otherwise than in breach of the agreement, if it both refused to supply the technology to another Party and refused to reprocess for it.

Whatever the intentions and the legal arguments about the bargain, the facts show that in this respect the existence of the Treaty has not made any difference. The situation—both in relation to the non-acquisition of nuclear weapons and the acquisition of nuclear technology—appears to be the same in all countries, whether they have joined the Treaty or not.

Take first the undertaking not to make or acquire nuclear weapons. One might have expected that at least some of the countries that refused to sign the Treaty—and therefore gave no such undertaking—would have by now made or acquired nuclear weapons. Yet, after 15 years, not one of the 42 non-members of the NPT has done so overtly. Even India, which detonated a nuclear 'device' in 1974, claims that the intention was to explore the peaceful applications of nuclear explosives. Israel and South Africa never admitted to having nuclear weapons. Pakistan strenuously denies that it is preparing nuclear weapons. The same applies to Argentina and Brazil. These six countries are generally denoted as 'potential nuclear-weapon States', but no suspicion has ever been levelled at the great majority of the countries which refused to sign the Treaty (Table 1). On the other hand, suspicions have been levelled at some countries that did sign the Treaty, such as Iraq and Libya.

Except for a few such cases, one may presume that even in the absence of the NPT, it is very unlikely that its present adherents would have decided to embark overtly on a nuclear weapons programme. Making of nuclear weapons is simply 'not on' in the present climate and this applies both to members and non-members of the NPT.

A similar conclusion is reached in relation to the other end of the bargain, the help in the development of nuclear energy. The criteria of nuclear facilities for peaceful purposes are not well defined. Many countries have research reactors, but these cover a very wide range of power outputs and degree of enrichment of the uranium. It is also not always clear to what extent these reactors are used, if at all. A criterion much better defined is the operation—actual or planned—of at least one reactor for the generation of electricity. In Table 2, the countries with such programmes are listed, sub-divided into three groups: with reactors already in operation, under construction, and being planned. Considering the time needed to build a reactor (which, on average, has increased during the last decade from six to ten years), this may be taken as the total number of States with nuclear power generation by the year 1995, when the NPT comes to the end of its present term.

Table 2 shows that 25 of the 125 countries that have signed the Treaty, that is 20 per cent, already have, or soon will have, or plan to have nuclear power for electricity. Among the countries that have not signed the Treaty, the corresponding figure is 8 out of 42, that is 19 per cent. We must conclude that despite the clamour for help by some countries, membership of the Treaty has not made a significant difference in this respect.

Another part of the Treaty is also relevant to this discussion. Under Article III, Parties to the Treaty agree to submit to IAEA safeguards. But such submission is not exclusive to members of the NPT. The IAEA safeguards have wider application: a number of countries which have not signed the NPT but have nuclear power programmes, have agreed to submit to the safeguards (they are marked with an asterisk in Table 1). The same applies to other agreements about supply of materials. So, once again, there is little difference between belonging or not belonging to the NPT. Indeed, there have been complaints that NPT members were treated worse than non-members.

It is also important to note that all five nuclear-weapon States—although not obliged by the terms of the Treaty—have voluntarily agreed to submit all or some of their civil nuclear programmes to IAEA safeguards.

3. The great importance of the NPT

The discussion in the previous section might lead one to conclude that the existence of the NPT did not make a significant difference to the major objectives for which it was set up and that therefore it is unnecessary. However, one can also come to the reverse conclusion: that the NPT did play a vital role and its continuation is most important for world security. It is this conclusion that is advanced in this paper.

In the NPT, three-quarters of all nations have put their signature to a solemn undertaking not to acquire nuclear weapons. They have all adhered to it faithfully during the past 15 years. This very fact has created a new climate in world opinion on nuclear issues, a climate hostile to the possession of nuclear weapons. As a result of this, any country—whether a member of the NPT or not—that openly declares that it has acquired, or intends to acquire, nuclear weapons would incur such an opprobrium, there would be such an outcry of public opinion, with possible economic and political repercussions, that only in extreme desperation, or due to the insanity or swashbuckling of a leader, would a country take such a step. Whatever the original motive may have been, the NPT has now become the formal expression of the instinctive feeling of people everywhere that nuclear weapons are evil and must be got rid of as soon as possible.

Even so, there is still the danger that the acquisition of nuclear weapons by one country—for one of the unlikely reasons mentioned above—could have a domino effect; neighbouring countries suddenly feeling threatened and compelled to take similar action, and so on. It is of the utmost importance to prevent such a situation. In this respect, an important step would be a declaration by 'potential nuclear-weapon States'—particularly Israel and South Africa, which do not discourage rumours that they already have nuclear weapons—that they do not intend to acquire such weapons. This would considerably allay fears in neighbouring countries.

Notwithstanding the initial reasons for the specific formulation of the Articles in the Treaty—the trade-offs and compromises between the negotiating Parties—there appears to have been a genuine and fundamental change since the sixties. We should build on that change in world opinion in proposing a new formulation of the NPT which would make it stand on its own feet; the renunciation of nuclear weapons would not have to be part of a bargain.

However strongly we may feel about the violation of Article VI, the present situation is still preferable to the alternative: no Treaty, or a weakened Treaty by the withdrawal of a significant number of its members. Such a step would signal the beginning of overt horizontal proliferation and we shall all be in a much more dangerous situation.

Not only must this be avoided, but we must concentrate our efforts on bringing in the 42 non-nuclear-weapon States that have so far refused to join the NPT. In the following sections reasons will be presented that should appeal to these States and make the Treaty truly universal. This, in turn, would make it possible to exert stronger pressure on the nuclear-weapon States to fulfil their obligations, and thus to achieve the ultimate aim of the Treaty, nuclear disarmament.

4. The changed situation since 1970

As already indicated, the situation in 1985 is in many ways radically different from that prevailing at the time the NPT was being negotiated. In most aspects the difference is such as to make it easier to draw up a more equitable Treaty, when the matter of its extension is decided in 1995. Four of these aspects will be reviewed here.

(*a*) *More suppliers of nuclear technology*

In the initial period, the nuclear-weapon States were—apart from Canada—the only ones capable of supplying nuclear technology to other countries. This ceased to be the case some time ago. Apart from members of the NPT, such as the Federal Republic of Germany, even non-NPT members, such as Argentina or Spain, are now suppliers of material, equipment and know-how. The terms offered are often more attractive, and carry fewer conditions—resented by many countries as restricting their sovereignty—than those stipulated by nuclear-weapon States. While we hope that this would not result in a lowering of standards of safeguards, the fact is that the link between Articles II and IV is now of little relevance.

(*b*) *Decreased importance of nuclear energy*

An even more important reason for the reduced emphasis on nuclear technology in the NPT is the changed attitude towards nuclear energy. In the earlier years, many Third World countries became convinced—to a large extent thanks to the promotional drive of the IAEA—that nuclear power would be the best solution to their energy problems. The glamour which was then attached to this new source of energy was an additional factor; some leaders of less-developed countries coveted the prestige which would accrue from the possession of the most advanced technology. And, of course, one cannot exclude the conscious or subliminal motive of having the means to convert the facilities of a peaceful nuclear power programme to military purposes, should the need for this arise.

All this has changed to a very large extent. Even industrialized countries have encountered many difficulties with their nuclear power programmes, especially since some aspects of it, such as waste disposal, are still unresolved and may remain so for a long time. The Three-Mile Island accident—even though it did not result in a disaster—has alerted the public to the possibility of human error leading to grave consequences; the need for more protection has contributed to the considerable increase in capital costs of reactors. For developing countries this has made the economic advantages of nuclear energy even more doubtful. Furthermore, there has been an upsurge of public opinion against nuclear energy, frequently linked with the mass movements against nuclear weapons. Finally, new technologies have emerged, such as genetic engineering, microcomputers, or space exploration that have replaced nuclear energy as the exciting frontier of science and in some cases have offered new economic and industrial avenues for progress.

The outcome of this, plus a number of other no less important factors, was a dramatic slow-down in the development of nuclear power in the world. The projected nuclear power programmes are now an order of magnitude lower than they were in 1970, with every projection being lower than the earlier one. Only about 20 per cent of all countries now have or plan to have nuclear power. Clearly, the need for assistance in nuclear technology can no longer serve as a general inducement to give up nuclear weapons.

(*c*) *Peaceful nuclear explosions—a non-issue*

At one time, another aspect of nuclear energy, namely peaceful nuclear explosions, was blown up into great prominence as offering important benefits in a variety of fields. Article V of the Treaty is devoted to this subject; it calls for all potential benefits from peaceful applications of nuclear explosions to be made available to non-nuclear-weapon States Party to the Treaty.

This Article may have been an obstacle to some nations to join the Treaty. For example, the 1974 nuclear explosion in India was ostensibly for peaceful purposes, but it would have been a violation of the Treaty—if India were a member—since it was not carried out under international observation and procedure.

As it turned out, however, peaceful nuclear explosions have very limited viable applications, and even where they have been considered, the benefits turned out to be only marginal. This aspect of nuclear technology can therefore be put in cold storage.

(d) Nuclear weapons do not offer security

The question of security offered by nuclear weapons is paramount. If the possession of nuclear weapons really afforded greater security to a State, then no international treaty would or could stop the acquisition of such weapons. Fortunately, the evidence points in the opposite direction: the history of the nuclear arms race is a clear indication that the possession of nuclear weapons gives less, not more, security.

Even though both super-Powers had long ago acquired a sufficient potential to fulfil the requirements of deterrence—to inflict unacceptable damage in retaliation for an attack—they still feel impelled to acquire new weapons. At no time was either side satisfied with what it already had in its arsenals. The dynamics of the arms race does not allow for a standstill. President Reagan's insistence on the Strategic Defense Initiative is a clear expression of the sense of insecurity in the United States, with all its 15,000 nuclear warheads.

France and the United Kingdom are also not able to rest on what they already have in their arsenals. They feel compelled to update them all the time—imposing a heavy burden on their economies—although it is difficult to imagine a situation when these countries would use, or threaten to use, nuclear weapons without the super-Powers being brought in, which would lead to an all-out nuclear war with catastrophic consequences to all.

5. The renunciation of nuclear weapons is in the self-interest of a State

The above discussion leads to the formulation of the principles on which a more equitable NPT should be based, and on measures to bring it about.

The most important principle is that the renunciation of possession of nuclear weapons is not a sacrifice but is in the self-interest of a State. This follows directly from the analysis in the previous section showing that the possession of nuclear weapons decreases rather than increases the security of a nation.

If this is accepted, then it becomes unnecessary to offer any compensation to a State that renounces nuclear weapons, such as help in developing a nuclear technology. The present Article IV (as well as Article V) will therefore become redundant.

Instead of the technological link between Articles II and IV, there should be a political link, namely a commitment by the nuclear-weapon States not to use nuclear weapons to endanger the security of non-nuclear-weapon States Party to the Treaty. If such a guarantee were to be restricted to States that do not have nuclear weapons on their territory, it would be an incentive to States with such weapons to demand their removal.

As mentioned earlier, in an all-out nuclear war it would not make much difference whether a country is or is not directly attacked with nuclear weapons. Nevertheless, such a guarantee would be conducive to a more relaxed atmosphere; this by itself might contribute to the lowering of the probability of a nuclear war.

As was pointed out earlier the main danger to the non-proliferation regime is that one nation may suddenly violate it and acquire—by one means or another—a nuclear weapon capability. A neighbouring country, that is not on friendly terms with it, may perceive this as a threat to itself and attempt to restore the balance by also acquiring nuclear weapons. It is therefore in the interest of every nation to ensure that its neighbours adhere to the NPT.

One way towards this is by establishing nuclear-free zones embracing all nations in a given zone. In view of the sensitive positions of Israel and South Africa it is most urgent to establish nuclear-free zones in the Middle East and in Africa. In Latin America, Argentina and Brazil should be persuaded to join the Tlatelolco Treaty. The recent changes in the regimes in these countries may be propitious in this respect. But the ultimate aim must be to ensure that all nations on the globe renounce nuclear weapons by joining the NPT.

One of the chief reasons for the persistent refusal of some States to join the Treaty is that in its present formulation it perpetuates the division of nations into 'haves and have-nots', the former being privileged by being allowed to have nuclear weapons. However, if we accept the premise that the self-interest of a State dictates the renunciation of nuclear weapons, then the whole situation can be viewed in an entirely different light. The nuclear-weapon States, far from being privileged, are in fact victims of their own folly; they became entangled in a web of their own making from which they are unable to extricate themselves. They deserve pity rather than envy.

All the same, since the consequences of that folly may gravely affect all other nations, these nations have the right to demand that the nuclear-weapon States take steps to reduce the danger, as stipulated in Article VI. Such a demand would carry much greater weight if it were the unanimous voice of all other nations, that is if all other nations joined the NPT.

To begin with, this demand should concentrate on the first two steps.

One is a comprehensive test ban, a step specifically named in the Preamble to the NPT. There do not appear to be sound technological reasons why the compliance with such a test ban could not be verified, down to one kiloton. A comprehensive test ban would bring the nuclear arms race to an effective halt and prevent a deterioration of the situation while negotiations are being conducted on arms reduction.

The second step is for France and the United Kingdom to give up their independent deterrents. One may ask, why not all five nuclear-weapon States? Realistically, one cannot expect—nor would it be feasible—for the two super-Powers to abolish their nuclear arsenals in one fell swoop. China is at the crossroads at the present time and it is difficult to see in which direction its policies might take it; for the time being it is expedient to leave China alone. But there is no such hesitation in relation to France and the United Kingdom. Both are in the Western camp and one cannot conceive any rational and likely situation in which either of these two countries might use nuclear weapons, or threaten to use them, outside their NATO involvement. The main reason why France and the United Kingdom have their own nuclear arsenals is historical and out of date. Charles de Gaulle said: 'No country without an atom bomb could properly consider itself independent.' For the United Kingdom, Ernest Bevin said: '[without the bomb] we would be going naked in the international conference chamber.' If these arguments were considered valid at the present time we would not now have five but 172 nuclear-weapon States.

At the Review Conference this year, strong pressure should be exerted on France and the United Kingdom to give up their independent deterrents, even though such a call is unlikely to be heeded just now. It is difficult to imagine Mrs. Thatcher moving in that direction, but the next British Government may do it, if the anti-nuclear movements in the United Kingdom gave high priority to this end. France is in a different situation, its insistence on the *force de frappe* seems to hold, irrespective of the political colour of its Government. But it would become difficult for France to remain intransigent if the United Kingdom gave up its own nuclear weapons. In any case, a campaign towards this objective should start now.

6. Safeguarding nuclear energy

Nuclear power programmes are likely to continue—albeit on a small scale—and therefore there is the need to maintain the safeguarding of sensitive technologies by the IAEA, as stipulated in Article III of the NPT. To avoid discrimination, the same safeguards should apply to all countries. All civil nuclear projects, whether in nuclear or in non-nuclear-weapon States, should be subject to full-scope IAEA controls.

However, additional measures should be taken to lessen the opportunities for the diversion of sensitive materials by terrorist groups or irrational leaders. One such important measure would be an agreement not to carry out the chemical processing of spent fuel elements from reactors in order to extract the plutonium from them. Instead, the fuel elements should be kept in the cooling tanks and later in storage tanks. With the present glut of uranium this would not have any adverse effect on the economy of the fuel cycle in thermal reactors. It would of course mean that the fast breeder reactor could not be developed on a commercial scale, but this is in any case not envisaged for the near future and may not become necessary even later if the next measure proposed here is implemented, namely the development of alternative sources of energy.

In parallel with the many difficulties encountered by the nuclear industry—as described earlier—there has been a growing realization of the initial mistake, made in the fifties, in singling out nuclear as the only energy source with which the family of nations should concern itself, as expressed by the setting up of the IAEA and the consequent neglect of other sources of energy. It is now generally recognized that alternative sources of energy have great potential and that some lend themselves to early practical application, but their development has been hampered by lack of a substantial research effort, most of which went into nuclear energy.

To remedy this, all nations should be encouraged to satisfy their energy needs from alternative sources. This would be achieved best by a co-ordinated international effort, for example, by setting up a World Energy Organization under the United Nations, along lines similar to those of the World Health Organization. The need for such a measure should be expressly stated in the revised Non-Proliferation Treaty.

TABLE 1

States that have not ratified the NPT

China	Democratic People's Republic of Korea	People's Democratic Republic of Yemen
France	Djibouti	Qatar
Albania	Guinea	Saudi Arabia
Algeria	Guyana	South Africa
Andorra	India	Spain
Angola	Israel	Trinidad & Tobago†
Argentina*	Kiribati	United Arab Emirates
Bahrain	Kuwait†	United Republic of Tanzania
Belize	Malawi	Western Samoa
Bhutan	Mauritania	Vanuatu
Brazil*	Monaco	Yemen Arab Republic†
Burma	Mozambique	Zambia
Chile*	Niger	Zimbabwe
Colombia*†	Oman	
Comoros	Pakistan	
Cuba*		

* accepted IAEA safeguards
† signed but not ratified

TABLE 2

Nuclear power in non-nuclear-weapon States

Countries with reactors in operation	under construction	being planned
A. NPT Member States		
Belgium	Mexico	Egypt
Bulgaria	Philippines	Iraq
Canada	Poland	Libya
Czechoslovakia	Romania	Thailand
Finland		Turkey
German Democratic Republic		
Germany, Federal Republic of		
Hungary		
Italy		
Japan		
Korea		
Netherlands		
Sweden		
Switzerland		
Taiwan		
Yugoslavia		
B. States outside the NPT		
Argentina	Cuba	Israel
Brazil		
India		
Pakistan		
South Africa		
Spain		

Cutting off Nuclear Weapons at the Source

DR. FRANK VON HIPPEL

Woodrow Wilson School of Public and International Affairs and Center for Energy and Environmental Studies, Princeton University

Dealing with the problem of proliferation requires a two-sided approach: political and technical.

On the political side, we are not going to stop proliferation as long as the super-Powers continue fantasizing that nuclear weapons are potentially usable militarily. If nuclear weapons are illegitimate for non-nuclear-weapon States, then they must be illegitimate for the nuclear-weapon States as well. That is, of course, the fundamental understanding on which the Non-Proliferation Treaty was based.

The problem is that the super-Powers *do not* believe that nuclear weapons are illegitimate. Indeed, each has pursued these weapons in part for very good reasons: the US to use as a threat to keep the Soviet Union from invading Western Europe, the Soviet Union to make US nuclear weapons unusable. These reasons still prevail and they drive the nuclear arms race.

The same logic drives nuclear weapons proliferation. The US and the Soviet Union are not the only nations in the world that feel threatened. Indeed, we see around the world today the potential for many replications of the US–Soviet 'balance of terror': between India and Pakistan, Israel and its neighbors, Argentina and Brazil, South and North Korea, China and Taiwan, South Africa and its neighbors, . . .

The problem of the nuclear arms race cannot therefore be separated from the problem of war which created the need for the balance of terror in the first place. Getting out of this situation will require more than nuclear arms control. It will require the reduction of the enormous confrontation of non-nuclear forces in Europe and it will require an end to military intervention in the Third World.[1]

Of course, nuclear weapons proliferation would have proceeded much more rapidly than it has, had not the possession of nuclear weapons been recognized as a danger to the owner as well as his adversaries. Before the US brought nuclear weapons into the world, we were completely safe from attack. Now we can be destroyed in less than an hour and, if we are destroyed, it will probably be either because we used our own nuclear weapons or because the Soviet Union thought that we were about to do so. Other countries looking at our situation might well wish to run the more limited

[1] Randall Forsberg, 'The Freeze and Beyond: Confining the Military to Defense as a Route to Disarmament', *World Policy 2*, Winter 1984, p. 285.

risks of old-fashioned war—especially as wars of conquest seem to be becoming less and less successful.

Nevertheless, the consensus in favor of non-proliferation would be strengthened if we could broaden its definition so that it is a coherent opposition to the creation of more nuclear weapons materials *anywhere*—that is inside the current nuclear-weapon States as well as among currently non-nuclear-weapon States. It is two steps in this direction that I would like to discuss in the remainder of my talk.

The first step is for the nuclear-weapon States to halt their production of fissile materials for nuclear weapons and put their remaining nuclear activities under the same type of international safeguards that the non-nuclear-weapon NPT signatories have accepted.

The second step is that the large-scale separation of plutonium from spent nuclear power reactor fuel be abandoned, for the time being at least, as a commercial activity as well as a weapons-related activity. The recovery of plutonium from nuclear power reactor fuel is completely unnecessary to nuclear power at this time and, by creating large stockpiles of this weapons-usable material in non-nuclear-weapon States, threatens to destabilize the non-proliferation regime.

In the remainder of my talk I will lay out the rationale for each of these proposals. I look forward to your reactions.

A cut-off of the production of fissile materials for nuclear weapons by the super-Powers

A cut-off in the production of fissile material for nuclear weapons by the super-Powers would put a ceiling on their nuclear arsenals at a time when it is becoming increasingly difficult to limit the missiles that can deliver nuclear weapons. We are currently on the threshold of a huge proliferation of the number of long-range cruise and ballistic missiles in the super-Power nuclear arsenals. A large number of these missiles are being advocated as 'delivery vehicles' for conventional explosives, but how will we be able to tell which are nuclear and which are not? At the same time, concern about vulnerability of land-based nuclear weapons has stimulated a trend toward small, mobile and less detectable land-based nuclear missiles.

Systems as ambiguous and concealable as these may soon make it more difficult to arrive at nuclear arms control agreements based, like SALT II, on verifiable counts of delivery vehicles. Agreements limiting and reducing the amounts of nuclear weapons materials available to the two sides may therefore increasingly become one of the principal remaining tools for limiting new nuclear weapons systems and reducing the sizes of the nuclear arsenals.

This is a good time to propose a fissile production cut-off agreement because the super-Powers have nuclear arsenals of approximately equal sizes. They also seem to have approximately the same amounts of weapon-grade plutonium—the most sought-after fissile material because its small critical mass allows the manufacture of compact nuclear weapons.

Although the amounts of plutonium in the super-Power weapons stockpiles are supposedly secret, it is possible to make good estimates on the basis of public data.[1] In the case of the US, this can be done simply on the basis of recently-released information on the power-history of US production reactors. (See Figure 1.)

An estimate of Soviet plutonium production can be obtained from the Soviet contributions to the atmosphere's inventory of radioactive krypton-85. This isotope is produced by fission and released principally from nuclear fuel reprocessing facilities. Krypton-85 accumulates in the atmosphere because it is chemically unreactive, and its distribution in the atmosphere is relatively uniform because of its relatively long radioactive half-life of 11 years. (See Figure 2.)

The upper curve shows the cumulative releases of Kr-85 to the atmosphere as a function of time, based on historical measurements of the atmosphere's Kr-85 concentration. The lower three curves show our estimate of the contributions from nuclear weapons tests, from nuclear fuel reprocessing in the US and from Western Europe and Japan. Most of the reprocessing in the US and the USSR has been done in order to recover plutonium for nuclear weapons. Most of that in Western Europe and Japan has been civilian.

We attribute virtually all the Kr-85 in the atmosphere not produced in the West to the Soviet Union. It will be seen, therefore, that the cumulative amounts of Kr-85 released by the two super-Powers to the atmosphere are comparable—although the production rate in the Soviet Union currently appears to be much higher. Therefore, the amounts of plutonium in the two nuclear arsenals are also probably roughly comparable—about 100 tonnes each.

From 1956 through 1969, the US repeatedly proposed a cut-off in the production of both plutonium and highly-enriched uranium for nuclear weapons. But the Soviet Union refused—presumably at least in part because its stockpiles at the time were much smaller. Finally, in 1982, Foreign Minister Gromyko announced that the Soviet Union was interested in a cut-off agreement. Unfortunately, by that time, the US had lost interest. Hopefully, this condition is only temporary.

The US made clear in 1969, the last time that it put forward the fissile material production cut-off proposal, that it believed that such a cut-off would be adequately verifiable if each of the super-Powers would only be

[1] Frank von Hippel, David Albright and Barbara Levi, *Scientific American*, September 1985, to be published.

willing to open up its nuclear energy facilities to inspection by the International Atomic Energy Agency (IAEA) on the same basis as the non-nuclear-weapon States do under the Non-Proliferation Treaty. Indeed, the US has made most of its civilian energy facilities available to the IAEA for inspection and the USSR has, since Gromyko's speech, also made a first small step in this direction.

If all facilities in the nuclear-weapon States that were processing significant quantities of fissile material not already in the weapons stockpiles were either subject to international monitoring or shutdown, the only remaining question about verification would be the possibility of secret production facilities. Here the US was confident in 1969 that any facilities capable of significantly increasing the size of one of the super-Power stockpiles of fissile materials would be quite easily detectable by national technical means. Two collaborators and I have recently reviewed this situation in a study that will be summarized in a *Scientific American* article in September. We are convinced that the 1969 US position on the verifiability of a cut-off is still valid.

Furthermore, the motivations for one of the super-Powers to violate such an agreement would not be large. No advantage could be derived that would be worth even a small risk of detection.

The problem of nuclear fuel reprocessing

I would now like to discuss the problem of commercial nuclear fuel reprocessing and explain why it has reached a point where I believe it may be on the verge of destabilizing the whole non-proliferation regime.

The non-proliferation situation has been relatively stable thus far because large quantities of weapon-usable fissile material have not been easily available. U-235, the chain-reacting isotope that destroyed Hiroshima, is present in nature—but safely diluted by more than one hundred times as much non-chain-reacting U-238. Virtually all of the uranium used for nuclear power reactor fuel is enriched to only a few per cent in U-235—much less than the 90 per cent that is used in nuclear weapons.

Plutonium, the chain-reacting element that destroyed Nagasaki, disappeared by radioactive decay long before the earth's material coalesced. To make significant amounts, one needs to bombard U-238 with neutrons in a high-power nuclear reactor. A great deal of plutonium is present in the irradiated nuclear fuel discharged from nuclear power reactors but because of the intense radioactivity of the fission products in this fuel, it is difficult to recover. (See Figure 3.)

Even with the advances in nuclear technology that have taken place during the past 40 years, it still takes a substantial and lengthy effort to produce weapon-grade material on a significant scale. As Pakistan has discovered in its now approximately thirteen-year-long all-out effort, it takes skilled personnel, time and money.[1]

The fact that the construction of a nuclear weapon cannot be accomplished quickly by a few people in the absence of easy access to weapon-grade fissile materials is enormously stabilizing. It means that the national leadership must be consulted and think seriously about the reactions of other groups who will certainly become aware of the program before it is completed. There were, for example, serious discussions of preventive nuclear war in the US when we became aware of the progress of the Soviet nuclear weapons program[2] and it has been asserted that the Soviets thought about attacking China at a similar stage of its nuclear weapons program.[3]

If the implementation of the decision to 'go nuclear' takes long enough, awareness of the dangers and costs of joining in the nuclear arms race can even bring a nation to reverse the decision. Recently we have learned that this is exactly what happened in Sweden. Apparently a nuclear weapons program was launched in Sweden in 1957 and largely abandoned in 1968. During that entire period, the principal obstacle delaying the program was the unavailability of plutonium.[4]

Unfortunately, the sobering length of time between the decision to go nuclear and the achievement of that goal is being dangerously shortened because of efforts to introduce separated weapons-usable plutonium as a fuel for nuclear reactors. Already, France and Britain are separating out of spent reactor fuel five tonnes of plutonium *each year*—enough to make hundreds of nuclear weapons. The fact that the plutonium being recovered is not 'weapon-grade' does not make a great deal of difference since the requirement of the bomb designers for weapon-grade plutonium is only a matter of convenience, not necessity.

Very little of the plutonium separated thus far has left the French and British nuclear fuel reprocessing plants. That situation will not last much longer, however. A first large shipment was recently delivered from France to Japan. This shipment, incidentally, ended up being guarded by warships because of fears of plutonium 'pirates'. This, of course, raises the spectre that terrorists might acquire nuclear weapons if plutonium enters widespread commercial circulation.

Before discussing how this situation might be stopped, I would like to discuss how it came about.

The plutonium breeder reactor—a fading dream

Currently, most of the energy released in nuclear power plants comes from the fission of the rare uranium isotope, U-235. But the amount of energy in

1 Leonard S. Spector, *Nuclear Proliferation Today* (New York: Vintage, 1984), Chapter II.
2 Gregg Herkin, *Counsels of War* (New York: Alfred A. Knopf, 1985), pp. 95–7.
3 H. R. Haldeman, *The Ends of Power* (New York, Times Books, 1978), pp. 88–94.
4 Christer Larsson, 'Build a Bomb!' *Ny Teknik*, 25 April 1985, pp. 55–83.

the U-235 in uranium ore of high enough grade to be economically mined is limited. Indeed, early in the nuclear program, it was thought that scarcity of low-cost uranium would limit the current types of U-235-burning reactors to a very small number. Since that time, we have learned that high-grade uranium ore is much more abundant than was thought.

In any case, whether the problem is near-term or long-term, the early atomic scientists quickly found a solution to it. The abundant uranium isotope, U-238, contains as much energy as U-235 and the energy can be made accessible by converting non-chain-reacting U-238 into chain-reaction plutonium by neutron bombardment in a nuclear reactor.

Current reactors convert some U-238 into plutonium—but not enough to replace the U-235 that originally produced the neutrons. However, reactors can be designed to produce as much or more plutonium as they consume. After these plutonium breeder reactors have been provided with a start-up supply of plutonium, they can be fueled by U-238. (See Figure 4.)

Plutonium breeder reactors could in principle be fueled from ordinary rock since the fission energy stored in the uranium in a ton of rock is equivalent to the energy stored in several tons of coal. Breeder reactors could therefore solve the energy problem for millenia. As Oppenheimer said about the Ulam-Teller design of the hydrogen bomb, the idea of the plutonium breeder reactor is 'technologically sweet'.

It was the US Atomic Energy Commission (AEC), led by Glenn Seaborg, the man who won a Nobel Prize for first isolating plutonium, that originally promoted the idea of a plutonium breeder reactor as the final solution to man's energy cravings. The AEC encouraged and assisted a number of nations, including India, in developing their capabilities to separate plutonium from nuclear reactor fuel. France followed suit with Israel and later only pulled back half way through a similar collaboration with Pakistan.

This technology has been used by India, Israel and perhaps soon Pakistan to obtain plutonium for nuclear weapons. However, after fast starts all over the world, programs to commercialize the plutonium breeder reactor are grinding to a halt. In the US, an intermediate-scale demonstration breeder reactor, the Clinch River Breeder Reactor, was cancelled after the pro-nuclear energy Reagan Administration concluded that it was uneconomic and premature.

France has become the international leader in breeder technology and hopes to put into operation a full-size breeder reactor soon, the Super-Phénix 1, but the capital cost of this reactor is twice that of a conventional light-water reactor of equivalent capacity and France no longer expects to switch to breeders for the foreseeable future. West Germany has just barely decided to complete its intermediate-scale demonstration breeder. Japan has decided to go ahead with its similarly-sized demonstration plant—but on a stretched-out schedule. The Soviet Union has been delaying its next breeder demonstration project.

Many factors have combined to reduce the economic interest of breeder reactors.

—The cost difference between conventional and breeder reactors and the cost of recovering plutonium from irradiated nuclear fuel are both much greater than previously expected. As a result, the cost of uranium would have to increase perhaps tenfold before the breeder would be economically justified.[1]

—With the end of declining electricity prices, the growth in electricity demand has slowed drastically to the point that, even if nuclear power were to supply *all* electricity in the future, there would still be much less required than was previously projected. (See Figure 5.)[2]

—As a result, the uranium resource situation is now seen as adequate to support current-generation nuclear power plants for a very long time. The already discovered uranium deposits (outside the Centrally-Planned Economies), available at recovery costs equivalent to about one dollar per barrel of oil or less would sustain the year 2000 nuclear capacity currently projected for these nations for 50 years and OECD analysts have estimated that a few times as much more uranium ore in this cost category remains to be discovered.[3]

The commercialization of plutonium as a nuclear fuel—a growing danger

It has been suggested that the 'invisible hand' of economics has saved the world from the dangers of the plutonium economy. Unfortunately, however, we have not been saved yet. As I have already mentioned, despite the fading near-term prospects for the breeder, France and Britain, heavily subsidized by the Japanese, have decided to exploit the expertise that they developed in their nuclear weapons programs to launch commercial operations for the recovery of plutonium from nuclear reactor fuel.

[1] H. A. Feiveson, Frank von Hippel and Robert H. Williams, 'Fission Power: An Evolutionary Strategy', *Science 203*, 26 January 1979, pp. 330–7. Although the economic assumptions used in this paper could be updated, the changes would be virtually all adverse to the breeder.

[2] The 1974 projection appeared in US Atomic Energy Commission, *Proposed Environmental Statement on the Liquid Metal Fast Breeder Reactor Program*, WASH–1535 (1974). The 1983 projection appeared in US Department of Energy, Office of Policy, Planning, and Analysis, *Energy Projections to the Year 2010* DOE/PE–0029/2 (October 1983), Table 5–11.

[3] *Uranium: Resources, Production and Demand* (OECD and IAEA, 1983). The WOCA nuclear capacity for the year 2000 is estimated as 504–558 Gwe (p. 42). The associated estimated annual uranium requirements (assuming light-water reactors operating on a once-through fuel cycle) are 67–82,000 tonnes U (p. 44). The estimated tonnages available at less than $130/kg are: 2 million tonnes or 'reasonable assured resources' (p. 19); 2 million tonnes in 'extension of well-explored deposits' and 'in well-defined geological trends or areas of mineralization with known deposits' (pp. 20, 23); and 9.6–12.1 million tonnes ('most-likely range') in deposits 'thought to exist mostly on the basis of indirect evidence and geological extrapolations' (p. 24).

They are being joined by Japan, West Germany and other European nations. By the year 2000, if current plans are carried through, these reprocessing plants will have separated enough plutonium out of civilian nuclear power reactor fuel to make 50,000 nuclear weapons—as many as there are in the super-Power arsenals. And, as if that were not bad enough, virtually every country with any nuclear program at all is arguing that it must have at least a small reprocessing facility of its own. (See Figure 6.)[1]

Originally the plutonium so recovered was to be used to start up plutonium breeder reactors, but now that that demand is not developing, France is urging its reprocessing customers to take the plutonium back and use it as a substitute for U-235 in their current reactors. With such 'plutonium recycle', the uranium requirements of current reactors could be reduced by 25-30 per cent.

If this reprocessing-recycle program is carried through, soon, any country with a nuclear power plant will have available to it huge quantities of readily-accessible weapon-usable plutonium. In many nations the length of time between the decision to go nuclear and its achievement on a potentially very large scale will have shrunk from years to weeks—thus making it easy for some opportunistic official to try for a *fait accompli* before his more cautious countrymen can stop him. The danger of plutonium finding its way into the hands of terrorists will also increase greatly.

It is obvious why France and Britain are embarking on commercial fuel reprocessing: they need the foreign exchange. But why are countries like Japan, West Germany, Sweden and Switzerland sending their spent fuel to France and Britain to be reprocessed? The reason is not economics.

Although plutonium recycle does reduce uranium and enrichment costs by about one quarter, the extra cost of reprocessing and then fabricating fuel containing plutonium is great enough so that the price of uranium would have to increase at least threefold before plutonium recycle became economical. On the other hand, the cost of nuclear power is dominated by the cost of the reactor and, if there are non-economic reasons to do so, one can switch to the plutonium fuel cycle at a cost penalty of only about five per cent. (See Figure 7.)

The two primary non-economic arguments that have been made for reprocessing are:

1. increased energy independence, and
2. reduction of the radioactive waste disposal problem.

Energy independence

There are no current plans to reprocess nuclear reactor fuel in either the US or Canada. However (as is pointed out by advocates of plutonium recycle)

[1] David Albright and Harold Feiveson, 'The Deferral of Reprocessing', in the Federation of American Scientists' *Public Interest Report*, February 1985, p. 9.

these countries are self-sufficient in uranium. In contrast, Japan and Western Europe are dependent upon uranium imports and they learned in 1973 and 1979 of the vulnerability that energy dependence can bring.

Nations are always learning the wrong lesson from history, however. Uranium differs from oil so much in cost and volume that vulnerability can easily be avoided by stockpiling. On an energy-equivalent basis, uranium for a conventional nuclear power reactor costs two per cent as much as oil today. A 25 years' supply for today's nuclear power plants could therefore be bought for the price of a six months' supply of oil for the equivalent oil-fired plant. The carrying charge for this stockpile would be less than the difference in costs between the once-through and plutonium recycle fuel cycles. On a tonnage basis, 25 years' uranium supply weighs only as much as *one day's* oil supply. Because of the low cost and ease of storage of uranium, a number of nations have already acquired, almost absent-mindedly, stockpiles equivalent to several years' uranium requirements—something that they could not dream of doing in the case of oil.

Waste disposal

Radioactive waste disposal has been a 'hot' political issue in some of the same countries: Japan, West Germany and Sweden, that have been France's and Britain's best customers for nuclear fuel reprocessing. And reprocessing has been sold as a major part of the solution to radioactive waste disposal because plutonium, the most feared of the radioactive elements in the radioactive waste, would be separated out and fissioned.

However, this argument has not stood up under analysis. Because of process losses during the repeated recycle of the average plutonium atom before it fissioned, significant amounts of plutonium would go into the radioactive waste in any case. And a significant fraction of the plutonium would be transmuted by neutron absorption into long-lived transplutonium isotopes which would end up in the wastes and increase their toxicity. [1] As a result, the waste from a plutonium recycle fuel cycle would be about as radioactive for as long a time as that from a once-through fuel cycle. And, since each processing of plutonium would contaminate equipment and buildings and thereby create new wastes, plutonium recycle would create a more complicated waste disposal problem. The countries that are sending their fuel to France and Britain are therefore just postponing their waste-disposal problems—not solving them. (See Figure 8.)

This argument has been accepted by now by the governments of many nations—the US, Canada, Sweden, and, most recently, that of the Federal Republic. The director of the FRG study which compared reprocessing with the direct disposal of spent fuel has been reported to have concluded that his

[1] Hartmut Krugman and Frank von Hippel, 'Radioactive Waste: The Problem of Plutonium', *Science 210* (1980), p. 319.

interim results show a 'certain, sometimes clear advantage of [direct disposal] over reprocessing with regard to radiation exposure for personnel and population, overall risk and economics'.[1] Nevertheless, inexplicably the FRG has nevertheless decided to proceed with the construction of its own reprocessing plant—giving the peculiar reason that it was necessary to become independent of other countries' reprocessing services. As in the case of the nuclear arms race, nations find it difficult not to pursue technologies that other nations are pursuing—even when these technologies appear to be wasteful and dangerous.

A modest proposal

In summary, the nuclear-weapon States continue to produce fissile material for nuclear weapons—even though their stockpiles are both excessive and unusable. Similarly, interest in and commitment to the separation of plutonium from spent nuclear power reactor fuel is increasing even though any benefits from such an activity have receded into the mists of the future and despite the great associated dangers of proliferation and nuclear terrorism.

This is why I suggest a 'package deal' in which both of these foolish activities would be ended. Such a package may be more feasible politically than either of its parts separately. A halt by the nuclear-weapon States of the production of fissile material for nuclear weapons should appeal to the non-nuclear-weapon States because it would be a first step toward halting the nuclear arms race. The abandonment of nuclear fuel reprocessing should appeal to the nuclear-weapon States because it would help retard the spread of nuclear weapons.

Here is a way to throttle the production of more nuclear weapons—*at the source*.

[1] *Hannoversche Allgemeine*, 29 May 1984.

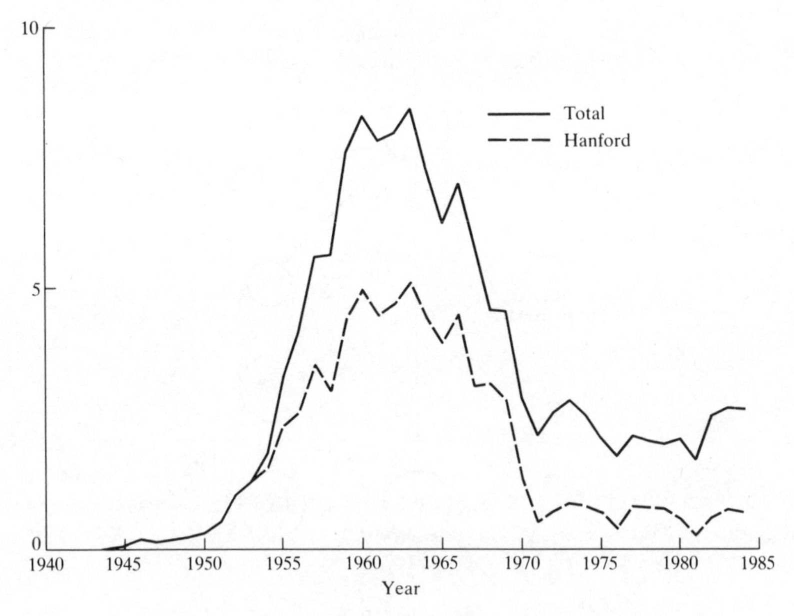

Figure 1. Heat output of US production reactors
(equivalent tonnes of U-235 fission per year)

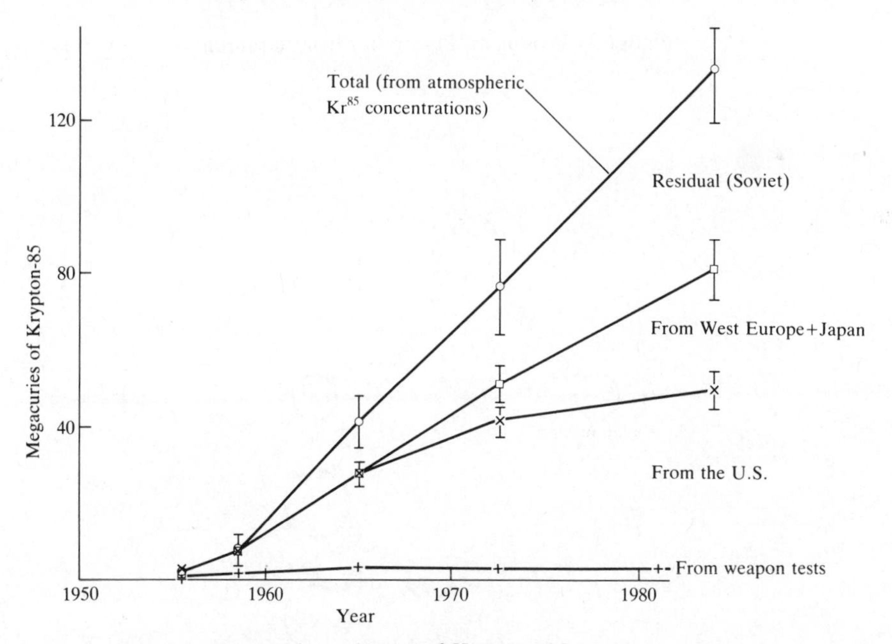

Fig. 2. Cumulative releases of Krypton-85 to the atmosphere
(undecayed)

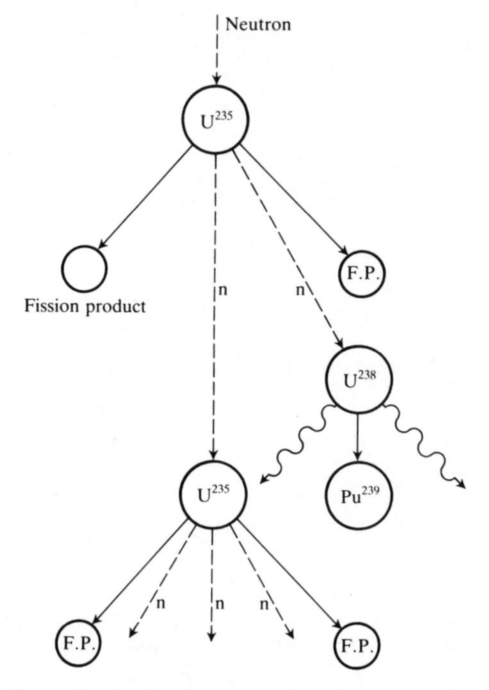

Figure 3. Producing Plutonium from Uranium

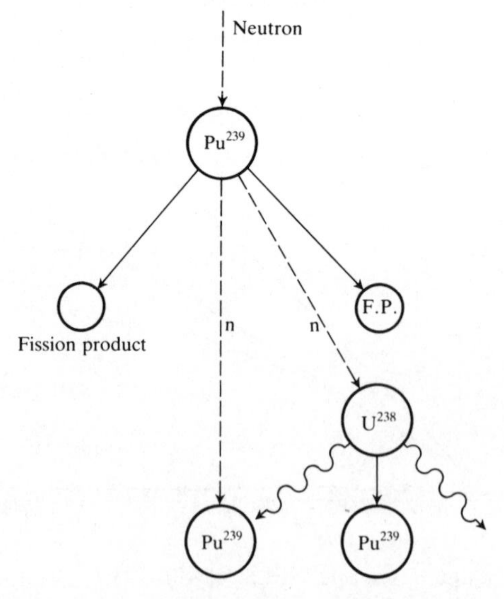

Figure 4. Using Plutonium to breed more Plutonium

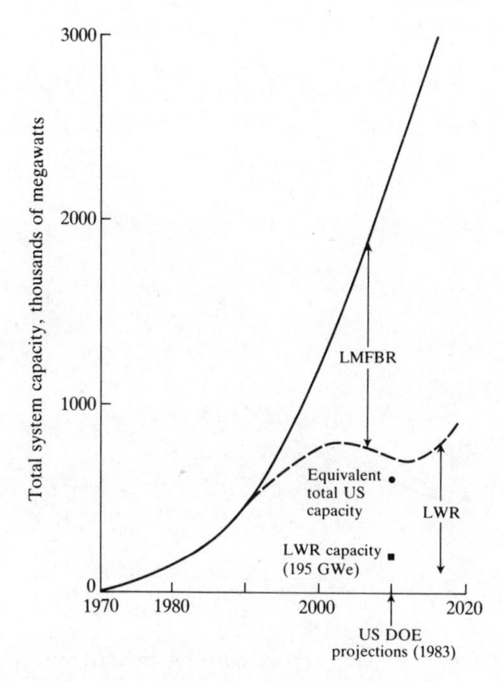

Figure 5. US AEC's 1974 nuclear growth projection (80 per cent average capacity factor assumed)

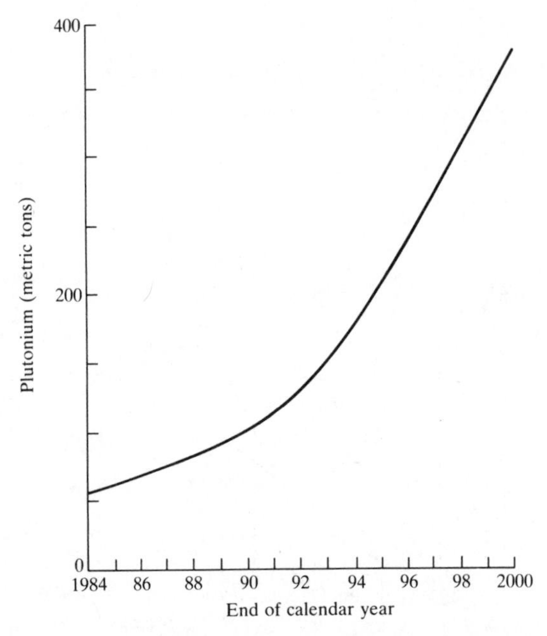

Figure 6. Cumulative plutonium separated (non-centrally-planned economies)

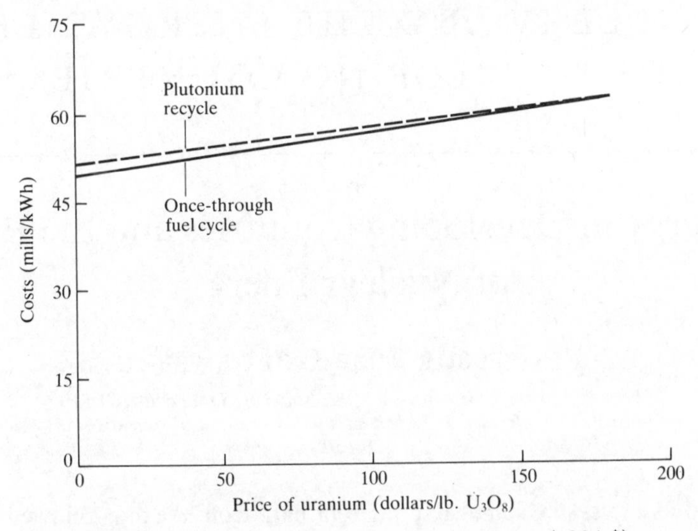

Figure 7. Generation costs of nuclear power (1984 $)

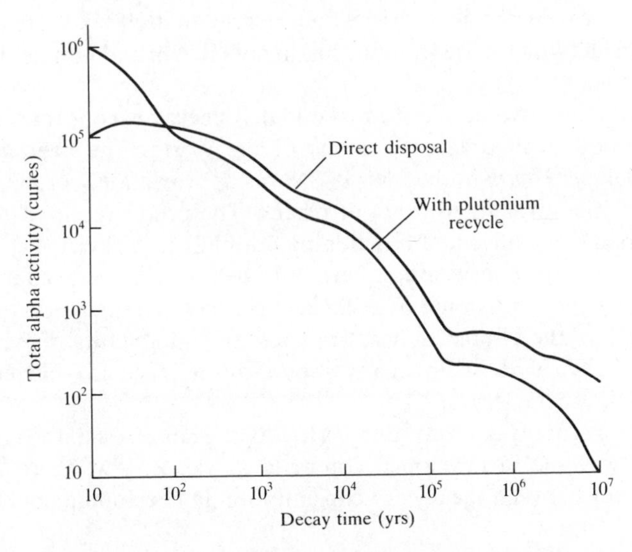

Figure 8. Radioactivity in light water reactor wastes

ARTICLE IV AND THE ENERGY NEEDS OF DEVELOPING COUNTRIES

Energy in Developing Countries and the Role of Nuclear Energy

PROFESSOR JOSÉ GOLDEMBERG

President, Energy Company of the State of Sao Paulo (CESP), Brazil, S.A., former President of the Association of Scientists of Brazil

I would like to take a somewhat different path from the one followed by the people that spoke before me. I would like to explain that the role of nuclear energy in developing countries is likely to be reduced in the near future and that is probably also true of most of the developed countries. As a consequence less emphasis on nuclear energy will in itself take care of a good many problems which arise from the mixing of civilian and non-civilian users of nuclear energy.

The first point I would like to make is that energy is consumed in vastly different amounts in different regions of the world. The average energy consumption *per capita* in the mid-1970s was approximately 42,000 kcal per day, which is equivalent to 2 kw of power. The power required to keep a naked human being alive and functioning normally is 0.1 kw.

Typical energy consumption around the world can change very significantly from a minimum of 2,300 kcal per day in Bangladesh to 243,000 kcal per day in the United States. So, while the inhabitants of Bangladesh barely stay alive with their energy input, the average US citizen uses a hundred times that energy.

The average energy consumption in developing countries in the mid-1970s was 0.86 kw while in developed countries it was 5.3 kw; there is thus a six-fold factor between the energy consumption in developing countries and developed countries.

The vast disparities between average energy consumption in developed and developing countries are a major international problem and a major cause of instability around the world.

In addition to that there is the problem of how this energy is distributed among different parts of the population within each country; the wide disparities in income so prevalent in developing countries are reflected in wide disparities in energy consumption. Usually in such countries 10–20 per cent of the population consumes 80–90 per cent of the energy according to the patterns of developed countries, leaving the rest of the population without the amenities available to the whole population in the developed countries.

World population is expected to increase to 8 billion people in the year 2030, which is double the present number. If *per capita* energy consumption around the world were to reach the present level of Western Europe, which is 5 kw, the total consumption would be 40 Tw (Terrawatts),[1] which is an enormous amount of energy. Present total consumption around the world is 8 Tw.

There has been a very large number of studies on future energy consumption of the world, conducted by many groups, including the World Energy Conference, the IIASA group in Vienna, which are rather similar in their predictions with characteristically 'hard' scenarios. They rely very heavily on the use of coal and nuclear energy. To reach such levels of consumption as I mentioned over the next 50 years, either one nuclear plant of 1 Gw(e) of generating capacity every 2 to 3.5 days or new fossil fuel production capacity equivalent to bringing on line a new Alaska pipeline of 2 million barrels of oil equivalent per day every one to two months, would be required. Anyone familiar with the problem of building new energy supply capacity will realize how difficult it would be to meet these production targets.

Furthermore, developing energy supply on a scale envisaged by these projections would be in strong conflict with many other global concerns, such as the amount of soot in the atmosphere and the problem of radioactivity and nuclear proliferation. Nuclear power projections in these studies imply a serious nuclear weapons proliferation risk: for example, the nuclear projections imply that by the year 2030 some 2.6 to 4.0 million kg of plutonium would be recovered from spent reactor fuel and circulated each year in global commerce. This is to be compared with the 5–10 kg required to make a nuclear weapon.

However, despite these gloomy predictions, it is feasible to evolve much lower energy demand scenarios consistent with the attainment of ambitious economic goals.

One of the driving forces for a low-energy future is the ongoing shift to less energy-intensive economic activities in industrialized countries, which is not adequately taken into account in the studies mentioned above.

The other major factor that makes such a future feasible is the wide range of opportunities for making more efficient use of energy in both developing and industrialized countries. Over the last four years, Amulya K. N. Reddy from Bangalore, India, Thomas B. Johansson from the University of Lund in Sweden, Robert M. Williams from Princeton University, and myself have

[1] 1 Tw = 10^{12} = 1,000,000,000,000 watts.

been working on a study which is called 'An End-use Oriented Global Energy Strategy'. What we have done in this study is to adopt the obvious point of departure that the use of energy is not an end in itself.

Energy is useful only in so far as it provides energy services like cooking, lighting, heating, refrigeration, mechanical work, personal and freight transport, etc., in ways that improve the overall quality of life. The focus of our analysis has been on understanding better the role of energy in society by examining in detail the patterns of energy end-uses, how and by whom different forms of energy are used today and how the energy end-use system might look in the future. I do not want to dwell on the details of the study, some details of which are given in the paper that will be distributed, but I will outline the main results.

The most important one is that in all likelihood it is possible to satisfy the energy needs of the developed countries and developing countries alike by the year 2020 with something like 11 Tw compared to 8 Tw being used at present.

This is obtained by reducing in half the *per capita* energy used in industrialized countries from 6.3 kw to 3.2 kw which can be done by the use not only of conservation measures but also by modern existing technology. I think the most dramatic example of how this can be achieved is the fact that in the United States the gross national product has grown approximately 20 per cent since 1975 although the total energy consumption has been constant since then.

In addition to that in Japan the gross national product has been growing steadily and the energy consumption since 1979 has reduced rather dramatically. Therefore the iron link that economists believed existed between gross national product and energy consumption is a thing of the past and it is not accepted any more by anyone who cares to look into the evolution of energy consumption over the last 10 years.

If the energy consumption in industrialized countries falls from 6.3 to 3.2 kw then it would be possible to increase the energy consumption in the developing countries to 1.3 kw, which is less than industrialized countries use, because one has to account for the fact that there are very significant differences in climate between industrialized and developing countries, since in general they are located in tropical climates of the southern hemisphere. Of course the 1.3 kw which would be used in the developing countries would be used with a much higher efficiency than the 1 kw used today. To give an example, one of the great problems of countries in Africa, as you well know, is the destruction of forests which are used for fuel cooking. It is an extremely ineffective system to use wood, since out of the energy contained in the wood, only approximately 5 to 10 per cent is used in effectively cooking the food. This is a technical problem. Most people in Africa have been living with that problem for thousands of years, but this is a problem that can be solved and it can be solved not only by using better cooking stoves but by abandoning cooking stoves altogether and using instead gas stoves. Any gas stove that is used in Europe or the United States today has an efficiency of 50 per cent. Wood can be transformed very efficiently to gas, so that as one transforms wood into gas there is approximately a tenfold gain in efficiency. There are a number of other points that can be made along the same lines.

I will give you now an indication of what are the energy futures of the world—40 years from now. The 'hard future' predictions, of which IIASA's is representative, indicate a large growth in the consumption of oil and natural gas, coal, and nuclear energy which becomes very, very important. The total energy consumption in such predictions lies in the range of 10 to 35 Tw.

In a more reasonable energy future, which is the one I and my colleagues have been working on—which makes use of energy conservation opportunities and new efficient technologies—the amount of oil would be reduced, natural gas would grow, coal would be reduced a little bit, biomass would grow a lot and nuclear energy will remain approximately the same as it is today.

What I think this leads to is that the energy future of developing countries has better options than a massive reliance on the use of nuclear energy and these options are preferred for a number of reasons, among them a reduction of the danger of mixing weapons and civilian nuclear programs.

I submit therefore that it is rather unlikely that nuclear energy will play a significant role in the economies of most of the developing countries. Many of them have more readily accessible, less controversial and less expensive energy sources. Even in the developed countries the role of nuclear energy in the future is probably limited and the number of reactors in operation in the future will probably not be bigger than twice the present number.

As a consequence, it is high time that the promotion of nuclear power in the developing countries—which has been made unashamedly by big companies in the developing countries—should stop and all the international organizations, such as the International Agency for Atomic Energy and others, should refrain from promoting nuclear energy without a thorough study of other existing options.

The application of Article IV of the NPT in my view is greatly perturbed by restrictions imposed by 'full-scope' safeguards, 'trigger lists' and other limitations, which, in effect, limit the sovereignty of smaller States. This of course applies to the developing countries—which are not many—who feel that they cannot foreclose the nuclear option. I think that the Ambassador of China has stated that very clearly here. It is—I am rephrasing what he said—amazingly arrogant for someone coming from the South to come here and to hear that one of our countries cannot have something that the countries of the North do have. It does not have any meaning to independent countries like ours, which have a long history and tradition of anti-colonialism, to be discriminated against.

In conclusion I would say that 'full scope' and other safeguards would be acceptable only if linked to very concrete steps towards effective nuclear disarmament among the great Powers. Only a revision of the NPT along these lines could attract some of the non-signatory nations to sign.

TABLE I

'Per capita' Energy Consumption in Selected Regions and Countries (mid 1970s)

Regions	Population (billions)	kal/day	Equivalent power (Kw)
World	4,0	42.500	2.04
Developed countries	1,05	110.000	5.3
Developing countries	2,95	18.000	0.87
Brazil	0,11	22.800	1.1
India	0,6	11.000	0.53
China	0,878	7.100	0.34
Bangladesh	0,08	2.300	0.11
United States	0,214	243.000	11.7

TABLE II

Energy and Population in 1980 and 2020

Type of country	Population (billions)		Energy consumption per capita (kw)		Ratio of energy consumption—industrialized/developing	
	1980	2020	1980	2020	1980	2020
Industrialized	1.11	1.24	6.3	3.2		
Developing	3.32	5.71	1.0	1.3	6.3	2.5
Total	4.43	6.95				

Source: José Goldemberg, Thomas B. Johansson, Amulya K. N. Reddy and Robert H. Williams, *An end-use Oriented Global Energy Strategy*.

TABLE III

Global primary energy supply scenario (in TW)

	1980	2020
Nuclear power[a]	0.22	0.75
Hydro[a]	0.19	0.46
Wind and photovoltaic electricity[a]	—	0.09
Fossil fuels		
Coal	2.44	1.94
Oil	4.18	3.21
Natural gas	1.74	3.21
SUBTOTAL	8.36	8.36
Biomass		
Organic wastes		0.79[b]
Plantations or woodfarms		0.79[c]
SUBTOTAL	1.49	1.58
TOTALS	10.3	11.2

[a] Nuclear energy is counted as the thermal energy released in fission (assumed to be 2.5 times the produced electricity in 2020); hydro, wind, and photovoltaic energy as the electricity produced.

[b] We estimate that in 1980 the global production of organic wastes (forest product industry wastes, crop residues, manure, urban refuse) amounted to 2.8 TW. We assume that the level will increase in proportion to the population, reaching 4.1 TW in 2020. Because of competition with other uses we assume that only 1/5 of these wastes are available for energy purposes in 2020.

[c] For an average yield of 10 tonnes per hectare per year, some 140 million hectares of plantations would be required by 2020.

TABLE IV

Global electricity supply scenario (in TW)

	1980	2020
Hydro	0.19	0.46
Wind and photovoltaic electricity	—	0.09[a]
Cogeneration		
Biomass	—	0.14
Fossil Fuel	—	0.13
Central Station		
Nuclear	0.08	0.30
Fossil Fuel	0.66	0.66
TOTALS	0.93	1.78

[a] Owing to the large uncertainties in the future of photovoltaics technology we do not specify how the wind/photovoltaics mix might be disaggregated. In the event that photovoltaics technology is not commercialized, all of this electricity would be provided by wind. However, if the promise of photovoltaic technology is realized its contribution could be considerable.

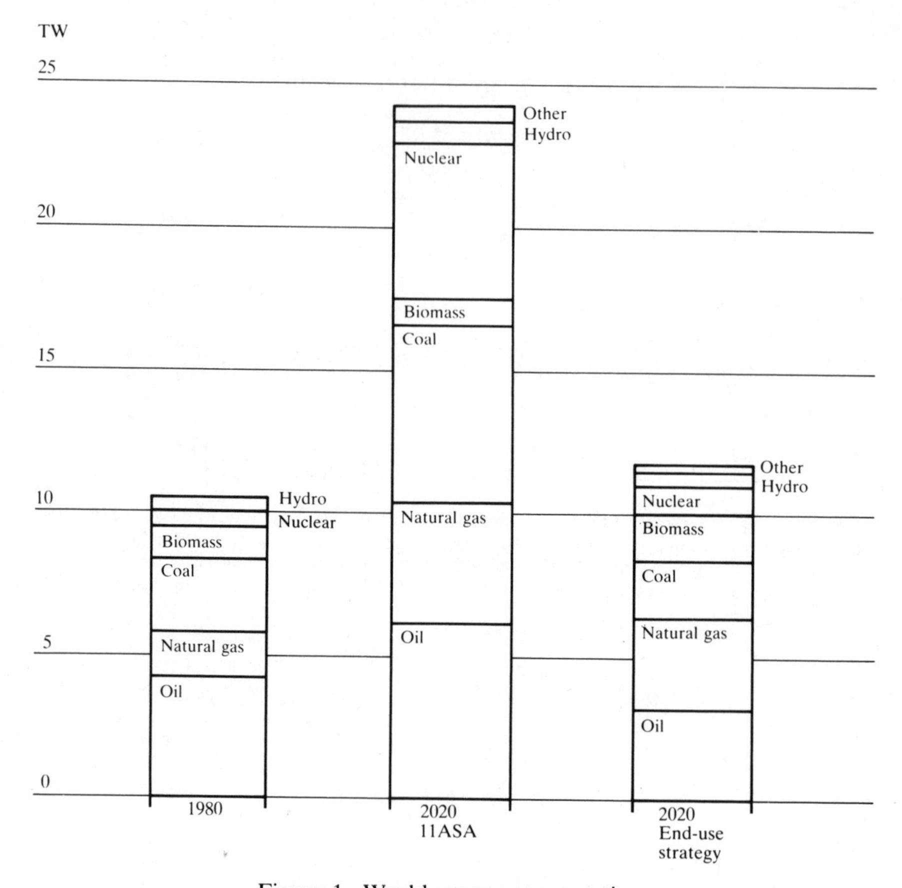

Figure 1. World energy consumption

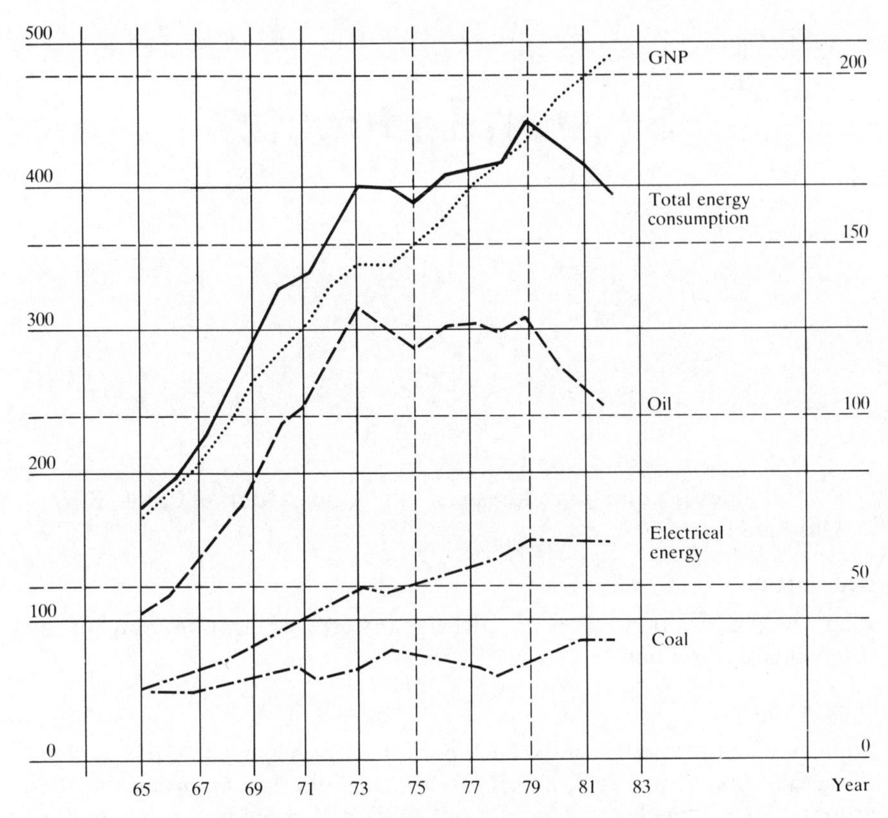

Figure 2. GNP and energy growth in Japan

Session I Debate

Chairman

First of all, there is a question addressed to the Ambassadors of China, Egypt and Sri Lanka.

Ove Nathan

What is the position of your country towards realization now of a comprehensive test ban?

Qian Jiadong

I think China fully understands the importance which many countries attach to the question of a CTBT, and it does not belittle this importance in the proposals it has made for a number of years calling upon the two major nuclear Powers to take a lead in stopping testing, production and deployment of nuclear weapons and drastically reducing their nuclear armaments; a nuclear test ban, in fact, is included in them. The question is how to achieve this objective. This year, the Chinese Delegation declared in the Conference on Disarmament that it would be prepared to participate in the subsidiary body on the item of NTB—if it is set up. This shows that China is willing to discuss this topic with all countries concerned.

Mohamed Shaker

Egypt would definitely be ready to sign a Comprehensive Test Ban Treaty. It was one of the very first countries to sign the Partial Test Ban Treaty in 1963 and it would do the same if a comprehensive test ban is agreed upon.

Jayantha Dhanapala

I shall be very brief. Sri Lanka would be ready to sign a Comprehensive Test Ban Treaty immediately.

Chairman

I now turn to the other questions addressed specifically to Ambassador Qian Jiadong.

Brian Fitzgerald

You spoke of China's refusal to sign the NPT as being based largely on the failure of the super-Powers to comply with Article VI. In the light of China's recent statement before the Conference on Disarmament expressing your country's willingness to join in negotiations toward a Comprehensive Test Ban Treaty, may I ask if the conclusion of a complete ban on nuclear weapons tests, which would address both horizontal and vertical proliferation, would make China reconsider its opposition to the NPT?

Qian Jiadong

I think I have already answered part of this question, but I want to reiterate here that the Chinese Government's criticism of the NPT is threefold: firstly, the lack of progress in the field of nuclear disarmament; secondly, so far no assurance has been given to the non-nuclear-weapon States regarding the use of nuclear weapons; and thirdly, the unwarranted restrictions in the field of nuclear co-operation for peaceful purposes. So a CTBT, important as it might be, is only just one step and it still falls short of the worldwide demand for the cessation of the nuclear arms race and nuclear disarmament. So even if a CTBT is achieved, would this suffice for China to change its opposition to the NPT? I am not so sure at the moment.

Simon Henderson

Are there, or have there been, circumstances in which China would compromise its views on proliferation in order to help Pakistan's nuclear development?

Qian Jiadong

China has been implementing nuclear co-operation for peaceful purposes for some time with a number of countries, including Pakistan, and I think China will continue its efforts in this direction. But to my knowledge the policy pursued by China in this field has been, and will continue to be, one of neither advocating nor encouraging nuclear proliferation, and one of not helping any country to develop nuclear weapons. I think this would be the consistent policy of the Chinese Government.

Angelo Miatello

Last month, the international press stated that China had 'recommenced' nuclear testing in the atmosphere. Is this true?

Qian Jiadong

I have no information of this sort at all.

Chairman

The next question is addressed to Ambassador Shaker.

Christopher Weeramantry

Nuclear winter findings take nuclear war far beyond genocide as a crime against humanity. It is within the power of the non-nuclear States by themselves to enter into a multilateral treaty, declaring the principle that the use of nuclear weapons in any circumstances is illegal. Such a treaty, signed by over 100 States, would be a powerful indication of international law as understood by the vast majority of mankind. Would this not be a useful additional restraint on both vertical and horizontal proliferation?

Mohamed Shaker

There have been attempts to sign a convention, or to agree on a convention, on the non-use of nuclear weapons—there have been several attempts here at the Conference on Disarmament—and certainly the signature of such a convention would be a very important step in curbing vertical as well as horizontal proliferation. But I believe that signature of such an agreement by the nuclear-weapon States would render it more credible. These are the countries which are producing nuclear weapons and therefore their commitment not to use them would be a very important step. However, I must say that there is some progress in this direction. First of all, during the NPT negotiations, there were a number of proposals to have a text or certain provisions in the Treaty banning the use of nuclear weapons. One example is the Kossygin proposal not to use nuclear weapons against States not having nuclear weapons on their territories, but it was not possible to agree on such a proposal under the NPT because of United States resistance to including it in the Treaty. Nevertheless, under the Tlatelolco Treaty the five nuclear-weapon States have undertaken not to use nuclear weapons against the members, or the Parties, to the Tlatelolco Treaty. I think we have achieved great progress in getting these undertakings. They will build up and later on will contribute towards efforts to reach a convention on the non-use of nuclear weapons.

Chairman

The next question is addressed to Ambassador Dhanapala.

Mariusz Kuklinski

Could you comment on an idea recently voiced by a representative of a huge, non-nuclear State of having a 'second league' of nuclear States with small, symbolic nuclear arsenals—a 'protest bomb'?

Jayantha Dhanapala

I would like to make three points in reply to that. The first is to repeat what the President of the Groupe de Bellerive said this morning and that is that a nuclear bomb in the hands of the weak is no less dangerous than a nuclear bomb in the hands of the strong. Consequently, as a result of having a second league of nuclear States—or a nuclear second eleven—the cure can be, in fact, as bad, if not worse, than the disease, and it will not make the world a safer place. The second point I would like to make is: what will the existence of these small, symbolic arsenals achieve? As I pointed out, it is not going to make the world safer. Will it in fact enable us to use nuclear threats in order to force the nuclear-weapon States Parties to disarm? Will it be a deterrent? We have already heard arguments—very persuasive ones—about the fact that deterrence is in fact a fallacious theory. So even a small nuclear arsenal will not be a deterrent. Thirdly, the question of a small arsenal: I think in this nuclear age, the important thing is whether one has a nuclear weapon or not, and a small bomb or a big bomb is still a nuclear bomb. It is a very dangerous thing to think that a limited nuclear arsenal is likely to prove a deterrent and that a protest bomb is going to make the world a safer place.

Chairman

The next question is addressed to both Dr. Blix and Dr. von Hippel.

David Lowry

If it is accepted that verification by physical oversight measures is the kernel both of international nuclear safeguards applied with reference to Article III of the NPT and bilateral safeguards applied by the IAEA (and also to nuclear and chemical-biological arms control agreements), why should the non-nuclear-weapon States believe the nuclear-weapon States, which only offer 'assurances' or voluntary limited safeguards, when they say that the civil (peaceful) nuclear power programmes are not being used to buttress their nuclear arsenals by a form of devious, if not illegal, diversion of nuclear materials in the reprocessing facilities? This applies especially to the United Kingdom, which excludes both IAEA and EURATOM safeguards inspectorates from Windscale.

Hans Blix

I am not quite sure that I understood all the sense of the question. First of all, I would say that I don't think that safeguards are the kernel of non-proliferation.I think that I, and most of those who have spoken before, have said that the political will is the decisive factor, that the Non-Proliferation Treaty and other treaties constitute legal barriers, that the restraints in transfer of technology may slow down a potential proliferator, but no more than that. There are no technical fixes that can stop proliferation. Safeguards as I describe them are in the nature of a very important confidence-building measure that will verify that there is no diversion and will also incidentally deter a potential proliferator. This applies to the non-nuclear-weapon States which wish to create confidence that they are not acquiring nuclear weapons.

When we apply safeguards in nuclear-weapon States, as I described, it does not of course have at all the same purpose as in the non-nuclear-weapon States. They are already nuclear-weapon States, so there is no direct effect in the field of non-proliferation; they made these voluntary offers for different reasons.One was the criticism among the non-nuclear-weapon States that they were submitted to commercial disadvantages in having to open up their peaceful nuclear industry, while the nuclear-weapon States did not have to do so. The nuclear-weapon States therefore said 'All right, we can open up as well. We are not worried about any commercial disadvantages.' Another reason why they opened up was to enable the IAEA to gain experience of different types of facilities which were not common or did not exist at all in non-nuclear-weapon States, and thus we have gained experience, for instance, in the United Kingdom in providing safeguards on the Dounreay breeder reactor. We have also provided inspection for nuclear fuel element factories, and in the United States, the centrifuge enrichment plant in Portsmouth—which the United States is no longer going ahead with—was also selected for inspection.

The third element in inspection in nuclear-weapon States, to which I attribute great significance, is the precedent that nuclear-weapon States will accept verification, will accept inspection on their territories.This is important, though I don't think it has been advanced as a reason why they have invited safeguards on their territories. It follows from this that the main purpose of these inspections is not to make sure that none of the peaceful part of the nuclear industry can yield any advantages for the military sector. In the case of Windscale, if I remember correctly, it is not as such submitted to inspection. It is a dual-purpose plant which also has some military aims and purposes. We do provide inspection of some spent fuel which comes from other countries to the United Kingdom for reprocessing at Windscale, and as regards these particular nuclear materials, I think we do provide certainty that none of it goes for any military purposes in the United Kingdom.

Frank von Hippel

In the line of my talk, I do think that non-nuclear-weapon States, signatory to the Non-Proliferation Treaty or not, should press the nuclear-weapon States to accept inspection of all their nuclear facilities as steps towards a total end to the production of additional fissile material for nuclear weapons. We can go to that directly, or we can go to it step by step, but the unsafeguarded production of fissile material should be cut off world-wide if we are ever to reverse the increase in the number of nuclear weapons in both the nuclear-weapon States and the non-nuclear-weapon States.

Chairman

The next question is also addressed to Dr. Blix.

Sheila Oakes

What proportion of each of their civil facilities are under IAEA safeguards in the United States, the USSR, the United Kingdom and France?

How many States Parties with research reactors or larger facilities are under partial safeguards or no safeguards?

How many more inspectors would be needed if all civil programmes were under full-scope safeguards?

How many more if the non-signatories also joined the NPT?

Hans Blix

The voluntary offers that we have from four nuclear-weapon States differ somewhat one from the other. The United States offer covers in principle the whole of their peaceful nuclear sector and the United States then itself defines which are the peaceful nuclear installations and which are those where they will not invite inspection. The United Kingdom is similar to the United States in that all of the peaceful nuclear sector, as defined by them, is open to safeguards. The French offer, if I remember rightly, requires that France will name a number of installations which would be open to safeguards and the Agency would thereafter decide and select those it wished to inspect. The Soviet offer will also name a number of installations among which the Agency could select some for inspection. It has to be kept in mind then that the purpose of safeguards in nuclear-weapon States is that the Agency should acquire experience in new types of facilities. They are not designed to prevent proliferation since we are already concerned with nuclear-weapon States. In fact, we only select for inspection a few installations in these States, notably those where we could acquire new experience on installations of which we did not have previous experience. Only a very small fraction of the installations in the United States or the United Kingdom are in fact selected.

The other part of the question related to what additional resources would be needed for inspection if we were to inspect all the peaceful nuclear facilities in all the nuclear-weapon States. To implement the idea that the Agency should inspect all peaceful nuclear facilities to make sure that there was no communication between the peaceful sector and the military sector in those countries would of course require much larger resources because the whole United States peaceful nuclear industry alone is a very big part. The same is true of the French industry, not to mention the Soviet and the United Kingdom industries. Inside the Agency we have not made any calculation regarding what additional resources would be needed. As I mentioned, we are now spending annually about $30 million on safeguards operations. Others have looked into this matter, not inside the Agency, but in governments, and a guess has been that resources would approximately have to double. That is to say that it would cost something like $60 million a year. These are probably very rough figures, but it is not tenfold, it is not just a small sum, but a doubling of the present amount.

The question was also asked: 'Which are the States Parties to the NPT where you have partial safeguards only for a part of the nuclear industry?' It is only in the nuclear-weapon States. The non-nuclear-weapon States Parties to the NPT have so-called 'full-scope' safeguards, that is safeguards over the whole of their nuclear industry. Of non-Parties to the NPT or to the Tlatelolco Treaty, there are a number who have safeguards over part of their nuclear industry. To be concrete, in the case of India, Pakistan, Israel and South Africa, we do implement safeguards over some of their nuclear facilities, not because they have made a voluntary offer to do so, but because when they imported nuclear technology it was a condition made by the exporter that the installations should be submitted to safeguards and the importing State in question accepted this as part of the deal. In those States, of course, we are responsible for guaranteeing that no diversion of fissionable material and no military use occurs in those installations which we safeguard, but we are not thereby pronouncing ourselves at all about installations in those States which are not under safeguards. With regard to those States that I have just mentioned—India, Pakistan, Israel, South Africa—the question was 'what additional resources would we need to cover their presently non-safeguarded installations?' It would not require a lot because their nuclear industry is not all that vast. India has a fair amount, Pakistan has not so much more, and South Africa and Israel would require a little more, but not vastly more. It cannot be compared with the increase in resources we would need if we were to safeguard the whole peaceful sector of the nuclear-weapon States as well.

Chairman

The following questions are to Professor Rotblat.

Bruce Adkins

You said that the Three-Mile Island accident had alerted people to the dangers of civil nuclear power. It is suggested that the Three-Mile Island accident, which harmed nobody apart from the power station's financial backers, has demonstrated the remarkable effectiveness of the in-built safety measures incorporated in all civil nuclear power plants.

Joseph Rotblat

First, maybe I should correct the statement just made. What I actually said about the Three-Mile Island accident was that it had alerted the public to the possibility of human error leading to grave consequences and the need for more protection had increased the cost of reactors. I don't think anybody would dispute this, it was the result. The fact is that because of this accident—and I did not say it was a disaster—people realized that there could be human error and that new safety measures would have to be introduced. All this has increased the cost of reactors and no doubt has contributed to the slowing-down of reactors, particularly in the United States, where there have been no new orders for a number of years now.

Secondly, I would not entirely agree with the questioner that no harm was done to anybody at all there, because, if you remember, people were evacuated. It resulted in quite a material loss to those people who had to be evacuated and a lot of anxiety was caused. It caused psychological damage to some people and all this was recognized in court. In fact, awards were made of up to something like $20 million. I don't believe the court would have made such awards if there had not been substantial grounds for believing that there was some damage, even if it was only of psychological value. We must not ignore the psychological aspect because how people perceive nuclear energy is very important too. In this case, there was the possibility that there could have been a more serious accident, a release of much larger amounts of radioactivity, and this is the reason why people were evacuated. Therefore, I don't think that people should gloat or take this as an example of how safe a reactor is.

Marjorie Thompson

In view of the fact that some countries persistently cite verification as a stumbling block getting in the way of support for United Nations resolutions on disarmament or other positive initiatives, could Professor Rotblat give details about requirements and/or procedures for verification down to 1 kilotonne?

Joseph Rotblat

It is quite true that problems of verification are a great stumbling block and they are going to be even greater for some types of weapon. For example, Cruise missiles are very difficult to verify and their introduction may in fact make the problem of reducing and eliminating such weapons very difficult. However, in the particular case cited, namely, the verification of a comprehensive test ban down to 1 kilotonne, I do not believe that verification is the stumbling block. By seismic means—which have been improved over the years—one can distinguish between natural earthquakes and seismic waves produced by nuclear explosions, and nowadays this need not be done by verification but by national means. For example, the United States should be able to use its national means to check whether a seismic wave is due to an earthquake or to a nuclear explosion. The question is how far can you go down to distinguish it? You come down to a level of explosion where the noise is so loud that one really cannot say which it is. I understand that with present techniques one could distinguish down to a level of certainly about 5 kilotonnes, and some people say even to 1 kilotonne, quite distinctly. Therefore, I do not think that verification should be used as an excuse for not introducing the Treaty. Moreover, there may even be possibilities of having proper international, not national, means of verification by using black boxes, and I believe that the Soviet Union agreed to this a long time ago. Therefore, I do not think that in this case the matter arises.

Sir John Hackett

So long as nuclear power generation depends upon fission, the deadly danger from nuclear weapons will persist, with little, if any, diminution. Only the application of fusion to the peaceful generation of energy can hold out real hope. How close is this?

Joseph Rotblat

To take the first part, I agree with Sir John that if one could get rid of all fission in the world, in nuclear power reactors and otherwise, it would to a large extent eliminate the danger, but not entirely, because any fusion reactor which may eventually be built but is not yet in existence is also a source of an extremely intense number of neutrons. Therefore, if a nation is intent on making nuclear weapons, it could simply take some uranium, put it around the fusion reactor, and then make plutonium inside the uranium. So there are ways of overcoming this problem, but again there is no technological fix to get over it. Another problem is that plutonium is mainly used in nuclear weapons as a trigger, it is a fission trigger that starts the hydrogen bomb. One could trigger a hydrogen bomb without the fission, because, after all, a hydrogen bomb is a thermonuclear reaction. I would not be too optimistic about the possibility of eliminating the danger of nuclear weapons by getting rid of fission and replacing it with fusion. Unfortunately, however, the prospects of fusion seem to recede all the time. From time to time, we have a breakthrough, then it turns out that it is a breakthrough in some aspects but not in others. I believe that at this present time nobody could come out and definitely say when we may expect fusion to be a practical proposition.

Christine Hudgins

If there is a NPT walk-out, which States are thought to be most likely to withdraw their participation?

Joseph Rotblat

The whole gist of my paper was the optimistic assumption that there would be no walk-out, that the Third Review Conference would lead to some positive results and not to any walk-out. I did not say that I believed there would be a walk-out, I said there are predictions that there may be. Therefore, I am inclined to be nervous about mentioning nations as such.

Chairman

The next question is addressed to Dr. von Hippel.

Dieter von Ehrenstein

What are your further comments concerning the special dangers of fast breeder reactors in view of the fact that these reactors might eventually supply great quantities of weapon-grade—or even super-grade—plutonium, i.e. a material almost purely consisting of the particularly dangerous weapon isotope Pu^{239}? (The IIASA study *Energy in a Finite World* projects in one of its scenarios for the year 2030 about 4,000 GWe by fast breeders.)

Frank von Hippel

Before I answer that question, I would just like to add one addendum to Dr. Rotblat's last answer, and that is that the ignition of nuclear weapons without fissionable materials has not been achieved as yet even by the most advanced nuclear-weapon States, so the control of fissionable materials continues to be a very effective way of controlling the spread of nuclear weapons.

In response to the question that was addressed to me, breeder reactors are dangerous because they require the separation of plutonium from nuclear fuel. Plutonium, as long as it is in the nuclear fuel, is protected by the highly radioactive fission products that are formed there at the same time as the plutonium. Current reactors do not require the separation of plutonium from nuclear reactor fuel and in that sense they are much safer from proliferation and the terrorist perspective than breeder reactors, so it is very fortunate that, you might say, the invisible hand of economics has been protecting us from the commercialization of the plutonium breeder reactors which have this undesirable characteristic. On the other hand, it is very unfortunate that we seem to be nevertheless determined to throw this advantage away by, despite economics, continuing with the separation of plutonium and using it in the current reactors where it too is uneconomic. As far as the difference between weapon-grade and non-weapon-grade plutonium is concerned, the uninitiated are often deceived into believing that one requires so-called 'weapon-grade' plutonium to make a nuclear weapon and that therefore the so-called 'reactor-grade' plutonium which is produced in power reactors operated normally is less of a danger, but that is not true. Weapon-grade plutonium is called weapon-grade plutonium because weapon designers prefer it, but not because they require it. They have repeatedly stated that they could do very well with reactor-grade plutonium in making nuclear weapons and that would certainly be true as well for nuclear terrorists.

Chairman

The next two questions are addressed to Professor Goldemberg.

Claude Bourdet

A few years ago there was a press conference in West Germany given by the Research Director of AEG; it was reported at length in the *Frankfurter Rundschau*. He said 'We are still making money with nuclear energy, but in the long run we are playing all our cards on solar energy. Our solar cells already make solar energy competitive in tropical countries, but, as their price is halved practically every two years, we will soon be competitive with other energy sources, even in temperate climates'. How do you feel about that prospect?

José Goldemberg

Unfortunately, the prospects did not materialize. Electricity produced from solar cells is still very expensive, about three to four times more expensive than energy produced from other sources, including nuclear energy. Therefore, it can be used only for very special applications such as satellites. However, there are other energy sources which are very promising in tropical countries, for example, sugar cane is converted into ethanol in Brazil in huge quantities and almost all of the automobiles run on solar energy via the conversion of sugar cane into ethanol, which is as good as gasoline.

Reinhard Spilker

As a nuclear physicist and energy expert, are you now saying that nuclear energy is bad for development? Is this the outcome of your experience with nuclear technology in your country?

José Goldemberg

I would not say that nuclear energy is bad for development in general, but it has proved to be inadequate in several developing countries, including Brazil. For example, hydroelectric power is much more successful than nuclear energy was, and in all likelihood this is not going to change in any foreseeable future. On the other hand, there are countries in which nuclear energy seems to play an indispensable role, like France, where a third of the energy is produced from nuclear reactors. It is a matter of national choice—regional choice maybe—and some countries can choose one solution while some choose another. In the small-sized and medium-sized developing countries, of which there are many, nuclear energy has just proved to be inapplicable because the big companies have not succeeded in producing small nuclear reactors and since, in their perspective, the market is there, the fact that they have not succeeded teaches us something. Brazil's experience has been a bad one which will certainly reflect on the fortunes of suppliers of nuclear equipment in the future because other people will be very careful before embarking on very expensive programmes which can fail or which can be expected to fail in some sense. I have never heard of hydroelectric power which did not succeed. There are one or two examples of hydroelectric power stations that have collapsed for some reason, but there are thousands around the world; they are very reliable and their technology is very well known. I do not think that nuclear energy should be condemned for what happened in Brazil, but it does make you alive to the fact that there are good choices and bad choices, and one should be very careful about making expensive choices. One can afford to make mistakes in inexpensive choices, but in expensive choices one has to be a lot more careful.

Chairman

There is another question addressed to Ambassador Qian Jiadong.

Jochen Benecke

Would Professor Goldemberg's statement also apply to China, that nuclear energy will not play a significant role in the future?

Qian Jiadong

As is known to everybody here, China is now engaged in a very arduous task of reconstruction and the so-called 'programme for modernization and energy' is one priority area about which we think enough to devote a lot of our development efforts to it. Apart from conventional energy sources, our choice at the moment would also include the development of nuclear energy. Many of us here know that we are in the process of building a few nuclear power plants and only recently we entered into agreements with some countries on the further promotion of nuclear energy co-operation. How big will that role be? Of course it is difficult for me to say at the moment, but in any case I will recommend to our departments concerned with energy that they should look into the statement made by Professor Goldemberg.

Chairman

We have two more questions for Dr. Blix.

Mycle Schneider

How many safeguards inspectors are actually working for the IAEA and how is their number developing?

Concerning MOX-fuel, some top representatives recently stated that one of the main lessons learned was that each client must accept the swap of part of his plutonium for equivalent plutonium already in the system, one of the reasons being the storage limits (*Nuclear Europe*, May 1985). Do you think that effective safeguards would still be possible under these circumstances, also in respect of the American Nuclear Non-Proliferation Act?

Hans Blix

I think I mentioned in my statement that we now have about 180 inspectors on active duty and that they are backed up by another 70 inspectors at

Headquarters. Attention is often focussed only on the number of inspectors, but of course the safeguards effort is a much bigger one. I mentioned the figure for how many nuclear data are reported to us and registered in our computers and how we, like accountants, check the data in the first place to see whether there is any diversion. The inspectors' role is to check, as it were, if the gold is in the bank vaults. So while their number is an important part of the safeguards effort, it is a much bigger effort than that.

On the evolution of the safeguards system, I think I also mentioned that there has been a very rapid growth. In fact, in 1981 we had 202 safeguards inspectors altogether, and in 1984 we had 253, an increase of 25 per cent. The safeguards budget in 1981 was about $20 million, in 1984 it was $27 million, an increase of 37 per cent. With regard to records in our computers, in 1981 we had 1.1 million records in the computerized safeguards data base, in 1984 it was up to 3.8 million records. I will not continue with this illustration, but it shows that there has been a very rapid growth in the safeguards operations, due in the first place to the fact that the nuclear installations to be safeguarded have increased. Many more nuclear reactors and other nuclear installations have come on stream and require safeguarding of resources on our side. There has also been a gradual improvement in the quality and consolidation of the safeguards effort. We are still of the view that we need more resources to carry out any inspection that we think will give perfectly adequate confidence in the statement that there is no diversion, when such a statement is issued.

On the other question that was asked regarding the MOX-fuel, it is perhaps both too technical for the audience and for myself. Perhaps another colleague who is technical would care to answer it.

Pierre Lehmann

Nuclear energy bears a relation to nuclear weapons; the very existence of IAEA bears witness to this fact. Besides, the nuclear practice is a very complicated way of providing energy with lots of dangers attached to it. It has never been proved, nor has it been generally agreed, that nuclear energy is really necessary to mankind. Wouldn't it be simpler, and also more realistic, to phase out not only nuclear weapons but also nuclear energy?

Hans Blix

I am not sure whether it has really been proved that gas is needed for mankind either; no one has tried to do that. I would mention three points: firstly, the world is not threatened by a few hundred nuclear reactors, but it is threatened by some 50,000 nuclear warheads and to suggest that you should phase out nuclear energy in order to stop the nuclear warheads is to look at the wrong end of the picture. Secondly, as I already said in my statement, even if you were to scrap all the peaceful nuclear energy in the world, all the nuclear reactors in the world, you would not get rid of nuclear weapons, nor would you get rid of the knowledge of how to construct nuclear weapons. Thirdly, at this stage it is not so easy to phase out nuclear energy. Today it provides about 13 per cent of the electricity in the world as a whole and in some countries in Europe it provides a great deal indeed: in France it is over 50 per cent and in certain other European countries around or over 40 per cent of the electricity, without contributing to the sulphur dioxide of the atmosphere, or the nitrogen oxide, or indeed, for that matter, increasing the carbon dioxide. Therefore, I don't think that it would be at all easy to phase out nuclear energy, nor do I think that it would help at all in stemming proliferation—neither vertical nor horizontal.

Chairman

We now have another question addressed to Professor Rotblat.

Claude Bourdet

I strongly approve of your proposal about Great Britain and France renouncing nuclear weapons. Regarding the de Gaulle–Bevin quotation, do you remember that the time of the greatest independence of French foreign policy (under de Gaulle) was when he had no nuclear weapons worth mentioning (at the time of his Phnom Penh speech, for instance)? Today, with a sizeable nuclear force, French policy is more aligned with the United States than it ever was. Isn't it a fact that the countries showing the greatest independence—Sweden, Yugoslavia (or even, in a deplorable way, Iraq and Iran)—are non-nuclear? Independence today equals non-alignment and non-alignment has little to do with nuclear weapons.

Joseph Rotblat

Firstly, I am very glad to realize that at least there is one supporter of my controversial proposal that Britain and France should give up their nuclear weapons. I do not remember this particular quotation from General de Gaulle and I was interested to hear about it. I want to agree with part of the third comment about the role of the non-aligned countries. We heard this morning from Prime Minister Olof Palme that Sweden, for example, did seriously consider at one stage whether it should have its own nuclear weapons. It came to the conclusion, which is completely in alignment with what I said in my paper, that it would be against its own interests to have such weapons and it decided not to have them. I hope that other countries too will reach this statesmanlike decision, but it should not necessarily be restricted to non-aligned countries. After all, even the aligned countries are not monolithic, they have different attitudes. For example, in NATO, you find that some countries refuse to have some of the weapons—intermediate-range nuclear weapons, for example—which other countries accept. Therefore, we should not just say that this is only a matter for non-aligned countries. I would like to see all countries, whether aligned or not, reach the same sort of decision.

Chairman

Another question for Professor Rotblat. It seems you have another supporter.

Constanze Eisenbart

Policy does not only work with arguments, power pressure and negotiations, it needs symbolic gestures. Why can the middle nuclear forces—China, France and the United Kingdom—not be persuaded to give up their strategically useless and politically detrimental nuclear arsenals?

Joseph Rotblat

All I can say is that we should try to persuade them. This is the reason why I put forward this proposal, not that I expected it to be accepted immediately by Mrs. Thatcher or President Mitterand, but I think we should at least begin to argue this issue out in the open. From what I see of Mrs. Thatcher's policies, I am convinced that she certainly would not agree. On the other hand, if the next Government were to be a Labour Government and if they followed the policies they now propose, it may well be that Britain would give up nuclear weapons—an independent nuclear deterrent. France, I think, is less likely to do so, whatever the colour of the Government, but should Britain give them up then the chances would also not be too bad for France. The thing to do is to try to advocate this idea, propagate it among the public, hoping that eventually it will be accepted.

Chairman

The next question is to both Ambassador Shaker and Professor Rotblat.

Wolfgang Biermann

Which countries that have not signed the NPT would join it if there were a halt to tests by the nuclear-weapon States?

Mohamed Shaker

First of all, let me say that a comprehensive test ban would be a very important measure as far as the Parties to the Treaty are concerned; it would help them to remain committed to the Treaty. As to non-Parties, for conceptual reasons, I doubt very much whether some of them would join the NPT because of a CTB. Let us take one example: India. I doubt if India will join the NPT because of a CTB. It objected conceptually to the Treaty because of the discrimination between nuclear and non-nuclear and it would have liked to see the NPT banning altogether the production of nuclear weapons, as well as the submission to safeguards of all nuclear activities in all States Parties. If you take other examples: Argentina and Brazil. They want to keep the option of using peaceful nuclear explosions for peaceful purposes. The Treaty bans the production of nuclear devices, whether they are peaceful or military. So I doubt also that countries like Argentina and Brazil would join the NPT because of a CTB. However, some other countries may join the NPT if there is real progress on disarmament, especially a CTB. I recall a statement made many years ago by the Foreign Minister of Zambia. He said that if there was progress on disarmament, his country would be ready to sign and ratify the NPT. However, I think that what is expected in the future, which would make it easier for other countries to abide by a non-proliferation regime, is to encourage the creation of nuclear-weapon-free zones. For example, Colombia is not a Party to the NPT, but is a Party to the Tlatelolco Treaty, and many others I think would abide by a non-proliferation regime which would bolster the NPT, but would not necessarily become Parties to the NPT because of disarmament measures. We have other examples: Pakistan is very active in the creation of a nuclear-weapon-free zone in South-East Asia; and Israel has expressed its readiness to join a nuclear-weapon-free zone in the Middle East. Therefore, I think that to bolster the NPT we ought to look into other measures which would complement and add to the provisions existing as a result of the NPT.

Joseph Rotblat

We have heard that most of the criticism of the NPT was about Article VI, that no progress had been made towards disarmament. I believe that a Comprehensive Test Ban Treaty would be a very important step towards that because it would effectively halt the nuclear arms race, and once you halt it, you have a better chance of beginning to reverse it as well. At the moment, whatever you do in negotiations, new weapons are developed and you end up worse off than you were before. For this reason, I believe that this step would be very important.

Looking through the list of the 42 countries which have not ratified the NPT, it seems to me that, apart from the few States mentioned by the Ambassador just now, most of them have not really any strong views about the NPT. They follow this criticism about Article VI and my feeling is that, should it really come about, a majority will join. I would not like to mention which, because of course I could not predict this, but I am sure that a majority will come in.

Chairman

I think that Professor Goldemberg would like to comment on this question.

José Goldemberg

I would like to make a clarification about the Tlatelolco Treaty which might be useful. It has a provision which allows for peaceful nuclear explosions; I can assure you that no one that I know of in Latin America takes that seriously, nuclear explosions for peaceful purposes are just an invention and nobody thinks of them seriously. Nevertheless, that provision is in the Tlatelolco Treaty and is interpreted as more acceptable to Latin American countries than the International Atomic Energy Agency. I don't want to be a spoiler, but the main reason why countries have signed the Tlatelolco Treaty and not the NPT is that the former is an empty Treaty. You will excuse me for my bluntness, but it is absolutely empty, because it has a clause—or many countries have added a clause—that states that it will only enter into operation when all the States concerned have signed it, which is somewhat impossible because there are more than 30 nations and Cuba is one of them. Puerto Rico has weapons because it has a special relationship with the United States, and Britain introduced weapons in the South Atlantic during the Malvinas war, so it is really a piece of paper and I don't think that one should keep propagating the idea that the Tlatelolco Treaty is an answer. It is not an example of a regional treaty which could replace the NPT. Having spoiled things a little bit, I want to take a very strong stand on the Comprehensive Test Ban Treaty, and I agree with Professor Rotblat that if Article VI were to be changed, then a very strong case would be made in some of the threshold States—Brazil, Argentina and many others—for joining the Treaty, because of the situation in any one of these countries, except maybe South Africa or Israel which have somewhat desperate problems of national insecurity. There is a very strong debate in the government, sometimes it is open, sometimes it is not, but nevertheless a debate exists and people use anti-colonialist arguments for not joining the NPT because of the colonial character, or at least the semblance of colonialism, that the NPT has—the discriminatory character of the Treaty. If that were removed and if the Treaty were made more symmetric, then I think that the case for the civilian authorities in several countries—Brazil, Argentina and some others—would be strengthened. So I believe that it is a very important consideration. To use it as a threat towards the great Powers doesn't seem to be very effective, because the great Powers are not frightened very easily. I see people so concerned because Pakistan will have a bomb, but people should be a thousand times more concerned because the big Powers have thousands of weapons. The asymmetry in treating these countries is very striking for someone who does not attend this type of meeting very often.

Chairman

I am afraid that we won't have time for all the questions. The final question is addressed to Ambassador Dhanapala and Professor Rotblat.

Christopher Lee

Could Ambassador Dhanapala, as the representative of one of the smaller States, and Professor Rotblat, as a long-time observer of arms control, please explain why anybody should believe that the super-Powers will ever take any notice of the neutral and non-aligned States, and therefore, what realistic chance is there of a Comprehensive Test Ban Treaty?

Jayantha Dhanapala

In general, it is tempting to adopt the cynical view that nothing which the non-aligned and neutral States do will have any impact on the super-Powers, it will be so much water off a duck's back. But I think we are talking specifically in the NPT context and, in the NPT context, the non-aligned and neutral States are the majority, and the rules of procedure do permit voting if consensus cannot be achieved. If the non-aligned and neutral States turn up at the Review Conference in sufficient number, it is possible that the threat of voting, if not voting itself, could change the situation within the NPT. The depositary States—the nuclear-weapon States—are aware of this and they do want to keep the *status quo*. The fact that there was no final declaration at the Second Review Conference was itself a demonstration by the non-aligned and neutral States of their impatience with the present situation. It is difficult to predict what will happen in the Third Review Conference, but the avenues for applying pressure are there for non-aligned and neutral States and will be used by them unless the nuclear-weapon States heed the demands being made by this group.

Joseph Rotblat

After this professional answer, I will just give an observer's answer. It seems to me that the super-Powers have got to take notice of what is going in the smaller countries in the Third World, not just for altruistic reasons, but simply because whatever happens in these countries may affect their security too. In the future, they may be drawn into a conflict that has arisen in these countries, and therefore I feel that they have got to take notice. As far as the Comprehensive Test Ban Treaty is concerned, to say that the super-Powers would not agree to it is perhaps not quite correct because I understand that one of the super-Powers at least has said that it will be willing to sign a Comprehensive Test Ban Treaty; therefore, we are only waiting for the other one, and I hope that its agreement will also be forthcoming.

II

The Spread of Nuclear Weapons among Nations: Militarization or Development

CHAIRMAN:

MR. JACQUES FREYMOND

Honorary Director of the Graduate Institute of International Studies, Geneva

THE LINK BETWEEN HORIZONTAL AND VERTICAL PROLIFERATION

The Nuclear Arms Race and the Danger of its Spreading to New Countries

PROFESSOR ANATOLY A. GROMYKO

Director of the Institute of African Studies of the USSR Academy of Sciences, Corresponding Member of the USSR Academy of Sciences, Member of the Soviet Scientists' Committee for Peace against the Nuclear Threat

A sober approach to nuclear weapons is needed

The vertical and horizontal proliferation of nuclear weapons can be regarded as tantamount to the loss of control over them. It is not accidental that this subject is particularly popular now with science fiction writers and cinema producers. Who has not read a book, or watched a movie, where some maniac, deciding to become the 'master of the world', would use for this purpose a submarine or even a spacecraft loaded with various kinds of mass destruction weapons? The rest depends on the author's imagination. But the most astonishing thing is that there is nothing particularly incredible in stories of this kind. It is probably this fact that makes them so dramatic.

The sophisticated nuclear-weapons systems, the product of research done by physicists, mathematicians and experts in chemical and mechanical sciences, have long since gone out of their control and now have a life of their own. Frequently the very characteristics sought by the military, e.g. increasingly self-contained operation and comparatively simple handling and maintenance of such weapons not only contribute to lowering the 'nuclear threshold' but are also conducive to the spread of their production far beyond the countries where those systems were first developed. Moreover, now that increased numbers of specialists in industrialized countries are acquiring computer skills, it is already not too difficult to find people for handling such systems. As for Cruise missiles, neutron weapons or 'backpack' nuclear mines, they might appear to be specially designed for adventurists of all kinds, from ordinary gangsters to paranoid dictators.

In the world of today, when so much is known of the possible effects of a thermonuclear catastrophe, a tranquillizing idea has appeared, almost as a matter of course, that no State leader would run the risk of initiating a nuclear war and that it can only result from a fatal error or accident. In short, quite a few respectable people seem to be convinced that what one should fear is just a short-circuited computer or a terrorist acting alone.

This kind of thinking is not so innocuous as it might seem at first glance. This was noted by, among others, the Independent Commission on Disarmament and Security Issues under the chairmanship of Olof Palme. Its report emphasized that such attitudes 'greatly hamper the effort to build the political constituents necessary to bring pressure to bear to halt the nuclear arms race'.[1]

Quite often a similar view is taken of the proliferation of nuclear weapons, as something inevitably resulting from technological progress. It is forgotten, however, that the 20th century, which has brought, on top of the supreme achievements of the human mind, the ever-present threat of mankind perishing under an avalanche of nuclear weapons, has also raised in the most dramatic terms one of the key questions of civilization, the question of whether man is ethically and morally capable of dealing with the increasing possibilities opened by his own creativity. The Russian and Soviet intelligentsia has traditionally addressed this problem.

This brings to mind, in particular, the words of Academician V. I. Vernadsky, an outstanding natural scientist of the 20th century. Looking with both hope and apprehension at the then only barely visible contours of the coming nuclear era, he said in the early 1920s: 'We are approaching a great turning point in the life of mankind, which has no precedent in anything it has experienced. The time will soon come when man will gain control of atomic energy, a source of power that will make it possible for him to build his life as he desires. This may happen in a few years, or in a hundred years. But one thing is clear—it must happen. Will mankind be able to use this force, for good purposes and not for self-destruction? Is man mature enough to use this power which science will inevitably place in his hands?'[2] Unfortunately not all mankind proved to be morally prepared to live with nuclear energy. Less than a quarter of a century stood between those prophetic words of V. I. Vernadsky and the nuclear explosions in Hiroshima and Nagasaki.

The realities of the nuclear age have made it necessary to rethink such basic concepts of political science as power, superiority, victory, and security. Nuclear war can no longer be regarded as 'a continuation of policy by other means'—there can be no winner in such a war. The direct relationship between the arms race and diminished national security is the central idea of

[1] *Common Security: A Blueprint for Survival.* Report of the Independent Commission on Disarmament and Security Issues under the chairmanship of Olof Palme. UN General Assembly document A/CN. 10/38, p. 41.

[2] V. I. Vernadsky, *Essays and speeches.* Moscow, 1922.

the already mentioned report of the Palme Commission: 'In the modern age, security cannot be obtained unilaterally. Economically, politically, culturally and—most important—militarily, we live in an increasingly interdependent world. The security of one nation cannot be bought at the expense of others . . . We face common dangers and thus must also promote our security in common.'[1] Unfortunately this reasonable approach has quite a few unreasonable opponents. And this is dangerous, for quite often they exercise political power and have control of vast military potentials. This poses a threat to peace and the survival of mankind.

A new logic resulting from the threat of nuclear 'overkill' has been acquiring crucial importance in international relations in the last decade of the 20th century. One cannot secure a unilateral advantage for oneself at the expense of someone else's security without ultimately prejudicing one's own interests. This logic was already well understood by the most far-sighted and sober-minded of those who witnessed the dawn of the nuclear era, at least by those who were not under the spell of various concepts of force. The starting point for developing a philosophy of mankind's survival is contained in the famous words of Albert Einstein about the necessity of a new manner of human thinking since the atomic bomb has changed the world radically and people are in a new situation to which their thinking must conform.

Few people realized at the time that the advent of weapons of mass destruction of the power that threatens to get out of control changes not only the role and attitudes to a war involving the use of such weapons, but also the order of priorities among mankind's major concerns. This became fully evident in the course of the 'nuclear race', whose entire history is vivid proof that attempts to ensure security through military superiority are futile. Each time the United States sought to achieve a unilateral advantage through the development and adoption of new types of arms, it forced the Soviet Union to take measures in response. The result was a new, more dangerous spiral in the arms race, which developed vertically, thus undermining international stability and security, including the security of the Americans themselves.

Nevertheless, the special responsibility of the nuclear-weapon States for the fate of the world is not the same as 'equal responsibility' of these States for heightened international tensions. For surely one cannot seriously equate the scientists who discovered atomic energy and the politicians who took the decision to drop the atomic bomb. The world has not forgotten the specific political situation in which this ominous decision was taken. It is recalled with a special feeling today, in the year of the 40th anniversary of the great victory of the united nations over German fascism and Japanese militarism in World War II.

The circumstances under which nuclear weapons were used by the United

[1] *Common Security: A Blueprint for Survival*, p. 12.

States against Japan were quite odd. The use of such weapons was not militarily justifiable. It was an indefensible, immoral action. By dropping the A-bombs on Hiroshima and Nagasaki, Truman and his people were just hastening to tell the world, and above all the Soviet Union, of their monopoly on the dreadful 'overkiller' weapon. The possession of atomic weapons was seen by them as guaranteeing a special role of 'world leadership'.

That was how the first pages of the philosophy of nuclear deterrence were written. It was to become the 'legitimate heiress' to the old political doctrines couched in terms of conventional military power and superiority. But since the pursuit of its speculative tenets would sooner or later result in the disappearance of any policy together with its advocates, the philosophy of nuclear deterrence is absolutely unusable in practical politics; figuratively speaking, it is the last chapter in the traditional system of relations built along imperial lines.

This by no means signifies that the philosophy and practice of deterrence have been abandoned. With an amazingly stubborn self-confidence its advocates are determined to pursue their old ways even at the risk of the death of the whole of mankind. For instance, in a book by Edward M. Kennedy and Mark Hatfield the authors write with unconcealed alarm that a considerable portion of the United States political and military élites believe that a nuclear war can be won.[1]

Trying to brush aside the fears, caused by the principle of the 'balance of terror', based on the presumption that in the event of a nuclear attack the other side would still have enough weapons remaining for a devastating retaliatory strike, the 'nuclear optimists' have found nothing better than to talk of than 'decapitating' nuclear strikes or of 'limited' or 'protracted' nuclear wars. It is supposed that such a war would be fought in the European theater. It is not mentioned, however, that the idea of a 'limited' use of nuclear weapons in Europe could also be applied to other regional crisis situations. Military experts are talking of the possibility of using in local conflicts the new high-precision weapons systems that are being developed to fit the concept of a 'decapitating' strike. If a 'limited' nuclear war is possible in Europe, why can it not be waged in any other part of the world, say, on the American continent or on any other?

There is a maxim that a pessimist is a well-informed optimist. I do not think that 'nuclear optimism' results from a lack of information. It is rather the opposite—an attempt to disregard the available scientific data concerning the nature of the effects of a nuclear war on the Earth's climate and its ecology.

Let me now address a subject that could be entitled 'Tropical palm-trees under nuclear snow'. Once again I will turn to science fiction. In his novel *Cat's Cradle*, the American writer, Kurt Vonnegut, has set forth his own

[1] Kennedy E. M., Hatfield M. O. *Stoppt die Atom-Rüstung*, Hamburg, April 1982.

version of a global catastrophe resulting from the spreading of a fundamentally new super-weapon called 'Ice 9'. Its developer was to solve a specific technical problem, trying to come up with a universal means for crossing swamps. Yet, the new chemical possessed one vexing quality, i.e. its ability to trigger an instantaneous chain reaction. A single crystal of 'Ice 9' was enough to freeze all liquid on the planet. Following a series of conflicts brought about by such, regrettably common, human qualities as ambition, cupidity and incredible light-mindedness, a capsule of 'Ice 9' ended up on a small god-forsaken island in the midst of the ocean. Due to the combination of a number of entirely accidental events, each and every one of which by itself could not in any way affect the fate of the planet—such as the absence of proper storage facilities, a pilot's error at a military parade and, finally, the nastiness of the island's dictator, who decided to time his death to the end of the world—'Ice 9' wound up in the ocean.

Credit should be given to the talented author whose insight makes one see more dramatically the global implications of the use of mass destruction weapons, whose use, even in small quantities, is capable of upsetting the fragile ecological balance of our planet; indeed, in many respects the author anticipated the well-substantiated scientific hypothesis of 'nuclear winter'.

Merely 10 or 15 years ago it was said that a nuclear war would kill hundreds of millions of people but the question of the survival of mankind was raised only by the writers of science fiction, if at all. The strictly scientific data available today is much grimmer than even their most dire predictions. This is not only because the nuclear arsenals have grown and continue to expand. We now possess more knowledge of and insight into the consequences of the use of nuclear weapons and the global nature of the impact of man's activities on his environment.

The nuclear weapons, which were developed in the quiet of secret laboratories by experts who often were unaware of the achievements in other areas of research, have quite recently become a subject of interdisciplinary analysis not just by physicists and mathematicians but also meteorologists, ecologists, biologists, physicians, economists and sociologists. Indeed, it can be safely said that never before have nuclear weapons been presented to mankind so starkly with their potential to destroy the human race.

On the basis of a mathematical model developed by Soviet scientists, a well-substantiated conclusion was made that the ecological consequences of a nuclear war would be no less dangerous than the direct effects of nuclear weapons. As was evident at the Soviet-American meeting of scientists on the global impact of a nuclear war on the Earth's environment, held in December 1983 in Washington, American experts had arrived at similar conclusions. A certain difference in approach mainly concerns the quantitative aspect, in particular in determining the threshold at which the effects of the use of nuclear weapons would become irreversible for the Earth.

However, even today one can clearly imagine the magnitude of the disaster which would strike our planet if only a small fraction, i.e. about 10–20 per cent, of the nuclear weapons accumulated thus far, were to be used. The tremendous force of the nuclear energy released thereby would destroy the ozone layer in the atmosphere up to the height of 20–30 kilometres and start forest fires that would sweep areas exceeding 1 million square kilometres. The cloud caused by the explosions and fires—and not only forests but also cities and industrial plants would be ablaze—would in two or three weeks envelop virtually the entire globe. The absorption of the sun's radiation by that smoke-and-dust cloud would result in the cooling of land by dozens of degrees. According to Soviet and American scientists, average temperatures would drop by 30 to 50 degrees Celsius. The fires in the areas of hostilities would result in freezing cold in the tropics. Climatic changes of global magnitude caused by thermonuclear war have become known in scientific literature as 'nuclear winter'.

The destruction of tropical forests by the 'nuclear cold' would increase many times over the reflective capacity of the areas covered by them at present. Even after the atmosphere's transparency is restored, those areas would receive much less energy from the sun. The energy structure of the Earth's climatic system would be qualitatively changed. The climate and subsequently the biosphere would be transformed into a new state whose characteristics are hard to predict. But even if man as a biological species were to survive somewhere on our planet, his socio-economic support system, fragile as it is—for here we are talking about what is now known as the developing countries—would be destroyed.

The ecological consequences of the nuclear catastrophe in the developing countries will be compounded by an almost total breakdown of their economic relations with industrialized countries, which for the most part will be destroyed. It is not difficult to imagine what this would mean, for example, for Africans, of whom 150 million are even now facing an imminent threat of death from starvation. In a nuclear war, the prospects for people in Latin America, Asia, Australia and Oceania would be no better.

The irreversible changes in the Earth's ecological character would not only rule out any possibility of a Third World country benefiting from the mutual nuclear destruction of the countries of the Northern hemisphere but would also call into question at least the survival of any such country as a sovereign entity.

Ironically, however, the increased threat of a global thermonuclear catastrophe, which ought to be a factor for a more stable non-proliferation regime, has so far not restrained the nuclear ambitions of some so-called threshold nuclear States.

The threat of an escalation in the nuclear weapons race increases not only with the emergence of new types of such weapons and the ripening of, so to speak, the material prerequisites for its horizontal proliferation. The threat is closely linked with the very spirit of the nuclear arms race, with the existence of the philosophy of nuclear deterrence.

Since the days when the atomic bomb was first developed and used and at all stages of the process of adopting new nuclear weapons systems, culminating recently in the US Strategic Defense Initiative, which calls for the militarization of outer space, NATO has been trying to justify the nuclear arms race by its 'concern for preserving peace'. It is sad and, indeed, tragic that the illusion of being able to live in peace and security under a 'nuclear umbrella' is still spreading much faster than even the nuclear weapons themselves; in the end, it becomes a kind of drug, an impulse driving some States to enrol in the nuclear club.

The disappointment caused by the failure of the attempts to contain the global arms race sometimes gives rise to ideas of the kind expressed by the African scientist Ali Mazrui in his book *A World Federation of Cultures* and his report 'Africa's Nuclear Future'.[1] Criticizing the Western powers for their 'chauvinism' in the arms race, Mazrui puts forward a demand for 'equality' in the arms race. In his opinion, only an armed Africa, and an armed Third World, possessing not only conventional but also nuclear weapons, can force the nuclear powers, who are the 'real war-mongers', to act more reasonably. Such thinking would make it impossible to prevent horizontal proliferation of nuclear arms.

The idea that the nuclear arms race can be halted if more countries participate in it is an extremely dangerous delusion. If new States acquire a few nuclear weapons and systems for their delivery, or even dozens of them, this cannot have a decisive impact on the global balance of nuclear arsenals that contain thousands of such weapons. On the contrary, this would make nuclear arms control more difficult, increase the global impact of the factor of uncertainty, breed distrust and mutual suspicions in international relations, and, I would say, would further strain the already tense 'nervous system' of nuclear politics.

At the same time some arguments worthy of attention have been put forward by a number of non-aligned States who criticize the non-proliferation regime for its inability in the present conditions to provide any guarantee against the danger of more States becoming nuclear and for not being an effective instrument for taking measures to limit nuclear arms and to achieve nuclear disarmament as stipulated in Article VI of the Non-Proliferation Treaty. One can also understand the growing disappointment of the non-aligned countries due to the fact that contrary to the provisions of the Treaty the Western nuclear powers have broken off the negotiations on a comprehensive nuclear weapons test ban.

[1] Mazrui Ali A. *A World Federation of Cultures*, N. Y., 1976; 'Africa's Nuclear Future', *Survival*, 1980, March/April.

While some are critical and others are complaining, still others, such as, for example, the prominent American expert on the developing countries, Ernest Lefevre, come to the conclusion based on the analysis of the military potential of just nine countries (India, Pakistan, Iran, Israel, Egypt, South Korea, Taiwan, Argentina and Brazil) that within the next two decades Third World countries will start to produce nuclear weapons, in spite of the huge expenditures and enormous political risks involved.[1]

It is obvious that breaches in the system of measures designed to ensure the non-proliferation of nuclear weapons are made by such States as South Africa, Israel, and Pakistan supported by Western countries, and above all by the United States. It is known, for example, that a uranium enrichment facility producing 10 tons of uranium a year has been operating in South Africa since 1977. According to some reports, it can produce up to 35 kilogrammes of highly-enriched uranium a year. The plant is not subject to IAEA control and, as can be understood from statements by the South African Government, it has no intention of placing it under the Agency's safeguards. This cannot but cause growing concern on the part of all countries that are interested in the non-proliferation of nuclear weapons and, in particular, South Africa's neighbours.

In the hands of the governments that, as a result of their own short-sighted policies find themselves in international isolation, are condemned by the international community and constantly have to face internal political instability, nuclear weapons may become a means of blackmail to be used at any moment as an argument of last resort in the struggle to preserve power. The very prospect of nuclear weapons appearing in such regions as the Middle East and southern Africa is not only making the settlement of tensions there more difficult but is also increasing the danger of their escalation into a large-scale confrontation.

Actions by nuclear States to deploy outside their own territory weapons of mass destruction and systems for their delivery constitute an equally serious blow to the non-proliferation regime. The military activities of the United States and other NATO countries pose a serious obstacle to the establishment of nuclear-free zones, which could become an effective means for strengthening the idea of non-proliferation. At present there are about 25 military bases used by the United States just on the territories of six African States—South Africa, Liberia, Morocco, Somalia, Kenya and Egypt, and on islands not adjacent to Africa. In the Mediterranean and in the Atlantic Ocean the United States has up to 60 nuclear submarines and at least 240 carrier-based attack aircraft capable of delivering nuclear weapons.

The deployment of American medium-range missiles in Europe, including Italy, constitutes a real threat to African countries. Suffice it to say that the range of the American nuclear missiles deployed in Sicily covers the whole

[1] Lefevre E. W. *Nuclear Arms in the Third World.* U.S. Policy Dilemma N.Y., 1980.

of northern Africa and the Middle East. A serious potential danger comes from the military activities of certain Western States, above all the United States, in the Indian Ocean, where a large formation of the US Navy is deployed. Hundreds of nuclear-capable attack aircraft are based on United States aircraft carriers deployed in this area. The island of Diego-Garcia, located in the middle of the Indian Ocean, has become a multipurpose base for the US Navy and Air Force, including its strategic air command.

The United States Central Command (CENTCOM), which was established in 1983 and which controls the rapid deployment force of up to 300,000 men, extends its zone of operation to 19 African and Asian countries. The many types of military equipment assigned to this Command include about 30 strategic bombers. There have been alarming reports that these forces, designed to suppress national liberation movements in the developing countries, could be equipped with neutron nuclear weapons.

I would also like to emphasize the fact that the danger of proliferation of nuclear weapons comes not only from the misguided intentions of some political leaders; it is also being stimulated by the official military doctrine of the United States whose actions have been preventing the establishment of nuclear-free zones. A vivid example in this respect has been the political, economic and diplomatic pressure brought to bear upon the New Zealand Government, which decided to ban access to its ports of ships with nuclear weapons on board.

The US plans for militarizing outer space bring the arms race to a qualitatively new level, demonstrating the direct link between the 'vertical' nuclear arms race and 'horizontal' proliferation. At the same time, while scientific studies have proved that controlling the destructive power of the weapons of mass destruction is not humanly possible and that the only way to survival is in preventing a conflict in which such weapons could be used, 'outer-space nuclear optimists' are trying to convince the world that just one more step remains to 'tame the nuclear genie', just one more effort to shut him up in the 'bottle' of military staff games and strategic concepts. For the United States 'curbing' the nuclear threat means threatening other nations and preparing for 'Star Wars'. Such has been the US response so far to the Soviet Union's unilateral obligation not to be the first to use nuclear weapons. The fact that under this obligation our country has taken steps to ensure strict control over nuclear weapons so as to preclude any possibility of their unauthorized use, is also being ignored.

It must be stated here that the analysis made by Soviet scientists of weapons systems under development in the United States, purportedly for the purposes of anti-missile space 'defence', shows that such systems could also be used for surprise attack against land and sea targets in various regions of the globe. Space-based weapons—'directed energy lasers', 'laser beams' or 'neutron particle beams'—could also be used to destroy targets on Earth.

There is another aspect worthy of attention here. Even at the present stage, which the American representatives call 'the research and development phase', the United States is trying to involve in preparations for a war in space not only its NATO allies but also States located in areas of actual armed conflicts. It is significant that Israel was among the first to express its readiness to join the plans of 'Star Wars'.

In scientific terms the consequences of the extension of the arms race into outer space are no less dangerous than in military terms. They would ruin the hopes for peaceful exploration of extra-terrestrial space in the interest of mankind. Moreover, although the 'Star Wars' programme is only in its initial stage, it is already disturbing the world, destabilizing global international relations and sharply aggravating the political and military confrontation.

Scientists cannot but feel concern for our future. While constantly thinking how to avoid disaster, one has to come to the conclusion that the policies of confrontation and the growing danger of nuclear war, overshadow, as it were, other global problems and sometimes impede the realization of their urgency. Figuratively speaking, in addition to the nuclear time bomb two other bombs have been placed under our common home, the Earth—the growing gap between the North and the South, the developed capitalist States and the developing countries, and the increasingly precarious ecological balance.

Of course, the arms race, particularly the nuclear arms race, is the most dangerous of the global problems—above all, because it threatens to destroy mankind. But even if the worst does not happen, still the 'nuclear marathon' will eventually bring mankind to a dead end, for it will deplete the strength and resources which are needed for defusing the other two bombs.

The growing gap in living standards between the industrialized and the developing countries exacerbates social and national conflicts and tensions in the Third World, leading to wars. It is quite clear that bridging this enormous gap between the North and the South and providing genuinely human conditions of existence for all people on Earth requires more than the implementation of a set of international political and economic measures envisaged in the programme for a new international economic order. The problem of ensuring harmonious development world-wide can only be resolved on the basis of the achievements of scientific and technological revolution placed at the service of peaceful causes and projects.

To illustrate this, I would refer to just one aspect of the problem of bridging the gap between the developing and the industrialized countries, i.e. the energy aspect. Socio-economic and technological backwardness cannot be overcome without finding reliable sources of energy. But even preliminary estimates indicate that if the whole of mankind were to consume the same amount of energy *per capita* as in the developed countries, the world's energy consumption would have to triple. In turn, such a global rate of energy consumption would not only result in the depletion of such traditional energy sources as oil, coal and gas, but would also bring about the danger of 'thermal pollution'.

Therefore, to solve the energy problem on a global scale new energy sources have to be found. There are a number of possible ways to solve the energy problem. One such possibility lies in outer space. One recalls in this context that the term 'high frontier' was used, long before President Reagan's 'Star Wars' plan, by the physicist G. O'Neil from Princeton University, who gave this name to his project of a solar power-generating station in space. Soviet scientists also point to the basic feasibility of energy production in space. The Russian scientist Konstantin Tsiolkovsky, who pioneered the study of space travel, pointed out long ago that it was ironic to look for new energy sources while the energy of the Sun is largely unused by man.

Energy generation in space is, of course, a new area of research, whose development will require vast material and intellectual resources. But experts believe that the expenditures involved would exceed the cost of the Strategic Defense Initiative programme. Mr. O'Neil estimated the cost of building a space power station, using spacecraft of the Shuttle type, to be 100 billion dollars, whereas the Reagan Administration is known to be planning to spend hundreds of billions of dollars on space militarization projects. United States Assistant Secretary of Defense R. Delauer has recognized that to build a large-scale space-based ABM system it is necessary to solve at least eight scientific and technological problems of no less complexity than the Manhattan project of developing the first atomic bomb.

Regardless of how approximate the forecasts are the fact remains that mankind's material and intellectual resources are not enough to tackle both the problems of social and economic progress and the requirements of the arms race. There was a time when experts were engaged in debate as to the role of politico-military needs in speeding up the general advancement of nuclear physics. Today the plans for militarizing outer space call into question the prospects of space exploration in the interests of humanity.

In today's world political leaders are confronted as never before with the most pressing choice—where should they channel peoples' energies and resources, to the arms race or to development? In the 1980s the Reagan Administration seems to be making a fundamentally wrong choice; instead of the programme of energy independence, which would benefit the American people, it opts for the strategic arms build-up programme, which is fraught with new dangers for the Americans and which would absorb the two trillion dollars that could ensure energy independence for the United States.

The arms race, above all the nuclear arms race, could become—to use a figure of speech—the last link in the socio-economic and ecological chain thrown around mankind's neck, that would strangle it to death. It has become more than the problem of politico-military relations between the East and the West or of economic relations between the North and the South; in the final analysis, it is driving the whole of mankind into a death trap.

The only way out of the present critical situation is to halt the arms race and to channel the resources thus released to the needs of development.

Only effective measures directed at an overall improvement in the international situation can ensure conditions for resolving the problems that face mankind, including that of blocking all avenues for the proliferation of the deadly nuclear arms on our fragile planet. The history of the 20th century contains numerous examples which prove convincingly that precisely the policy of peaceful coexistence among States with different socio-economic systems is the only reasonable formula for international relations. What is needed is to learn to live with each other rather than against each other. Of special value here is the already existing positive experience of the practical implementation of this formula. The alliance of the States of the Anti-Hitlerite coalition was one example of political realism. Forty years ago the Soviet Union and the United States were allies in the struggle against the common enemy that threatened to enslave mankind—German fascism and Japanese militarism. Today they have to become allies in the struggle against the monster of nuclear weapons. Either we, the inhabitants of the Earth, shall destroy it or it will destroy us. It would be foolhardy, to say the least, to pretend that such a catastrophe is impossible.

I do not share the view that '*détente* is dead'. History has shown that the 'cold war' period of the 1950s and 1960s was an attempt to destroy the system of relations which emerged as a result of the historic victory of the forces of the Anti-Hitlerite coalition, a kind of turn away from the path of political realism to the quagmire of the illusions of power. The current aggravation of tensions in the relations between the countries of East and West which, due to the policies of the philosophers and practitioners of deterrence, have retrogressed in a number of aspects, cannot reflect the logic of history either. Rather, it is a political anomaly. In particular, it would be wrong to believe that any conflict outside Europe should automatically bring about a crisis of detente in Europe. If such automatic linkage between problems existed, *détente* would not be possible at all. At the same time its experience has shown that when there is concord in Europe, the whole world can breathe more easily.

The non-use of force as a fundamental principle of contemporary international relations implies the pursuit of increasingly active foreign policy by all States of the world without exception, regardless of their economic potential or military power. The six non-nuclear-weapon States—Argentina, Mexico, India, Tanzania, Greece and Sweden—who in May 1984 issued a joint declaration calling for a complete cessation of the development, production and deployment of nuclear weapons and delivery systems and for freezing and starting to reduce nuclear arsenals, are regarded by us as realists striving to create a healthier international environment.

As is known, the Soviet Union has put forward a concrete programme of action for freezing nuclear armaments, which has a great deal in common with the ideas expressed by the leaders of the six countries. The idea of the inadmissibility of nuclear war in any form lies at the basis of a realistic approach to international relations in the nuclear age. This is the essence of the Soviet Union's foreign policy and its military doctrine. All nuclear States should renounce first use of nuclear weapons. The Soviet Union has already assumed such an obligation. The nuclear powers should guarantee that they will not use nuclear weapons against those States which do not have such weapons on their territories. The Soviet Union has undertaken an obligation in that respect, too, and it is ready to record it in treaty form. It is important to prevent the extension of the nuclear arms race to new areas and, naturally, no weapons of any kind should be allowed in space.

A major new step was taken by the Soviet Union when it instituted as of 7 April 1985 a unilateral moratorium on the deployment of medium-range missiles. The Soviet Union is also ready to resume the tripartite negotiations, suspended in 1979, on a complete nuclear weapons test ban.

The vertical and horizontal proliferation of nuclear weapons can and must be stopped.

The first simple and natural step for mankind to take in order to break the diabolic circle of the arms race is to freeze the nuclear arsenals. The Soviet Union has proposed this and it is ready for a freeze in military potentials on the basis of reciprocity with the United States.

The second step is to renounce the development and production of new types and systems of weapons of mass destruction. The Soviet Union has proposed that a treaty be concluded regarding this problem too.

The third step is to reach agreement on a step by step reduction of nuclear and conventional arms on the basis of reciprocity, equality and equal security. Proposals for this have been made by our country on a number of occasions.

There are, unfortunately, some people who believe that every generation should travel its own road of trial and error—should itself, so to speak, carry the burden of history. They believe that there are things more important than peace. I am afraid that in the nuclear era such a view is hopelessly obsolete, for there will be no one left to learn from the mistakes that our generation risks making. Whether we have enough wisdom and courage to halt the vertical nuclear arms race and to close the channels for its horizontal proliferation is not an academic question. The fate of mankind and of each individual hinges on its solution.

The Link between Horizontal and Vertical Proliferation

DR. KRISHNASWAMI SUBRAHMANYAM
Director, Institute for Defence Studies and Analyses, New Delhi

Proliferation is today a much abused term. According to the Concise Oxford Dictionary 'proliferate' means 'reproduce itself, grow, by multiplication of elementary parts, increase rapidly'. Nuclear proliferation is essentially a problem relating to those countries which are multiplying nuclear weapons rapidly both in qualitative and quantitative terms. It is an abuse of the English language to term acquisition of a few nuclear weapons by a new country as proliferation. Be that as it may, in the literature on nuclear proliferation vertical proliferation refers to development and multiplication of newer categories of nuclear weapons incorporating qualitative improvements, while horizontal proliferation refers to acquisition of nuclear weapons by a country which had not hitherto been in possession of such weapons. But these two conceptual definitions alone are inadequate to explain the phenomenon of nuclear proliferation. They do not include two other kinds of proliferation which have been of great significance. First of these is the spatial proliferation of nuclear weapons, namely, the introduction and deployment of nuclear weapons in new areas where they had not been earlier deployed. Cases in point will be deployment of nuclear weapons in the Indian Ocean area and introduction of SS–21s and SS–22s in Eastern Europe. The second category of proliferation not dealt with in the strategic literature is the horizontal proliferation within the armed forces of a nuclear-weapon Power or those of its non-nuclear allies, which process has been continuously taking place. This horizontal proliferation refers to the ever-increasing number of authorities who acquire the power to decide on the firing of the nuclear weapons in the event of war. While horizontal proliferation in terms of new nations acquiring nuclear weapons has not taken place, at least in an acknowledged manner, the other kind of horizontal proliferation has not only been taking place but has not even been recognized as a problem in the strategic literature.

When the problem of linkage between vertical and horizontal proliferation in the conventional sense is analyzed there is a major difficulty. There has been no horizontal proliferation in the conventional sense since 1964, unless Israel and South Africa are counted as nuclear-weapon Powers. So far the five established proliferating nations have not done so. India which conducted a peaceful nuclear test at a time peaceful nuclear tests were very much in vogue does not consider itself a nuclear-weapon Power, nor do the established nuclear weapon nations. In the case of Pakistan, so long as it does not conduct a test of a nuclear weapon at least the US law will not treat it as a nuclear-weapon Power and the Pakistani authorities assure us repeatedly that it is not their intention to acquire a nuclear arsenal. There are no signs today that this situation is likely to change significantly in the near future. Horizontal proliferation in the conventional sense does not appear to be as grave a problem as the horizontal proliferation within the armed forces of proliferating nuclear-weapon Powers. Having a number of nuclear devices with the last wire unconnected and without having tested them at least on one's own soil is not a violation of the so-called Non-Proliferation Treaty.

According to the study *First Strike* by Robert C. Aldridge (Pluto Press, 1983, Boston), submarines have no outside controls on their weapons such as the permissive action links. 'Instead they have a verification code which is changed hourly. It is transmitted to the submarine along with the launch order and must be verified by the submarine skipper, the executive officer and the weapons officer. But for those three men to be able to verify the code there has to be prior knowledge of what it is and that implies someone else knows the key. It could be possible that some one in the Pentagon might usurp the authority and send the command.'

That the nuclear submarines can fire off their missiles without a central national direction has been highlighted in the article 'Nuclear subs: on their own' by Joseph Volz and Alton Slagle in their article in *Daily News* (New York, 19 October 1983). Paul Bracken in his book *The Command and Control over Nuclear Forces* (Yale University Press, New Haven, 1983) refers to the control of the at sea SSBN force as the greatest source of ambiguous command. Every nuclear missile submarine amounts to an independent authority with untramelled powers to launch their weapons.

There appears to have been at least one other case of horizontal proliferation in the conventional sense on the part of a nuclear-weapon Power. The Canadian strategic interceptor aircraft CF-101B Voodoo is deployed as part of North American Air Defense Command (NORAD) and it was armed with two Genie (Air-2A) nuclear armed missiles. According to *Nuclear Weapons Databook, Volume I: US Nuclear Forces and Capabilities*, Genie did not have any permissive action link safeguard and was probably armed by inflight insertion of nuclear materials. Vice-Admiral Gerald Miller (Retired), former deputy commander of the joint Strategic Target Planning Staff, told a Congressional committee in 1976 that the 'NORAD Commander has been delegated such authority only under severe restrictions and specific conditions of attack.' The fact remains he has delegated powers to use nuclear weapons (Robert Aldridge, *First Strike* p. 247). The Canadian Prime Minister Trudeau claimed in the First United Nations Special Session on Disarmament that his country had become not only the first country to choose not to manufacture nuclear weapons when it had the capability to do so but also the first country to give up nuclear weapons. The Prime Minister elucidated this by adding that he had ordered the Canadian aircraft on patrol not to fly any more with nuclear weapons. This appears to be a reference to the Genie nuclear-tipped missile carried by the Canadian 101B carrier under the control of NORAD. It is absurd to think of an air-to-air missile being under locking devices while on patrol and during the flight it should have been entirely under the control of the Canadian pilot. This appears to be a case of horizontal proliferation in clear violation of Articles I and II of the NPT highly recommended to the rest of the world by the US and Canada.

The NATO Allies of the United States have access to a number of nuclear-weapon systems in case of hostilities, though during peacetime the US functions as a custodial power. These systems include B-28, B-43 and B-61 nuclear bombs, Honest John, Nike, Hercules, Pershing and Lance missiles, 155 and 203 mm. artillery shells. The non-nuclear countries which have access to such nuclear weapons are Turkey, Greece, Italy, Netherlands, Belgium, UK and the Federal Republic of Germany. The widely projected impression is that the nuclear weapons in the allied territories are under strict control of the President of the US and the first use of nuclear weapons will require his specific authorization. However some recent publications on the subject tend to raise doubts about such popular images.

According to Aldridge 'a 1975 Library of Congress report points out that the authority to release nuclear weapons 'may be delegated to subordinate officers in the chain of command virtually without limitation.' The report goes on to say that because nuclear weapons can wreak unprecedented havoc it is popular belief that the President has tighter limitation on delegating authority for their use, but 'we have been unable to find any constitutional or statutory basis supporting [that belief]. According to the report, delegation of authority to use nuclear weapons would be secret. Nevertheless, there is substantial evidence that others than the President have access to the nuclear button.' (*First Strike* p. 247.)

Daniel Ellsberg revealed at a May 1978 Whistleblowers' conference in Washington that he had personal knowledge that launch authority had been delegated to major overseas commanders during the Eisenhower and Kennedy Administrations and expressed his conviction that such delegation had remained in effect while Presidents Johnson, Nixon and Ford were in office. When the White House was asked if launch authority was delegated under President Carter the reply was, 'under existing law, the President alone has the basic authority to order the use of nuclear weapons. This authority may be delegated to subordinate officers in the chain of command virtually without limitations.'

Lord Zuckerman has hinted at the existence of delegated authority. He said in the Pugwash symposium held at Toronto (published in *Dangers of*

Nuclear War, edited by Franklyn Griffith and John C. Polanyi, University of Toronto Press pp. 164–5): 'What Admiral Miller (former Deputy Director of Joint Strategic Target Planning Staff, USA) has told us about the chain of command in the control of the use of nuclear weapons makes it inevitable that if the concept of tactical warfare were to have any meaning at all there would have to be the authority for "prior release" as soon as hostilities begin.'

Paul Bracken has gone into this issue in great detail. He writes,

> As a practical matter, we must seriously discount the prospect that centralized political command could intervene in a large conventional war to maintain detailed control over nuclear weapons. Political leaders would have little ability to respond in the very short decision times that characterize modern combat, and, even if there were sufficient time, these leaders would lack detailed information on local conditions and knowldge of how to operate combined arms forces. Decisions of this sort cannot even be made at a high level inside the military command structure; they must be delegated lower in the hierarchy to division and brigade level. The development of nuclear weapons has done nothing to change this organizational feature of conventional forces, and we should be skeptical of purported technological solutions to problems that have deep organizational roots.
>
> Specifically, the electronic locks that are on these weapons, known as permissive action links (PALs), do nothing to alleviate the organizational and environmental pressures to decentralize and delegate control of most theater nuclear weapons. While it may be technologically possible to lock weapons against unauthorized use, this is hardly the issue in a European crisis. The same effect as an unbreakable lock would come from removal of the weapons from Europe altogether. For, if weapons were sent into battle while political authorities retained control of the codes needed to unlock them, there could be no guarantee, not even a likelihood, that all of the codes could be matched with their respective weapons in the confusion of a conventional or perhaps a chemical-nuclear war. The political command, or any centralized depository for the codes, could be attacked, thereby paralyzing the military's ability to strike back. Practically speaking, a strong pressure exists to release any needed codes at the same time that the weapons are dispersed from their storage sites. In peacetime planning, this pressure can be ignored, and elaborate enforcement can be devised to keep the tactical nuclear weapons locked until they are just about to be fired. But even a moderately intense military crisis in Europe will expose the vulnerability of such procedural schemes. Sending thousands of locked weapons into the fog of war flies in the face of every known military tradition. The peacetime controls for preventing unauthorized use of nuclear weapons would then be swept away as irrelevant to the new condition of a real possibility of war. Then, in order to field a viable force either *ad hoc* controls would be devised or previously established verbal understandings would be employed.

Bracken compares the command and control procedures to a safety catch preventing the other triggers from firing and points out that its function is not to act as a trigger to launch nuclear weapons. The existence of pre-delegated authority to various command centres and below is designed to protect the command system from a decapitating attack. As NATO goes on alert beyond a certain level the nuclear weapons will be disbursed from the storage sites to operational points from which they are intended to be used. At this stage the locks are unlocked and the delegated authority starts operating at various levels. The extent of delegation is a secret but it is not possible to rule out that it would include commanders of other NATO nationalities besides US and it might go down to the level of a battalion Commander. These aspects are never discussed in public since as Paul Bracken put it 'What government can possibly announce that its security is dependent on turning nuclear weapons over to a battalion Commander who just might pull the trigger even if he were not authorized to do so?'

The so-called non-nuclear-weapon countries of NATO will get nuclear weapons at the time of high alert when they actually would have to think of using them and one of the nationals other than those of the five nuclear-weapon Powers will be in a position to fire the nuclear weapon and initiate a nuclear war under delegated authority. The NATO procedures according to the above-quoted literature envisage rapid horizontal proliferation at the time of high alert and once that point is passed and the weapons are disbursed the centralized control of custodial power will no longer be operative and any of the commanders of forces belonging to a country other than the nuclear Power can initiate a nuclear war under the delegated authority.

Such horizontal proliferation of nuclear weapons among the armed forces of NATO countries and correspondingly of the Warsaw Pact countries is a direct result of the vertical proliferation phenomenon continuously taking place. The increasing accuracy of the missiles and other delivery systems, the reduction of time of flight between launch and impact and more efficient target acquisition capabilities have together made possible a decapitating strike on command centres and brought about a situation when every commander in charge of nuclear weapons will face the agonizing dilemma of either using the weapon immediately or losing it to a strike by the adversary. A decapitating strike would in fact destroy the safety catch mechanism and transform every command structure in possession of nuclear weapons into an independent and sovereign user of it. That will be the ultimate in horizontal proliferation. Yet this is what PD-59 strategic doctrine is reported to aim at. According to Thomas Powers (Choosing a strategy for World War III, *Atlantic Monthly*, November 1982) 'PD-59 placed heavy emphasis on the communications and intelligence needed to fight a nuclear war over a period of months; it implied a theory of nuclear attrition; and it promised Soviet leaders that they would be hunted down in their new blast-hardened shelters if things went the limit. It may have been only words, but it marked a sea change in official American attitudes toward nuclear war'. It is quite logical that faced with such a threat the threatened side would have further decentralized and delegated authority to use nuclear weapons in case the leadership was destroyed.

There have also been mentions in strategic literature of putting the nuclear response on machine intelligence (*First Strike*, p.520) in the light of the reduction in warning time between launch and impact. This will be yet another step in horizontal proliferation as the machine will become an additional independent decision-maker to unleash the nuclear retaliation.

Literature available on the subject of nuclear war clearly reveals the impossibility of controlling rapid escalation of a nuclear war between the industrialized nations once the first few shots have been fired. Paul Bracken raises the more pertinent question (in his book *The Command and Control of Nuclear Forces*) whether nuclear alerts can be controlled since these alerts when they go beyond a level lead to horizontal proliferation of the type mentioned earlier. A comparison of the risks of horizontal proliferation of of the conventional sense discussed in the strategic literature—of new nations acquiring some primitive arsenals—with the risks involved in the horizontal proliferation that will be caused by a nuclear alert of a status involving dispersal of forward-based weapons among the allied forces would make it quite obvious that the latter exceeds the former by orders of magnitude. Usually the literature on conventional proliferation highlights the safeguard measures incorporated in the nuclear weapons of the five nuclear-weapon nations (such as permissive action link, command disable, unique signal generator and so on) and the command and control system and their redundancies to point out how primitive arsenals without such features are more risky.

However, an elementary analysis shows that nuclear arsenals at primitive stages (air-droppable bombs or just a few missiles) are more easily controllable and may permit easier war termination than the highly-sophisticated arsenals in vast numbers in respect of which the escalation cannot be controlled once the weapon exchange begins. This is not meant to justify or advocate nuclear proliferation of the conventional type to new nations. It is, however, necessary to debunk the myths built around the safety of nuclear arsenals in the hands of established nuclear-weapon Powers and to focus attention on the comparative risks of nuclear war breaking out and ending civilization on earth due to the existence of vast and highly-sophisticated arsenals and that of primitive arsenals so that the world gets its priorities right as to which horizontal proliferation needs prior attention. While horizontal proliferation in the conventional sense has not taken place in the last two decades—at least in an acknowledged manner—the risks of horizontal proliferation taking place among the armed forces of nuclear-weapon Powers and their allies have increased manifoldly and these risks have hardly attracted any attention in the strategic literature.

The nuclear war doctrines and the vertical proliferation in the industrialized world have crossed all bounds of rationality. The entire nuclear strategy is based on the threat of a possibility of rationality breaking down and ending human civilization. The proliferation of nuclear arsenals in qualitative and quantitative terms has increased the risks of unstoppable escalation in case a nuclear war breaks out. Admiral Noel Gayler has pointed out that 'There is no sensible military use of any of our nuclear forces. Their only reasonable use is to deter our opponent from using his nuclear forces'. Field Marshal Carver says, 'To initiate use of nuclear weapons . . . seems to me to be criminally irresponsible.' Lord Mountbatten and several other retired British Chiefs of Defence Staff have indicated that under no circumstances would they have recommended that NATO initiate the use of nuclear weapons. President Reagan has admitted that a nuclear war cannot be won and should never be initiated.

Yet the qualitative and quantitative proliferation goes on in respect of these unusable arsenals. There are plans in the USA to produce an additional 28,665 warheads between 1983 and the mid-1990s (*Nuclear Weapons Databook*, Volume 1, p. 16) and it is to be presumed that there are similar efforts under way in the Soviet Union and other nuclear-weapon powers.

Instead of the irrationality of building up arsenals which are either unusable or if used will end human civilization being debunked, it has been sought to build a mystique around the proliferation process and a cult has been established on the basis of certain unprovable belief systems. The believers of this cult argue that deterrence exercised through the build-up of nuclear arsenals has preserved peace among industrialized nations for 40 years while in the developing world—where deterrence does not operate in the absence of nuclear arsenals—there have been more than 150 major instances of inter- and intra-State violence. The cultists believe that the continuous process of vertical proliferation has sustained deterrence and one of the deadly weapons under development has been named the 'Peace maker'. Possession of nuclear weapons has been vested with prestige and, instead of non-proliferating nations policing proliferating nations, the proliferators assert their right to police non-proliferating nations and to indulge in unlimited proliferation to maintain their status as high priests of the nuclear weapons cult. The so-called Non-Proliferation Treaty codifies the dogmas of this cult.

Those who believe that the doctrine of deterrence operates effectively against their adversaries are themselves liable to be deterred by their perceptions of the adversary's capabilities. This has been the history of the last four decades. Vertical proliferation is an attempt to gain an image of superiority and to reassure oneself that the adversary will not be able to gain such an image. The nuclear strategy of the last four decades has been one of formulating perceptions of possible capabilities of adversaries and projecting images of one's own capabilities through development and deployment of increasingly sophisticated nuclear hardware. The underlying reality, if any, of the nuclear strategy can never be tested without risking human civilization.

It is to be noted that the majority of industrialized nations base their security doctrines on the doctrine of nuclear deterrence. Though the Warsaw Pact nations have voted along with the non-aligned nations to declare the use of nuclear weapons as a crime against humanity and to have a convention to prohibit the use of nuclear weapons, yet they appear to believe that so long as the Western industrialized nations subscribe to the doctrine of deterrence they ought to be deterred by projecting a nuclear capability by which they lay so much store. It is only logical to deter a believer through operating on his own belief system. The same logic appeals to some of the countries outside the military blocs who are capable of developing very modest nuclear arsenals.

If the industrialized nations have come to develop fervent belief in the efficacy of the doctrine of deterrence, consider it essential to pursue vertical proliferation to sustain that deterrence, have built a mystique around nuclear arsenals and emphasize that nuclear deterrence has preserved peace in the industrialized world, these perceptions and behaviour patterns of the dominant nations of the world are bound to have their impact on the world outside industrialized nations.

There is an increasing awareness regarding the unusability of nuclear arsenals. Deterrence is exercised today not merely through projection of factors of certainty but by emphasizing the various factors of uncertainty associated with the use of nuclear weapons in war. This too has had its impact on nations outside the military blocs. Lastly, it is also understood that the exercise of deterrence is mostly a matter of perceptions and projection of images. Among the nations outside the military blocs in the industrialized world deterrence can be generated at much lower levels of nuclear capability or even by an ambiguous image of a nation being suspected to have a modest capability. Limited nuclear arsenals outside the military blocs can be used in war and there can also be war termination, no doubt at the cost of large casualties. Such use of weapons on a limited scale will not mean the end of human civilization. Hence the deterrent effect of such suspected arsenals enveloped in ambiguity is much higher than the unusable arsenals of the military blocs, which if ever used will destroy human civilization.

These perceptions have perhaps led to or are likely to lead to nuclear proliferation without testing of weapons, proliferation enveloped in ambiguity and proliferation without acknowledging the possession of nuclear weapons. Such proliferations are not likely to be many and their risks on the whole are much lower than those inherent in continuing vertical proliferation among established nuclear-weapon Powers with the compulsion to proliferate horizontally within their own armed forces and of their allies in case of nuclear alert.

The so-called Non-Proliferation Treaty which was primarily intended to vest legitimacy in the nuclear arsenals of nuclear-weapon Powers and license their unlimited proliferation, has no relevance to either kind of horizontal proliferation. In fact the Treaty today serves no purpose. Article I is not being observed by the weapon Powers. Article VI is a dead letter. Nations have found a way to circumvent Article II. It is time the nations of the world discarded this dysfunctional document and focussed on a strategy of non-proliferation which would stop the engine of proliferation in the proliferating nations instead of having their attention diverted away to stopping proliferations which are not likely to take place.

The World is Constantly Threatened by Two Dangers: Order and Disorder[1]

MR. RÉGIS DEBRAY

Maître des Requêtes au Conseil d'Etat

First, I have a confession to make: I am not going to speak as a civil servant or as a propagandist. I have no system and I do not belong to any party, nor am I going to speak as a poet or an ideologist, but simply as a Frenchman faced with reality. Although I am not here to defend or explain my country's official standpoint, which experts much better qualified than I can describe in detail, it would not be honest of me to evade it. It so happens that I agree with it, morally and intellectually. It is rare for a country's national interests to concur with the security of all other countries, therefore, the coincidence must be welcomed. Do not think that my job is easy; on the contrary, there is a strong likelihood that I will shock you.

France has not signed the Non-Proliferation Treaty—a major legal instrument prepared by the Russians and the Americans and signed on 1 July 1968. And yet in 1983, 119 countries had signed it. At first glance, then, France appears to be one of the virtual suspects which constitute the non-signatories. But, in fact, it had nothing to gain by abstaining as it had already been on the 'good side'—if I may use that expression—for seven years, namely on the side of the nuclear Powers—those which had already carried out a nuclear explosion before 1 January 1967 and which, under the Treaty, were completely free to develop their nuclear weapons without any IAEA control measures, the latter being reserved for non-nuclear-weapon Parties to the NPT. France has been a member of the IAEA in Vienna since its establishment, and has always occupied its place on the Board of Governors and, since 1968, has acted as though it had signed the Treaty: its exports are placed under peaceful-use control (although it refuses to use nuclear co-operation as a pretext for requiring a State to submit all its nuclear activities to IAEA control unless that State has so agreed in advance). In 1974 and 1975, it took part in preparing the 'London Directives' and complies with their provisions scrupulously.

Neither did France sign the 1963 Moscow Treaty banning nuclear testing in the atmosphere—in explanation, I can say that it was then tackling the most critical part of its military programme, the hydrogen bomb, which could be tested only by aerial explosion. Like China, France refused the

[1] Paul Valéry.

discriminatory principle whereby the super-Powers had a monopoly on nuclear weapons. As Bertrand Goldschmidt, one of the French atomic energy pioneers, and a former Chairman of the IAEA Board of Governors said, the treaty was not a disarmament treaty, but a treaty to prevent unarmed countries from arming. Since 1968, France has shown that it has no desire to encourage other countries to manufacture nuclear weapons: it supports the non-dissemination of plutonium reprocessing and uranium enriching plants. Since 1974, it has restricted itself to underground tests not exceeding 150 KT; in other words, it complies with the 1974 American-Soviet treaty on underground tests without acceding to it formally.

Between 1945 and 1982, SIPRI in Stockholm recorded 1,375 nuclear explosions, including 700 American, 500 Soviet, 113 French, 35 British and 26 Chinese and Indian. In 1984, of the 53 underground explosions detected by the Stockholm Institute, the USSR carried out 27, the USA 15, France 7, Great Britain 2 and China 2. You will see that a country cannot sign the NPT and conduct itself more soberly than others in so-called vertical proliferation. I shall also remind you that in 1983, France became the first military nuclear Power to open its experimental site to foreign scientists, Australians and New Zealanders, so that they could see for themselves the virtually complete restriction of radioactivity to the Mururoa atoll subsoil and the normal radiological situation of terrestrial, air and maritime environments. Let us hope that this unprecedented breakthrough will lead to healthy emulation in the community of comparable countries. That is up to them: they are sovereign States. The right to security is one of the rights of peoples and it must be exercised respecting security of all. France, which is merely ensuring that it has the means to secure its independence and has nothing to hide on that score, has no reason to beat its own breast and so refrains from beating those of its neighbours.

Between order and disorder, imposed security and dangerous anarchy, the path is narrow: it lies between discrimination and proliferation. My country refuses both, because discrimination is the surest way towards proliferation. Brutal discrimination, such as imposing total control on countries wishing to acquire nuclear capacity for peaceful uses is counter-productive. In fact, experience shows that politically unacceptable discrimination results in co-operation between countries which escape all controls (China–Pakistan, China–Brazil, South Africa–Israel). As Mr. André Petit, one of the senior officials of the Commissariat à l'Énergie Atomique (the Atomic Energy Commission) has said, 'the strength of political commitments is in inverse proportion to the political pressure exerted to obtain them . . . The more Parties there are to the NPT the better. But if everyone accedes to the NPT because it is impossible to do otherwise, the NPT will be worthless as there is no way of knowing which of the signatories has acceded in good faith'. Countries cannot be judged on the sole basis of a signature (it is not because

Libya is a signatory of the NPT that a centrifuge can be sold blindly to Colonel Khadafi), any more than on their level of development. There is no reason to call the developing countries who set up an electro-nuclear programme 'bad' or 'suspect' and the industrialized countries who do the same 'good' or 'reliable'. It is often the least well-endowed countries that have a critical need for energy, which only nuclear power can supply. The criminal and evil aura surrounding this abundant and cheap source of energy which takes up little space, is less polluting than coal or oil, and has fewer occupational hazards than the footwear or ship-building industries, must not lead us astray: in both the South and the North, rightly or wrongly, nuclear power must be used if we are to modernize at all. And incidentally, transformation from civilian to military capacity requires not only an exceptionally strong political will, but also a series of technical, scientific, financial and human resources which are not easy to assemble.

So France has attempted to ally, in co-operation designed to facilitate access for all States to peaceful use of nuclear energy, an effective non-proliferation policy with respect for national sovereignty.

The French Government applies a certain number of specific rules to its nuclear technology and materials exports. Hence, French sales to non-nuclear-weapon countries are accompanied by an intergovernmental agreement providing for exclusively peaceful use of the products exported, placing them under IAEA control and, finally, physical protection measures for the materials, particularly to guard against hijacking. For the most sensitive products there are also supplementary provisions concerning re-exportation.

In addition, in 1976 the French Government decided unilaterally to restrict exports of the most sensitive products and technologies and, in particular, to suspend exports of irradiated fuel processing plants which pose special proliferation dangers.

Finally, considerable research efforts have been undertaken in France with a view to developing 'non-proliferating' technologies.

As a result, it is now producing a low-enriched uranium fuel (about 20 per cent) for research reactors which will replace the highly-enriched uranium used previously.

Similarly, the Commissariat à l'Énergie Atomique is developing a uranium-enriching process through chemical means which is much more difficult than the present gaseous diffusion and, particularly, centrifugation processes to transform it into highly-enriched fuel for military uses. But action designed to limit the risk of proliferation must be accompanied by broad co-operation aimed at giving all States which need it the chance to profit, with maximum guarantees, from the peaceful applications of nuclear energy.

France, for its part, is ready to guarantee the safety of nuclear fuel supplies to the power stations it supplies and to respond to legitimate needs for access to technology. It is also prepared to furnish any fuel cycle services which might be requested. At the international level, France gives full support to the IAEA in perfecting its safeguard techniques and developing non-proliferating processes. It tries, in any case, to advocate co-operation methods likely to receive the widest consensus among all the States concerned.

France is not a contender in the quantitative arms race and does not substitute vertical proliferation for horizontal non-proliferation: its strategic doctrine is sufficiently modest and firm to preserve it from that. As President Mitterrand reiterates, it believes that the balance of forces is a guarantee of peace but that this balance must and can be established at the lowest level: at the extreme, and as an illustration, it would be enough for each of the opposing forces to have one intercontinental rocket aimed at the other's capital for them to respect each other. There are two kinds of strategic deterrence. The first, which is the oldest and commonest, is to be stronger than one's opponent so as to prevent him from taking action: this leads to an endless arms spiral. The second, which is cheaper and more in keeping with the nuclear age, is called from the weak to the strong; it consists simply of making the cost of any aggression by the stronger against the weaker prohibitive or the risk higher than the stakes: this conception, which does not aim at parity with the possible adversary, entails no more than maintaining constant belief in one's own reprisal capacity against the adversary, in accordance with the principle of sufficiency. Each super-Power has about 10,000 nuclear warheads—a dangerous and technically unnecessary surplus. France has about 150 heads and autonomy of decision, which is enough to guarantee its security. For France, the arms race is purely qualitative and means ensuring that its various launching facilities are invulnerable and have adequate penetration capacity, in accordance with the others' technological progress and constantly improving counter-measures. While awaiting general, controlled disarmament, that eminently desirable objective which is constantly referred to but which, it must be admitted, present developments do not really bring any closer—making war irrational or suicidal is still the least awful way of making it impossible. I think that nuclear deterrence is like political democracy, the worst possible system, apart from all the others.

We all know that it is not weapons which explain international insecurity and tensions, but the reverse: the accumulation of arms contributes to instability and aggressive vertigo, but the real cause of conflict must be sought. 'In a paradoxical chain reaction,' said President Mitterrand, speaking at the United Nations, 'the troubled international economic system strengthens the need for security and at the same time fuels the arms race, which, in turn, once more sparks off disequilibrium'. What is the point of spending more and more to have less and less security? From this springs the idea of putting disarmament at the service of development, taking into account the increasing debt service burden which strangles the economies and crushes the societies of the Third World. How then? It would be possible to levy a tax on the military budgets of the major industrial countries. But on what criteria would countries be selected? Should they be chosen exclusively in the West (when the USSR accounted for 21.9 per cent of the world arms market in 1984—half as much as the USA but twice as much as France)? And how would the various military budgets be assessed objectively? How would the domestic and foreign effects of increased military expenditure be assessed? How would the relationship between the evolution of military expenditure and the main causes of international economic disorder be evaluated? How would the resources made available be used in the collective interest (for health, agricultural development or other productive investments)? And how would redeployment of the contributing countries' military industries be encouraged? At the thirty-eighth session of the United Nations General Assembly, President Mitterrand declared that France was prepared to host in Paris an international preparatory conference bringing together the chief military Powers to discuss these issues. The response to this proposal from those concerned was far from enthusiastic.

Calculations of the balance of forces are always haphazard and fluctuating, dependent as they are on the parameters adopted and the statistical and geographical divisions chosen. Regional or circumstantial dissymmetry of panoplies must not mask the essential, which is the *stability* of reciprocal deterrence. For it is only the security of the second-strike force which can nullify the temptation for either side to make the first strike or encourage a last-chance dialogue.

There is a risk at present that this mutual vulnerability or balance of weakness—what used to be called the 'balance of terror'—will be upset by the development of the so-called defensive systems (ABM and ASAT) brought to the forefront both by the Soviet capacity and by the so-called 'Star Wars' research programme. The possessor of an impenetrable anti-missile shield (supposing it could exist) would in fact acquire a first-strike capacity, since such a space shield, whether or not impenetrable, would shelter its possessor from reprisals by the enemy, whose retaliation capacity would hypothetically be already downgraded and scattered by a pre-emptive anti-force strike. The SDI appears to be an unprecedented destabilization factor in the deterrence system guaranteed until now by the 1972 ABM limitation treaty.

Strangely enough, this project stems from a very popular and sympathetic legitimate concern—some would say demagogic—to turn a new leaf in the nuclear era, to put an end to the nightmare of populations held to ransom, and to consign to pre-history the spectre of a general holocaust. If this demarcartion line were ever to be crossed, it is a fair bet that we would then feel an unconquerable nostalgia for the nuclear age and a constant terror of the so-called 'guaranteed mutual survival' system. For by giving up what we have for the unknown, we would have traded the impossibility of world war for the likelihood (especially in Europe) of a limited war. The bomb indexes security on risk. The shield would revive risk on the basis of false security. One of the disadvantages of public danger is that it hides another danger, less well-known but more threatening. With regard to world peace and the stability of political balance, the danger of nuclear proliferation seems much less dreadful than the danger of proliferation of non-nuclear weapons. The first, restricted and monitored, forced into secrecy, is acknowledged to be harmful and almost criminal: the offender would be subjected to world opprobrium. The second, very officially planned and without the slightest supervision by an international body, is acknowledged to be legitimate and truly enviable. The worst does not always come to pass—as demonstrated by the fact that despite so many sombre prophecies, 40 years after Hiroshima still only the five permanent members of the Security Council possess effective nuclear armaments and since the Chinese explosion twenty years ago in 1964, the world has not witnessed a further military explosion (if the Indian experiment in 1974 is taken to be civilian). But it is when the worst dresses up as the best that it becomes the least improbable.

It should not be necessary to praise the bomb any further. And yet circumstances encourage me to take up this exercise again, as paradoxical and disagreeable as is the bomb itself, which only prevents war provided it is not banned in advance; whose only use is that it will not be used, and which only achieves its aim by never hitting the target.

Let us banish fancies for a moment and restrict ourselves to facts. For 40 years now the world map of war has matched up with the denuclearized zones or those covered by the nuclear deterrent. It is true that the nuclear Powers no longer wage war with each other, and with good reason: they have granted themselves 'asylum'. The 140 or more international conflicts which have led to over 20 million victims since the end of the Second World War have bypassed the central zones stabilized by the nuclear deterrent. Preventing war at the higher level, deterrence may perhaps stimulate vicarious violence in the surrounding areas. But if Vietnam had had the bomb in 1965 or Afghanistan in 1979 it is doubtful whether they would have suffered what they did. Soviets and Americans do not kill each other and China was not punished nor decapitated by its vast northern neighbour in the worst of the 1969 Sino-Soviet conflict. The East and the West are prevented by the deterrent in the North and transfer their conflicts to the South—as though the communicating vessels of war worked to the detriment of latecomers to and abstainers from nuclear power and as though the nuclear-weapon continents were also the most peaceful on earth.

It is also a fact that in no country has the military establishment hailed with joy this essentially anti-militarist weapon (in France, the resistance of the military establishment to General de Gaulle's nuclear project was common knowledge). This passive and abstract object, with no style or gallantry, which would make armies virtually passive, deprives the cavalry of their armoured mounts, sailors of their finest surface fleet and all warriors of their dreams of adventure; all these are deprived of their favourite toys by the bomb and its budgetary priorities. I do not know whether, as MacNamara claims, the bomb has no military value, but it does devalue the profession of arms in the traditional, feudal or savage sense, because it civilizes and intellectualizes it. The nuclear tool is a violence inhibiter which ridicules muscle power, making it subject to brain power; it short-circuits military responsibility in the field by making the holder of civilian power the sole commander-in-chief directly in charge of operations and the users of the major weapon mere instruments at the end of the chain. It makes the traditional manoeuvre forces subject to the dictates of the deterrent, an algebraic probability which devalues, or even replaces, the old dictates of blood. It is one thing to manage crises, but quite another to win battles. It is understandable that at present military staffs are exalted by all the new systems in theatre or tactics which are likely to re-introduce the joys of conventional warfare into the strategic austerity of pure deterrence: Cruise missiles, the neutron bomb, 'nuclear artillery' (with firing responsibility delegated to the military commander), precision guided munitions (PGM), etc . . . all offer increased manoeuvre potential to the professionals. But it is not certain that peace will gain from the proliferation of peri-, para- or infra-nuclear facilities.

It is still a fact that the atom, which upsets alliances and destroys empires, cures bloc discipline and slackens submissions. Our various Big Brothers have learned it to their cost, some with France, others with China. The weapon of political sovereignty which prevails over the sovereignty of arms democratizes power by virtue of the 'equalizing power of the atom'. It assists the weak since it no longer makes strength depend on numbers—as Pakistan can tell itself in confronting India . . . ; it is disastrous to hierarchies and established natural situations, since the gross physical size of a country—by population or wealth—is no longer the decisive classification factor—as Israel can tell itself in confronting the Arab-Muslim world . . . the emancipating atom has already upset the condominial game of spheres of influence in the world. It is a constant feature in history that Empires and their order ensure peace in their own way; that nations against Empires make for disorder, with their rebellions and squabbles (how peaceful the Middle East was under the Ottoman Empire!). Shall it be a *Pax Americana et Sovietica* or a deluge of national wars? A nuclear duopoly or a proliferation of twenty (since there are estimated to be around 15 countries with a high enough level of technology to carry out nuclear arms experiments, even if it takes at least 15 years to progress from this initial act to a panoply of effective carriers)? Order or disorder—which is the lesser evil? The nuclear weapon, the only one which is not shared with anyone, which no country can transfer to another, is the ambiguous weapon of nationalism—the major force of our times—both liberating and ethnocentric, democratic and anarchical, capable of stabilizing regional order while destabilizing world order. The astonishing fact is that the horizontal proliferation of sovereignty in the world, where the number of States has doubled in 30 years, has not been paralleled by an equal proliferation of nuclear weapons, despite the world energy crisis. And surely this ambivalence of nuclear power is reflected in the ambivalence of the campaign against horizontal nuclear proliferation, the only permanent and active area of collaboration between the Soviet Union and the United States (it is understandable why, for the masters of the game, the question of whether or not the transfer of intermediate or tactical-operation nuclear *missiles* to third countries is an act of proliferation is rarely raised). This convergence is interesting, rather than suspect. The anti-nuclear proliferation campaign serves the cause of peace and collective security; it certainly does not harm the cause of the existing blocs, whose phobia of 'third forces' and taste for discipline is well known. Let us be allowed to share in the vigilance of the great Powers—the stakes are too high—without swearing moral allegiance to any particular protector.

To summarize: atomic weapons have caused no deaths since Hiroshima. The most dreadful instrument of death operates in reverse, as a weapon for peace. If the peace movement were logical, would it not transform itself into pro-nuclear movement? With the slogan: 'To save peace, save the bomb' or 'bombs for all, but at home'. It is not possible to make war on war and at the same ban the bomb which prevents war. If these common-sense notions make your hair stand on end and run counter to your preconceptions, let us agree at least that in over-castigating nuclear arms in the name of morality (but has a technique ever been mastered by renouncing it?) we are unconsciously admitting the use of all other weapons—conventional, as well as chemical and bacteriological ones. As though the horror of Hiroshima cancelled out the 84,000 deaths caused by the incendiary bombs launched on Tokyo on 9 March 1945.

Because Hiroshima happened, because we all know that today there are one million Hiroshimas in stock throughout the world and that a single nuclear match *can* light the fuse, these stocks self-destruct simply because they exist. Justified horror at 'the day after' must not—and is not likely to—end up by making the 'day-to-day' of war less horrible and almost attractive. Should carnage become 'clean', ecological and nice just because it is conventional? Let us take care that the abstract possibility of a horrible end to our species in a nuclear winter does not detract from the constant horror of the present.

Undoubtedly, in their time, Mao-Tse-Tung and our General Gallois pushed provocation a bit too far when they stated that proliferation was desirable as a factor in increased regional stability which, moreover, would tend to reduce the influence of the imperialist Powers. The pleasant surprise has been that, whether desirable or dreadful, the threatened proliferation has not taken place, at least within the time expected. Vertical proliferation is galloping ahead but horizontal proliferation is crawling. For every single person on earth today, there are four tonnes of explosive (TNT equivalent), but the number of persons stockpiling it underground or under the sea remains principally the two main ones (altogether they are five). Let us say that these two—or these five if you prefer it—are strong enough to have persuaded 120 others that the main danger comes not from themselves (they possess thousands of *megatonnes* already) but from those who as yet have none but who reserve the right to have a few *kilotonnes* one day or another. The net result, which demonstrates the strength of public opinion and moral factors at historical crossroads, is all the more praiseworthy given that there are about three hundred nuclear power stations in the world and that there is no such thing as a completely secure technological lock preventing access to the entire fuel cycle, from the extraction of natural uranium to the production of plutonium. Legal locks are the only existing ones and are inherently precarious and revocable: no one can prevent a State that has accepted existing international controls from denouncing them one day and setting up a military programme. At the very most, we know that it cannot do so on the quiet—it must do so openly and suffer worldwide disapproval. This may not seem much, but it is enormous. It is enough, added to the virtual certainty of reprisals and regional escalation among neighbouring States, to have dissuaded many who might have done it. We must congratulate ourselves on it. Horizontal proliferation, especially in the Third World, would give a new impetus to vertical proliferation, and particularly to the race, within the club, for anti-ballistic defence weapons, always harmful to deterrence. By helping to make nuclear weapons commonplace, the use threshold could be lowered in the short term; and it would become politically difficult for certain industrialized countries which have renounced nuclear weapons, either through bans, like Germany and Japan, or through deliberate abstinence, like Canada, Sweden or Italy, not to rejoin the pack.

A nuclear Sarajevo is the most likely scenario, in the abstract, for a chain reaction involving the super-Powers, in a regional conflict of strike and counter-strike. With a more-or-less operational bomb, it is very easy to imagine a psychotic leader lighting the fuse. More than once, history has confounded political fiction. Power sends people mad but can nuclear power not make them sane? There is no certainty that those new to power, once given the supreme weapon, will not become adult, and therefore moderate, like the others. The bomb strangles adventurism and can make national entities become self-deterrent. It could even—and why not—promote a certain positive neutrality status. The nuclear wand, certainly, would not change a Mussolini into a de Gaulle but its hypothetical wielders could gain in prestige what they lost in vainglory, realizing to their chagrin that the ultimate weapon is the hardest one to use: against those who have it, for that means physical suicide; or against those who do not have it, for that means moral suicide. France, which has signed the two protocols to the Tlatelolco Treaty, has stated several times that it refuses any actual or threatened use of its nuclear arms against a State in a non-nuclear zone (except, of course, in the event of agression in association or alliance with a nuclear State). These optimistic considerations on human nature—and I repeat, the worst does not always come to pass—do not alter the fact that everything possible must be done so as to avoid the Third World nations wasting their assets on building up nuclear forces, which are damaging to regional stability and to their own economic development. Taking into account demography and the unequal value attached to human life, the strongest religious forces for and against, the acknowledged weakness of civilian authorities and the weakest technical and political link in chains of command, it is not a sign of neo-colonialism or arrogance to infer from all these factors that military nuclear power is a greater danger in the Third World than in the large, industrialized countries. But it is precisely in the Third World that are to be found the potential proliferating countries exposed to the greatest temptation: Pakistan, India, Iraq, Taiwan, South Africa, Israel, South Korea, Iran, Argentina and Brazil. If we note that most of them belong to the same ideological camp, it is even easier to explain the attitude of the Soviet authorities in supervising transfers of technology and of fuel (for which they are already very restrictive in their own camp).

Today, the best guarantee for non-proliferation is not of a technical or legal nature—it is strategic. Everything which serves to make nuclear horror a commonplace notion contributes to its proliferation. War is too human and the bomb is inhuman: do not let us humanize it; do not let us tame the monster. We must keep our fear of the holocaust weapon intact so that it continues to be a weapon of peace, the only real one. When people talk about 'limited nuclear war', when they start to play with the idea of 'tactical nuclear power' as a decision to be taken in the field rather than the ultimate warning, then we are heading towards the irrevocable. Everything which, conversely, maintains in force and on guard the strategic arrangements of horror, guaranteed and recognized as such, escalation or joining forces, ensures that war would be unlimited, and therefore that a 'limited war' would be impossible. The nuclear monster can be tamed only by refusing to turn it, even in words, into a domesticated animal. The ultimate alien is amongst us, and no one is going to make it disappear with the stroke of a pen: it can be denied access in one place or another but once it has taken up residence somewhere there is no going back. Has anyone realized that there is really no 'denuclearized' zone in the world? The places we call that—Latin America and Antarctica—never were 'nuclearized'. The only way to 'neutralize' this silent spectre is to refuse to be on familiar terms with it.

Donoso Cortes said that man could avoid a war but did not have the power to eradicate war. I shall add that in dreaming of eradicating war, he has caused more than one war: he has imbued or still imbues with that power a collective myth or a technical artefact, be it the League of Nations or the Maginot Line, non-proliferation or space defence. In order to wager your life and win, you have to know that you are in danger of death at any moment. There is no magic formula to relieve our human community, which since 1945 has 'held its death in its hands', of having to decide, every day, without benefit of insurance policy or right of appeal, whether to live or to wipe itself out.

Europe: The Third Nuclear Super-Power, and its Role in the Creation of a Universal Non-Proliferation Regime

MR. MICHEL DE PERROT

Physicist, Research Fellow, Geneva International Peace Research Institute (GIPRI)[1]

Summary

Fast breeders and the associated nuclear fuel cycles can destroy the very foundations of the non-proliferation regime and bring about the final breakdown of the Soviet-American arms control structure.

Europe is moving inexorably towards becoming the third nuclear super-Power. It has a unique opportunity of obtaining a drastic reduction in the nuclear arsenals of the two other super-Powers and setting up a universal non-proliferation regime.

1. The breakdown of the non-proliferation regime

At the United Nations in 1953 Eisenhower launched his 'Atoms for Peace' programme and laid down the principle of a clear and distinct separation between civil and military nuclear power. This principle lies at the very basis of the entire American non-proliferation regime, and the national programme for the development and export of commercial nuclear technology is subject to it. The separation of civil and military nuclear power is also the keystone of the Treaty on the Non-Proliferation of Nuclear Weapons (NPT) with regard, at least, to the activities of the non-nuclear-weapon signatory States.

However, with the arrival of the commercial fast breeder and the associated industrial fuel reprocessing in Europe and the Soviet Union, the distinction between civil and military nuclear technology has become increasingly blurred.

One of France's atomic energy pioneers, the former adviser to the French Atomic Energy Commission (CEA), Mr. Bertrand Goldschmidt, recently stated that he was 'certain'—a word on which he laid great stress—that Super-Phénix, the first European commercial-type fast breeder to be installed in France, would be used for weapons production purposes.

In 1978, less than a year after the construction of the Super-Phénix had been undertaken, General Jean Thiry, adviser to the Managing Director of

[1] The views expressed here are those of the author.

the French Atomic Energy Commission (CEA), wrote: 'France will be able to build atomic weapons of all kinds and within every type of range. At relatively low cost, she will be in a position to produce large quantities of such weapons, with fast breeders providing an abundant supply of the plutonium required. Lucky Europe and lucky France—at long last in a position to engage in an enlarged nuclear deterrent of their own, thus guaranteeing their security.'

In Britain, British Nuclear Fuels has just redefined 'military plutonium' as plutonium intended for military use, regardless of whether it comes from a civil or military reactor. Furthermore, a spokesman for the European Commission recently told the European Parliament that official inspectors from Euratom and the International Atomic Energy Agency have been refused access to one area of the Sellafield reprocessing plant on grounds of national security.

The Soviet Union has no specifically military reactors, which means that fuel from its entire nuclear power generation programme is directed both ways. Only two types of reactor, the VVER-440 and the VVER-1000, have just been placed under international safeguards, and this is only because they are intended for export to countries that are required to accept safeguards. The highly respected German periodical *Atomwirtschaft* stated in its February 1983 issue that the USSR is using the plutonium produced by its fast breeders for military purposes.

Commercial-type fast breeders also introduce a new kind of proliferation which might conveniently be termed *oblique proliferation*. Let me explain this. Around France, Britain and the Soviet Union revolves a constellation of non-weapon NPT signatory States which depend on one or other of these three nuclear Powers for the reprocessing of spent fuel. There are therefore two plutonium economies, one geared to the Soviet Union and the other to France and Britain. In their turn these nuclear Powers are vitally dependent on their non-nuclear partners for the supply of the plutonium needed for the operation of their fast breeders and even for the partial or total financing of these fast breeders and the reprocessing plants. This applies, for instance, to Super-Phénix and the UP-3 plant in France. No country is, in fact, capable of undertaking such a commercial programme on its own.

As the option of using plutonium from fast breeders for weapons purposes is being kept open by the nuclear-weapon States, the non-nuclear-weapon States involved in the two plutonium economies are being marched willy-nilly towards the same military goal. 'Oblique' proliferation then, is the contribution of non-nuclear-weapon States to the direct or indirect production of nuclear weapons in the nuclear States—so-called 'vertical' proliferation.

This process is leading to the technical and strategic integration of both Western Europe and the Eastern bloc in the production of nuclear weapons.

One of the consequences of the transcontinental breakdown of the distinction between civil and military power will be the collapse of the entire non-proliferation regime. With such a precedent being set in Europe, it is hard to see what reasons the United States can put forward for subjecting fast breeders, or any other nuclear installation, to safeguards in the Third World.

This brings us, then, to a first conclusion: the commercial-type fast breeder now constitutes the Gordian knot of the non-proliferation regime.

2. The breakdown of the arms control structure

The time of France's 'baby-bomb' and a strategically negligible British force is now over. France and Britain plan to increase the number of their nuclear warheads from 162 (or about 300, taking into account submarine-borne weapons) to 1,200 by 1992. Furthermore, the current plans for PWR reprocessing in Europe will produce sufficient plutonium to build 50,000 nuclear warheads by the end of the century. With the introduction shortly of laser isotopic separation the availability of high-quality plutonium will no longer be a problem.

The Super-Phénix I fast breeder (1200 MWe) will be commissioned in September 1985 and will be capable of converting PWR plutonium into military-grade plutonium at a rate of 300 kg, or the equivalent of 60 nuclear warheads, a year. The detailed plans for Super-Phénix II (1500 MWe) will be available by the end of 1986 or 1987. The agreement between France, the United Kingdom, Italy, Belgium, Luxembourg and the Federal Republic of Germany, dated 10 January, 1984, for 'a long-term European programme of co-operation on fast breeders and the associated fuel cycles' completes the technocratic integration of the European plutonium economy. This momentum is further increased by Britain's recent proposal to its European partners to build a reprocessing plant at Dounreay.

The plutonium requirement for the new French nuclear weapons programme—around 5 tonnes, or 10 if the neutron bomb is to be produced in large numbers—will not be met by the production from military reactors alone. Super-Phénix is therefore essential to support the technical base for France's *force de frappe*.

The negotiations on intermediate range nuclear missiles (INF) foundered on the question of whether French and British nuclear forces should be taken into account. *Yet the nuclear programme that has just been outlined will promote Europe to the rank of a nuclear super-Power because it will have the capability to destroy at least one of the super-Powers.* This will inevitably have a profound effect on the current fragile structure of arms control between the super-Powers and may, within the next five years, ultimately lead to its breakdown.

3. Europe, the third nuclear super-Power

The emergence of Europe as a nuclear super-Power is evidenced by more than the proposed weapons programme. There is currently a strong campaign for a European defence and some American encouragement of its allies, against a background of isolationism, to acquire and directly control their own nuclear weapons.

However, not all the proposals under discussion can necessarily be brought to fruition because of various international treaties in force, and especially, until 1995, the NPT. The form of European defence that would be permitted under the terms of the NPT is therefore very important.

The transfer (including the ownership) of nuclear weapons or their control (the finger on the button) to third parties or to a multilateral entity are forbidden. The NPT would not bar, however, succession by a new federated European State to the nuclear status of one of its former component States, such as France or Britain. There is one precondition to be met: this federated European State would have to control all of its external security functions, including defence and all foreign policy matters relating to external security. It would not, however, have to be so centralized as to assume all ordinary governmental functions.

The Milan Summit taking place today (28 June) is discussing the French/West German proposal which takes the form of a draft treaty of European Union, which envisions the development of common foreign and security policies co-ordinated by a secretary-general. Before the Summit, Chancellor Kohl declared it is 'critical that we pave the way for a common European foreign policy'.

The United States has assured the Federal Republic of Germany that the NPT would not prevent the establishment of a European nuclear force if political unification of Western Europe took place. It was on this condition that West Germany ratified the NPT in 1974.

Clearly, we are moving in the direction advocated by Mr. Helmut Schmidt before the Bundestag in June, 1984, i.e. a strengthening of the Paris–Bonn axis and an extension of the French nuclear umbrella to West Germany. A view supported by Mr. Valéry Giscard d'Estaing: 'the use of French nuclear capabilities may be "approved" beforehand by our partners without being subject to a joint decision'. Approval 'beforehand' is in accordance with the provisions of the NPT.

The joint decision is thought to be one of the consequences of the uncertainties concerning the doctrine of the deployment and use of the new HADES prestrategic missiles, which have a range of 450 km. Only East Germany can be a target of the HADES missiles. But then there is the incontrovertible fact that West Germany would be covered by the French nuclear umbrella with all the consequences that brings, starting with the preliminary agreements which would appear to be necessary between the French and German Governments on the deployment and use of these weapons.

Over the last few years, France has become more and more outspoken in favour of a European defence, or at least a strengthening of the European pillar of the Atlantic alliance. France has refused to integrate the French forces into comparisons between NATO and the Warsaw Pact, proposed a new fillip to the Western European Union and, to counterbalance Mr. Reagan's 'Star Wars' plan, launched the Eureka project to expand the 'common technological stream which waters both the civilian and the military', as the French Minister of Defence has said. These, then, are indeed two- or three-speed initiatives aimed at widening the concept of independence so dear to General de Gaulle's heart, to embrace Europe as a whole.

The European nuclear infrastructure means that France and Britain can already provide themselves with the necessary strategic nuclear facilities.

In this connection, I feel that the virulent attacks by President Giscard d'Estaing and Chancellor Schmidt on President Carter were largely motivated by his policy of non-proliferation and a ban on the reprocessing of spent fuel because they reduced the chances of Europe becoming independent in nuclear technology, strategy and geopolitics.

4. A unique opportunity for a universal non-proliferation regime

To summarize the situation, *firstly* the European fast breeder and reprocessing programme can destroy the existing non-proliferation regime. One of the many consequences of this will be to bury finally the American nuclear industry, the political survival of which depends upon the fundamental distinction between the civil and the military. *Secondly*, the European fast breeder and reprocessing programme, backed by the French and British strategic plan for the next seven years, gives Europe virtually the status of a third nuclear super-Power.

Europe's strategic potential is even in a fair way to rival that of the Soviet Union. The result will be an escalation of the arms race, which would be extremely expensive for the USSR in a period of economic difficulty. By increasing the economic pressure on Warsaw Pact countries, this arms race will also lead to the speeding up of the centrifugal movement within the Eastern bloc.

This situation puts Europe in an unprecedented position of influence in making the two great Powers see reason. One can imagine a scenario where the leaders in London and Paris invite the negotiators from the Kremlin and the White House to come to their table and persuade them to agree to reduce their arsenals to a new ceiling of 1,000 nuclear warheads each within five years. On this condition, France and Britain, together with the United States and the Soviet Union, agree to subject their civil and military nuclear fuel cycles to international inspection (full-scope safeguards).

The United States will thus have a choice between maintaining its nuclear overkill capability and the survival of its nuclear industry. The Soviet Union will be faced with the alternatives of either withdrawing a considerable proportion of its threat to Europe, and its overkill capability, or exhausting its economic resources in a new arms race.

This solution will increase the security of Europe, the United States and the Soviet Union while reducing the risks to everyone. In fact, 1,000 nuclear warheads are already enough to ensure the total destruction of a super-Power, let alone the 25,000 now held by each side.

The solution would also set up a new, universal non-proliferation regime and save the NPT. The 1990 NPT Review Conference will provide an opportunity of reviewing the results of the negotiations and of laying the best possible foundations for a new non-proliferation regime to be set up after 1995, when the NPT expires.

Only Europe can take the part of the third super-Power in limiting the nuclear arms race in the near future. Moreover, as the review of the NPT next September will put the super-Powers on the defensive, it is the ideal opportunity for the European countries to support this Franco-British initiative for negotiations. In addition, France and Britain will gain tremendous prestige in many Third World countries where there is growing alarm over the hitherto unsuspected horrors of nuclear winter and the failure of the super-Powers to come to grips with the arms race.

Time is short, of course, but governments can reach agreement quickly in emergencies. It should also be remembered that all the European States involved in the plutonium economy have signed the NPT and that the Treaty requires all Parties to 'negotiate in good faith on effective steps to stop the nuclear arms race'. Only France has not signed the NPT, but it undertook in 1968 to behave 'in future in this field in exactly the same way as the States which decide to accede to it'.

In five years time such an initiative will be pointless. Europe's nuclear arsenal will be aligning itself with those of the two great Powers and the Soviet Union will have reacted strongly. What is at stake, therefore, is national and global security and the future of the non-proliferation regime. What is possible is nothing less than an end to the nuclear arms race itself.

Further Reading

(It seemed more logical to set references out in chronological order in a field which is in constant evolution.)

Non-Proliferation Treaty, Hearings before the Committee on Foreign Relations, United

States Senate, ninety-first Congress, first session on Executive H. 90th Congress, second session, Treaty on the non-proliferation of nuclear weapons, part 2, 18 and 20, 1969.

L. Lammers, 'Le choix fera le destin', ENERGIES, Revue hebdomadaire de l'équipement national et d'informations économiques, ISNN 0395—3866, No. 1298, 23 April 1982.

Michel Genestout et Yves Lenoir, 'Quelques vérités (pas toujours bonnes à dire) sur les surgénérateurs', *Science et Vie*, October 1982, No. 781.

Michel de Perrot, 'Le surgénérateur et le risque de prolifération des armes nucléaires', 27 October 1982, paper read at the Colloquium of the Institut national genevois, in *Energie et Société: Les surgénérateurs, vrai ou faux problème?*.

Atomwirtschaft, February 1983 (see especially Dr. Stoll's analysis).

Richard Garwin, 'Technical opportunities and inopportunities versus domestic and international politics of the arms race', in *European Security: Nuclear or Conventional Defence?*, IVth International Colloquium organized by the Groupe de Bellerive, 8/10 December 1983, Pergamon, Oxford, 1984.

Michel de Perrot, 'Commercial fast breeders: towards an integrated European nuclear force?', IVth International Colloquium organized by the Groupe de Bellerive, 8/10 December 1983, Pergamon, Oxford, 1984. This article and its French translation, 'Surgénération commerciale ou intégration techno-stratégique d'une Europe nucléire?' have also been published by the GIPRI (Geneva International Peace Research Institute, 41, rue de Zurich, CH 1200 Geneva).

Michel de Perrot, 'Le surgénérateur et l'option franco-européenne de dissuasion. Les implications pour le TNP', in *Armes nucléaires et droit international/Nuclear War and International Law*, proceedings of the Colloquium on 1 February 1984, GIPRI, Geneva, 1985.

Michel de Perrot, 'Commercial fast breeders and the European military implication', *Journal of World Trade Law, Volume 18, No. 3, May/June 1984.*

Jean-Pierre Pharabod, 'La France et la prolifération nucléaire', *Assises européennes contre la surgénération*, Lyon 26–27 May 1984, in *Superpholix*, January 1985.

La documentation française—problèmes politiques et sociaux, No. 434, 1982, p. 30 (dossier sur la non-prolifération) quoted by Zidiane Mériboute, 'La surgénération et le traité de non-prolifération', *Assises européennes contre la surgénération*, Lyon 26–27 May 1984, in *Superpholix*, January 1985.

Louis Puiseux, 'Superphénix atteint par le doute', *Le Monde diplomatique*, October 1984.

Dominique Finon,'L'avance technologique: atout décisif ou coûteux inconvénient?', *Le Monde diplomatique*, October 1984.

Michel de Perrot, 'Le passage du civil au militaire: surgénération commerciale ou option d'une force nucléaire européenne', *Le Monde diplomatique*, October 1984.

Ignacy Sachs, 'Des Superphénix pour le tiers-monde?', *Le Monde diplomatique*, November 1984.

Martine Barrère, 'Quand les experts tiennent les citoyens à l'écart', *Le Monde diplomatique*, November 1984.

Alain Joxe, 'Technostratégie et démocratie', *Le Monde diplomatique*. November 1984.

'Westminster: vibrant appel de M. Mitterand au désarmement', *Journal de Genève, 25 October 1984.*

Bertrand Goldschmidt, 'Interview with Paul Leventhal', *Nuclear Fuel*, 31 December 1984.

Ernest van den Haag, 'A case for enlarging the nuclear club', *International Herald Tribune*, 11 February 1985.

US–Euratom Agreement, 1972, article XI, para. 3, quoted by R. J. S. Harry (Netherlands) in *Bulletin of Atomic Scientists*, March 1985.
'France would sell India atomic fuel', *International Herald Tribune*, 9 April 1985.
Harold Jackson, 'Waiting for Britain to close nuclear gap', *The Guardian*, 29 May 1985.
Pierre Lellouche, *L'avenir de la guerre*, Magazine, Paris, 1985.
Melvyn B. Nathanson, 'Soviet reactors to open for international inspection', *Bulletin of the Atomic Scientists*, June/July 1985.
Steven J. Dryden, 'European Community discusses Reform before Iberian Entry', *International Herald Tribune*, 29/30 June 1985.
'Europe, le Tandem franco-allemand à l'Epreuve', *L'Express*, 5 July 1985.
'Le débat sur la défense de l'Europe, le PS pour une dissuasion élargie à l'Allemagne fédérale', Jacques Isnard, *Le Monde*, 4 July 1985.
'France, in Strategy Shift, Takes On Defense of West Germany', *International Herald Tribune*, 6–7 July 1985.

Annex

Fast breeder reactors in operation, under construction or planned

Country	Unit name	Power (MWth/MWe)	Startup date
Operational			
USA	EBR-11	62·5/20·0	1963
USSR	BOR-60	60/12	1969
USSR	BN-350	1000/150*	1972
France	Phénix	605/270†	1973
USSR	BR-10‡	10/0	1973
UK	PFR	670/250	1974
Germany Fed Rep	KNK-11	58/21	1977
Japan	Joyo	100/-	1977
USSR	BN-600	1470/600	1980
USA	FFTF	400/-	1980
Under construction			
France	Super-Phénix 1	3000/1242	1985
Germany Fed Rep	SNR-300	762/327	1986
India	FBTR	42/15	1985
Italy	Pec	118/-	1989
Japan	Monju	714/280	1991
Planned			
France	Super-Phénix 11	3600/1500	
Germany Fed Rep	SNR-2	3420/1300	
India	PFBR	1250/500	
Japan	DFBR	2550/1000	
USSR	BN-800	2100/800	
USSR	BN-1600	4200/1600	
UK	CDFR	3300/1250	

* 150 MWe+120000 m^3/d desalinated water

† The design basis power level was 568/250. Good performance and precise fuel management permitted an increase in the output without changing the installation

‡ Originally the BR-5 (5 MWth) which started operation in 1958

Source: *IAEA Bulletin* Vol. 26, No. 4; *ATOM* No. 344, June 1985

SPACE WEAPONS

Nuclear Security, Disarmament and Development

PROFESSOR MOHAMMED ABDUS SALAM

Nobel Prize Winner, Director, International Centre for Theoretical Studies, Trieste

1

The world's stock of nuclear weapons, which was three in 1945, has been growing ever since and is 50,000[1] in 1985; *nearly one trillion dollars of the public funds have been spent over the years to improve their destructive power, and the means of delivering them.* One indicator of the awful power of these weapons is that the explosive yield of the nuclear weapons stockpiled today by the US, USSR, UK, France, and China is equivalent to *one million Hiroshima bombs.* Less than 800 of these 50,000 weapons could destroy the USA and the USSR. A thousand more of these in an all-out nuclear exchange could destroy the world as a habitable planet, ending life for the living and the prospects of life for those not yet born, sparing no nation, no region of the world.

Hannes Alfven has suggested that the word 'annihilators' should be used for nuclear weapons, to bring home to mankind their real nature. The awful point about nuclear annihilators is that their destructiveness has only superficially sunk in. We continue to think of a nuclear war in terms of the historical experience of mankind with wars in the past. Thus, though it is recognized that the only value of nuclear weapons is deterrence, how many weapons are necessary for deterrence has never been made clear by either super-Power. Can the objective of deterrence be expressed in absolute terms? Does it represent a minimum of 10 city-destroying weapons or 1,000? How many lives, what proportion of the enemy's industrial capacity, have to be assured of extinction? The uncertainty of what the opponent may do next encourages the worst-case assumptions and makes the competition *open-ended.*

[1] These numbers include 'strategic', 'intermediate' and 'tactical' weapons. The average yield is 1/3 megatons of TNT per weapon.

The military strategists have gone on from the doctrine of 'deterrence' to 'damage limitation'. 'Damage limitation' meant that nuclear weapons must be given the capability to destroy other nuclear weapons before they could sow death and destruction. Thus one could justify unremitting efforts at modernization: goals of pinpoint accuracy, an MX with the power to blow up missiles in their silos, the ultimate 'Star Wars' defense through satellite systems.[1]

2

I should not be misunderstood; I am not criticizing one super-Power versus another. I will mostly use the US figures in this article only because they are the most readily available. The truth is that both super-Powers, equally, as well as all members of the nuclear club, stand indicted before the bar of humanity. A most pertinent question in this regard has been asked by the United Nations Secretary-General in his speech to the General Assembly on 12 December 1984, voicing the thoughts of all humanity:

> As I look across this Hall, I see the delegations of 159 member nations. Almost all the world's peoples are represented here. And all of them—all of us—live under the nuclear threat. As Secretary-General of this Organization, with no allegiance except to the common interest, I feel the question may justifiably be put to the leading nuclear-weapon powers: by what right do they decide the fate of all humanity? From Scandinavia to Latin America, from Europe and Africa to the Far East, the destiny of every man and every woman is affected by their actions. The responsibility assumed by the great Powers is now no longer to their populations alone: it is to every country and every people, to all of us.
>
> No ideological confrontation can be allowed to jeopardize the future of humanity. Nothing less is at stake: today's decisions affect not only the present, they also put at risk succeeding generations. Like supreme arbiters, with our disputes of the moment we threaten to cut off the future and extinguish the lives of the innocent millions as yet unborn. There can be no greater arrogance. At the same time, the lives of all who lived before us may be rendered meaningless. For we have the power to dissolve in a conflict of hours or minutes the entire work of civilization, with all the cultural heritage of humankind.
>
> At a time of uncertainty for the young and despair for the poor and the hungry, we have truly mortgaged our future to the arms race—both nuclear and conventional. The arms trade impoverishes the receiver and debases the supplier. Here there is a striking resemblance to the drugs trade. Yet we continue on the same course even when faced with the silent genocide of famine that today stalks millions of our fellow men and women. The international community has to focus and act on the link between disarmament and development. We should take concrete and far-sighted steps towards the conversion of arms industries from military to civilian production. And we should begin to redress some of the enormous imbalance between research on arms and research on arms limitation and reduction.

[1] I have used extensive quotations from Ruth Leger Sivard's excellent book, *World Military and Social Expenditures*, 1983.

3

In the context of nuclear security, it is pertinent to reflect the view from the point of view of developing countries.

Security for us in the developing world means not only security from a nuclear winter which may be unleashed on mankind by accident or through the design of 'homicidal maniacs', but also security from conventional wars waged on our soils. Since 1945, there have been 105 wars (with deaths of 1,000 or more per year), with or without super-Power involvement. These have been fought in 66 countries—*all of them in the Third World.* Twelve of these are being waged today, in more than one-third of which the richer countries are implicated. On the average, each has lasted three and a half years. They have caused 16 million deaths, the majority of them in Asia. Cambodia lost 2 million, over one-quarter of its population; Vietnam 2.5 million or 6 per cent of its population; Nicaragua, by the end of 1983, had lost 1.5 per cent of its population with 35,000 deaths and El Salvador 45,000 deaths with 1 per cent death toll. Most of these deaths took place among civilians with incalculable material and social costs; for example, in Iran, where damage to the civilian economy may be over $100 billion; or in Afghanistan, where, with already four out of five adults illiterate, 17,000 schools have been destroyed.[1] Thus, loss of security for us in the developing world is something which is more immediate, something we constantly live with.

4

Regarding the military expenditures, conventional and nuclear, reduced to numbers, the world's arms race and its effects on human life easily lose touch with reality. The current global war-budget is around $700 billion per year, out of a total global GNP of 12,000 billion. Of this expenditure, 550 billions is attributable to the developed and 150 billion to the developing countries.

Twenty-five million men are under arms; one billion—one quarter of humanity—live under military-controlled governments; and more than nine million *civilians* have been killed in 'conventional' wars since Hiroshima.

How much are the super-Powers spending on war today? At $855 per capita in 1982, military expenditures in the US are to be compared with $75 in comparable prices just before World War II. The military effort has risen faster than GNP, with US spending 6.5 per cent of GNP as compared with one per cent pre-war. The implications this has in respect of diminishing social expenditures need not be spelled out. Similar figures, even more stark in proportion, apply to the USSR.

Between 1960 and 1981, the world as a whole spent some $5 trillion (out

[1] *Ibid.*

of a total GNP of around $97 trillions) on military expenditures. Of this, $3.2 trillion were spent by the two super-Powers, $1 trillion by other industrialized countries, and around $0.8 trillion ($800 billion) by developing countries, mostly by the OPEC countries. (As I said earlier, $1 trillion of this $5 trillion total has been spent on nuclear weapons.) 'While military expenditures of developed countries (including the centrally-planned) rose by more than $400 billion, their foreign economic aid rose by no more than $25 billion.' In 1982 the super-Power military expenditures were 17 times larger than their extensions of aid to countries in need.

And it is not just the super-Powers which have spent lavishly on war. With the rich countries' drive to sell arms, the developing world has been equally profligate; among the 25 countries which since 1981 have had to negotiate to reschedule their debt six had spent more than $1 billion each for arms imports, in the five preceding years. Between them the 25 piled up a bill of $11 billion for arms in that period. Among 20 countries with the largest foreign debt, *arms imports* between 1976 and 1980 were equivalent to 20 per cent of the increase in debt.

5

What does this military expenditure mean in terms of unmet global human needs? Again I quote from Ruth Leger Sivard:

Poverty. 2,000 million people live on incomes below $500 per year.[1] At least one person in five is trapped in absolute poverty, a state of destitution so complete that it is silent genocide.

Jobs. In the Third World, one in three who wants to work cannot find a regular job.

In all countries it is the young people who are hardest hit by unemployment; in the US half of black teenagers are jobless.

Food. 450 million persons—one-tenth of mankind—suffer from dire hunger and malnutrition.

There are an estimated 15 million deaths yearly from malnutrition and infection, conditions which are preventable and which society has both the knowledge and means to prevent.

Every minute 30 children die for want of food and inexpensive vaccines and every minute the world's military budget absorbs $1.3 million of the public funds.

Education. 120 million young children of school age have no school they can go to. Educational neglect in fact begins at the earliest ages. One-third of the children between the ages of 6 and 11 are not in school. Over 250 million children in the world have not received even a basic education. To get a comparative estimate, the cost of a single new nuclear submarine equals the annual education budget for *160 million school-age children* in 23 developing countries.

[1] Of these 1/2 billion live on incomes below $100 per year.

6

I shall not go on labouring these points, but concentrate on just a set of proposals which had been made from time to time at the Forum of the United Nations by the Governments of France, Mexico, Senegal, USSR, and others, as well as by the Brandt Commission, to redress this balance. The proposals concern the creation of an International Disarmament Fund whose proceeds would be used for development tasks. It is hoped that such a fund may discourage war spending. In any case, it would ease warring humanity's guilt-feelings and its conscience. The most detailed proposal is that from France presented by its President, Mr. Giscard d'Estaing, in his address to the United Nations General Assembly in 1978. This proposal, elaborated in a memorandum by the French Government (United Nations Document A/S-10/AC. 1/28), envisioned the fund as a new United Nations specialized agency which would constitute a practical manifestation of the relationship acknowledged by the world community to exist between disarmament and development. Contributors to the fund would be those States which were both most heavily armed and most developed; beneficiaries of the fund would be those States which were least heavily armed and least developed.

In principle, the fund would be based on the disarmament dividend approach, that is, on resources released by disarmament measures. However, the French proposal also provided for a transitional phase of the fund with an initial one-time endowment of $1 billion, until resources derived from disarmament savings could become its long-term basis. In its transitional phase, contributions to the fund would be assessed on the basis of a State's level of armament, measured by the possession of certain types of weapon systems the existence of which, according to the proposal, could be objectively determined. The fund would make grants or loans to developing countries, utilizing as much as possible existing international agencies for the administration of its loan and grants.

Various criteria could be used in the transitional stage to identify the richest and most heavily armed countries. Assuming that the five permanent members of the Security Council would be automatically included, the following criteria have been suggested: (1977 statistics in 1977 US dollars):

—As a criterion of wealth: a per capita GNP of more than $1,000;
—As criteria of armaments: a level of military expenditure in excess of 2 per cent of GNP; a volume of military expenditure in excess of $1.5 billion.

Of the sum foreseen as the contribution during the transitory stage, amounting to $1,000 million, 50 per cent should be based on the States' nuclear armaments and 50 per cent on conventional armaments. The criterion used to determine the relative contributions[1] for the nuclear sector of the

[1] For conventional armaments the following contribution is proposed: 20 per cent from the

United States of America and the Union of Soviet Socialist Republics could be their number of vehicles, based on the SALT Agreement. The joint participation of these two countries would amount to 80 per cent of the whole sum. China, the United Kingdom and France would jointly contribute 20 per cent.

7

One may disagree with the details but the intention of setting up such a fund is clear and commendable. For today's discussion, I propose that we should spend our time discussing the modalities of setting up such a fund and its uses. I believe the two questions are linked. My remarks are mainly addressed to the last issue.

Why have such proposals for disarmament funds so far fallen by the wayside? Is it that such resolutions at the United Nations fora among delegates to United Nations bodies seldom bear fruit? If this is so, I believe that for effectiveness, we must engage the young men and women—particularly in the developed countries—in the crusade of getting their governments to act. The public outcry, focused principally against nuclear weapons, is today firmly backed. How soon it will begin to affect government priorities is not yet clear but it has already become a healthy counterweight to *official policy that has lost touch with reality*. It is imperative that this movement would embrace the constructive issue of development in addition to nuclear and conventional disarmament.

But to effect this, we must remember that the young people today are not moved by the *totality* of global development tasks in development or employment; nor always by dangers of unchecked population increase, of polarization of poverty and riches and by world illiteracy. I believe that what immediately moves the young today are (1) environmental problems; (2) death from hunger; and (3) possibly the desirability of eradication of dread diseases like leprosy and trachoma. My feeling is that if we ask for funds for eradication of illiteracy or generally for bridging the gap between the rich and the poor or for solving the energy problems of the world—however worthy all these causes may be—it is unlikely that we shall succeed in getting enough public support. I would therefore like to argue that—at least at the outset—we should set out the goals of a Disarmament Fund to deal with

Navy—using large units as a criterion; 40 per cent from the Army—using the number of heavy armoured vehicles as a criterion; 40 per cent from the Air Force—using the number of combat planes as a criterion. Data relating to this material would be supplied by statistics most frequently used internationally.

In the second and final stage, contributions would be determined by arms reduction agreements. The States which would be parties to these agreements would, through negotiations, determine what is for them the optimum security threshold, the level of which could be gradually lowered by subsequent negotiations. (*The Relationship between Disarmament and Development*, United Nations Publication, New York 1982.)

(1) problems of global environment; (2) death from hunger; and (3) eradicable human diseases.

8

Consider global environment: the biosphere has been likened in its thinness to 'dew upon an apple'. Its survival intact is mankind's survival. Take one aspect of its health, connected with the preservation of rainforests situated in the Third World. According to the Report presented to President Carter giving global projections for the year 2000, significant losses of world forests—particularly those in the tropics—are predicted for the next 20 years, principally as demand for fuelwood and food, both from the poor and the rich, increases. The world's forests are now disappearing at the rate of 18–20 million hectares a year (an area half the size of California), with most of the loss occurring in the humid tropical forests of Africa, Asia and South America. The projections indicate that by the year 2000 some 40 per cent of the remaining forest cover in less developed countries will be gone.

I wish to emphasize that an important factor in this disappearance is man's greed. According to a recent study made by Catherine Caulfield:

> In the face of big business, the environment would seem to stand little chance of survival. The beef-producing industry provides a perfect example. Because Latin American beef is half the price of America's own home-produced grass-fed variety, more and more of the land is being turned into pasture—much of it at the expense of the rain forests.[1]

The question should be asked: Is the saving of this global heritage to be left to the poor impoverished countries of the South only? Should this not be a charge on a global fund—possibly linked with disarmament?

Why is the disappearance of the tropical forests, proceeding now at 2 per cent of the forest per annum, disastrous for mankind as a whole? One of the many ecological reasons is the anticipated annihilation of a large fraction of species and organisms which inhabit these forests.

Approximately 1.5 million kinds of organisms have been named and classified, but these include only about half a million from the tropics. Many tropical organisms are very narrow in their geographical ranges and are highly specific in their ecological and related requirements. Thus, tropical organisms are unusually vulnerable to extinction through disturbance of their habitats. Since more than half of the species of tropical organisms are confined to lowland forests, and since, in most areas, these forests will be gone within the next 20–30 years; and with them most of the 3 million of these organisms.

With the loss of organisms, we give up not only the opportunity to study

[1] *The Rainforest* by Catherine Caulfield, published by Heinemann, 1985.

them, but also the chance to utilize them to better the human condition, both in the tropics and elsewhere. The economic importance of wild species, a tiny proportion of which we actually use, has been well documented. Suffice to say that the entire basis of our civilization today rests on a few hundred species out of the millions that might have been selected, and we have just begun to explore the properties of most of the remaining ones. Unfortunately this process of extinction cannot be reversed.

But how does a Global Development Fund come into this? In a recent issue of the *Bulletin of Atomic Scientists*, P. H. Ravan has argued that if the West cannot find the means to eliminate real poverty in the ecologically devastated areas, the people living there will topple any government; be it friendly or unfriendly! Thus it is no coincidence that El Salvador is ecologically the most devastated of all countries of Central America and yet the authors of the Kissinger Report pay no attention to the ecological problems which force peasants to shift to and destroy permanently, through cutting of forest cover, the productivity of their marginal lands. One may in this context ask if it is not the concern of the environmental groups in the developed countries to help to preserve this global heritage? Should they not come to the rescue of the developing countries? Should this type of global assistance not be a first charge on the international communities and on a Global Development Fund?

9

A second area for which such a Fund may be used is freedom from hunger, with the Ethiopian tragedy still on the public conscience. Favourable climate, water, good arable land and chemical inputs are the four factors essential for enhancing food production. According to the Carter Report the global area of arable land will increase only 4 per cent by the year 2000, so that most of the increased output of food will have to come from higher yields. During the same period expected increases in world population are nearly in the 30–40 per cent range—from 4.5 billion to 6 billion. Unfortunately, to feed this enhanced population, and to avoid recurrence of other Ethiopias, most of the elements which contribute to higher yields of food crops—fertilizer, pesticides, energy for irrigation, and fuel for machinery—depend on the scarce resources of oil and gas.

To make the problem more difficult, regional water shortages will become more severe. In the 1980–2000 period population growth alone will cause requirements for water to double in nearly half the world. Still greater increases would be needed to improve standards of living. In many less developed countries, water supplies will become increasingly erratic by 2000 as a result of extensive deforestation. Development of new water supplies will become more costly virtually everywhere.

'Unless action is taken, serious deterioration of agricultural soils will occur worldwide, due to erosion, loss of organic matter, desertification, salinization, alkalinization, and waterlogging. Already, an area of cropland and grassland approximately the size of the State of Maine is becoming barren wasteland each year, and the spread of desert-like conditions is likely to accelerate.' Offices of India's Planning Commission reported recently, 'We in India are on the verge of an enormous ecological disaster, with our water reserves drying up. What is happening in Africa is going to happen in India within a few decades.'

10

So far as the chemical inputs for enhanced agriculture are concerned, in December 1982 in the Philippines, under the auspices of the International Union of Pure and Applied Chemistry, 600 top-ranking chemists of the world met and drew up a plan of action where chemistry could be utilized to raise world food productivity through chemical inputs in 15 years—the goal being to increase world food productivity by 50 per cent by the year 2000. A number of world institutes for teaching, training and research of chemists from the Third World were to be created. If they are not, it will mainly be because of shortage of funds.

11

The World Resources Institute of Washington, DC has made a list of some of the truly serious ecological problems which are deserving of wide international attention:

1. Loss of crop and grazing land due to desertification, erosion, conversion of land to non-farm uses, and other factors. The United Nations reports that, globally, farm and grazing land are being reduced to zero productivity at the rate of about 20 million hectares a year.
2. Depletion of the world's tropical forests, which is leading to loss of forest resources, serious watershed damage (erosion, flooding, and siltation), and other adverse consequences. Deforestation is projected to claim a further 100 million hectares of tropical forests by the end of this century.
3. Mass extinction of species, principally from the global loss of wildlife habitat, and the associated loss of genetic resources. One estimate is that more than 1,000 plant and animal species become extinct each year, a rate that is expected to increase.
4. Rapid population growth, burgeoning Third World cities and ecological refugees. World population will most likely double by the early decades

of the next century, and almost half the inhabitants of developing countries will live in cities—many of unmanageable proportions.

5. Mismanagement and shortages of fresh water resources. Water-borne diseases are responsible for perhaps 80 per cent of all illness in the world today.
6. Overfishing, habitat destruction, and pollution in the marine environment. Twenty-five of the world's most valuable fisheries are seriously depleted today due to overfishing.
7. Threats to human health from mismanagement of pesticides and hazardous substances and from pathogens in human wastes and aquatic vectors. An estimated 1.5 to 2.0 million persons in developing countries suffer acute pesticide poisoning annually and pesticide-related deaths are estimated at 10,000 a year.
8. Climate change due to the increase in 'greenhouse gases' in the atmosphere. The steady build-up of carbon dioxide and other gases in the atmosphere, due principally to fossil fuel burning, is predicted to create a 'greenhouse effect' of rising temperatures and local climate change—the question increasingly is not 'if?' but 'how much?'. For a variety of reasons, poor countries are likely to suffer disproportionately from the consequences of climate change.
9. Acid rain and, more generally, the effects of a complex mix of acids, ozone and other air pollutants on fisheries, forests, and crops.
10. Mismanagement of energy fuels and pressures on energy resources, including shortages of fuelwood, the poor man's oil. Although the energy crisis is in temporary remission in the developed countries, the high costs of oil imports and fuelwood shortages continue to plague much of the developing world.

12

And this brings me finally to one of the most crucial charges on a Disarmament Fund—relevant scientific research in the areas of global environment, food and dread disease.

At the cutting edge of the military competition between the major Powers is a mobilization of research resources without parallel in history. The results of this research provide an irresistible momentum to the arms race. The post-war take-off in weapons research was even more spectacular than the rise in military expenditures in general. In the US, government-financed military R & D jumped from $1.7 billion in fiscal year 1947 to $22.1 billion in fiscal year 1983 (both in 1980 prices). The thirteenfold increase in research expenditures was four times as fast as the already very rapid growth in US military spending over the same period.

The stark fact is that one half of mankind's research effort is on military R & D. The scientific talents of these men and women together with the resources devoted to military R & D might have been spent on research on ecology, climate, food and disease.

In this context, consider ecology and climate studies. I do not know whether one can really hope to change the climate; but surely it is a scandal that there is no scientific study of the climate of the Sahelian area over a long-term period. The universities in these areas have Departments of Meteorology but these Departments are weak, ill-organized and without any funds. They could be made stronger. Can one hope for a Global Disarmament Development Fund to organize the building up of indigenous scientific communities for carrying out such studies in the countries concerned? The truth is that mankind is already engaged in 'the Third World War'—the war against our heritage of resources—against life on planet Earth. And we are winning it.

13

Strategic Defense Initiative

One of the military projects which is still more likely to divert scientific resources away from global projects is the Strategic Defense Initiative. Again, I do not wish any mistake to be made about what I am saying. If the desire is not nuclear aggression, I have no doubt that a *partial* defensive system against nuclear weapons can be built after more than a decade. But at what cost in material terms and at what cost to the global scientific effort of mankind? Why could the super-Powers not agree to a straightforward elimination of their nuclear arsenals instead?

The estimates for material cost to each super-Power are open-ended, starting with a minimum of $1 trillion upwards. (Recall that the atomic weapons have so far cost mankind about $3 trillion over the last 25 years.) To estimate the number of scientists and technologists needed, it is perhaps good to remember that 10,000 scientists are supposed to be working just in the research establishments on laser technology in the USSR. The numbers of scientists and engineers needed to design and build the satellites and other interceptors will not be less than several hundred thousand. If deployed on the global projects I have mentioned before (and with a trillion dollars available), such an effort could transform our sick planet.

To give you an idea of what is needed for the Strategic Defense Initiative, let me mention the tasks first, then the strategies suggested, and finally, the countermeasures possible.

The tasks

1. Number of nuclear weapons on both sides—around 25,000 each with an average yield of 1/3 megaton.
2. Number of ICBMs—around 1,000-1,400 each side.
3. Number of weapons which would suffice to destroy each super-Power—at most around 400 each.
4. Minimum megatons needed for the onset of nuclear winter—600 megaton exchange.

The strategic defense initiative

1. The *boost phase* with the use of lasers as the killers of rising enemy ICBMs (which will last a few minutes).
2. The bus deployment phase.
3. The mid-course phase.
4. The terminal phase with rockets as the killers.

The boost phase

In the boost phase, lasers would be needed, mounted on a battle station, the rising ICBMs before they have mirved or released the decoys and the dummies. The lasers could be either of infra-red wavelength or ultra-violet or X-ray wavelengths.

Now both infra-red and X-ray wavelengths would be absorbed in the atmosphere and must be used outside. To take an example, an infra-red hydrogen fluoride laser, producing a beam of 2.7 microns wavelength, could be mounted on a battle station. Its power needs would be around 25 megawatts. (The best lasers available today can deliver no more than 1/3 megawatts of power, and are some 200 metres in length. This beam would have to be aimed by a perfect 10 metre diameter mirror (the best terrestrial telescopes are nowhere near this figure). These mirrors should be able to focus the beam on a spot with a diameter of less than a metre at a distance of a few thousand kilometers with an intensity sufficient to burn through the shell of a booster, within 5 seconds or less. All this could be developed, perhaps within a decade, but the development effort and its costs would naturally be colossal.

The number of battle stations required to destroy all 1,400 of the Soviet ICBMs would depend on a number of factors and is a matter of controversy at the present time. The figures quoted range between 100–1,500 such battle stations orbiting the earth but most experts say that a minimum of 300–400 battle stations would be needed to cover the Earth. Such deployment is expected to cost in the order of 1/2 trillion dollars.

The best use of X-ray lasers (which would be nuclear explosion-powered) would not be in space but probably in a mode suggested by Teller. On warning of an enemy attack, a submarine could send these nuclear-bomb-powered killer X-ray lasers into space. One of the difficulties involved in this is the time that it would take for the defence missiles to reach sufficient height to hit the boosting missiles. The optimum place for the stationing of X-ray laser-carrying submarines would be in the Indian Ocean to hit boosting Soviet missiles. Since the Earth is curved, this laser could not be effective till 200 seconds have elapsed after the warning, while the Soviet missiles would have needed only 120 seconds to reach this height.

At least this makes for an uncertainty in the sureness of the kill.

Finally, the ultra-violet lasers—excimers—may be used. This laser light can penetrate the atmosphere. The best suggested use for these lasers is ground-based, with a geosynchronous mirror—36,000 kilometers above the Earth—which would reflect the laser beam to low orbiting mirrors used for the kill itself.

The perfect geosynchronous mirror necessary for the operation is considered likely to be a sitting duck, for a pre-emptive attack.

It should also be noted that these interlocking systems, in order to work as a system, will need computer power of an order hitherto unimagined and unachieved. The computer software needed to launch and integrate these systems would be so enormous that new whole generations of computers which could write such software would have to be developed. Considerable difficulties in completing credible peacetime tests of such software are anticipated. Since there will be no time left for human decision-making, the decision to attack a perceived attack would have to be made autonomously. This would certainly be a new situation in our affairs where the crucial decisions of mankind's survival would depend on computers sensing and rightly interpreting whatever they see.

One may also mention that the nuclear explosions carried out in space would affect the present generation of computers deleteriously while their circuits are affected by electromagnetic radiation. To counteract this, it has been suggested that a sixth generation of computers should be developed to work with photons only. This may happen in one or two decades but certainly not in the immediate future.

But the real difficulty with the Strategic Defense Initiative is that counter measures can be easily devised. Some of those suggested for the boost phase are:

1. Harden the missiles a few more millimeters against laser attacks.
2. Launch the missile in less time, i.e., shorten the boost phase time.
3. Interfere with the very exact mirror alignment.

The mid-course phase

If the ICBMs have not been shot down in the boost phase, or the short bus-deployment phase, then in mid-course the enemy would be deploying a vast number of decoys and metal balloons, in addition to warheads. There could be many more metal balloons than warheads—about 100 times as many, with the warheads hidden in the balloons. The defence involves either destroying all the balloons or else detecting which balloons are carrying the warheads. X-ray bombs could be effective for destroying these except if the enemy counters these by using his X-ray lasers.

The final opportunity for a defence to counter the warheads would be in the terminal phase after re-entry of the warheads. This phase is again very short, lasting less than one minute. Homing rockets have been suggested as the means for countering the warheads. Such a defence could be countered by very high altitude nuclear explosions of some of the warheads prematurely, before they are in the range of the defence. This would interfere with the detection of the rest of the warheads, which would come in behind the explosion.

To summarize, even if a strategic defence system could be built with 99 per cent efficiency, it may still allow in the order of 100 weapons to get through and ensure unacceptable destruction of the invaded country. I do not think any country could really rely on a defence system. In any case, in view of the fear that the enemy can always build up their offensive capability much more cheaply than defence capability, 'strategic defence' is more likely to cost much more to the country which relies on it, than to its adversary.

The Defense Initiative *can* be implemented in time, to provide partial defence at a colossal cost. One, however, asks in despair: But why? For whom is this being done? Why not the simplest alternative of agreeing to a diminishing of the numbers of and eventually the outlawing of nuclear weapons and nuclear missiles? That surely should be the goal of nuclear statesmanship.

Nine hundred years ago, a great physician of Islam, Al Asuli, living in Bokhara, wrote a medical pharmacopoeia which he divided into two parts: 'Diseases of the Rich' and 'Diseases of the Poor'. If Al Asuli were alive and writing today about the afflictions wrought upon itself by mankind, I am sure he would divide his pharmacopoeia into the same two parts. One part of his book would speak of the affliction of nuclear annihilation inflicted on humanity by its richer half. The second part of his book would speak of the affliction which poor humanity suffers from—underdevelopment, undernourishment and famine. He would add that both these diseases spring from a common cause—excess of science and technology for the case of the rich, and a lack of science and technology for the case of the poor. He might also add that the persistence of the second affliction of mankind—

underdevelopment—was the harder to understand, considering that the remedies for it are readily available in that the world has enough resources—technical, scientific, and material—to eradicate poverty, disease and early death for the whole of mankind, if it wishes to do so. It has only to eschew deployment of these resources towards aggravating the first affliction.

TABLE

Summary of Global Expenditures (1960–1981)

	Industrialized countries ($\frac{1}{3}$ of mankind)	Developing countries (including OPEC countries, $\frac{2}{3}$ of mankind)
GNP	$70 trillions	$8 trillions
Military expenditures	$4 trillions	$0.8 trillions (OPEC 0.3 trillions)
Nuclear expenditures (Super-Powers only)	$1 trillion	
Development aid	$0.3 trillion	$0.06 trillions (OPEC)

NEW NUCLEAR WEAPON STATES AND THEIR IMPACT ON THIRD WORLD REGIONAL CONFLICTS

PROFESSOR ALI A. MAZRUI
Department of Political Science, University of Michigan

I will be dealing with issues in a slightly different way than I had originally intended. There are some questions here that I will simply pose. One issue is nuclearized South Africa! Is it a short-term nuisance for the rest of Africa but a possible long-term advantage? Is the first black-controlled nuclear system going to be South African when the blacks take over? In other words, will the blacks be inheriting white South Africa's bomb, possibly before the end of the century?

Another issue is nuclear terrorism. Will Israel be the first target of such an exercise? Is this partly related to not pushing the Arabs or the Muslims too far?

A third issue concerns a strange alliance between potential nuclear proliferation in the Third World and women's liberation in the Northern Hemisphere. Are these two trends much more relevant for the quest for a nuclear-free world than we currently realize? Then there is the issue of nuclear 'macho' and nuclear castration, the psychology of military power. Is there a factor connected with macho in the desire to acquire nuclear capabilities? Is it a continuation of primordial instincts that have just taken a more advanced technological form? And is the danger of the nuclearization of macho part of the total peril for the human race right now?

Those are some of the questions I worry about and some of them will emerge as I elaborate on these issues. On the question of cultural differences on one side and sexual imbalances on the other, I start from this premise that the most revolutionary forces in the twentieth century and possibly for the first half of the twenty-first century (assuming we are still alive then) are still the forces of Marx's ideology and commitment to transformation, on one side, and the resurgence of Islam and commmitment to revivalism, on the other. So if those are the two most important revolutionary forces, Marxism on one side and Islam on the other, it is possible that Marxism is more likely to reconcile itself to preserving the *status quo* than radicalized Islam? In other words, the symptoms we see in a Soviet commitment to maintain the present order may be an indication of the greater readiness of the Marxist stream to accept accommodation with the *status quo*. In contrast, there is evidence that Islam is impatient for change and suffers from a sense of wounded dignity. Therefore, the possibility of an increasing desire on the part of an increasing number of Muslims to change this *status quo* has to be taken into account. The Marxist revolution is a revolution of rising aspirations, but the Islamic resurgence is partly a revolution of resurrecting a lost status. The Marxist revolutions have tended to be ones of 'how have the lonely risen and the underprivileged come up?'. The Islamic anger concerns 'how are the mighty fallen?'. Marxism is perhaps in search of a new order. Islamic fundamentalism is in search of resurrecting a more important phase of Islamic order. A Marxist revolution is at its best innovative; Islamic revolution is revivalist.

Islam has not done well by the nuclear age. The twentieth century generally has not been kind to Islam politically and that may be a major factor as to why Muslims are dissatisfied with the *status quo*. First, the colonization of Islam by Europeans from Egypt to Indonesia in the first half of the twentieth century; secondly, the collapse of the Ottoman Empire, a mixed blessing admittedly, but creating a leadership void in the Muslim world, and thirdly, the psychology of the Ataturk revolution in Turkey, which implied that Islam had failed in modern terms.

The fourth disaster was the creation of the State of Israel in the teeth of almost universal worldwide Muslim opposition and revealing the vulnerability of Muslims in the twentieth century. Then there was the coming of the nuclear age itself at a time when Islam was technologically backward and therefore emphasizing a significant marginality.

Then came the nuclearization of Israel, potentially creating a permanent stalemate between the Arabs and the Jews in the Middle East. Nor must we forget the nuclearization of India and its possible consequences for Indo-Pakistani relations. Underlying them all has been the continuing triumph of European culture and civilization as a soil for technological innovation. The successes of the Israelis in the Middle East are not due to the fact that they are Jews: they are due to the fact that a large number of them are of European extraction. If the population of Israel had consisted primarily of Middle Eastern Jews, the Arabs would have won every war in that confrontation by sheer margin of numbers. But it is precisely the difference in technological and organizational power characteristic of the Western Jews that tipped the scale in favour of the Israelis.

In the face of this sense of insecurity, will there be a nuclearization of Islam? A lot of discussions have focussed on Pakistan and whether it is on its way there. There is also speculation about the possible marrying of Gulf petrol resources on one side and Pakistani and Egyptian expertise on the other. Islam in anger could be forced to the nuclearization of its military ambitions. After all, powerlessness corrupts and absolute powerlessness can corrupt absolutely, even to the extent of creating nuclearized terrorism in the Middle East.

As for my own continent, black Africa, that is scientifically marginal, economically at the moment desolate, militarily peripheral. The African continent remains on the periphery of the nuclear age. It is true that uranium from Africa was an important aspect of the early phases of calculating the raw material of the nuclear age. African uranium is still relevant. It is true that the French used the Sahara for their own nuclear tests and Africa tried to protest at the beginning of the sixties, but ultimately it may well be in the Republic of South Africa that Africa's most direct experimentation with nuclear power will attain some degree of maturity. Curiously enough, nuclear weapons are less relevant for the survival of the Apartheid system than they are for the survival of Zionism in Israel. After all, the greatest danger to the Apartheid system is from within and it is unlikely that the South Africans will use nuclear devices in dealing with rebels within their own territory in the streets of Soweto or their equivalent. And if they did, they would implement one of their true nightmares; one nightmare is: 'The blacks are coming!'. The other is: 'The whites are leaving!'. Using nuclear devices within the Republic of South Africa would be a sure guarantee of a large-scale exodus of whites as a result. At any rate, the South African whites have decided to invest in a nuclear capability. This is bad news to some extent for black Africans for the time being, but South Africa's nuclear capability will be inherited by a black government after the confrontation takes place before the end of the century. Black South Africans will change from being the most humiliated blacks of the twentieth century to possibly the most powerful ones of the twenty-first century.

Then there is the case of Egypt within Africa. Egypt can be re-radicalized, either in the direction of Islamic fundamentalism or in the direction of left wing secular radicalism. If that did happen, the possibility of Egypt withdrawing from NPT and embarking once again on nuclear ambitions cannot be ruled out.

But is all this bad news? There are occasions when horizontal proliferation can be a cure for vertical proliferation, that the increasing number of countries with nuclear weapons can create enough of a scare among the big Powers to create additional motives for nuclear disarmament. After all, what made the peaceful uses of nuclear energy more suspect in the United States was in part the alarm caused by the accident on Three-Mile Island. We need a culture shock to induce earnest pursuit of a denuclearized world. And one approach to that culture shock is precisely the image of one or two Idi Amins doing war dances with nuclear devices. The lunatics of the North that we have had in this century are at least as alarming as any Idi Amin. We have had the horrors of Hitler and Stalin and there was also the danger that Nixon was approaching the same direction when he ordered a world-wide nuclear alert in 1973. The capacity of planetary destruction in the hands of Northern lunatics is far greater than the capacity that could even be approximated by Southern deviants.

And finally let me insist that it is not enough to seek conferences on nuclear disarmament. The genie of nuclear power and its possible military uses is already out of the bottle. The chances are that the genie cannot be effectively put back into the bottle and thrown back into the deep blue sea. Some additional fundamental changes are needed. My question is: what kind of fundamental social revolution could stabilize a denuclearized world permanently? And to ask that question, I then ask the following: what has been the most persistent characteristic of war in all societies across millenia and across cultures? No, not the consistency of motives, Gold, God and Glory, that is definitely one set of triumvirate of motives, but war motives have varied from capturing women to defending national dignity. Some have gone to war because one of their citizens has had his ear cut off: the War of Jenkin's Ear. There have been wars connected with football rivalries. Clearly, motivation for war is not the most consistent characteristic. What about similarity of weapons? We know that the weapons of war vary from very sophisticated, surface-to-air missiles to spears and swords. What about climatic consistency? We know all hell has broken out in tropical hot areas as well as in cold areas. What about the technology of war? This can be the basis of organization as well as weapons. But technologies of warfare have also varied enormously across time and cultures. The most persistent relevant attribute of war has been its masculinity. Societies otherwise vastly different from each other have used their sons rather than their daughters for war across time, across cultures. Do I assume that women are less violent than men? Well, they are certainly less experienced in large-scale slaughter. Men and women are admittedly both active in causing birth, but men have been by far more active in causing death. Women are perhaps senior partners in the process of pregnancy and baby-making, but men have definitely been senior partners in the game of destruction and corpse-making. Iron ladies like Golda Meir, Indira Gandhi as well as Margaret Thatcher succeed because it is a male dominated world and these ladies have pursued their own nuclear credentials. Only the women who approximate masculine criteria of toughness stand a chance of success in the power game of today's world. For the time being we have no real women equivalents of a Hitler or a Stalin or a Pol Pot or an Idi Amin or the more brutal architects of a party. Nuclear weapons may still be macho symbols. Behind the macho is the masculinity of warfare. With the coming of the nuclear age war has become too dangerous to be left to men alone. The power system needs to be androgynized. Nuclear disarmament is not enough, we have to reduce the risk of war. The only thing we have never experimented with is a gender revolution, a balanced sharing of responsibility for peace between men and women. So when all the talk is finished about how to disarm, the remaining agenda is how to stop killing by whatever means, because if we do not stop killing by whatever means the nuclearization of suicide will persist as a global danger. Security may not work with the androgynization of military power. We do not know, because we have never experimented on that scale. The gender revolution is the only social revolution that has had no real implementation in the annals of war. Let us try it out—just in case.

ARMS OR DEVELOPMENT: A MORAL CHOICE FOR SURVIVAL

PROFESSOR THEO C. VAN BOVEN

Professor of Law, Limburg University, Maastricht, and Chairman, Commission of the Churches on International Affairs of the World Council of Churches

When 40 years ago the Charter of the United Nations was signed at the close of the Conference of San Francisco on 26 June 1945, this act was a solemn expression of the determined wish of 'we the peoples of the United Nations to save succeeding generations from the scourge of war'. The preamble of the same Charter also reaffirms faith in fundamental human rights, it seeks to maintain justice and respect for the obligations arising from treaties and other sources of international law, as well as to promote social progress and better standards of life in larger freedom. It would be tempting to analyse and assess at this juncture of the fortieth anniversary of the United Nations to what extent the system of international co-operation and common security as embodied in the organization of the United Nations has proved to be a viable proposition and reality. It would also be tempting to reflect on the promises and ideals of a world whose peoples would enjoy fundamental rights and freedoms, the fruits of justice and the benefits of progress and development. Any such stock-taking of today's realities in the light of perceptions and assumptions of 40 years ago would present a disturbing picture which does not correspond to the promises of those earlier days.

The issues facing us today and which constitute the main theme of this Colloquium are potentially more dramatic and fateful than the authors of the UN Charter could have envisaged. Forty years ago the explosion of atomic bombs with their devastating effects demonstrated the terrible hazards of the atomic age. Today we are facing what might become the militarization of space and we are being warned that we find ourselves at the edge of perhaps the most far-reaching military threshold since the beginning of the atomic age. Precious as the notions of peace and justice may be and will be, the keyword now is the very basic notion of *survival*. I will revert to this.

It sometimes occurs to me to wonder—and the reference in the preamble of the UN Charter to 'succeeding generations' has led me to this thought—how future generations succeeding us will judge our lifetime, our policies and priorities and the manner in which we acted as stewards of the world's human, natural and other resources. If there will be human survival, and if objective conditions should exist to reach an overall judgement of the predominant policies and priorities of our times, the verdict by future generations cannot be but harsh. How can it be explained and justified under any standards of justice that huge and ever-increasing amounts of resources be allocated to the production and the trade of the most destructive conventional and nuclear arms, while at the same time some one billion people are lacking the most basic needs and struggling daily for their survival? Although it would be too simplistic to assume that everything that could be saved by limiting military expenditure could easily be diverted into development efforts, there is nevertheless such an enormous disproportion as regards allocations of resources aimed at meeting basic human needs in comparison with resources directed at what are supposedly military security interests, that this situation is bound to be judged as a scandal by present and future generations.

We are all aware that there is no lack of plans, programmes and blueprints for new and enlightened economic, social and political priorities. They were developed, on the basis of solid research and studies, by United Nations bodies and independent commissions and institutions with high repute for their scholarship, expertise and dedication. A wealth of information and insight is for instance presented in the report of the United Nations Group of Governmental Experts on the Relationship between Disarmament and Development[1] and in the report of the Independent Commission on International Development Issues under the Chairmanship of Willy Brandt and entitled *North–South: a Programme for Survival.*[2] Churches and other religious bodies guided by theological motivations and moral imperatives, call in prophetic and cogent terms for new ethical approaches, for the integration of human rights standards in national and international policies. They challenge the present world order with its patterns of superiority and inferiority, its structures of power and poverty, its reliance on deterrence and its uncalculated risk of total destruction. These expressions of grave concern, these deep-felt notions of responsibility which are also in the minds of those who organize this Colloquium, these enlightened calls for new policies and priorities are gaining momentum and urgency. They affirm the pertinent but unheeded words which President Eisenhower spoke in his 1961 farewell address when he—who was eminently qualified to speak on the subject—warned against the military-industrial complex. After having exposed the all pervasive influence and impact of the immense military establishment and the large arms industry, he said: 'In the councils of government, we must guard against the acquisition of unwarranted influence, whether sought or unsought, by the military-industrial complex. The potential for the disastrous

[1] UN doc. A/36/356.

[2] *North–South: A Programme for Survival*, Pan Books, London and Sydney, 1980.

rise of misplaced power exists and will persist. We must never let the weight of this combination endanger our liberties or democratic processes.'[1] The issues raised by Eisenhower some 25 years ago have not lost any of their significance. On the contrary, they are now more important than ever before and they do not only apply to one system of government and power but to all. What factors and what interests are pushing the arms race to ever unprecedented levels? Who decides on these issues, and on what basis, and is there any effective democratic control on the development, production and employment of weapons? It is not too bold an assumption to state that to a large extent these vital issues of decision-making and these processes leading to a military build-up are in most societies, if not in all, withdrawn from effective democratic and public control. As Eisenhower observed quite rightly, the question of liberties and democratic processes within our nations is at stake and in this respect we face a serious human rights issue. Equally, negotiations and other dealings between nations on disarmament and arms limitation are cut off from the political and economic life to which they are important. As the Brandt Commission reported: 'They continue as exchanges between armaments experts, attempting to reach binding and policeable agreements on highly technical issues, with the inherent danger that politics becomes the prisoner of technological developments.'[2] Again democratic and public control is lacking as regards decision-making and processes which affect vital interests of humankind.

In international relations and within many societies, the philosophy of the survival of the fittest, and the dictates of the strongest, are prevailing over the demands of peace and justice for all. The arms race and the aims of development have to be approached in their mutual and competitive relationship. While the frantic race towards nuclear conflagration and the imminent spread of nuclear weapons among nations poses a grave threat to the survival of humankind, this should not obscure the fact that for many millions the most immediate threat to survival is posed by various local, national, and international conflicts which rage around the world, and by the lack of the most basic needs of existence. As the World Council of Churches stated in 1983 at its sixth Assembly in Vancouver: 'The intersection of East–West and North–South conflicts results in massive injustice, systematic violation of human rights, oppression, homelessness, starvation and death for masses of people. Millions have been rendered stateless, expelled from their homes as refugees or exiles . . . Even without war, thousands perish daily in nations both rich and poor because of hunger and starvation. Human misery and suffering as a result of various forms of

[1] Dwight D. Eisenhower, *Waging Peace, The White House Years, A Personal Account*, New York, Doubleday and Co., 1965, p. 516.
[2] *North–South: A Programme for Survival*, pp. 118–19.

injustice have reached levels unprecedented in modern times.'[1] This leads to the inescapable question of today's global priorities which appear to be gravely distorted, inasmuch as present priorities are largely determined by fallacious concepts of security. In this respect I would again refer to pertinent observations by the Brandt Commission and the World Council of Churches. They expressed their views on a new concept of security more aptly than I could, and I will therefore quote from their statements and reports. The Brandt Commission stated:

> Our survival depends not only on military balance, but on global cooperation to ensure a sustainable biological environment, and sustainable prosperity based on equitably shared resources. Much of the insecurity in the world is connected with the divisions between rich and poor countries—grave injustice and mass starvation causing additional instability.[2]

And in the same vein the World Council of Churches declared in Vancouver:

> No nation can pretend to be secure so long as others' legitimate rights to sovereignty and security are neglected or denied. Security can therefore be achieved only as a common enterprise of nations but security is also inseparable from justice. A concept of 'common security' of nations must be reinforced by a concept of 'people's security'. True security for the people demands respect for human rights, including the right to self-determination, as well as social and economic justice for all within every nation, and a political framework that would ensure it.[3]

I am quite aware that the laws of morality count very little for those who defend the laws of force. But I am also convinced that the laws of force which are at the basis of patterns of domination and policies of deterrence are, apart from being morally condemnable and ethically unjust, not capable of safeguarding peace and security in the long run. There are eminent scientists who in good conscience put to themselves and to the world pertinent questions about the effects of their research on humanity and on the natural and biological environment. These questions touch upon issues of fundamental existence and survival. There are leading economists who are questioning the priorities which are dictated by rampant militarism and by uncontrolled demands of the military-industrial complex.[4] The same economists have offered schemes for the conversion of military expenditure to civilian production which would serve the rights and interests of the peoples of both developed and developing countries. There are conscientious lawyers who strive to give normative content to the right to peace and the right to development as a basis for international co-operation. In this respect

[1] *Gathered for Life*, Official Report of the VI Assembly of the World Council of Churches, Vancouver, Canada, 24 July–10 August 1983, edited by David Gill, Geneva-Grand Rapids, pp. 131–2.

[2] *North–South: A Programme for Survival*, p. 124.

[3] *Gathered for Life*, p. 134.

[4] Jan Tinbergen, 'What Road to Survival?', World Press Review, August 1984, pp. 25–8.

it may also be recalled that a body of legal experts from all parts of the world, entrusted in the framework of the United Nations with the implementation at an international level of the International Covenant on Civil and Political Rights, adopted in autumn 1984 by consensus in connection with its interpretative comments on the right to life the following statement: 'The production, testing, possession, deployment and use of nuclear weapons should be prohibited and recognized as crimes against humanity'.[1] Lawyers, philosophers and theologians have in the past developed doctrines of a 'just war', a concept often abused and now largely written off as legally unacceptable and to be substituted by the concept of a 'just peace'. New emphasis and a new orientation is being directed at what a 'just peace' means and what it requires. It is definitely not the peace of a graveyard.

All these efforts—and many more can be cited—have only to a limited extent, if at all, made an impression upon those who reign in the various political and economic power centres of the world. Norms of morality and justice, the laws of humanity and human rights, as defined by the United Nations in international instruments and embodied in plans for a new political, economic, social, and human order, are largely being ignored by those power centres. But as a sign of hope and as a matter of faith, we are witnessing the emergence of a broad popular peace movement in various parts of the world. A movement that challenges in various ways present unjust structures and practices and that in a variety of forms and actions works for peace and justice. This popular movement needs the support of all those who, guided by their conscience, their expertise, their influence, and their enlightened interests, are prepared to engage themselves in serious efforts to develop new economic and political priorities as viable alternatives aimed at bringing about common security, economic conversion, and 'just peace'. These are ingredients for a common survival. And in conclusion I cannot resist quoting one sentence from the Brandt report which appears simplistic but which derives its strength and its power of persuasion from solid analysis and profound conviction: 'More arms do not make mankind safer, only poorer'.[2]

[1] UN doc. CCPR/C/21/Add. 4.
[2] *North-South: A Programme for Survival*, p. 117.

Session II Debate

Chairman

First of all, a number of questions have been addressed to Professor Gromyko.

Angelo Miatello

Why do you state that the USSR will not be the first to use nuclear weapons when Article 2.4 of the United Nations Charter prohibits all use of force or arms in the settlement of international disputes?

Anatoly Gromyko

Without any doubt, the Charter is a very important document in safeguarding peace and I can assure Mr. Miatello that in my country we have great respect for it. For me, how could it be otherwise when a relative of mine signed the Charter? I would like to lay emphasis on the question of whether we must look at the Charter as the only safeguard in the modern world. Must we not help, by additional agreements, to strengthen the ideas of the founders of the Charter which was signed in San Francisco? International obligations are also very important and the international obligations which help to strengthen the Charter are the documents which would stabilize international relations, especially when States and their supreme bodies—legislative bodies I mean—make an obligation before the whole world not to be the first to use nuclear weapons. Would it be better if every nation declared that it would use nuclear weapons first, especially if we see this spread of nuclear weapons throughout the world which some might think would not be very detrimental to the balance—to the stability—of the world? It seems to me that we must create an atmosphere of mutual trust that would be upheld by new international agreements, including national declarations, and this would help to create a political climate that would be quite different from the climate of the 1980s, especially after the Reagan Administration came to power.

Andreas Kohlschütter

With reference to Dr. Subrahmanyam's thesis of the danger of horizontal proliferation inside the armed forces of the nuclear powers, what is the degree of central control of tactical nuclear systems in the field in Eastern Europe, with Warsaw Pact forces facing NATO?

Anatoly Gromyko

I will be quite frank in answering this question. I am not a military expert, although I am familiar with some aspects of the military situation. There is very, very strict control of technical nuclear systems in Eastern Europe, but still the situation there is very dangerous. No matter what control you have there, you must keep in mind that the flight time of current military delivery vehicles is so short that one may presume that any sort of control may be helpless in the event of some misguided action or some technical failure. Even grenades sometimes explode in West Germany during military manoeuvres. One can see that if such things happen in dealing with rockets, if Pershing IIs explode, why can we not envisage a situation where there would be some very horrible event which would make the other side think that it was being attacked, either from the East or the West? From the East—I can assure you this is my personal, deep conviction, which is shared by my countrymen—an attack would never come. That is why we openly took the obligation and we are very proud of it. I would add that no matter how strict is the control of this very region that has been mentioned, in my opinion, one has to adopt additional measures such as, for example, the creation of nuclear-free zones. Why should we not create a nuclear-free zone in Central Europe where all those nuclear weapons of middle-range which worry Mr. Kohlschütter would be taken out of this context of a six or seven minutes' flight, or even much shorter, because six or seven minutes is the flight of a rocket coming to the USSR or Western Europe. In my opinion, the best way to get rid of the apprehensions which surround Mr. Kohlschütter's mind, as well as ours, is to get rid of nuclear weapons in Europe. Why shouldn't we get rid of nuclear weapons in Europe, why shouldn't we freeze them, then drastically reduce and eliminate them? As far as I remember, but I am not a walking encyclopaedia, our country has proposed that we should get rid of all nuclear weapons in Europe. What would be bad about such a situation? Personally, I really cannot understand the logic of people who say that nuclear weapons are to stay with us in Europe all the time, in our lifetime, our children's time, our grandchildren's time. I think it is an insane approach to nuclear weapons. I could continue answering this question, but I will turn to a further question.

Altaf Gauhar

It is suggested that nuclear weapons are of no military use. This suggestion overlooks the fact that nuclear weapons cease to serve any military purpose only after contesting nuclear States have acquired equal capability. So long as either side has a clear advantage over the other, nuclear weapons continue to serve a decisive military purpose. Hence the continuing arms race.

Anatoly Gromyko

My comment is that, of course, equal capability—the military balance—is very important, and I would agree with Mr. Gauhar in the sense that in the present situation, when we have a military balance that in general is based on equality and equal security, we do not have a perfect—not an ideal—situation. I would also say it is a dangerous situation, but one which we have lived with more or less for many years, and it seems to me that to be realistic this balance is to be preserved in order that nuclear weapons should not be used. A military balance between the United States and the Soviet Union does exist now, and all the serious military experts agree with this. So there is no desire, on the part of some adventurers perhaps, to use the military potential of, for instance, the United States, because they know for sure that they would receive a blow that they could not withstand. But we come to another aspect of this question: if the situation is changed, of course, we all understand that in the minds of certain people there may arise a temptation to strike first. I can assure you that the whole strategy that we now see—and we shall not be deceived by sweet words coming from Washington when we watch their deeds—is that they want to create a situation for a limited war in Europe to defend the United States. When I say the United States, I don't mean the American people, because you cannot defend all the system, all the cities with all the kinds of exotic weapons that some of their scientists are trying to acclaim, though the majority of American scientists disagree with their views. It seems to me that if this equilibrium is disturbed, a real danger of nuclear war would appear. For our part, the Soviet Union will never allow this to happen. We shall do everything so that there is a balance of power based on equality and equal security.

In concluding, I would like to say that of course we want to change the situation in the sense that we want this balance to be frozen, then we want to have an agreement that all production of new weapons systems of mass destruction would also be prohibited, and that there would be a drastic reduction of all nuclear weapons. For example, we propose that middle-range nuclear weapons in Europe should be reduced by 25 per cent or even more. If there is going to be a freeze, all kinds of agreements are possible, but in order to achieve a freeze one must be in favour of not going into the cosmos with new weapons. Unfortunately, as you know, the Americans—the present Administration—have other views. They think that they can assure the security of the United States by getting new weapons into the cosmos, but the security of the United States does not lie in new weapons in the cosmos—first-strike weapons against the Soviet Union and other countries—it is based, believe it or not, on agreement with the USSR which would take into account Soviet security as well as American security.

Giorgio Cantini

What general conditions, international legislation and world-wide enforcement should be met and would be considered satisfactory by the USSR in order to agree to global total disarmament?

Anatoly Gromyko

I will be quite brief: if the Americans agree, as well as others of course, to global total disarmament, the Soviet Union will agree to the most comprehensive international control. Control should not go before disarmament measures, that would be like putting the cart before the horse. Control and disarmament should go together hand in hand. Just to clarify this point still further: in a situation where there was comprehensive control without comprehensive total disarmament measures hand in hand with the control, one of the sides could come to the other after the most comprehensive and total control but before disarmament and say 'Sorry, but I have changed my mind. Thank you for the comprehensive control, but I think that the disarmament measures at the moment are not likely, due to your behaviour'. You would thus have a very simple situation in which there would be a gathering of intelligence data without any adequate disarmament measures. My answer to this is that we in the Soviet Union—the scientists, the research workers—think that it is a very sane idea that we should first of all reach total disarmament. Nowadays our minds are in a sort of nuclear siege and everybody only seems to be thinking of how to live with nuclear weapons and how to create stability with them, but somehow we must break this nuclear siege of our minds. We are humans, if we have the political will, we are capable of doing away with this nuclear siege of our mentality. Maybe we cannot reach a radical solution in one, two or three years, but it involves total, complete nuclear disarmament, perhaps followed by other disarmament measures under the most strict and comprehensive international control.

Bruce Adkins

Why can the USSR not work, in collaboration with the United States, to develop orbiting satellites that could automatically destroy any missile—nuclear or otherwise—launched anywhere in the world, including from their own bases? By rendering all missiles useless, could this not turn 'Star Wars' into heaven-guaranteed peace?

Anatoly Gromyko

This is a very complicated question and it would take me several minutes to answer. I would say that in our approach to such matters we are besieged either by pessimists or by optimists. We quite often have a pessimism of intellect when we study such important issues as the ones we are now considering. We are also experiencing a political optimism: we feel that we may manage to do away with the problems before us. I would say that to a large extent the answer to this question lies in the field of optimism getting the upper hand over pessimism. In order to achieve the heaven the questioner is speaking about, it is better not to carry out this collaboration in space at all. It would mean the organization of space by two super-Powers, as the USSR is sometimes also called, and this condominium would not be a phenomenon that would meet with the approval of the majority of nations. My point is that it is better not to have any sort of Soviet-American co-operation in space in the sense that together they would introduce weapons and hypothetically they would be able to control the behaviour of others. I do not think this is a realistic idea due to many factors, but I will not go into detail now.

The other point I would like to mention while answering this question is that one cannot make all missiles useless. It would take quite a lot of time to explain this, but one cannot make all missiles useless. Any cosmic 'Star Wars' system can be destroyed. Missiles may become more sophisticated, and they are going to be much more sophisticated if the present United States Administration goes ahead with its militaristic plans. I would also emphasize that this idea of the 'weaponization' of the cosmos would not only mean new weapons being introduced into space, but also a grave change in the global strategic situation that would undermine the security of mankind, even more than the invention and the use of the atomic bomb. This is my strong opinion and I would urge my colleagues present to think really seriously about it.

Heaven-guaranteed peace will be a reality not with nuclear weapons, but without them. Let us ask ourselves what we can do in order to leave heaven in peace and not to weaponize it. In forthcoming years, would we all like to see the sky filled with artificial stars moving in geometrical directions? What sort of sky would we be looking at? My personal proposition is that the stars must not belong to the generals or to the political maniacs, but to people—especially people in love—and I hope all the women present here will support me.

Chairman

We also had a brilliant demonstration of SDI from Professor Abdus Salam. A few questions for Dr. Subrahmanyam.

Richard Perle

How would India react to a 'peaceful nuclear test' by Pakistan identical in every way to the 'peaceful nuclear test' conducted by India?

Krishnaswami Subrahmanyam

From the very beginning—from the 1950s—India has been emphasizing that a peaceful nuclear explosion technique is possible. At that time, it was the received wisdom, both in the United States, where textbooks had been written, and in the Soviet Union, where textbooks had also been written. Therefore, we insisted on that during the time of the negotiations on the Non-Proliferation Treaty, and subsequently. All the time we emphasized that we would get into that technology when we were ready, and we did so in 1974.

The position in respect of Pakistan is totally different. Pakistan did not contribute to the view that there was a peaceful nuclear technology. In fact, in 1970 or 1971, Pakistan tabled a paper in the Conference on Disarmament stating that there was no difference between the two and therefore they were one and the same. Pakistan contributed to the wisdom of those Powers which said that there was no difference between the two. Therefore, it is not possible for Pakistan to conduct a peaceful nuclear test identical to the Indian peaceful nuclear test because the declaratory policies of the two countries have been very, very different. As of today, the Pakistani leaders say that there is no difference. If they still conduct their peaceful nuclear tests, one will have to draw appropriate conclusions with regard to the discontinuity of their declaratory policies.

Manuel Tello

How can you make a difference between a nuclear device that is destined for peaceful purposes and one that can destroy a city? If there is really a difference, why do you need to stockpile devices that have no military use?

Krishnaswami Subrahmanyam

First, of course, you can use dynamite to blast a well in addition to killing people by dropping bombs. You can use a matchbox to light a cooking fire as well as to start an arson. So it is not the technology that makes the difference, it is the application, whether peaceful or not. Therefore, there is a distinction in how it is applied. If there is a difference, would you need to stockpile devices that have no military use? I don't think we are stockpiling any such devices.

Patricia Lindop

Would you tell us what, in your opinion, should be the response of India if it became clear that Pakistan had developed a nuclear weapon capability?

Krishnaswami Subrahmanyam

Since I am speaking personally, I am of the view that Pakistan most probably has developed nuclear weapon capability. My recommended response is that India should also make it clear that it has a nuclear weapon capability.

Klaus Gottstein

Where did you get the information that the authority to use nuclear weapons could be delegated to non-American NATO commanders in the field?

According to information given to me, every single shot of a nuclear weapon in case of war would have to be authorized by the US Supreme Command, and only US officers attached to the units of the other NATO allies have the key necessary for releasing these weapons.

Krishnaswami Subrahmanyam

Firstly, I got the information from a book by Paul Bracken, the commander in control of nuclear forces. He argues that the key that unlocks the weapons has to be given when the weapons are issued in case a particular state of alert is reached. The weapons are usable and after that they are not unlocked. Secondly, there is no other way, as is argued convincingly; if the keys are still with the American officers, there is no need to keep such nuclear weapons in Europe, because you cannot use them; you might as well take them away. Thirdly, Lord Zuckerman, who as scientific adviser to the United Kingdom Ministry of Defence conducted many exercises, has said that a tactical nuclear war in Europe cannot be conducted unless there are pre-release orders. By that he implies that there are pre-release orders. Of course he is not in a position to say so, because he would be violating the Official Secrets Act; he can only hint that there must be, this is the logical effect. Anybody who says that the orders are with the Americans will have to work out how the missiles will be used in war. As I mentioned, at least in the case of the Canadian air-to-air missiles, they were under Canadian control, and I have a feeling that similar air-to-air nuclear missiles are under the control of the countries which are flying with those weapons. It can't be somebody else, otherwise they need not fly those particular planes. They could as well be without those weapons or, if they are flying patrols, those patrols are of no use.

Christopher Weeramantry

If it can be argued that nuclear war is a crime against humanity, those who knowingly contribute towards it, including scientists, are participants. Would not a declaration of scientific responsibility in relation to the making of nuclear weapons be useful in helping to cut off the proliferation and improvement of nuclear weapons at source?

Krishnaswami Subrahmanyam

The latter part is not quite clear, but with regard to the declaration of scientific responsibility, the Pugwash Movement has done quite a lot in this respect; they have come out with policy declarations regarding the responsibility of scientists. Considerable work has already been done in this area. There are various other scientific organizations such as the Hearing of Concerned Scientists, and Physicians for Social Responsibility. All the others have also been moving in this direction and a considerable body already exists which supports this kind of view and has been trying to achieve this.

At the same time, the practical difficulties in this respect have to be accepted. I believe that in a plant in Amarillo, Texas, where they were making fuses for the various bombs, the local Catholic bishop issued a circular saying that it was sinful to do this and therefore urged the population to desist. However, even though they were good Catholics, the population had to earn a living and they just couldn't accept that. So the practical aspects of this also have to be taken into account.

Chairman

The next questions are addressed to Mr. Debray.

Pierre Lehmann

France is one of the largest exporters of conventional weapons and uses human misery to balance its budget. Does this not contradict your statement that possession of the atomic bomb, by France in particular, should reduce the need for conventional weapons?

Régis Debray

Let me clarify the statement that France is one of the largest exporters of conventional weapons. Looking at the figures, this is praise we do not merit. According to SIPRI, the United States supplies about 43 per cent of the conventional weapons market, the Soviet Union 21.9 per cent, and France 10.8 per cent. You can see that its place is quite modest.

France 'uses human misery to balance its budget': it is true that we use the misery of Saudi Arabia, Kuwait and the Gulf States, which account for approximately three-quarters of the French arms market. 'Does this not contradict' my statement: I do not believe that we used the misery of Nicaragua when it requested a certain number of weapons in 1981. I did not say that the atomic bomb reduced the need for conventional weapons, I said that it reduced the margin for manoeuvre and action by conventional forces. However, it is obvious that conventional weapons are needed: first of all to protect the sites, the silos and the nuclear weapons themselves; secondly, there are zones outside deterrence, that is to say, areas in the Third World where regional conflicts are taking place. This is the reason why France has a rapid deployment force whose objectives, although they are not specified, cover both Europe and the rest of the world. I simply said that it seems to me that the atomic weapon is an anti-macho weapon, to use a current expression. It is a weapon that can calm the itch for adventure and moderate unconsidered threats.

Sheila Oakes

Would Mr. Debray accept that it would be reasonable for any or all other sovereign States to develop and/or deploy their own national minimum but credible deterrent using the same arguments as he uses for France, thus adding to the nuclear weapon proliferation of the United States, the USSR, the United Kingdom, France and China?

Régis Debray

I did not say that it was reasonable to disseminate nuclear weapons. In this respect, I would not go as far as an interesting paper I read after having written my own where it was stated that 'More may be better'. It is a serious paper written by a highly competent professor at the University of California (Berkeley) who is a nuclear-weapon specialist. I would not go as far as he does, I would simply say that, for a number of reasons, it is not certain that there will be an apocalypse. Firstly, it would be illogical to inflict a humiliating defeat on an adversary possessing nuclear weapons, because everyone knows that, in the event of panic, the temptation to use nuclear weapons would be great. It is therefore conceivable that two nuclearized States can practically be prevented from carrying offensives or wars to extremes. Nevertheless, the danger of pre-emptive strike remains; for example, if a State sees that its adversary is acquiring nuclear weapons, it might be tempted to use its own. I believe this aspect was mentioned in the press in 1969 during the Sino-Soviet conflict. I don't know whether the information was correct, but I note that a pre-emptive strike did not take place. Such strikes would be unlikely because, if no-strike can be considered serious, strike itself is illogical. How can one take the risk of one's enemy possessing a residual or existing second-strike capability? Since such a danger cannot be eliminated, this factor, however marginal, is capable of ensuring deterrence among Third World nuclear-weapon States.

France is opposed to the dissemination of plutonium-reprocessing and uranium-enriching plants. I emphasize that French policy is not the dissemination of nuclear weapons, but the best possible collaboration with IAEA so as to prevent proliferation or to make it very difficult.

Mycle Schneider

What considerations prevent the French Government from declaring once and for all that the Super-Phénix fast breeder will never be used for military purposes? Naturally, this would not imply renunciation of French policy whereby it is not revealed which French installation is used for and by the military!

Régis Debray

The same considerations that incite the American, Soviet, Chinese and British Governments not to reveal which of their nuclear installations are used for military purposes. I do not see what purpose would be served by such a declaration since, in any case, whether the plutonium comes from Super-Phénix or elsewhere, we know that France has a military programme.

Claude Bourdet

Mr. Debray's optimistic vision conforms to that of the French chiefs of staff, despite the 'darts' he throws at them. It gives rise to a considerable number of questions that call for a real debate; I will only ask the following:

1. He mentioned that the Mururoa site had been opened for observation by countries in the Pacific; is he aware of the report by CFDT engineers, which was cited in the *Sunday Times* in summer 1981? It stated that Mururoa had sunk by 1 metre, that there are vast fissures in the basaltic strata, storms have destroyed the bituminous base destined to cover the products of fission so that a large part of these poisons has flowed into the lagoon and the ocean.
2. He has rightly referred to the dangers of tactical nuclear weapons, which tend to make a so-called 'limited' war possible. Does he know that the French Government has practically decided upon the construction of a neutron bomb—a decision that will be made public at the end of the parliamentary recess? Does he agree that this bomb cannot be a 'final warning', that its use presupposes delegation of the decision to the lowest level, and that it will necessarily bring about the escalation and transformation of any commencement of war into a 'limited' nuclear war and then into a nuclear war itself?

Régis Debray

In reply, I would state that, having visited Mururoa, I did in fact note that some subtle changes, but not accidents, had taken place in the atoll's geological situation. Incidentally, the atoll was uninhabited until the beginning of the 1960s. These changes are not as serious as the engineers' report appears to suggest. There has been a slight sinking of the atoll's coral reef in certain places; a wave did break up a bituminous base, that is a fact. However, it has not prevented almost 3,500 volunteers from living on the atoll for approximately 20 years. They are never the same people, so almost 50,000 people have lived there and there has never been a major accident.

With regard to the second question, I am less well-informed than my friend Claude Bourdet. I have no knowledge of this decision, which, I must say straightaway, would not shock me personally in view of the purely defensive nature of the neutron bomb. It is not a battlefield weapon, but a weapon aimed at preventing battle and without the attendant destruction. That being said, this calls for a technical discussion which is not my domain. I would merely say that French policy is to elevate the nuclear threshold as high as possible. It therefore rejects the concept of nuclear artillery or tactical nuclear weapons and it has renamed its tactical nuclear forces, *Pluto* and soon *Hades*, 'pre-strategic forces' to show clearly that it rejects the concept of a nuclear battle. This must be seen in the light of the weaker party to the strong strategy of deterrence. The weaker party does not seek to impose his will on the strong, he merely refuses to submit. This is where deterrence from the weaker party to the strong differs from that of the strong to the strong. Concepts of duels or escalation therefore do not make sense. It is a strategy with a negative goal (I do not want) rather than a strategy with a positive or aggressive goal (I oblige you to do what I want). In other words, it means exposing a major risk through the pre-strategic forces. However, this is a discussion that others can sustain in more depth.

David Lowry

When you say that nobody has been killed by nuclear weapons since Hiroshima, why don't you consider the nuclear pollution caused at places like Windscale, Savannah River, Cap de la Hague and Kytsym in producing nuclear explosive materials, as well as the nuclear pollution caused by testing nuclear weapons? If these tests are so safe, as we are informed, why not bring them from the Pacific to just outside Paris?

Régis Debray

I was often asked this question when I was in the Pacific. I have been there many times—to Australia, New Zealand and the Pacific islands affected by French nuclear policy. Therefore, it does not really take me by surprise. It is a question that we do not have time to go into in detail, but first of all let me cite the facts: the atoll of Mururoa lies 1,200 km. from Papeete, the capital of French Polynesia. The latter is under French sovereignty and, up to the present, the local government—which has internal autonomy—has never officially demanded France's departure. Furthermore, the atoll is probably a lot further from the nearest inhabited land than Las Vegas or Los Angeles are from the Nevada site. Underground explosions require a specific geological structure, broadly speaking a basaltic structure, which in France is only to be found in the Massif Central. It is perfectly feasible to carry out underground explosions in France in the Massif Central without endangering lives, but with risks for the highway infrastructure—bridges, viaducts, roads, etc. It would entail a considerable financial problem and would imply major infrastructural work, whereas the Mururoa site has existed for 20 years without causing any deaths in the Pacific, nor any pollution, as all those who visit the site can see.

Marjorie Thompson

Mr Debray claims that nuclear weapons are no longer used for coercion and that nuclear bombs have killed no one since Hiroshima. As someone with an interest in, and experience of, developing countries, could he comment, in the first instance, on the context of American nuclear policy and the achievement of foreign policy aims using Central America as a surrogate field of confrontation, and, in the second instance, would he care to comment on his country's testing programme in the Pacific, which has already killed people and is making many others very ill?

Régis Debray

I do not understand the object of the question. I do not believe that the United States envisaged using nuclear weapons against Nicaragua or any other Central American country. It would be strategically and politically stupid. I really do not see how such a question could arise. The United States obviously has no need of this type of weapon to reach their political and military objectives in the region.

With regard to the second question, the information is incorrect. The underground explosions have killed no one, just as the Chinese explosions have killed no one according to our information, but we know very little. In any case, the Soviet and American explosions, which amount to approximately fifty times the number of the French explosions, have killed no one.

Jenny Hartland

If Mr. Debray is so comforted by nuclear deterrence, and is so horrified by 'conventional' warfare, why is he reluctant to allow developing countries the comfort of a modest nuclear arsenal?

Régis Debray

I stated that proliferation was not the apocalypse, but neither is it salvation, as certain people believe. The politically unstable conditions in the Third World mean that, while the emergence of new nuclear decision-makers in these regions is not a catastrophe in itself, it is not a goal to be pursued. This seems obvious to me. Neither is it a chimera or hallucination that obscures our vision. I believe that it would be inadvisable to encourage this development, even if one deems it inevitable in the long run.

William Howard

What is Régis Debray's view of the position France should take on moving towards a comprehensive world-wide freeze on the testing, production and deployment of additional nuclear weapons, perhaps with a comprehensive test ban as a first step?

Régis Debray

In other words, what is France's position on the CTB? It has been stated a number of times; it is the position stated by President Mitterrand before the United Nations. When those States we consider to be over-armed have significantly reduced their strategic and tactical weapons, France will be ready to take an active part in a policy of multilateral, verifiable and controlled disarmament. What does 'significantly' mean? Perhaps half for the super-Powers' arsenals, from 10,000 to 5,000 strategic nuclear warheads. In any case, France has approximately 150 and it does not believe that it should take the first step. The same applies to the 'Comprehensive Test Ban Treaty'. It would not be reasonable to ask France to start by implementing a prohibition that has not been previously adopted or followed by those who, between 1945 and 1982, carried out 1,200 nuclear tests, i.e. the Americans and the Soviets. China might be expected to give a very similar reply.

Chairman

Perhaps those people whose questions have not been answered in public due to lack of time could take them up directly with the speakers or could attend the subsequent press conference. I would hope nevertheless that you will find time to reply to Ambassador Shaker, who raised a fundamental question.

Mohamed Shaker

In the light of France's declaration that it would behave as if it were a Party to the NPT, do you think that France should abstain from assisting Israel in the introduction of nuclear power as long as Israel does not accept full-scope safeguards?

Régis Debray

I agree that it is a fundamental question and I would like to say publicly that I share Ambassador Shaker's concern. Such transfers should be subject to maximum guarantees.

Chairman

Mr. de Perrot, the following two questions are addressed to you.

Dieter von Ehrenstein

What are your comments concerning the triggering of the use of nuclear weapons as retaliation for large-scale contamination after destruction of civil nuclear installations by conventional weapons?

Michel de Perrot

Although I am not a jurist, I believe that the additional protocols to the Geneva Conventions prohibit bombing a civil reactor or a nuclear installation. Even if they have not been ratified, in the case cited it is clear that where military and civilian objectives are combined—as might be the case with Super-Phénix—the reactor itself could become the object of a conventional attack and the question put by Mr. von Ehrenstein would be relevant. The question should be put to Mr. Gromyko, I do not know how the super-Powers would react; would it be by a nuclear attack because their country had been contaminated? Personally, I don't have the answer.

André Petit

Mr. de Perrot said that Mr. Goldschmidt had stated that he was certain that Super-Phénix would be used for military purposes. I was present during the meeting at which several people affirmed that Mr. Goldschmidt had made such a statement and I can testify that it is incorrect. On several occasions, Mr. Goldschmidt himself has contradicted those who attributed such words to him.

Michel de Perrot

First of all I would like to cite my source. It is an interview with Mr. Goldschmidt by Paul Leventhal which was published in *Nuclear Fuel* on 31 December 1984. I should be happy to read Mr. Goldschmidt's remarks or denial. However, it is not the only declaration and the sources are numerous. In particular, an article published in 1978 and signed by the former Adviser to the Atomic Energy Commission, Mr. Jean Tirry, who at the time was a general. He stated that France was in a position to make atomic weapons of all types and all sizes. At relatively low cost, it could manufacture large quantities as soon as the fast breeders provided enough of the necessary plutonium. Other statements along these lines have also been made; editions of the *Energie de l'EDF* review specifically refer to Super-Phénix as support for the French nuclear strike force. At the juridical level—the question was put to Mr. Debray—the military option remains open until proof is produced to the contrary. In order to be under EURATOM's control the promoter of Super-Phénix would have to make a declaration explicitly informing the European Commission that the irradiated fuel in the Super-Phénix blanket—the weapon-grade plutonium—is to be used solely for civil purposes. I believe that we will wait a long time for such a declaration.

Furthermore, even in the Swiss Government there is strong feeling regarding this question. Questions were raised in Parliament and the replies given by the spokesman for the Federal Council implied that the option remained open because the Swiss Government admitted the principle of military use of Super-Phénix. In addition, Phénix, which is the existing prototype reactor, does not come under EURATOM's control and is used for military purposes, and here we have thoroughly reliable sources from the Atomic Energy Commission.

Chairman

The following questions are addressed to Professor Mazrui.

Margaret Jacobs

In this last year of the United Nations Decade for Women, it seems surprising that not one woman is represented in the Groupe de Bellerive nor in the list of speakers. Nuclear war would have grave consequences for all humans;

nuclear proliferation is having serious social and economic effects on women, and men, right now. Why are women not represented in a discussion of issues that are so important to all human beings?

Ali Mazrui

The question is partly addressed to me, but it is also addressed to the Colloquium's organizers. I suspect this is partly the lethargy of centuries of sexual division of labour, as well as the assumption—even sometimes subconscious—that on issues of war and peace the experts around are disproportionately male and therefore let us corner them from different parts of the world. It may be subconscious lethargy rather than intended malice.

Marjorie Thompson

Following on from his refreshing and radical presentation, why does Professor Mazrui think no women are addressing this Colloquium? Does this reflect the truth of his remarks, and would he go further and say that, while women are a majority in grassroots protest movements, there will never be any direct participation in decision-making by the élite until his gender revolution has taken place?

Ali Mazrui

I think I am in sympathy with that reasoning. I would go further and say that in general the gender revolution I have in mind will have to include a considerable female participation in the actual combat forces, because in order to have sufficient weight in decisions on war and peace, it is not enough to be in the political Cabinet of a country. I am afraid the revolution has to be so fundamental that female 'tokenism' in the armed forces will not do; they really have to be in commensurate numbers in the war machinery in order to exercise sufficient leverage over the decision-making concerning war and peace.

Yoshiaki Iisaka

There seems to be too much optimism about nuclear arms in the hands of Black Africa, considering the ever-recurring tribal and other conflicts. What is your comment on this?

In your assessment of the future, the vision of the role of non-Islamic Asia—China, Japan and others—is lacking. What is your opinion on this aspect?

Ali Mazrui

Firstly, in general you have to make up your mind conceptually whether nuclear war is more likely in situations of high propensity for inter-State conflict or high propensity for internal conflict. Africa has a high propensity for internal, political conflict, although when you look closely it only concerns a minority of countries, but anyhow those are enough. There is a good deal of internal incidence of conflict, but in reality there is a very low level of potential inter-State conflict within Africa, remarkably, in spite of the artificiality of the boundaries. One of the factors that have contributed to military coups in Africa is that the soldiers have no real sense of military purpose *vis-à-vis* neighbours, so they are not preparing for a potential conflict with Ghana next door, or with the Ivory Coast next door. So the low conflict potential at the inter-State level makes nuclear weapons slightly safer in an African situation than in those situations where inter-State conflicts are more immediate. In general, I would say, safer than, say, South Asia or the Middle East, and ultimately even in East-West relations.

One of the things that strikes me forcibly and unpleasantly is how often we congratulate ourselves that we have kept the peace for 40 years without a world war. That we have got to the stage that if we only have two world wars in a century it is a matter for self-congratulation is really remarkable. I think that the fact that we have escaped a third world war is no special issue of congratulation. We are constantly in danger of a trip-up. Because East-West relations carry greater propensity for inter-State conflict than African relations with each other, I am not sure that nuclear weapons are more dangerous in Africa than elsewhere.

With regard to the second question, Japan is particularly interesting because it seems to be the only country that has neutralized its macho factor, however temporarily, partly because of its experience of nuclear weapons and partly because of the imposition of American occupation after the war. There has been at least a temporary disengaging from the nuclear game and for the time being in no country of the world is the issue of going nuclear more sensitive than it is in Japan. But it would be harsh to conclude that the only way we can convince the world that nuclear weapons are bad is to have a Hiroshima in every country of the world. It is too expensive a way of learning the lesson.

As for China, of course it has ambitions to be a great Power, which it will be. Its acquisition of nuclear status in 1964 confirmed its ranking among the five veto members of the United Nations Security Council, but apart from that its nuclear capability is still relatively modest. I didn't mention Argentina or Latin America generally either. I am myself very curious to know about the probable impact of the humiliation over the Falklands for the future nuclear ambitions of Argentina. The chances are that it has more relevance than we are at the moment aware of.

Mohamed Shaker

1. Could you substantiate your statement that Egyptians are helping Pakistan in its nuclear activities?

2. You have said that Egypt may withdraw from the NPT in case it turns to Islamic fundamentalism or to the radical left. How would you explain Iran's continued affiliation to the NPT, as well as the socialist countries' strong support for it?

Ali Mazrui

There are Egyptian scientists working with Pakistanis, with the encouragement of Libya. It may or may not be the case, but the point I was making was very different: God, in his wisdom, had decided that for the time being in the Muslim world the countries with a concentration of economic wealth be separate from countries with a concentration of scientific expertise. The only exception being possibly Iran, which is trying to combine both economic wealth and scientific expertise. The two other leading Muslim countries with scientific expertise are in fact Egypt and Pakistan, but they are not economically wealthy. The point I was making is that a convergence of scientific resources in Egypt and Pakistan with financial resources in the oil-rich countries could be part of the exploration of nuclearizing Islam.

Iran, as a regional foe or enemy, is also affiliated to the NPT, but Egypt's regional enemy in the event of re-radicalization will presumably continue to be the State of Israel, which does not commit itself to that. That is one important difference as to why a post-Sadat-legacy Egypt could conceivably move towards a greater nuclear interest. As for the socialist countries, it is quite clear that within the alliance itself there is a policy to restrict nuclear weapon production to the Soviet Union, and it seems to be a policy that also aids the whole doctrine of proletarian internationalism. You can imagine the difficulties the socialist countries would have faced in 1968 if Dubcek had been fully equipped with nuclear weapons so that he was able to make threats. The denuclearization of the rest of the socialist world within Europe is part of an alliance policy and the safeguarding of socialism, and is not in itself a refutation of what I had in mind.

Robert Betchov

Many suicide attempts fail. Psychiatric treatment shows that the act was really a cry for help, an admission of failure. Could one nation be driven to such despair?

Ali Mazrui

I assume the question means in relation to nuclear weapons. I think the answer is 'Yes', that is why I raised the importance of the psychology of wanting to enter games of this kind. I paraphrased Lord Acton when I said that powerlessness also corrupts and absolute powerlessness corrupts absolutely. The retreat into despair as a factor of readiness to invoke the ultimate weapon cannot be ruled out. I have been anxious about the implications of despair in the Middle East, partly because of that particular consideration. In addition, in Shiite Islam there is what has been called the 'martyrdom complex'; not suicide for its own sake, but suicide as an instrument of combat, as a weapon of struggle; Jihad in a manner where you are ready to give up your life for the sake of a bigger cause, the Kabala of Hussein legacy of Shiite Islam. It has been reactivated in recent times and sometimes it is a case of despair finding new ways of self-expression.

Chairman

There is a question to Mr. van Boven.

Paul Sieghart

Is there anything in international law which makes it unlawful:

(a) to possess nuclear weapons in peacetime;

(b) to threaten the use of nuclear weapons at any time;

(c) to use nuclear weapons against a conventional attack;

(d) to use nuclear weapons against a nuclear attack?

If not, what can be done to outlaw these things unconditionally in international law?

Theo van Boven

Perhaps there are better authorities on international law than I who would be better qualified to speak on the subject. I would like to say the following in this context: firstly, international law in order to be effective should be accepted by the international actors; secondly, it should be able to be enforced.

Unfortunately, in international relations, we often deal with Powers that consider themselves above the law in many respects or they adhere to the laws of the jungle. Insofar as the question of nuclear weapons is concerned—the possession and the use of nuclear weapons—the credibility of the law is at stake since you might say that, under certain circumstances, the international actors have agreed to outlaw petty offences, but they are not prepared for the time being to outlaw huge crimes. I think that, in effect, undermines the credibility of the law. To be more specific, to my knowledge there is no particular general international agreement that would forbid the possession of nuclear weapons or their use under certain circumstances. There is at least one United Nations General Assembly resolution to that effect dating from the early 1960s, but it was adopted by a divided vote. I think the Western Powers at that time voted against such a resolution. I do not think that it has already entered into the realm of law.

It would seem to me that in most instances, if not in all, at least the use of nuclear weapons would have an indiscriminate effect and would cause unnecessary suffering to mankind. It could also affect the environment, and in that respect I would say—and I would insist—that the use of nuclear weapons would in most instances be incompatible with the general principles that underlie international humanitarian law. These principles have quite recently been reaffirmed in the 1977 Geneva Protocol that was mentioned a moment ago in another context. However, much to my regret, a number of Powers entered into these negotiations by insisting that nuclear weapons would fall outside the scope of that Protocol and outside the scope of what was to be agreed under that Protocol. In effect, a number of countries in ratifying the Protocol now unfortunately make explicit reservations to that effect. In spite of that, I would insist that use of nuclear weapons in its effects would be contrary to the general principles of humanitarian law which are already of a long-standing nature.

Finally, the question 'what could be done in order to outlaw these things unconditionally in international law?'. I referred in my statement to experts from all parts of the world—responsible experts, lawyers—who unanimously here in Geneva last November agreed that the possession, deployment and use of these weapons should be outlawed as crimes against humanity. But who are individual experts after all? They may have more wisdom than those who are in power. It all depends on the political willingness, perhaps of the super-Powers to start with, and also of other major Powers, to start negotiating on that issue. You can outlaw weapons, but they can still be produced, they will still exist, there is the technological know-how. For that purpose any system of effective international control would be indispensable to enforce such a part of international law.

Chairman

This very Colloquium is at least representative of the efforts which we are all making for the improvement of international law. On the Protocols, I would say that one should not forget that, even if they have not been ratified by a number of nations, the fact that they have been signed is already something and one can also further and encourage behaviour before formal ratification.

III

Global Effects of a Nuclear War

CHAIRMAN:

MR. OVE NATHAN

Professor of Physics, Rector of the University of Copenhagen

REGIONAL CONFLICTS AND NUCLEAR-WEAPON STATES INVOLVEMENT: COULD A REGIONAL CONFLICT TRIGGER A NUCLEAR WAR BETWEEN THE SUPER-POWERS?

A View from the Muslim World

HIS ROYAL HIGHNESS CROWN PRINCE HASSAN BIN TALAL, THE HASHEMITE KINGDOM OF JORDAN

I come here from a part of the world where moderation is increasingly viewed as a sign of weakness and might is often considered right. The Rule of Law is replaced by the law of the jungle in the name of political necessity or military expediency. Some commit acts of aggression and call them pre-emptive actions. Others commit acts of violence and call them heroism.

When nations and individuals start following dual principles and apply double standards, when traditional values begin to erode and myopic opportunism replaces far-sighted policy, then chaos follows, bringing in its wake death and destruction. The pattern is well-known in human history. But never before has *homo sapiens* faced the prospect of total annihilation. Regrettably, the nuclear age has brought man more knowledge, but no more wisdom.

I speak here in my personal capacity as a human being deeply concerned by what we are doing to ourselves and to the planet we inhabit. It is this concern which led me to initiate, along with His Highness Prince Sadruddin, the formation of an Independent Commission on International Humanitarian Issues. In that framework, we have discussed the humanitarian dimension of the nuclear dilemma. I wish to express my deep appreciation to him for the energy and time he has devoted to organizing this timely meeting to precede the NPT Review Conference later this summer. I also welcome this opportunity provided by the Groupe de Bellerive to comment on specific aspects of the nuclear problem relating to the Muslim world.

In the volatile Middle East to which I belong and where a global confrontation could well begin, we must think even more than elsewhere about the problem of nuclear proliferation. Although I hasten to add that the spiral of violence and the resulting loss of human life in the region makes even this awesome prospect fade into insignificance. However, meetings such as this one where most individuals can freely express their concerns are helpful in crystallizing thinking at international and inter-governmental levels. I sincerely hope that this meeting will have constructive thoughts to offer to the NPT Review Conference.

I have been asked to present a view from the Muslim world relating to nuclear weapons and regional conflicts. Let me start by saying that there is no single view from the Muslim world. The view largely depends upon the geographical and strategic position of the viewer. There is, consequently, a whole range of views, of perceptions, and misperceptions. In fact, if I were to assert that the Muslim world is divided in its attitudes and policies, I might be credited for having made 'the understatement of the year'. I hasten to add that the Muslim world is certainly not divided in its aspirations and its pursuit of unity and cohesion, however elusive that goal may be.

Before addressing the specific question whether regional conflicts can trigger nuclear war between the super-Powers, some general remarks relevant to the Muslim world might be in order.

The Muslim world today is not a single entity. Muslims are spread around the globe, from Indonesia to Afghanistan, from Iran to Sudan, covering the whole of the Middle and Near East and much of Africa. The Arab world, in population terms, is only a small part of the Muslim world although in the minds of many in the West, Muslim and Arab worlds are almost synonymous. I suspect that, for the common man, the word Muslim evokes the image of oil rather than Islam.

In addition to the Muslim countries as such, there are very large minorities of Muslims, numbering tens of millions, in important countries such as China, the Soviet Union and India. The Muslim world, consequently, is composed of very disparate historical, cultural, political, economic and social backgrounds. Unfortunately, sweeping generalizations and distorted images have led to a situation where for countless millions, Muslim means fanatic, Arab means oil, Palestinian means terrorist, Shiite means fundamentalist and so on. Such hackneyed notions and ill-founded clichés are serious impediments to constructive dialogue and to promotion of peace and security. What binds the Muslim world together are the tenets of Islam whose primary source is the Koran. It lays down clearly basic principles relating to warfare although their interpretation in terms of modern armed conflicts is not as adequate as it could be. Let me give a few examples. In Surah II, verse 190, it is said: 'Fight in the way of God against those who fight against you, but begin not hostilities.' Translated into nuclear jargon, this means 'No first strike.' If all States were to follow this injunction, logically it should mean 'no war'. Unfortunately, there are certain modern notions such as pre-emptive strike and legitimate self-defence which have been twisted into justifications for aggression. As far as the Muslim world is concerned, in the nuclear field, there is no shred of evidence that any State intends to go against this injunction. In any event, the question for the time being is theoretical since no Muslim State has nuclear weapons.

The Surah continues (191, II) 'And drive them out of the places whence they drove you out, for persecution is worse than slaughter.' This is very relevant to the situation in the Middle East, but not so much to the nuclear context. I will, therefore, pass on without comment to the next verse (194, II) 'And one who attacketh you, attack him in like manner.' In nuclear terms, it could mean retaliation with atomic weapons. But here, proper interpretation is important. The established Muslim humanitarian law and practice since the times of the Prophet forbid indiscriminate killing. In a nuclear exchange, this is impossible. This aspect which relates to mass destruction weapons leads me to my third general remark.

The most disturbing and tragic aspect of contemporary warfare is the increasing lack of respect for humanitarian norms and for the legal framework so painstakingly built. And here I am referring not to the Geneva Conventions and Protocols but also to the injunction of Islam which has been followed since its outset. There should be no indiscriminate killing of civilians, no mass destruction, etc. In contemporary armed conflicts, on the contrary, it is the innocent civilians who pay the highest price in terms of loss of life and property. The use of nuclear or even non-nuclear mass destruction weapons practically means writing off the whole system of humanitarian law. Legal norms have their importance even though politicians and military strategists sometimes tend to look down upon them. This is why, a few days ago, we in the Independent Commission issued a special appeal to governments to adhere to the international instruments in their own interest. It is worthwhile noting in this connection that certain members of the nuclear club made reservations at the time of signing the Protocols Additional to the Geneva Conventions in respect of nuclear weapons.

The nature of armed conflicts has changed considerably over the last few decades. Undeclared interstate wars or internal conflicts, often aided by external factors are now widespread. Violence and terrorism have become a part of military strategy. They are used by governments as much as by non-governmental factions. In such a chaotic situation, it is not inconceivable that nuclear devices, however crude, may become available to groups of terrorists who may consider nuclear blackmail a viable option to achieve their goals.

I wish to point to the incompatibility between nuclear non-proliferation and Western commercial interests. If the North does not wish horizontal proliferation, it must not only take effective measures in this regard but also resist the temptation to make money. This means not only a greater control of the dealings of nuclear industry but also greater vigilance with regard to the sale or theft of materials that can be used for production of nuclear weapons.

While our preoccupation with nuclear proliferation is fully justified, it is equally important to pay attention to the so-called near-nuclear weapons. Development and proliferation of mass destruction non-nuclear weapons is as hazardous to man's future as nuclear weapons. Perhaps even more so, since these weapons can be more easily produced or become more easily accessible.

Bearing in mind these general considerations, I would now turn to the specific question of regional conflicts and the possible involvement of nuclear-weapon States. I have chosen to concentrate on the Middle East rather than the Muslim world—which I understand provoked heated debate during this morning's session—because it seems to me to be the area where regional conflicts are more likely to trigger off a nuclear war. Such an eventuality is conceivable either on the basis of a conventional armed conflict degenerating into a nuclear exchange or a nuclear first strike by a small country on account of perceived threat to its national security. In both cases, it may not be easy to confine the conflict within regional limits. For over two decades, the possibility of a nuclear exchange has been envisaged in the Middle Eastern context. There are many concrete reasons for this:

First, the frequency of armed conflicts in the region: in addition to major Arab-Israeli wars in 1948, 1956, 1967, 1973 and 1982 and the ongoing Gulf War, there have been numerous armed actions, provocations and acts of terrorism or violence. To say that the area is vulnerable and accident-prone would be to understate its recent history.

Secondly, the intractability of the Arab-Israeli conflict: it has become more complex and resistant to solution over time. In fact, time seems to be against solutions and against healing of wounds.

Thirdly, the super-Powers have been deeply entangled, if not directly in the conflict then certainly in the conflict resolution processes, in all the major Arab-Israeli wars and in most other local conflicts. Middle East conflicts have led to super-Power confrontations in the past. These Powers are also known to have been involved in transmitting nuclear materials to the area.

Fourthly, the importance of the Middle East to the super-Powers and to other industrialized countries both in commercial and historical terms, continues to be immense. The political commitment of the super-Powers is as deep as ever. In the United States, the salience of Middle Eastern issues in domestic policies has never been as high. On the other hand, Soviet commitment to a Third World country has reportedly seldom exceeded its present involvement in Syria.

Finally, nuclear weapons are already in the Middle East. The United States maintains nuclear weapons in Turkey and aboard nuclear-armed submarines in and around the waters of the Middle East. More significantly, Israel possesses nuclear capability and is known to deploy nuclear missiles. Its nuclear programmes have benefited from the direct or indirect support of nuclear and near-nuclear powers including South Africa.

I do not wish to be the prophet of doom. I would rather opt for hope and optimism. The fact is, nonetheless, that it is not unrealistic to consider the Middle East as the area which is most vulnerable to nuclear confrontation. In a purely academic spirit and in order to facilitate discussion, let me elaborate on three possible scenarios.

First, let us consider the possibility of the use of nuclear arms by Israel which is the only power in the region to possess them. There is no 'balance of terror' in the Middle East. It is, therefore, unlikely that Israel would simply opt for a surprise nuclear attack on an Arab country. There is no military or political advantage for Israel to do so. There are, however, two factors which could lead to a possible consideration of the nuclear option. One is the possibility of yet another conventional Arab-Israeli war which drags on, degenerating into a war of attrition. The continued loss of life and the internal political pressures may lead Israel to consider the possibility of cutting short the conflict by nuclear means. If so, there is no guarantee that the Soviet Union would not come to the rescue of the Arab side, thus leading to general conflagration. The other factor could be the deployment and use of increasingly sophisticated missiles of mass destruction in the region which may invite nuclear retaliation under intense internal political pressure.

The second hypothesis represents a departure from the traditional patterns. It is conceivable that within the foreseeable future, miniaturized nuclear devices, crude but nonetheless lethal in urban areas, become available in the market place. Suppose these are acquired by a group which finds the Middle East a fertile ground for trying out its own twisted design of social order. The nuclear dimension gives to these radicalized groups the rare chance of holding the world to ransom. Due to mutual mistrust, the situation could conceivably degenerate into a wider conflict.

The third scenario I propose is not altogether hypothetical since it almost happened in 1973. There is nothing to suggest that it could not happen again. During the last decade, political alignments and personalities have changed, so have military capabilities. But the fundamental situation has not. In 1973, different perceptions of the situation and other factors unrelated to the actual position in the field led the super-Powers to the brink of nuclear exchange. The limited ability of either super-Power to control its regional allies and the pace of hostilities with the possibility of miscalculation, are factors which can bring about a situation comparable to 1973. The details of the 1973 situation are too well-known for me to tax your patience further. The point

I wish to emphasize is that no basic change has occurred in the Middle East since 1973.

I have suggested these scenarios not because I underestimate the caution that the super-Powers may exercise in the event of another war in the Middle East. After all, despite their differences, the super-Powers also have common interests and shared responsibilities. They know better than others what a nuclear exchange can mean. I also do not underestimate the abilities of the regional Powers. The point though is: if one knows one cannot use a weapon, why have it? The question may sound naive, but it is not any more naive than to build up the capacity to annihilate the human race twenty-five times over when one knows that doing so once would be more than sufficient.

Turning now to the Non-Proliferation Treaty, which is the focal point of this meeting, let me say that the countries which are viewed by some as troublesome—Iran, Iraq, Libya, Syria, and of course my own country—are all Parties to the NPT. Let us hope that others can follow their example. Adhesion to the NPT is a measure of a country's good faith with regard to the use of nuclear power. International agreements and treaties by themselves do not suffice to safeguard what they contain. It is the political will and shared perceptions which give them real meaning. Experience has shown that in times of war, international agreements are either misinterpreted to suit the circumstances or conveniently forgotten. The problem is that man has not yet learnt to think in global terms. Parochial, national interests or simply national pride and desire for power are allowed to prevail upon the interest of mankind. This is true for the North as much as it is for the South. Specifically in the nuclear case, horizontal proliferation cannot be avoided if vertical proliferation is not contained. The legitimate expectations of the South must not be frustrated if the hopes of the North are to be realized.

In this context, let me venture a few concluding remarks.

1. NPT must not be allowed to wither away, due to the debate on horizontal and vertical proliferation.
2. The International Atomic Energy Agency should be strengthened and given the mandatory and financial means to carry out more effectively its safeguarding task. In this connection, it would be worthwhile to re-examine the proposal for the establishment of an international satellite monitoring agency (ISMA).
3. There should be a moratorium on nuclear tests at the global level, with an adequately effective system to single out those who may directly or indirectly violate it.
4. Even though NPT does not directly encourage regional denuclearized peace zones, it would be worthwhile to consider more actively their establishment as a tangible proof of non-nuclear intentions by the countries concerned. This would naturally require adequate guarantees

of national security. In this context, I wish to reiterate the need for a nuclear-free zone of peace for the Middle East. The proposal has been discussed in recent years without much progress. It can become possible if the foundations for a just and durable peace are laid.

In the final analysis, the only effective constraints on conduct of States are those which are self-imposed and are dictated by conscience and international morality. There is an urgent need to develop and respect a code of conduct which deters misconduct and safeguards peace and security.

Likewise, in the nuclear field, the moral responsibility of scientists must be emphasized. What is the use of knowledge whose main purpose is to destroy? Why develop technology which can only serve to kill those who develop it and all others as well? Why spend $2 million per minute on military expenditure when we know that arms have never brought about a durable solution to any problem? Why have an arms race which cannot be won and which can only enhance the danger of total annihilation?

These questions may sound simplistic. But they do call for convincing answers. Arms industries must undergo conversion to the extent possible. This will not be easy but those who live on arms must have alternative means of profit. Similarly, the inner dynamic of the war machine needs to be turned to peaceful goals.

To the North I say: the world needs food, not bombs. To the South I say: let us turn swords into ploughshares.

I for one firmly believe that peace is possible. It can become a reality if there is adequate political will, not only at regional but also at international levels.

In the nuclear context, the formula 'If you want peace, prepare for war' is outdated, unrealistic and entirely unacceptable if one cares for the future of mankind. I believe that whatever the justification—balance of power or deterrence or national security—going nuclear for military purposes is opting for collective suicide.

A Nuclear-Weapon-Free Middle East

PROFESSOR JOSHUA JORTNER

Tel Aviv University

I. Introduction

This presentation alludes to the issue of regional conflicts and nuclear-weapon States involvement. I would like first to address the grave question of whether a regional conflict in the Middle East could trigger a nuclear war between the super-Powers. In my opinion, such a scenario is most unlikely, highly improbable and almost impossible, as I believe that global and local responsibility of the super-Powers precludes the escalation of a local conventional conflict in the Middle East into a nuclear war between the two super-Powers. It is true that nuclear arsenals of the great Powers have not prevented scores of wars all over the globe, but whenever the use of nuclear weapons was contemplated the idea was abandoned. This is also an outcome of *realpolitik*. The state of nuclear parity, which has prevailed since the early sixties, between the USA and the USSR has resulted in nuclear nullity. No super-Power could regard nuclear exchange as a realistic military option. This exclusion principle renders the huge nuclear arsenals not as weapons of war but rather as a means of global deterrence, whose use would not give ascendency to any of the super-Powers in global and local conflicts.

The Middle East constitutes one of the most sensitive areas in the world, and the conventional arms race in that area is staggering. It is a fact that Saudi Arabia is the biggest arms importer in the Third World, followed by Libya. A conventional arms race creates the initiative for more sophisticated and powerful weapons. Such a situation could eventually encourage attempts to procure nuclear weapons. Accordingly, I strongly believe that removing the threat of nuclear proliferation in the Middle East is a currently highly acute task. Unconventional and imaginative solutions are required to achieve this goal. For this purpose, *credible* measures of restraint and constraint have to be undertaken and implemented. Before engaging further in this discussion, it will be helpful to consider some aspects of Middle Eastern conflicts.

II. Comments on the Middle Eastern situation

Four aspects of the Middle Eastern situation are relevant for the issues of nuclear proliferation and of international agreement in this area.

II.1. Ubiquity of conflicts

It should be recognized that the presence or absence of Israel makes little difference to peace in the Middle East. A cursory examination of the relations between States in the region reveals a changing pattern of alliances and hostilities which exist apart from the issue pertaining to the Israel–Arab conflict. There exist: (i) inter-Arab conflicts, e.g., Syria and Iraq oppose one another; Jordan officially seeks arms to defend itself against Syria; Libya is opposed to Egypt; and (ii) inter-Muslim conflicts, e.g., Iran and Iraq are now at war. There is a trend to disregard all conflicts in this area except one.

II.2. Agreements have short lifetimes

The contemporary history of the region is fraught with agreements, which have had short lifetimes. Notable examples are the creation of the United Arab Republic by the fusion of Syria and Egypt some 25 years ago, which was dissolved, or the Union of Iraq and Syria, soon to be followed by hostility which has persisted since that time. These examples illustrate the transient nature of solemn pledges and agreements in this area.

II.3. Adherence to international treaties does not always prevail

Iraq has recently employed chemical warfare in its war with Iran. This kind of weaponry is strictly outlawed by a Treaty to which Iraq is a solemn signatory. Despite Iraq's denials, a team of experts, appointed by the Secretary-General of the United Nations did unanimously 'substantiate the allegations that chemical weapons have been used'.

II.4. Israel has a small margin of error

Contrary to appearances, Israel has a vanishingly small margin of error, the stakes being its existence and survival. No other country's survival is at stake. Except for supplies, Israel has to rely solely on itself for defence.

III. The NPT and the Middle East

The aspects alluded to above are pertinent for the value of international undertakings, such as NPT, as a means of curbing nuclear proliferation in the Middle East. In this context, it will be useful to consider some notions of the NPT, as viewed by those Israelis who take an interest in nuclear developments in this area.

The virtues of the NPT are:

(i) It is supposed to generate a general feeling of reassurance with respect to nuclear policies of its adherents.
(ii) The adherents formally commit themselves not to acquire or develop nuclear weapons.
(iii) The adherents accept IAEA inspection.

(iv) Only safeguarded export of nuclear materials to non-nuclear States is permitted.

It is my view that any Israeli Government should be extremely reluctant to accede to the NPT in its present form. Rather, it should urge the establishment of more credible alternatives for preventing nuclear proliferation in the Middle East. The following general and specific components of the NPT seem to be inapplicable to the problem at hand.

(a) The NPT cannot serve as a reassurance in an unstable area where warlike threats exist. A central assumption of the NPT is the existence of the conditions of peace which, unfortunately, do not prevail in the Middle East. With the exception of Egypt, the Arab States do not recognize the right of Israel to exist and, since its inception in 1948, have fought its existence by all means at their disposal, e.g., diplomatic, economic, military, etc. Furthermore, a number of Arab States have added reservations to their signatories of the NPT with regard to Israel.

(b) No State confides its security to its own or to another State's adherence to the NPT. None of the 20 to 30 countries which are technically able to develop a nuclear weapons programme and are also signatories to the NPT is solely responsible for its defence. Rather the most advanced among these countries shelter under alliances, i.e., NATO and WTO. The stability of these alliances guarantees the security of these countries. It should be noted that the adherents to the NPT were quite content to live with the inherent limitations of its safeguard system, at most advocating a gradual review of it, and that the failure of the Second Review Conference in 1980 did not visibly alarm the world community. This cannot be the attitude of States whose security solely depends on the effectiveness of the system.

(c) Imperfect Safeguards. On the workings of the safeguards system, Dr. Hans Blix, the Director-General of the IAEA made the following cautious comments:[1]

> The safeguards do not, of course, reveal what future intention the State may have. It might change its mind on the question of nuclear weapons and wish to produce them despite possible adherence to the NPT. Neither such adherence nor full-scope safeguards are full guarantees that the State will not one day make nuclear weapons.

(d) The NPT can be subverted. The limitations of the NPT in the context of the Middle East are of paramount concern in Israel. In support of this attitude, let me recall Article 10 of the NPT, which states:

> Each Party shall in exercising its national sovereignty have the right to

[1] Introductory remarks by Dr. Hans Blix, Director-General of the IAEA, at the meeting with representatives of the media, on 11 December 1981.

withdraw from the Treaty if it decides that extraordinary events, related to the subject matter of this Treaty, have jeopardized the supreme interests of the country. It should give notice of such withdrawal . . . three months in advance.

NPT permits a State to withdraw from the Treaty upon three months' notice. On this provision, Dr. Rudolf Rometsch, former Deputy Director-General of the IAEA, remarked in 1977:[1]

> the 'abrogation risk' has to be understood and accepted. This is a new notion in the non-proliferation discussion. It designates the risk that a Sovereign State might at any time—according to the rules or by breaking them—abrogate a safeguards agreement or a treaty partnership. We have to live with such risks.

These reservations assume the character of escape channels which may be adhered to by committed adversaries. Libya and Iraq, for instance, are Parties to NPT. It is accepted that Libya still opts under NPT for the acquisition of nuclear technology, which is highly significant for nuclear proliferation, after vainly trying to buy bombs. A similar attitude regarding nuclear proliferation was adopted by Iraq, also a Party to NPT. Current assessments attribute proliferation risks to Iraq, Iran and Libya, despite their adherence to NPT.

IV. Israel and the NPT

The position of Israel with respect to the NPT can be summarized as follows:

(a) On 12 June 1968, Israel voted in favour of United Nations Resolution 2373, which endorsed the text of the NPT.

(b) Israel has persistently insisted since 1974 on negotiating a nuclear-weapon-free zone in the Middle East as a more credible alternative to NPT. On 30 October 1980, Israel submitted to the 35th Session of the United Nations General Assembly a draft resolution (A/C.1/35/L.8) calling upon,

> all States of the Middle East and non-nuclear-weapon States adjacent to the region, which are not signatories to any Treaty providing for a nuclear-weapon-free zone, to convene a conference at the earliest possible date with a view to negotiating a multilateral treaty establishing a nuclear-weapon-free zone in the Middle East.

(c) In a letter of 9 June 1981 to the Secretary-General of the United Nations, Israel formally requested all States of the Middle East and States adjacent to the region to:

> indicate in the course of 1981 their consent to the holding of a preparatory conference to discuss the modalities of such a conference of States of the Middle

[1] R. Rometsch, 'Fuel Cycle Safeguards': Remarks at Annual Meeting of the Institute of Nuclear Materials Management, Arlington, VA. June 1977.

East, with a view to negotiating a multilateral treaty establishing a nuclear-weapon-free zone in the Middle East.

(d) The declared policy of Israel has been that it would not be the first to introduce nuclear weapons into the Middle East. The Foreign Minister of Israel, speaking to the General Debate of the United Nations General Assembly on 1 October 1981 stated that:

> Let me take this opportunity to reiterate Israel's policy that it will not be the first country in the Middle East to introduce nuclear weapons into the region. Faced as it is with the stark realities of the Middle East, Israel must insist on distinguishing between spurious and genuine safety . . . the NPT cannot effectively prevent such a country (Iraq) from resorting to nuclear weapons so as to achieve what more conventional means have failed to do . . . The only genuine way to remove the nuclear threat to the Middle East can be found in the establishment of a nuclear-weapon-free zone, freely and directly negotiated among the countries of the region and based on mutual assurances, on the pattern of the Tlatelolco Treaty of Latin America.

(e) Israel has not signed the NPT for reasons spelled out in Section III.

(f) Given a political decision, Israel is supposed to have the technical capability to produce a nuclear weapon.

V. Nuclear potential and intentions in Arab countries

The assessment of a proliferation threat should be based on evaluation incentives and capabilities. In an area of ongoing military conflicts, the incentive exists for the creation of nuclear capabilities. The potential of Arab countries will now be summarized, relying on non-Israeli sources.

Egypt is a Party to NPT, has an ambitious programme for the installation of several power reactors, and is acquiring a sound technological base. Its potential capability will be high within a few years.

Iraq's present capability is low but its incentives and potential capabilities are high. On Iraqi intentions, I quote:[1]

> In 1977, after the conclusion of the nuclear contracts with France and Italy, Naim Haddad, also a member of Iraq's Revolutionary Command Council, reportedly stated at a meeting of the Arab League, 'The Arabs must get an atom bomb. The Arab countries should possess whatever is necessary to defend themselves.' Haddad's unqualified enthusiasm for nuclear weapons at a time when Iraq was building a large nuclear programme that would provide it with virtually all of the necessary components caused considerable concern in Israel and other countries. Three years later, in July 1980, the London Times quoted Saddam Hussein, by now Iraq's President, as saying, 'We have no programme concerning the manufacture of the atomic bomb.' The article went on to state, however, that: 'President Hussein implied several times that Arab nations would be able to use atomic weapons', adding—after

[1] Leonard S. Spector, *Nuclear Proliferation Today*. A Carnegie Endowment Book, page 173.

his denial of any intention to make a bomb—that, 'whoever wants to be our enemy can expect that enemy to be totally different in the very near future.' Circumspect though this phrase may appear, it is no secret that Iraq's nuclear reactor was expected to be commissioned in five months' time.

While not a direct contradiction of his disavowal of nuclear weapons, Hussein's statements raised serious doubts as to its credibility.

Regarding *Libya's* attitude, the following information[1] is enlightening:

Libyan Intentions. As the dealings with Pakistan and India unfolded, a high-ranking Libyan official openly confirmed his country's continuing interest in obtaining nuclear arms—despite its ratification of the Non-Proliferation Treaty. According to Jeremy Stone, Director of the Federation of American Scientists, during a late 1978 Libyan-sponsored Conference in Tripoli, Ahmed 'el-Shahati, Head of the Foreign Liaison Office of the Libyan People's Congress, stated 'unequivocally that Libya is seeking nuclear weapons'. As Stone later wrote: 'That evening I dined privately with Shahati and his group of Western-trained people-to-people entrepreneurs. I opened the discussion by saying that our scientists were often quite tolerant of anti-American statements and widely varying politics. But we did draw the line at the use of science for killing innocent people. Were they going to persist in supporting terrorists, and were they seeking an atomic bomb? They were.

Shahati made no bones about it, saying they would seek all weapons with which to defend themselves. To be sure I understood, I asked again were they seeking to maintain the right to get a bomb or actually trying to get the bomb itself? It was the latter.' The Federation subsequently wrote an open letter to the Soviet Ambassador, Anatoly Dobrynin, urging the Soviet Union to reconsider its planned power reactor sale to Libya on the ground that Tripoli could not be relied upon to honour its renunciation of nuclear weapons under the Non-Proliferation Treaty. While it is unlikely that this letter was an important factor in Soviet decision-making, the Soviets have repeatedly postponed transferring the facility to Tripoli, as noted earlier, quite possibly out of concern over Khadafi's nuclear intentions.

Also, one cannot discount the various co-operation agreements to which Libya is a party, each of which purports to enhance its nuclear potential. Such agreements exist with Argentina. Co-operation with two Belgian firms (Belgatom and Belgonucleaire) caused the US to make representations to the Belgian Government, without success. Libya's financial support for the Pakistan nuclear effort in conjunction with an unsafeguarded shipment of uranium purchased in Niger were widely reported and assumed to imply nuclear technology transfer in return.

It is likely that Iraq, Libya, Iran and other Arab countries will wish to develop a nuclear weapons capability, irrespective of their formal adherence to the NPT.

[1] *Ibid*, page 154.

VI. Towards a nuclear-weapon-free zone in the Middle East

Israel has constantly and persistently proposed that the countries in the region negotiate a nuclear-weapon-free zone. The guiding idea is derived from the Treaty of Tlatelolco, which established a nuclear-weapon-free zone in South America. Agreements at such a regional level deserve special attention and effort in providing credible alternatives to the NPT. The Israeli proposal further rests on the recommendation of the Independent Commission on Disarmament and Security Issues (the so-called Palme Commission) adopted by the United Nations General Assembly.[1] It said:

> The Commission believes that the establishment of nuclear-weapon-free zones on the basis of arrangements freely arrived at among the States of the region or sub-region concerned, constitutes an important step towards non-proliferation, common security and disarmament. They could provide mutual reassurance to States preferring not to acquire or allow deployment of nuclear weapons as long as neighbouring States exercise similar restraint. This would improve the chances for the region not to become enveloped in the competition of the nuclear-weapon States. The nuclear-weapon States would have to undertake a binding commitment to respect the status of the zone and not to use or threaten to use nuclear weapons against the States of the zone.

The obvious advantages of the proposed nuclear-weapon-free zone in the Middle East are:

1. Negotiations among the parties will be conducted without prejudice to any technical, political or legal claim and without any pre-conditions.
2. Such negotiations between the parties concerned will serve as a central principal genuine confidence-building measure. It will contribute towards a gradual diminution of hostilities in the area.
3. The commitment to a nuclear-weapon-free zone will preclude conventional warfare in the region. It seems inconceivable that the States in the region will contemplate military engagements and at the same time place their faith in the loyal administration of a nuclear-weapon-free zone. This proposed arrangement will provide a significant step towards reduction of a conventional arms race in the Middle East.
4. The establishment of a nuclear-weapon-free zone in the Middle East will substantially contribute to the global aspects of world peace.

Israel's proposal had no support from the Arab countries. Nevertheless, Israel voted in favour of Egyptian draft resolutions, which called for the signing of the NPT, accepting full-scope safeguards which go with it and last 'pending the establishment of the zone, the States declare their support for establishing such a zone and deposit this declaration with the Security

[1] Resolution 37/99B adopted by the United Nations General Assembly on 13 December 1982 and distributed as document UNGA A/CN. 10/38 of 8 April 1983.

Council for consideration'.[1] This resolution does not contain any reference to direct negotiations between the Parties at any time. While voting for the Egyptian draft resolutions, Israel reserved its stance on the modalities, insisting that the priorities of regional initiative and the principle of negotiations should be adhered to. Israelis read the Egyptian proposal as a strong indication that the Arab countries would not negotiate with Israel, would wish to ascertain that Israel's adherence to NPT did invalidate a potential capability arising from its technical competence in the nuclear realm, that Israel could eventually be dealt with, with impunity, and that ultimately there would never be a need to arrive at the stage of negotiating a nuclear-weapon-free zone. This reaction to Israel's proposal introduced a further measure of reluctance to its adherence to NPT. Israel's earnest attitude to avert the threat of a nuclear arms race in the Middle East was never put to the test. When a nuclear-weapon-free zone is agreed to in the Middle East, Israel would, I believe, accede to the NPT.

It is scientists who should undertake a major contribution to the needs of contemporary mankind. Among the major roles of the scientific community is that of underlining specific steps towards arms reduction and to ensuring local and global peace in the world.

If a group of pioneering scientists arises in the Middle East, irrespective of nationality and political background, who share a common concern for the future of the region, their contribution to peace could be invaluable. They could and should convey the message that it is imperative for the States in the region to undertake concrete steps towards the establishment of a nuclear-weapon-free zone in the Middle East.

[1] UNGA Resolution 37/75 adopted on 9 December 1982.

MEDICAL EFFECTS ON HUMAN POPULATIONS

PROFESSOR SUNE BERGSTRÖM

Nobel Prize Winner, Karolinska Institutet, Stockholm

In May 1981, the World Health Assembly of WHO, composed of the Ministers of Health of the world, adopted a resolution which stressed 'the contribution of health to the socio-economic development of countries, particularly developing countries, as well as to the preservation and promotion of peace as the most significant factor for the protection of peoples' life and health'.

The Director-General was requested 'to continue collaboration with the Secretary-General of the United Nations and with other governmental and non-governmental organizations, to the extent required, in establishing a broad and authoritative international committee of scientists and experts for comprehensive study and elucidation of the threat of thermonuclear war and its potentially baneful consequences for the life and health of peoples of the world'.

A committee, of which I had the honour to be Chairman, was appointed, and two years later submitted its first report to the Assembly. The report is now available in eight languages and those interested can find therein detailed descriptions of the various medical consequences of atomic warfare. I will only touch here on the summary.

The Committee studied three scenarios:

1. The detonation of a one-megaton bomb over a large city would kill probably about a million and a half people right out and injure a similar number.

   The number of killed and injured depends on many factors, the main one being the height of the explosion (Figure 1). In a detonation involving the surface, the effect of radiation dominates that of blast and heat, whereas in an air burst, the blast effect predominates over that of heat and radiation. An estimate of the numbers under these two conditions is indicated in Figure 2. In both cases, the number of victims would be in the hundreds of thousands seriously injured by heat, blast or radiation—or a combination—numbers that would overwhelm the health services of any country or region.

The other two scenarios are worse:

2. A limited nuclear war, similar to that described in AMBIO some years earlier in which 20 megatons of tactical weapons aimed at 'military' targets in Central Europe were used, estimated to result in nine million killed or severely injured. However, it is significant that of these nine million, eight million would be civilians.
3. Finally, an all-out nuclear war with 10,000 megatons, which might produce 1,000 million deaths. At that time, we had only heard rumours of the traumatic climatic effects that will be discussed later today that would add a new dimension to the effects of atomic warfare.

The scenario with the one-megaton bomb detonated over a large city is enough to make it clear that in atomic warfare no health services can give any significant help and the catastrophic conditions of the other scenarios are really difficult to comprehend.

The conclusion of the Committee was therefore that the only approach was what in medicine is called primary prevention, i.e. prevention of atomic war.

The Committee concluded that 'WHO can make important contributions to this process by systematically distributing information on the health consequences of atomic warfare and by continuing and expanding international co-operation in the field of health'.

I will return to the last part of that paragraph, which I think contains some important implications. However, I maintain that preventing a large-scale 'conventional' war is also of paramount importance. Even if the desired strengthening of the NPT is achieved and a comprehensive test ban is instituted, the reduction of the nuclear stockpile will certainly take a long time, and even a small fraction of the present stockpile is enough to cause devastating damage and drastic climatic changes. Furthermore, during this time, research and development is continuing on conventional, as well as on biological and chemical, weapons.

Clearly, prevention of any type of warfare is necessary. In addition to the information efforts that are now proliferating, what is needed is more active and systematic work to promote trust and friendship among nations. In my opinion, the only way to speed up this process is to develop active co-operation between the nations in a systematic way and by all possible means. An obvious and non-controversial area is health, including nutrition.

Previous speakers have referred to the famine in Africa which is now catching the interest of the media. I will make a few remarks on the general health status of the developing countries as a background to this tragedy.

Sweden has a unique population record dating from 1750 and at the top of Figure 3 you can see the ages of those dead during one year in the middle of the eighteenth century. Fifty per cent of the dead are less than five years old and the rest have a random distribution like an animal population. The lower part shows that 200 years later there are very few young children among the dead and most people have a long life.

The tragedy now is that more than half of the population of the world is in a situation like that of the industrialized countries 200 years ago. Figure 4 illustrates that death before the age of five is indeed common in large areas of the world whereas low infant mortality is limited to the industrialized countries.

One of the main diseases in early childhood is diarrhoeal disease. In addition, it is estimated that there are 150 million cases of malaria and 200 million of schistosomiasis in this world. It is not catching the media's attention that every single year something like a million small children die from malaria in Africa (Figure 5).

These facts led the advisory research committees of WHO in the various regions of the world to agree that efforts to get better therapeutic or preventive methods for these tropical diseases had to be started. This programme, which I will describe very briefly, is an example of international co-operation in health research involving scientists and health workers in most countries of the world.

The main object is research and development to get improved tools for control of tropical diseases plus training and strengthening of medical research capabilities in developing countries. The unique thing about this programme is that it is run by outside scientists and not like a traditional United Nations programme. Each of the six diseases has its own 'scientific working group' for chemotherapy, vaccine development and field work, i.e. it has its own international research council that is planning and deciding what projects to fund (Figure 6). A similar group is strengthening selected laboratories and clinics in the developing world after reaching an agreement with the government that they will take over after five or ten years (figure 7). The whole programme is controlled by a committee of representatives from 27 governments, plus the World Bank, the United Nations Development Programme and WHO. This committee is in effect an international scientific sub-committee of the United Nations system for these six tropical diseases. The governments listed were represented on that committee in 1983—a majority from the developing world (Figure 8).

Just to give a few examples of how the programme works: resistant falciparum-malaria is spreading all over the world (Figure 9). The location of funded projects is illustrated in Figure 10 showing that work is really going on where the problem is. In filariasis (river blindness belongs to that group) Figure 11 illustrates the location of the co-ordinated work of laboratories and industries around the world involved in chemical synthesis, screening, metabolism, clinical trials and field trials. The latter are more often located in the industrialized countries because of their greater scientific capability for developing vaccines or drugs. The work will shift to the areas of the disease quickly when clinical trials can be started. Figure 12 shows the distribution of leprosy projects. After five years of work, a new vaccine has been produced and it has just been tested for safety in Norway. This fall long-term studies will start in India. This illustrates worldwide co-operation in the production of leprosy bacteria, their purification, production and clinical trials, a co-ordination that WHO is uniquely competent to sponsor.

Figure 13 shows all the places where long-term commitments have been made for training and equipping laboratories in the developing countries. I do not know any better controlled and effective transfer of knowledge and resources from North to South.

The budget of the Tropical Diseases Programme is close to $30 million (Figure 14). Similar programmes for diarrhoeal diseases and for human reproduction have been organized by WHO (Figure 15). The total budget of these three 'special' programmes approaches $50 million, which means that together they spend about the same amount of money in one year that is spent on the military while I am speaking here.

I think this is an absolutely unique endeavour in the United Nations system, and it can play its fundamental role as the point of crystallization of international co-operation by different groups of experts in the member countries. The work is led and executed by the scientific experts of the world, like a research council, but on an international scale.

Hopefully, more resources will gradually be diverted from bilateral aid to this type of multilateral endeavour in research and development in many other fields that would benefit from such an approach.

I think active international co-operation is the only approach that can dissolve the two threatening shadows that Prince Sadruddin referred to in his opening remarks, but it will require systematic and hard work to organize and sustain.

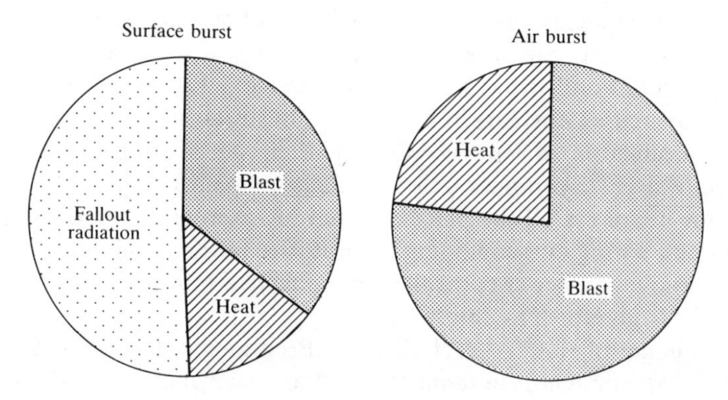

Figure 1. Distribution of casualties from the detonation of a 1–Mt bomb

Casualties from a 1-Mt bomb detonated over London

	Low altitude (580 m)		High altitude (2500 m)	
	Dead	Injured	Dead	Injured
Blast	500 000	700 000	1 000 000	1 500 000
Heat	400 000	100 000	600 000	100 000
Radiation	900 000	900 000	—	—
Total	1 800 000	1 700 000	1 600 000	1 600 000

Figure 2

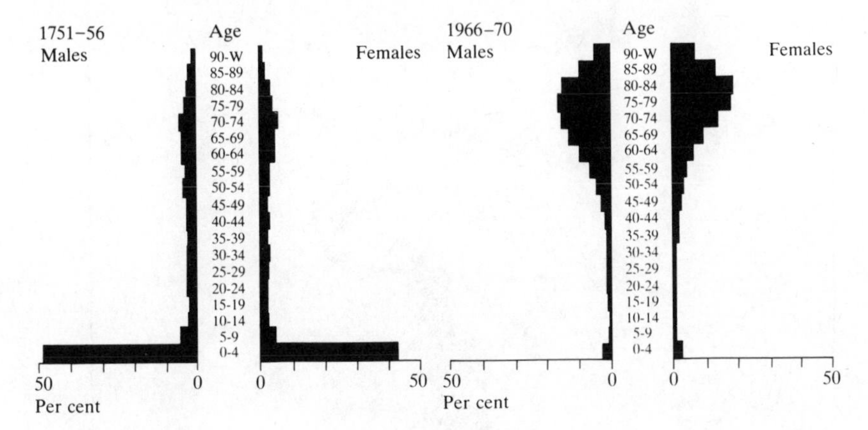

Figure 3. Age of death in Sweden 1751–56 and 1966–70

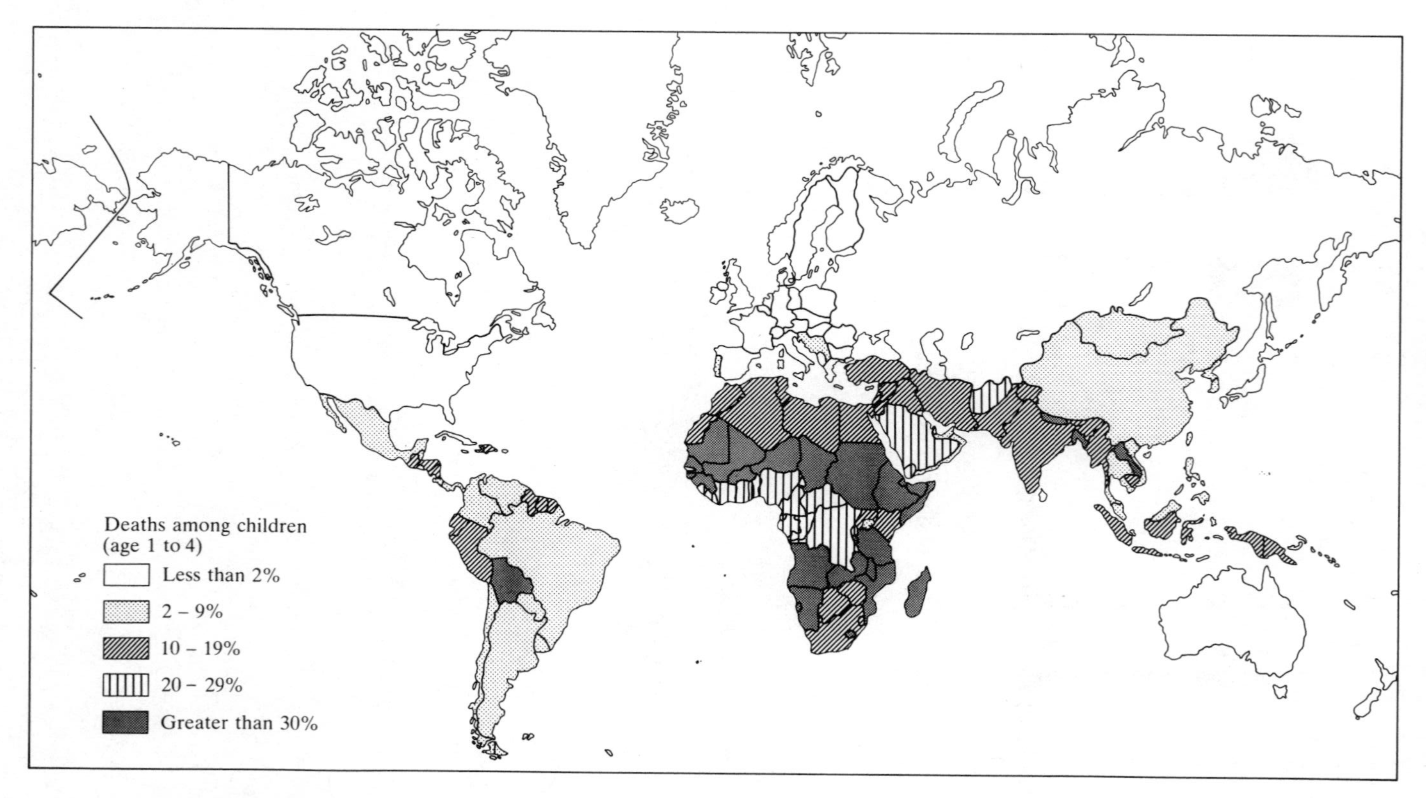

Figure 4. Childhood mortality in the late 1970s

Prevalence of Tropical Diseases

Disease	Millions
Malaria	150
Schistosomiasis	200
Chagas' Disease	10
Leprosy	11

Figure 5

WHO Tropical Disease Programme

Disease SWG	
Malaria	Vector Biology & Control
Trypanosomiasis	Epidemiology
Filariasis	Social & Economic Research
Schistosomiasis	Biomedical Research
Leishmaniasis	
Leprosy	
(1) Chemotherapy (2) Immunology (3) Field Research	

Figure 6

WHO – TDR

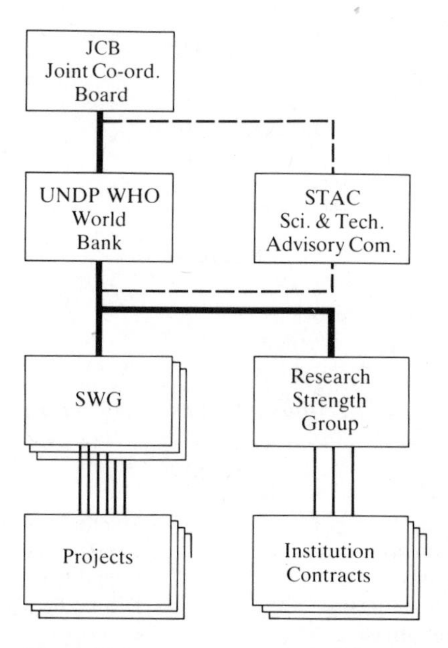

Figure 7.

TDR: Joint Coordinating Board

UNDP	World Bank	WHO
Australia	Belgium	Brazil
Burma	Canada	Denmark
Egypt	France	Germany, Federal Republic of
India	Liberia	Netherlands
Madagascar	Malaysia	Pakistan
Nigeria	Norway	Switzerland
Philippines	Sweden	United States of America
USSR	United Kingdom	
Venezuela		

Figure 8

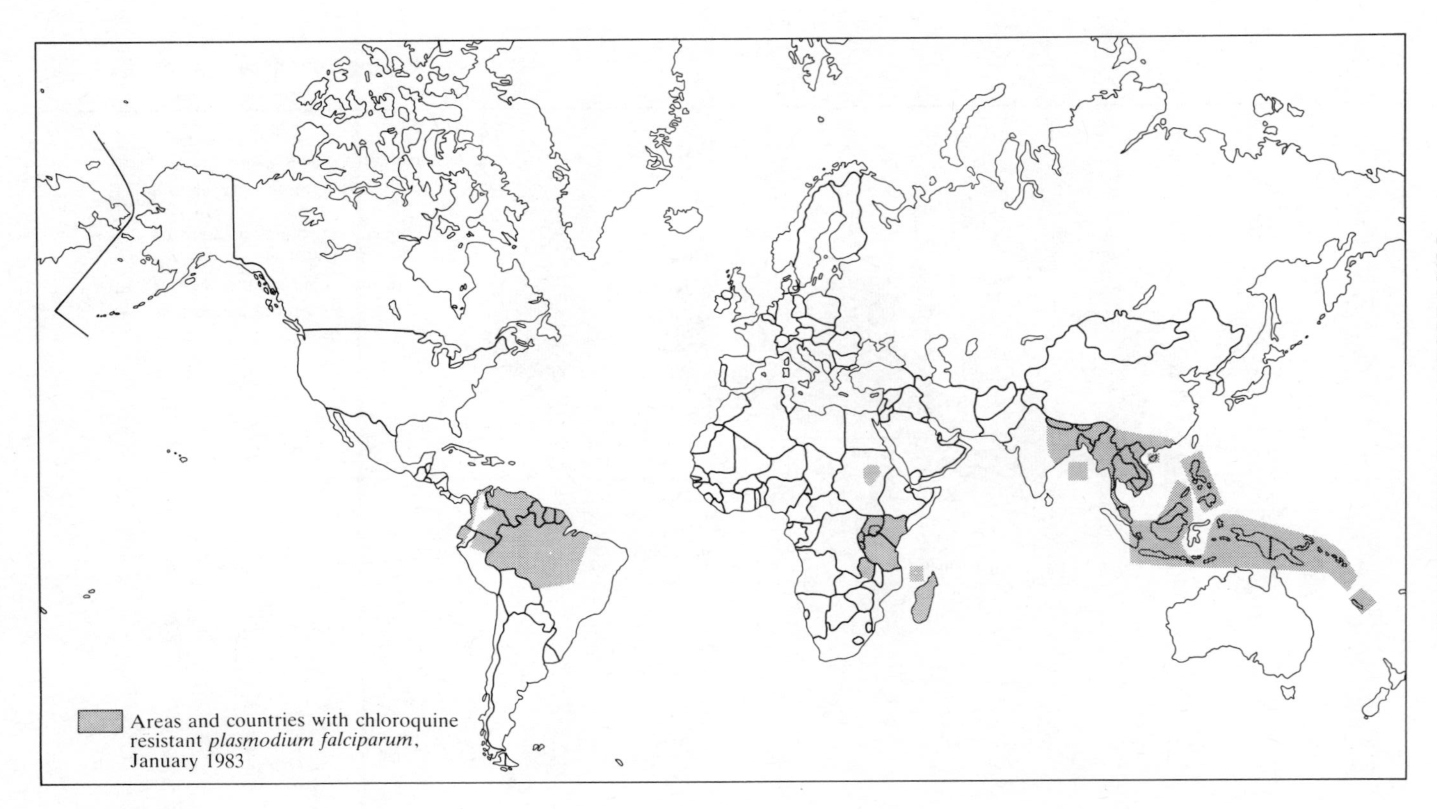
Areas and countries with chloroquine
resistant *plasmodium falciparum*,
January 1983

Figure 9.

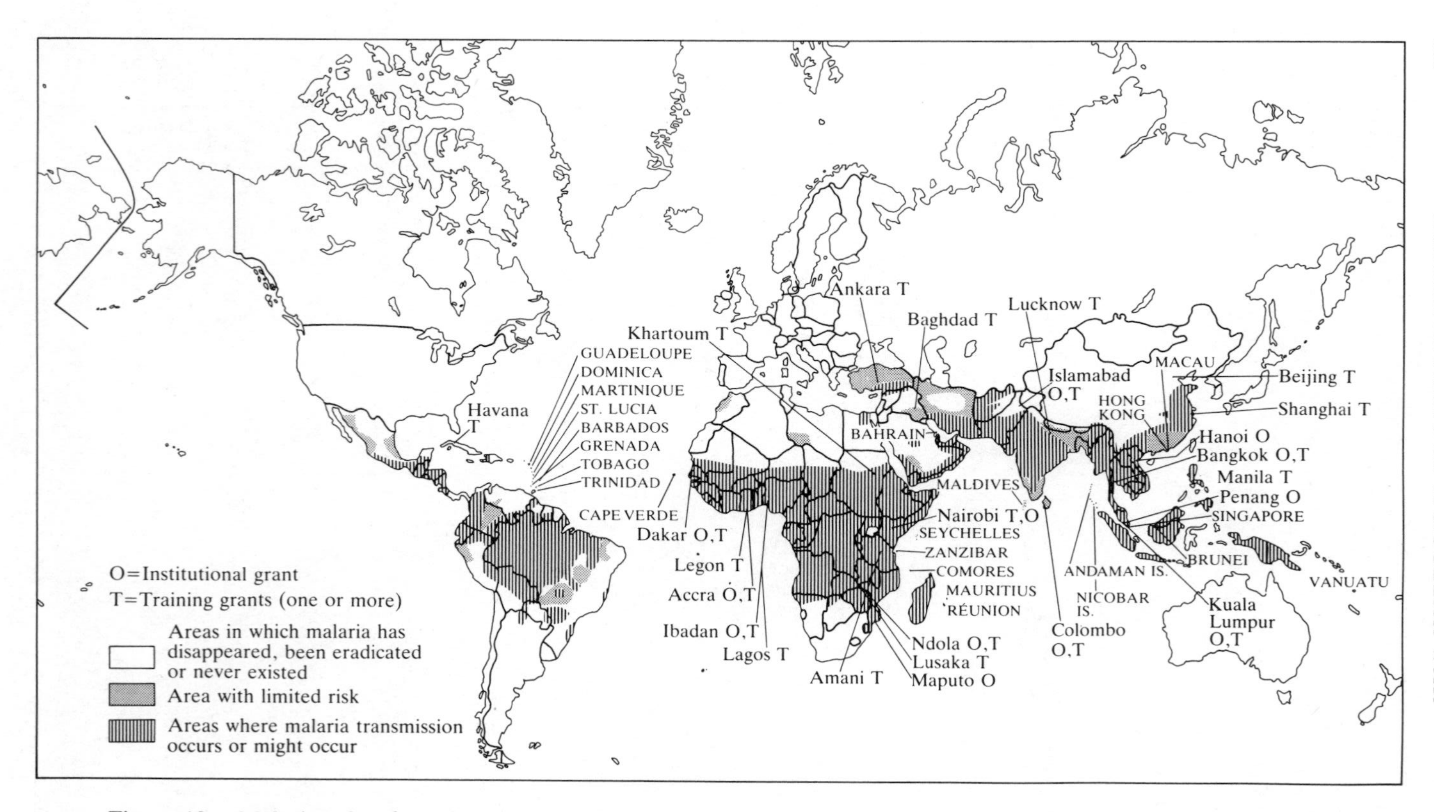

Figure 10. Malaria-related grants

Field trials
Clinical trials
Screening
Synthesis
Metabolism
Other Activities

Figure 11.

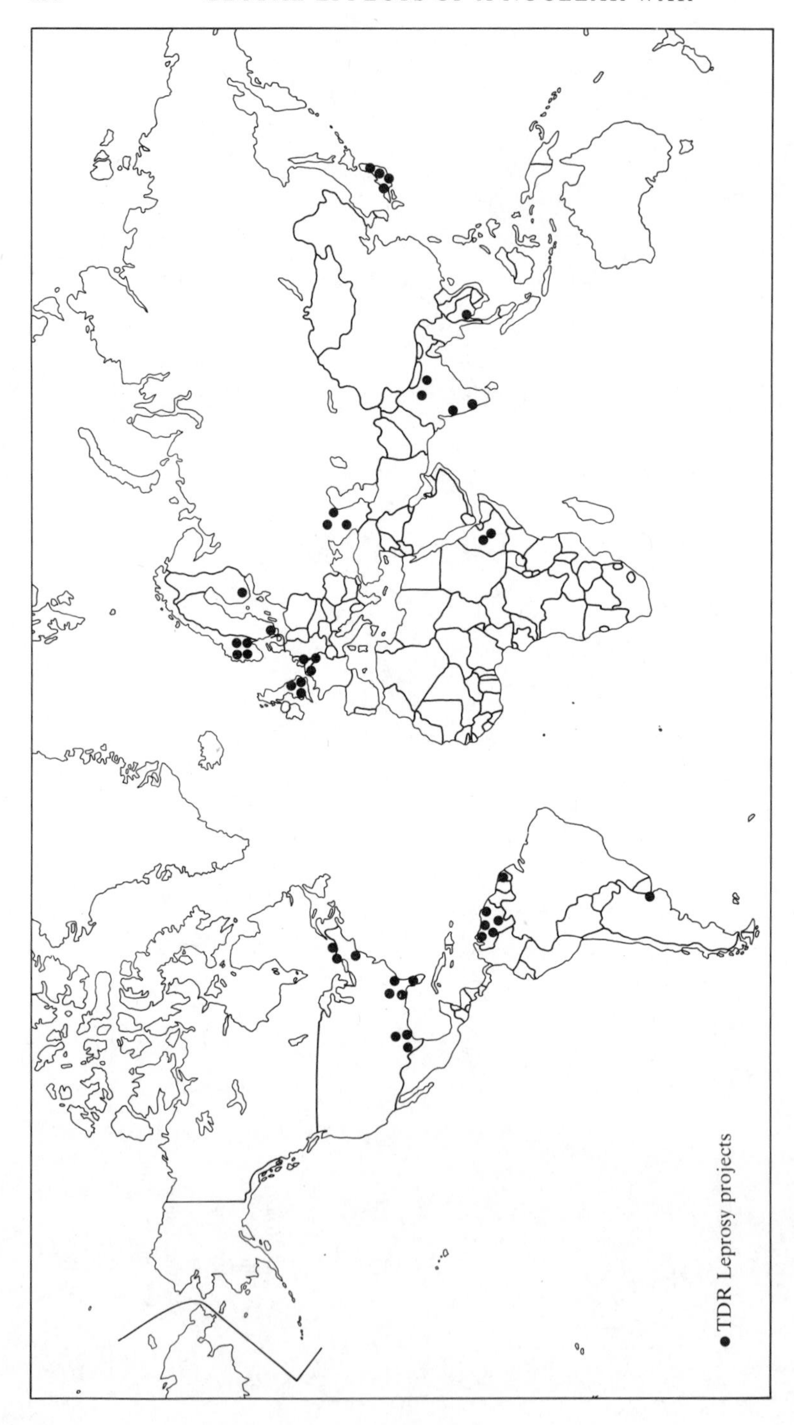

Figure 12.

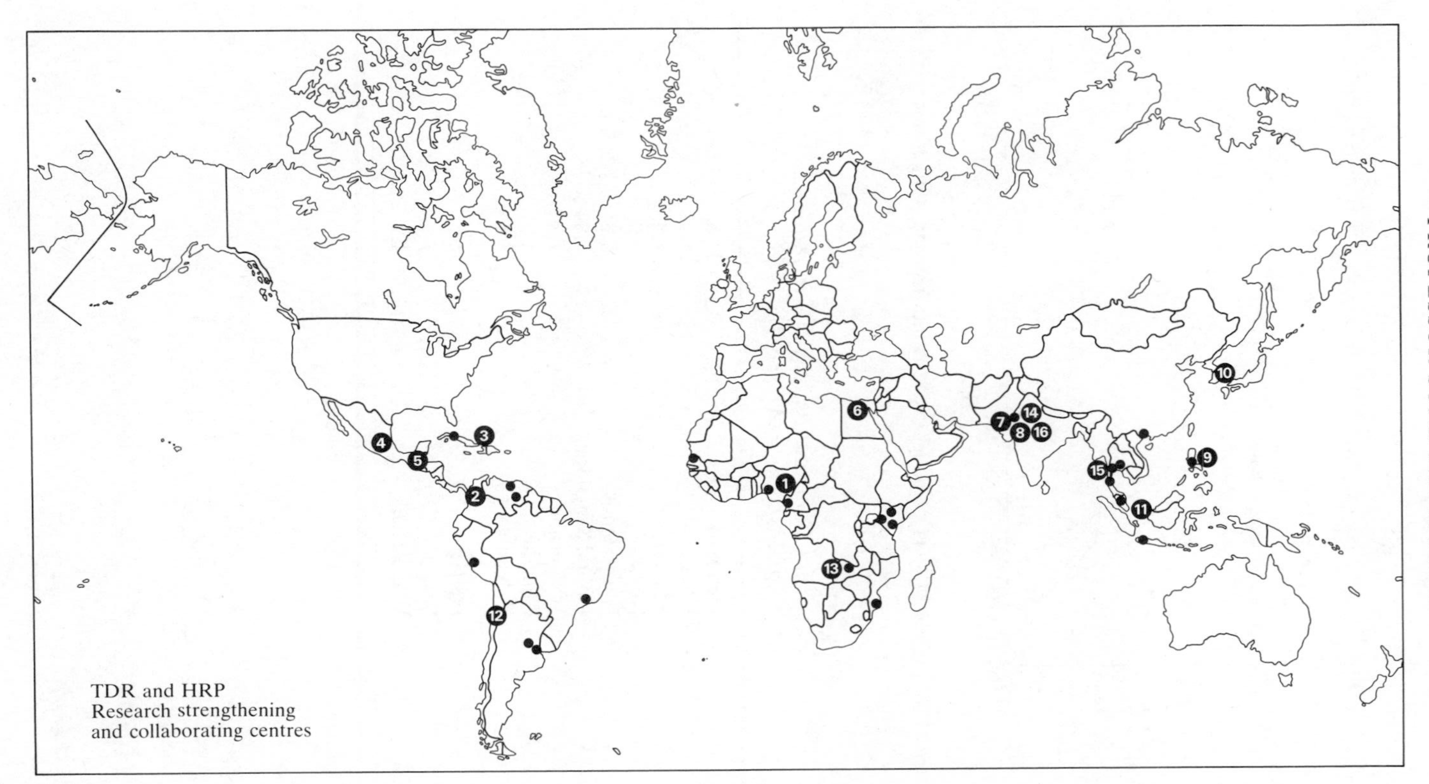

TDR and HRP
Research strengthening
and collaborating centres

Figure 13.

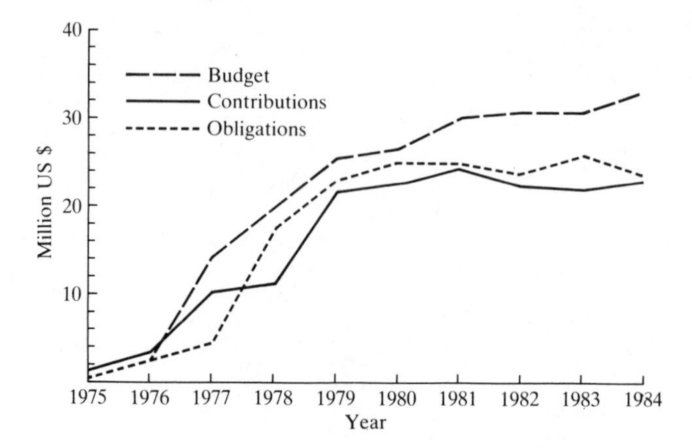

Figure 14. TDR budget, contributions, and obligations

Financial Contribution to TDR in millions of US $ up to March 31, 1983

Denmark	22.6
USA	15.4
Sweden	14.8
Norway	6.0
Netherlands	6.0
United Kingdom	4.8
W. Germany	4.8
Canada	3.6
Belgium	3.1
UNDP	9.3
WHO	7.7
World Bank	4.9

Figure 15

Nuclear War and Climatic Catastrophe: Some Policy Implications[1]

DR. CARL SAGAN

Center for Radiophysics and Space Research, Cornell University

It is not even impossible to imagine that the effects of an atomic war fought with greatly perfected weapons and pushed by the utmost determination will endanger the survival of man. (Edward Teller, *Bulletin of the Atomic Scientists*, February 1947)

The extreme danger to mankind inherent in the proposal by [Edward Teller and others to develop thermonuclear weapons] wholly outweighs any military advantage. (J. Robert Oppenheimer, *et al. Report of the General Advisory Committee*, AEC, October 1949)

The fact that no limits exist to the destructiveness of this weapon makes its very existence and the knowledge of its construction a danger to humanity . . . It is . . . an evil thing. (Enrico Fermi and I. I. Rabi, Addendum, *ibid.*)

A very large nuclear war would be a calamity of indescribable proportions and absolutely unpredictable consequences, with the uncertainties tending toward the worse . . . All-out nuclear war would mean the destruction of contemporary civilization, throw man back centuries, cause the deaths of hundreds of millions or billions of people, and, with a certain degree of probability, would cause man to be destroyed as a biological species . . . (Andrei Sakharov, *Foreign Affairs*, Summer 1983)

Apocalyptic predictions require, to be taken seriously, higher standards of evidence than do assertions on other matters where the stakes are not as great. Since the immediate effects of even a single thermonuclear weapon explosion are so devastating, it is natural to assume—even without considering detailed mechanisms—that the more or less simultaneous explosion of 10,000 such weapons all over the Northern Hemisphere might have unpredictable and catastrophic consequences.

And yet, while it is widely accepted that a full nuclear war might mean the end of civilization at least in the Northern Hemisphere, claims that nuclear

[1] Copyright 1983 by Carl Sagan. First published in *Foreign Affairs*, Winter 1983/84, *62*, 258–292.

war might imply a reversion of the human population to prehistoric levels, or even the extinction of the human species, have, among some policymakers at least, been dismissed as alarmist or, worse, irrelevant. Popular works that stress this theme, such as Nevil Shute's *On the Beach*, and Jonathan Schell's *The Fate of the Earth*, have been labeled disreputable. The apocalyptic claims are rejected as unproved and unlikely, and it is judged unwise to frighten the public with doomsday talk when nuclear weapons are needed, we are told, to preserve the peace. But, as the above quotations illustrate, comparably dire warnings have been made by respectable scientists with diverse political inclinations, including many of the American and Soviet physicists who conceived, devised and constructed the world nuclear arsenals.

Part of the resistance to serious consideration of such apocalyptic pronouncements is their necessarily theoretical basis. Understanding the long-term consequences of nuclear war is not a problem amenable to experimental verification—at least not more than once. Another part of the resistance is psychological. Most people—recognizing nuclear war as a grave and terrifying prospect, and nuclear policy as immersed in technical complexities, official secrecy and bureaucratic inertia—tend to practise what psychiatrists call denial: putting the agonizing problem out of our heads, since there seems nothing we can do about it. Even policymakers must feel this temptation from time to time. But for policymakers there is another concern: if it turns out that nuclear war could end our civilization or our species, such a finding might be considered as a retroactive rebuke to those responsible, actively or passively, in the past or in the present, for the global nuclear arms race.

The stakes are too high for us to permit any such factors to influence our assessment of the consequences of nuclear war. If nuclear war now seems significantly more catastrophic than has generally been believed in the military and policy communities, then serious consideration of the resulting implications is urgently called for.

It is in that spirit that this article seeks, first, to present a short summary, in lay terms, of the climatic and biological consequences of nuclear war that emerge from extensive scientific studies conducted over the past two years, the essential conclusions of which have now been endorsed by a large number of scientists. These findings were presented in detail at a special conference in Cambridge, Massachusetts, involving almost 100 scientists on April 22-26, 1983, and were publicly announced at a conference in Washington, DC, on October 31 and November 1, 1983. They have been reported in summary form in the press, and a detailed statement of the findings and their bases will be published in *Science*.[1] The present summary is designed particularly for the lay reader.

[1] R. P. Turco, O. B. Toon, T. P. Ackerman, J. B. Pollack and Carl Sagan (TTAPS), 'Global Atmospheric Consequences of Nuclear War', *Science*, in press; P. R. Ehrlich, M. A. Harwell,

Following this summary, I explore the possible strategic and policy implications of the new findings.[1] They point to one apparently inescapable conclusion: the necessity of moving as rapidly as possible to reduce the global nuclear arsenals below levels that could conceivably cause the kind of climatic catastrophe and cascading biological devastation predicted by the new studies. Such a reduction would have to be to a small percentage of the present global strategic arsenals.

II

The central point of the new findings is that the long-term consequences of a nuclear war could constitute a global climatic catastrophe.

The immediate consequences of a single thermonuclear weapon explosion are well-known and well-documented—fireball radiation, prompt neutrons and gamma rays, blast, and fires.[2] The Hiroshima bomb that killed between 100,000 and 200,000 people was a fission device of about 12 kilotons yield (the explosive equivalent of 12,000 tons of TNT). A modern thermonuclear warhead uses a device something like the Hiroshima bomb as the trigger—the 'match' to light the fusion reaction. A typical thermonuclear weapon now has a yield of about 500 kilotons (or 0.5 megatons, a megaton being the explosive equivalent of a million tons of TNT). There are many weapons in the 9 to 20 megaton range in the strategic arsenals of the United States and the Soviet Union today. The highest-yield weapon ever exploded is 58 megatons.

Strategic nuclear weapons are those designed for delivery by ground-based

Peter H. Raven, Carl Sagan, G. M. Woodwell, *et al*, 'The Long-Term Biological Consequences of Nuclear War', *Science*, in press.

[1] For stimulating discussions, and/or careful reviews of an earlier version of this article, I am grateful to Hans Bethe, McGeorge Bundy, Joan Chittester, Freeman Dyson, Paul Ehrlich, Alton Frye, Richard Garwin, Noel Gayler, Jerome Grossman, Averell Harriman, Mark Harwell, John P. Holdren, Eric Jones, George F. Kennan, Robert S. McNamara, Carson Mark, Philip Morrison, Jay Orear, William Perry, David Pimentel, Theodore Postel, George Rathjens, Joseph Rotblat, Herbert Scoville, Brent Scowcroft, John Steinbruner, Jeremy Stone, Edward Teller, Brian Toon, Richard Turco, Paul Warnke, Victor Weisskopf, Robert R. Wilson, and Albert Wohlstetter. They are however in no way to be held responsible for the opinions stated or the conclusions drawn. I deeply appreciate the encouragement, suggestions and critical assessments provided by Lester Grinspoon, Steven Soter and, especially, Ann Druyan, and the dedicated transcriptions, through many drafts, by Mary Roth.

This article would not have been possible without the high scientific competence and dedication of my co-authors on the TTAPS study, Richard P. Turco, Owen B. Toon, Thomas P. Ackerman, and James B. Pollack, and my 19 co-authors of the accompanying scientific paper on the long-term biological consequences of nuclear war. Finally, I wish to thank my Soviet colleagues, V. V. Alexandrov, E. I. Chazov, G. S. Golitsyn, and E. P. Velikhov among others, for organizing independent confirmations of the probable existence of a post-nuclear-war climatic catastrophe, and for helping to generate a different kind of climate—one of mutual concern and cooperation that is essential if we are to emerge safely from the trap that our two nations have jointly set for ourselves, our civilization, and our species.

[2] Samuel Glasstone and Philip J. Dolan, *The Effects of Nuclear War*, 3rd ed., Washington: Department of Defense, 1977.

or submarine-launched missiles, or by bombers, to targets in the adversary's homeland. Many weapons with yields roughly equal to that of the Hiroshima bomb are today assigned to 'tactical' or 'theater' military missions, or are designated 'munitions' and relegated to ground-to-air and air-to-air missiles, torpedoes, depth charges and artillery. While strategic weapons often have higher yields than tactical weapons, this is not always the case.[1] Modern tactical or theater missiles (e. g., Pershing II, SS-20) and air support weapons (e.g., those carried by F-15 or MiG-23 aircraft) have sufficient range to make the distinction between 'strategic' and 'tactical' or 'theater' weapons increasingly artificial. Both categories of weapons can be delivered by land-based missiles, sea-based missiles, and aircraft; and by intermediate-range as well as intercontinental delivery systems. Nevertheless, by the usual accounting, there are around 18,000 strategic thermonuclear weapons (warheads) and the equivalent number of fission triggers in the American and Soviet strategic arsenals, with an aggregate yield of about 10,000 megatons.

The total number of nuclear weapons (strategic plus theater and tactical) in the arsenals of the two nations is close to 50,000, with an aggregate yield near 15,000 megatons. For convenience, we here collapse the distinction between strategic and theater weapons, and adopt, under the rubric 'strategic', an aggregate yield of 13,000 megatons. The nuclear weapons of the rest of the world—mainly Britain, France and China—amount to many hundred warheads and a few hundred megatons of additional aggregate yield.

No one knows, of course, how many warheads with what aggregate yield would be detonated in a nuclear war. Because of attacks on strategic aircraft and missiles, and because of technological failures, it is clear that less than the entire world arsenal would be detonated. On the other hand, it is generally accepted, even among most military planners, that a 'small' nuclear war would be almost impossible to contain before it escalated to include much of the world arsenals.[2] (Precipitating factors include command and control malfunctions, communications failures, the necessity for instantaneous decisions on the fates of millions, fear, panic and other aspects of real nuclear war fought by real people.) For this reason alone, any serious attempt to examine the possible consequences of nuclear war must place major emphasis on large-scale exchanges in the five-to-seven-thousand-megaton range, and

[1] The 'tactical' Pershing I, for example, is listed as carrying warheads with yields as high as 400 kilotons, while the 'strategic' Poseidon C-3 is listed with a yield of only 40 kilotons. *World Armaments and Disarmament, SIPRI Yearbook 1982*, Stockholm International Peace Research Institute, London; Taylor and Francis, 1982; J. Record, *US Nuclear Weapons in Europe*, Washington: Brookings Institution, 1974.

[2] See, e.g., D. Ball, Adelphi Paper 169, London: International Institute for Strategic Studies, 1981; P. Bracken and M. Shubik, in *Technology in Society*, Vol. 4, 1982, p. 155.

many studies have done so.[1] Many of the effects described below, however, can be triggered by much smaller wars.

The adversary's strategic airfields, missile silos, naval bases, submarines at sea, weapons manufacturing and storage locales, civilian and military command and control centers, attack assessment and early warning facilities, and the like are probably targets ('counter-force attack'). While it is often stated that cities are not targeted *per se*, many of the above targets are very near or co-located with cities, especially in Europe. In addition, there is an industrial targeting category ('counter-value attack'). Modern nuclear doctrines require that 'war-supporting' facilities be attacked. Many of these facilities are necessarily industrial in nature and engage a work force of considerable size. They are almost always situated near major transportation centers, so that raw materials and finished products can be efficiently transported to other industrial sectors, or to forces in the field. Thus, such facilities are, almost by definition, cities, or near or within cities. Other 'war-supporting' targets may include the transportation systems themselves (roads, canals, rivers, railways, civilian airfields, etc.), petroleum refineries, storage sites and pipelines, hydroelectric plants, radio and television transmitters and the like. A major counter-value attack therefore might involve almost all large cities in the United States and the Soviet Union, and possibly most of the large cities in the Northern Hemisphere.[2] There are fewer than 2,500 cities in the world with populations over 100,000 inhabitants, so the devastation of all such cities is well within the means of the world nuclear arsenals.

Recent estimates of the immediate deaths from blast, prompt radiation, and fires in a major exchange in which cities were targeted range from several hundred million to 1.1 billion people—the latter estimate is in a World Health Organization study in which targets were assumed not to be restricted entirely to NATO and Warsaw Pact countries.[3] Serious injuries requiring immediate medical attention (which would be largely unavailable) would be suffered by a comparably large number of people, perhaps an additional 1.1 billion.[4] Thus it is possible that something approaching half the human population on the planet would be killed or seriously injured by the direct effects of the nuclear war. Social disruption; the unavailability of electricity, fuel, transportation, food deliveries, communications and other civil services; the

[1] National Academy of Sciences/National Research Council, *Long-term Worldwide Effects of Multiple Nuclear Weapons Detonations*, Washington: National Academy of Sciences, 1975; Office of Technology Assessment, *The Effects of Nuclear War*, Washington, 1979; J. Peterson (Ed.), *Nuclear War: The Aftermath*, special issue *Ambio*, Vol. 11, Nos. 2-3, Royal Swedish Academy of Sciences, 1982; R. P. Turco, *et al.*, *loc. cit.* , footnote 2; S. Bergstrom, *et al*, *Effects of Nuclear War on Health and Health Services*, Rome: World Health Organization, Publication No. A36. 12, 1983; National Academy of Sciences, new 1983 study in press.

[2] See, e.g., J. Peterson, *op. cit.* footnote 7.

[3] S. Bergstrom, *op. cit.* footnote 7.

[4] *Ibid.*

absence of medical care; the decline in sanitation measures; rampant disease and severe psychiatric disorders would doubtless collectively claim a significant number of further victims. But a range of additional effects—some unexpected, some inadequately treated in earlier studies, some uncovered only recently—now make the picture much more somber still.

Because of current limitations on missile accuracy, the destruction of missile silos, command and control facilities, and other hardened sites requires nuclear weapons of fairly high yield exploded as groundbursts or as low airbursts. High-yield groundbursts will vaporize, melt and pulverize the surface at the target area and propel large quantities of condensates and fine dust into the upper troposphere and stratosphere. The particles are chiefly entrained in the rising fireball; some ride up the stem of the mushroom cloud. Most military targets, however, are not very hard. The destruction of cities can be accomplished, as demonstrated at Hiroshima and Nagasaki, by lower-yield explosions less than a kilometer above the surface. Low-yield airbursts over cities or near forests will tend to produce massive fires, some of them over areas of 100,000 square kilometers or more. City fires generate enormous quantities of black oily smoke which rise at least into the upper part of the lower atmosphere, or troposphere. If firestorms occur, the smoke column rises vigorously, like the draft in a fireplace, and may carry some of the soot into the lower part of the upper atmosphere, or stratosphere. The smoke from forest and grassland fires would initially be restricted to the lower troposphere.

The fission of the (generally plutonium) trigger in every thermonuclear weapon and the reactions in the (generally uranium-238) casing added as a fission yield 'booster' produce a witch's brew of radioactive products, which are also entrained in the cloud. Each such product, or radioisotope, has a characteristic 'half-life' (defined as the time to decay to half its original level or radioactivity). Most of the radioisotopes have very short half-lives and decay in hours to days. Particles injected into the stratosphere, mainly by high-yield explosions, fall out very slowly—characteristically in about a year, by which time most of the fission products, even when concentrated, will have decayed to much safer levels. Particles injected into the troposphere by low-yield explosions and fires fall out more rapidly—by gravitational settling, rainout, convection, and other processes—before the radioactivity has decayed to moderately safe levels. Thus rapid fallout of tropospheric radioactive debris tends to produce larger doses of ionizing radiation than does the slower fallout of radioactive particles from the stratosphere.

Nuclear explosions of more than one-megaton yield generate a radiant fireball that rises through the troposphere into the stratosphere. The fireballs from weapons with yields between 100 kilotons and one megaton will partially extend into the stratosphere. The high temperatures in the fireball chemically ignite some of the nitrogen in the air, producing oxides of nitrogen, which in turn chemically attack and destroy the gas ozone in the middle stratosphere. But ozone absorbs the biologically dangerous ultraviolet radiation from the Sun. Thus the partial depletion of the stratospheric ozone layer, or 'ozonosphere', by high-yield nuclear explosions will increase the flux of solar ultraviolet radiation at the surface of the Earth (after the soot and dust have settled out). After a nuclear war in which thousands of high-yield weapons are detonated, the increase in biologically dangerous ultraviolet light might be several hundred per cent. In the more dangerous shorter wavelengths, larger increases would occur. Nucleic acids and proteins, the fundamental molecules for life on Earth, are especially sensitive to ultraviolet radiation. Thus, an increase of the solar ultraviolet flux at the surface of the Earth is potentially dangerous for life.

These four effects—obscuring smoke in the troposphere, obscuring dust in the stratosphere, the fallout of radioactive debris, and the partial destruction of the ozone layer—constitute the four known principal adverse environmental consequences that occur after a nuclear war is 'over'. There may be others about which we are still ignorant. The dust and, especially, the dark soot absorb ordinary visible light from the Sun, heating the atmosphere and cooling the Earth's surface.

All four of these effects have been treated in our recent scientific investigation. [1] The study, known from the initials of its authors as TTAPS, for the first time demonstrates that severe and prolonged low temperatures would follow a nuclear war. (The study also explains the fact that no such climatic effects were detected after the detonation of hundreds of megatons during the period of US-Soviet atmospheric testing of nuclear weapons, ended by treaty in 1963: the explosions were sequential over many years, not virtually simultaneous; and, occurring over scrub desert, coral atolls, tundra and wasteland, they set no fires.) The new results have been subjected to detailed scrutiny, and half a dozen confirmatory calculations have now been made. A special panel appointed by the National Academy of Sciences to examine this problem has come to similar conclusions. [2]

Unlike many previous studies, the effects do not seem to be restricted to northern mid-latitudes, where the nuclear exchange would mainly take place. There is now substantial evidence that the heating by sunlight of atmospheric dust and soot over northern mid-latitude targets would profoundly change the global circulation. Fine particles would be transported across the equator in weeks, bringing the cold and the dark to the Southern Hemisphere. (In addition, some studies suggest that over 100 megatons would be dedicated to equatorial and Southern Hemisphere targets, thus generating fine particles locally.) [3] While it would be less cold and less dark at the ground in the

[1] R. P. Turco, *et al.*, *loc. cit.* footnote 2.

[2] National Academy of Sciences, 1983, *loc. cit.* footnote 7.

[3] J. Peterson, *op. cit.* footnote 8.

Southern Hemisphere than in the Northern, massive climatic and environmental disruptions may be triggered there as well.

In our studies, several dozen different scenarios were chosen, covering a wide range of possible wars, and the range of uncertainty in each key parameter was considered (e.g., to describe how many fine particles are injected into the atmosphere). Five representative cases are shown in Table I, below, ranging from a small low-yield attack exclusively on cities, utilizing, in yield, only 0.8 per cent of the world strategic arsenals, to a massive exchange involving 75 per cent of the world arsenals. 'Nominal' cases assume the most probable parameter choices; 'severe' cases assume more adverse parameter choices, but still in the plausible range.

Predicted continental temperatures in the Northern Hemisphere vary after the nuclear war according to the curves shown in Figure 1. The high heat-retention capacity of water guarantees that oceanic temperatures will fall at most by a few degrees. Because temperatures are moderated by the adjacent oceans, temperature effects in coastal regions will be less extreme than in continental interiors. The temperatures shown in Figure 1 are average values for Northern Hemisphere land areas.

Even much smaller temperature declines are known to have serious consequences. The explosion of the Tambora volcano in Indonesia in 1815 led to an average global temperature decline of only 1°C, due to the obscuration of sunlight by the fine dust propelled into the stratosphere; yet the hard freezes the following year were so severe that 1816 has been known in Europe and America as 'the year without a summer'. A 1°C cooling would nearly eliminate wheat growing in Canada. [1] In the last thousand years, the maximum global or Northern Hemisphere temperature deviations have been around 1°C. In an Ice Age, a typical long-term temperature decline from pre-existing conditions is about 10°C. Even the most modest of the cases illustrated in Figure 1 give temporary temperature declines of this order. The Baseline Case is much more adverse. Unlike the situation in an Ice Age, however, the global temperatures after nuclear war plunge rapidly and take only months to a few years to recover, rather than thousands of years. No new Ice Age is likely to be induced by a Nuclear Winter.

Because of the obscuration of the Sun, the daytime light levels can fall to a twilight gloom or worse. For more than a week in the northern mid-latitude target zone, it might be much too dark to see, even at midday. In Cases 1 and 14 (Table 1), hemispherically averaged light levels fall to a few per cent of normal values, comparable to those at the bottom of a dense overcast. At this illumination, many plants are close to what is called the compensation point, the light level at which photosynthesis can barely keep pace with plant metabolism. In Case 17, illumination, averaged over the entire Northern Hemisphere, falls in daytime to about 0.1 per cent of normal, a light level at

[1] National Academy of Sciences, 1975, *op. cit.* footnote 7.

which plants will not photosynthesize at all. For Cases 1 and especially 17, full recovery to ordinary daylight takes a year or more (Figure 1).

As the fine particles fall out of the atmosphere, carrying radioactivity to the ground, the light levels increase and the surface warms. The depleted ozone layer now permits ultraviolet light to reach the Earth's surface in increased proportions. The relative timing of the multitude of adverse consequences of a nuclear war is shown in Table 2.

Perhaps the most striking and unexpected consequence of our study is that even a comparatively small nuclear war can have devastating climatic consequences, provided cities are targeted (see Case 14 in Figure 1; here, the centers of 100 major NATO and Warsaw Pact cities are burning). There is an indication of a very rough threshold at which severe climatic consequences are triggered—around a few hundred nuclear explosions over cities, for smoke generation, or around 2,000 to 3,000 high-yield surface bursts at, e.g., missile silos, for dust generation and ancillary fires. Fine particles can be injected into the atmosphere at increasing rates with only minor effects until these thresholds are crossed. Thereafter, the effects rapidly increase in severity. [1]

As in all calculations of this complexity, there are uncertainties. Some factors tend to work towards more severe or more prolonged effects; others tend to ameliorate the effects. [2] The detailed TTAPS calculations described here are one-dimensional; that is, they assume the fine particles to move vertically by all the appropriate laws of physics, but neglect the spreading in latitude and longitude. When soot or dust is moved away from the reference locale, things get better there and worse elsewhere. In addition, fine particles can be transported by weather systems to other locales, where they are carried more rapidly down to the surface. That would ameliorate obscuration not just locally but globally. It is just this transport away from the northern mid-latitudes that involves the equatorial zone and the Southern Hemisphere in the effects of the nuclear war. It would be helpful to perform an accurate three-dimensional calculation on the general atmospheric circulation following a nuclear war. Preliminary estimates suggest that circulation might moderate the low temperatures in the Northern Hemisphere predicted in our calculations by some 30 per cent, lessening somewhat the severity of the effects, but still leaving them at catastrophic levels (e.g., a 30°C rather than a 40°C temperature drop). To provide a small margin of safety, we neglect this correction in our subsequent discussion.

There are also effects that tend to make the results much worse: for example, in our calculations we assumed that rainout of fine particles

[1] The climatic threshold for smoke in the troposphere is about 100 million metric tons, injected essentially all at once; for sub-micron fine dust in the stratosphere, about the same.

[2] The slow warming of the Earth due to a CO_2 greenhouse effect attendant to the burning of fossil fuels should not be thought of as tempering the nuclear winter: the greenhouse temperature increments are too small and too slow.

occurred through the entire troposphere. But under realistic circumstances, at least the upper troposphere may be very dry, and any dust or soot carried there initially may take much longer to fall out. There is also a very significant effect deriving from the drastically altered structure of the atmosphere, brought about by the heating of the clouds and the cooling of the surface. This produces a region in which the temperature is approximately constant with altitude in the lower atmosphere and topped by a massive temperature inversion. Particles throughout the atmosphere would then be transported vertically very slowly—as in the present stratosphere. This is a second reason why the lifetime of the clouds of soot and dust may be much longer than we have calculated. If so, the worst of the cold and the dark might be prolonged for considerable periods of time, conceivably for more than a year. We also neglect this effect in subsequent discussion.

Nuclear war scenarios are possible that are much worse than the ones we have presented. For example, if command and control capabilities are lost early in the war—by, say, 'decapitation' (an early surprise attack on civilian and military headquarters and communications facilities)—then the war conceivably could be extended for weeks as local commanders make separate and uncoordinated decisions. At least some of the delayed missile launches could be retaliatory strikes against any remaining adversary cities. Generation of an additional smoke pall over a period of weeks or longer following the initiation of the war would extend the magnitude, but especially the duration of the climatic consequences. Or it is possible that more cities and forest would be ignited than we have assumed, or that smoke emissions would be larger, or that a greater fraction of the world arsenals would be committed. Less severe cases are of course possible as well.

These calculations therefore are not, and cannot be, assured prognostications of the full consequences of a nuclear war. Many refinements in them are possible and are being pursued. But there is general agreement on the overall conclusions: in the wake of a nuclear war there is likely to be a period, lasting at least for months, of extreme cold in a radioactive gloom, followed—after the soot and dust fall out—by an extended period of increased ultraviolet light reaching the surface. [1]

We now explore the biological impact of such an assault on the global environment.

III

The immediate human consequences of nuclear explosions range from vaporization of populations near the hypocenter, to blast-generated trauma

[1] These results are dependent on important work by a large number of scientists who have previously examined aspects of this subject; many of these workers are acknowledged in the articles cited in footnote 2.

(from flying glass, falling beams, collapsing skyscrapers and the like), to burns, radiation sickness, shock and severe psychiatric disorders. But our concern here is with longer-term effects.

It is now a commonplace that in the burning of modern tall buildings, more people succumb to toxic gases than to fire. Ignition of many varieties of building materials, insulation and fabrics generates large amounts of such pyrotoxins, including carbon monoxide, cyanides, vinyl chlorides, oxides of nitrogen, ozone, dioxins, and furans. Because of differing practices in the use of such synthetics, the burning of cities in North America and Western Europe will probably generate more pyrotoxins than cities in the Soviet Union, and cities with substantial recent construction more than older, unreconstructed cities. In nuclear war scenarios in which a great many cities are burning, a significant pyrotoxin smog might persist for months. The magnitude of this danger is unknown.

The pyrotoxins, low light levels, radioactive fallout, subsequent ultraviolet light, and especially the cold are together likely to destroy almost all of Northern Hemisphere agriculture, even for the more modest Cases 11 and 14. A 12° to 15°C temperature reduction by itself would eliminate wheat and corn production in the United States, even if all civil systems and agricultural technology were intact.[1] With unavoidable societal disruption, and with the other environmental stresses just mentioned, even a 3,000 megaton 'pure' counterforce attack (Case 11) might suffice. Realistically, many fires would be set even in such an attack (see below), and a 3,000 megaton war is likely to wipe out US grain production. This would represent by itself an unprecedented global catastrophe: North American grain is the principal reliable source of export food on the planet, as well as an essential component of US prosperity. Wars just before harvesting of grain and other staples would be incrementally worse than wars after harvesting. For many scenarios, the effects will extend (see Figure 2) into two or more growing seasons. Widespread fires and subsequent runoff of topsoil are among the many additonal deleterious consequences extending for years after the war.

Something like three-quarters of the US population lives in or near cities. In the cities themselves there is, on average, only about one week's supply of food. After a nuclear war it is conceivable that enough of present grain storage might survive to maintain, on some level, the present population for more than a year. But with the breakdown of civil order and transportation systems in the cold, the dark and the fallout, these stores would become largely inaccessible. Vast numbers of survivors would soon starve to death.

In addition, the sub-freezing temperatures imply, in many cases, the unavailability of fresh water. The ground will tend to be frozen to a depth of about a meter—incidentally making it unlikely that the hundreds of millions of dead bodies would be buried, even if the civil organization to do so existed.

[1] David Pimentel and Mark Sorrells, private communication, 1983.

Fuel stores to melt snow and ice would be in short supply, and ice surfaces and freshly fallen snow would tend to be contaminated by radioactivity and pyrotoxins.

In the presence of excellent medical care, the average value of the acute lethal dose of ionizing radiation for healthy adults is about 450 rads. (As with many other effects, children, the infirm and the elderly tend to be more vulnerable.) Combined with the other assaults on survivors in the post-war environment, and in the probable absence of any significant medical care, the mean lethal acute dose is likely to decline to 350 rads or even lower. For many outdoor scenarios, doses within the fallout plumes that drift hundreds of kilometers downwind of targets are greater than the mean lethal dose. (For a 10,000-megaton war, this is true for more than 30 per cent of northern mid-latitude land areas.) Far from targets, intermediate-timescale chronic doses from delayed radioactive fallout may be in excess of 100 rads for the baseline case. These calculations assume no detonations on nuclear reactors or fuel-reprocessing plants, which would increase the dose.

Thus, the combination of acute doses from prompt radioactive fallout, chronic doses from the delayed intermediate-timescale fallout, and internal doses from food and drink are together likely to kill many more by radiation sickness. Because of acute damage to bone marrow, survivors would have significantly increased vulnerability to infectious diseases. Most infants exposed to 100 rads as foetuses in the first two trimesters of pregnancy would suffer mental retardation and/or other serious birth defects. Radiation and some pyrotoxins would later produce neoplastic diseases and genetic damage. Livestock and domesticated animals, with fewer resources, vanishing food supplies and in many cases with greater sensitivity to the stresses of nuclear war than human beings, would also perish in large numbers.

These devastating consequences for humans and for agriculture would not be restricted to the locales in which the war would principally be 'fought', but would extend throughout northern mid-latitudes and, with reduced but still significant severity, probably to the tropics and the Southern Hemisphere. The bulk of the world's grain exports originate in northern mid-latitudes. Many nations in the developing as well as the developed world depend on the import of food. Japan, for example, imports 75 per cent of its food (and 99 per cent of its fuel). Thus, even if there were no climatic and radiation stresses on tropical and Southern Hemisphere societies—many of them already at subsistence levels of nutrition—large numbers of people there would die of starvation.

As agriculture breaks down worldwide (possible initial exceptions might include Argentina, Australia and South Africa if the climatic impact on the Southern Hemisphere proved to be minimal), there will be increasing reliance on natural ecosystems—fruits, tubers, roots, nuts, etc. But wild foodstuffs will also have suffered from the effects of the war. At just the moment that surviving humans turn to the natural environment for the basis of life, that environment would be experiencing a devastation unprecedented in recent geological history.

Two-thirds of all species of plants, animals, and microorganisms on the Earth live within 25° of the equator. Because temperatures tend to vary with the seasons only minimally at tropical latitudes, species there are especially vulnerable to rapid temperature declines. In past major extinction events in the paleontological record, there has been a marked tendency for tropical organisms to show greater vulnerability than organisms living at more temperate latitudes.

The darkness alone may cause a collapse in the aquatic food chain in which sunlight is harvested by phytoplankton, phytoplankton by zooplankton, zooplankton by small fish, small fish by large fish, and, occasionally, large fish by humans. In many nuclear war scenarios, this food chain is likely to collapse at its base for at least a year and is significantly more imperilled in tropical waters. The increase in ultraviolet light available at the surface of the Earth approximately a year after the war provides an additional major environmental stress that by itself has been described as having 'profound consequences' for aquatic, terrestrial and other ecosystems. [1]

The global ecosystem can be considered an intricately woven fabric composed of threads contributed by the millions of separate species that inhabit the planet and interact with the air, the water and the soil. The system has developed considerable resiliency, so that pulling a single thread is unlikely to unravel the entire fabric. Thus, most ordinary assaults on the biosphere are unlikely to have catastrophic consequences. For example, because of natural small changes in stratospheric ozone abundance, organisms have probably experienced, in the fairly recent geological past, ten per cent fluctuations in the solar near-ultraviolet flux (but not fluctuations by factors of two or more). Similarly, major continental temperature changes of the magnitude and extent addressed here may not have been experienced for tens of thousands and possibly not for millions of years. We have no experimental information, even for aquaria or terraria, on the simultaneous effects of cold, dark, pyrotoxins, ionizing radiation, and ultraviolet light as predicted in the TTAPS study.

Each of these factors, taken separately, may carry serious consequences for the global ecosystem: their interactions may be much more dire still. Extremely worrisome is the possibility of poorly understood or as yet entirely uncontemplated synergisms (where the net consequences of two or more assaults on the environment are much more than the sum of the component parts). For example, more than 100 rads (and possibly more than 200 rads)

[1] C. H. Kruger, R. B. Setlow, *et al.* , *Causes and Effects of Stratospheric Ozone Reduction: An Update*, Washington: National Academy of Sciences, 1982.

of external and ingested ionizing radiation is likely to be delivered in a very large nuclear war to all plants, animals and unprotected humans in densely populated regions of northern mid-latitudes. After the soot and dust clear, there can, for such wars, be a 200 to 400 per cent increment in the solar ultraviolet flux that reaches the ground, with an increase of many orders of magnitude in the more dangerous shorter-wavelength radiation. Together, these radiation assaults are likely to suppress the immune systems of humans and other species, making them more vulnerable to disease. At the same time, the high ambient-radiation fluxes are likely to produce, through mutation, new varieties of microorganisms, some of which might become pathogenic. The preferential radiation sensitivity of birds and other insect predators would enhance the proliferation of herbivorous and pathogen-carrying insects. Carried by vectors with high radiation tolerance, it seems possible that epidemics and global pandemics would propagate with no hope of effective mitigation by medical care, even with reduced population sizes and greatly restricted human mobility. Plants, weakened by low temperatures and low light levels, and other animals would likewise be vulnerable to pre-existing and newly arisen pathogens.

There are many other conceivable synergisms, all of them still poorly understood because of the complexity of the global ecosystem. Every synergism represents an additional assault, of unknown magnitude, on the global ecosystem and its support functions for humans. What the world would look like after a nuclear war depends in part upon the unknown synergistic interaction of these various adverse effects.

We do not and cannot know that the worst would happen after a nuclear war. Perhaps there is some as yet undiscovered compensating effect or saving grace—although in the past, the overlooked effects in studies of nuclear war have almost always tended toward the worst. But in an uncertain matter of such gravity, it is wise to contemplate the worst, especially when its probability is not extremely small. The summary of the findings of the group of 40 distinguished biologists who met in April 1983 to assess the TTAPS conclusions is worthy of careful consideration: [1]

> Species extinction could be expected for most tropical plants and animals, and for most terrestrial vertebrates of north temperate regions, a large number of plants, and numerous freshwater and some marine organisms . . . Whether any people would be able to persist for long in the face of highly modified biological communities; novel climates; high levels of radiation; shattered agricultural, social, and economic systems; extraordinary psychological stresses; and a host of other difficulties is open to question. It is clear that the ecosystem effects *alone* resulting from a large-scale thermonuclear war could be enough to destroy the current civilization in at least the Northern Hemisphere. Coupled with the direct casualties of perhaps two billion

[1] P. Ehrlich, *et al.*, *loc. cit.* footnote 2.

people, the combined intermediate and long-term effects of nuclear war suggest that eventually there might be no human survivors in the Northern Hemisphere.

IV

Furthermore, the scenario described here is by no means the most severe that could be imagined with present world nuclear arsenals and those contemplated for the near future. In almost any realistic case involving nuclear exchanges between the super-Powers, global environmental changes sufficient to cause an extinction event equal to or more severe than that at the close of the Cretaceous when the dinosaurs and many other species died out are likely. In that event, the possibility of the extinction of *Homo sapiens* cannot be excluded.

The foregoing probable consequences of various nuclear war scenarios have implications for doctrine and policy. Some have argued that the difference between the deaths of several hundred million people in a nuclear war (as has been thought until recently to be a reasonable upper limit) and the death of every person on Earth (as now seems possible) is only a matter of one order of magnitude. For me, the difference is considerably greater. Restricting our attention only to those who die as a consequence of the war conceals its full impact.

If we are required to calibrate extinction in numerical terms, I would be sure to include the number of people in future generations who would not be born. A nuclear war imperils all of our descendants, for as long as there will be humans. Even if the population remains static, with an average lifetime of the order of 100 years, over a typical time period for the biological evolution of a successful species (roughly ten million years), we are talking about some 500 trillion people yet to come. By this criterion, the stakes are one million times greater for extinction than for the more modest nuclear wars that kill 'only' hundreds of millions of people.

There are many other possible measures of the potential loss—including culture and science, the evolutionary history of the planet, and the significance of the lives of all of our ancestors who contributed to the future of their descendants. Extinction is the undoing of the human enterprise.

For me, the new results on climatic catastrophe raise the stakes of nuclear war enormously. But I recognize that there are those, including some policymakers, who feel that the increased level of fatalities has little impact on policy, but who nevertheless acknowledge that the newly emerging consequences of nuclear war may require changes in specific points of strategic doctrine. I here set down what seem to me some of the more apparent such implications, within the context of present nuclear stockpiles. The idea of a crude threshold, very roughly around 500 to 2,000 warheads, for triggering the climatic catastrophe will be central to some of these considerations. (Such a threshold applies only to something like the present distribution of yields in the strategic arsenals. Drastic conversion to very low-yield arsenals—see below—changes some of the picture dramatically.) I hope others will constructively examine these preliminary thoughts and explore additional implications of the TTAPS results.

1. *First Strike.* The MIRVing of missiles (the introduction of multiple warheads), improvements in accuracy, and other developments have increased the perceived temptation to launch a devastating first strike against land targets—even though both sides retain a powerful retaliatory force in airborne bombers and submarines at sea. Much current concern and national rhetoric is addressed to the first-strike capability of extant or proposed weapons systems. The mere capability of a first strike creates incentives for a preemptive attack. Launch-on-warning and simultaneous release of all strategic weapons are two of several ominous and destabilizing innovations contrived in response to the fear of a first strike.

The number of US land-based strategic missiles is about 1,050; for the Soviet Union, about 1,400. In addition, each side has at least several dozen dedicated and alternative strategic bomber bases and airstrips, as well as command and control facilities, submarine ports and other prime strategic targets on land. Each target requires—for high probability of its destruction—two or perhaps three attacking warheads. Thus, a convincing first strike against land targets requires at least 2,200 and perhaps as many as 4,500 attacking warheads. Some—for example, to disable bombers that succeed in becoming airborne just before the strike—would detonate as airbursts. While many missile silos, especially in the United States, are surrounded by farmland and brush, other strategic targets, especially in Europe and Asia, are sufficiently near forests or urban areas for major conflagrations to be set, even in a 'pure' counterforce attack. Accordingly, a major first strike would be clearly in the vicinity of, and perhaps well over, the climatic threshold.

A counterforce first strike is unlikely to be completely effective. Perhaps 10 to 40 per cent of the adversary's silos and most of its airborne bombers and submarines at sea will survive, and *its* response may not be against silos, but against cities. Ten per cent of a 5,000-warhead strategic arsenal is 500 warheads: distributed over cities, this seems by itself enough to trigger a major climatic catastrophe.

Such a first-strike scenario, in which the danger to the aggressor nation depends upon the unpredictable response of the attacked nation, seems risky enough. (The hope for the aggressor nation is that its retained second-strike force, including strategic submarines and unlaunched land-based missiles, will intimidate the adversary into surrender rather than provoke it into retaliation.) But the decision to launch a first strike that is tantamount to national suicide for the aggressor—*even if the attacked nation does not lift a finger to retaliate*—is a different circumstance altogether. If a first strike gains no more than a pyrrhic victory of ten days' duration before the prevailing winds carry the nuclear winter to the aggressor nation, the 'attractiveness' of the first strike would seem to be diminished significantly.

A Doomsday Machine is useless if the potential adversary is ignorant of its presence. [1] But since many distinguished scientists, both American and Soviet, have participated vigorously in recent studies of the climatic consequences of nuclear war, since there appears to be no significant disagreement in the conclusions, and since policymakers will doubtless be apprised of these new results, it would appear that a decision to launch a major first strike is now much less rational, and therefore, perhaps, much less probable. The better political leaders understand the nuclear winter, the more secure are such conclusions.

If true, this should have cascading consequences for specific weapons systems. Further, the perceived vulnerability to a first strike has been a major source of stress and fear, and thereby a major spur to the nuclear arms race. Knowledge that a first strike is now less probable might make at least some small contribution to dissipating the poisonous atmosphere of mistrust that currently characterizes Soviet-American relations.

2. *Sub-threshold War*. Devastating nuclear wars that are nevertheless significantly below the threshold for severe climatic consequences certainly seem possible—for example, the destruction of 10 or 20 cities, or 100 silos of a particularly destabilizing missile system. Nevertheless, might some nation be tempted to initiate or engage in a much larger, but still reliably sub-threshold nuclear war? The hope might be that the attacked adversary would be reluctant to retaliate for fear of crossing the threshold.

This is not very different from the hope that a counterforce first strike would not be followed by a retaliatory strike, because of the aggressor's retention of an invulnerable (for example, submarine-based) second-strike force adequate to destroy populations and national economies. It suffers the same deficiency—profound uncertainty about the likely response.

The strategic force of the United States or the Soviet Union—even if they were all at fixed sites—could not be destroyed in a reliably sub-threshold war: there are too many essential targets. Thus, a sub-threshold first strike powerfully provokes the attacked nation and leaves much of its retaliatory force untouched. It is easy to imagine a

[1] The term 'Doomsday Machine' is due to Herman Kahn, *Thinking About the Unthinkable*, New York: Horizon Press, 1962.

nation, having contemplated becoming the object of a sub-threshold first strike, planning to respond in kind, because it judges that failure to do so would itself invite attack. Retaliation could occur immediately against a few key cities—if national leaders were restrained and command and control facilities intact—or massively, months later, after much of the dust and smoke have fallen out, extending the duration but ameliorating the severity of the net climatic effects.

This, however, may not be the case for such nations as Britain, France or China. Because of the marked contiguity of strategic targets and urban areas in Europe, the climatic threshold for attacks on European nuclear powers may be significantly less than for the United States or the Soviet Union. Provided it could be accomplished without triggering a US-Soviet nuclear war, first strikes against all the fixed-site strategic forces of one of these nations might not trigger the climatic catastrophe. Nevertheless, the invulnerable retaliatory capability of these nations—especially the ballistic-missile submarines of Britain and France—makes such a first strike unlikely.

3. *Treaties on Yields and Targeting*. I would not include this possibility, except that it has been mentioned publicly by a leading American nuclear strategist. The proposal has two parts. The first is to ban by treaty all nuclear warheads with yields in excess of 300 or 400 kilotons. The fireballs from warheads of higher yields mainly penetrate into the stratosphere and work to deplete the ozonosphere.

The reconversion of nuclear warheads to lower individual yields would reduce (although not remove) the threat of significantly enhanced ultraviolet radiation at the surface of the Earth, but would in itself have no bearing on the issue of climatic catastrophe, and would increase the intermediate-timescale radioactive fallout. Within the present strategic arsenals, there is no mix of yields that simultaneously minimizes ionizing radiation from fallout and ultraviolet radiation from the Sun.

As delivery system accuracy has progressively improved, there has been a corresponding tendency toward the deployment of lower-yield warheads, although not through any concern about the integrity of the ozonosphere. There is also a trend toward higher fission fractions, implying more radioactive fallout. Limitations on the sizes and therefore, to some extent, on the yields of new warheads are part of recent US arms control proposals. With the bulk of Soviet strategic warheads having yields larger than their US counterparts, however, treaties limiting high yields place greater demands on Soviet than on US compliance. Moreover, to enforce a categorical yield ceiling seems to imply verification problems of some difficulty.

The second part of the proposal is to guarantee by treaty that cities would not be targeted. Then the worst of the climatic effects might be avoided, although the climatic consequences of 'pure' counterforce exchanges can still be extremely serious (Figure 1). The encoding of targeting coordinates, however, is in principle done remotely, and involves different coordinates for each warhead. Even if we could imagine international inspection teams descending unannounced on Soviet or American missile silos to inspect the targeting coordinates, an hour later the coordinates could be returned to those appropriate for cities.

Targeting policy is among the most sensitive aspects of nuclear strategy, and maintaining uncertainty about targeting policy is thought to be an essential component of US deterrence. The proposal is unlikely to be received warmly by the US Joint Strategic Targeting Staff or its Soviet counterpart. It is also difficult to understand how those skeptical of the verifiability by reconnaissance satellites of SALT II provisions on the deployment of missiles ten meters long can rest easy about verification of treaties controlling what is encoded in a microchip one millimeter long. Nevertheless, a symbolic, unverifiable targeting treaty, entered into because both sides recognize that it is not in their interest to target cities, might have some merit.

4. *Transition to Low-Yield High-Accuracy Arsenals.* A conceivable response to the prospect of climatic catastrophe might be to continue present trends toward lower-yield and higher-accuracy missiles, perhaps accompanied by development of the technology for warheads to burrow sub-surface before detonating. Payloads have been developed for the Pershing II missile that use radar area-correlators for target recognition and terminal guidance; the targeting probable error is said to be 40 meters. [1] It is evident that a technology is gradually emerging that could permit delivery accuracies of 35 meters or better over intercontinental ranges.

It is evident as well that burrowing technology is also under rapid development. [2] A one-kiloton burst, two to three meters sub-surface, will excavate a crater roughly 60 meters across. [3] Clearly, high-accuracy penetrating warheads in the one-to-ten-kiloton range would be able, with high reliability, to destroy even very hardened silos and underground command posts.

Low-yield sub-surface explosions of this sort cannot threaten the ozonosphere. They minimize fires, soot, stratospheric dust and radioactive fallout. Even several thousand simultaneous such detonations might not trigger the nuclear winter. Similar technology might be used for pinpoint attacks on military/industrial targets in

1 *Aviation Week and Space Technology*, May 15, 1978, p. 225.
2 *Ibid.*
3 S. Glasstone and P. J. Dolan, *op. cit.* footnote 4.

urban areas. Thus, the TTAPS results will probably lead to calls for further improvements in high-accuracy earth-burrowing warheads.

There are, I think, a number of difficulties with this proposal, as attractive as it seems in a strictly military context. A world in which the nuclear arsenals were completely converted to a relatively small number of burrowing low-yield warheads would be much safer in terms of the climatic catastrophe. But such warheads are provocative. They are the perfect post-TTAPS first-strike weapon. Their development might well be taken as a serious interest in making a climatically safe but disabling first strike. Greatly expanded deployment of anti-ballistic missiles might be one consequence of their buildup.

Retaliation from surviving silos, aircraft and especially submarines, as discussed above, is likely, whatever the disposition of yields in a first strike. Also, arsenals cannot be converted instantaneously. There would be a very dangerous and protracted transition period in which enough newer weapons are deployed to be destabilizing, and enough older weapons are still in place to trigger the nuclear winter.

However, if the inventories of modern higher-yield (more than ten kiloton) warheads were first brought below threshold, a coordinated US–Soviet deployment of low-yield burrowers might be accomplished in somewhat greater safety. On many launchers, each with a single warhead, they might provide a useful reassurance to defense ministries at some points in the transition process. At any rate, the dramatic reduction of arsenals necessary to go below threshold before large-scale burrower deployment is indistinguishable from major arms reduction for its own sake (see below).

5. *Consequences for the Developing World.* Before the TTAPS calculations were performed, it was possible to argue that the developing world would be severely affected by secondary economic consequences, but not fundamentally destroyed by a northern mid-latitude nuclear war. Now it seems more likely that nations having no part in the conflict—even nations entirely neutral in the global confrontation between the United States and the Soviet Union—might be reduced to prehistoric population levels and economies or worse. Nations between 70°N and 30°S, nations with marginal economies, nations with large food imports or extensive malnutrition today, and nations with their own strategic targets are particularly at risk.

Thus, the very survival of nations distant from any likely nuclear conflict can now be seen to depend on the prudence and wisdom of the major nuclear Powers. India, Brazil, Nigeria or Saudi Arabia could collapse in a nuclear war without a single bomb being dropped on their territories.

Quite apart from any concern about the deflection of world financial, technical and intellectual resources to the nuclear arms race, the prospect of nuclear war now clearly and visibly threatens every nation and every person on the planet. The diplomatic and economic pressure accordingly placed on the five nuclear Powers by the other nations of the world, concerned about their own survival, could be at least marginally significant.

6. *Shelters.* The usual sorts of shelters envisioned for civilian populations are ineffective even for the nuclear war consequences known before the TTAPS study. The more ambitious among them include food and water for a week or two, modest heating capabilities, rudimentary sanitary and air filtration facilities and no provisions for the psychological burdens of an extended stay below ground with unknown climatic and ecological consequences propagating overhead. The kinds of shelters suitable for prolonged sub-freezing temperatures, high radiation doses, and pyrotoxins would have to be very much more elaborate—quite apart from the question of what good it would be to emerge six or nine months later to an ultraviolet-bathed and biologically depauperate surface, with insect pests proliferating, disease rampant, and the basis of agriculture destroyed.

   Appropriate shelters, able to service individual families or family groups for months to a year, are too expensive for most families even in the affluent West. The construction of major government shelters for civilian populations would be enormously expensive as well as in itself potentially destabilizing. The prospect of the climatic catastrophe also heightens the perceived inequity beween government leaders and (in some cases) their families, provided elaborate shelters, and the bulk of the civilian population, unable to afford even a minimally adequate shelter.

   But even if it were possible to build perfectly effective shelters for the entire populations of the United States and the Soviet Union, this would in no way address the danger to which the rest of the world would be put. Shelters for the combatant nations under circumstances in which only their citizens are threatened are one thing. Shelters for the combatant nations when gravely threatened noncombatant nations have only rudimentary or non-existent shelters are a very different matter.

7. *Ballistic-Missile Defense Systems.* It might be argued that the prospect of a climatic catastrophe strengthens whatever arguments there may be

The distribution of the coldest regions will vary with time and geography. In one recent but still very crude three-dimensional simulation of the nuclear winter, the temperature has, by 40 days after the war, dropped by 15 to more than 40 centrigrade degrees over much of the globe, including a vast region extending from Chad to Novosibirsk, from the Caspian Sea to Sri Lanka, embracing India, Pakistan and western China, and having its most severe effects in Afghanistan, Iran and Saudi Arabia. V. V. Alexandrov and G. L. Stenchikov, preprint, Computing Center, USSR Academy of Sciences, Moscow, 1983.

for ground-based or space-based ballistic missile defense (BMD) systems, as proposed by President Reagan in his March 23, 1983 'Star Wars' speech. There are grave technical, cost and policy difficulties with such proposals.[1] Even advocates do not envision it being fully operational in less than two or three decades.

Optimistic informed estimates of porosity or 'penetrance' (the fraction of attacking missiles successfully detonating at their targets despite the BMD) are no lower than 5 to 30 per cent. The present world arsenal of strategic warheads is so much greater than the threshold for climatic catastrophe that, even if 5 to 30 per cent of attacking missiles get through in something like a full exchange, the catastrophe could be triggered. And most competent estimates put the porosity—at least for the foreseeable future—at 50 per cent to 99 per cent. Further, one likely response to an adversary's anticipated deployment of BMD systems would be a proportionate increase in the stockpiles of offensive warheads in compensation.

There are three phases in the trajectories of incoming missiles when they might be attacked: boost phase, midcourse phase, and terminal phase. Boost-phase and midcourse interception would, at best, require an untried technology deployed at scales never before attempted. Only terminal-phase BMDs exist at the present time (anti-ballistic missiles or ABMs), and even they, ineffective as they are, may require ruinous capital investments before they can provide meaningful levels of defense. Developments in terminal-phase manoeuverability of attacking warheads are likely to raise the price tag of an effective BMD sharply again. Even in the best of circumstances, offense will be more effective and less costly than defense.

Finally, terminal-phase interception, generally effective only for hard-target defense, is characteristically designed to occur at very low altitudes. There would be an advantage to the offense if it fused the incoming missiles so they would explode if attacked ('sympathetic detonation'). In some schemes, the BMD itself involves nuclear warheads exploded near the ground. A fair fraction of hard targets, especially in Europe and the Soviet Union, are within a few tens of kilometers of cities or forests. Thus, the most readily deployable BMD suffers the disability, when it works at all, of generating fires contributory to a climatic catastrophe, quite apart from its porosity.

8. *Other Possibilities*. There are a number of other conceivable responses to the climatic catastrophe, some even more desperate than those discussed above. For example, a nation might relocate its silos and mobile

[1] Richard Garwin, testimony before the Subcommittee on International Security and Scientific Affairs of the House Committee on Foreign Affairs, US Congress, November 10, 1983; Hans Bethe, manuscript in preparation.

launchers (the latter inviting barrage attack) to cities and forests to guarantee that a barely adequate counterforce first strike by its adversary would trigger a global climatic catastrophe with high confidence. Or nations with small nuclear arsenals or marginal strategic capability might contemplate amassing a threshold arsenal of some 500 to 2,000 deliverable warheads in order to be taken seriously in 'great Power' politics.

But these and similar contrivances increase the probability of nuclear war or the dangers attendant to nuclear war sufficiently that they are likely to be rejected by the nation contemplating such moves or, failing that, by other nations. Major relocations of strategic weapons systems or the deployment of new strategic arsenals are readily detectable by national technical means.

V

None of the foregoing possible strategic and policy responses to the prospect of a nuclear war-triggered climatic catastrophe seem adequate even for the security of the nuclear Powers, much less for the rest of the world. The prospect reinforces, in the short run, the standard arguments for strategic confidence-building, especially between the United States and the Soviet Union; for tempering puerile rhetoric; for resisting the temptation to demonize the adversary; for reducing the likelihood of strategic confrontations arising from accident or miscalculation; for stabilizing old and new weapons systems—for example, by de-MIRVing missiles; for abandoning nuclear-war-fighting strategies and mistrusting the possibility of 'containment' of a tactical or limited nuclear war; for considering safe unilateral steps, such as the retiring of some old weapons systems with very high-yield warheads; for improving communications at all levels, especially among general staffs and between heads of governments; and for public declarations of relevant policy changes. The United States might also contemplate ratification of SALT II and of the 1948 United Nations Convention on the Prevention and Punishment of the Crime of Genocide (ratified by 92 nations, including the Soviet Union).

Both nations might consider abandoning apocalyptic threats and doctrines. To the extent that these are not credible, they undermine deterrence; to the extent that they are credible, they set in motion events that tend toward apocalyptic conclusions.

In the long run, the prospect of climatic catastrophe raises real questions about what is meant by national and international security. To me, it seems clear that the species is in grave danger at least until the world arsenals are reduced below the threshold for climatic catastrophe; the nations and the global civilization would remain vulnerable even at low inventories. It may even be that, now, the only credible arsenal is below threshold. George Kennan's celebrated proposal [1] to reduce the world arsenals initially to 50 per cent of their current numbers is recognized as hard enough to implement. But it would be the only first step toward what is now clearly and urgently needed—a more than 90 per cent reduction. Kennan proposed an ultimate reduction of more than 84 per cent—adequate for strategic deterrence, if that is considered essential, but unlikely to trigger the nuclear winter. Still further reductions could then be contemplated.

The detonation of weapons stockpiles near or above threshold would be, we can now recognize, in contravention of the 1977 Geneva Convention on The Hostile Use of Environmental Modification Techniques, signed by 48 nations and duly ratified by the Soviet Union and the United States. [2] And Article VI of the 1968 Nuclear Non-Proliferation Treaty requires the United States and the Soviet Union, among other signatory states, 'to pursue negotiations in good faith on effective measures relating to cessation of the nuclear arms race at an early date and to nuclear disarmament . . . ' I do not imagine that these treaties can, by themselves, play a determining role in producing major reductions in the world strategic arsenals, but they establish some sense of international obligation and can at least expedite urgent bilateral and multilateral consultations.

VI

We have, by slow and imperceptible steps, been constructing a Doomsday Machine. Until recently—and then, only by accident—no one even noticed. And we have distributed its triggers all over the Northern Hemisphere. Every American and Soviet leader since 1945 has made critical decisions regarding nuclear war in total ignorance of the climatic catastrophe. Perhaps this knowledge would have moderated the subsequent course of world events and, especially, the nuclear arms race. Today, at least, we have no excuse for failing to factor the catastrophe into long-term decisions on strategic policy.

Since it is the soot produced by urban fires that is the most sensitive trigger of the climatic catastrophe, and since such fires can be ignited even by low-yield strategic weapons, it appears that the most critical ready index of the world nuclear arsenals, in terms of climatic change, may be the total

[1] George F. Kennan, 'The Only Way Out of the Nuclear Nightmare', *Manchester Guardian Weekly*, May 31, 1981. This is Kennan's acceptance speech for the Albert Einstein Peace Prize on May 19, 1981, in Washington, D. C.

[2] Article 1, paragraph 1, states: 'Each State Party to this Convention undertakes not to engage in military or any other hostile use of environmental modification techniques having widespread, long-lasting or severe effects as the means of destruction, damage, or injury to another State Party.' Paragraph 2 goes on: 'Each State Party to this Convention undertakes not to assist, encourage or induce any State, group of States or international organization to engage in activities contrary to the provisions of paragraph 1 . . . '

number of strategic warheads. (There is some dependence on yield, to be sure, and future very low-yield, high-accuracy burrowing warheads could destroy strategic targets without triggering the nuclear winter, as discussed above.) For other purposes there are other indices—numbers of submarine-launched warheads, throw-weight (net payload deliverable to target), total megatonnage, etc. From different choices of such indices, different conclusions about strategic parity can be drawn. In the total number of strategic warheads, however, the United States is 'ahead' of the Soviet Union and always has been.

Very roughly, the level of the world strategic arsenals necessary to induce the climatic catastrophe seems to be somewhere around 500 to 2,000 warheads—an estimate that may be somewhat high for airbursts over cities, and somewhat low for high-yield groundbursts. The intrinsic uncertainty in this number is itself of strategic importance, and prudent policy would assume a value below the low end of the plausible range.

National or global inventories above this rough threshold move the world arsenals into a region that might be called the 'Doomsday Zone'. If the world arsenals were well below this rough threshold, no concatenation of computer malfunction, carelessness, unauthorized acts, communications failure, miscalculation and madness in high office could unleash the nuclear winter. When global arsenals are above the threshold, such a catastrophe is at least possible. The further above threshold we are, the more likely it is that a major exchange would trigger the climatic catastrophe.

Traditional belief and childhood experience teach that more weapons buy more security. But since the advent of nuclear weapons and the acquisition of a capacity for 'overkill', the possibility has arisen that, past a certain point, more nuclear weapons do not increase national security. I wish here to suggest that, beyond the climatic threshold, an increase in the number of strategic weapons leads to a pronounced *decline* in national (and global) security. National security is not a zero-sum game. Strategic insecurity of one adversary almost always means strategic insecurity for the other. Conventional pre-1945 wisdom, no matter how deeply felt, is not an adequate guide in an age of apocalyptic weapons.

If we are content with world inventories above the threshold, we are saying that it is safe to trust the fate of our global civilization and perhaps our species to all leaders, civilian and military, of all present and future major nuclear Powers; and to the command and control efficiency and technical reliability in those nations now and in the indefinite future. For myself, I would far rather have a world in which the climatic catastrophe cannot happen, independent of the vicissitudes of leaders, institutions and machines. This seems to me elementary planetary hygiene, as well as elementary patriotism.

Something like 1,000 warheads (or a few hundred megatons) is of the same order as the arsenals that were publicly announced in the 1950s and 1960s as an unmistakable strategic deterrent, and as sufficient to destroy either the United States or the Soviet Union 'irrecoverably'. Considerably smaller arsenals would, with present improvements in accuracy and reliability, probably suffice. Thus it is possible to contemplate a world in which the global strategic arsenals are below threshold, where mutual deterrence is in effect to discourage the use of those surviving warheads, and where, in the unhappy event that some warheads are detonated, there is little likelihood of the climatic catastrophe. [1]

To achieve so dramatic a decline in the global arsenals will require not only heroic measures by both the United States and the Soviet Union—it will also require consistent action by Britain, France and China, especially when the US and Soviet arsenals are significantly reduced. Currently proposed increments in the arsenals at least of France would bring that nation's warhead inventory near or above threshold. I have already remarked on the strategic instability, in the context of the climatic catastrophe only, of the warhead inventories of these nations. But if major cuts in the US and Soviet arsenals were under way, it is not too much to hope that the other major powers would, after negotiations, follow suit. These considerations also underscore the danger of nuclear weapons proliferation to other nations, especially when the major inventories are in steep decline.

Figure 2 illustrates the growth of the American and Soviet strategic inventories from 1945 to the present. [2] To minimize confusion in the Figure, the British, French and Chinese arsenals are not shown; they are, however, as just mentioned, significant on the new scale of climatically dangerous arsenals. We see from the Figure that the United States passed the Doomsday Threshold around 1953, and the Soviet Union not until about 1966. The largest disparity in the arsenals was in 1961 (a difference of some 6,000

[1] Since higher-yield tactical warheads can also be used to burn cities, and might do so inadvertently, especially in Europe, provision for their elimination should also eventually be made. But initial attention should be directed to strategic warheads and their delivery systems.

[2] The total warheads calculated in Figure 2 include strategic and theater weapons, but not tactical weapons. Not all published sources are in perfect agreement on these numbers. The principal sources used here are the *Report of the Secretary of Defense [Harold Brown] to the Congress on the FY 1982 Budget, FY 1983 Authorization Request and FY 1986 Defense Programs*, Washington: Department of Defense, 1981; and *National Defense Budget Estimates*, FY 1983; Office of the Assistant Secretary of Defense, Comptroller, March 1982.

Beyond 1983, projected increases in arsenals are shown for US and Soviet arsenals as nearly vertical dashed lines, with the sum of these arsenals as the line at the top of the Figure terminating in an arrowhead. The data are from Frank Barnaby in the special issue of *Ambio* cited in footnote 7, pp. 76–83. See also *Counterforce Issues for the US Strategic Nuclear Forces*, Congressional Budget Office, January 1978.

Figure 2 shows three regions: an upper region in which the nuclear winter could almost certainly be triggered; a lower region at which it could not be triggered; and a transition zone, shown shaded. The boundaries of this transition zone are more uncertain than shown, and depend among other things on targeting strategy. But the threshold probably lies between several hundred and a few thousand contemporary strategic weapons.

warheads). At the present time the disparity is less than it has been in any year since 1955. A published extrapolation of the present strategic arsenals into 1985 is shown as dashed, nearly vertical lines, accommodating new US (Pershing II, Cruise MX and Trident) and Soviet (SS–21,–22,–23) strategic systems. If these extrapolations are valid, the United States and the Soviet Union would have almost identical numbers of inventories by the late 1980s.

The uppermost (dash-dot) curve in Figure 2 shows the total US and Soviet arsenals (essentially the world arsenals) climbing upward since about 1970 with a very steep slope, the slope steepening still more if the projection is valid. Such exponential or near-exponential runaways are expected in arms races where each side's rate of growth is proportional to its perception of the adversary's weapons inventory; but it is likewise clear that such rapid growth cannot continue indefinitely. In all natural and human systems, such steep growth rates are eventually stopped, often catastrophically.

It is widely agreed—although different people have different justifications for this conclusion—that world arsenals must be reduced significantly. There is also general agreement, with a few demurrers, that at least the early and middle stages of a significant decline can be verified by national technical means and other procedures. The first stage of major arms reduction will have to overcome a new source of reluctance, when almost all silos could be reliably destroyed in a sub-threshold first strike. To overcome this reluctance, both sides will have prudently maintained an invulnerable retaliatory force, which itself would later move to sub-threshold levels. (It would even be advantageous to each nation to provide certain assistance in the development of such a force by the other.)

As arsenals are reduced still further, the fine tuning of the continuing decline may have to be worked out very carefully and with additional safeguards to guarantee continuing rough strategic parity. As threshold inventories are approached, some verifiable upper limits on yields as well as numbers would have to be worked out, to minimize the burning of cities if a nuclear conflict erupted. On the other hand, the deceleration of the arms race would have an inertia of its own, as the acceleration does; and successful first steps would create a climate conducive to subsequent steps.

There are three proposals now prominently discussed in the United States: Nuclear Freeze, Build-Down, and Deep Cuts. Their possible effects are diagrammed in Figure 2. They are by no means mutually exclusive, nor do they exhaust the possible approaches. A negotiated Freeze would at least prevent the continuing upward escalation in stockpiles, would forestall the deployment of more destabilizing systems, and would probably be accompanied by agreement on immediate annual phased reductions (the curved lines in the middle to late 1980s in Figure 2). To reduce the perceived temptation for a first strike, de-MIRVing of missiles during arms reduction may be essential.

The most commonly cited method of following the Freeze with reductions is incorporated in the Kennedy-Hatfield Freeze Resolution: percentage reductions. Under this approach, the two sides would agree on a percentage—often quoted as being between five per cent and ten per cent—and would agree to decrease deployed warheads by that percentage annually. The percentage reduction method was proposed to the Soviet Union by the United States at the Vienna Summit in June 1979 and was to be applied to the limits and sub-limits of the SALT II accords until these reached a reduction of 50 per cent.

The Build-Down proposal is one in which modernization is permitted, but each side must pay a price in additional reductions of warheads for each warhead mounted on a modernized missile. In many current versions of the proposal, it would also require both sides to decrease their total warhead inventories by about five per cent a year (again, the percentage annual reduction approach), to ensure that at least some reductions would take place even if modernization did not. The rate of decline for Build-Down illustrated in Figure 2 is essentially that of Representative Albert Gore (D.-Tenn.), in which rough parity at 8,500 warheads each is adopted as a goal for 1991-92, and the levels are reduced to 6,500 warheads each by 1997. [1]

There is concern that the 'modernization' of strategic systems that Build-Down encourages might open the door to still more destabilizing weapons. It is also by no means clear that all proponents of Build-Down envision further reductions below the interim goal of about 5,000 warheads each for the United States and Soviet Union. If this rate of Build-Down continued indefinitely, the two nations would not cross back below threshold until about the year 2020. As dramatic a change from the present circumstances as this represents, in light of the present global crisis, it is, I think, too leisurely a pace.

Deep Cuts, originally advocated by George Kennan and Noel Gayler [2] as an initial halving of the global arsenals in some relatively short period of time, proposes the turning in of the fission triggers of thermonuclear weapons, deployed or undeployed, to a binational of multinational authority, with the triggers subsequently gainfully consumed in nuclear power plants (the ultimate in beating swords into plowshares). A highly schematic curve for something like Deep Cuts is also shown in Figure 2, starting from Gore's assumption of parity by 1991-92. Halving of the present global arsenals would then occur around 1995, and the global arsenals would return to below the Doomsday Threshold by the year 2000.

The actual shape of these declining curves would very likely have kinks and wiggles in them to accommodate the details of a bilaterally—and eventually

[1] *Congressional Record*, August 4, 1983, Vol. 129, No. 114.

[2] George F. Kennan, *loc. cit.*, footnote 24; Noel Gayler, 'How to Break the Momentum of the Nuclear Arms Race', *The New York Times Magazine*, April 25, 1982.

multilaterally—agreed-upon plan to reduce the arsenals without compromising the security of any of the nuclear Powers. The Deep Cuts curve shown has a rate of decline only about as steep as the rate of rise beginning in 1970. Much steeper declines may be feasible and should be considered.

No one contends it will be easy to reverse the nuclear arms race. It is required at least for the same reasons that were used to justify the arms race in the first place—the national security of the United States and the Soviet Union. It is necessarily an enterprise of great magnitude. John Stuart Mill said: 'Against a great evil, a small remedy does not produce a small result. It produces no result at all.' But if the same technical ingenuity, dedication and resources were devoted to the downward slopes in Figure 2 as to the upward slopes, there is no reason to doubt that it could be negotiated safely.

In the deployment of more stabilizing weapons systems, in the possible development—especially in later stages of arms reductions—of novel means of treaty verification, and (perhaps) in the augmentation of conventional armaments, it will, of course, be expensive.

But, given the stakes, a prudent nuclear Power should be willing to spend more every year to defuse the arms race and prevent nuclear war than it does on all military preparedness. For comparison, in the United States the annual budget of the Department of Defense is about 10,000 times that of the Arms Control and Disarmament Agency, quite apart from any questions about the dedication and effectiveness of the ACDA. The equivalent disparity is even greater in many other nations. I believe that the technical side of guaranteeing a major multilateral and strategically secure global arms reduction can be devised and deployed for considerably less—perhaps even a factor of 100 less—than the planet's direct military expenditures of $540 billion per year. [1]

Such figures give some feeling for the chasm that separates a prudent policy in face of our present knowledge of nuclear war from the actual present policies of the nuclear Powers. Likewise, nations far removed from the conflict, even nations with little or no investment in the quarrels among the nuclear Powers, stand to be destroyed in a nuclear war, rather than benefiting from the mutual annihilation of the super-Powers. They too, one might think, would be wise to devote considerable resources to help ensure that nuclear war does not break out.

VII

In summary, cold, dark, radioactivity, pyrotoxins and ultraviolet light following a nuclear war—including some scenarios involving only a small

[1] Ruth Leger Sivard, *World Military and Social Expenditures*, Leesburg (Va.): World Priorities, 1983.

fraction of the world strategic arsenals—would imperil every survivor on the planet. There is a real danger of the extinction of humanity. A threshold exists at which the climatic catastrophe could be triggered, very roughly around 500–2,000 strategic warheads. A major first strike may be an act of national suicide, even if no retaliation occurs. Given the magnitude of the potential loss, no policy declarations and no mechanical safeguards can adequately guarantee the safety of the human species. No national rivalry or ideological confrontation justifies putting the species at risk. Accordingly, there is a critical need for safe and verifiable reductions of the world strategic inventories to below threshold. At such levels, still adequate for deterrence, at least the worst could not happen should a nuclear war break out.

National security policies that seem prudent or even successful during a term of office or a tour of duty may work to endanger national—and global—security over longer periods of time. In many respects it is just such short-term thinking that is responsible for the present world crisis. The looming prospect of the climatic catastrophe makes short-term thinking even more dangerous. The past has been the enemy of the present, and the present the enemy of the future.

The problem cries out for an ecumenical perspective that rises above cant, doctrine and mutual recrimination, however apparently justified, and that at least partly transcends parochial fealties in time and space. What is urgently required is a coherent, mutually agreed upon, long-term policy for dramatic reductions in nuclear armaments, and a deep commitment, embracing decades, to carry it out.

Our talent, while imperfect, to foresee the future consequences of our present actions and to change our course appropriately is a hallmark of the human species, and one of the chief reasons for our success over the past million years. Our future depends entirely on how quickly and how broadly we can refine this talent. We should plan for and cherish our fragile world as we do our children and our grandchildren: there will be no other place for them to live. It is nowhere ordained that we must remain in bondage to nuclear weapons.

An Addendum

CARL SAGAN

For the foreseeable future, horizontal proliferation does not seem to increase much the dangers of nuclear winter. It seems very unlikely that anyone can produce major nuclear winter effects with, for example, a dozen nuclear warheads—even with perfect delivery systems and the *intent* to produce nuclear winter. But vertical proliferation is quite another story: here we have the extraordinary circumstance that the United States and the Soviet Union each have arsenals that are many times, perhaps many tens of times, more than seems adequate to generate at least a hemisphere-wide climatic catastrophe (Figure 2).

As the delegate from China properly pointed out at this meeting, the responsibilities placed on the adhering non-nuclear-weapon States by the Non-Proliferation Treaty are very specific, while the responsibilities of the adhering States that have nuclear weapons are much more vague. Nevertheless, the requirements on the nuclear-weapon States are sufficiently explicit as to make it clear that the United States and the Soviet Union are in flagrant non-compliance with Article VI of this Treaty, which they have solemnly signed and ratified. We hear complaints about non-compliance with treaty obligations on telemetry encoding, and environmental tents, and phased array radars—some of which are disputes about ambiguously phrased provisions in unratified treaties. But we do not hear anything from the United States and the Soviet Union about their most ominous violation of Article VI of the Non-Proliferation Treaty.

If the United States and the Soviet Union had fulfilled their obligation in the late 1960s and made massive reductions in their strategic arsenals, consider how much easier it would have been to bring the stockpiles below the rough threshold for nuclear winter (Figure 2). Instead, since the Treaty's ratification, more than 10,000 strategic weapons have been added to these grotesque arsenals—enough to destroy our global civilization surely, and possibly everyone on the planet.

Because of the connection between vertical and horizontal proliferation, because of the increased danger of nuclear war with so many weapons so widely distributed, and because of the prospect of nuclear winter, all nations—but especially the United States and the Soviet Union—would be well served if the so-called super-Powers reversed their history of systematic and sustained violation of the Non-Proliferation Treaty and got down to the urgent business of massively reducing the stockpiles of strategic weapons.

TABLE 1

Nuclear exchange scenarios

Case	Total Yield (MT)	% Yield Surface Bursts	% Yield Urban or Industrial Targets	Warhead Yield Range (MT)	Total Number of Explosions
1. Baseline Case, countervalue and counterforce[a]	5,000	57	20	0.1–10	10,400
11. 3,000 MT nominal, counterforce only[b]	3,000	50	0	1–10	2,250
14. 100 MT nominal, countervalue only[c]	100	0	100	0.1	1,000
16. 5000 MT 'severe,' counterforce only[b,d]	5,000	100	0	5–10	700
17. 10,000 MT 'severe,' countervalue and counterforce[c,d]	10,000	63	15	0.1–10	16,160

[a] In the Baseline Case, 12,000 square kilometers of inner cities are burned; on every square centimeter an average of 10 grams of combustibles are burned, and 1.1% of the burned material rises as smoke. Also, 230,000 square kilometers of suburban areas burn, with 1.5 grams consumed at each square centimeter and 3.6% rising as smoke.

[b] In this highly conservative case, it is assumed that no smoke emission occurs, that not a blade of grass is burned. Only 25,000 tons of the fine dust is raised into the upper atmosphere for every megaton exploded.

[c] In contrast to the Baseline Case, only inner cities burn, with 10 grams per square centimeter consumed and 3.3% rising as smoke into the high atmosphere.

[d] Here, the fine (submicron) dust raised into the upper atmosphere is 150,000 tons per megaton exploded.

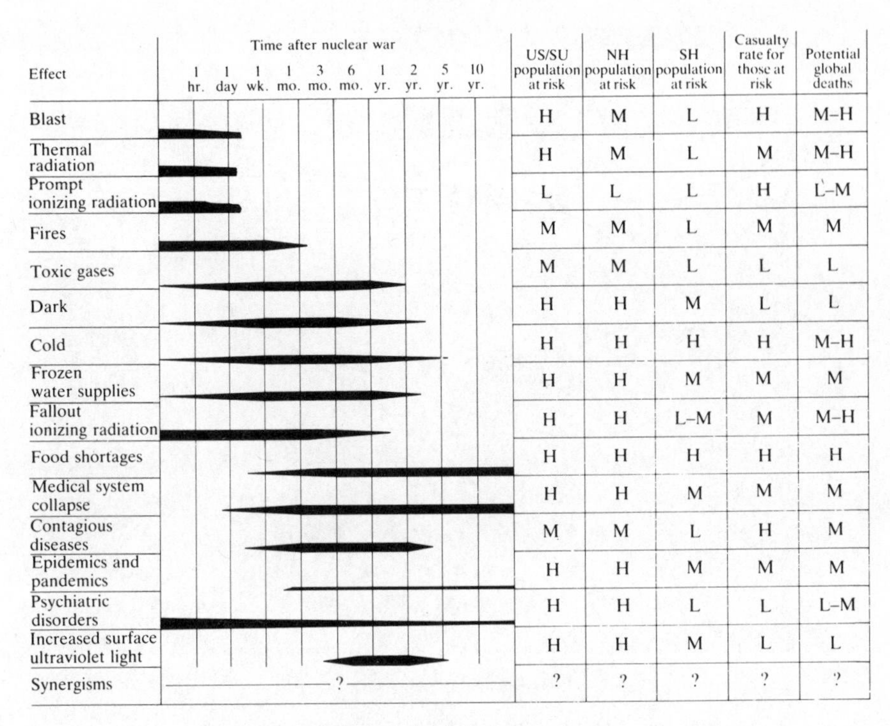

Effect	US/SU population at risk	NH population at risk	SH population at risk	Casualty rate for those at risk	Potential global deaths
Blast	H	M	L	H	M–H
Thermal radiation	H	M	L	M	M–H
Prompt ionizing radiation	L	L	L	H	L–M
Fires	M	M	L	M	M
Toxic gases	M	M	L	L	L
Dark	H	H	M	L	L
Cold	H	H	H	H	M–H
Frozen water supplies	H	H	M	M	M
Fallout ionizing radiation	H	H	L–M	M	M–H
Food shortages	H	H	H	H	H
Medical system collapse	H	H	M	M	M
Contagious diseases	M	M	L	H	M
Epidemics and pandemics	H	H	M	M	M
Psychiatric disorders	H	H	L	L	L–M
Increased surface ultraviolet light	H	H	M	L	L
Synergisms	?	?	?	?	?

Table 2. Effects of the baseline nuclear war

Note: This is a schematic representation of the time scale for the effects, which are most severe when the thickness of the horizontal bar is greatest. The columns at the right indicate the degree of risk of the populations of the United States and the Soviet Union, the Northern Hemisphere, and the Southern Hemisphere—with H, M, and L standing for High, Medium, and Low respectively.

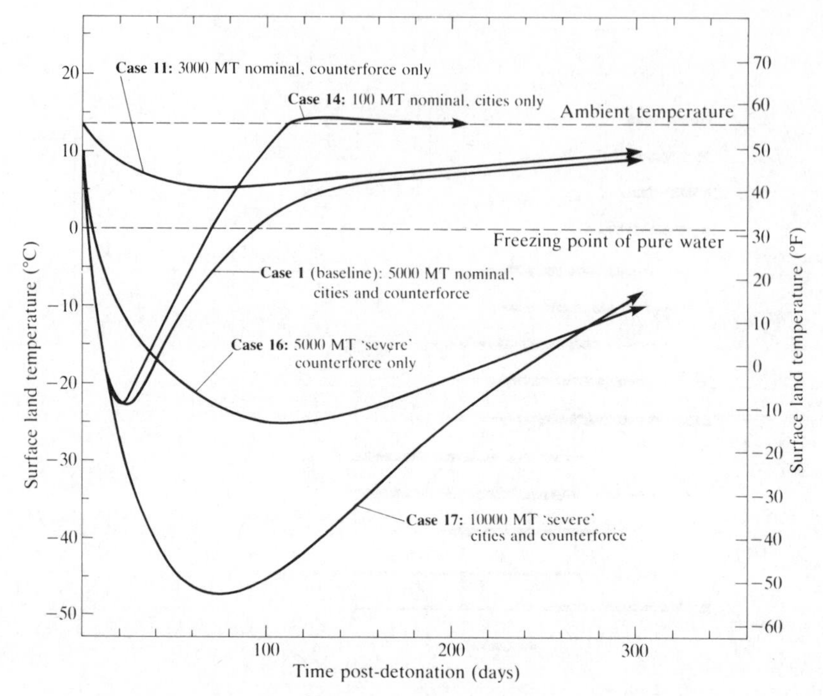

Figure 1. Temperature effects of nuclear war cases

Note. In this Figure, the average temperature of Northern Hemisphere land areas (away from coastlines) is shown varying with time after the five Cases of nuclear war defined in Table 1. The 'ambient' temperature is the average in the Northern Hemisphere over all latitudes and seasons: thus, normal winter temperatures at north temperature latitudes are lower than is shown, and normal tropical temperatures are higher than shown. Cases described as 'nominal' assume the most likely values of parameters (such as dust particle size or the frequency of firestorms) that are imperfectly known. Cases marked 'severe' represent adverse but not implausible values of these parameters. In Case 14 the curve ends when the temperatures come within a degree of the ambient values. For the four other Cases the curves are shown ending after 300 days, but this is simply because the calculations were not extended further. In these four Cases the curves will continue to the directions they are headed.

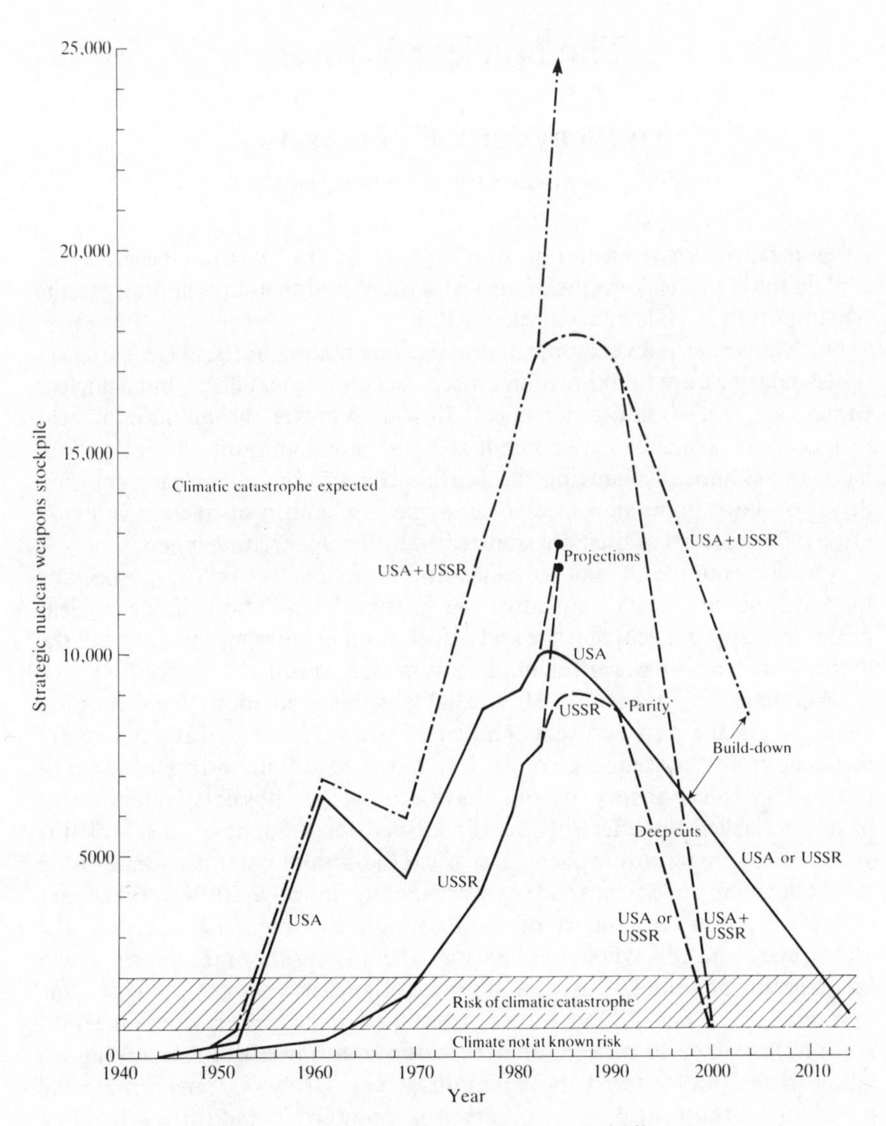

Figure 2. Past and future nuclear stockpiles

The Nuclear Winter

DR. YEVGENY P. VELIKHOV

Deputy Director, Academy of Sciences of the USSR

After the brilliant presentation of Professor Sagan, it is not necessary to explain more of the concepts of nuclear winter. I address myself firstly to the two important problems connected with it.

Nuclear winter is an example of possible secondary effects, and if we speak of secondary we are thinking of small-scale second-order effects, but a nuclear winter is not a second-order effect. If you calculate the amount of heat produced by a nuclear explosion, it is a very small amount which does not have any chance of changing the Earth's climate, but a nuclear explosion drives or starts some new mechanism—the mechanism of nuclear winter—after 100 megatons of dust are transferred to the upper atmosphere.

Another example of such amplification is radioactive fall-out, especially long-life radioactive fall-out after the possible elimination of the nuclear power industry, nuclear storage and distribution of storage waste around the globe. This is a very powerful amplification mechanism.

Of course, the question is: 'How reliable is this prediction?' This question has arisen in the past two years and stems from the circle of those who are sceptical of any consequence of nuclear war. First of all, in this criticism of the nuclear winter theory, we only have examples of possible factors which have diminished the effect of fire, diminished the amount of dust which is going to the upper atmosphere. But if we look more carefully—and in the USSR Academy of Science today we are looking more carefully at the theory of fire formation, the theory of mainly non-linear interaction between the atmosphere and this whole mechanism—there is another mechanism which increases the amount of dust and the effect of nuclear winter. I will give some examples: pyrolysis—wood in the forest and in towns. If you take into account just 30 or 40 per cent of all the enormous power of nuclear weapons going to the photons and these photons cause pyrolysis, transforming the wood into carbon substance; if afterwards a powerful wind turns this into a fireball and the fireball transfers this to the upper atmosphere, it is possible to calculate that perhaps the same amount of dust is being caused by such a mechanism, in addition to the simple fires.

Another example: in all calculations one very important question is the question of the ocean's influence. The ocean is a very large heat source—heat storage in 100 metres of ocean water. But after the development of a nuclear winter it is very probable that there will be another development of very powerful winds between ocean and continents, because of big differences in temperature and the density of the air above the continents and oceans. This wind produces great turbulence and mixes the ocean waters. As the mixture is quite high, quite fast, the very cool deep ocean waters with 4 centigrade temperatures move up and have a considerable cooling effect.

There are many other problems which it is necessary to discuss in connection with the development of all nuclear winter theories. Of course, the best way to address the problem is to carry out experiments. Already all the experiments which we carry out are done with 10 to 11 joules per second which means quite a large amount of power: all the fires of the last war and historical fires. But if you calculate the requirement for the scale of this experiment, it may be 100 kilotons, not less, in order to have some chance of being representative. I personally like large-scale experiments, but this is very big and in our Academy we are now discussing how to proceed. One problem is not only the scale of the experiment but the probability of having really representative results. Such very big experiments cost tens of millions of dollars and may not be enough to answer all questions, but we must be sure of all the consequences of a nuclear winter.

We are coming to the principal question: it is very difficult in a nuclear age to have exact knowledge of many consequences of our action because of the scale of impact; we only have probabilities. However, in such cases, the problem is not of probability, but how to evaluate productive probability. What is at stake is life on this planet. This so-called 'mathematical expectancy' really is enormously big, much bigger than we can live with. This is the principal question that is not only connected with the nuclear winter, but with many other aspects of the strategic and other doctrines of the nuclear age. For example, all doctrines of limited nuclear war, counter-force theories or prevailing nuclear war, controlled nuclear war, are always connected with this major question. In the early 1950s and 1960s people tried to solve it with a simple calculator, for example, the Rand Corporation bomb-damage effect calculator. Today, with a very sophisticated machine, there is no improvement because really it is not a problem of mathematical simulation, it is a problem of experience. In the old type of war, as you know from Clausewitz's theory, it was the friction of war which changed all the plans. Today it is not friction, it is large-scale turbulence which completely changes the results and we have no chance of knowing exactly what happens after any large-scale disturbance and crisis.

Another example is the so-called 'space-based anti-ballistic missile system', the Strategic Defense system. If we have some chance of proceeding along a difficult and dangerous path and succeeding—which is very questionable—in building such a shield, such an astro-dome around, for example, the United States, how do we test this extremely complicated system? The only possible test is the real test, but there you have the same problem of expected failure.

If probability of fall-out is minus 4, the value is infinite. In such a case there is no real possibility of just testing the system. I am not stating that it is impossible to build it, but that we have no way of testing it. Such a case, I think, is not very new for mankind.

Since the beginning of this century we have met this problem in Heisenberg—a relation of uncertainty. If you try to measure the position of an electron in an atom, if you have a chance to measure this position, you destroy the atom and this is the core of the uncertainty principle. Today we have the same principle of uncertainty in the nuclear age. We cannot know exactly what really happens in such very complicated systems, and what is the real consequence of the nuclear age. If we have knowledge, it is probable that we have no people, if we have people we have no knowledge. This is a fundamental question, and there is only one answer—it is necessary to get out of nuclear weapons. But how? It is not a very difficult problem, although the way is not easy because for 40 years we have not succeeded, we have only continuously built up this arsenal. If we are going to reach a state of equilibrium and follow a stable path, step by step, I see no problem because of the common wisdom of mankind. Nevertheless, today there are real obstacles in the way and the most terrible is this open conspiracy of the so-called 'Strategic Defense Initiative' against the anti-ballistic missile strategy. It is conspiracy, as in criminal law, because it is action directed against the Anti-Ballistic Missile Treaty of 1972; it is the real fundamental obstacle in the path of nuclear disarmament. The only way for survival is disarmament. Building an impenetrable shield is first of all a very unstabilizing and hopeless way, it is not the way to disarmament but the way to increased rearmament.

What is the reason for such erroneous development? Of course the simplest explanation today, which I believe is another misleading and wrong explanation, is the so-called theory of 'symmetrical responsibility' of most so-called 'super-Powers'.

The USSR has no fundamental interest in the increase of tension because we have no sizeable foreign market. We are not too dependent on foreign trade. We are completely self-sufficient in energy and mineral sources, and nobody is hurt very much if there is some foreign trade problem. Principally, the USSR has no real interest in increasing tension. Cannon, speaking of this relation said: 'There is no issue in this State which can ever justify resort to nuclear weapons'. Speaking as a political scientist and a physicist, I ask myself what is the driving force today for this situation of high tension and disruption of the arms talks and arms control process? I have only a simple zero-order magnitude answer, but it is this: after the Second World War, the United States twice embarked on the solution of a cold war. What is the reason for this? My feeling is that there is only one, the possible loss of global dominance, not only in the military sense but in the economic sense. If the

United States lost its dominance in the economic sense, not compared with the USSR, but with Japan, Europe, and the Third World, there is only one solution for big businesses: resort to higher tension. There is one reason and driving force—maybe not only one, but an important reason—to drive the situation to confrontation; the United States has organized the weapons market, organized the necessity for other countries—Europe and Japan ask for military support in times of high tension—and this reason, and I think only this reason, causes the second cold war and the so-called 'Strategic Defense Initiative' aimed in this direction.

My conclusion is this. We live, of course, in a very dangerous and critical period, we have no technological escape from the terrible reality of the nuclear age. There is only one real way to disarmament, but it is necessary to face reality and take a most important step on the way to survival.

Session III Debate

Sheila Oakes

I wonder whether His Royal Highness would be so kind as to spell out some way that it might be possible to start this process of not necessarily a zone of peace in the Middle East, but at least a nuclear-weapon-free zone.

Crown Prince Hassan bin Talal

I thank you for your very demanding question, which has puzzled and perplexed superior intellects to mine. I think that the problem of spelling out the concept of a nuclear-free zone is of course assailed by the fact that we are speaking of the Middle East, and you will have noticed that I made reference earlier to the Near and the Middle East. We are speaking consequently of at least three hot-spots in the region. With the completion of the lateral oil pipelines from the Gulf to the Red Sea and the export of two-thirds of what formerly went through the Straits of Hormuz, there is an inter-related Eastern Mediterranean–Red Sea Theatre. Secondly, we are of course speaking of the context of the Gulf war and the fact that the Gulf, with its resources, represents a form of Arab Ruhr Valley. The separation of the resources of the Gulf from the political and human aspirations of the people who neighbour Arab oil in its hinterland is one of the greatest challenges that the Arab and Muslim peoples face, and consequently the concerns over the ongoing Gulf conflict do extend to a considerable degree of worry over the future of super-Power relations in that region.

I would like to say that, as far as the Indian Ocean and the Arabian Sea are concerned, the Brezhnev doctrine called for a generalized peace zone in that area. However—and I think that the point should be made in context—with the exception of United Nations mediation, inasmuch as Mr. Palme reflects the will of the Security Council, there has been very little comment by other Security Council members as to the possible ways of ending that particular conflict, which in terms of certain surface-to-surface missiles could evolve into the nuclear option missiles which already exist in the region. I think that the possibility of evolving a nuclear-free zone, or indeed a conflict-free zone, in that area is directly thwarted by the absence of any apparent desire to engage in discussion over this war in its fifth year and the feeling one gets that somehow the Gulf will fall into two units, the southern Gulf States and possibly the northern Gulf States.

The third area of potential conflict, of course, is the South Asian context, and as I believe Professors Abdus Salam and Subrahmanyam have already given this subject adequate venting, I don't feel that I should comment on it further. But it is my feeling as someone coming from the region that, unless we use platforms such as this to emphasize politics where people matter and to de-emphasize politics where strategic concerns alone matter, it is going to be very difficult for the issue of war and peace to be discussed with adequate commitment by the Powers that represent the nuclear club.

I am sorry if I have offered more questions than answers to your extremely demanding question, but I would just like to say that we can only live in hope and attempt through abiding by conventions, through participating in independent thought-exercises such as this, to come closer to universal truth.

Simon Henderson

In the war with Iran, Iraq has broken its commitment to the banning of chemical weapons. Under this sort of circumstance what chance has the NPT?

Crown Prince Hassan bin Talal

I believe that the extremely outrageous use of weapons of war on both sides in the Gulf conflict make the chances of NPT, conflict-free zones or nuclear-free zones being implemented in the region very slim. I would like to say, however, that the sovereign States to which I referred, including Iraq and Iran, have abided by conventions. To mix the two issues for the purposes of press coverage of this meeting and to put me on the spot with a question of this nature is of course a welcome opportunity for the *Financial Times*, but I would like to point out that in terms of outrage and outrageous use of weapons, the recent spiral of violence, including terrorist hijackings, genocide of one form or another, either in the Gulf war or the Eastern Mediterranean, by whatever use of weapons, makes the whole NPT issue in terms of people in the region pale into insignificance. I would say that coming to a meeting such as this probably means quite a lot if I put a foot wrong in terms of press sensation in the Western world, but it does not mean terribly much in terms of the general public in the region of which we speak. I think that the general feeling of helplessness is directly related to the fact that international mediators in the context of the Iraq–Iran war have looked at maritime issues, have looked at the economic significance of the Gulf, have looked at ways and means of securing oil, whether from source or at outlets—new outlets such as the Red Sea—but have not considered the Gulf in human terms. I would like to say to the gentlemen and ladies of the media that it frustrated me a great deal to be in the United States during the week of the Falklands crisis, where we supported the British on the issue of self-determination, to find that 30,000 people were killed in one of the sporadic offensives—Iraqi or Iranian offensives—and that no mention was made of this aspect. Consequently, to wring our hands about the uses of this or that form of outrageous weaponry is all very well and I share the sentiment with you and say that there is very little hope of peace and resolution, but at the same time I would like to ask how many of you have considered these forms of conflict in terms of the damage that they are doing, not only by referring to the fact that these weapons are employed, but to the fact that a whole generation has been decimated over the past five years? I would also like to ask what degree of political will and resolve we have collectively in facing these continuing and tragic conflicts?

Mariusz Kuklinski

Do you think that the attack by a threshold country in your area on a safeguarded nuclear facility in a NPT-member country was sufficiently dealt with in terms of international law as to dissuade further infractions on the NPT from without?

Crown Prince Hassan bin Talal

I feel that the kind of initiative taken in eliminating the nuclear reactor is an extremely grave and worrying prospect for the future. I relate that point to the question asked earlier, what hope is there for NPT if States Parties are faced with this military option? I would also add that the legal aspect in terms of dealing with the problem—and I referred to code of conduct earlier—is effectively not an aspect taken terribly seriously by countries in the region. In terms of the possession of nuclear weapons, countries that have been subjected to attacks of this nature are not likely soon to possess nuclear weapons. However, to the extent that we perceive an unending threat by more technologically advanced countries, I do feel that this continuing menace will not lightly relinquish the monopoly on nuclear weapons in the region. I think that the offer of the nuclear weapon first-strike capability is one that we should speak about seriously, although in reference to this particular strike on the nuclear reactor it was a conventional method. Here I would like to say that little is known about Israeli tests of its nuclear weapons. However, one report has it that United States satellites did pick up one test, probably held in co-operation with South Africa, over the South Atlantic in 1979. My sources here are articles in the *Washington Quarterly* in the summer of 1980 and in *Aerospace and Defense Daily* in May 1985. However, deployment of the missile has been under way for some time. I am not digressing from the question, but I would like to say that it will not only be through the use of conventional weapons that such an attack could take place; it could be through the use of near-nuclear weapons, and it certainly could be through further use of SSMs which are currently in use in the conflict between Iran and Iraq.

Paul Sieghart

Among the dangerous scenarios which His Royal Highness outlined in his, if I may so, immensely informative and very peaceful and peace-seeking talk, it seems to me that far and away the most dangerous one arises if the only nation in that region which has the technical capability to construct a nuclear weapon is at the same time in such a state of anxiety and fear, not only of having its back to the wall, but of being literally driven into the sea, that it may feel that it needs to resort to the use of such a weapon as a weapon of ultimate last resort, in order to preserve its very existence. The fear is not entirely irrational, because it is constantly fed by the less responsible statesmen in the Muslim world who do speak of driving that particular people into the sea, and one has to remember that it is a people which over the centuries has been much persecuted, not in fact by Muslims but very largely by Christians. So far as I know, only one of its Muslim neighbour States has so far formally recognized its existence and said out loud that it is willing to live at peace with it. Does His Royal Highness see any prospect of any of that country's other Muslim neighbour States following that example?

Crown Prince Hassan bin Talal

I would just like to say that we are currently engaged in an extensive dialogue with the United States Administration, and to a very large extent with the interested but rather more lethargic United States Congress, on the subject of upping the priority of the Middle East conflict. As we understand it, in terms of super-Power discussions of late, the nuclear issue, international terrorism, the question of Afghanistan, and subsequently the question of the Middle East, have been the order of priority.

I don't know how familiar you are with His Majesty King Hussein's initiative of 11 February, taken jointly with the PLO leadership, to move closer to a dialogue with the United States, which hopefully in the months to come could lead us to a first step towards a wider peace process. In terms of this desire, I would like to remind you of the fact that we live in an extremely pivotal situation, and I say we—the Jordanians and the Palestinians—because in a sense we are caught between extremes of both sides. Consequently, that sense of beleaguerment is not limited to Israel in the traditional context.

I would like to say with reference to beleaguerment and nuclear capability that in *Time* magazine of 12 April, 1976, in a story entitled *How Israel got the Bomb*, Israel was reported to have prepared to deploy nuclear weapons in the early stages of the October 1973 war at a time when Israeli forces were doing poorly on both fronts. In terms of the pivotal role that we are attempting to play in focussing on problems of people, in focussing on the plight of 1.3 million Palestinians in the occupied territories on the West Bank and in Gaza, we are in international terms finding lukewarm support, not so much on the part of governments, but to a very large extent on the part of the media, which I think has taken the issues—the sensational issues of the moment—very much to heart. Hijacking, for example, has covered up very conveniently the ongoing genocide in the Palestinian refugee camps in Lebanon. It is the only new story today and presumably if we commit political suicide by entering—as is envisaged by some liberal-minded citizens—into direct negotiations without any preamble or infrastructure, this would also be the sensation of the moment, but would it achieve peace? Peacemaking is an extremely intricate and difficult task if we are not only speaking of an event but of a lasting solution. As far as Jordan is concerned, and I feel that as far as many countries in the Arab world are concerned, the desire for peace is there, but the problem is, given those three regional hot-spots, given the fact that we are kept occupied every possible waking hour, that it is extremely difficult to envisage moving towards developing political centrism, not only on the part of the Arab countries but also in Israel itself.

Gwyn Prins

You have spoken with feeling and some implied pessimism about curbing the commercial drives within the arms-manufacturing nations. The Middle East has the largest single concentration of arms purchasing power outside the super-Powers. Can you conceive of that power being used to impose conditionality in a sellers' market as one way in which the Middle Eastern States could act to promote the arms conversion which you advocated?

Crown Prince Hassan bin Talal

In terms of the moral imperative being exercised by the sellers' market, I could only wish that this could apply, and I am speaking here as a non-nuclear, non-oil-producing Jordanian. Our country tries to produce manpower, trained manpower, and I hope constructive and possibly controversial thought. I would like to point out that the meeting I am going to next is with the Director-General of the International Labour Organisation to talk about complementarities between oil-producing countries and their neighbours in terms of the enormous question marks that we have in mind over the future of the hinterland that surrounds the oil-producing region and includes countries such as Sudan, where I am told that over 4 million children are threatened with extinction in the coming six weeks if something is not done to provide aircraft to move supplies from A to B. I do know that the petrodollars, the Arab dollars of our region, represent a significant source of support to the budget of the United States, for example, as indeed they represent a sizeable and voluminous exchange with many of the countries of Europe, but in terms of the conditionality and in terms of the moral imperative of focussing on regional issues, it seems that that factor on its own is not enough. We are not yet demanding constituents from within the American scene and it seems that we have not yet got our priorities clearly defined. Consequently, I would say that, in terms of the purchase of hardware, the relatively little emphasis on software that should accompany it, the relatively little emphasis on building up local management and regional management capabilities and consequently affecting the transfer of our technology, even in the most modest of beginnings, all of this does emphasize to us the fact that the sellers' market is as much involved with the buyers' disregard for the priorities of which we speak. I do hope that in terms of the Middle East, in terms of the use of finances from the region, the less cynical view could develop, if not from within the region itself then alternatively from the financial centres, and the financial centres are basically the portfolio managers in the well-known centres of this world. But to speak collectively about a new moral imperative that would lead us effectively to turning swords into ploughshares, I think that this is a long way off.

Chairman

We have a number of questions addressed to Professor Jortner.

James Thompson

In your opinion, are Middle East conflicts territorial, religious or racist, or all three?

Joshua Jortner

Dr. Thompson is correct in alluding to Middle East conflicts in the plural. They are definitely not racist, this is an unacceptable term for the Israelis. The long history of the Jewish people and their contemporary tragic history in Europe makes any approach which rests on racial discrimination unacceptable. I trust that the Arab and Muslim countries will endorse this point of view. The religious aspects are often raised by some Muslim countries, such as Iraq recently in relation to Arab fundamentalism, and this prevailed in inter-Muslim conflicts. Regarding the Israeli–Arab conflict, both Iraq and Iran recently claimed that the road to Jerusalem, which is holy to the Arabs and of course to all three religions, passes through the other State's capital. Geography is of course on the side of Iran in this issue, but to be serious, let me hope that, with the development of the Middle East, such arguments based on religion will fade out. Territorial conflicts do exist of course in the Middle East, the Iran–Iraq conflict is one example. The Israeli–Arab conflict has territorial aspects. The only solution to territorial conflicts, in my opinion, is not military but political, and a political solution through negotiation has to be found.

Altaf Gauhar

Has Israel developed any kind of nuclear weapons?

Joshua Jortner

Let me reiterate what I said: Israel is supposed to have the technical capability to produce nuclear weapons, and it has declared that its policy has been that it will not be the first to introduce nuclear weapons into the Middle East. This approach, in conjunction with the programme for a nuclear-weapon-free zone in the Middle East, constitutes Israel's basic approach.

Chairman

I will now give the floor to Ambassador Shaker, who wants to make a brief comment on Professor Jortner's remarks concerning a nuclear-weapon-free zone in the Middle East.

Mohamed Shaker

Several references were made concerning Egypt's position on a nuclear-weapon-free zone in the Middle East and on the NPT. I would just like to say that Egypt's proposal was made in the early 1970s, at first with Iran and then separately, when Egypt presented this resolution to the General Assembly each year. I would like to explain why the formula that Professor Jortner was referring to was Egypt's choice in the draft resolution submitted to the General Assembly. The formula was that each country in the region would make a statement saying that it accepted in principle the idea of the establishment of a nuclear-weapon-free zone in the Middle East and would deposit this statement or declaration with the Security Council. As Professor Jortner rightly said, we felt that the time was not yet ripe. Most of the Arab countries would not now agree to sit at one table with Israel and discuss the creation of such a zone, as Latin American countries did in relation to the Tlatelolco Treaty. Therefore, the situation is very tense in the area, and we thought that until the time comes when everyone can sit down with each other and discuss the creation of such a zone, we ought quickly to find an interim solution, and this was by resorting to such a formula. I think that the Tlatelolco Treaty is an excellent model for future nuclear-weapon-free zones, but I don't think that the way towards such a zone should necessarily be the way that the Parties to the Tlatelolco Treaty have followed. That is why we have suggested this formula to start with.

We went further in the General Assembly this year. Egypt proposed that the Secretary-General should contact all the countries of the region to seek their views on the establishment of the zone. So we keep the matter alive and we keep the parties interested in such a zone, and therefore we expected the report of the Secretary-General this year would be a very important one which would give us some reflections on this important issue.

As far as Egypt's ratification of the NPT is concerned, Egypt in fact ratified the NPT because it was particularly encouraged by the Israeli position on our idea of a nuclear-weapon-free zone. In fact, the resolution was adopted by consensus, and therefore we were encouraged by Israel's position on our resolution. One reason why we said we would go ahead with our ratification of the NPT was that it might also encourage Israel in the long run to ratify the NPT—to follow us—because in fact Egypt was the last country—the last immediate neighbour of Israel—which had not yet ratified the NPT in 1981. We thought that this step would engender more security in the region and would maybe induce Israel some time after to think over its ratification.

If Israel ratifies the NPT, it would be a gigantic step. Professor Jortner was speaking about President Sadat's step, and I think that this step by Israel would be greatly appreciated, not only in the region, not only by its neighbours, but by the whole world. I believe that many other countries which are potential nuclear-weapon Powers would also follow suit. This tactic by Israel would engender a great sense of security, not only in the region but in the world. I think that ratification by Israel of the NPT should come soon, and it would in fact calm the worries of many countries, not only in the area but in the world, and this calming down of tension would increase security here and there.

Chairman

Thank you very much, Ambassador Shaker, for illuminating this very intricate question of zones and adherence to the Treaty in the Middle East region. Perhaps, if you would allow me and without letting this develop into an especially long debate, I will give Professor Jortner the chance of a very quick reply.

Joshua Jortner

It was really encouraging for me to hear the Egyptian Ambassador. According to another Middle Eastern term, one has to keep the momentum going. Let me say that is why it is a pity that Israel's attitude towards averting the threat of a nuclear arms race in the Middle East has not yet been put to the test. There is hope that we shall really find a credible solution and establish a nuclear-weapon-free zone.

Chairman

As far as I can see there are no further questions on the Middle East problem so questions will now be put to Professor Bergström.

Pierre Lehmann

African people have succeeded in staying alive for thousands of years before anyone from the so-called 'developed' world enquired into their health. Isn't the misery in today's Africa a result of European influence and, if so, wouldn't it be better to phase out progressively international interference in this continent?

Sune Bergström

Certainly Africa has been populated for a long time, but the point now is that Africa has one of the highest population growth rates anywhere. From the moral point of view, it is well known that unless health problems are resolved there will never be a population balance. The African population has a right to be treated properly in health matters. It would be a disaster if they were separated from world development.

Dorothy Rowe

Nuclear weapons are created because people believe that they must protect themselves from their enemies. Neither the nuclear nor the ecological problems which threaten the future of the human race can be solved unless all of us can give up having enemies.

Do you think it is possible for human beings to change so that we can live without enemies?

Sune Bergström

No, and I think the word 'peace' gives a wrong impression of political peace. I think that a peaceful world would be much more noisy than now. There would be an enormous increase in travel and discussion and possibly in personal enemies, diplomatic language would disappear and we would use abusive language in national politics, but we would not start a war.

Chairman

We now have a number of questions addressed to Professor Sagan.

Bernard Anet

It is simply a question of scientific honesty to state that nuclear winter can only be considered a potential effect. Other values of the model parameters may give other effects (from no winter up to deep freeze). Furthermore, it must be pointed out that the nuclear winter as presented is based on the apocalyptic AMBIO scenario of a full-scale exchange of 5,000 megatons.

Other less dramatic cases haven't been studied. At the moment the nuclear winter is only a speculation, which nevertheless has to be taken seriously. Would you agree with these comments?

Carl Sagan

The original nuclear winter study—the first one to do any temperature calculations—was the TTAPS calculation that I referred to earlier; TTAPS standing for Turco, Toon, Ackerman, Pollack and myself. We did some 50 different cases, different nuclear war scenarios and different variations of uncertain parameters through their plausible range and we found, of course, that if you blow up one nuclear weapon you will not produce a nuclear winter. But for a surprisingly wide range of cases we found a nuclear winter was the result.

With regard to the second comment, I am afraid that it is also equally wrong, for the same reason. As I said, there are some 50 different cases down to a 100 megaton case, which represents 0.8 per cent of the strategic arsenals. That was a hundred down-towns burned and was adequate to produce a major nuclear winter effect.

Joseph Rotblat

What is your opinion about the following version of SDI: country A attacks country B with nuclear weapons just up to the 'nuclear winter' threshold. This would make A invulnerable to a nuclear attack, without the need for space weapons, unless B commits suicide?

Carl Sagan

This is a case where the uncertainties come to our rescue. The threshold is uncertain, certainly to within a factor of two or three, and depends very much on targeting doctrine, on the mix of high-yield and low-yield weapons, air bursts and ground bursts, and targeting of cities. No one can know where the so-called 'threshold' lies to that degree of accuracy. So there is the uncertainty of calculations. This is not a problem which lends itself to experimental verification, at least not more than once, and few of us wish to perform the experiment. So for that reason alone, I think this is not something that has to be worried about too much.

Marjorie Thompson

As a result of his findings on the nuclear winter, does Dr. Sagan believe that an independent British deterrent serves any useful purpose or could an initiative taken by Britain to rid itself of its nuclear arsenal start to turn the curve (as shown in his chart)?

Has Dr. Sagan been able to see any change in NATO or Warsaw Pact strategies as a consequence of the new knowledge of nuclear winter? For instance, a change in the strategies of air-land battle or deep strike?

Carl Sagan

How shall I answer this? When we were first producing the original nuclear winter findings it was clear that there was something very serious here, even for small nuclear wars. I thought that I saw a range of policy implications, some of which I mentioned today, and so we were able to call a small private meeting of experts in the field—senior practitioners of the dark arts—in Washington and I submitted the scientific results. I presented what I imagined were the policy implications and one senior practitioner responded as follows: 'Look, if you think that the mere prospect of the end of the world is enough to change thinking in Washington and Moscow, you clearly have not spent any time in those places.' By that standard, we maybe have made some progress, certainly high levels in the American and Soviet Governments have acknowledged at least the possibility of nuclear winter, but I cannot say that I have yet seen any change in policy strategy tactics or doctrine from either of the so-called nuclear super-Powers in response to nuclear winter. Maybe we shouldn't be too impatient, the stakes are, however, high.

Anne Rhoads

If some form of space 'defence' eventually does prove possible and was deployed, could the destruction of intercontinental nuclear missiles in flight touch off a nuclear winter? What about the destruction of Cruise or other low-flying missiles carrying nuclear charges?

Carl Sagan

The answer to the first question is 'No'. The problem is fundamentally the following: if a nuclear weapon is exploded at high altitude, whether it detonates its nuclear charge or not, the burning of the ground, the digging out of a crater and the injection of the fine particles into the atmosphere tend not to happen. There may be distribution of radioactivity, which of course would be dangerous, but nuclear winter requires the explosion to be relatively near the ground.

Mycle Schneider

Could the destruction of a big number of nuclear power plants in the event of a conventional world-wide military conflict create effects of a nuclear winter, or what would be the impact?

Carl Sagan

This is a similar question. The destruction of a nuclear power plant does not put disproportionate amounts of fine particles into the atmosphere, thus it does not disproportionately create nuclear winter. What it does do is to put large amounts of radioactivity into the atmosphere and that can be extremely dangerous. Academician Velikhov alluded, I think, to some work of Joe

Knox at Livermore Laboratory, in which he calculated what would happen if nuclear fuel reprocessing plants and power reactors were targeted world-wide, and his conclusion was that a simply colossal dose of radioactivity would be spread all over the planet. I happen to know that Joseph Rotblat does not believe it, but that is Knox's conclusion. There is a debate on this issue.

Joseph Rotblat

It is not Knox's conclusion. It will be increased by about a factor of three—the intermediate and long-term fall-out; it will not affect the local fall-out.

Carl Sagan

I wasn't talking about local fall-out. I was talking about intermediate and long-term fall-out, but there Knox calculates we get up to hundreds of rads and so that is close to the mean lethal dose for humans.

David Lowry

Is it possible to trigger the nuclear winter by pulverization of the northern hemisphere coal and oil stockpiles by conventional weapons in a strategic attack or by a small number of tactical nuclear weapons or back-pack nuclear devices?

Carl Sagan

I don't know that any detailed studies have been done on this. I do know of some studies on the possibility that coal seams would be pulverized by the usual sort of nuclear war, and the tentative conclusion was that this was not the best way of making nuclear winter if you were intent on making nuclear winter. As far as the difference between conventional and nuclear weapons in generating nuclear winter is concerned, nuclear weapons do two things that conventional weapons don't: one is that the energy is so large that the fine particles are put very high up into the atmosphere; the second is that it is the most likely means by which large numbers of cities would be simultaneously burnt, but in principle, in a mad planet, it would be possible to imagine burning hundreds of cities simultaneously by conventional means, which would have some comparable effect. I think this is one of the few things that we don't have to worry about.

Chairman

There are a number of questions for Professor Velikhov.

Yevgeny Velikhov

First of all, I will start with the same question which was addressed to us by Ms. Rhoads concerning some form of space defence. It is very difficult to build a complete space defence against nuclear weapons, because it has to be an invulnerable 99.99 per cent efficient system. We are going through a stage in which it is possible to build inefficient, vulnerable and very dangerous space defence. This is just part of the first strike because, if you have a small number of space stations, it is not enough to stop an unpredictable nuclear attack, but theoretically it is possible to make a concentration of the battle station just after the first strike. We are going through a very dangerous and very destabilizing stage and it involves all the consequences connected with nuclear winter.

Robert Betchov

Konstantin Tsiolkowsky, father of the space age, predicted in a book for young people that by the year 2017 the planet would be ruled by a single federal authority, able to control all problems, except for the ever-increasing population. Would you like to comment?

Yevgeny Velikhov

I prefer the reverse, to control population but not to control all other problems!

In reply to Dr. Rowe's question on whether human beings can live without enemies, which was also addressed to Professor Bergström, I am not a philosopher and don't know whether it is possible or not, but I think the general solution is that today we have only one important enemy—nuclear weapons. If all of us understood this and subjected all other problems to this one, it would give some chance for survival.

Altaf Gauhar

Knowing that Israel has the technical capability to develop nuclear weapons, knowing also that it is Israel's declared policy not to introduce nuclear weapons in the Middle East, would you say that Israel does not possess any kind of nuclear weapon at present?

Yevgeny Velikhov

I have some suspicion, but I have no real knowledge.

Paul Sieghart

Do you agree that a few hundred warheads are enough for either the United States or the USSR to inflict unacceptable damage on the other? If so, could not either of them unilaterally reduce its arsenal by, say, 90 per cent, without suffering any disadvantage? Would the USSR be willing to take the lead?

Yevgeny Velikhov

It is a very complex question. From our historical experience, the United States only started to talk with us after we had achieved some sort of equilibrium with it. From the point of view of the 90 per cent without any disadvantage, maybe it is too much, but maybe 'Yes'. It is a much more complex question than I can answer straightaway. I would require some time for reflection.

Carl Sagan

I would like to say something about that 90 per cent unilateral reduction question. Clearly, it would be better if the United States and the Soviet Union by treaty divested themselves of nuclear weapons than if it was done unilaterally. Unilateral moves run political risks; unilateral arms reductions are vulnerable to claims that the nation making the reduction is weak. The reason is that we have not heeded Einstein's warning that nuclear weapons have changed everything except our way of thinking. We persist in pre-1945 thinking that the more nuclear weapons you have, the safer you are. In the United States, it is always easier for a politician to be re-elected on the grounds that he or she will make the country stronger by building up more weapons than by saying that there are simply an obscene number of nuclear weapons in the arsenals both of the United States and the Soviet Union and that the only rational move is to reduce them. But from my own point of view, it is desirable to do it either way and it is possible to imagine a succession of non-negotiated unilateral actions in which the United States and the Soviet Union in effect have a major divestment of nuclear weapons. For example, in 1963, just such a thing happened in the preliminaries leading to the limited test ban treaty. After some informal consultations via intermediaries between President Kennedy and Premier Khruschev, the President of the United States announced in his American university speech that the United States was henceforth ceasing above-ground nuclear tests. A few days later, I think maybe one day later, the text of the President's speech appeared in both *Pravda* and *Izvestia*, and within the week Premier Khruschev announced that the Soviet Union was unilaterally stopping its above-ground nuclear testing provided the United States did the same and a *de facto* treaty was in existence. Ambassador Harriman was then despatched to Moscow after consultations to negotiate a *de jure* treaty. He was greeted by a reporter from *Tass* who said that, considering the difficulty of the negotiations, did Ambassador Harriman not imagine that he would be in Moscow for a long time? Ambassador Harriman replied that if Premier Khruschev wished this treaty half as much as President Kennedy, he—Ambassador Harriman—would be on the airplane in two weeks. Thirteen days later the Treaty was signed. This is an example of what can be done by largely non-negotiated unilateral action on both sides where there is goodwill on both sides, an important pre-condition.

Chairman

Professor Velikhov, would you like to comment on the question of reducing by 90 per cent?

Yevgeny Velikhov

This is such an important question and it is necessary not to depart from reality. I think reality is much worse today because we are not decreasing weapons, we are increasing them. This is connected with the development of offensive and defensive programmes, which I have already discussed, and the first important step is to change direction. But we need to have real assurances for the future, because, for example, if we are going to decrease the number by 90 per cent and afterwards the other side builds so-called 'defensive' systems, what is the result? I agree with Professor Sagan that it is necessary first of all to have the will of both sides to go in the same direction and then it is possible to go to half of 90 per cent, and to zero, but of course there are many questions arising in this connection: equilibrium, stability, nuclear powers ever agreeing to a 90 per cent reduction and so on. I think the only hope for mankind is in any case to exterminate nuclear weapons.

Chairman

May I just take the liberty of adding another comment on this question of unilateral moves towards a large reduction. I think one of the most pertinent United States comments on this can be found in the last chapter of a book called *Race to Oblivion* written in 1970 by Professor Herbert York. As you may remember, Professor York was the first Director of Livermore and he made some very pertinent remarks in that book saying that honestly the United States side has by and large been leading in building up nuclear power arsenals and the Soviets have been following, and therefore, in his opinion, the United States has a kind of moral responsibility to take the lead in the reduction too. Of course this is a question you can dispute, but I think that at least that chapter of his book is really worth reading, even today 15 years after it was written.

Chairman

The next question is directed to Professor Sagan and/or Professor Velikhov, but it could I think be directed to any of the speakers here.

Konstantin Volkov

The mass media have a definite responsibility for giving reliable information. The latter is vital today in the framework of the World Nuclear Disarmament Campaign. Could you comment on this problem?

Yevgeny Velikhov

Of course I think the most important question today is disseminating the truth of the whole problem connected with the nuclear issue. To give an example, in the USSR we held a seminar on nuclear winter; there was a televised conference between 300 scientists in Moscow and 600 in the United States, including Professor Sagan and myself. The conference was fully covered by nation-wide television for approximately 150 million people. We have had many articles on nuclear winter. For instance, this month the very popular magazine *Science* has carried a full discussion of all these problems. I do not know exactly the situation in the United States, but I believe that scientific journals cover the question, although I am not sure about television. In any case, a large degree of responsibility lies on the shoulders of the mass media to disseminate the truth and understanding of reality to the population.

Paul Sieghart

I would like just to follow up my question about unilateral reduction of the gross overkill capacity which both the super-Powers have, and I am grateful to Dr. Sagan for pointing out the constraint upon the American President that he lives in a democracy and may not get re-elected if he does something which looks at first sight politically unpopular. But that constraint does not operate in the Soviet Union, and I don't insist on 90 per cent first time round. However, might one not achieve a reversal of direction by the Soviet Union unilaterally saying 'All right, we will throw away 20 per cent of our arsenal; we don't need it anyway; it can make no difference to us; in fact it will improve our already over-strained economy'? Now of course if the United States does not respond within a reasonable time, you can build it up again, but that would give the President of the United States the opportunity of running a huge campaign saying 'We will make it 25 per cent' and then you can have a splendid reverse or negative arms race. Why not?

Yevgeny Velikhov

We have another historical experience. In August 1983, Andropov proposed a halt to the American Congress and the American Government and we unilaterally stopped any testing, any development of space weapons, but America did not follow us. Why, in such a case, did the President not use this opportunity?

Paul Sieghart

Try again!

Yevgeny Velikhov

We tried again just recently with the medium-range, we tried with no-first-use. It is not very easy and maybe we should not try too many times if the situation is against us.

Carl Sagan

In today's *International Herald Tribune* there is a story that the United States Congress yesterday voted not to go ahead with the testing of anti-satellite weapons so long as the Soviet Union adheres to its unilateral moratorium, so this is perhaps an example which is working. Perhaps if the Soviet Union had not made a unilateral moratorium on anti-satellite weapons, Congress would have felt itself required to support testing of them, so this may be an example going the other way.

Georgi Arbatov

I would like to make a couple of comments on what you said. The first thing is that you demand that we try by destroying our weapons, or many of them. If it does not work, we can build them again, and you speak about this doing good to our economy! It simply does not fit. The second point is based on logic, and I think the nuclear arms race has long ago surpassed and transcended any logic and therefore what the weapons are built for is a question which cannot be answered on the basis of logic. So I don't think you should approach it in this way. I would also say that, for us, we have certain memories and certain attitudes towards the United States and if the President of the United States promises to throw us out on the ash heap of history, we understand that our own chance is that it reflects more his intentions than his real possibilities. If he had the possibility, I think we would share the fate of Grenada.

Chairman

Mr. Sieghart, do you wish to reply to this or should we end the round on the unilateral moves?

Paul Sieghart

I am sad, at the end of the second day of this Colloquium, to hear as prominent a Soviet negotiator as Mr. Arbatov tell us that even he, and even his country, cannot reintroduce logic and rationality into the arms race.

Georgi Arbatov

Like many things, the arms race resembles the tango, you need two to do it and it is true also for the arms race and for peace.

Chairman

There was after all a glimpse of optimism in all this in the remarks of Professor Sagan and I think we shall conclude our session here in a spirit of mild optimism.

IV

The Nuclear Arms Race and Arms Control

CHAIRMAN:

DR. MARTIN M. KAPLAN

Former Director of Medical Research, WHO, Director-General, Pugwash Conferences on Sciences and World Affairs, Geneva and London

Opening Remarks

THE HONORABLE GEORGE BUSH
Vice-President of the United States

At the outset, may I just express my profound respect for and gratitude to Prince Sadruddin Aga Khan for sponsoring this most constructive conference, for inviting such distinguished speakers as those that you heard this morning, and others that you have met with earlier on. My only regret is that I was not able to attend the whole conference.

Our host invited me to just make some brief remarks and that I shall do, and I am always reminded of the comments after the speaker who gets up and says: 'I will make some brief remarks', goes on for about 45 minutes and then suddenly someone says: 'I would hate to hear that guy make a real speech.' So I will try—I know you are at the end of a long morning—to make just some observations that hopefully bear on some of the discussions you have had here today. I am very sorry I will miss the exchange between Dr. Arbatov and Senator Stevens, because I expect that I, like everyone here, might well have learned a good deal from that discussion. But I have just come from a meeting with the Soviet negotiating team, the arms control delegations, and there my mission was not to negotiate on anything of that nature. My mission was simply to reaffirm our President's commitment to arms control. To review briefly: that means our abiding interest in deep cuts in the number of strategic weapons threatening mankind. It means either the elimination of these intermediate nuclear force weapons or, failing that, deep cuts to equal numbers in INF missiles. Last month our President took a major step, going an extra mile to make these talks succeed when he ordered the dismantling of the Poseidon submarine in spite of what we feel, on our side, was clear and disturbing evidence of violations of the SALT II limits. We hope that the Soviet side will respond in an appropriate fashion and that this gesture of good faith helps us move ahead with the important work of negotiating real arms reductions in the nuclear arsenal.

I have a feeling, and I have not travelled in Eastern Europe that much, but I have travelled in I think 64 foreign countries since I have been Vice-President of the United States, and I have the distinct feeling that men and women from all walks of life, from all countries, with all systems, really do want to see the type of arms reductions that our President has pledged to achieve through negotiation.

Shortly before I left on this trip I addressed a conference on the subject of non-proliferation—that was held at Brookings in Washington—and there I outlined the basic points in our approach to non-proliferation, and I might review that—lay it out as the three official points of our policy. One, that there are important peaceful uses of the atom: medicine and agriculture, for example, and this is atoms for peace and it is important that peaceful uses of the atoms be available to all who need them. Second, peaceful atomic technology must not be diverted into making bombs: we want to discourage nations that do not have the atomic bomb from getting the atomic bomb. And, thirdly, the United States cannot stop proliferation alone: we work with other nations and we work with the International Atomic Energy Agency. Also at the Conference I proposed that the United States, on a reciprocal basis, allow an inspector of Soviet nationality to be a member of an Agency team conducting a safeguards inspection of a United States nuclear power site, and I repeat that proposal here today. The world has been made more aware of the threat of terrorism this week and that ties into your discussions. The ultimate act, I guess, of terrorism would be nuclear terrorism, and preventing proliferation is part of what we must do to prevent nuclear terrorism. Stopping terrorism is the other part. Everywhere we travelled this past week—and we have been to five countries now—terrorism has been on the front burner, almost the first topic of discussion. As some of you may have heard, it appears now that the TWA hostages—the hostages held in Beirut—are now on their way to Syria, on their way out of Beirut, and if indeed things go forward, Barbara and I will be there to greet those American hostages in Germany when they arrive there late tonight. Some asked me to quantify my emotions about this good news, and I guess you know joy at the release of my fellow countrymen, sadness that a young kid, Robert Steedham, because he was a member of the armed forces travelling on a civilian airliner, was brutalized and killed. Senator Mathias, he and I with Barbara stood there when that young man was returned in his coffin and I tell you, it really wracked the emotions of the American people. And then, maybe still another emotion, still a sense of outrage that seven of my countrymen are still held hostage somewhere around Beirut.

But anyway, this question of terrorism was on everybody's mind and leaders such as Craxi and Kohl related personal experiences about prominent friends murdered by terrorists. Everywhere there was sympathy for the victims of the latest round of violence and everywhere, though, the encouraging thing—and I expect it is true from every country represented here—promises of more cooperation, this need to have closer cooperation. For our part, the President has asked me to head up a task force to look at ways to get our own act together, to be sure that our vast government bureaucracy is coordinating as best it can, and then to work for closer international cooperation. It is absolutely essential if we are ever to overcome this modern version of piracy. The number of terrorist incidents each year has been increasing—about 500 in 1983, 700 in 1984, and perhaps 1,000 in

1985 if present trends continue. Approximately 30 to 35 per cent of these incidents occur consistently in Western Europe, and not only has the violence been increasing, but the terrorists have become more imaginative in their violence in order to capture the world's headlines. Not long ago, seizing embassies and car bombs were unheard of as terrorist acts. The latest addition to the terrorists' repertoire has been the taking of hostages from a hijacked plane. Before the TWA 747 hijacking, that had not been attempted in such a bold manner. We must be prepared for other more dramatic acts of terrorism in the future. And although we so far have been spared the terrible spectre of nuclear terrorism, that does not mean that we do not need to begin addressing this problem, and we are. In particular, our President made a proposal to the Soviet Union in 1983 for agreeing on measures to combat nuclear terrorism; recently headway has been made on that in talks with the Soviets, and we welcome that. We believe it is necessary to broaden that out and find other ways to have that kind of cooperation. I note that yesterday the United Nations Associations of the USA and USSR called upon the leaders of both countries to develop a consensus that terrorists who use or threaten to use nuclear weapons be dealt with jointly and swiftly.

As I look around this room—and I see so many people with whom I have interacted in the past, whether it was at the United Nations years ago or in China or in various capacities that I have had in the United States—I see a roomful of commitment, commitment to peace, commitment to lowering the level of terror that is presented to mankind by nuclear weapons.

And so, my appeal today in these remarks is simply to say: expand your thinking, if you will, to include the threat of terrorism: the worst act, of course, would be nuclear terrorism, but this seems to me to be a problem that working-together, civilized people really can solve.

Thank you very much for your attention and thank you, Sir, for giving me this opportunity to appear before this most prestigious forum.

THE NUCLEAR ARMS RACE

A View from the South

H E Carlos Andres Perez

Former President of Venezuela

On 8 June this year I visited Hiroshima. Moved by the memory of that dreadful event of 40 years ago, when I was still in my early twenties, I went up to lay a wreath at the foot of the simple yet majestic monument to the holocaust. My heart was racing in my breast. Confused feelings overwhelmed me. My perception of the moment was influenced by a rush of conflicting mental reations. I visited the museum housing the remains of that horrifying hecatomb. This actually happened? Could it have happened? And it is now a monument to peace! A fine, noble gesture on the part of Japan, giving it to the world, not as a visible expiation of past deeds but as dramatic proof of the destructive capacity of man and confronting it with the sublimity of the state of mankind, of the common masses, victim of the egoism, unhealthy nationalist sentiment, thirst for grandeur and power, hegemony and conceit of which man is capable.

Why, I thought, instead of Geneva, that beautiful, quiet Swiss town cradled by its magnificent lake, is not Hiroshima the venue for talks on disarmament by the two super-Powers? In the presence of the holocaust, whose irresistible emotional violence rocks man's very fibres, could they perfidiously hold talks on how many missiles each possessed and was deploying? Could they ignore the fact that in their silos of terror they store warheads which could turn the whole world into a Hiroshima twelve or more times over and have the human race disappear from the face of the earth?

Forty years have gone by since the first atomic bomb was dropped on Hiroshima. Shortly after that the United Nations was born as a staunch hope for peace and understanding among all nations to eradicate war, the traditional scourge of mankind, put an end to arms rivalry and devote man's endeavour and the resources of the earth to the development, progress and well-being of all mankind.

And now, 40 years later, what do we, the people of the Third World, the underdeveloped nations of the universe, have to say? 600 million people suffering from malnutrition, 800 million people illiterate, 250 million children not attending school. And amidst all this, over these 40 years, some 10 per cent of the earth's resources have gone towards armaments. Today, over $600,000 million are invested each year for military purposes.

The sad reality is that over the 40 long post-Hiroshima years, we have come to the brink of self-destruction; not only for those rash enough to go to war but everybody else and, beyond that, for any life which might come after us.

Nobody can be unaware of this but we must nonetheless repeat it obstinately. After the bombs of Hiroshima and Nagasaki scientific research has shown us—and the super-Powers are aware of this—that all life on earth would be affected by the dreadful consequences of a nuclear war. We have all read and heard of the dangers of the nuclear winter which would lay waste the earth. Notwithstanding this, the arrogance and madness of war is pushing us towards an arms race in outer space.

Until a few years ago the countries of the Third World looked upon nuclear capacity as something alien which could not affect us directly. We now know how wrong we were. Our countries have thrown themselves into the struggle to protect human civilization, for it is not merely a question of the evil which the use of resources for warlike ends does to our nations, but our own survival and that of generations to come is at stake.

We comprise the majority of the world, we live in countries without nuclear arms and have the inalienable right to demand that nuclear rivalry cease and that nuclear arsenals be progressively reduced until they disappear completely.

The worst fallacy of man, the hypocrisy of our times lies in what its proponents call 'nuclear dissuasion' or what has been more harshly defined as 'the balance of terror'. It is both false and cynical to say that it has been an element of security. On the contrary, we are witnessing increased insecurity.

Today, under the reign of terrorism—the great scourge of our times—the world is expressing its indignation at the 40 innocent United States hostages in Beirut. But what is this 'balance of terror' if it is not the treatment of all mankind as hostages? Would it not be worth investigating and considering to what extent this terrorist madness of today is being psychologically nurtured by that insecurity which is overwhelming us? What is the moral basis of a society founded on the doctrine of terror?

On 28 January 1985, a message of peace and hope went out to the world from New Delhi. In addition it announced the presence of five continents, and thereby the active participation of the Third World, in the struggle against nuclear armament. Two Presidents from Latin America, one from Asia and one from Africa, together with the Prime Ministers of Greece and Sweden, announced to the world a truth, a denunciation and a declaration of peace to wage decisive battle against nuclear madness. From the New Delhi Declaration, which marks the Third World's resolute participation in the struggle against nuclear armament as a fundamental cause of the evils afflicting mankind, I would like to read some paragraphs which are already making history:

> Almost imperceptibly, over the past four decades, each nation and each human being has lost ultimate control over his own life and death. For all of us, it is a small group of men and machines in distant cities which may decide our fate. Each day which we remain alive is like a day of grace, as though mankind as a whole was imprisoned in a death cell waiting for the uncertain moment of execution and, like any person innocently accused, we refuse to believe that the execution may one day be carried out.
>
> Outer space is to be used for the benefit of mankind as a whole, not as a future battlefield. We therefore appeal for the development, testing, production, deployment and use of all space weapons to be banned. An arms race in outer space would not only be vastly expensive but would also certainly have a destabilizing effect. It would put a large number of agreements on arms limitation and disarmament in danger.
>
> To put an end to the arms race has become essential. Only by this means can we ensure that nuclear arsenals will not increase while negotiations continue. It must be immediately followed by a substantial reduction of nuclear forces, aimed at the complete elimination of nuclear armament and the ultimate proposition of general and complete disarmament. In parallel with this process it is urgent and necessary for precious resources which are today squandered on military use to be transferred for use in social and economic development. The strengthening of the United Nations must equally be an essential part of this task.
>
> It is essential for us to find a remedy to the existing situation whereby hundreds of thousands of millions of dollars, corresponding to an amount of appoximately one and a half million per minute, are destined for arms. This contrasts dramatically with the poverty and in many cases misery in which two-thirds of the world's population live.

In Athens on 31 January this year, I had the honour to take part in the meeting called to support the initiative of the five continents, promoted by the six Heads of State already mentioned, thereby launching a major public campaign to have the world join forces against self-destruction.

This is the first time I am attending this open discussion of the Groupe de Bellerive in the face of what is the most dramatic challenge to mankind: nuclear armament. It is in the same spirit and conviction with which I took part in the meeting in Athens that I attend this meeting here in Geneva, moved by the same sentiments which filled my whole being at the Hiroshima monument.

This international discussion on 'Nuclear War, Nuclear Proliferation and their Consequences' is taking place in a year when so many expectations of very contradictory indications hang over the world. Talks on nuclear disarmament are being resumed by the United States and the Soviet Union in a climate of increasing pessimism and protest. The forthcoming Third Meeting (in September 1985) of the 124 States signatory to the

Non-Proliferation Treaty of 15 years ago will carry out a follow-up and review, against the background of the harsh reality of the most flagrant violation and non-observance. Neither the Soviet Union nor the United States has pursued 'negotiations in good faith on effective measures relating to cessation of the nuclear arms race at an early date' as Article VI of the NPT states. The Soviet Union which in 1970, when it signed the Treaty, had 2,000 nuclear weapons now has 9,000 and the United States when then had 4,000 now has 11,000. The latter, in the face of universal protest, is assuming the responsibility of starting an accelerated arms race in outer space. Meanwhile, in the developing countries thousands of children are dying daily of hunger, pneumonia or enteritis while the world is spending a million and a half dollars in arms each minute!

However, we have not gathered here to lament over this inconceivable moral crisis in the world. We wish to say, as in the New Delhi Declaration, that we are not resigned to hoping that the two super-Powers reach an agreement on nuclear disarmament. We know that both have made solemn declarations on their objectives to eliminate nuclear arms. However, we also know that this formulation of objectives has no date limit. The world is looking for tangible results. This is a struggle for the right to life, which belongs to all nations, all peoples, those of today and those of the future. And only with the co-operation of all of us, all human beings, can we achieve that. This is what we have to say over and over again from all corners of the earth to the governments of the super-Powers and we seek their peoples' alliance.

Each day pacifist movements become stronger in the developed countries, particularly in Europe, which is the nearest and most privileged for the initial holocaust. These movements must have profound repercussions in the world and must meet with the solidarity of the peoples of the Soviet Union and the United States. They are already making themselves felt in the latter and the United States Congress may represent a formidable tribune for the aims of this great people. Although a different system does not allow us to know their reactions, similar sentiments and proposals no doubt dwell in the hearts of the Soviet and Eastern European peoples. Let us hope that the re-opening of discussions is a result of these pressures.

I am aware that distinguished persons from the great nuclear Powers are listening to me here. My words are not proposals for confrontation. The leaders of these nations have our consideration and respect and we cannot cast doubt on their fine proposals. However, we have to confront reality with open eyes. We are working for international peace: it is not merely a matter of principle but of our own national interest.

The peoples of the Third World are therefore uniting in this universal coalition; we are claiming our right to live free of the threat of succumbing in a nuclear hecatomb. We in Latin America can see dangers in increased armament beyond the already preoccupying and absurd figures of weapons and arms expenditure by our nations. We saw in the absurd Falklands Islands war that British ships were carrying nuclear devices. This year, in this Latin American island, territory of the Argentine Republic, a strategic military airport has been opened which can receive planes with nuclear loads. Is the Southern Atlantic becoming militarized? Articles in the press refer to negotiations between the Chilean dictator, Pinochet, and the United States Government to do the same in the Easter Islands in the Pacific. Thus the Treaty of Tlatelolco, an all-important and most welcome initiative on the part of the Latin American countries, would also seem to be threatened.

The persistence of such present tendencies is not unconnected with the concern expressed in United Nations reports on the increase of the nuclear club, which is also destroying our hope of a Latin America free of nuclear devices.

I cannot conclude without referring to the dramatic economic circumstances of the Third World, which are a consequence not only of exaggerated conventional armament which plays an important role in the question of the immense foreign debt hanging over it but also the cost to the world in development for the benefit of the arms race of the great Powers. We contribute to financing it through exactions of all types imposed upon us by the powerful economies of the industrialized nations, as is shown in the continued increase in prices of capital goods and other manufactures imported from the industrialized countries and in the continuing decline in the value of basic commodities from developing countries. Not even oil is safe from this process. It is calculated that for this reason alone the value of exports from Latin America decreased by 25 per cent in 1984.

Deteriorating terms of exchange is a constant factor in trade relations with the Third World and is in reality a means of plunder.

The Third World's $900,000 million debt represents an intolerable and non-negotiable burden under present terms with the increasing decapitalization of the developing nations, which have become net exporters of capital.

Another serious and imminent threat to world peace is to be found in the intolerable imbalance between North and South.

If the enormous amounts of money which are being invested in the terrifying nuclear arms race and in arms in general were to be used for peaceful purposes to alleviate the Third World's crushing burden, the economic recovery of the developed and developing nations would not be long in coming and the dangerous tension between East and West—which, directly and indirectly, is increasingly affecting the Third World and aggravating conflicts, as in the case of the Middle East and Central America to cite but the two most important, to the point of seeing the developing countries over the past three decades as the theatre of most of the violence in the world—would be alleviated.

It is today undeniably true that security and the very existence of nations are interdependent, there can be no partial solutions nor can there be any hope that the problems between East and West and between North and South will be rapidly resolved. The first essential step is to have confrontation give way to understanding, for a start to be made on reducing the risk of war, limiting arms and declaring a moratorium on the nuclear arms race in order to discuss gradual reduction leading to the final disappearance of this terrifying weapon; to initiate a process towards economic and social development, progressively mitigating those forms of injustice which have their roots in years of colonization and oppression of the Third World countries and which have established profound economic differences and continued systems of exploitation and impoverishment of our peoples.

The Third World rejects such abominable persisting forms of colonialism as apartheid in South Africa and the permanent genocide in Namibia and has a deep wish for *détente* between East and West, for these tensions disturb, complicate, interfere with and aggravate regional or local conflicts or serve as pretext for disagreement over the search for solutions between the industrialized world and the developing nations. Dialogue between North and South has come to a standstill; this deterioration in relationships is apparent in the irrational conduct of the governments of OECD countries in relation to the southern nations' debts, that time-bomb which can bring the psychological climate of uncertainty to exploding point, shake the foundations of international politics and increase the risk of war.

It is not possible either to establish the security of one nation at the expense of the others nor to deal unilaterally with the economic and social problems of mankind. Just as there is interdependence of problems so there is interdependence of solutions. The inter-relationship of the global economy is an inseparable part of peace talks and will also bring us either closer to or further from the risk of nuclear war. International security will in the final instance depend on whether the vast differences in the living conditions of peoples are reduced. Prosperity for all is a determining factor of peace.

Never before has mankind had to meet such a dangerous challenge. Science and technology in the service of the arms race has provoked an unhealthy imbalance between the pace of international justice and that of the increasing sophistication of weapons. Economic resources are channelled by the same frenzy of the forces unleashed and a halt to this race can only be achieved by applying urgent, effective measures of disarmament. It is an axiom, and therefore requires no proof, that the attainment of disarmament would advance development. For as long as the nuclear arms race persists in the world it is not possible to look to the future with any confidence, morale will be so profoundly affected that it will transform and degrade the conduct of man and nations, as we see today in the savage, inhuman and atrocious expression of terrorism and the increasing violation of the rules of international law.

We trust that hope will prevail over terror and that the memory of the 40 years which have gone by since August 1945, the Hiroshima holocaust, and since 24 October 1945, the fortieth anniversary of the United Nations, will awaken mankind to international peace and justice.

A View from the East

DR. GEORGI ARBATOV

Director, Institute of the USA and Canada, Academy of Sciences of the USSR

Very soon we will get over the first forty years of coexistence between nuclear weapons and human beings. The problems posed by it won't go away. They are growing. The rapid accumulation and constant improvement of the first weapons in human history which can in a matter of hours end all human history is called the nuclear arms race. It has two main dimensions. On the one hand, it is a race between East and West, primarily between the United States and the Soviet Union. The other and, perhaps, more meaningful dimension is that it is a race between man and Frankenstein's monster, man and the means of his own destruction which he created with his own hands.

My subject, however, is not Apocalypse nor philosophy, but the East-West dimension of the nuclear arms race. From the East, from the Soviet Union in particular, its logic looks quite simple: we didn't start it, we didn't want it, but we had to catch up or perish and we have been trying to stop it all the way.

I am aware that this may sound one-sided to some of you and that there are different views on this subject. Some think that the fault lies with the eternal source of evil—communism—others would divide the blame for the arms race at least equally between the US and the USSR, but I am to report on our view, not Mr. Perle's nor Mr. Kohl's nor Mrs. Thatcher's.

Let me start with the very beginning. In our deep conviction, the purpose of the atomic bombing of Hiroshima and Nagasaki was not so much to defeat the enemy—Japan—as to intimidate the ally—the Soviet Union. Thus started what was later called 'atomic diplomacy'—American attempts to use nuclear weapons to bring the Soviet Union down on its knees. There were people even then who knew where it would lead to, and not only in the Soviet Union, but also in the West. Truman's Secretary of War, Henry Stimson, was one of them. He urged the President to adopt a more co-operative policy towards the Soviet Union. 'For if we fail to approach them now,' he wrote in September 1945 in his memorandum to Truman 'and merely continue to negotiate with them, having this weapon rather ostentatiously on our hip, their suspicions and their distrust of our purposes and motives will increase'. That attitude, he warned, would lead to an 'armaments race of a rather desperate character'.[1]

[1] William A. Williams, *Americans in a Changing World*, N.Y., 1978, p. 358.

It was a different time, and a very different secretary of war, but think how relevant it sounds now, 40 years later, as we try to identify the roots of the arms race and prevent it from entering a radically new and even more perilous stage.

Let us get back to history. At first it was a rather peculiar nuclear arms race—only the Americans were racing. During the first four years of the nuclear age they stockpiled dozens of atomic bombs, built up a mighty fleet of strategic bombers and a huge network of military bases from which it was possible to reach almost any target in the USSR.

It should be admitted that we felt more than uncomfortable in this situation, particularly given the growing hostility of United States policy. The nuclear monopoly definitely intoxicated many heads in Washington with the notion of *Pax Americana*, but there was more to it than growing arrogance and Messianism. The Soviet Union was explicitly declared enemy number one while the whole of United States policy was getting increasingly militaristic both in form and content. Of course, the official American rhetoric pictured it differently: believe it or not, we were the clear and present military danger threatening that main stronghold of 'freedom' and the 'free world', the United States of America.

Such rhetoric could only increase suspicions in Moscow. For there it was well understood that the real Soviet interests and goals had nothing in common with the Cold War mythology propagated by Washington and its allies. Our country could not be a major military threat if only because it was devastated by the war—20 million dead, 1,700 cities and towns in ruins. We demobilized our armed forces, bringing their number down from 11.5 million to 3 million men. We were faced with an enormous task of rebuilding the country. That real situation, as we thought, could not be anything but obvious to US policy-makers.

I refer to this only to explain our feelings and perceptions back then. We did think at the time that Washington could go very far indeed in its anti-Soviet policy. Decades later, when some American Government papers were declassified, our suspicion was confirmed. The first plan for an American atomic bombing of the Soviet Union was drawn up two months after the end of the Second World War. As the American nuclear arsenal grew, new plans appeared. The 1948 plan, for instance, called for the atomic destruction of 70 Soviet cities. Eight bombs were allocated for Moscow, seven for Leningrad, and so on—a total of 133 bombs. Nor could we have any real hope that the United States would agree to ban nuclear weapons and destroy its stockpiles.

This makes it clear why the Soviet Union made liquidation of the American atomic monopoly its high priority, working tirelessly towards that end. By 1949 we succeeded, the Soviet Union had developed its own atomic bomb. That did not mean, of course, that we immediately became equal to the

Americans in our strategic power, but still it was a crucial moment and from then on Washington had to take into account that if it ever used the bomb against the Soviet Union, the latter would respond in kind. The new situation, however, failed to bring Washington to what seemed to be a logical conclusion—to stop the nuclear arms race there and then. Obviously, nuclear weapons were already too ingrained in American strategic thinking, and the emergence of the Soviet Union as the second nuclear power spurred Washington on to keep and increase its nuclear superiority over the Soviet Union. The Truman Administration soon decided to develop the hydrogen bomb counted upon to restore the American advantage. The nuclear arms race speeded up.

Until the late 1950s, the US had not only many more nuclear weapons than the USSR, but also an overwhelming superiority in the means of delivery—the US strategic bomber fleet had no rivals. So the situation was rather peculiar—deprived of nuclear monopoly, the United States still had a clear superiority and fear of losing it made some US strategists only more reckless, and their ideas more adventurist. In retrospect, one could assume that the threat of nuclear war reached its height in 1953–4.

The situation changed only when the USSR moved closer to parity and the watershed here was creation by the Soviet Union of the intercontinental ballistic missile. That was the beginning of strategic parity—at first qualitative if not quantitative. American territory was now just as vulnerable to our nuclear weapons as our territory had been to American nuclear weapons since 1945.

We regarded the liquidation of the United States atomic monopoly and achievement as the absolute imperative of our defence policy in the nuclear age. The years of American nuclear monopoly and then of overwhelming American superiority were a time when US official anti-Sovietism was at its height and assumed its most extreme forms, while the military danger was, by our estimates, at a maximum.

At the same time it became clear rather early that each step toward strategic parity between the USSR and the USA would only spur Washington on to new attempts to get ahead. Thus appearance of Soviet ICBMs was followed by a new huge American military build-up—both in nuclear and conventional weapons—started by the Kennedy Administration. Just as in the past, the build-up was accompanied by the wildest rhetoric about the alleged 'Soviet threat', to be used as a justification for new US arms programmes.

But the 1960s were destined to become a time for changes, including the US approach to the nuclear arms race. The Caribbean crisis of October 1962 demonstrated how close the world moved to the brink of nuclear death. Later, the war in Vietnam exposed the whole US approach to foreign policy as dangerous, misguided and counterproductive. Thus, both the nuclear dimension of the Cold War and its broader political-military dimension became subjects of serious political debates in America. Those debates helped identify several key misconceptions of the Cold War design which had effectively brought US foreign policy to a deep crisis by the late 1960s.

Firstly, it was the idea that America could and should shape the world economic and political systems according to its interests and preferences. Once the *Pax Americana* became the operational outlook of US policy-makers, US foreign policy inevitably became militarized, intolerant and ideologically obsessed.

Secondly, refusal to accept the Soviet Union's legitimacy as a country with a different social system, ideology and political organization. To fit into the *Pax Americana* design, the USSR had to undergo major changes—in fact, stop being the USSR, or else simply disappear. Much of US foreign policy in the post-war period was aimed at achieving just that.

Thirdly, a belief in military superiority based on nuclear weapons as the main tool of pressure on the Soviet Union and its allies—and also as a natural right of the United States, simplifying its task of shaping world events.

Fourthly, a belief that 'meaningful' military superiority was achievable. Underestimating the Soviet capacity for competition with the United States has surprisingly enough been compatible with the familiar picture of the omnipresent 'Soviet threat'.

Fifthly, the Cold Warriors have stubbornly refused to recognize that the nuclear stalemate, which came into being when neither of the two sides could hope to use its nuclear weapons without committing suicide, created a radically new situation in the world. A situation in which many traditional notions and concepts, such as military victory, superiority, security achieved by military means, are losing their old meaning or at least their former significance.

The United States path to the realization of the realities of the nuclear age has proved to be extremely difficult, for Americans had to overcome their old perceptions of the world and of their place in it, sometimes even to overcome themselves. We were in quite a different situation, having been introduced to those realities before; introduced, shall I say, from the 'position of weakness', that of a target and not of an arrow. This did not mean that we had nothing to learn and nothing to leave aside, including some outdated concepts in the military-political and strategic spheres.

A perception of a danger is a prerequisite of actions to prevent it. This was also the case here.

The period of the late 1960s–early 1970s was an extremely important time. Even though the nuclear arms race was not reversed, at least we began to create a certain framework to restrain it. The strong and widespread critique of Cold War policies, the emergence of Soviet–American strategic parity, a general improvement in the political atmosphere—all this opened a 'window of opportunity' for arms control, for positive changes in this sphere.

Still, SALT I negotiations were extremely difficult. Their success demanded something new and unusual from both sides: a practical ability to view their own security as dependent to a considerable extent on the security of the other side, to work out agreements which would restrain their military efforts in the most sensitive area—strategic nuclear weapons.

The negotiations also required a lot of effort at mutual understanding and adjustment—both on the American and on the Soviet side. All in all, both sides managed to meet that challenge then.

Of course, those first steps may look rather modest today, but their true significance was that they were practical steps and, as first successful steps, they opened up a whole new road. In the 1970s, arms control became the centrepiece of Soviet-American relations, with SALT I, SALT II, and other agreements that were reached.

Frankly, it was difficult to imagine five or six years ago that the results of such complex and important work would be wasted with such ease, as seems to be happening in recent years. As we see it, the main reason lies in a convergence of a number of powerful factors on the American side, which has led to a reversal of US foreign policy to the Cold War mode.

Intentionally, I do not want to go into much detail concerning the reasons for so dramatic a turn. To be persuasive, a history of any significant event must be based on a lot of facts and an extensive analysis of their various interpretations, but this would require time and space, which, alas, are not available to me today. Therefore, I will limit myself to one observation which is unlikely to hurt anyone's feelings. Each serious policy turn is by nature very difficult. It is more difficult by an order of ten if it is a turn which means a break with centuries-old traditions of the politics of force and violence, with views of military force and war as 'the King's last argument'. But the turn from the Cold War and unlimited arms race to *détente* and arms control meant just that, therefore, one may view that turn as requiring a lot of time, and compare it with a grand battle, in which there are triumphs and disappointments, assaults and retreats, frontal offensives and bypassing manoeuvres.

If we treat the nuclear age as a certain whole, we can trace the following trend: as early as the 1950s, it began to be understood in both East and West that the Cold War, unmitigated hostility and the arms race were leading not only to a dead end, but also to oblivion, and it was then that attempts began to turn away from that path. Eisenhower and Khrushchev tried to do it, but soon failed. After the Caribbean crisis of 1962, those attempts led to the first agreement to curb the nuclear arms race—the partial test ban treaty, but then the work stopped—largely because of the war in Vietnam. The late 1960s-early 1970s brought new progress—more substantial, deeper, involving a broader front. We hoped that the watershed had come between the old and the new, between the past and the future. Unfortunately, it turned out not to be the case. Forces of the past turned out to be too powerful and stubborn. The dead were grasping the living and stopping them, but we hope, not forever.

Be that as it may, we are back in a period of cold war, which is sometimes called Cold War 2. Its results are already evident: the danger of nuclear war has increased; the nuclear arms race is accelerating its tempo; the existing structures of arms control are being eroded; the arms control talks are up against the obstacles which today seem almost insurmountable.

Let me now turn from history to nowadays, to Soviet views of the Reagan Administration's policies in the area of the nuclear arms race.

Firstly, we are becoming increasingly convinced that the Reagan Administration set itself a goal of fully dismantling the limitations regime established by the existing treaties and agreements—SALT I and SALT II, the ABM Treaty, and others. What is more, it is attempting to liquidate the whole process of arms control and get back to the times of an unlimited arms race.

Earlier, during the 1980 election campaign and in the first year of the Reagan Presidency, that goal was openly talked about. Treaties with the USSR, especially SALT II, were declared contrary to American interests. The Republican leaders stressed that they would be ready to reopen talks with the Soviet Union only after they had built up enough weapons to gain military superiority and a position of strength. It was not before they were confronted with opposition to such policies both inside America and among the allies, that the Reagan Administration had to commit itself to observing the existing treaties and announced its intention to resume talks with the USSR. But the ensuing years showed that the Administration's goals remained the same and that it was more of a manoeuvre than anything else. Seeing that it was impossible to do away in one strike with the agreements and treaties, and with the very idea of arms limitation, Washington switched over to 'salami tactics', according to which treaty commitments are liquidated slice by slice, as if cutting salami.

Strange as it may seem, this impression was confirmed after the Gromyko-Shultz agreement in January 1985 on the beginning of talks on space and nuclear weapons. The US stepped up its old propaganda campaign about alleged Soviet 'violations' of existing treaties (who will go about branding his partner as a 'cheat' while intending to negotiate seriously?). Meanwhile, the very fact of the agreement was used, under the pretext of 'strengthening the American hand at the Geneva talks', to obtain from US Congress additional military appropriations, including for the MX, and from the allies (Belgium, in particular) consent to the stationing of missiles. And on 10 June,

President Reagan announced the 'conditions' which the US would now attach to its consent not to break SALT II.

I have been watching with surprise how different are the interpretations of that statement by President Reagan. Quite a few people saw in it almost nothing less than a victory by the 'moderates' over the extremist faction in the Administration. After all, goes the reasoning, Reagan decided not to renounce the SALT II Treaty and promised to observe many of the limits prescribed by it. We in the Soviet Union cannot agree with such reasoning. In our view, the statement of 10 June is yet another big step toward the full erosion of the arms control regime. The reason is that by attaching conditions to its intention to observe SALT II, the US arbitrarily violates important provisions of the Treaty. According to one of them, there must be no development or deployment of more than one new ICBM. I would also like to note the President's claim to a right to decide at his will whether the United States should observe limitations on the overall number of strategic launchers in connection with the activation of new American systems, such as Trident 2 submarines and Cruise missiles. The 10 June decision is a a new serious blow to the SALT II regime and to the arms control process as a whole. This is further proof that the Administration is consistently moving toward a rejection of arms control treaties by means of biting off piece by piece.

If there are people who praise the Administration for its 'moderation' and 'commitment' to the Treaties, this only testifies to the high achievements of the current US leadership in the skill which they value so much—public relations. At first, there was a big fuss about the impending doom—full rejection of SALT II. There was increasing alarm in Congress, among America's allies, in public opinion. Resolutions were adopted, letters were sent to the President not to break off the Treaty. And then the President heeded the call, and made a statement which amputated . . . only a couple of limbs from the Treaty. But, since the Treaty's head is still in place, everyone is happy, and the President is praised.

Secondly, I would like to make a general observation on the Administration's nuclear policy. This Administration took a big step backwards also in the attitude toward nuclear war. Contrary to the past solemn statements and even treaty commitments, Washington concentrated its efforts on trying to find a way out of the nuclear stalemate and somehow revive the situation when one could wage war with impunity and hope to gain victory in it. Again, at an earlier stage, this attitude was quite frank. I have in mind the 1980 Republican platform, the numerous statements by Defense Secretary Weinberger and his lieutenants, by William Clark and other Administration officials, as well as official documents like *The 1984–88 Defense Guidance*. The keynote of all those statements and papers is that

America must regain a capability to win in a nuclear war. Just as frankly, they spoke in the early 1980s of plans for a limited nuclear war in Europe.

Later, when concern rose in the US and allied countries, the rhetoric was moderated, but the policy stayed the same. I might tell you that in the Soviet Union, at the level of both military and civilian experts, the purpose of the main military programmes launched by Washington is seen exactly as regaining a capability to wage war without risking suicide—in strategic jargon, a 'first-strike capability'.

If US military programmes are analysed in detail, such an impression gets a striking confirmation. The American missiles recently deployed in Europe have a minimal flight time—eight to twelve minutes—which makes them an ideal weapon for the much-advertised American strategy of 'decapitation', that is a pre-emptive strike at all the command, control and communications centers. The MX and Trident 2 missiles and the new warheads on Minuteman 3 missiles can be designed for pre-emptive strikes at the Soviet missile silos. What little remained after those strikes would be intercepted by the ABM system which the US has now begun to develop.

This is how it looks from Moscow and you will understand that our concerns cannot be allayed by the oft-repeated assurances by Reagan supporters that the Russians have nothing to be afraid of, since the United States is so evidently peace-loving that no one should even for a moment imagine that it can ever attack anyone. Such words don't work with us. And not only because we remember the foreign invasion of 1918–20, in which the US took part. That was long ago, after all, but we have not forgotten Vietnam, and we see what is happening in and around Nicaragua. We cannot ignore President Reagan's calls to throw us out on the 'ash heap of history', even as indications not of his capabilities but of his intentions. And if the capability were to appear, we would most certainly share the fate of Grenada.

The *third* aspect of the Reagan Administration's policy I would like to discuss now reflects the first two in a concentrated form. I mean the so-called 'Strategic Defense Initiative', or SDI, which in my deep conviction is meant to become at first the main weapon to wreck the arms control process, and then a key tool for the first-strike capability. These two things define the danger of the 'Star Wars' programme.

I would like to start with something which has been repeated many times, but which needs to be emphasized again. The official rationale for the SDI—to create a weapon to do away with the nuclear threat and to lead mankind to a shining future for all (or in the words of President Reagan 'to move away from a future that relies so heavily on the prospect of rapid and massive nuclear retaliation and toward greater reliance on defensive systems which threaten no one')[1] is totally preposterous.

What did the President count on as he tried to sell this science-fiction

[1] *Weekly Compilation of Presidential Documents*, 7.1.85, page 8

project to his compatriots who are usually praised for their practicality and pragmatism? I would think that he counted on the traditional American faith in technology. Appealing to that faith, President Reagan promised to find a technical solution to the problem of security, and he blasted those who have doubts about his approach, stating that the history of technology argues strongly against the notion of the impossibility of something.

I would like to emphasize, first, that the proposition that any problem lends itself to a technical solution is wrong. It is wrong even in the narrow technical sense. For instance, it is impossible, even with the best technology available or thinkable, to create a *perpetuum mobile*, to overcome the action of the laws of physics, to make man physiologically immortal.

Likewise, what President Reagan promises with his 'Star Wars' programme is unthinkable. Of course, one can imagine that with some new types of defensive weapons, some mysterious rays, super-super-computers and so on, in some future, maybe in 30, 100 years or even more, it may become possible to build a defensive system which would rather effectively shoot down the existing missiles, but by that time the 'existing' missiles will be different too, won't they?

The main mistake here is that the US President disregards a self-evident truth: the same brains, the same research resources, the same machines which will work on those 'defensive' weapons, will at the same time be engaged in creating weapons to overcome the 'defence' in one way or another. In this sense, there can be no absolute weapons—to borrow a favourite phrase from SDI advocates, you can't stop technology. Thus, scepticism about Reagan's 'Star Wars' reflects not any lack of faith in human intelligence, science and technology, but just the opposite, the greatest faith that their onward movement will not stop. Unless, of course, we manage, by conscious efforts and political will, to stop the development of dangerous technologies of mass annihilation. That is, unless we succeed at arms control.

If technology by itself cannot provide for security, it is not because technology is weak, but because the problem of security is not technological but political by nature. To prove it, there is no need to launch yet another colossal military programme. It has already been proved quite amply. History itself has answered the simple-minded question which is asked in order to mislead naive people: why not give it a try? One should also be aware of the price that will have to be paid for such curiosity. For the question here goes far beyond research, or even development and testing of new weapons systems. The question is about a new, and possibly unprecedented in both scale and danger, round of the arms race.

Just think about the scale of the project—$70 billion plus for eight years. This is about five times the cost of the Manhattan Project (in current prices), and more than twice the cost of Project Apollo. Therefore, even if we grant that these means will be used largely for research and development, that will mean an unprecedented mobilization of funds, brains and all kinds of resources for a qualitatively new leap in war technology. The leap would cover all areas: defensive and offensive, nuclear and conventional weapons, weapons to be used in space, ray guns, kinetic energy and many other weapons. It would be a leap toward new and unknown dangers, which would far surpass the dangers of military nuclear technology—those which are already known, but which humanity has not yet managed to cope with. Are we prepared for such a leap into uncertainty? Do we want it? No one has answered this question yet. In fact, the problem has not yet been discussed from this angle.

They attempt to reduce the problem to a far safer and simpler formula—why not try and see what comes out of it? Why not do some research and then decide what to do? But 'then' it will be too late to decide anything—for a number of reasons. One reason is that the so-called 'research' will itself cost, in addition to the $70 billion, a huge political price. One of the first victims of this programme is most likely to be the Soviet-American talks on arms limitation. Their goal was defined in January of this year as prevention of an arms race in space and its termination on earth, however, it is now being clarified that the US will under any circumstances work on SDI in order to see if the system will work or not, and when they do find out (according to their current estimates that is not supposed to happen before 1993), a decision will be made: to deploy an ABM system or not. If they decide to deploy it, they will then consider whether they should break the ABM Treaty unilaterally or try to persuade the Russians to castrate it so that it would not interfere with implementation of US arms programmes.

What an amazing approach! If such is the intention of the US Government, then what is it that the USSR is supposed to discuss with the US at the negotiating table for eight or more years, while the Americans are moving towards their own decision on whether to seek an agreement or not, a decision which would depend on the success of their work on military technology? Clearly, nothing can be achieved before such a decision is made. Such a US posture makes space weapons virtually non-negotiable, but in that case it is pointless to discuss offensive weapons. Let me remind you that already more than a decade ago, in the late 1960s–early 1970s, both sides came to a mutual decision that there could be no limitation, much less reduction, of offensive weapons without limiting defensive ones. The 'Star Wars' project does not at all cancel that inexorable strategic logic. It is difficult to escape the conclusion that the United States has no intention of negotiating seriously for the next eight or more years and views the talks as a propaganda ploy, a foreign policy public relations exercise.

This makes 'Star Wars' the most destructive mine laid under the whole arms control process. Another conclusion is that 'Star Wars' is a powerful engine driving the arms race and destabilizing the world military-political situation.

All this must be said despite all the inconsistency and unfeasibility of the idea to create some kind of 'impenetrable shield' capable of doing away with the nuclear threat. The thing is that even an imperfect ABM system for the territory of the United States may become, as has already been said, a component of what is being designed as the arsenal for the 'first strike'. All the more so since the development of the new ABM system is accompanied by further intensification of efforts at all kinds of offensive weapons—MX, Midgetman, Trident 2, B-lB, Stealth, and others.

As we see it, all this will only increase the nuclear threat. The Soviet Union will be compelled to take countermeasures, which, judging by the precedents, will be effective enough. Those measures, again judging by the precedents, will cause a new American response, which can be expected to lead to a new response from the Soviet side, and so on and so forth. There will be more and more arms, and less and less security. This paradox has been in evidence for many years already, and it tends to become ever more ominous.

This is why the 'Star Wars' programme should be expected to cause serious problems very soon. Problems for all of us—the USSR, the United States, Europe, the whole world—in spite of the fact that the technical and political feasibility of the programme will be studied for many years to come. This is yet another paradox.

To keep peace, one has to do real things. To undermine it and push humanity off the brink, one can do with illusions alone. 'Star Wars' *is* an illusion, as almost any serious expert on the matter will testify. It is an illusion from the point of view of feasibility of 'absolute defence' against the nuclear threat—the notion clearly borrowed from science fiction movies (even though major science fiction writers are sceptical about SDI: Arthur Clarke calls it 'technological obscenity', Isaac Asimov has said 'I don't think "Star Wars" is feasible and I don't think anybody takes it seriously. It's just a device to make the Russians go broke. But we'll go broke too.'.[1] It is an illusion also in terms of the quality, seriousness and credibility of the project. It looks much more like a hodge-podge of hare-brained schemes and half-baked ideas, poorly connected with each other—a hodge-podge which they are desperately trying to turn into something like a long-term plan.

One is prompted to ask 'Why such a hurry?' I think one answer could be this. For President Reagan himself, 'Star Wars' may have indeed become an object of faith—fanatical faith that banishes any doubt. But already among his close aides, I don't think you can find many true believers who support SDI unequivocally. Maybe two or three people, hardly more. Pragmatic designs of the rest are quite different from the offical promises of the

[1] *International Herald Tribune*, 2–3.3.85.

President. Those designs may be different with different people, but there seems to be a common theme.

The Reagan Administration, no matter where it may place itself on the US ideological spectrum, occupies a place on it which is very near its far right end. Those people are very ideological, which means that when their ideas collide with reality, they are more inclined to tamper with reality than modify their ideas. I think there is growing alarm among them that, no matter how big the margin of their victory over Mr. Mondale and Mrs. Ferraro, their time is running out. Meanwhile, they do want to leave a big imprint on history, to leave a lasting heritage to their successors.

'Star Wars' is a way to do just that. The Administration may be pushing the scheme so hard because it wants to make irreversible a new round of the arms race—irreversible due to the inertia of the military programmes now being launched, and the weighty clusters of economic and political interests being formed around them.

Summing up, let me draw some general conclusions.

Firstly, the nuclear arms race has long ago overstepped the bounds beyond which it does not make any sense. It is a race in the production of weapons which can't be used, a race in the creation, on more and more of a mass scale, of ever more advanced tools of suicide.

Secondly, the nuclear arms race cannot be won, and attempts to solve the problems it creates, by means of new technology, are doomed to failure

Thirdly, today, the nuclear arms race has turned from a consequence of poor political relations, distrust and enmity, into their fundamental cause.

Fourthly, the problem of security, political by nature, can be solved only by political means.

The political way is far from easy. At stake is a thorough restructuring of our political thinking, of the whole international system, of traditions and patterns of international behaviour.

War, the arms race, even mere absence of international understanding and co-operation are turning into luxuries which we can no longer afford.

I do not want to minimize the difficulties inherent in breaking with those age-old traditions, even though the nuclear age demands such a break under the threat of a global death penalty. Historical experience has not yet answered the question whether it would be possible or not, but we cannot afford to be fatalists. War is different from earthquakes or floods in that, with regard to war, people can be not just objects, but active moulders of events. The hovering threat can and must evoke such impulses for self-preservation in humanity which will be on a par with the danger. I am talking about conscious efforts by all of us. The hope is that those efforts will be strong and effective enough. I would add that it is the only hope.

A View from the United States

THE HONORABLE TED STEVENS

Senator for Alaska (Republican)

Ever escalating, the arms race now threatens to absorb the total product of man's ingenuity, depriving future generations of the genius of their productivity. They will be saddled with the burden of paying most of the bill for this generation's military expansion.

United States Senators are sworn to defend our Nation 'against all enemies, foreign and domestic'—an oath we take most seriously. For me, there is no alternative to assuring our ability to deter any potential aggressor. However, in view of the inexorable trend toward larger and larger defense expenditures—funds which I said are borrowed from future generations—I am convinced there *must* be a way to limit such costs. Surely, the Soviets must be reaching the same conclusion.

Greater reductions in weapons and costs can be made at the Geneva negotiating table than we can ever make at conference tables in our respective countries.

Despite the fact that the US strategic nuclear weapons stockpile is at its lowest level in 20 years; its megatonnage is at its lowest level in 25 years; 1,000 tactical warheads have been removed from Europe since 1979 with another 1,400 planned for removal, I share the viewpoint of many here that even the current stockpile of weapons on both sides of the ideological dispute is an indication of the madness of our times. The doctrine of mutually assured destruction fosters escalation in the arms race at a critical time in our world's history, making it imperative that there be progress in the negotiations taking place here in Geneva.

The Soviet Union and the United States are committed in these negotiations, not just to limit arms for the future but to bring about a radical reduction in nuclear armaments. SALT I took almost four years to complete; SALT II stretched out over six and one half years. Surely, we must be patient with the current bargaining sessions—these talks involve three separate negotiating areas, each more complex and more in need of mutual understanding than any of the previous attempts to limit arms.

It is the subject of mutual understanding that I address today.

The gravity of the undertaking to seek radical reductions in nuclear arms is apparent. Equally obvious is the fact that in recent years the lack of understanding of, or, indeed, overt malice between, our nation and the Soviet Union has almost destroyed the ability of men and women who represent our two nations to eliminate distrust and suspicion from these talks which mean so much to us all.

We often speak of 'confidence building measures'. To many such a phrase perhaps means joint naval consultations, such as those cancelled last week because of the unfortunate Soviet shooting of Major Nicholson. To me, confidence building measures should convey to individual members of our societies the feeling that each government is trying its best to relieve existing tensions.

The United States is now in a unique position, having announced we will not undercut the concepts of SALT II despite the almost unanimous conclusion in our country that the Soviets have repeatedly violated some of its terms. We know the Soviets have not reduced warheads as required by SALT II; there are other allegations too numerous to detail here; but, the foremost and most worrisome one is the ABM Treaty violation in the Krasnoyarsk radar.

Being from Alaska, if the Soviets were to argue that strict compliance with the Treaty would be too expensive in their Arctic, and had not been as clandestine in regard to all aspects of this new radar, I would not, personally, be as worried as I am over that installation. It *appears* to be a battle management radar, capable of marshalling their new mobile missiles into a territorial ABM mode. Clearly, such an installation is the most flagrant violation of the ABM Treaty to date *if* it is what it appears to be. We have no way to really determine what it is without being there. Mr. Arbatov has been quoted in our press as having said that in some instances on-site inspections, and I quote, 'would be necessary'. Surely, this is one of those instances. While in Atlanta with former Presidents Carter and Ford in their Symposium on Arms Control, Senator Nunn and I indicated that we would welcome an opportunity to take our Arms Control Observer Group of US Senators to Krasnoyarsk, with our technical people, to view that installation. An on-site inspection of that Krasnoyarsk radar could bring a new era in our mutual relationship. From my point of view *that* would be a confidence building measure.

Another matter has now become a festering sore between our two nations. In 1969, the United States and the Soviet Union agreed to permit one another to build new Embassies. These were to be roughly equal in cost and available for simultaneous entry. Under our system, the Soviets leased the most prominent hill in our Nation's capital. They have constructed a gigantic Embassy; also homes for their diplomatic officials, which we have already permitted them to occupy. In Moscow, our new Embassy is in the process of being rebuilt. What was to be a $75 million edifice, now has an estimated cost of $167 million. One of the most significant reasons for the cost overruns is that the building must now, as I said, be completely reconstructed.

An announcement by the new Soviet Leader that past practices which led to the delay of this building will be abandoned and the United States will be able to complete and occupy its new Embassy in Moscow would be a notable confidence building measure to me.

There are similar steps the United States could take. I am personally reviewing the Threshold Test Ban Treaty and the Peaceful Nuclear Explosions Treaty. Neither has been formally approved by our Senate, yet both could be if Mr. Arbatov's concept that on-site inspections 'may be necessary' were incorporated into those agreements. On-site inspections are envisioned by the Peaceful Nuclear Explosions Treaty and should be in each and every Treaty.

To me, the most important confidence building measure would be for both sides to cut through the rhetoric and distrust and commence the process of reconciliation by a meeting of our two leaders. This need not be a Summit; the mere fact that such a meeting took place would reduce world tensions and would, I feel, be a signal to negotiators here in Geneva that progress would be welcome in both Washington and Moscow. Such a meeting could take place in two sessions—one on the Soviet East Coast: the developments there are largely unknown to the West, but those of us who have visited that area of the Soviet Union have great respect for the modernization taking place there. The second session, I would hope, could take place in my state—Alaska. We live closer to Russia than any Americans, and, in the past had great rapport with our neighbours. As late as 1973 Alaska Airlines flew to Leningrad and Khabarovsk. We would welcome an opportunity to restore that relationship and lessen the tension that exists in the area of the North Pacific and Bering Sea.

It would be helpful if both countries would step up efforts to recommence cultural and academic exchanges—these activities have been revoked on various occasions for political reasons. Unfortunately, the cultural dialogue that is lost when the exchanges cease leaves a virtual vacuum in non-official contact between the Soviet Union and the United States. We should take the first step toward re-establishing these exchanges and that would be a good starting point toward normalizing relations.

Lastly, the rhetoric of the past ought to be left in the Archives. We constantly hear references to our role in 1917 or to the period of time it took our country to recognize the Soviet Union. The Soviets do have a point when they say we should do more to recognize their contribution to the defeat of Hitler. But, we seldom have an opportunity to comment in other than a negative vein. Although Mr. Arbatov and many other Soviets often have appeared on our US television news programs for completely open expression of their points of view, Soviet television and news media are seldom available to us. As a matter of fact, they are not available to us. From the preoccupation of Russian young people with everything Western—from blue jeans to rock music—it would seem that we might begin by including some of the advocates for greater understanding of what the West is all about to the Soviet news media.

We welcome the opportunity to join once again in a dialogue in which the Soviets participate. It is my hope that others here, including the Soviets, will articulate what they believe are confidence building measures. Unless a climate of reasonable trust and confidence is restored, hope for radical reductions in the fearsome weapons already deployed is nil.

But I believe there is reason for hope. The Russian people have a new Leader. He apparently enjoys widespread popular support. Our President demonstrated his support only last November with the largest mandate ever achieved in the 200 years of our Republic. These two men can do more for the future of the world than any of their predecessors.

As a father of six children and a grandfather of three, I join each of you here, I hope, in prayers for guidance to those who have the power to make the decisions which can remove from those future generations the fear of nuclear weapons that now plague this world.

TECHNICAL INNOVATIONS, ARMS CONTROL AND THE ARMS RACE

THE HONORABLE RICHARD PERLE

Assistant Secretary, United States Department of Defense

I am pleased and honoured to have been invited to address this distinguished gathering of men and women whose dedication to peace is so admirably reflected in the public lives and careers of those assembled from all over the world in this place so long associated with the search for peace. There is no higher calling than the search for peace and freedom and there is no path to their attainment more important than free and open discourse conducted with clarity and candour. I shall endeavour in these remarks to be both clear and candid. I should prefer to be diplomatic as well—in this city of diplomacy—but in the 20 minutes allotted to me there is no time to treat, in the gingerly manner customary in international diplomacy, those ideas and arguments, some of which we have heard yesterday and again this morning that are misleading, or malicious, or just simply false.

Yesterday morning Professor Gromyko contributed arguments of all three types, and Dr. Arbatov has done so again this morning. In a single breath, Professor Gromyko managed to celebrate 'the great victory over Japanese militarism in World War II' while condemning as 'an indefensible, immoral action' President Truman's use of atomic weapons to bring that war to a close. The use by the United States of the atomic bomb against Japan came at a moment where the Soviet army was busy consolidating its hold over the countries of Central and Eastern Europe that it continues to occupy to this day. And it was motivated, not as Professor Gromyko suggests, to impress upon the Soviet Union that the United States had succeeded in developing the atomic bomb (a charge repeated by Dr. Arbatov this morning) but to save the lives of the hundreds of thousands of Americans and Japanese who would doubtless have perished in the prolongation of a bitter war. Professor Gromyko referred in his speech to President Truman's desire to exhibit the American monopoly of nuclear weapons in order to acquire for itself 'a special role of world leadership'. But nowhere did he acknowledge that, in a manner unprecedented in human history, the United States never used its unique possession of atomic weapons to attack, or threaten, or intimidate any other nation. It is fair to ask whether Joseph Stalin or his successors would have done the same, or whether Germany or Japan would have been spared with atomic weapons in Soviet hands in 1945.

Professor Gromyko would have us believe that the Soviet build-up of strategic nuclear weapons has been forced upon them by American efforts to achieve what he calls 'unilateral advantage'. But it is the Soviet Union, alone, that today possesses a force of intercontinental ballistic missiles with a combination of yield and accuracy sufficient to attack and destroy hardened military facilities that are essential elements of the American nuclear deterrent. The United States has no comparable hard-target offensive capability. It is the Soviet Union alone that has deployed a system of anti-ballistic missile defense. It is the Soviet Union alone that has a fully tested and deployed anti-satellite system. It is the Soviet Union alone that has mobile missiles with multiple warheads of intercontinental range. And until the North Atlantic Alliance began a modest offsetting deployment of intermediate ballistic missiles in Europe a year ago, it was the Soviet Union alone that possessed such weapons, which it continues to deploy in numbers that vastly exceed the American equivalence. We know, from Dr. Andrei Sakharov—a man whose immense personal courage and internationally recognized scientific and moral stature stands in sharp contrast to the deplorable cruelty and isolation he has experienced at the hands of his own Government—we know from Andrei Sakharov that he was drafted to begin work on the Soviet hydrogen bomb a full year before President Harry Truman made the decision to proceed with the development of an American hydrogen weapon.

While I am on the subject of US and Soviet weapons developments, let me cite a few examples of the different US and Soviet trends in weapons development over the past two decades. The last of our B-52 bombers rolled off the production line in 1962, 23 years ago; and some of our active fleet of strategic bombers were built as far back as 1956. We began deploying our newest land-based intercontinental ballistic missiles 15 years ago. And during the same year we began deploying the Poseidon submarine-launched ballistic missiles. We did not field another new strategic system until 1978, when we began deploying the Trident I submarine-launched missiles. Since then we have begun to deploy air-and sea-launched Cruise missiles and to build the Trident I ballistic missile carrying submarine at the rate of about one a year. By contrast the Soviet Union has, since 1971, deployed at least three, and probably four, new types of ICBMs, eight improved versions of existing ICBMs and SLBMs, long-range Cruise missiles, and we are about to see a new intercontinental bomber. The Soviet Union is continuing to develop new strategic weapons of all types. Professor Gromyko told us yesterday that the deployment of American medium-range missiles in Europe 'constitutes a real threat to African countries' and the Middle East. And yet the Cruise missiles to which he refers are, as I trust he knows full well, targeted on the Soviet

Union. Indeed their guidance system is such that they can only be directed against targets that have been surveyed and stored in their guidance computers. And there will be, at most, 464 of them if an agreement is not reached in Geneva, as we hope one will be, to limit the deployment of medium-range systems by both the United States and the Soviet Union.

But can the same be said of the Soviet SS-20? There are now well over 1,200 warheads on Soviet SS-20s, (probably closer to 2,400 if one counts re-fire missiles) and the range of them is twice that of the American Cruise missiles. They can reach well into Africa and the Middle East; and unlike the American Cruise missiles, there is no technical limit on their targeting. And while the United States would gladly abandon its entire force of medium-range missiles, as President Reagan has proposed, the Soviet Union has rejected the proposal to eliminate this entire class of weapons on both sides. The effort to frighten countries in Africa and the Middle East by raising the false spectre that American missiles, reluctantly deployed in Europe, and in the interest of European security, might be used against them, is propaganda pure and simple, as is Professor Gromyko's suggestion that the forces of the United States Central Command might be equipped with neutron weapons.

Dr. Arbatov this morning, even while invoking the name of George Orwell, has rewritten post-war history in a manner that reminds one of Orwell's description of the Soviet Union as 'a place where yesterday's weather can be changed by decree'. I doubt that Orwell's writings are widely available in the Soviet Union, but Dr. Arbatov is privileged to read what he likes; I wonder whose political system he thinks serves as the model for *Animal Farm* or the awesome totalitarian State depicted in *1984*?

We in this room, and most of the world, accept an image of the strategic relationship between the United States and the Soviet Union that is characterized by a spiralling arms race. And yet the facts are significantly different. The United States has today, deployed around the world, some 8,000 fewer nuclear weapons than we had deployed in 1967. And as Senator Stevens indicated earlier, the megatonnage of this diminished American force is barely one-quarter of what it was in the late 1960s. Moreover, the Western Alliance agreed, at a meeting in Canada a little over a year ago, to reduce further, by 1,400 weapons, the number of our nuclear weapons deployed in Europe. By contrast, we have seen in recent years consistent additions to Soviet nuclear forces; 8,000 new strategic warheads alone since 1969, when the SALT I negotiations got under way, 4,000 of which have been added since 1979 when the SALT II Treaty was signed.

Not only have the Treaties of the past failed to achieve the limitations that we in America, and I trust most of you, had hoped for, but even those agreements that have been reached are now being violated. The SALT II Treaty, for example, permits the deployment of one new type of ICBM. The

Soviets are presently deploying two new types of ICBMs and there are strong indications that we will see further new types as time goes on. The SALT regime has required (and it has been understood well on both sides) restraint in the concealment of information so that we might verify performance under the agreements. And yet the Soviet Union has consistently been obscuring the information upon which clear judgments necessary for verification must be based.

Senator Stevens has already referred to the radar Krasnoyarsk, a radar that practically completes the comprehensive radar coverage of the Soviet Union in a manner that would permit a rapid deployment of short-lead time, and highly mobile elements of a comprehensive territorial defense. Now Dr. Arbatov has said this morning that the radar Krasnoyarsk is for space-tracking purposes. Radars for space-tracking purposes are oriented towards space, where the objects to be tracked are to be found. The radar Krasnoyarsk is not oriented toward space; it is oriented towards the horizon which is precisely how one would orient a radar that was intended, in due course, to support the infrastructure for a nation-wide system of anti-ballistic missile defenses. The radar at Krasnoyarsk is identical to a radar already completed at Pechora, a radar that the Soviets have acknowledged is for the purpose of long-range detection of ballistic missiles. And the Krasnoyarsk radar happens to be situated, in violation of the Treaty, in the precise location that one would have anticipated if one were looking for comprehensive radar coverage of Soviet territory. With respect to space-tracking, there are many other radars in the Soviet Union that can perform the space-track function far more efficiently and effectively than the radar at Krasnoyarsk. Space-track radars, unlike radars that may become part of a system of anti-ballistic missile defenses, are not surrounded by thousands of tons of concrete and hardened to resist the blast over-pressures of a nuclear war.

I was not surprised that Dr. Arbatov reserved most of his remarks for the American program on strategic defense. And I must say to you that Soviet comment on the American strategic defense research program has yet again, in his remarks, reached an extravagant hypocrisy. In the spring of 1983, a few days after President Reagan's speech announcing the initiation of the American program, there appeared in *Pravda*, reprinted elsewhere in other papers around the world, an open letter from a group of Soviet scientists deploring the American SDI, deploring the use of science for military purposes, and in passing, suggesting that it would not be possible to achieve an effective result. There was a large number of signatories to the letter; let me recall some of them to you: one was Mr. P. D. Grushin, who was the Head of the Design Bureau responsible for anti-aircraft and ABM systems in the Soviet Union. Another was V. S. Semenkhin, a leading figure in the development of command, control and communications systems for anti-aircraft and ABM use. Another was B. V. Bunkin, an important figure in the development of radars and other key components of weapon systems for strategic defense. I can go on, the list is long. For among the signers of that letter were the principal architects of the Soviet SDI program, a program that has been under way since the mid-1960s, at increasing levels of investment and research following the ABM Treaty of 1972.

The Soviet Union has long been working on directed energy weapons, on particle beam weapons, on lasers both ground- and space-based. And this Soviet effort, far from tapering off when the United States and the Soviet Union agreed to abandon anti-ballistic missile defense in 1972, has increased significantly ever since. In January, in this city, Secretary of State Schultz met with Foreign Minister Gromyko. It was agreed by the Soviet Foreign Minister that there is a Soviet research program on SDI and that it will continue just as the Soviets expect the American research program will continue. And the Soviet Foreign Minister acknowledged that it is impossible to verify research.

In my judgement, Soviet insistence in the various disarmament negotiations now under way that the United States abandon its SDI research program, as a precondition for progress in other areas—something they know we will not do—is simply a device for justifying the unrelenting build-up of offensive weapons and Moscow's refusal to move towards satisfactory agreements limiting those offensive weapons. Dr. Arbatov has said this morning that it is impossible to overcome the laws of physics. I assure you, Dr. Arbatov, that we will bear your advice in mind and instruct our scientists accordingly that they should conduct their research with the laws of physics firmly in mind.

I should like to conclude with a few words about arms control. Throughout the first Reagan Administration, there were questions from a number of quarters, including at home, about the Administration's commitment to arms control. I might say in passing that the program of today's event, which describes the morning presentations as 'A View from the South', 'a View from the East', and 'A View from the West', must contain a typographical error. There is the view from the East, and you have heard it from the Soviet delegation, but there are *many* views from the West. And some of the criticism of the new Administration's approach to arms control came from within the West, and questions were raised about the seriousness and the sincerity of the United States in its approach to arms control. By now, I think the record of our proposals speaks for itself. Because on one issue after another, on a wide variety of issues of disarmament and arms control, the United States has put forward proposals that we believe could and should lead in the normal course of negotiation to agreements that are militarily significant, verifiable, fair and equitable. We believe that such agreements would achieve greater stability than we would expect to achieve in the absence of a collaborative effort. We have, as many of you know, proposed deep reductions in offensive nuclear forces in the START talks. Dr. Arbatov now says that it will not be possible to reach an agreement along those lines because the United States is continuing its program on strategic defense. But we saw no progress in achieving significant reductions in those offensive forces before we announced our program of strategic defense research in 1983. And I am sorry to say that the Soviet Union seems determined to cling to its large and growing force of intercontinental ballistic missiles and has thus been unwilling to respond positively to the American proposal to reduce to the still awesome level of 5,000 the number of such warheads on the ballistic missiles on both sides. In the negotiations on intermediate nuclear forces, as you know, we have proposed to eliminate them entirely. And when the Soviets rejected that proposal, we offered to reduce them to *any equal level* that the Soviet Union would accept.

With respect to chemical weapons, again in Geneva, the United States has proposed to ban them completely and the only thing that stands in the way of concluding a treaty banning chemical weapons is the difficult issue of verification. And in this regard we have made an unprecedented proposal: that inspectors organized internationally should be permitted to go anywhere, at any time, in order to verify suspicion that one side or the other is violating that ban. The Soviets reject this proposal for international inspection.

I think I should say at this point that, much as we might desire far-reaching arms control, the obsessive secrecy of the Soviet Union puts real and practical limits on the extent to which it is reasonable to expect the West to accept the risks of uncertainty associated with broad and comprehensive approaches to arms control, especially where issues of research or qualitative limitation are concerned. And if we didn't think that before the last year or two, we surely do now, following the determination, after careful study by all agencies of the United States Government, that the Soviet Union is violating major provisions of most of the Treaties that exist between us.

With respect to nuclear testing, which was mentioned a number of times this morning and yesterday, the United States believes that there is a good likelihood that Soviet tests have exceeded the 150 kiloton threshold limit that now exists between us. For this reason, we have made a simple proposal: that we permit the scientists of each other's country to go to the areas where these tests are conducted and take the appropriate measurements of yield so that we could be confident that ratification of that treaty would be justified. Those of you who are familiar with the testing establishments of the two countries will recognize that in those remote locations there is no conceivable military intelligence that could be obtained by technicians with measuring devices to establish yields. Thus far the Soviets have not responded favorably.

I regret that I have found it necessary, considering what was said earlier by Professor Gromyko and Dr. Arbatov, to say some things in direct response that some will regard as too explicit for diplomatic dialogue; but I believe we will not get very far in our deliberations here if we obscure the fundamental differences of fact on which we and the Soviet Union disagree. I hope that we will find mechanisms for resolving those differences in fact, and still other mechanisms, however difficult it may be, for composing the relationship between us, based on a common understanding of what forces are possessed on both sides leading to a radical reduction of those forces. The world has far too many nuclear weapons. The reductions that are possible on both sides could be dramatic; and there is now no obstacle except the artificial Soviet linkage between reductions in offensive forces and a demand that the US terminate its SDI research, that stands in the way of those deep reductions.

Postscript

Upon reading the transcript of these remarks I am struck at the apparent absence of hope, or optimism, in my exchange with the Soviet speakers. I suspect that this derives, at least in part, from the ease with which Professor Gromyko and Dr. Arbatov yielded, in their presentations (which preceded mine), to the temptation to propagandize their audience. I like to believe that in the privacy of the negotiations between us, in Geneva and elsewhere, a more constructive dialogue may be found and agreements reached.

The Politics of Arms Control: the American Context

PROFESSOR JOHN KENNETH GALBRAITH
Harvard University

In the summer of 1976, while working on a television series for the BBC on the past and future of economics, I persuaded the producer, Adrian Malone, to come to Death Valley in California with his crew. There we sought to give a picture of how the terrain between New Haven and Philadelphia would look after the explosion of a mere four twenty-megaton bombs. Such destruction is, we must agree, a wholly plausible part of the economic prospect; the filming in the Valley seemed a useful way of advancing awareness of the dangers to which we are now subject and the need for making progress toward effective arms control.

I am not sure how much our exercise accomplished; the post-nuclear terrain of Death Valley did make a strong impression on me. In the years since, I have concerned myself with the threat of nuclear conflict and its economic consequences and with the belief that such a war could serviceably defend an economic and social system. It would not. Both capitalism and Communism are sophisticated products of a long process of economic development. Neither, in anything resembling their modern form, could survive a nuclear attack. Not even the most committed ideologue will be able to tell the ashes of capitalism from the ashes of Communism, although, if they survive, there are some who will certainly try.

In these years I learned also of one of the major problems in winning awareness of the threat of nuclear devastation. That is the depression that one suffers after meetings devoted to the subject; how great is the psychological denial which causes one to put the issue aside, seek return to the comfortable norms of ordinary life. I came also to appreciate the nature of the whole public and political task of winning escape from the nuclear horror. As it is viewed in the United States, it involves four major steps. It is my purpose in this paper to describe these four steps and to tell of the progress being made in the United States in winning public and political support and of the task that remains.

The four requirements for escape from the nuclear terror consist, first, of winning a full appreciation of the effects of nuclear war, as just mentioned. Second, there is the need for an arms control design that is within the realm of popular understanding—that removes the issue at least partly from the people who have made such policy and negotiation their highly private possession. Third, there is the need to have the civility and confidence in our relations with the Soviet Union that allows of negotiations—negotiations that proceed in the belief that both sides are serious, that neither hopes to emerge with some major advantage in weaponry and that the resulting agreements will be observed. We must hope, needless to say, for similar civility and restraint on the Russian side.

Finally, there must be recognition that there are forces in both the United States and the Soviet Union that are economically, professionally and bureaucratically averse, even hostile, to an effective arms agreement. This, broadly speaking, is the military power; among other things it has need for a plausible enemy. Without such an enemy the position of the military power, including its claim on public resources, is greatly reduced.

All of these steps, as I have noted, are essential for ultimate success against the arms race. I now turn to our present state of progress in the United States on each of these steps with further thought as to what is needed in the future.

Public appreciation of the consequences of nuclear war, including the now widely accepted prospect of the nuclear winter, has been greatly enhanced in recent times. Few Americans now believe that a nuclear war is survivable or that surviving would be worthwhile. Influential organizations—Physicians for Social Responsibility, the Council for a Livable World, the Union of Concerned Scientists, SANE, Business Executives for National Security (BENS) and many other groups all win credit for this achievement. Also the writing of Jonathan Schell, Carl Sagan, Theodore Draper, Harold Willens and, again, many others. The first instinct of one of my countrymen on encountering some threat is to form an organization to combat it. The next, for many, is to write a book about it. A democracy, it is assumed, must always be responsive to enlightening information.

This may be too optimistic. As the present case of the 'Star Wars' initiative indicates, government and the military power can be resistant to all but unanimously adverse judgment. An organization or a book—or a speech—is not a substitute, we are coming to see, for solid political influence. Nor can we accord all credit to organizations, books and meetings for such progress as we have now made in realizing the horrors of nuclear war. The present Administration in Washington has also contributed with great effect to public consciousness on this matter. But in according credit to the Administration, one cannot say that the achievement was fully intended.

In the early years of the new Administration in 1981 and after, we had a flood of statements on the acceptability of limited nuclear war, on prevailing in full-scale nuclear war, on winning a protracted nuclear war and on various civil defense strategies for surviving nuclear war. This last included the death-defying promise from one exuberantly optimistic official that, with a thrown-down door and enough earth on top, 'almost everyone could make it'. Some thought that on Park Avenue in New York City there might be a shortage of both doors and earth. In my own community of Cambridge, Massachusetts, the normal academic calm was broken by a Civil Defense Advisory calling on us, in the event of an atomic emergency, to mount our automobiles and proceed westward 100 miles to the small town of Greenfield, Massachusetts. We were told to take our credit cards with us. That our universities, libraries and museums would have to be left behind was not emphasized. In consequence of this Advisory the City Council of Cambridge, not previously involved in matters more compelling than rent control, condominium conversion, zoning-law changes and a new tax assessment, decided, in what may have been an unduly sanguine mood, to have the city declared a nuclear-free zone.

That my fellow-Americans are now well-aroused to the danger of nuclear war is reasonably certain. In a recent Yankelovich survey more than 80 per cent said that such a war could not be won, limited or survived. However, a continuing awareness of our danger is still required. We must not allow ourselves to relent or relapse, as one is so tempted, into psychological denial.

Our second needed step was to find a formula for arresting the arms race that would bring the public at large into support of the necessary action. Over nearly all of the last 40 years, our policy on nuclear weapons, including our arms control policy, has been in the hands of a small group of arms control specialists. To speak with any influence on the subject, even have a position, it was held that knowledge was necessary on the weapons and weapons systems involved; on what was technically possible as regards new weapons; on Soviet weaponry, possibilities and intentions; on the problems and possibilities as to verification. Some of the needed information was subject to security classification—secrecy; some was subject to modification, interpretation or emphasis that would serve the policies sought by those involved. In consequence, not more than a few hundred people were thought qualified to speak on arms control. Those who regarded themselves as so qualified regularly and indignantly dismissed any larger public intrusion as uninformed and thus irresponsible. There was to the nuclear theologians, as they have been called, an extraordinary delegation of power. Death and taxes have anciently been associated as the two most certain, least pleasant fates of humankind. We had a delegation of power over death that no American would dream of allowing as regards taxes.

Further, the nuclear theologians to whom this delegation was accorded were subject to intense political, bureaucratic and personal rivalries.[1] The one certain consequence of such rivalries is inaction or delayed action. Arms control, not surprisingly, has been a subject on which bureaucratic discussion has far outweighed affirmative initiative.

However, we have also had success in these last years in the effort to take arms control policy away from the nuclear theologians and put it in the

[1] Strobe Talbott has told of this in his book *Deadly Gambits*.

hands of the public at large. This was the service of the bilateral freeze movement—of the campaign for the cessation by both the Soviets and ourselves of the production, testing and deployment of nuclear weapons. It was a step the Russians say they would accept. In association with the rather less portentous step of disavowing any first use of nuclear weapons, the freeze made arms control policy for the first time a matter of massive public involvement, debate and political action. The monopoly of policy by the nuclear theologians was drastically invaded.

Five years ago this summer, if I may enter a personal note, I went to the Democratic National Convention in New York City to speak for a resolution supporting the bilateral freeze. We had won enough support to bring it to the convention floor. I shared the platform with Mr. Harold Brown, then the Secretary of Defense, who was there to speak for the MX missile. He and I exchanged some acerbic words on each other's enterprise. The MX, supported by a letter to each of the delegates from President Jimmy Carter, was voted in by a big margin. The freeze lost overwhelmingly. Now after five years the MX still evokes strong opposition and is still not fully approved. The freeze—supported, polls show, by 70 per cent or more of the population and with strong congressional support—was accepted by the Democrats at San Francisco a year ago with little opposition. A *Los Angeles Times* poll showed it had a majority support among the delegates at the Republican Convention in Dallas. So here, too, there has been progress.

The freeze movement, nonetheless, has weaknesses. It did challenge the monopoly of the issue by the nuclear theologians. It did bring the American public into the arms control issue in a highly practical way. However, at best, it is a first step. It would leave in place the terrifying arsenals that already exist. It is also vulnerable to the belief that the Russians will always cheat and that compliance cannot be verified. Individuals well-informed on these matters—Herbert Scoville, a former Deputy Director of the CIA, and others—hold to the contrary, saying that there is very little that goes on in the Soviet Union of which we in the United States are unaware. And, a *much-neglected calculation*, while there are risks associated with possible noncompliance with arms control agreements, these must be set against the near-certainty of disaster if the arms race continues and accelerates unchecked.

Finally, the freeze has shown itself vulnerable to other efforts, real or simulated, to achieve arms control. As negotiations have recently resumed here in Geneva, there has been an undoubted tendency to relax—to say, in effect, they must be given a chance.

This, I am forced to say, I regret. We must continue to exert strong pressure for an arms control measure that takes the issue away from the specialists. It was the threat of the freeze that helped to get the Geneva talks under way. We must in the United States continue to have the freeze as an alternative to bureaucratic inaction or simulated action as against genuine intention and effort.

The third requirement for successful arms control requires a civil relationship between the United States and the Soviet Union. There is little prospect for success in an atmosphere of mutual insult, condemnation, recrimination and associated mistrust. Much remains to be done to improve our public expression. These last years have brought some highly damaging anti-Communist, anti-Soviet rhetoric from Washington; that the present Administration disapproves of the Soviet system has been more than sufficiently established. But here, too, we are hearing countering voices. The National Conference of [American] Catholic Bishops in their 1983 pastoral letter stressed the point: 'Negotiation on arms control agreements in isolation, without persistent and parallel efforts to reduce the political tensions which motivate the build-up of armaments, will not suffice.' The bishops went on to urge 'maximum political engagements' to reduce areas of friction. Arthur F. Burns, President Reagan's Ambassador to West Germany, said a few months ago that 'it is particularly important that the United States . . . extend to the Soviet Union the constructive attitude, the civility and the consideration that are necessary for a useful dialogue'. He added, reasonably, the hope that 'the Soviet Union will behave in a similar fashion'. As a one-time ambassador myself, I yearn to believe that ambassadors are heard in Washington. In an academically careful study of ways to avoid nuclear war, colleagues of mine at Harvard University have stressed that 'arms control must be accompanied by some improvement in US–Soviet relations if humanity is to cope with its nuclear predicament'. Averell Harriman, George Kennan, Barbara Tuchman and others have made the same point in more affirmative language. The American Committee on East–West Accord, with which I have long been associated, has found increasing support for its advocacy of civil relations with the Soviets.

We cannot, as Ambassador Kennan and many others have pointed out, expect that the Soviets will approve of the American economic, social and political system. Or we in the United States of theirs. But there can and must be a commitment to the common concern for survival. The alternative to coexistence is now none at all. We give up nothing when we eschew references to Russian depravity or wickedness. Most of these references are less to advise the Soviets of their sins than to rejoice one wing of the American right.

We also know that on these matters changes in our official mood are possible. Twenty years ago Communist China was, in the accepted Washington view, the world's leading international menace. All references were then to the Sino-Soviet bloc, the Chinese enjoying the first mention. Armed with nuclear weapons, they were held to have designs on all of Asia. Now in a matter of a mere two decades, Presidents and Secretaries of State must, as a matter of high obligation, make a pilgrimage of friendship to Beijing. Mr. Reagan made reference recently to the '*so-called* Chinese Communists'. China has become an honorary exponent of free enterprise.

It is our hope that the pressure of public opinion will, sooner or later, bring similar movement as regards Russia. Of late the adverse rhetoric has diminished—at least slightly. Prior to the last election there was a strong competition to be agreeable to Mr. Gromyko—something that must have surprised him a little. Now there is talk of a meeting between Mr. Reagan and Mr. Gorbachev. The Administration has recently proposed a crisis control center—a very important step that could appreciably reduce the risk of war by accident. This is progress.

Yet there is still a long way to go. The individual who urges better relations can still be stigmatized, if not as pro-Communist, then as being unduly gullible. Life with us is still easier if one avoids such matters. In the last quarter century in China, North Africa and with the rise of the Euro-Communist party in Italy, Soviet influence has been manifestly in retreat. In Africa the Marxist Governments of Ethiopia and Mozambique are not showpieces of achievement. (Marx was adamant in his view that there could not be socialism before capitalism; he would have been horrified at the idea of a socialist Ethiopia.) The standing of the Soviet Union in Eastern Europe is not visibly high. Nevertheless, and aided by the misguided action in Afghanistan, relentless Soviet expansionism is still assumed. 'Isms', our symbol of evil, can survive a great deal of adverse evidence.

To have relations with the Russians that allow of negotiation must remain a major point of emphasis. It faces, however, another grave obstacle. That is the need of the modern military power for an enemy. To this, as a final matter, I now turn.

In a recent speech to the National Science Foundation of the United States, Jerome Wiesner, the former Science Adviser to Presidents John F. Kennedy and Lyndon Johnson, former President of the Massachusetts Institute of Technology and a quiet-spoken scholar, held that our country 'has been overtaken by the social cancer of a runaway militarism from which only widespread understanding and decisive action can save us'. He added the more encouraging thought that, 'Even while the government has been engaged in a vast anti-Soviet campaign and a major arms build-up, understanding has gone forward'. These are hard words, the expression of optimism notwithstanding. They echo those of President Dwight D. Eisenhower a quarter of a century ago warning of the emergence of power of the military-industrial complex. It is here—in the fourth of our steps back from Armageddon—that we have the greatest distance yet to go.

The military establishment in the United States, as in other countries, is presumed to serve the defense of the nation. Criticism of it, by slight extension, is criticism of one's country and thus unpatriotic. No one—

congressman, commentator, columnist, scholar—wishes to be thought unpatriotic or so to consider himself. In consequence, the politician who essays a complaint on the Pentagon budget or a criticism of some proposed weapons system must always explain that he is, nonetheless, in favor of a *strong* defense. In the last election Walter Mondale in his campaign for the presidency agreed with President Reagan that the military budget would have to grow substantially after adjustment for inflation; the difference between the two candidates on this issue was all but microscopic. Conservatives must currently show they are strong as to defense; liberals must show they are not weak.

The military power also derives its strength from its unequalled access to all or nearly all of the sources and instruments of power in the modern economy and polity. The sources of power in any social situation are three: personality, financial resources and organization. This is not an age of charismatic military personality in the United States. Almost no one knows the names of the Joint Chiefs of Staff or even of their Chairman. There is no Eisenhower, MacArthur or Bradley to command attention and respect. Of the Vietnam era and after, only General Westmoreland will be remembered, and that will be for his libel suit.

However, in both financial resources and the scale and effectiveness of organization, the military power is unparalleled in our time. Its budget for the fiscal year of 1985 is $285 billion; that proposed for 1986 is around $300 billion. As of last September 30, there were 2,138,157 men and women in the services and 1,099,100 in the civilian bureaucracy in the Pentagon and elsewhere. This is an organization, military or civilian, of exceptional discipline. To substitute the goals and methods of the organization for one's own is a prime virtue; it is what military training is designed to ensure. The marked and surprised attention we accord to the occasional Pentagon whistle-blower shows how great also is the civilian discipline—how general the acceptance of organization goals and behavior in the civilian bureaucracy as well.

Nor is this all. Extending out from the Pentagon are the great weapons firms—the firms that, along with their Washington agents, provide a major part of the present civilian leadership of the Department of Defense. The exercise of authority extends on to recipients of political contributions and to advocacy by businessmen and politicians in communities dependent on defense employment.

There is a further source of authority; this, as it may be called, is social and political conditioning. It is the persuasion that is bought by highly available money, manpower and the natural access of high officialdom to the public. It includes extensive control, enforced by law, over the information that reaches the public. It includes the power to emphasize, perhaps even invent, information or prediction serviceable to the military power. This management of information is not perfect; an exceptionally healthy tension exists as between the Pentagon and the news media. Distinction, as also grave rebuke, accrues to the reporter who identifies something particularly flagrant in news management or suppression. Yet of its overall effect there can be no question.

Constitutional principle in the United States has always held that the military power should be subject to a stern restraining civilian control. That such control is now effective one cannot easily believe. High civilian defense officials, without exception, are enthusiastic spokesmen for the military power; in advocacy they regularly outdo the soldiers, sailors, even the airmen. (Nor is this new. In the past, American liberals have felt it necessary when taking high Pentagon positions to prove their muscular commitment to military objectives.) Presidents have, traditionally, been resistant to the military power, President Eisenhower being a notable case. President Reagan, all agree, is a fully convinced exponent. It is hardly surprising that no informed American has lately been heard to speak seriously about civilian control of the military establishment.

As there is a major concentration of power in the military in the United States, so, we must assume, there is a counterpart concentration in the Soviet Union. I am not given to unilateral interpretation, blame or action. Arms control must be by negotiation—by addressing the common threat of nuclear devastation. But it must be our effort as Americans to understand our own case; we must be assured that our Government is not subordinate to the military power. We must now ensure that it can accept and lead in effective arms limitation. And we must be sure that our initiatives in weapons development and deployment are not the propelling factor in the arms race. In the view of nearly all independent authorities, including the two presidential Scientific Advisers—Dr. Wiesner, just mentioned, and the late Dr. George Kistiakowsky, who served President Eisenhower—we have since the atomic bomb been the initiating force in weapons development. And so now with 'Star Wars'. From this comes the particular responsibility that we have for leadership in control and restraint.

On the military power we are also making progress. That power is being recognized. So also the absence of effective executive control. The military budget in these last years has been in sharp and highly publicized conflict with social programs and needs. And with a responsible fiscal policy. This has attracted sharp attention. There has been an increasingly critical view of specific weapons systems—the MX and the Strategic Defense Initiative. Finally, some highly publicized incompetence and corruption in the granting of military contracts has added to the opposition. There is still a long way to go in achieving a full restraint on the military power—on fully coming to terms with what Dr. Wiesner has called the military culture. But here too there is at least progress.

During World War II, Low, the British cartoonist, had Colonel Blimp, his most famous character, take notice of the extensive current concern with post-war planning. All of this planning, Blimp said, was leading to chaos, adding the cheerful thought that chaos did give maximum scope for free enterprise. So it is now in the the United States in response to the threat of nuclear war. Organizations, scores in all, are addressing themselves to one or more of the four steps here mentioned—to pressing the horrifying dangers of nuclear war, to urging the freeze, to working for better relations with the Soviets and to developing an appreciation of the military-industrial complex which President Eisenhower first brought to public attention. In all this effort there has been, at a minimum, the chaos that allows of free enterprise.

Needed, however, is an understanding and acceptance by all so involved that no one of the four steps here outlined is sufficient in itself. Effective arms control—assurance that the Government will take all possible measures to that end—will come when there is a compelling pressure on all four fronts. For escaping the nuclear terror, we must see and act on the whole task.

And there is another need. That is for political commitment. We will not be fully successful until representatives, senators and presidential candidates are not only persuaded but taking the lead effectively on the issue of arms control. This requires not passive expressions of concern but active political effort. In this political advocacy we must not be confined by traditional political or ideological lines. All people, rich and poor, white and black, liberal and conservative, are equally at risk in the arms race. The affluent, we know, are more conservative in their political views than the less rich and the poor. While there is some psychiatric argument to the contrary, it seems likely that enjoyment of life increases, *pari passu,* with increasing income. Accordingly, conservatives, with more of life's pleasures to lose than liberals, should, if anything, be more resistant to the prospect of nuclear annihilation.

A final point: it will be said that after all the effort—after full popular and political persuasion—we may well find the Soviets reluctant. This, for what it may be worth, I do not believe. It is my strong impression that they are no more given to suicide than we. The Russians have the history or the memory of three great invasions—those of Napoleon, of World War I and of Adolf Hitler. All, but especially the last two, brought devastating death, sorrow and great deprivation for those who survived. In consequence, the Russians see themselves as victims in any war-induced disaster. We in the United States, on the other hand, are part of that small group on the earth's surface that has largely escaped the horrors of war. We, if anything, are therefore more sanguine in our tendency, a view that is confirmed by others more informed on the Soviet scene than am I.

One thing, in any case, is sure: next time we will not escape. No one will escape. So we must be certain that the responsibility for continuing or increasing the risk of nuclear war is not ours. We have no slight distance yet to go; I hope you will not doubt the determination with which those of us so concerned intend to address the remaining miles and miles before we sleep.

Session IV Debate

Chairman

I have a first question addressed to President Perez.

Freimut Duve

You mentioned the military nuclear interest of Argentina. Would you or your political friends organize a regional move in Latin America to reach regional agreement against proliferation?

Carlos Andres Perez

I said that there is a danger of militarization in the South Atlantic, that Great Britain has built a strategic military airport which can supply aircraft with nuclear facilities in the Falkland Islands, which are under Argentine sovereignty. In connection with the Non-Proliferation Treaty in Latin America, during my term of office Venezuela acceded to the Treaty. It is one of the 124 countries which have signed it and we are also signing the Treaty on Safeguards. We have carried out an extensive campaign in Latin America, where the Tlatelolco Treaty is also operative and has been signed by all our countries, to make Latin America a denuclearized zone and we shall make all possible efforts there. President Raul Alfonsin of Argentina took part in the Five Continents Peace Initiative, even though Argentina has not yet signed the Non-Proliferation Treaty. We hope that in the future this Treaty will be signed by all Latin American countries.. But we are also concerned about it and hope that the United States, Great Britain, the Soviet Union and France will keep the promises they have made in this Non-Proliferation Treaty which will be reviewed next September here in Geneva.

Chairman

I have another question addressed to Professor Arbatov and Senator Stevens.

Constanze Eisenbart

Even the very moderate speakers of the Third World at this conference were unanimous in stressing the growing impatience of non-nuclear-weapon States with the unrelenting attitude of the five nuclear-weapon States as regards cuts in their nuclear arsenals. How would the super-Powers react if a significant number of threshold countries walked out of the Review Conference, denounced their membership in the NPT according to Article I, and refused to renegotiate a new treaty. Would that have any impact on their own rather harmonious non-proliferation policy? Would it influence their armament policy?

Georgi Arbatov

This growing concern and pressure exerted by the Third World countries, and not only by Third World countries but by all non-aligned and neutral countries and others allied to different blocs, is a very important phenomenon. The more active this becomes, the more chance there will be for the arms race to be halted. At the same time, abandoning the NPT would not be a useful contribution to this struggle, and I think that this point of view is shared by the majority of developing countries. But we cannot make a distinction between good and bad countries, and I would not say that all non-nuclear-weapon States are of snow-white innocence. That is why every country—nuclear and non-nuclear, big and small—must exercise the utmost responsibility towards the problems we are facing today. The nature of nuclear war, taking into account such consequences as a nuclear winter and other effects, is such that it is right to call for a halt to a situation where the fate of all countries is decided by a small group of people, and I quote the New Delhi Declaration: 'a small group of men and machines in cities far away'. This is really an unbearable situation and we must be aware of it, it is our common cause. Without strong pressure from all countries, we are highly unlikely ever to achieve the goal about which we are speaking here: disarmament. I am growing old and I am also a historian, and I have come to the conclusion that people are very lazy by nature; they only take action when it is really necessary, when it is impossible not to do something. Now it is urgent to do something about the arms race and it is everybody's task. I don't want to say that we in the Soviet Union are opposed to the participation of developing countries in this process, we warmly welcome their participation, we are in favour of it.

Theodore Stevens

I should think that it would be very unfortunate if the other nations of the world were to walk out of the one forum in which they have such a great reception from the nuclear Powers. It is the one area where we are working together in which the Third World countries have been heard very forcefully.

If we are to make the gains that we believe we can make in bringing about a radical reduction in existing nuclear weapons, it would be counter-productive to have a signal from the Third World that they are no longer committed to the concept that there should not be a proliferation of nuclear weapons. This would constitute a signal to the United States that would be very different to that coming from the rest of the world, namely, that the United States should use all its powers to try and bring about a radical reduction in the nuclear threat to the world. I would hope that they do not take such a step.

Chairman

The next question is addressed to Dr. Arbatov.

Ove Nathan

Does the Krasnoyarsk installation in your opinion constitute a violation of the Anti-Ballistic Missile Treaty, as suggested by Senator Stevens? Can the USSR accept on-site inspection in this case?

Georgi Arbatov

In our opinion, and we have said so repeatedly, the construction of radar stations in Krasnoyarsk is not in itself a violation of the ABM Treaty. I would also like to say that, taking into account the widespread discussion on the problem in the United States, people ignore the reality. A radar station is being built and approximately 40 to 45 per cent is finished. Our experts say that when the construction is finished, everybody—including the Americans—will see that it is not intended for anti-ballistic missile defence, but that it is designed to track space objects, satellites launched by our country and by the United States, and all activities in space. The construction of this station is not accompanied by any measures to build up a regional system of ABM defence or to create any new ABM defence elsewhere, except where allowed by the ABM Treaty, that is to say around Moscow. Americans have complained about its construction, but they also have other complaints. We too have complaints about the Americans, including radars; several of them in Texas, for example, are directed to the north, and in some other states as well. This was discussed in a special commission set up for the purpose. We did not open a campaign to discredit the United States, and I must say that when this campaign began a couple of weeks after the agreement reached between Mr. Gromyko and Mr. Shultz on the resumption of talks and the American Government officially published complaints that the USSR was violating the Treaties, I took it as a bad sign. If somebody wants to engage in negotiations and on the very first day declares his partner a liar not deserving any credibility, then I think it is a sign that that person does not want to be seriously engaged in the negotiations nor conduct them seriously.

We are not opposed to on-site inspection in principle, but we maintain a different viewpoint. We think that inspection measures must correspond to the arms reduction measures listed in the agreement, which refers to arms reduction and not to facilitating the intelligence of the other side. The wider the reduction measures, the wider will be the verification measures. We are also interested in these measures because we do not trust the Americans any more than they trust us. This question of verification and on-site inspection is a pretext rather than a reason for not concluding an agreement.

I would like to tell you a Russian joke. There was a very jealous husband who suspected that his wife was not faithful. Once he said that he was going on a trip, but he stayed. When he came home unexpectedly, he saw his wife with another man, talking and drinking, then they went to another room and switched off the light. Next morning he complained to his friend 'Again this damned uncertainty. They switched off the light and I did not see anything'. I think that in the spirit of this joke one should not overestimate this problem of inspection. It should be regarded realistically and not as an exercise in rhetoric. It is an important problem, but it is a derivative of treaties and agreements.

Chairman

Senator Stevens would you like to comment on that?

Theodore Stevens

The simple comment really is that if it is a space-tracking radar, then what military secrets would be disclosed if a group of United States Senators visited it? We visit each other's space-tracking stations, we do not visit Soviet military installations. There has been no indication that we would be welcome to inspect that station, and where it is located—just the very fact of where it is located—is a violation of the ABM Treaty. The way it is being constructed is fearsome because it means that the Soviets are going to a new generation of battle management that would be breaking out of the ABM Treaty within another two to three years. It is something that the Soviets had better address because it is the most worrisome thing so far as the Senate is concerned.

Chairman

I will turn to a question addressed to Dr. Arbatov.

Bruce Adkins

Yesterday Professor Gromyko repeated the USSR's declaration that the Soviet Union would never use nuclear weapons against a non-nuclear weapon country. But the Soviet Union has agreed with other expert authorities that a nuclear war would be equally disastrous for all countries in the world. What therefore is the practical significance of the promise not to attack, at least with nuclear weapons, non-nuclear-weapon countries?

Georgi Arbatov

I don't know whether the esteemed gentleman would feel happier if we were to withdraw this commitment and say that we will use nuclear weapons, that we will be the first to use nuclear weapons. Of course we have not in general come to grips with the hard fact of nuclear winter. This is not the only Soviet proposal. Everybody could make a commitment to no-first-use of nuclear weapons. This is actually part of an official agreement between Mr. Gromyko and Mr. Shultz to do away with nuclear weapons in general, as a final end, and this would be the only radical solution, here I would agree with you. But in the interim period I think all commitments—self-imposed or imposed by Treaty limitations—are very welcome.

Chairman

The next question is addressed to Senator Stevens.

Niall MacDermot

Do you agree that the SDI is incompatible with the ABM Treaty, and would the United States be prepared to abandon the SDI programme if satisfied by on-site inspection that the Krasnoyarsk complex does not violate, or no longer violates, the ABM Treaty?

Theodore Stevens

The SDI, which is really a composite of a series of research programmes that have been going on now for a substantial period of time, is not incompatible with the ABM Treaty at the stage it is at now. The Soviets have been engaged in similar research since 1966; they have ongoing research in particle beam weapons, in laser weapons, they even have an airborne laser weapon that they are demonstrating now, all of these are related to ABMs. We are both conducting research. As far as the relationship between the Krasnoyarsk radar and the SDI is concerned, as I said, if it is a space-tracking station, it has no business where it is. Under the ABM Treaty, it should have been on the periphery of the nation, but it is in the centre of the nation and the way it is aimed indicates to us that it is to be a battle management station for mobile anti-ballistic missiles. Under the circumstances, I just don't see the relationship, as the question implies, between our desire to accept the Soviets at their word that it is a space-tracking station and asking to visit a space-tracking station. If it *is* a space-tracking station, I don't understand the refusal to let us see it; if it isn't, then the world had better worry.

Georgi Arbatov

You know, it is not so easy, Senator Stevens. You voice suspicions that something is wrong and demand on-site inspection. If we create a precedent, then you will become insatiably curious about all sorts of things. You are yourself very strict about measures and you have strict regulations. You don't even sell us primitive—rather primitive by present standards—computers and other kinds of technology; you even brutalize your allies if they do something of this kind, so what is the fuss about? Please don't play the innocent child here.

With regard to SDI, in your contract law you have such a concept as anticipated breach. You are not simply carrying out innocent research programmes, you are doing other things. You have proclaimed that, if you have the technical opportunity to do so, you will create a massive anti-ballistic defence system to cover the whole territory of the United States. This is an absolute anticipated breach of the ABM agreement and this is what people are concerned about. As to allegations that the Soviets have done this or that, does the United States have a perfect record? The bomber gap in the 1950s, the missile gap in the 1960s, the civil defence gap, now you have the research gap, and I think it simply has no credibility.

Chairman

A further question addressed to Dr. Arbatov.

Catherine Guicherd

I suppose that Dr. Arbatov would agree with Senator Stevens that one of the main priorities is to restore a climate of confidence between the super-Powers as a prerequisite to any arms control or disarmament agreement. Senator Stevens listed some possible confidence-building measures. Does Dr. Arbatov agree with these proposals and what kind of measures would he suggest?

Georgi Arbatov

I think that any confidence-building measure, any measure to normalize Soviet-American relations, would be most welcome and should not be ignored. Although it has to be understood that there are no easy ways of carrying out the very difficult task of bringing Soviet-American relations on to the rails again. Somehow it is difficult for me to believe in what Senator Stevens has said, although I don't doubt his personal honesty, but I simply think it represents a one-sided view of the question. If he speaks about some minor things which could improve our relations then forgets that what we actually have with the United States is the worst relationship in many, many years in the economic field, with the one exception of grain, where we—as I firmly believe—do more of a favour to the United States than they do to us, helping their farmers and farming states which are really in a bad situation. We are almost in a state of economic warfare, with all the discriminatory measures, with United States attempts to persuade its allies to impose export control provisions and not to give us loans, etc., not to mention discriminatory rules in the United States; we are discriminated against on the American market.

If you take the psychological atmosphere, if you are reminded constantly that you are an evil empire which should be thrown out on the ash heap of history, if you are compared with the Nazis, if, in a speech devoted to the Second World War, the President of the United States simply forgets to mention the Soviet Union, it doesn't increase confidence. We take these words as a manifestation of intentions. It is not possible to throw us out on the ash heap of history, but there is a desire to do so and, therefore, we had better beware so as not to share the fate of Grenada, as I mentioned yesterday.

Chairman

The next question is addressed to both Senator Stevens and Dr. Arbatov.

Sheila Oakes

Recognizing that neither of you believe that your country is in any way responsible for the nuclear arms race, what actions, nevertheless, could your country undertake to reduce the fear the other has of your country's increasingly sophisticated nuclear weapons?

Theodore Stevens

I can't accept the basic premise. I think that the Soviet Union and the United States have to accept responsibility for the arms race; we are the two participants in it basically, and I think we are trying to reduce the fear of the other country. I sincerely believe that our President means it when he says that if our research indicates that it is possible to have a non-nuclear response to nuclear missiles, then we will share that information with the Russians and we would ask them to make the same commitment. We believe that we should find a way to reduce the fear of those missiles, and that if we do that we would share that information with the Soviet Union. In addition, in the current talks we have tabled a proposal that was there when the strategic talks broke up, when the Soviets left the last negotiations, and to my knowledge there has been no response, there has been no indication from the Soviet Union as to what they mean by a reduction of offensive weapons. I do believe that we are prepared to make substantial reductions in our nuclear weapons, and in my judgment the SDI concept is on the table too at these negotiations. I don't see what we can do further than that to show that we are prepared to change the course of history as far as the nuclear threat is concerned.

Georgi Arbatov

I think we can do a lot of things to reduce the nuclear threat: we can stop nuclear testing, we are ready to do it immediately; we can have a freeze. I know that this word has become unpopular in the United States, but I firmly believe that there is no way to circumvent it. If you are running like hell forwards, you have to stop before you start going backwards. It is just the law of physics and it is the law of policy. We face a very interesting situation when military technology develops tremendously quickly and the diplomatic process drags on. This means that we are really discussing yesterday's problems. I think it is necessary to introduce a freeze, not as a final goal but as a measure to create some elementary conditions for the talks. Senator Stevens was not very encouraging when he said that these talks will last for a very long time and indicated that the SALT talks lasted six and a half years, so these will maybe last more. If this situation continues, I am sure that we will soon find ourselves in a non-negotiable world where, even with the best on-site inspection available, you will be unable to verify; it will become a nightmare even to calculate what the balance is, with all the different weapons and growing asymmetries, proliferation and other things which will come as a natural result of this. So something has to be done. As to the promise which we heard from the United States: if you are successful with SDI, you will give all the technology to the Russians, excuse me, but I don't believe it. I don't believe it and if it demands such an amount of mutual goodwill and trust, if we can mobilize it, why not just start to annihilate all the offensive nuclear weapons right now, rather than circumventing everything and postponing it to God knows what time?

Chairman

The next question is also addressed to Dr. Arbatov.

Ginna Lewis

You mentioned a US nuclear bombing plan of the Soviet Union shortly after World War II. Does the Soviet Union have, or has it ever had, a bombing plan for the United States, before or after World War II, nuclear or conventional?

Georgi Arbatov

I am not at the button so it is not very easy for me to answer such questions. I am sure that people in our Ministry of Defence do what is needed for our strategy of deterrence and this provides for some plans of this kind. The Americans must know—not from talks, but from the positions of weapons—that if they attacked there would be retaliation which would cause such damage that it would make the attack against us prohibitive. This is the way we live now, and we would like to change the situation. This no-first-use pledge by the way is not simply words, it can be seen and tracked because it also demands a different positioning of military force. Of course we have weapons, I am sorry to say it, and of course they can destroy a lot of people in case of war. This is the harsh reality in which we live, but we don't want to live in it and we believe that if it goes on for a long enough time, there will be a very sad end; therefore, we are concerned about things as they are now.

Chairman

Another question addressed to both Dr. Arbatov and Senator Stevens.

Daniel Lack

Would Senator Stevens and Dr. Arbatov not agree that the answer to the concerns about the SDI would be a joint super-Power research project, the first phase of which would be devoted to the feasibility of SDI at the theoretical level?

Theodore Stevens

Dr. Arbatov doesn't believe our commitment to share with him once the research project reaches the stage of feasibility. I am not sure that he would accept any comment I might make about any joint research project, but I want to repeat that the Soviets have been conducting this research which we now call SDI for almost 20 years and they have ongoing demonstration projects, which we do not have, in the particle beam and laser areas. With regard to the attack that they are making on the SDI, I even had a call from an Ambassador in Washington concerning a message he had received from his country's Ambassador to Moscow in which the latter claimed that the Soviets had informed his nation that the space weapons that we were working on had the power to destroy hardened targets on the ground. That is absolutely false, we are not working on any weapons that could hit the ground, we are working on the concept of trying to intercept weapons that are in the air with non-nuclear, non-explosive weapons, and it is, by the nature of what we are talking about, not directed at the earth. The extent of the Soviet propaganda effort concerning SDI is overwhelming. For myself, there is nothing in SDI that is new, research projects have been ongoing, the President has put a special effort behind them because of the Soviet Union's fantastic deployment in the last few years of very heavy land-based weapons capable of delivering a first-strike capability against our country. I agree with the basic assumption of the question that we would be better off if there were more sharing of research and I, for one, would be willing to urge initiation of such a concept in the area in which we know we are both conducting research now. I think it might be possible to start that seed of co-operation in terms of the concept that the Soviets would join us in the effort to bring about radical reduction in the first-strike weapons in the first place.

Georgi Arbatov

Regarding the question of whether the Americans have already had tests, I am afraid, Senator Stevens, that your Government has secrets from you! I already told you that there are people who know that the United States has tested some components of this ABM. However, it is not the main point in what was asked, and what was said by Senator Stevens.

I think it is very dangerous and misleading to depict SDI in such a harmless manner, especially because SDI is going forward not alone but in the good company of a lot of new, very dangerous offensive weapons. If you build armour around a tank and in addition you modernize its gun, nobody will trust nor believe that it is just to defend the poor driver! It is a weapon, and this is what makes us concerned. As stated yesterday by Professor Velikhov, even if SDI is very primitive and not very effective, it can become part of a first-strike capability. If you have Pershing IIs as decapitation weapons—a very popular strategy in the United States nowadays—against control, command and communications centres, with a short flying time of six to eight minutes, you will hardly have time to get dressed. You have Trident IIs, MX and Minuteman III with the new warheads which can take care of a big part of the Soviet retaliatory arsenal, and what will be left will be dealt with by this imperfect, not very good, ABM system which is being built. This is how we understand the effort. It is not absolutely harmless.

I remember a time when the situation was reversed; Mr. McNamara tried to persuade the late Prime Minister Mr. Kosygin that defence was not always harmless. Mr. Kosygin and our leadership were very quick learners, they came to this conclusion very soon. I hope the same will happen with the Americans now.

Chairman

We now have a question addressed to Mr. Perle.

Frank von Hippel

Is the Reagan Administration willing to stop *any* weapons programme if the Soviet Union would verifiably do the same?

Richard Perle

I think the answer to that is clearly 'Yes', and a number of the proposals that we have put forward would have precisely that effect; I referred to some of them earlier. We are prepared to ban chemical weapons totally, we are prepared to eliminate intermediate missiles totally, we have, as you know, already forsworn any development of biological weapons, and I think the Soviet Union will find that there is a willingness on the part of the United States to reciprocate any programme that we can find. I think it is important to recognize that, however much we may wish that the degree of trust necessary to proceed without confidence in the behaviour of the other side will one day arrive, it has not arrived yet. As a practical matter, we find it necessary to insist that there be adequate means of verification. In these areas, that is difficult, but we think it is possible, and we believe that the proposals we have put forward are adequately verifiable and will lead to precisely the results suggested by the question.

Chairman

The next two questions are addressed to both Mr. Perle and Professor Galbraith.

Paul Sieghart

It has been said that a few hundred nuclear warheads, out of the thousands in the arsenals of the two super-Powers, are more than enough to inflict 'unacceptable damage' on the other, and that the use of more would anyway risk a suicidal nuclear winter. If that is so, what would you advise your Government to do if the USSR unilaterally (and credibly) retired 1,000-2,000-3,000 of its strategic warheads?

Richard Perle

I would not have the slightest hesitation in applauding such a development and urging that the United States follow suit. Indeed,. it is fundamental to the position that we have taken in the negotiations here in Geneva that we are prepared significantly to reduce the number of weapons in our arsenal even beyond those unilateral reductions that have been made in the years since 1967.

Kenneth Galbraith

I would not like to forgo any conceivable opportunity to agree with Secretary Perle.

Yoshiaki Iisaka

You said that the A-bombs were dropped on Hiroshima and Nagasaki to save American and Japanese lives. At the time of the dropping, the United States knew full well that the Japanese war-executing capability was almost drained and that it had already started exploration of surrender talks. Moreover, bombs were dropped on the densely populated cities. Do you still justify the dropping?

Richard Perle

I was about four years old at the time and not able to judge for myself. My impression is that, whether it has turned out to be right or wrong, it was widely believed in the United States and believed by the President that the behaviour exhibited by Japanese forces in the war up until that point suggested that the invasion of the Japanese homeland would produce very large numbers of casualties on both sides. We'll never know, I am afraid, whether that was true or not, and in responding as I did to the suggestion that those bombs were dropped to make a political point, I sought only to clarify the record insofar as I think an understanding of the President who made that decision—a thoroughly decent man—needed to be said.

Kenneth Galbraith

This is a complicated matter in history, it could lead to a long discussion. One of the major documents—perhaps the major document—on the subject was a report called 'Japan's Struggle to End the War' by the US Strategic Bombing Survey to which I referred earlier, the principal guiding voice of which was Paul Nitze, who is not regarded as a radical on these matters. That report concluded in fact that the atomic bombs had ended the war about two weeks earlier than it would otherwise have ended. However, that was not known to the people who were associated with the action. Two things were relevant there: first, that the military operations had by that time in the Pacific, as earlier in the bombing of Dresden in the European theatre, developed a dynamic of their own in which specific questions were unfortunately not asked. Perhaps this was inevitable. Secondly, the actions that were then being taken in the Japanese Cabinet—the famous Cabinet meeting called by the Emperor to quiet the disconsolate forces that were arguing for suicidal action—were not known. Nor was the enormous destructiveness of this weapon really known; it certainly wasn't appreciated. George Ball, subsequently Under-Secretary, came back to Germany that summer to tell me that we had a weapon that had been tested—it's an indication of how good our information was—either in South Dakota or North Dakota, and had destroyed a considerable part of the whole state. But this was something we didn't believe; the destructive power of the bomb was not imagined. Having said all this, if we were going to use it, we certainly should have used it on some unoccupied territory.

Chairman

I would like to ask Professor Rotblat, who was involved in the Los Alamos affair, if he would make some comments on this point.

Joseph Rotblat

As perhaps the only one present here who was involved in the Manhattan Project, I would like to make one comment from my own experience. In March 1944, I was involved in a conversation with General Leslie Groves, who was the Head of the Manhattan Project, and he said in Los Alamos 'You realize, of course, that the whole purpose of making the atom bomb is to subdue our chief enemy, the Russians'. Now this was said, you remember, in March 1944. He subsequently repeated this remark about ten years later during the Oppenheimer hearings. This was his view, I don't say that it was the official view of the Administration, but certainly of the head of the Manhattan Project.

With regard to the reasons for dropping the bomb—both bombs—to end the war so soon, perhaps I should remind you of the thesis put forward by Professor Blackett, who said in his book that the main reason why two bombs were used when only one would bring the war to a finish immediately was because it was feared that the Soviets would bring their armies to the Far East, to Japan, if time was allowed for the war to be prolonged, and it appeared that the armies were being transferred much faster than the Western leaders thought and this would mean that the Soviets would have occupied Japan. Therefore, it was politically imperative to finish the war as quickly as possible.

Chairman

A footnote on that: you will recall that the physicists who were associated with the development in the Manhattan Project pleaded and tried to arrange the dropping of a demonstration bomb on an uninhabited island to show its destructiveness before it would be used on a civilian population. Unfortunately, that did not gain acceptance in Washington.

There are two questions that are associated, both on the Comprehensive Test Ban Treaty, and they are addressed to Mr. Perle and Senator Stevens.

Eric Fersht

Please explain the reasoning behind the current United States policy that concluding a Comprehensive Test Ban Treaty at this time would make achievement of bilateral deep strategic arms reductions impossible.

Erica Parra

Why does the United States not take up the Soviet offer to stop all nuclear testing if the United States will, and write a Comprehensive Test Ban Treaty?

Richard Perle

I believe the premise in the first question to be wrong. I am unaware of any linkage between the prospects for reductions in strategic forces and the question of a comprehensive test ban. We have one important problem with the prospect of a comprehensive test ban and that is we cannot verify compliance with that ban at low levels of nuclear testing. Beyond that, a number of the developments in the United States in recent years that have required nuclear testing have had the effect of permitting weapons that are considerably improved with respect to safety and security, necessary elements in any comprehensive programme to protect against nuclear terrorism. I frankly believe that the potential for the development of new nuclear weapons, even with the prohibition on testing, is really quite considerable, given the ability to extrapolate from the existing data bases that exist on both sides. And so I do not believe that a ban on nuclear testing would be followed—even if it could be verified and were fully adhered to—by an end to the further development of nuclear warheads.

Chairman

The next question is addressed to Mr. Perle.

Enrique ter Horst

Does the international economic crisis, i.e. the debt question, protectionism, international monetary instability and the effect it has on social and political stability in the world, enter into your strategic considerations and, if so, how?

Richard Perle

It is the policy of the Government of the United States, and not just this Administration but previous Administrations as well, to recognize that instability, poverty, a rate of economic development in many places in the world that is unsatisfactory, are potential causes of conflict and dispute, and potentially causes of conflicts and disputes that could escalate and embroil the super-Powers. So, of course, we view with concern economic difficulties around the world. While we don't do all that we might, or in my view all that we should, to give assistance to countries that are in difficulty and need help, I think we do reasonably well by international standards and would hope we could do better in the future.

Chairman

Professor Anatoly Gromyko has asked for a few minutes to respond to some of the remarks that were made earlier about him by Mr. Perle.

Anatoly Gromyko

Frankly speaking, to some extent I am satisfied that Mr. Perle has criticized some points and observations of my report. When an American hawk criticizes a Soviet professor who favours disarmament and the ideas of Einstein and Russell, believe me, Mr. Perle, you made me feel happy. So from the bottom of my heart, I thank you for your remarks and comments, though at the same time I must stress another important point. It is not Academician Arbatov who is rewriting the history of post-war relations between the United States and the Soviet Union, it is you, and people higher than you, who are trying to rewrite the history. One can have one's own judgement about this. Perhaps you are convinced that we are trying to rewrite post-war history, but in fact it is the Reagan Administration and people like you who are trying to rewrite history, but this cannot be done, Mr. Perle. History will stay as it was, and no amount of speeches can change what happened after the Second World War. To speak of Hiroshima and Nagasaki, of course, some American soldiers' and officers' lives were saved, I would agree on this, but is it a price that was to be paid by killing hundreds of thousands of innocent civilians, children, women? Have you ever seen pictures of this terrible experience, Mr. Perle? Would you like your own children to be under such an academic review as you gave of this period? I hesitate to say so, but it seems to me that perhaps you could again answer whether you personally, as a person present among us, not as a historian, condemn the use of weapons against civilians; whether you think that it is a crime. I must remind you that after the Second World War the Nazi leaders were hanged at Nuremberg for crimes against civilians and civilian populations, not for military warfare, but for crimes against civilians. So this is really a moral question, and to dodge it by saying that Mr. Truman was a decent person is, in my opinion, perhaps not to answer the question itself.

For a long time, Mr. Perle, beginning with the time when you served with the late Senator Jackson, you have been trying to undermine Soviet-American relations. Not only the tone, but also the substance, of your report show that being a part of the military-industrial complex you are in favour of the armaments race and not disarmament, and your speech today convinced me that for Soviet-American relations, for the people who are in favour of developing Soviet-American relations, it would be impossible, either in the present or in the future—this is my personal opinion, and I would be very happy if I am wrong—to deal with such a kind of approach as you have demonstrated here. It even seems to me that, in your opinion, the worse Soviet-American relations are, the better for the United States. I think that the security of the United States is not based on any new weapons system, which only undermines it. Believe it or not, Mr. Perle, the security of the United States, as well as our security, is based on real compromises with the Soviet Union. One should think about real compromises and not just stone-walling policies which, as far as I understand, you are happy about.

Chairman

The next question is addressed to Dr. Arbatov and Mr. Perle.

Mohamed Shaker

Now that we are approaching the Third NPT Review Conference, what in your view would be the most appropriate action to be taken by the two super-Powers with regard to Article VI before the convening of the Conference? Do you think that the ongoing negotiations between the two super-Powers in Geneva may yield some results before the Review Conference?

Georgi Arbatov

I think that actually we could announce that we will stop all nuclear testing; it would be a very proper thing to do and it is absolutely verifiable. I am astonished at what Mr. Perle said here. With the very serious advances in seismography and other scientific methods of detection—you can talk to all the specialists, I have done so with American, Soviet and British specialists—you can be absolutely sure about verifying even the smallest nuclear explosion in the world. If we could manage to announce a freeze, let us say for a year, on all space and nuclear weapons, this would also be a tremendously important contribution to the non-proliferation regime in the world. There are a lot of possibilities, but what is really needed is political will. You do not even need to strain your imagination very much, all of it has already been discussed many times. It is very clear, and I would use this opportunity to make one very short comment: I do not want to address Mr. Perle in the way he addressed me, and I understand that, long before the advent of Mr. Perle on the political scene, Russell said that there are three kinds of lies—lies, damned lies and statistics. I think that Mr. Perle contributed to our conference in a very great way, because what he did is just what represents absolutely accurately the policy of this Administration: the Soviets are so bad that you cannot trust them at all, they cheat, they lie, so you just cannot do any business with them, and you cannot have agreements with them. This is what he proved in a very eloquent way today, and this is what concerns me most and this is what I talked about. I see no progress under such circumstances.

Richard Perle

As you know, we now have negotiations under way in Geneva and highly competent negotiators on both sides. A great deal of work has been done in both countries to understand the details of these issues, and they are complex. It is clear that if there is any hope at all for progress before the NPT Review Conference, it will come in those negotiating forums where competent negotiators are prepared to conclude agreements. We will not be able to achieve agreement in that time or for so long as it is the position of the Soviet Union that there can be no agreement unless and until the United States terminates a research programme that it knows well we are not prepared to terminate and for reasons, not least of all, having to do with the nature of the Soviet comparable programme and the impossibility of verifying compliance with the ban on research.

I do not want to be left in the position that Professor Gromyko sought to put me in, suggesting that I am somehow callous or indifferent to the loss of civilian life from nuclear weapons or weapons of any kind. I responded, as you know, to what I thought was an unfair charge, that the motives of the President of the United States in using the atomic bomb were to demonstrate that the United States possessed it and to use that weapon to intimidate other countries. I thought I had responded to that point by observing that in the whole of the period that the United States uniquely possessed nuclear weapons, they were never used for that purpose. I think the historical record on that stands, but I am glad that it was possible to join these issues, and I would hope that we could find occasions on which to review the history of the misunderstandings that have developed between us, because I have a strong sense that much of the doubt and much of the suspicion that now clouds the relationship has its roots in the interpretation of historical events about which interpretations differ. I hope that in my comments—I certainly know that I tried—I refrained from characterizing the individuals whose remarks I commented upon. I tried to address myself to what had been said previously, but I do not think it reasonable to expect me to come out somewhere in the middle, a luxury that Professor Galbraith managed to use most eloquently, having first listened to the accusation that my country does not desire arms control, that it is preparing for limited nuclear war in Europe, that it has neutron bombs associated with its central command and the several other allegations to which I felt bound to respond.

Chairman

The next question is addressed to Mr. Perle.

Gwyn Prins

Would you be good enough to confirm or deny that the views expressed in those portions of *Defense Guidance 1984–1988*, now in the public domain, and to which Dr. Arbatov referred earlier, reflect accurately the long-term strategy for United States-Soviet relationships held by the Administration in which you serve?

Richard Perle

I am sorry to say that it is difficult to comment on that rather lengthy document without specifying more precisely which statements in it I would be expected to confirm or deny. It is, like all documents, an atrocious bureaucratic product that has little bearing on our actual defence policy. So I can only respond to a more precise question, but I can sum up the policy of the United States by saying that it is to maintain nuclear forces for the purpose of deterring an attack against the United States and its allies, and for that purpose alone.

Chairman

Congressman Markey, could I ask you to comment for a couple of minutes on some of the points made this morning? I think that you are an expert in some parts of this field.

Edward Markey

I believe that if the nuclear Powers are unwilling, as a minimum requirement, to abandon military deterrent strategies which contemplate the first use of nuclear weapons to deter conventional as well as nuclear threats, then the appeal of nuclear weapons in world politics is certain to become universal. After all, if nuclear weapons really do confer immunity from conventional attack, why should every nation not have one? One cannot chant the mantra of nuclear deterrence with unbridled enthusiasm and at the same time attempt to silence other nations when they seek to add their voices to the nuclear chorus. The old double standard of nuclear deterrents for the few and nuclear denial for the many has obviously run its course in this world, so for those outside the super-Power conflict or who would somehow manage to see beyond it, the two-way tunnel vision of the Soviet Union and the United States is truly stupefying. While the Reagan Administration wastes time here in Geneva trying to sell the Soviet Union on the President's vision of a stabilizing defensive arms race in space, and while the Soviet Union responds by becoming utterly engrossed in deflating some space war fantasies, some 260 commercial power reactors worldwide are churning out 45 tonnes of bomb-usable plutonium every year, the equivalent of 6,000 nuclear weapons. If present trends continue, by the year 2000 there could be as much as 400 tonnes of bomb-usable plutonium circulating in world commerce—nearly twice the combined plutonium stockpile of the two super-Powers. I do not believe that the world is ready for widespread traffic in separated plutonium, I do not believe that the world will ever be ready for widespread traffic in plutonium. So the United States and the Soviet Union have to bite the bullet if they expect the other countries of this world to do so. Those who still harbour dreams of breeding plutonium as a boundless source of power must give up their cherished illusions, we must deny political terrorists even the possibility of building or attaining nuclear bombs and that means stopping the world-wide spread of nuclear-weapons-usable materials—plutonium and highly-enriched uranium—as well as the technology to produce it.

I wind up with a question to Dr. Arbatov and Mr. Perle, which I hope that they can address here this morning, and that is that as long as the super-Powers remain transfixed by the coercive possibilities of nuclear weaponry and obsessed in many ways—and I believe that this is how the world looks at it—with the minutiae of the nuclear balance, in the light of the fact that both countries have the capacity to destroy the other many times over, how can we possibly expect other nations not to develop the very same obsession and will they not pursue nuclear arms with the same tenacity that the super-Powers continue to demonstrate, and will the horizontal arms race ultimately outstrip the vertical arms race as the real danger to the stability of this planet?

Georgi Arbatov

I agree with you.

Richard Perle

Knowing well the sentiments in this room, it would be easy to say that the pressures for horizontal proliferation are a function, or largely a function, of the armaments of the super-Powers. I will not say that because I believe that it is too easy an excuse, too easy a justification for the many separate efforts that are under way around the world by countries which wish to acquire nuclear weapons for purposes that are largely local and regional in nature, and whose desire to acquire those weapons would in my judgement not be significantly diminished even if the United States and the Soviet Union were extraordinarily successful in arriving at negotiated arms control agreements. The desire to acquire nuclear weapons elsewhere did not diminish much when, in 1972, agreements were reached between the United States and the Soviet Union and greeted with enormous, and I am sorry to say, subsequently disappointed, optimism.

On the question of plutonium, I agree with you entirely. There is no place for the spread of plutonium around the world in any sensible policy aimed at restricting the proliferation of nuclear weapons and I think that traffic in plutonium ought to be halted and halted absolutely.

Georgi Arbatov

In essence, I agree with you, this is a great danger. I think we have to see that it is not a direct function of automatic consequences of a vertical arms race that it will be horizontal, but it makes it most probable and maybe inevitable. I will say that, just as with the problem of international terrorism, all of it is connected with this high-tension style of political relations which exists now between East and West—the United States and the Soviet Union—not in the sense which was popular in your country to look for the hand of Moscow behind any mischief which occurs in the world. The whole atmosphere of tension, of suspicion, of armament, of expectation of a war to come, of some calamities, catastrophes, makes inevitable such hectic and very painful events as the manifestation of terrorism and also proliferation of nuclear armaments. The problem is much deeper than that. In order not to have nuclear war, it is not enough to give a solemn oath that we will never push the button; it is necessary to reconstruct the whole system of international relations, the whole atmosphere, our attitudes, our modes of foreign policy behaviour. As a species, we are the first to make instruments which can destroy us as a human species and up till now we have quite honestly lived by the law of the jungle in international relations. He is right and we have to understand this, that all of this is incompatible with the instruments of mutual annihilation which we possess now.

Chairman

There is one more question addressed to Dr. Arbatov and Mr. Perle.

Harald Müller

What would your reaction be:

1. If the Western Europeans made the acquisition of an independent satellite monitoring capability a high priority area of the EUREKA programme?
2. If they assisted the United Nations in acquiring such a capability, in accordance with the French proposal of 1978?

Chairman

I might say that I have a self-interest in this question because Pugwash made the first analysis of the costs of such a peace-keeping satellite. We have had two meetings in France on this and it would be very interesting to hear the comments of both Dr. Arbatov and Mr. Perle on how it would be viewed from the standpoint of the two big Powers. The idea is to have a peace-keeping satellite for monitoring purposes to monitor the adherence to treaties by the neutral and non-aligned countries or the European countries.

Georgi Arbatov

As an idea it deserves serious analysis and is negotiable. It can be done only following the agreement of all parties concerned, and I don't believe that it will solve all the problems facing us, but it might be found deserving of serious consideration. I don't know.

Richard Perle

We are an open society and I would not be in the least troubled at the prospect that third countries would have a surveillance capability that would permit them to observe military activities in both the United States and the Soviet Union. Indeed, I think it would solve one of the problems we now have which is that there is insufficient information available to the international community in detail about what is going on in our respective countries, so from that point of view I would see no problem with it whatsoever. I think it would run into difficulty, however, if the satellite were to make observations in some regions of the world where conflicts exist and where participants in such conflicts would be very uneasy indeed at the dissemination of information about the disposition of their military forces to others, including their potential enemies. I think the idea has practical problems, but as far as my own country is concerned, if third Powers or United Nations institutions were in a position to verify compliance with arms control agreements we might have a higher standard of compliance and that would be a very positive development.

V

The Nuclear Non-Proliferation Treaty and its Future

CHAIRMAN:

MR. PAUL SIEGHART

Barrister. Trustee, European Human Rights Foundation. Chairman, Executive Committee, British Section of the International Commission of Jurists

ARTICLE VI AND THE IMPORTANCE OF A COMPREHENSIVE TEST BAN TREATY

Non-Proliferation and Nuclear Arms Control

THE HONORABLE EDWARD M. KENNEDY

Senator for Massachusetts (Democrat)

I want to thank the Groupe de Bellerive for your kind invitation to speak today. You have assembled a distinguished group of individuals from around the world who share a deep interest and concern for the problems of nuclear war and nuclear proliferation. I want to pay special tribute to Prince Sadruddin Aga Khan for his leadership and commitment in bringing together statesmen, scientists and experts to discuss these vital questions. Since its founding the Groupe de Bellerive has provided a widely respected forum for the challenging issues of peace in our environment that face the world today.

We meet at an auspicious time. For Monday marks the 17th anniversary of the signing of the Non-Proliferation Treaty by the United States, the Soviet Union and 60 other nations. This September the Third NPT Review Conference will convene here in the City of Peace. One hundred and twenty-nine countries which have now ratified the NPT will come together to discuss the past and the future of this historic agreement. The NPT is a linchpin in our effort to halt the spread of nuclear weapons and ultimately to put an end to the nuclear arms race.

Perhaps most significant of all, on 6 August, we will observe the 40th anniversary of the dawn of the nuclear age—four decades since the mushroom cloud at Hiroshima changed the face of war for all time.

The immediate horror of Hiroshima has faded; its survivors are fewer and fewer. An entire generation of humanity has been born since that fateful day. The leaders of tomorrow have come of age in the nuclear era. The world has learned to live in the shadow of nuclear war, but sadly, we have done too little in these four decades to eliminate the possibility that nuclear weapons will ever again be used—by accident or in anger. The nuclear stockpiles of the United States and the Soviet Union have spiralled up to the point that together we now possess 50,000 warheads. And even our modest efforts at arms control threaten to unravel amid allegations of cheating, bad faith, and impatience with their constraints.

And always there is the ever-present danger of the proliferation of nuclear weapons. In these unstable times, when regional conflict and international terrorism flash across the globe, the importance of limiting the spread of nuclear weapons has never been more obvious. The Non-Proliferation Treaty has contributed substantially to that goal—but not substantially enough. In recent years a number of non-signatory States have edged closer to the production of nuclear weapons. Unless this fearful trend can be reversed, the nuclear peace of the past 40 years could easily be broken.

The complex problem of maintaining stability with the small number of nuclear-weapon States we have today is difficult enough; with more extensive proliferation, the task could become unmanageable. For this reason, it is critical that the NPT should be extended, not dismantled. And the nuclear-weapon States bear a special responsibility to prevent its demise by living up to their own commitments to one another and to the non-weapon States.

Part of that commitment consists of the Article I obligation not to participate in the transfer of nuclear weapons and weapon materials to non-weapon States. But equally important is the obligation set forth in Article VI, which calls on the Parties to 'pursue negotiations in good faith on effective measures relating to cessation of the nuclear arms race at an early date and to nuclear disarmament'.

The central importance of Article VI to the success of the Treaty was well-recognized at the time the NPT was negotiated. As America's Ambassador to the United Nations, Arthur Goldberg noted: 'My country believes that the permanent viability of this Treaty will depend in large measure on our success in the future negotiations contemplated in Article VI.' And President Johnson stated: 'The non-nuclear States have wanted their renunciation of nuclear weapons to be matched with a binding pledge by the nuclear Powers to negotiate a halt in the arms race. The obligations of the Non-Proliferation Treaty will reinforce our will to bring an end to the nuclear arms race. The world will judge us by our performance.'

Seventeen years later, what judgement has the world given? Four major arms control treaties have been negotiated since the NPT was signed. Three—the Threshold Test Ban Treaty, Peaceful Nuclear Explosions Treaty and SALT II—have never been ratified by the US, although both Parties have pledged to abide by their terms. The fourth agreement—SALT I, which includes the ABM treaty—is jeopardized by actions on both sides. Some Soviet activities appear to violate the Treaty; and the United States has now declared its intent to develop a 'Star Wars' system that could not be implemented without violating the Treaty.

The stockpile of nuclear warheads grows while stability is undermined by the modernization that brings greater accuracy, shorter warning time and increased effectiveness. Since the US terminated CTB negotiations in 1982, the US and the USSR have set aside the active pursuit of an end to nuclear testing—an important pre-condition for an end to the arms race and ultimately for nuclear disarmament.

The US termination of CTB negotiations jeopardizes efforts to stop the arms race by halting so-called vertical proliferation. Equally important is the role CTB plays in holding the NPT regime together—the problem of 'horizontal proliferation'. Indeed, the preamble to the NPT explicitly recognizes the link by reaffirming the bold commitment expressed in the Limited Test Ban Treaty—'to seek to achieve the discontinuation of all test explosions of nuclear weapons for all time'.

For three decades, every American President until now has sought to limit nuclear testing. President Eisenhower proposed a halt to nuclear testing in 1957 and he later called the failure to achieve it the greatest disappointment of his Presidency. Two decades ago, President Kennedy said in his commencement address at American University in 1963, 'The conclusion of a [test ban] treaty, so near and yet so far, would check the spiralling arms race in one of its most dangerous areas. It would place the nuclear powers in a position to deal more effectively with one of the greatest hazards which man faces, the further spread of nuclear arms. It would increase our security—it would decrease the prospects of war'.

This judgment was shared by President Nixon who stated that 'an adequately verified comprehensive test ban would be a positive contribution to moderating the arms race'. And just a few months ago, Presidents Ford and Carter reiterated their view of the importance of achieving a CTBT.

By 1979, the United States, the Soviet Union and Great Britain had made substantial progress in negotiating a test ban. But those talks were suspended in the wake of the Soviet invasion of Afghanistan that year. In 1982, the Reagan Administration announced its withdrawal from the test ban negotiations altogether. They also indicated that they would not seek ratification of the two previously negotiated treaties, unless the Soviets agreed to reopen them and provide additional verification procedures.

Administration spokesmen contend that a test ban remains a 'long-term objective of the US'. But they are unwilling to pursue such negotiations now, until more is accomplished with respect to 'broad, deep and verifiable arms reductions, maintenance of a credible nuclear deterrent, expanded confidence-building measures and improved verification capabilities'.

It is difficult to understand why progress on a test ban must be conditioned on successful arms reductions. An end to nuclear testing would slow the arms race and make the climate more conducive to achieving deep reductions. But if both sides race forward with a new generation of nuclear arms, an agreement will be far more difficult to achieve.

I am particularly troubled by the Administration's second argument for breaking off CTB negotiations—the need to 'maintain a credible nuclear deterrent'. We possess enough nuclear weapons today to make Soviet rubble bounce all the way from Moscow to Vladivostok. To suggest that we need to test and develop more weapons to 'maintain a credible deterrent' is the kind of contorted logic that will guarantee a never-ending arms race in which both sides will be the losers.

I find no merit in the claim that a test ban cannot adequately be verified. Improvements in seismology have made adequate verification a reality. The Soviets have already agreed to on-site inspection in earlier negotiations. Rather than prejudge what specific provisions they will accept, let us present our proposals and judge their response.

The time now is ideal to complete the unfinished business of a CTB. We have begun to emerge from the dangerous period of recent years, when the US terminated the CTB talks and the Soviets walked out of the INF and START negotiations.

I welcome President Reagan's decision to resume discussions on arms reductions and preventing a space arms race in the talks here in Geneva. He has an historic opportunity to create the most important arms control agreement of our time, if both sides show the requisite flexibility.

I am also encouraged that the President has rejected the counsel of right wing opponents of arms control, and has agreed to abide by the SALT II limits. These are small, but important steps.

In this context, CTB negotiations could be a significant additional step in improving the climate for a far-reaching agreement to end the nuclear arms race now and for all times.

Yet, as Secretary Weinberger has indicated in testimony before our Senate Armed Services Committee, the issue of CTB is not part of the current Geneva arms talks. Perhaps not, but there is no reason why the talks, which neared fruition in the late 1970s, should not be resumed. An agreement is within reach—while the complex three-cornered negotiations continue on strategic arms, INF and space.

And if President Reagan were also to announce his personal support for ratification of the Threshold Test Ban Treaty and the Peaceful Nuclear Explosions Treaty—it would signal a new era of cooperation between the United States and the Soviet Union. It would demonstrate to the rest of the world—and to the NPT signatories in particular—that the nuclear super-Powers are serious about their obligations under Article VI.

A decision by American and Soviet leaders to undertake new initiatives against nuclear testing would receive broad, enthusiastic and bi-partisan support among the American people. Last year, the United States Senate overwhelmingly approved a resolution I offered with Senator Mathias, calling on the President to submit the two pending treaties for ratification—and to resume CTB negotiations. An identical resolution passed the House Foreign Affairs Committee last month and the House of Representatives is expected to take up this resolution in the near future. It is my hope that President Reagan will respond to Congress' call, and make known to the Soviets that the United States stands ready and willing to pursue a Comprehensive Test Ban.

I do not advocate unilateral or unverifiable measures. But, at the same time, the difficulties associated with verification cannot be made an excuse to evade negotiations entirely. Both sides agreed in principle to on-site verification in the last round of CTB negotiations. A broad consensus exists in the seismological community that with appropriate on-site inspection and in-country sensors, high confidence verification of a test ban treaty could be achieved down to a level of 1 kiloton or less—sufficient to drastically minimize, if not eliminate, the mililtary utility of testing.

The same broad support for a test ban treaty will be felt at the third NPT Review Conference in September. The delegations will carry with them the words of the First Review Conference—which concluded that 'a treaty banning all nuclear weapons tests is one of the most important measures to halt the nuclear arms race', and which urged nuclear-weapon States, 'to make every effort to reach agreement on the conclusion of an effective comprehensive test ban'. The halls still echo with the pointed challenge of the President of the First Review Conference, Ambassador Thorsson of Sweden, who addressed both Moscow and Washington when she said:

> You should not be allowed to turn the nuclear armament spiral one or several rounds upward only in order to put yourself in a better bargaining position while the world is crying out for nuclear disarmament.

How true her words ring today, when both sides seek to justify new and more dangerous rounds of nuclear escalation as 'bargaining chips'.

I have focussed my remarks today on the contribution that a test ban could make toward strengthening the NPT. But there are many other avenues that must also be pursued to achieve that goal. One important step is to close the loopholes and clarify the ambiguities in the ABM Treaty that may lead to the Treaty's erosion. Increased attention to conventional defenses would raise the nuclear threshold and reduce our dependence on nuclear arms. Confidence-building measures and advances in crisis control could limit the risk of accidental nuclear war.

The arms race is not simply a narrow competition between the two super-Powers, or among a handful of nuclear-weapon States. As we learn more about the nuclear winter that would follow even a partial nuclear exchange, our knowledge reinforces the obligation that we owe not only to our own citizens but to all the peoples of the earth. Arms control can never be the private preserve of the super-Powers, their generals or their wizards in their weapons labs. Ordinary citizens, in my own country and around the globe, have become increasingly outspoken and active in challenging their political leaders to bring the world back from the nuclear precipice. And those leaders will be held accountable for their progress.

Ten years ago I came to Geneva as a member of the US delegation to the first NPT Review Conference. I said at that time: 'Let us therefore challenge both super-Powers to break the old habit of seeing problems of nuclear weapons solely in terms of US–Soviet relations; let us seek to break the cycle of arms competition that feeds upon itself—to no benefit for either side. Neither super-Power gains from continuing the nuclear arms race; they will both lose if their own actions call forth nuclear arms races among other nations'.

As we go forth today, let us renew that challenge. The US and Soviet delegations meeting in this city on arms control have the obligation—and the opportunity—to act for the benefit of all humanity. The Non-Proliferation Treaty is a dramatic statement of our universal and indivisible stake in the maintenance of peace in the nuclear age. If we fail, there will be no survivors to record our mistakes. But with sufficient commitment, and goodwill, we shall succeed.

As President Kennedy observed in proposing a nuclear test ban treaty, 'never have the nations of the world had so much to lose, or so much to gain'. I am grateful to all of you for inviting me here. We share a common commitment to the cause of peace, and to a future free from the fear of nuclear war.

THE NPT: THE VIEW OF THE DEPOSITARIES

The Non-Proliferation Treaty

THE RT. HON. DR. DAVID OWEN MP

Leader of the British Social Democratic Party

The Non-Proliferation Treaty signed in 1968 and entering into force in 1970 puts two major obligations on the nuclear-weapon States. Under Article V they agree to make any benefits available from the peaceful use of nuclear explosions and under Article VI to enter into good faith negotiations on effective arms control and disarmament. The nuclear-weapon States have regrettably not lived up to these obligations. Of that there can be no doubt. The critics amongst the non-nuclear-weapon States and particularly the signatories to the Non-Proliferation Treaty have every right to feel let down by the nuclear-weapon States. But it is too simplistic to ascribe the movement towards horizontal proliferation among the non-nuclear-weapon States as being primarily a response to the vertical proliferation amongst the nuclear-weapon States.

History tells us that political leaders decide to acquire nuclear weapons either because they perceive the need for nuclear deterrence or their political ambitions need to be buttressed by their nation becoming a nuclear-weapon State. If one examines the political-military situation of the countries most likely to have or to become nuclear-weapon States in this decade, namely, India, Pakistan, Libya, Iraq, North and South Korea, Taiwan, Brazil, Argentina or Israel, one can see both national and regional political and military pressures combining to extend proliferation. Nuclear proliferation is therefore not an abstract but a very specific problem. The technical complexities and the political-military realities dictate that only a limited number of non-nuclear-weapon States can be considered as likely candidates for going nuclear.

Global non-proliferation instruments, such as the Non-Proliferation Treaty, only have a limited effectiveness in solving each of these, in their own way, unique situations. Sadly, it is a fact that the national political and military situation is by far the strongest influence on the decision to go nuclear, whatever the rest of the international community does or says.

Despite the rhetoric of many international conferences on the implementation of Article VI of the Non-Proliferation Treaty, there is little connection between the decision of say, Pakistan, to go nuclear and the current status of the Geneva negotiations between the United States and the USSR. Whether the super-Powers limit their warheads to 7,500 each will not make much difference to the Pakistani President, whose security concerns—and political objectives—are far removed from the minutiae of these negotiations, and are primarily driven by regional and national pressures. The one action by the super-Powers that would influence the Pakistani President would be the announcement of an immediate moratorium on all nuclear testing.

Security guarantees by nuclear-weapon States appear to have only marginal influence on some of the nuclear candidates. Super-Power guarantees have had an influence in East and West Europe but in truth no country in Europe once France became a nuclear-weapon State has shown much interest in developing nuclear weapons. In the case of Taiwan and South Korea, and in a different way, Pakistan and Israel, the relationship with the US has at times delayed the acquisition of nuclear weapons. Taiwan and South Korea, when it was discovered that they were in the process of acquiring nuclear weapons, were actually stopped by the United States. The Soviet Union has an excellent record in controlling proliferation and has blocked countries within the Warsaw Pact from acquiring nuclear weapons. When exporting nuclear power stations it has been able to insist on a totally closed fuel cycle. Yet if any of the Western democracies had been so strict, they would have been accused of colonial exploitation. The slackness of the Western democracies over the fuel cycle, which has fed proliferation, has not just been due to mercantalist attitudes but has also had an element of colonialist guilt. The Soviet Union has more room for manoeuvre on these sorts of issues than the United States. President Carter's Administration soon learnt, after it decided in 1977 to withdraw US troops from South Korea, that the relationship then changed. No longer could the US be so certain that their influence on nuclear and other matters would remain. China may have lost influence on North Korea's nuclear aspirations when it dramatically improved its bilateral relations with the US. US arms deliveries at varying times to Israel, Pakistan, Taiwan, Brazil and Argentina did not prevent any of these countries from contemplating—or working towards—acquiring nuclear weapons. To state such hard, and maybe for some, unpalatable realities, does not mean however that efforts aimed at improving the security and political stability in the candidate nuclear-weapon States are without value. They can be critical factors in dampening the aspirations to become a nuclear-weapon State. Nor do these realities excuse the obscene increase in nuclear warhead numbers that the nuclear-weapon States continue to produce, far in excess of what is needed for any credible strategy of nuclear deterrence.

The link between a comprehensive test ban and the reinforcement of the NPT is challenged by some who argue that none of the non-signatories will ever now sign up for the NPT. They go further and argue that even for those who have signed the NPT the decision to develop nuclear weapons is of such national importance that their governments will not be deflected from taking a decision of such overriding importance by the existence of a CTB. Yet a nuclear test is a political as well as a military threshold as we saw at Hiroshima. Incidentally, the first nuclear arms race was not between the US and the USSR. It was between the US, the UK and Canada, fearful of Nazi Germany acquiring nuclear weapons, an ever-present fear for a few throughout the Second World War.

If the maintenance of a CTB by the nuclear-weapon States was made conditional on no further proliferation, the political leverage of the nuclear-weapon States to halt proliferation would be vastly enhanced. The consequences of a total test ban, in addition to curbing proliferation, would be to slow the technological nuclear weapons race in the particular and important area of warhead design. But we should be realistic. Banning tests would not stop nuclear warhead development. Given the simulation capacity of the nuclear-weapon States' large computers, warhead modification will go ahead even after a CTB. But a CTB would be a step back, though in scope a modest step back, from the ever increasing sophistication and numbers of nuclear warheads and delivery systems. It would also greatly improve the political atmosphere between the super-Powers and make it far easier to achieve 'deep cuts' in strategic weapon systems, maintain the ABM Treaty and avoid deploying defensive systems in space.

To maintain the ABM Treaty while the US and the USSR continue to research into space defence, we should strengthen the ABM Treaty by extending the period of warning for its abrogation from the present ridiculously short period of six months to a five-year notice of abrogation. That would be a considerable safeguard against a sudden breakthrough in SDI research followed by deployment within six months. Though one can have a warning period for deploying observable defence, a warning period after a nuclear explosion is worthless for whoever can observe the deployment of nuclear weapons. It is the political significance of crossing the nuclear test threshold in the next year or so that holds the potential to deal an irreparable blow to the already fragile credibility of the NPT.

The argument for a CTB once the furore over the 1974 Indian test died down has tended to be somewhat abstract. The situation in the Indian subcontinent now makes the arguments a matter of vital practical politics. Kahuta, the Pakistan Institute of Nuclear Research, 20 miles south of Islamabad, mainly built underground and now surrounded by Crotale surface-to-air missiles is designed to produce nuclear weapons. There is little doubt that the point will soon be reached when Pakistan's scientists and military will be asking President Zia-ul-Haq for permission to carry out a nuclear test. India, which in 1974 carried out its own nuclear test in the Rajasthan Desert, is not alone in believing that Pakistan is very close to becoming a nuclear-weapon State. Even though India claims it is not a nuclear-weapon State and that its test was purely for peaceful purposes, its Prime Minister Rajiv Gandhi has made it clear that if Pakistan becomes a nuclear-weapon State, that will completely change the military balance in the subcontinent. He has said that at no cost will India allow its 'integrity and security to be compromised' and that India might resume testing and perhaps even start to stockpile nuclear weapons. No longer can the United States credibly claim that its relationship with Pakistan will of itself be sufficient to hold President Zia back from testing a nuclear device. Perhaps the only preventative action that President Zia would find hard to override would be an immediate agreement to a moratorium on testing involving initially the United States, the Soviet Union and Britain, to be followed by a Comprehensive Test Ban Treaty hopefully to be signed by those three, as well as China and France.

In addition, with the supply of 810 Kryptons from the United States to Israel, which can be used as part of the trigger mechanism for nuclear bombs, there is renewed evidence of Israel's status as a nuclear-weapon State. With the leak of information and further speculation over a possible South African nuclear test in 1979, there is a growing belief that South Africa is also a nuclear-weapon State. There is strong evidence that Israel and South Africa have combined together to share nuclear materials and information. There is less likelihood than with Pakistan of either making a test explosion but it cannot be ruled out. All of this makes the case for urgently reopening the CTB negotiations very strong. Indeed one wonders what other events have to happen to demonstrate the urgency to the US Administration.

The milestones on Pakistan's quest for nuclear weapons are political as well as military and illustrate the interconnection between the pursuit of civil nuclear power and the possession of nuclear weapons. Pakistan first began its civil nuclear programme in 1955. By 1965 it had its first nuclear research reactor supplied by the United States with international safeguards. Yet in that same year its most formidable post-independence politician, Zulfikar Ali Bhutto, warned that 'If India builds the bomb, we will eat grass or leaves, even go hungry. But we will get one of our own'. It was Bhutto as President in 1972 who in great secrecy, in the wake of Pakistan's defeat in the third war involving India and Pakistan, launched the drive to become a nuclear-weapon State. Interestingly, 1972 was the year when US–Soviet nuclear diplomacy was at its most successful. The year when it could be argued with justice that the two super-Powers were more closely fulfilling their obligations under Article VI of the NPT to halt their vertical proliferation than either before or since. This well illustrates the danger of falling prey to the escapist assumption of some of the non-nuclear-weapon States that there would be no proliferation were it not for the super-Powers' nuclear arms race. Pakistan has also followed the clever policy of diversifying its nuclear power relations so as to gain greater flexibility and access to nuclear-weapon-related technology by forcing a relaxation of safeguards under the market pressures put on competing nuclear-power-providing States. Pakistan obtained a Canadian commercial reactor with natural uranium as its fuel. Then in 1976 it entered negotiations with France for a commercial plutonium reprocessing plant which then went ahead despite President Giscard d'Estaing formally pulling out of the project in 1978. Meanwhile Pakistani scientists deliberately sought employment worldwide in the nuclear field, the most striking example being the present head of their Kahuta installation working on the gaseous diffusion technology for URENCO.

All of this undermined the international safeguard procedures. It is, however, not just preventing access to enriched uranium or even plutonium. In 1978, Britain, France, Germany and the United States decided on the fiercest ever clamp-down on all supplies of nuclear-weapons-related equipment and know-how to Pakistan. Yet despite that we have seen Pakistan still able to get critical nuclear-weapon-making material. In 1984 Pakistan was just thwarted from buying 50 Kryptons from the US, but the depressing lesson from this period is that safeguards will not stop nations determined to go nuclear. What safeguards may better do is to constrain individuals or terrorist groups acquiring the capacity to build a suitcase nuclear weapon. Safeguards are therefore still of critical importance and need to be further tightened, but they cannot stop nations cheating and circumventing.

President Zia in 1977 did fortunately break the hitherto strong link between Pakistan and Libya, but that was not before Libya had been given a head start on its own nuclear programme. In the longer term it may be as significant that Saudi Arabia replaced Libya as a source of financial help for the Pakistan nuclear weapons programme. Following the Israeli 1981 surgical air strike against the French-built Tammuz nuclear reactor in Iraq and Saudi Arabia's financial support for Iraq in the Iraq–Iran war, one cannot rule out a Pakistani–Iraq nuclear relationship developing. Pakistan, through its close relationships with China, has ensured an alternative access to a nuclear-weapon State should the US link be destroyed. In the wake of the Soviet Union's invasion of Afghanistan, US–Pakistan relationships improved with President Reagan massively increasing US arms supplies. Meanwhile India, of course, retains its close relationship with the Soviet Union, not that that has produced access to nuclear-weapon technology but it certainly maintains a super-Power rivalry on the continent and all five of the nuclear-weapon States are supplying conventional arms to the Indian subcontinent.

In looking in detail at the history of Pakistan's movement towards becoming a nuclear-weapon State, one can see the significance of the actual public revelation of a nuclear test. The Indian nuclear test explosion was the critical justification for Pakistan's nuclear programme in 1974 even though its programme had started two years earlier. If there is a Pakistan nuclear explosion it will be the public trigger that will be used by India to justify it becoming a declared nuclear-weapon State. Israel's more openly acknowledged status as a nuclear-weapon State could well be used to justify Iraq and Saudi Arabia's involvement in nuclear weapons. The political threshold of a publicly acknowledged nuclear test is therefore vital.

It was Eisenhower who said that the greatest regret about his presidency was the failure to convert the 1958–1961 US–Soviet comprehensive test moratorium into a formal treaty prohibiting all forms of nuclear test. That a most distinguished military, and later political, leader should single out this issue in this way is an illustration of its gravity. The search for a total test ban is still the most formidable challenge facing us all and particularly so for the Soviet and American leaders. Yet before they can sign such a ban as responsible leaders they will have to satisfy three essential questions.

1. Whether a ban would damage the safety and reliability of their existing nuclear stockpiles.
2. Whether a ban would prevent them undertaking new weapon development as part of assuring their citizens that their nation can retain at the very least an invulnerable second strike capability.
3. Whether a test ban can be verified to give a sufficiently credible guarantee that the super-Power they most fear will not be able to cheat.

These three questions are not semantic quibbles or excuses for inaction. They have hitherto bedevilled the achievement of a comprehensive test ban. They cannot be wished away, they have to be addressed and analysed in detail, particularly now if we are to restart the CTB negotiations so unwisely stopped by the US with UK acquiescence in 1982.

Firstly, the stockpile or shelf-life argument. This is the least substantive of the three questions. It only surfaced within the context of a CTB as a major issue in 1977–8. Suspiciously only when, for the first time, it looked as if the breakthrough in the negotiations over verification was such that a CTB looked as if it might be signed. Until then, not a single US or British nuclear test had been undertaken in order to confirm the reliability of stockpiled weapons. The shelf-life argument was then, and I said so within Government, a deliberate diversion, the protection of a vested interest by the nuclear-testing laboratories at Los Alamos, Livermore and Aldermaston. The US and UK scientists lobbied hard inside the military and political establishments to check progress towards a CTB. They were even prepared to argue that the nuclear stockpile would become so unreliable that the warheads would lose their utility as a deterrent. The lobbying nonetheless was so successful that President Carter felt, by the middle of 1978, that he could not get Congressional agreement to both a CTB Treaty and SALT II. This political decision in Washington was far more important than difficulties in the negotiations such as the rather odd attempt by the Soviet Union to force the UK to accept the same number of seismic stations as for themselves and the US. President Carter, when deciding rightly to give SALT II priority, sadly ensured that the political push behind the principle of CTB began to weaken.

The quality and value of a CTB was unfortunately already weakened when in negotiations at US insistence the period of the Treaty was shortened to only three years. The UK only accepted this at the negotiating table once the Soviets had reluctantly gone along with the US position. What would happen to the laboratories' expertise, it was asked, if a CTB Treaty was extended indefinitely? In fact, given computer simulation techniques, a design team would probably be maintained after a CTB for some time until confidence was firmly established and certainly simulation activity could continue. All that might be lost would be the experimental physicists who would probably drift away in the US and UK under market and job satisfaction pressures. In the Soviet Union admittedly experts could be retained more easily than in the US and UK. Yet there was never any reason why craftsmen trained in the art of dealing with weapon-grade materials should not be retained to service stockpiles.

Behind the second argument over whether a CTB would prevent new weapon development lies a tendency amongst the nuclear scientists to exaggerate the extent of recent technical advances. In fact no significant breakthroughs have taken place in the US or UK weapons laboratories since the hydrogen bomb. Some argue that testing has helped to refine the warheads in terms of size, safety and reliability, but these changes are more a reflection of metallurgical and design advances and could and would have been introduced irrespective of a testing programme. A ban would undoubtedly involve some sacrifice of NWS capability but it is a miniscule technical and scientific loss in comparison with the wider political gains of a Comprehensive Test Ban Treaty for both NWS and NNWS. It would, however, be foolish to pretend to the NNWS that a CTB would halt vertical proliferation.

In the US and the Soviet Union there is such a vast backlog of detailed and wide-ranging knowledge of all likely new warhead designs that there would be few inhibitions to their developing a new weapon system. The UK too has sufficient in-depth knowledge of single warhead design to manufacture unaided. It is probably true that the French, hitherto totally uninterested in a CTB, no longer need tests to produce new warheads for any of their likely new weapon systems and they are encountering strong environmental criticisms from their test programme. The Chinese for their part lag behind in warhead design but appear less interested in having sophisticated nuclear warheads and might be persuaded to sign a CTB.

The third question relates to verification. This has been all along the most serious obstacle to negotiating a CTB Treaty. In the CTB negotiations up to 1980, only seismic techniques had been discussed. Yet everyone knows that seismic observations would always be supplemented by intelligence from satellites. Glenn T. Seaborg, Chairman of the US Atomic Energy Commission from 1961–71 and a Nobel Prizeman, has since written that the breakdown in negotiations for a CTB in the early 1960s was wrongly brought about by US insistence on obligatory on-site inspection. 'With each passing year since then, the ability to monitor compliance with a CTB has become more assured' Seaborg wrote in 1983. 'At this time, tests above one kiloton have a high probability of being detected and identified, whether through seismic or satellite means, or through intelligence sources. Even more than in the 1960s, it seems unlikely today that the Soviets would take large political risks for the chance of making the insignificant military gains they could achieve through clandestine tests under a CTB.' That view of one of the most eminent US scientists is mirrored by the view of others knowledgeable in seismology, also leading US and UK warhead scientists who have worked at Los Alamos, Livermore and Aldermaston.

Yet despite this, the US in particular, but with Britain closely involved, has blocked the resumption of CTB negotiations. It is one of the most short-sighted decisions for which President Reagan and Prime Minister Thatcher, in marked contrast to President Kennedy and Prime Minister Macmillan, must accept the main burden of responsibility. Distinguishing between earthquakes and nuclear explosions is now achievable, though some still cast doubt on this. On-site stations, inspections on request and satellite surveillance have made the possibility of cheating by masking an explosion in a large cavity much less likely. Though a large cavity in the ground can fairly easily be dissolved out of a salt deposit, the effluent is detectable. Even exploding a device in dry alluvium—a remote option—is now much more open to detection. The possibility of hiding test signals in those of an earthquake not only risks discovery but the coincidence has to be exact and neither the US nor the Soviet Union could seriously plan a warhead development programme which relied for testing on the random occurrence of convenient earthquakes. A world-wide network of seismic stations would also ensure that a hitherto non-nuclear-weapon State would also be hard pressed to conduct a clandestine explosion.

The only remaining justification for concern over a CTB are explosions below one kiloton and although many seismologists are pretty confident of detecting these, it has to be admitted that the old data base they are using is insufficient for total confidence. Ensuring far greater confidence in existing data would therefore be a significant advance. US scientists, though not UK scientists, have been concerned for some time that the Soviet Union is breaking the 150 kiloton threshold test ban. Certainly the Soviets, like the US and the UK, have been testing right up to that limit. President Reagan, speaking to the United Nations General Assembly on 24 September 1984, proposed in a strikingly specific passage that 'we find a way for Soviet experts to come to the United States' nuclear test sites, and for ours to go to theirs, to measure directly the yields of tests of nuclear weapons. We should work towards having such arrangements in place by next spring'. We are now well past that spring date and it appears nothing has happened. Indeed it is unclear whether there has been any follow-up of the idea. The US seems to be giving very little priority to this field. Yet it could be the one area of arms control that might show early progress if because of SDI the Geneva negotiations stall.

If the Soviet Union would agree to something along the lines of Reagan's proposal it would give a reference point to a mass of geophysical knowledge that is at present derived only by inference. It would give a crucial boost to confidence in the existing verification capacity and open the way to real progress in starting to hold back the arms race and curbing proliferation.

Calibration of three tests in a range from, say, 150, 50 and 5 kilotons, on the designated test sites of the US and Soviet territory would give the sort of guarantee for the future that would allow President Reagan to reopen, on the prospect of such calibration tests, negotiations for a total test ban and to agree that this be preceded by a three-year moratorium. During the moratorium the results of these specific tests could be evaluated, and both parties could commit themselves in advance to the serious intention of negotiating a CTB Treaty of indefinite duration. Also the US Congress could immediately ratify the Threshold Ban and the Peaceful Nuclear Explosion Treaty which would restore Soviet confidence in the process of bilateral negotiations.

Before the CTB talks were adjourned by the US in 1982, direct negotiations between the US, the USSR and the UK had achieved considerable progress and this progress is worth summarizing. It was agreed that 10 seismic stations each would be sited in the US and the Soviet Union and tentative agreement had even been reached on their locations. The technology of the seismic stations has since then been proved, with five actually operating at present in the US. There remains some difficulty over the inexplicable Soviet insistence that the UK, which currently tests in the US and has only ever tested on territory which it now no longer controls, should also have 10 sites. Probably the UK will have to accept three sites on territory it still controls, for appearance's sake, but there is no seismic justification for this demand. One station on the Falkland Islands would give information on tests in Latin America, but Hong Kong would not give information on Chinese tests, and as for sites in the UK, they would only have symbolic value. A world-wide seismic station network would mean that a total test ban could be monitored.

The Soviet Union has argued about the over-sensitivity of the proposed specifications for internal seismic stations. Covering the full scale of the seismic spectrum, it appears that it is worried that these stations would detect ground vibrations from non-nuclear activities such as tank and missile manoeuvres, naval exercises with depth charges and civil engineering with chemical explosives. A solution to this Soviet fear would be to employ internal stations tuned to the low frequency, or long period end of the seismic spectrum, which is inaccessible to external stations but which it is essential to pick up before the nature of the source can be verified. This could be achieved by measuring the amplitude, or energy ratio high frequency/low frequency content of the signal. The high frequency signal is already accessible to distant external stations.

The concept of on-site inspections by invitation has been agreed whereby any signatory to CTB Treaty could request a visit if their instrumentation had recorded a doubtful explosion and they were suspicious. In almost all cases such a visit would be able to establish the truth. Again, if this could be widened to cover all nations this would greatly strengthen a universal total test ban.

Data transmission from the sensitive stations was initially a problem in the negotiations because of the mass of data and the fact that the law requires that no data leaves the Soviet Union uncensored. A delay of at least 24 hours was anticipated and there were questions as to whether this would be time enough for the Soviets to remove traces of a secret test. The Soviets were embarrassed by their technical incapacity to manage the enormous and continuous flow of data and offers to help were not received with enthusiasm. Now a data management and analysis centre in Washington is capable of dealing with international exchanges of seismic data received via the global telecommunications network (GTN) of the World Meteorological Organization. This is the well-established, well-organized and computerized network for circulating weather data by land line and satellite to and from every country in the world. Through the good offices of the CCD in Geneva, the *ad hoc* group of experts of the CCD is experimentally testing these communications for exchanging seismic data in support of CTB studies by the CCD. The US, the Soviet Union and the UK have already agreed to much of the treaty language for international exchanges under a CTB. What is now needed is a political stimulus. Perhaps the US Congress should pass its own legislation based on this language independent of the Administration and force its hand.

Also the improvements in satellite photographic resolution have drastically improved the capacity to spot activities which must follow a decision to cheat. Even the overt photography of the earth resources satellite reveals ground effects of tests. Attempts to hide these by testing at greater depth increases the probability of detections by seismographs, since the deeper explosions are more seismically coupled by surrounding rocks. Military satellite surveillance with its higher resolution could be intensified by ground direction based on the seismic location of any doubtful or suspicious data findings. This is a lot of technical detail but it is over resolvable technical questions that a CTB is stalled. Exposing the frailty of the technical case against a CTB focuses attention on the political inhibitions, which are in fact dominant.

Resistance to an immediate moratorium and a later test ban from nuclear-weapon scientists and military strategists is predictable. Just because it does represent the most fundamental challenge to the present course of ever-increasing nuclear warhead sophistication to which the scientists and strategists have either become resigned or enthusiastically advocate.

Politicians must, however, realize that to go on proliferating and expanding nuclear stockpiles is to head towards doomsday. It is long since time that the technicalities of a CTB Treaty were faced, mastered and the language of a treaty negotiated and implemented. The fact that this has not yet happened serves only to emphasize the old truth that where there is no vision the people perish.

An American perspective[1]

AMBASSADOR LEWIS A. DUNN

Assistant Director, US Arms Control and Disarmament Agency

In a little over two weeks, we shall mark the 40th anniversary of the atomic age. On 16 July 1945, the first test of a nuclear explosive at Alamogordo, New Mexico, demonstrated a new weapon of unprecedented destructiveness. Throughout the ensuing decades, the community of nations has faced the challenge of finding ways to neutralize the military threat of the atom while harnessing nuclear energy for peaceful purposes.

Both bilateral and multilateral arms control and disarmament negotiations have been undertaken. Their goal has been, and remains, the eventual elimination of nuclear weapons and in the interim at least drastic reductions of nuclear arsenals to ensure greater stability and safety for all countries. At the same time, peaceful nuclear cooperation around the world, in areas ranging from nuclear power generation to nuclear medicine, has burgeoned since President Dwight D. Eisenhower's Atoms for Peace Program was initiated in 1953. In addition, the world's nations have adopted increasingly stringent measure to prevent the spread of nuclear weapons to additional countries.

Since its entry into force in March 1970, the Treaty on the Non-Proliferation of Nuclear Weapons (NPT) has played a central part in this decades-long endeavor. The Treaty's specific undertakings have been carefully crafted to serve its three major objectives. The first, which was the driving force behind the initial push for the NPT, is to prevent the further spread of nuclear weapons. The second is to foster peaceful nuclear cooperation under safeguards. The third objective, added during the multilateral negotiation of the NPT, is to encourage good faith negotiations to end the nuclear arms race with a view to general and complete disarmament.

The treaty: goals and undertakings

The first two Articles of the Treaty seek to help prevent the further spread of nuclear weapons, thereby strengthening the security and well-being of all countries. Under Article I, the nuclear-weapon States Party to the Treaty undertake not to transfer nuclear explosives to any other State and not to assist, in any way, non-nuclear-weapon States to manufacture or acquire

[1] An earlier version of these remarks appeared in *Disarmament* (Winter-Spring, 1985).

such devices. In turn, under Article II, more than 120 non-nuclear-weapon States have renounced the right to seek to acquire or manufacture nuclear explosives.

Article III obligates the non-nuclear-weapon States Party to accept international safeguards, including on-site inspection by the International Atomic Energy Agency (IAEA). These safeguards verify fulfilment of these States' obligations under the Treaty and help to deter diversion of nuclear materials from peaceful purposes to the manufacture of nuclear explosives. Acceptance of safeguards is also an important confidence-building measure which can help lessen suspicions that could lead regional rivals to acquire nuclear explosives. This Article also contributes to the objective of preventing proliferation by requiring safeguards on nuclear exports to non-nuclear-weapon States.

An effective safeguards system is at the same time a critical pre-condition for the peaceful uses of the atom promoted by Article IV. That Article's objective is to facilitate the fullest possible dissemination of nuclear equipment, materials, and scientific and technological information for peaceful purposes. Thus, nations which forswear nuclear weapons and accept safeguards, and especially less-developed ones, should receive special consideration in tapping the benefits of the peaceful atom. And should there be any potential benefits of nuclear explosions for peaceful purposes, these benefits are to be made available under Article V on a non-discriminatory basis to the non-nuclear-weapon States Party.[1]

Article VI commits all Parties to pursue negotiations in good faith on effective measures leading to the cessation of the nuclear arms race and on general and complete disarmament. As such, this Article complements the other parts of the Treaty. It equally provides legitimacy and an imperative for reinvigorated measures to reduce existing nuclear arsenals as the first step toward its goal of an end to the arms race.

The Non-Proliferation Treaty, however, is more than its particular Articles. With more than 125 Parties, the Treaty also embodies a powerful international norm of non-proliferation.

In the 1950s and early 1960s, it was common to find references to the 'prestige' associated with developing nuclear weapons. In some quarters, it was feared that by the mid-1970s all countries with major military capabilities would have acquired nuclear weapons. Instead, world opinion has increasingly come to regard the acquisition of nuclear weapons as no longer legitimate, with the accompanying conviction that such acquisition does not enhance either a nation's prestige or security. Not least, there is a growing

[1] The United States and most other countries have maintained that there is no essential technical difference between nuclear explosives, whether used for weapons purposes or for peaceful purposes.

recognition, evidenced in steadily growing adherence to the NPT, that a world of many nuclear powers is not the inevitable wave of the future.

More is not better

A prime impetus for the Non-Proliferation Treaty was the widespread belief that the further spread of nuclear weapons would undermine all countries' security and threaten world order. More recently, however, it has become fashionable in some academic circles to question this belief.

Critics of the 'conventional wisdom' contend that the introduction of nuclear weapons to conflict-prone regions, rather than risking a local nuclear conflict, would lead to restraint on the part of regional rivals. In their view, fear of escalation to nuclear destruction would contain minor clashes and foster more basic stability—if not peace settlements—among long-standing enemies. In the words of one analyst, 'more may be better'.

These views are based on a simple, and false, extrapolation from the non-use of nuclear weapons by the United States and the Soviet Union to their future non-use in quite different circumstances. That extrapolation overlooks the very particular mix of geopolitical and technical factors that have ensured nuclear peace over the past decades: the presence of cautious leaders; the fact that neither national survival nor ideological purity was immediately at stake; the lack of common borders, thereby lessening flash points for conflict and impeding escalation; and adequate technical means to prevent nuclear weapons accidents or the unauthorized seizure or use of nuclear weapons. Without these circumstances, the fear of atomic destruction, though itself important, might not have sufficed.

The spread of nuclear weapons to conflict-prone regions is far more likely to exacerbate long-standing suspicions and tensions among rivals than to lead to better relations. It is more likely to add to the risk of war than to encourage the peaceful settlement of traditional disputes.

Preventive military action may be taken by one country in a region to keep its rivals from matching its progress towards the acquisition of nuclear weapons. Moreover, throughout these regions, past experience has repeatedly shown the great risk that limited conflict or border clashes could escalate to wider conflict. And the stakes of many Third World conflicts are high, often calling into question an opponent's legitimate claim to national survival or involving pursuit of over-arching religious-ideological goals.

Thus, in evaluating the risks of nuclear proliferation, the lingering Persian Gulf war between Iran and Iraq is a better and more appropriate model than the post-war political competition between East and West. In this war, both sides have violated international norms: Iraq has used chemical weapons and Iran refused to allow the Red Cross into its prisoner-of-war camps. Recently, both sides have conducted deliberate shelling, air, and rocket attacks against civilians. Only the relative military weaknesses of these two countries have dampened this conflict. More would not be better.

Preparations for the 1985 NPT Review Conference

As provided for by Article VIII(3), in both 1975 and 1980, the Parties to the Treaty met to review its implementation. Preparations have now been concluded for the Third Review Conference to take place in September 1985.

In a cooperative and constructive spirit, the three preparatory meetings have resolved the necessary procedural issues, including rules of procedure, a proposed agenda, dates of the Conference, and financing. A candidate for President of the Review Conference—Ambassador Mohamed Shaker of Egypt—has been proposed by the non-aligned and neutral nations and met with widespread support.

At the third preparatory meeting last April, there also was considerable formal and informal discussion of the tasks of the Review Conference. Virtually all delegations stressed that the Review Conference should undertake a full and honest assessment of how well the Treaty's goals have been met overall. How the substantive results would be reflected was left for the Conference itself to determine.

The preparations for the Conference also have involved intensified efforts to increase adherence to the NPT. In cooperation with many other countries, the United States has waged, and will continue to wage, a diplomatic campaign around the world to convince other countries to join the Treaty. Since 1980, moreover, 14 new countries have adhered. Each one brings the Treaty closer to universality and further strengthens the norm of non-proliferation.

As the 1985 Conference approaches, various proposals are being informally considered to implement more effectively the provisions and goals of the Treaty. A full and complete debate of these ideas is needed. But it also is important to remember the delicate balances and carefully negotiated compromises embodied in what is the most widely adhered-to arms control treaty in history. If changes to the Treaty itself are pursued, the process of amendment could get out of control, with many inconsistent proposals being offered.

Broad consultations and a continued cooperative approach among all NPT parties will greatly assist in assessing proposals to strengthen the Treaty and, more broadly, in its full review. Thorough consultations, bringing together neutrals and non-aligned, Socialist and Western countries, the United States and the Soviet Union, developed and developing countries, can help identify common concerns and ways to meet them. Such consultations reflect the fact that all parties at the Review Conference have a vital stake in the Treaty and that we must work together to promote a constructive review and to strengthen, not undermine, the NPT regime.

The main task at the Review Conference itself, however, will be a full and honest Article-by-Article review of the operation of the Treaty. Woven throughout that review and ensuing debate, there will be four major questions. First, has the Treaty strengthened the security of the Parties by helping prevent the further spread of nuclear explosives? Second, how well has the Treaty facilitated cooperation in the peaceful uses of nuclear energy and what can realistically be done to buttress further that cooperation? Third, what has been done to bring the nuclear arms race to an end? And, most important of all, weighing each of these considerations, has the NPT been a success?

Ending the nuclear arms race

There is little doubt that the implementation of Article VI, which provides for 'good faith negotiations' to end the nuclear arms race, will be a considerable part of the discussion at the 1985 Review Conference. The United States welcomes a full debate on this important Article, and shares the concern of all States—non-nuclear and nuclear-weapon States alike—that greater progress be made to realize fully its vision.

Since the earliest days of the post-war era, the prevention of nuclear war has been the most critical of concerns. A nuclear war cannot be won and must never be fought. For that reason, as President Reagan stressed at the United Nations last September, there is an urgent need for 'redoubled efforts to meet the legitimate expectations of all nations that the Soviet Union and the United States will substantially reduce their own nuclear arsenals.' This is the first step toward the eventual total elimination of nuclear weapons.

To achieve that goal what is needed is the negotiation of effective, concrete agreements. Only with such agreements can we ensure the precision of undertakings, the equality or equivalence of forces and the necessary verifiability essential if these agreements are to serve truly the security of all countries.

Consistent with its commitment to Article VI, the United States sought, in the early 1980s at the Strategic Arms Reductions Talks (START), major reductions of ballistic missiles, their warheads, and their destructive potential. These are the weapons already in existence which pose the most immediate threat. Similarly, in the parallel Intermediate-Range Nuclear Forces (INF) talks, the United States tabled proposals aimed at the elimination of an entire category of nuclear weapons.

Most recently, the United States and the Soviet Union, in March 1985, began new negotiations with the objective of working out effective agreements aimed at preventing an arms race in space and terminating it on earth, at limiting and reducing nuclear arms, and at strengthening strategic stability. We have agreed that our ultimate objective is the eventual elimination of nuclear arms everywhere. The second round of these negotiations is now underway here in Geneva.

The issues are complex and the road ahead long. The United States approaches these talks seriously and flexibly; we are ready for the give and take that can alone produce results. We are convinced that through constructive and persistent dialogue agreements can be reached which would serve both the United States' and other countries' security and well-being.

The United States recognizes the great interest of many nations in a comprehensive nuclear test ban. A ban on all nuclear tests remains a long-term goal of the United States, in the context of improved verification and of broad, deep and verifiable reductions of nuclear weapons. But in the view of the United States, the highest priority should be placed now on achieving radical reductions in existing nuclear arsenals and strengthened stability.

A comprehensive test ban of itself would not reduce the threat of nuclear war because it would leave untouched existing nuclear arsenals. A comprehensive test ban could delay nuclear force reductions by undermining confidence in the reliability of deterrence. Making a complete nuclear test ban the litmus test of arms control diverts energies away from the negotiation of deep and meaningful arms reductions. Only those reductions are the true first step towards a world in which the threat of nuclear war no longer exists and towards elimination of the discrimination between nuclear-weapon States sought by Article VI.

Elsewhere in the nuclear-testing area, the United States has proposed discussions with the Soviet Union on improvements to verification capabilities for the Threshold Test Ban Treaty and the Peaceful Nuclear Explosions Treaty, since these Treaties cannot now be effectively verified. In addition, President Reagan in his 24 September speech at the United Nations General Assembly suggested that 'we find a way for Soviet experts to come to the US nuclear test site, and for ours to go to theirs, to measure directly the yields of tests of nuclear weapons.' The purpose of such an exchange, the President continued, would be 'to establish the basis for verification of effective limits on underground nuclear testing.'

In addition to pursuing negotiations for deep reductions, the United States with its allies' support also has taken unilateral steps to meet the goals of Article VI. After consultations within NATO, 1000 short-range nuclear warheads were removed from Europe in 1980. In October 1983, in a similar step, NATO decided to reduce the number of nuclear warheads in Europe by another 1400 warheads.

In 1981, the United States ratified Protocol I of the Treaty of Tlatelolco. Under this Protocol, the United States agreed to apply the basic denuclearization provisions of the Treaty to those territories in the zone for which it is responsible.

Redoubled efforts to make greater progress in reaching the objectives of Article VI clearly are needed if we are yet to realize fully the expectations of the Treaty. But of equal importance, in reviewing the Treaty we should not lose sight of the important gains made in achieving the Treaty's other goals and of the need to assess the Treaty as a whole.

Strengthened security

The Non-Proliferation Treaty is a cornerstone of international efforts to erect and sustain effective barriers to the further spread of nuclear weapons. In the more than 15 years since its entry into force, the Treaty has successfully buttressed political constraints to the bomb's spread, helped check the growth of regional suspicions that can encourage a slide toward a nuclear explosives capability, and reinforced the technical obstacles to acquiring nuclear weapons. Not least, by strengthening the norm of non-proliferation, the continuing vitality of the Treaty has contributed to a global climate at odds with steps to seek nuclear explosives. As a result, since 1970, only one additional country is known to have detonated a nuclear explosive device. This success has served the security of all of the parties, indeed of all countries.

For its part, the United States, as called for by Article I, has not transferred nuclear weapons, nor assisted any non-nuclear-weapon State to build or acquire a nuclear explosive device. As noted earlier, we also have sought to increase adherence to the Treaty.

Consistent with Article III, the United States also has exported nuclear material and equipment to non-nuclear-weapon States only under international safeguards. We have also cooperated with other countries to increase the effectiveness of IAEA safeguards and to upgrade the so-called 'trigger lists' created to help the Parties meet their safeguards responsibilities under Article III on nuclear exports. These export constraints have not hindered access by NPT Parties to the peaceful benefits of nuclear energy; they have made it harder for countries seeking a nuclear explosives capability to reach that goal.

Moreover, in recent years, the United States has refused to enter into new commitments to supply significant quantities of nuclear material or equipment to non-nuclear-weapon States that do not accept IAEA safeguards on all their peaceful nuclear activities. We also have urged other suppliers to adopt this policy. Agreement to such full-scope or comprehensive safeguards would help equalize the treatment of Parties and non-Parties to the NPT. Further, the job of the IAEA would be made easier, and greater assurance provided of peaceful purposes.

Finally, in the spirit of Article III, the United States also concluded a voluntary safeguards agreement with the IAEA in 1980. Under this agreement, the IAEA has the right to apply safeguards to all nuclear material in all US nuclear facilities, excluding only those facilities associated with activities having direct national security significance. The list of eligible facilities provided to the IAEA includes more than 230 private and government-owned fuel cycle facilities.

Realizing the atom's peaceful promise

A vision of the potentially great peaceful benefits of nuclear energy in meeting needs for power, in the field of health care and medicine, in science, industry, and agriculture, also helped create the NPT. And the Treaty has helped its Parties, including developing countries, to realize that vision.

Peaceful nuclear cooperation has expanded steadily since 1970 when the Treaty entered into force. Many developing countries Party to the Treaty have set out on the road to use nuclear energy for peaceful purposes.

Tens of thousands of students from these countries have been trained in nuclear and related sciences. Dozens of developing country Parties now have research reactors and a growing nuclear scientific establishment. Still more Parties make use of radioisotopes and radiation in medicine, agriculture, and industry. Significantly, there are several developing nations such as Mexico, Romania, Yugoslavia, the Republic of Korea, the Philippines, Taiwan, and Egypt which already have significant nuclear power programs or are committed to that objective in the near future. And still others will follow.

Since President Eisenhower's historic Atoms for Peace message in December 1953, the United States has worked with other developed countries to create the needed world-wide pattern of cooperative arrangements and institutions to foster these peaceful uses of atomic energy. The non-proliferation assurances and safeguards provided by the Treaty have been essential to this expanding process.

As one of the original proponents of the NPT, moreover, the United States has long recognized that Parties to the Treaty should receive special benefits in international civil nuclear cooperation. The specific record of US nuclear cooperation as well as broad US policy reflects that approach. Let me note a few examples. Since the 1980 Review Conference:

—all new or amended agreements for cooperation with non-nuclear-weapon States entered into by the United States have been with Parties to the NPT or the Treaty of Tlatelolco;

—virtually all US exports of enriched uranium (nearly 12 million kg) were to NPT Parties;

—virtually all nuclear export financing (totalling well over $100,000,000) provided by the US Export-Import Bank went to NPT Parties;

—'sister laboratory' and 'joint committee' arrangements to foster technology transfer have been concluded only with Parties to the NPT or the Treaty of Tlateloco;

—well over 90 per cent of all Type 11 Fellowships for training granted by the United States under the IAEA and totalling more than $5 million have been for NPT Parties;

—all of US-funded IAEA 'Footnote A' technical assistance projects—111 projects for more than $4.5 million, have been for developing country NPT Parties; and more broadly

—nearly $22 million was pledged to the IAEA's Technical Assistance Program, which benefits primarily developing countries, while the United States has continued to support Agency efforts to train manpower, strengthen technical infrastructure, and exchange scientific and technical data.

In addition, increased US preferences for NPT Parties is also dramatically reflected in US law and regulations.

US law now limits exports of fissionable materials, reactors, and major reactor components to those non-nuclear-weapon States that have all of their peaceful nuclear activities under IAEA safeguards. Nations that adhere to the NPT clearly meet this criterion through a formal, binding international legal commitment. In turn, US regulations for licensing exports of fuel, reactor components, and so-called dual-use items have been changed to benefit NPT Parties. Similar changes also have been made in Department of Energy procedures for exports of nuclear technology and know-how.

Further, the United States has endeavored to be a reliable and predictable nuclear supplier. Better ties with key nuclear trading partners, including Japan and Euratom, have been developed; the United States has joined the search in the Committee on Assurances of Supply of the IAEA for a sound consensus on principles for nuclear trade. This, too, indicates our commitment to Article IV.

The NPT and global security: an arms control success

Over the past decade and one-half, the Non-Proliferation Treaty has steadily grown in membership and significance. With now over 125 Parties, it is, as I noted earlier, the most widely adhered-to arms control treaty in history. But numbers are only one measure of the Treaty's success.

Of greater importance is the contribution of the NPT to global security and well-being. Here, the fact that there has been less progress than expected—or hoped—towards the goal of ending the nuclear arms race should not lead us to overlook that the Treaty has been essential to international cooperation in the peaceful uses of nuclear energy and in checking what many once feared would be an inevitable spread of nuclear weapons. Those who doubt that the Treaty is an unprecedented arms control success need only consider the consequences for their own security of a world without the Treaty.

The Treaty's unravelling would fuel heightened suspicion in many quarters about neighboring countries' nuclear intentions. The belief would grow that a world of dozens of nuclear-armed States would be unavoidable. As a result, countries would hedge their bets by seeking a nuclear-weapons option. Political constraints on acquiring nuclear weapons would diminish. Over time, nuclear weapons would spread, adversely affecting regional and global peace and security.

Moreover, without the NPT, one of the legal, institutional, and normative foundations of nuclear export restraint would vanish. As a result, countries seeking nuclear explosives might face fewer technical obstacles to acquiring a nuclear explosive capability. And in this new supplier environment, there again would be heightened pressures not to be left behind regional rivals.

Weakening of the Non-Proliferation Treaty would also greatly set back global peaceful nuclear cooperation, affecting adversely many countries' economic security. Under the pressure of anti-nuclear domestic political forces some supplier countries would be forced to cut off nuclear cooperation, save with closest allies. Peaceful nuclear ties would look too dangerous in this more uncertain environment. The international safeguards system also would be undermined. As a result, nuclear suppliers now relying on the safeguards system to provide credible peaceful use assurances would have to put into place a system of bilateral safeguards or discontinue nuclear exports.

Further, despite concern about more limited progress than hoped for in implementation of the Treaty's Article VI goals, those goals remain a legal, political, and moral imperative in today's world. The nuclear-weapon States do recognize the need, as President Reagan stated, 'to meet the legitimate expectations of all nations that the Soviet Union and United States will substantially reduce their own nuclear arsenals.' But if nuclear weapons were to spread, pressures to reduce existing nuclear weapon arsenals would be far less.

The 1985 Review Conference: a prognosis

Two months from now the Parties to the Treaty will get together to review its implementation. Clearly, as the past days' discussion indicates, some tough questions and hard issues will be raised. The prospects for a successful review depend on many things: the readiness of non-nuclear and nuclear-weapon States, developing and developed countries to continue working together cooperatively; the state of US–Soviet relations; a realism about what can be accomplished; and readiness for an honest, fair, and balanced appraisal of how well each Treaty goal has been met.

In the final analysis, however, each Party will have to answer for itself whether taken as a whole the NPT continues to contribute to international peace and security. In the view of the United States, the Treaty's contribution to all countries' safety and security is even more important today than when the Treaty was signed.

The NPT: The View of the Depositaries

Dr. Andrey Kokoshin

Vice-Chairman, Committee of Soviet Scientists for Peace Against Nuclear Threat; Deputy Director, Institute on USA and Canada Studies, USSR Academy of Sciences, Moscow

I am the last speaker and that is probably an unfavourable position in some senses, but at the same time I would like to try to exploit some advantages of being the last one, and if you do not mind, I would like to address some issues which were raised during the previous session of our Colloquium. And at the same time, listening to previous distinguished speakers, I have been excluding piece by piece some points in my text related to the Non-Proliferation Treaty *per se*.

I would say that the attention paid to our Colloquium and the very impressive list of its participants manifest in themselves the importance of the problem of nuclear weapons non-proliferation for contemporary international relations. And I would tell you that this subject is a high priority issue of USSR foreign policy. As to the Non-Proliferation Treaty, the Soviet Union regards it as a significant success and an important contribution to common security.

I would also like to underline the complex nature, in the good sense of this word, of the Treaty and of its regime of non-proliferation based on three principal elements: obligations of the States for non-proliferation of nuclear weapons, international co-operation in the field of peaceful uses of atomic energy, and the realization of measures on limitation of the arms race and disarmament. In view of new tendencies in the latter area which mark the first half of the 1980s I would like to dwell at length on this subject.

One of the fundamental phenomena in international relations in the last 15 years is the attainment by the USSR of approximate military-strategic parity—balance—with the United States, and between Warsaw Treaty organizations and NATO, in spite of all the differences in structures and capabilities of the particular weapons systems. Such a situation was reached and we maintain it, making great efforts despite all the attempts of the other side from time to time to acquire any kind of superiority in the nuclear sphere. A strategic parity is attained and the situation of nuclear stalemate, I would say, plays the role of a certain restriction to direct use of military force as an instrument of our policy.

Certainly such a situation does not suit those who seek to restore the role of military force in international relations and ensure further build-up of various types of weapons.

In the 1980s we are confronted with the fact that certain forces in the United States are trying more actively to break the military-strategic balance, to eliminate the nuclear stalemate, to increase again the role of force in international relations, to get again some kind of strategic superiority. And it is possible, in my view, to define at least three directions towards this goal.

Firstly, there is the adoption of various military concepts, aiming at making nuclear war again thinkable, and envisaging different forms of use of nuclear weapons as a means of conduct of combat operations. First of all, I mean 'limited' nuclear war, protracted nuclear war, different kinds of 'surgical' nuclear strikes, and so on. And military technologies are being developed in certain directions as well (Pershing II, enhanced radiation weapons, MX, D-5, etc.). Today, the concept of 'limited' nuclear war includes plans of 'selected nuclear strikes' on the USSR territory and 'limited' nuclear war in Europe. It projects the use of nuclear ammunition in the operations of rapid deployment forces in a zone of developing countries. You can understand that the latter fact has specially direct implications on the problem of non-proliferation of nuclear weapons.

Soviet political thought and our military doctrine completely reject the idea of the 'limited' nuclear war. Marshal S. F. Akhromeev, Chief of our General Staff, pointed out recently that in contemporary times, when both sides possess thousands and thousands of nuclear warheads, a limited war is not possible. Should a nuclear war break out it will inevitably become universal with all the possible implications. The theory of limited nuclear war acceptable to the public and to convince people that a nuclear conflict could allegedly be conducted with the observance of some previous set of rules is groundless.

The Soviet Military Encyclopaedia clearly states that the concept of limited nuclear war is regarded by Soviet military thought as groundless since it is practically impossible to keep a nuclear war within a previous set framework.

I would say that behind given statements and estimates lies a deep understanding of the essence and the nature of war in general and nuclear war in particular. Such an understanding of this phenomenon is derived from our vast experience of the past most horrible wars and scientific apprehension of nuclear-age realities.

Secondly, to get out of 'nuclear stalemate', influential forces in the Western countries, and in the United States in particular, direct their efforts towards development of conventional non-nuclear means to conduct war and general-purpose forces on the basis of the latest technological achievements—so-called 'emerging technologies'. Considering the combination of all factors, it is possible to say that under US pressure the development of conventional forces and armaments is going on in such a manner that already before the year 2000 some of them may equal some types of weapons of mass annihilation in their destructive capacities.

Yet, a conventional war in the Centre of Europe under present conditions, while there are huge stocks of hydrocarbons, numerous atomic power plants, a build-up of waste products of the chemical industry, etc., would mean a disaster comparable with the effect of the use of different types of nuclear weapons.

Thirdly, now the international community pays increasing attention to such an attempt to disturb the established balance of power, strategic stability, as the activities of the United States aimed for global anti-missile systems, different types of space weapons. Moreover, one should not neglect a series of other US so-called defensive measures including the accelerated development of means and forces of strategic anti-submarine warfare.

The proponents of large-scale anti-missile systems try for demagogic purposes to exploit the natural human desire to seek protection against all destructive nuclear weapons. And they try to hide their strategic realities and all negative and dangerous consequences of building such a system.

The Working Group of the Committee of Soviet Scientists for Peace against Nuclear Threat has carried out a special study on this subject, and the study has confirmed once more the conclusion which was arrived at earlier by the members of the Soviet Academy of Sciences. I cite this conclusion: 'In reality, the attempt to create so-called defensive weapons against strategic nuclear forces of the other party will inevitably lead to the emergence of one more element reinforcing American first-strike capability. Such defensive weapons would give almost nothing to a country under a surprise massive attack since it cannot obviously protect the overwhelming majority of the population. The use of anti-missile weapons is above all suitable for the attacking side, trying to minimize the strength of the response.' The conclusion also was that it cannot fully protect against the retaliatory strike too—especially taking into account the broad range of potential countermeasures of the other side.

One of the most important conclusions made by the Working Party of Soviet Scientists lies in the fact that many vital components of the anti-missile system would be rather vulnerable to different countermeasures, both active and passive. Furthermore, the effective network of such means could be established much faster and would cost much less than the anti-missile system—in money terms the cost of the effective network of countermeasures could only amount to a few per cent of the cost of the global anti-missile system. The vulnerability of such an anti-missile system can only multiply its destabilizing effect. The thing is that this system, not providing effective protection from the massive first strike (inflicted at the same time with the use of all countermeasures), can give rise to the most dangerous illusion of having the capability to secure protection from the retaliatory strike, when the weakened enemy would encounter more difficulties taking countermeasures against, for example, orbital combat stations.

The USSR, having tremendous scientific, technological and economic potential, is able to do all that is necessary to prevent breaking up the strategic parity and the other side should not have the slightest illusion as to the possibility of acquiring the capability of unpunished first strike. And in doing so, the Soviet Union would choose the actions that highly respond to the true interests of its security and the security of our allies, and tasks of social and economic development of our country and not those to which present Washington officials would like to persuade it. Scientific and technological works are carried out in the Soviet Union but they are not directed to the creation of space weapons—they are connected with the perfection, for example, of space early warning, reconnaissance, intelligence-collecting and navigation systems, as was recently stated by our Minister of Defence. The Soviet Union does not develop space weapons or anti-missile systems for the comprehensive territorial defence of the country. The Soviet Union firmly adheres to the terms of the ABM Treaty of 1972.

The analysis of concepts for the development of space-based anti-missile systems, which are at present under elaboration in the United States, leaves no doubt that many components of this system would be designed not just for hitting strategic missiles or satellites, but for hitting a wide range of objects on the surface of the earth, in the air etc. as well. The circumstances betoken in a most direct way again that the question of deployment of weapons in space affects the interests of all members of the international community and could be very closely connected with the non-proliferation issue.

Now I should like to address some of the points raised by Senator Stevens this morning. He said the weapons which will be developed according to the SDI programme will be non-nuclear weapons. In this connection I shall cite the official State Department document on SDI issued on 4 June 1985. It says: 'We will continue to explore the promising concepts which use nuclear energy to power devices which could destroy ballistic missiles at great distances.' This quote definitely says that there are plans to use nuclear devices for this so-called defence and it would mean one new step to 'vertical proliferation' of nuclear weapons. Regarding the issue of the use of these weapons against different types of targets besides launched ICBMs or SLBMs, our study concluded, and it corresponded with the results of the independent analysis of other groups of scientists in the West, that different types of space weapons, which would be deployed according to this programme, could be used against so-called soft targets and some of them even against hardened targets practically in any part of the world.

All these three directions of activities aimed at escaping from 'nuclear stalemate' seem to be illusory and at the same time very dangerous attempts to achieve some narrow selfish goals using unilateral military and technical measures. In this respect, the statement that scientific developments of several emerging technologies 'now do offer the possibility of defence that did not exist and could hardly have been conceived earlier' seems to be completely unfounded—I cite again the same State Department document of 4 June 1985.

Serious analysis shows that there is a very basic fact that many types of 'emerging technology' would be equally or even more successfully utilized not just for defensive but for offensive weapons.

The only way to strengthen international security is the process of arms limitations, arms reduction and disarmament on the principles of equality and equal security. These measures are very closely associated with the common interests of all States and peoples, with the aim first of all to prevent a nuclear catastrophe. In the present situation, there is no other way but progressive reductions, including substantial ones of nuclear weapons, keeping the parity at any given moment but at a lower level, moving towards the ultimate goal of elimination of nuclear weapons. A nuclear freeze in qualitative and quantitative terms by all States that are in possession of these weapons would be an important step towards this kind of goal. The Soviet Union and the United States could be the first to make such a step as a kind of example for other nuclear States. The idea of nuclear freeze enjoyed large-scale support in the world community, including many scientists who were carrying out appropriate investigations.

The creation of nuclear-free zones in different parts of the world, including Central Europe, free from battlefield nuclear weapons, and nuclear-free zones in the North of Europe, the Balkans and other parts, can play an important role in strengthening international security, including the regime of non-proliferation.

This would also have been the aim of an agreement on a moratorium on nuclear explosions which was recently proposed by the Soviet Union and an agreement on complete prohibition of all nuclear weapons tests. The Soviet proposals on limiting naval activities, including those of aircraft carriers, and anti-submarine activities, are also aimed at strengthening international security and strategic stability.

I would like now also to say a few words about the Soviet approach to the issue of verification. It was very strange for me to hear from some speakers today that the Soviet Union is entirely against such measures as on-site inspection. The Soviet Union has demonstrated many times that, when a particular important agreement requires it, it is ready for a broad spectrum of verification measures according to the national technical means, which includes different kinds of on-site inspection. It was mentioned, for example, that the Peaceful Nuclear Explosion Treaty of 1978 precludes some particular types of on-site inspection. Our approach to a Comprehensive Test Ban Treaty, our proposals in the Vienna talks on limitations of arms and armaments in Central Europe and in other arms control forums include different kinds of verification procedures, including various forms of on-site inspection. Definitely, it is not an obstacle to any serious constructive business-like agreement between the Soviet Union and the United States, or to multilateral agreements.

Finishing my presentation, I would like to say that in general there is no doubt that if the interests of mutual and common security are met, many opportunities arise for significantly reducing military and political tension and for advancing towards nuclear disarmament.

Session V Debate

Chairman

Before I turn to the written questions, I am going to give the floor very briefly to the representative of a class of countries that has not actually yet had an opportunity of talking to us at all. We have heard from the non-nuclear-weapon Third World, we have heard from the nuclear-weapon States, particularly today, but we have not so far heard from any Western industrialized State that is a member of the NPT. We are very fortunate in having with us Mr. Freimut Duve, who is a member of the West German Parliament, and is in the position of being able to speak, at all events for those who elected him, in a country which certainly has the technological capability to develop nuclear weapons; it is nonetheless a State Party to the Non-Proliferation Treaty and yet has experience of nuclear weapons stationed on its soil.

Freimut Duve

First, I should like to make a personal remark as a Western European parliamentarian. I always thought that the initiatives taken by both President Giscard d'Estaing and my own Chancellor and Party friend Helmut Schmidt against Carter's initiatives on non-proliferation were a secular error. At the time I had the feeling that we should have done otherwise. This is all past, but I had to say this in the presence of so many American friends.

Secondly, I am convinced that we will not have any steps forward without peace movements, without people taking part in this process, and therefore I congratulate this Conference—and especially our host—for having invited so many groups representing people who take an interest. This nuclear matter should never go back into the clandestine hands of the nuclear expert where it has been for 20 years.

Thirdly, I was a bit sad when I witnessed the verbal confrontation of this morning. As a Western European parliamentarian who has to live very close to what is called 'the other side', it saddens me that a member of the American Government—a Government which has a global responsibility which no government in the world ever had before in the whole of history—should speak to us in the tone we heard this morning. But I am grateful that other speakers, especially Senator Edward Kennedy, showed us that there is still hope in this global responsibility of the United States.

Fourthly, I think we should be a bit more realistic, and I know that many people feel the same, regarding the notion of a sharp division between the peaceful use of nuclear plants and nuclear arms. By now we know that this very sharp distinction is not possible. At present, when the economic contradictions of the peaceful use of nuclear energy are so apparent, my own country—and I am not very happy about this—is very eager to take part in world-wide trade or export of nuclear plants. We are witnessing world-wide trade in nuclear materials which is at present controlled, but I don't know how long it is going to be controlled as it should be and must be, so we must be careful. We have learnt from this Colloquium the urgency of a comprehensive test ban as a minimum to show the serious willingness of the nuclear-weapon States to stick to their obligation under Article VI of the NPT. As Edward Kennedy proved this afternoon, a test ban can be easily verified with modern means. I can tell you that 200 members of the German Bündestag are supporting this test ban move. Let us ask the super-Powers to take the historic example of President Kennedy's approach to the Limited Test Ban Treaty, which was introduced by a unilateral halt to nuclear testing by the United States in 1963. Why should one of the super-Powers not take a real practical first step to stop testing for one year, ask the other super-Power to follow this example, and then conclude with a Comprehensive Test Ban Treaty at a later date? This would be a convincing signal to the participants in the Third Review Conference.

Finally, regarding the treaty to replace the present NPT when it expires in 1995, it is not too early to start talking about such a conference and if the idea comes out of this Colloquium, it would be a very successful result.

Chairman

I am going to begin the debate with a question that is addressed to all three speakers, but unfortunately since Senator Kennedy has had to leave he will not be able to reply.

Sheila Oakes

Given the information Dr. Owen shared with us on verification of a Comprehensive Test Ban Treaty, would he personally agree that Britain should agree to a moratorium on nuclear tests immediately?

David Owen

Yes, I did in 1978 and I would do now, and I say that as somebody who is prepared and who believes that, without some significant change in the arms control climate, Britain ought to continue as a nuclear-weapon State. So that could present problems to me in the sense that I would not go ahead with Trident, but I would replace Polaris, and that would mean that I would have to rely on computer simulation for any warhead design, but I would be prepared to do that.

Lewis Dunn

I am sure it will come as no surprise to anyone here that my answer is 'No'. My answer is 'No' both personally and as an official of the Reagan Administration and is based partially on the grounds that I do not believe that the questions of verification have been solved. As we all talk about this seismology, my own experience has been that mostly the seismologists don't understand each other and that the questions remain serious.

Secondly, in terms of a moratorium, I think back to the last moratorium from 1958 to 1961, which had an unfortunate end, and I believe that if we are going to have real arms control it is important to have written agreements and not unilateral moratoriums, because only in written agreements will we have the precision and equality that are needed.

Finally, I would say 'No' to the notion of an immediate moratorium on nuclear testing, because I believe that where we need to put emphasis now is not on the idea of a stop to nuclear testing at a point when you can choose your own number, whether you want to choose 50,000 warheads, or 40,000 or 30,000, but at a number where, as Richard Perle said today, we can at least all agree that there are too many warheads in the world. The place to focus is not on the notion of a test ban, which is not going to deal with this problem, but on the reduction of those weapons through agreements which will be effective, which will be implemented, and which will serve our long-term security.

Chairman

I have a supplementary question on this subject.

Ove Nathan

Talking about the comprehensive test ban, you mentioned that verification problems are serious. Can you amplify this statement? Does your statement apply only to yields below one kiloton or does it apply to all explosions independent of yield?

Lewis Dunn

Not being a physicist, I have to listen to what the physicists tell me, and I am told that verification of a comprehensive nuclear test ban involves major problems. I am told this by people I have confidence in, people who have long experience in this business. It is a problem, not simply a load problem, and not just with one kiloton, it is generally a problem.

Chairman

I repeat Sheila Oakes' question to Dr. Kokoshin.

Andrey Kokoshin

Maybe I am in a more favourable position than Ambassador Dunn because our country has already made such a proposal and has agreed with a group of Western activists on public movement on this issue. We propose to start the moratorium after 6 August. I have many contacts with Soviet, American and Western European scientists, and being an engineer I try to understand the details. Of course, there are disagreements among scientists, among different laboratories, and sometimes it does not matter from which country they are, but in general there is widespread understanding that we have very substantial achievements in detecting practically all types of explosion above approximately five kilotons explosive power, and, with slightly lower probability, even much smaller explosions. Therefore, from this point of view, I don't see any reason not to believe in such scientific findings. It is my personal view as a scientist dealing with these politico-military issues that the major reason why there are some people—very influential people—in the United States against this test ban is that they hope for some breakthrough in the development of nuclear weapons of the next generation. It is much talked about in the American scientific community and even amongst some officials. For example, the X-ray laser for the purposes of SDI. Maybe that is one of the major reasons, and there is also work under way to produce more and more nuclear warheads. Even if we have much smaller numbers of warheads and launchers than we have now, the remaining warheads will be replaced with more sophisticated, and in many respects more dangerous, warheads. Therefore, there is an interrelation between a moratorium and a comprehensive test ban on the one hand and prospects of substantial reductions of nuclear weapons on the other. I don't see any contradiction between this and the idea of a moratorium, if they were parallel, and I am quite sure that agreement on a moratorium would help and would substantially improve the climate of Soviet-American relations in such a way that it would contribute to the success of the ongoing negotiations in Geneva.

Chairman

I have another question for Dr. Kokoshin.

Ove Nathan

Has the USSR stopped all research of its own related to SDI-type systems? The question refers explicitly to research and not to development or testing.

Andrey Kokoshin

First of all, the Soviet Union does not have such a programme. We don't have a programme for comprehensive territorial defence, and that is our official position and it is a very strong position. We don't have research aimed at the creation of any kinds of space weapon. We have the research which I already mentioned connected with the improvement of different space-based early-warning systems, navigation and intelligence, which are used as a national technical means of verification and play a stabilizing role for the contemporary strategic balance.

Chairman

Let me now turn to a question which is addressed to Dr. Kokoshin and Ambassador Dunn jointly.

Jayantha Dhanapala

You are no doubt aware of the proposals that will be made by the non-nuclear-weapon States Party at the Review Conference out of a genuine concern to strengthen the Treaty. These range from a Comprehensive Test Ban Treaty to a voluntary fund to assist developing countries to develop peaceful uses of nuclear power. Do you have any proposals of your own to strengthen the NPT?

Lewis Dunn

It is clear that there are a number of ideas which have been circulating about how to strengthen the Non-Proliferation Treaty, and for those of you who may not be cognizant with this process, let me just mention a few of them: the search for ways to facilitate improved access to the peaceful atom on the part of the developing countries, some type of technical assistance co-operation; the principle of a tax on peaceful nuclear facilities; the principle of full-scope safeguards as a supply condition; the idea of trying to establish as an international principle the notion that the very least the nuclear-weapon States should do is keep their civil and military nuclear fuel cycles separate.

In the United States we have been looking at these; some of them we think have merit, others we are less convinced about. For example, we think that it is important to try to see if we can do something in the area of technical assistance and peaceful nuclear co-operation.In the area of separating civil and military nuclear activities, for the better part of 40 years we have tried to maintain the maximum separation possible because we think that it is important for non-proliferation.

I would like to talk about the point which came up during earlier comments about the expiration of the NPT. The Treaty does not expire in 1995; in 1995, the Parties to the Treaty get together to decide whether to continue it indefinitely or continue it for fixed periods of time. As we look down the road to 1995, we would argue very strongly that the best way to strengthen the Non-Proliferation Treaty at this point in time is not to think about amendments to it, nor about a conference to establish a new Treaty, because it is a very unique Treaty, but to make sure that when we get to 1995 we can all sit here and say that all three goals of the Treaty are being fully met. We should get to 1995 and say that the expectations and hopes of Arthur Goldberg and of Lyndon Johnson are being met, as well as the expectations and hopes in terms of peaceful uses and in terms of the security part of the Treaty. I think that is the real answer—to work at what needs to be done in all three parts.

Chairman

Dr. Kokoshin, does the USSR have any proposals to strengthen the NPT?

Andrey Kokoshin

My answer will be shorter. I do not have personal proposals, but I have no doubt that our delegation will bring some.

Chairman

I will now turn to the three questions addressed to Dr. Owen.

Gwyn Prins

In view of your strong remarks about the position in the Indian sub-continent, would you therefore also agree with the view expressed last Wednesday in the British House of Lords by former Chief of the Defence Staff, Field Marshal Lord Carver, that Britain's strategic nuclear weapon was without significant value in maintaining the defence of the realm, but rather was the expression of a nuclear delusion of grandeur?

James Thompson

Surely, as a supporter of nuclear weapons in the United Kingdom, you should welcome Pakistan's eventual nuclear contribution to deterrence?

Pierre Lehmann

Would unilateral nuclear disarmament, for instance, by the United Kingdom, be an effective step towards general nuclear disarmament?

David Owen

When Clement Attlee made the decision for Britain to become a nuclear-weapon State, I was aged eight, Pakistan was part of India and India was still part of the British Empire. If you ask me 'Did he make the right decision?', I think he did, and if I had been there at the same time I hope I would have made the same decision. I think there were a lot of good political and strategic reasons for making that decision. If you ask me,'Would you make that decision now, in 1985, if Britain had no history of being a nuclear-weapon State, and go to a nuclear explosion for the first time?', the answer would be 'No'. Does the fact that Britain is a nuclear-weapon State by implication mean that it is humbug for us to talk about Pakistan not being a nuclear-weapon State (which is really the purport of the question, although it has not been framed in quite such brutal terms)? The answer is that I do not think it does. If you wish to put that, I think in honesty you ought to put it to all five of the *declared* nuclear-weapon States. The reason why I am against Pakistan testing and going through the threshold is the same reason that I was against India going through the threshold of a nuclear explosion in 1974 and the same reason that I am against Israel now being a nuclear-weapon State, and in my judgement South Africa being a nuclear-weapon State. They all depend on a regional interpretation. I think it is tough on Pakistan, in the light of India's nuclear explosion, albeit peaceful, allegedly. It must be seen by its neighbour as being the opening to a nuclear-weapon State, but I still think that Pakistan should hold back. I think there is a deterrent already in the knowledge, which India obviously has, that Pakistan is on the threshold, but, for all the dangers of Israel and South Africa becoming nuclear-weapon States, I think there has been positive advantage in them never declaring it through a nuclear explosion, although I put a square bracket round the possible explosion in 1979 of a South African nuclear device, about which I still think we do not quite know the true answer.

On the question of whether Britain should be a unilateral nuclear disarmer, I do not believe so. I do not think it would make a contribution to world peace. 'Why?' comes back to what Lord Carver is alleged to have said. Lord Carver may have said that, but as a politician I am somewhat sceptical about commenting on remarks that I have not heard. If he did say that, he did not say it when he was Chief of Defence Staff in the early 1970s, and on balance I prefer the people who say one thing in Government, when they hold responsibility, to say the same thing when they are in opposition. I supported nuclear weapons while I was in Government and I will continue to support them while I am in opposition. I do so not because I think a British nuclear weapon is of itself a deterrent, it is a contribution to the NATO deterrent. I think there are advantages in the European nuclear deterrent and the nuclear deterrent strategy of NATO being maintained by the United States not being the sole nuclear-weapon State. I therefore see some important political advantages in France and Britain both being minor nuclear-weapon States with a minimum deterrent contributing to the overall NATO deterrent. The French in the audience would violently disagree that the French nuclear deterrent in any way contributed to NATO and would argue that it is totally and completely outside. I personally am sceptical about the actual consequences of France having nuclear weapons, but Britain is firmly within the NATO deterrent strategy and as such, I think, adds substantially to its political credibility. I do not think it is so easy for the United States to walk away from its nuclear guarantee, it involves the United States and Britain in a great deal of more intimate nuclear discussions. On occasions it has allowed Britain to argue with the United States to good purpose. Throughout the 1977–9 period when I was Foreign Secretary and Jim Callaghan was Prime Minister, we were passionately in favour of a comprehensive test ban. I think that the British influence was helpful within that tripartite discussion, mostly on the United States—because obviously that is the private and intimate contact—but also in part on the Soviet Union. There are merits and I would wish that France would join in those comprehensive test ban negotiations, and indeed China.

For all that variety of reasons, I remain, I am afraid, unrepentantly a believer that Britain should remain a nuclear-weapon State as long it does not cripple us financially, and there will obviously come a time when it will make such an indent into our conventional deterrence that I would not do so. You have to look at it in the broad ambit of politics, and I do not think there is anything the slightest bit humbug in anything that I have said in relation to the comprehensive test ban, nor do I think that is the argument against people in the Soviet Union and in the United States wanting to see the number of nuclear-weapon States kept down to the absolute minimum.

Chairman

The next few questions are all addressed to Ambassador Dunn.

Eric Fersht

What will the United States Government do to encourage adherence to the NPT by key nuclear-threshold States such as India, Pakistan, Israel and South Africa?

José Goldemberg

Although 128 countries have joined NPT, of which many are small developing countries, a significant number of medium-sized countries have not joined and show no intention of doing so, for example, Israel, Pakistan, Brazil, Argentina, South Africa, etc.

Are the depositary countries going to make any gesture to attract these countries at the NPT Review Conference, or just describe the niceties of the Treaty? These qualities are very hard to perceive for anyone coming from a non-signatory nation due to the discriminatory character of the Treaty.

In the name of what principle, except the one that the powerful can do what they wish, can the 'two caste' system of the Treaty be justified?

Lewis Dunn

I think the 'two caste' system of the Treaty can be justified in terms of recognition that the world does have five nuclear-weapon States and the world would not be any safer with six, seven, eight, nine, ten, eleven or twelve nuclear-weapon States. It is not a nice world with five nuclear-weapon States, maybe it would have been a better world with two nuclear-weapon States, maybe it would have been a better world with no nuclear-weapon States, but that is the world we have, and it will not be any safer with six, seven, eight or nine. As to whether the countries that are not now Parties would be any safer with six, seven, eight or nine, I do not think so. In a world in which nuclear weapons had spread openly into the Middle East and the Israelis found themselves surrounded by two or three other countries with nuclear weapons, the Israeli situation would be worse. In a South America in which nuclear weapons had spread, turning what is now basically political rivalry of some sort between Argentina and Brazil into a nuclear military rivalry, Argentina and Brazil would be no safer. I think that stands whether or not there are nuclear weapons in the United States, in the Soviet Union, in France, the United Kingdom and China. This is not to say that we should not be trying to reduce, and eventually eliminate, those nuclear weapons in the five, but I am just saying that it is a fact of the world, and we would not be any safer with more.

As to the question of what the United States has been doing with regard to adherence to the Treaty, we have worked to try to convince some of the key non-signatory countries to join the Treaty, but they are reluctant to do so for one reason or another. I have suggested some.

Dieter von Ehrenstein

What is your opinion concerning the dangers of projected large-scale world-wide construction of a number of fast breeder reactors in the next decades?

Sebia Hawkins

Please comment on Richard Perle's statement that traffic in plutonium ought to be halted and halted absolutely. Does this represent the Reagan Administration's view?

Lewis Dunn

With regard to the last question, this is a situation where I wish I could say what Dr. Owen has just said with regard to the comment in the House of Lords, that since he was not there when it was said he was not quite sure whether to believe it or not. It is the reason I pass and go on to the substance of the problem.

Both of these questions point to a world in which there is some use of plutonium as a civilian nuclear fuel. At this point in time, if your country is setting out to make nuclear weapons, you basically need two things: some type of nuclear-weapon material and a design. So, plutonium, which is a nuclear-weapon material, is clearly a very dangerous material. It is a material which this Administration—and the past Administration and I believe future Administrations—seeks to control tightly; the Reagan Administration recognizes that. It is important to try to limit the use of plutonium as a civil fuel to as few places as possible to try to ensure that any use of plutonium as a civil nuclear power fuel is under as tight safeguards and other physical protection conditions as possible. But the Reagan Administration also acknowledges the need to deal with the world as it is, rather than the world that we might like to have. In the world today, there are countries that believe that the use of plutonium as a civil fuel is important for their energy security. Some of these are very important countries. These countries have an ability to make that decision, whatever the Reagan Administration says. Much as some might like, the United States cannot dictate to the rest of the world. Thus, what it is necessary to do with regard to the use of plutonium is to recognize that it is dangerous, recognize that it is going to be used in some places and try to work with those countries that are going to use it to make its use as safe and as limited as possible, because I do not think we can 'halt traffic in plutonium absolutely'. We do not have that control over the world and I do not think we ever did.

Pierre Lehmann

What makes you believe that nuclear energy is good for the world, particularly the so-called 'under-developed' countries? Don't you think that they need food and a sound environment rather than a dangerous technology which provides energy for a few years but radioactive waste for centuries?

Lewis Dunn

I think what energy source a country uses clearly depends upon the particular country. In some developing countries, nuclear power may make sense, in others it may not make sense. What we have to recognize, and this is the basis of my own statement here, is that all energy sources have problems of one sort or another. What is happening to the West German forests suggests that there are some types of problem with coal. What is happening politically—or what happened politically—in the course of the mid-1970s suggests that there are some real problems with oil. Nuclear energy does have a problem, it has a problem in terms of managing waste, but it is a problem that can be handled and thus, in certain situations, nuclear energy is not a dangerous technology. I also happen to believe that nuclear energy is a safe technology. In contrast to what many believe, the Three-Mile Island accident in the United States demonstrated that it was a safe technology because those people did their best to have a major nuclear power accident and did not succeed. They did everything wrong and they could not have a major accident. To my mind, that suggests that it is a much safer technology, that the redundancies built in do exist.

Chairman

The next question is also addressed to Ambassador Dunn, but Dr. Owen is invited to add his comments.

David Lowry

Does Ambassador Dunn believe that the proposed launch of the USS Alaska Trident II submarine for sea tests in mid-September, in the middle of the NPT Review Conference—a happening we know about because of the open information policy in the United States as compared to the Soviet Union—will be interpreted by the non-nuclear-weapon States Party to the NPT as part of negotiations in good faith towards the cessation of the nuclear arms race?

Lewis Dunn

As you all know, this decision was made in the context of a broader review of what United States policy would be with regard to the SALT II and SALT I limits. The President made the decision that he would not undercut the SALT limits, despite reasons for doing something else. The President also decided that, when it goes to sea, the USS Alaska will lead to the Poseidon boat being taken out of service and dismantled in accordance with SALT II. The President did this because, as he himself put it, he wanted to go the last mile to demonstrate that we want big reductions of nuclear weapons, that we are ready to negotiate seriously, we are ready to negotiate flexibly. We have sent negotiators over here with an awful lot of material in their portfolios. You will have to ask a non-nuclear-weapon State how it would react, but if somebody asks me what it suggests, it suggests to me that the United States does take its obligations seriously and responsibly and that it is making a good faith effort and intends to continue doing so.

David Owen

I think it is rather important to comment as a European, because the Europeans have been extremely critical of President Reagan's negotiating stance more or less since he came into office, I believe with some justice. But the realities of politics are that that man won the presidential election in 1979 on a 'rubbishing' of the SALT II Treaty. I did not agree with it, but that is what happened. Despite all the problems of the first-term presidency, the United States did maintain the SALT II Treaty. For many of us in Europe, the critical test of whether the United States was approaching these negotiations in Geneva seriously was whether or not it was going to keep to the SALT II limits. I think that it is an extremely significant decision, not just that he decided to keep to the limits but the way that he kept to them, because there was quite a lot of pressure from moderate opinion in the United States to the effect that 'Well, we could live with putting the Poseidon submarine into dock, opening it, taking the missiles out, but not dismantling it.' The fact that he did go as far as to commit to dismantle it, which is the strict interpretation of the SALT II Treaty, was significant. What was perhaps even more significant was that the Chief of Staff apparently advised that he should do so, and that is perhaps the best signal that we have had of seriousness of intent in the Geneva negotiations. Although we are very unlikely to see any immediate breakthrough, I still remain reasonably optimistic that some movement on deep cuts and reductions will come next year and will justify the maintenance of a belief that the real strategy in arms negotiations is to cut warhead numbers; it is not to spend a couple of years in negotiating a verifiable freeze, but to negotiate a verifiable reduction in armaments.

Chairman

In order to balance that last question, a question to Dr. Kokoshin.

Henning Wegener

Is Dr. Kokoshin aware that a complete test ban was in effect from 1958 to 1961 and that it was unilaterally broken by the Soviet Union?

Andrey Kokoshin

I remember quite a different story. First of all, on 31 March 1958, the Supreme Soviet of the Soviet Union announced a unilateral moratorium on all kinds of atomic and thermonuclear weapons by the Soviet Union, and the United States and Great Britain were invited to join. But in April 1958 the United States and Great Britain again started testing and in October 1958 the Soviet Union declared that it also had the right to start its testing and to have a one-to-one ratio to the tests of the United States and Great Britain. Later, there were continuous efforts by the Soviet Union to conclude a really comprehensive test ban, but there was very serious resistance on the part of the other partners in these negotiations—I mean the United States and Great Britain—to a really comprehensive test ban, and finally we got a partial test ban in 1963. That was what happened at that time.

Chairman

Two views of history. I am now going to take up one more question which I hope will be wholly uncontentious and I trust that all our speakers will be able to agree with it wholeheartedly.

Jacques Mühlethaler

You have proved that we are condemned to live in peace, otherwise we shall all die. Therefore, why not envisage education for peaceful coexistence and also the necessary financial resources to make such education possible?

David Owen

In a sense that is what the Helsinki Final Act is about and if it had been fully implemented there would have been a very much greater dialogue like this. I do think that I have been critical of the Soviet Union, but perhaps more so of the United States. The opening up of Soviet society is an extremely important part of confidence-building, and the more we see this sort of conference taking place in the Soviet Union, the more we see the sort of dialogue and debate that is taking place here on Soviet television and involving Soviet citizens, the greater confidence we will have in any form of agreement and I believe greater trust will exist between the nations. There is a lot to be said for more being spent in our own countries, in Western Europe and in the United States, on education and explaining Soviet attitudes, and I strongly endorse the view that has already been expressed on this platform that the United States and my own country, and others in Europe, but particularly the United States and Britain, were not generous enough in the commemoration of the 1945 victory regarding the major role played by the Soviet Union. It was a great mistake not to make that an international commemoration and to link together those forces that had fought together as allies. I do not believe it would have been offensive to opinion in the Federal Republic of Germany, which was obviously the country we were most sensitive to, and I think it would have been a good demonstration, getting through to Soviet citizens that we did understand the sacrifices that they had made during the war. There is a lot to be done in explaining to our people and allowing the differing views to be on display, and I believe this to be an invaluable part of this Colloquium. But I do think there is a problem in that the Soviet Union is still too closed a society.

Lewis Dunn

I would only respond that it would seem to me that there are many areas in which the common interests of the United States and the Soviet Union can be served through negotiation and through the achievement of agreements, and one of those areas where I do believe that there are common interests is in the whole area of reducing nuclear weapons. By education for peace, if you mean the notion of the existence of these common interests and the importance of trying to achieve negotiated results, that sounds good to me at this hour of the afternoon!

Andrey Kokoshin

I should say that I am very much in favour of peace education. There are many different forms of it already in existence in my country. For example, on 1 September, every school year begins with a lesson of peace.

Regarding the issue of celebration of the allied victory over the Nazis and the militarism of Japan, I would agree with Dr. Owen that we could do more together, and it is not our fault. We also recognize the substantial impact of our allies, especially in the Pacific. We had some very important events during the celebration of our victory over the Nazis: the Head of the German Democratic Republic was in Moscow and we celebrated it as a joint victory with all the democratic forces and the German people. There is no contradiction between this kind of approach and the event of an allied victory.

Regarding the issue of the closed society, I cannot answer this. I would say that it is some kind of a cliché and I regard it as a totally wrong cliché of our society, though of course in many, many ways of expressing our opinion we differ from Western European countries and from the United States. But we have very active debates on many vital issues and millions and millions of people participate in them. We also appreciate the participation of foreign colleagues, for example, scientists, in such debates. In recent years we have had several television bridges with the United States in which Soviet and American scientists talked about, in particular, the consequences of nuclear war. One of these television bridges was mentioned by my colleague, Professor Velikhov, and it was watched by about 150 million people in the Soviet Union. We know that in the United States it was not shown by the national networks and the number of people watching it was about ten times less than in the Soviet Union. There are many other examples of the same kind. I would like to stress once more that the nuclear winter issue and all the consequences of nuclear war are the most vital issues and are the issues and concerns of everybody.

Closing Statement

PRINCE SADRUDDIN AGA KHAN
President, Groupe de Bellerive

We are coming to the close of this meeting. We have done a lot. And I thank all of you.

Pressures for proliferation are growing; the nuclear threat is unabated. We were here principally to discuss the Non-Proliferation Treaty. Although what we have heard underlines how urgent it is to turn back the impetus towards nuclear militarization, there is no escaping the truth that the Treaty alone is not enough for that.

Yet, in this Bellerive meeting the menace of the bomb has forged one voice. It no longer had the exclusive, often strident, accents of East–West but the deeper tones of a world collectively at risk. I, a Muslim, am as much in danger as a Christian, Jew, Buddhist, Hindu or a non-believer. These weapons are no respecter of creed, political belief or geography. We are as one before the bomb.

The standard answer for why the NPT cannot hold down proliferation is that we are suspicious of each other, we disagree too much; our interests are in conflict; our military competition too strong to be contained by lip-service to an imperfect piece of paper.

But what we heard was not for the most part an emphasis on differences, but what we shared: if this conference had a body language, it was frustration. Every speaker acknowledged the danger of the bomb, its powers of mass destruction; and nobody, I think, thought the chances of its being used were lessening. All saw that in one arena or another, super-Power, regional or terrorist, the likelihood of a nuclear attack is growing.

Yet there was frustration, because of a sense of the irreversibility of it all. It is often said, and it has been here, that people everywhere are against the bomb but that politicians, caught in their own concerns, press ahead. That the bomb has a life separate from public opinion. But in the last few days I detected the same angry impotence, in the face of this nuclear destiny, amongst the politicians. Amongst the Northerners as much as Southerners. A common helplessness in the face of the nuclear momentum.

Why is this momentum so seemingly irreversible? Again the clue lies in what we have heard here. Proliferation, both vertical and horizontal, is driven not so much by competition as by a sense of insecurity. Competition allows the privilege of choice; you can opt in, or out. Insecurity, particularly in a nuclear age, forces its own response: a military, and increasingly a nuclear, build-up. From the most powerful country to the weakest, there is a sense of vulnerability. That the bomb and national security cannot be delinked. We are trapped on an escalator on which we cannot find a way off.

May I, on behalf of my fellow members of the Groupe de Bellerive, try to draw together from our deliberations, the strands of a new safety net for those with the courage to make the leap; a way back to sanity, security and survival. We envisage an overlapping series of securities.

1. The maintenance and strengthening of the Non-Proliferation Treaty. Work that must go forward at the September Review Conference. In particular the International Atomic Energy Agency should be reinforced. Its modest $30 million budget for inspection, and its team of 180 inspectors to cover almost 900 facilities, should be increased; and so should the range of what it inspects.
2. Remove the inequalities of the NPT. The search for a universal non-proliferation regime, however, will continue to founder on the imbalances of the Treaty. We have heard powerful statements of its inherently unequal treatment between the nuclear haves and have-nots. But my experience in the international field has convinced me: if a signed and ratified agreement is imperfect, do not scrap it, improve it. Building multilateral treaties and institutions is a long, slow and painful business; we rarely, if ever, have the luxury of scrapping them and starting again. They may fall, like the League of Nations, because they are overwhelmed and pushed aside by events. But their friends should never take them apart.
3. If the NPT is an international corner-stone, regional and inter-super-Power security are the building blocks of disarmament and non-proliferation.

   I will deal with super-Power nuclear conflict first. As the debate on the nuclear winter again demonstrated, we would all bear the lethal effects of their war. Article VI of the NPT is unequivocal:

   > Each of the Parties to the Treaty undertakes to pursue negotiations in good faith on effective measures relating to the cessation of the nuclear arms race at an early date and to nuclear disarmament, and on a Treaty on general and complete disarmament under strict and effective international control.

   Where is that Treaty, where are even negotiations towards that Treaty?
4. Even if super-Power good example was in place, it would be naive to think that nuclear proliferation elsewhere would then be suppressed. We heard many strong statements of the regional security pressures for proliferation. Nuclear weapons are too serious a business to be solely a matter of emulation. So what good is an NPT with 124 signatures, if a handful of States particularly prone to such pressures stay out?
5. Several of our speakers would deny any linkage between horizontal and

vertical proliferation. And having listened to the debate, and knowing only too well from my own region how deep-rooted the tentacles of local conflict are, I would say that a measure of super-Power disarmament would by itself only be a pre-condition rather than the only vehicle for stemming horizontal proliferation. It would remove the dangerous legitimacy proliferation gathers to itself in an over-armed world.

6. But it is now clear that super-Power arms reduction can only follow on from a much more substantial reduction of tensions than some arithmetical fix on numbers of warheads. The real link between the super-Power and regional arms races is not emulation, but the fact that 40 years of nuclear stand-off in Europe seems to have led to the export of conflict to other regions. This process has exacerbated, rather than healed, historic local tensions. It has now brought all of us to the brink.
7. Nor in all this should we overlook the link between arms and development. Increasingly, I fear that it is an 'either/or' choice. The massive diversion of resources from development to arms; the apparent confusion of motives in some national nuclear energy programmes, that are uneconomic by a developmental criteria, are all part of a military and nuclear brutalization of development. It must stop.

   We are united in our wish to reverse this frightening nuclear momentum. There are a number of initiatives which could take us down the road I have outlined on behalf of the Groupe de Bellerive. These go beyond simple arms control to political confidence-building.
8. On the part of the super-Powers, a political accommodation that would allow massive negotiated reductions in armaments to the level of minimum deterrence is regrettably far off. Nevertheless this would be a measure that would pass like a tidal wave through a world, jumbled by conflict and instability. But the speakers have outlined much more modest proposals which at least start us down this long road.
9. On the part of the regions, the danger of historic conflicts in the nuclear age must be acknowledged and acted upon. Bold exercises in peace-making are needed. I was encouraged to hear regional opponents making common cause in the case for nuclear-free zones.
10. And for us all, nuclear and non-nuclear States, a ban on testing. We have heard the arguments for this forcefully put this afternoon. There remain those who doubt whether verification of such a test ban is possible. The common thread to all these measures is removing that sense of national insecurity which provides the nuclear drive. Such doubts must be removed. A test ban treaty which fed mutual suspicions, and hence insecurity, would be counter-productive. But if there are remaining technical constraints on verification, there are surely ways to overcome them—where there is a political will to do so.

We live in a world where rivalries threaten us all. Yet old politics linger on. We neither turn back to our moral and ethical foundations to seek support against the weapons we have created nor do we look forward to a world managed in the interest of our mutual survival. Where is the innovative multilateralism seeking reduction of tensions between States?

The Groupe de Bellerive, and I as its President, hope that we can go on providing a forum for ideas and actions to stir the international community into life.

As we close this meeting, I urge you to grasp our common concern, the common humanity we share. This oneness has been richly demonstrated in the friendships that we have shared in the last few days across boundaries and ideologies. Let us go forth from here and put that united purpose to work.

CONTRIBUTION *IN ABSENTIA*

The Spread of Nuclear Weapons among Nations: Militarization or Development

DR. A.Q. KHAN

Research Laboratories, Rawalpindi, Pakistan

1. Introduction

The present Colloquium organized by Prince Sadruddin Aga Khan, which is being attended by world-ranking civil servants, politicians, nuclear physicists, political scientists, writers, philosophers, theologians and professors, is going to provide a unique opportunity to draw world attention to the menace of nuclear proliferation and will allow the 121 nations who have signed the Non-Proliferation Treaty to encourage and press the super-Powers, at the Third Review Conference to be held in Geneva in September 1985, to take concrete and sincere steps for nuclear disarmament, as required and agreed upon earlier by the super-Powers under Article VI of the Treaty. It will also provide an opportunity to scrutinize the effectiveness and future of this whole non-proliferation regime. To remind us all of the commitments made under Article VI of the NPT, I reproduce the said Article:

> Each of the Parties to the Treaty undertakes to pursue negotiations in good faith on effective measures relating to cessation of the nuclear arms race at an early date and to nuclear disarmament, and on a Treaty on general and complete disarmament under strict and effective international control.

Article VI is certainly the most important by-product of the NPT and one of its most important provisions.

So much has been written and published, and so much has been said, about the need to control the spread of nuclear weapons that one hesitates to say anything more on this subject. But the matter is serious, and the threat is so real that there should not be any slackening of attention towards the most dangerous and serious threat to mankind.

Even though only five States have so far openly admitted that they have nuclear weapons, India is the sixth country which has tested a nuclear device, and it has unfortunately been engaged in the rhetoric of the peaceful nuclear explosion, which is no more than a blatant insult to the intelligence of all educated people. We all know that there is no such thing as a peaceful nuclear explosion. All nuclear explosions generate shock waves, heat, fire and radiation—tools of destruction—and it is only an academic question whether a nuclear test is dubbed as peaceful or non-peaceful. How can a firearm be classified as peaceful? Although no other nation has exploded its first nuclear weapon since 1974 and none of the nuclear-weapon-threshold countries have accumulated for the first time the fission materials required for the manufacture of nuclear weapons, unfortunately all of the threshold countries have refused either to sign the NPT or to allow their unsafeguarded facilities to be inspected. It is therefore high time to debate rationally the coming nuclear threat that is already overhanging everybody. One can only hope that good sense and security will prevail and that both the nuclear and near-nuclear States will see the grave danger to humanity and to this beautiful world of ours and will get down to serious thinking and negotiations to avoid a nuclear holocaust or the predicted nuclear winter.

For those who have been working relentlessly and are dedicated to stopping the spread of nuclear weapons the last few years have been nerve-wracking and bad. They could have been much worse. However, it is not all that black and there have been some positive developments, which I will discuss later.

History has shown us that most technologies have acted as a double-edged sword, double-edged because advances that promised to better the lot of some human beings often not only threatened, but actually harmed, others in the process. When the threat got rather serious, drastic action on the part of the threatened was the result. Following Murphy's classical law that a thing will happen if it can happen, the proliferation of nuclear weapons has taken place and is going to continue to take place if good sense and intelligence do not prevail on those involved in this mad race towards global destruction.

This has put great strain on the entire non-proliferation regime and many challenges to the NPT are to be expected at the NPT Review Conference. The last decade has not been very successful in containing the potential threat of proliferation of nuclear weapons.

Throughout history, humanity has always concentrated all its efforts on developing new technologies and their special applications. Even though all these technologies were initially developed for peaceful purposes, all ended up being used for killing fellow human beings. The work on fission by Hahn and Strassman and related work by Fermi, Bohr, etc., was of a purely academic nature, but the sudden terror of war and butchery unleashed by the Nazis forced the scientists (Oppenheimer, Szilard, Teller, Frisch, Peierls, etc.) to use this technology, which offered so much to humanity, for the destruction of that same humanity. Never in the history of mankind were such talented manpower and so many resources used for such a terrible weapon of destruction as the atom bomb. Victory in World War II was won by an alliance of the United States, the USSR and the United Kingdom, and its contribution to the defeat of Fascism was crucial and essential. Even though differing technologies and interests were involved, the allies succeeded in hammering out a real framework for future international security in the form of the United Nations Organization. The end of the War made increasingly evident the inherent differences between the allies. The use of the bomb had fundamentally changed the nature of the military conflict and the balance of power. It gave the United States the unrivalled position of a prime arbiter of international affairs. The USSR, having suffered so much initially at the hand of the Nazis, got down to safeguarding its interests and to breaking this monopoly, and developed its own nuclear weapons. The Berlin blockade, the detonation of a nuclear bomb by Russia and the Korean War started a trail of mistrust and the nuclear arms race, which is still going on and has engulfed more States. The mistrust was not confined to the United States and the USSR, it has also played a big role in the development of nuclear weapons by the United Kingdom and France. These two countries did not want to accept the role of second-rate Powers and be ignored in international politics. The same mistrust forced the People's Republic of China to go all out for nuclear weapons. Chairman Mao had earlier described the philosophy of politics that 'political power grows out of the barrel of a gun' and Marshal Chen Yi, feeling rather ineffective as a Foreign Minister without the weight of a nuclear force, lamented that as Foreign Minister, he could not straighten his back. The Marshal said that 'even if we have to pawn our pants, China should develop a nuclear arsenal so it can start on equal terms with other nuclear powers'. A country of 700 million people (now over 1 billion) had to exert itself and not be treated as a second-rate Power.

Moreover, the industrial fall-out of the nuclear weapons programme was so attractive that even President De Gaulle was forced to say 'A weapons programme gives a technical rub-off that makes you compete on the world market in a thousand other ways'.

2. Nuclear weapons promotion and proliferation

The first nuclear bombs produced by the United States were manufactured as a noble cause. All those involved worked with a sense of duty and as a means of safeguarding humanity from Fascism. The development of these awful weapons by the Soviet Union was to protect its security after the bitter experience of the Nazi invasion and the butchery of millions of its citizens. The production of nuclear weapons by the United Kingdom and France was not based on reasons of danger to their security, but more to gain status and weight in international affairs. The same reasons can be attributed to the development of the Chinese and Indian nuclear devices.

In the past 40 years since the first nuclear bomb was dropped on Japan by the United States, five additional States, mentioned above, have detonated nuclear devices and all have developed and deployed (India has not deployed so far) very sophisticated and costly nuclear-weapons delivery-systems. Lack of technological and financial resources has stopped many nations from acquiring this capability and many nations have chosen to refrain from doing so despite having all the necessary facilities at their disposal. Even though the arsenal of nuclear weapons has become awesome—vertical proliferation—the record showed that at least for those countries which were in a position to develop or acquire nuclear weapons, either the motivations to do so were not very strong or the disincentives have been even stronger. What are these incentives and disincentives which can lead to, or dissuade from, nuclear weapons?

2.1 Motivation to manufacture nuclear weapons

The dominant nuclear incentive for many States is the requirement to enhance their prestige and status at regional as well as at the international levels, followed by the requirement to protect their security. Every country considers that its first and foremost duty is to protect its territory from outside aggression, its sovereign independence from political and military threats, and its interests from foreign Powers. There is a great incentive to become a nuclear Power as it can increase a country's influence on regional security arrangements as well as in the United Nations agencies, including the Security Council and the IAEA.

2.2 Lack of motivation to manufacture nuclear weapons

A number of incentives can be given to those countries which are in a position to make, or feel compelled to undertake, the production of nuclear weapons, to refrain from going nuclear. Security Council Resolution 255 is meant to deter the use of nuclear weapons and thus, indirectly, to deter their manufacture and possession. Unfortunately, this has not been very successful. The Security Council should undertake to come to a general consensus on a modified Resolution 255 to prohibit the acquisition of nuclear weapons as such. In this matter, the United States and the USSR could play a major and constructive role, as most of the countries of the world are directly or indirectly under their spheres of influence. In virtually all cases, these two super-Powers are in a position to influence the policies of these countries. In principle, India, Iraq and Libya can be persuaded by the Soviet Union, while Pakistan, Israel, South Africa, Argentina, Brazil, South Korea and Taiwan could easily be influenced by the United States. A sort of security umbrella and some form of mutual security pact with one of the super-Powers could easily provide incentives to most of these nations to refrain from acquiring nuclear weapons and to concentrate on national development projects. Super-Power security guarantees (NATO, Warsaw Pact, etc.) have provided a sense of security to these countries, and the industrial progress of the countries concerned is exemplary. Even though the super-Powers will be inclined to pursue conflicting objectives, it is high time that they realized that acquisition of nuclear weapons by developing non-nuclear nations will result in serious risks for their own security. One can appreciate that such a mutually acceptable system is extremely difficult to chart out because of their differences and priorities, but it is in the interest of humanity that such a system should be evolved. Another incentive to reduce or eliminate incentives for nuclear weapon acquisition is to encourage regional security or friendship treaties to avoid confrontation and the quest for more powerful weapons, including atomic bombs.

3. Proliferation sources

The biggest and most potential source of nuclear weapons material is the civil nuclear power industry, which also provides the necessary training and experience for the technical personnel. Any country engaged in a well-founded nuclear power programme would need much less time to switch over to a weapon programme, if ever it decided to do so. Naturally, the time required to do it would depend on the facilities (uranium enrichment, fuel reprocessing) the country has in operation. All of us are fully aware of the close connection between a nuclear power industry and weapons proliferation. The example of India's switch over from a civil to a weapon-oriented programme is the biggest eye-opener. The development of the civil power programme is making huge quantities of plutonium available for potential risk of misuse or diversion for the manufacture of nuclear weapons. In the last decade the risk has increased considerably due to large quantities of plutonium produced in these facilities.

Since the early 1960s, the successful manufacturing and operation of gas centrifuges has further enhanced the danger of proliferation. It has a qualitative advantage over the gaseous diffusion plant (used by the United States, the USSR, the United Kingdom, France and China) and has great potential. Even though no nation has so far claimed to have enriched uranium to weapon-grade concentration, the theoretical possibility is there. Moreover, the next generation of enrichment processes such as laser and plasma techniques are undergoing intense development efforts. If one succeeds in mastering them, the danger of nuclear proliferation will be enhanced greatly. Uranium enrichment technology has become very important for countries which are interested in keeping their options open on nuclear and thermonuclear weapons. The NPT is unable to stop the spread of uranium enrichment facilities. It has also failed to safeguard the proliferation of this technology as it is outside the scope of the NPT.

4. The failure of the NPT

After World War II, the undiminished nuclear arms race between the United States and the USSR, the resulting radiation contamination and the enhanced danger of nuclear proliferation, resulted in a large number of countries taking an initiative that culminated in 1968 in the NPT, which took effect in 1970. By this time, concern about nuclear proliferation had decreased considerably. However, because no universal consensus was reached on the NPT, its scope was seriously limited. As the NPT is highly discriminatory with regard to the application of safeguards and discriminates in its privileges and obligations between nuclear-weapon and non-nuclear-weapon States, it has brought no diminution of nuclear weapons proliferation and the arms race. It has failed to prohibit the possession of nuclear weapons by those countries which have stockpiled large nuclear arsenals. In addition, the NPT does not contain any provision on security guarantees to non-nuclear-weapon States against a nuclear threat or attack, nor any retaliatory measures against violators of the Treaty. The fundamental hope that the NPT would be able to create an adequate barrier between peaceful and non-peaceful uses of nuclear energy through the IAEA has failed due to the absence of an international consensus. Of the several non-nuclear-weapon States with substantial nuclear programmes which have not signed the NPT, India is the only country which exploded a nuclear device in 1974 based on plutonium produced in a Canadian-supplied research reactor for peaceful purposes and using heavy water supplied by the United States. India thus became the first manifest proliferation case after the NPT entered into force in 1970. It shattered a very tender and delicate *status quo* and encouraged a dangerous precedent.

The First Review Conference of the NPT in 1975 made it evident to non-nuclear-weapon States that the weapon-possessing member States of the Treaty (the United States, the USSR, the United Kingdom—France and China are not members) had not taken any substantial and serious measures to halt vertical proliferation, nor were they prepared to make definite commitments to specific measures to that effect, such as the Comprehensive Test Ban Treaty prepared by the non-aligned States. The failure of the NPT was further manifested by the Second Review Conference held in September 1980, which demonstrated the failure of the nuclear-weapon States to fulfil their obligations to good faith negotiations and to stopping the nuclear arms race as soon as possible. No measurable progress was made between the First and Second Review Conferences, no Comprehensive Test Ban Treaty had been agreed upon and the SALT II agreement had not been ratified. On the contrary, vertical proliferation by the nuclear-weapon States continued unabated with more powerful and sophisticated nuclear and thermonuclear weapons. It was in this atmosphere that the Second NPT Review Conference was not even able to produce a Final Declaration. The present Colloquium is meant as a sincere effort to urge the nuclear-weapon-possessing Powers, especially the United States and the USSR, to do their utmost to make the Third Review Conference a success.

4.1 Vertical proliferation

In spite of all the vocal preaching and rhetoric to the contrary, the nuclear-weapon States have expressed their confidence in the value and usefulness of nuclear weapons in the most unambiguous manner by investing billions of dollars in enhancing the already massive stock and in new generations of all kinds of usable nuclear weapons. This way they have shown the hypocrisy of their own commitments to NPT and have made a mockery of good faith efforts at nuclear disarmament. Their actions have made nuclear weapons more attractive (and less expensive compared to the large regular requirements of conventional weapons) to many nations which face potential threats to their sovereignty and security. Thus, vertical proliferation by the nuclear-weapon States continues unabated and provides incentives to near-nuclear and non-nuclear States to press for acquisition of these awesome and monstrous tools of destruction. There is a great danger that if the United States and the USSR show no progress in limiting their own nuclear arms race, major non-nuclear threshold Powers may quit the NPT and go nuclear in the near future. That would mean the death of the NPT. If there is continued nuclear stockpiling by the super-Powers and observance of the Treaty by non-nuclear Powers, the latter see the strong getting stronger and the weak getting weaker. This is the main reason why the non-nuclear-weapon States have insisted upon a Review Conference every five years to keep up the pressure on the super-Powers to reach agreement. The Third Review Conference is for this purpose, and this Colloquium is a serious and sincere attempt to make the super-Powers aware of their duties towards humanity.

4.2 Horizontal proliferation and its relation to vertical proliferation

In the past 30 years, since nuclear technology first became available for peaceful purposes, most advanced and semi-advanced countries of the world have gained access to at least some of this technology. This access, together with the trained manpower and the seemingly attractive advantages in prestige, status and security, have made the task of non-proliferation of nuclear technology and materials very difficult and important. Only a very few countries with the ability, and incentive, to manufacture a nuclear bomb have not signed, but even this proves a great danger for horizontal proliferation. If one of these countries goes nuclear, others are bound to follow. The appreciation by the threshold countries that nuclear weapons confer enormous advantages upon the country having them and can affect the imbalance in manpower, natural resources, industrial potential and military strength, is a very big incentive for nuclear proliferation and has contributed a lot to the desire of these countries to keep all options open. India's persistence and continuing quest for international recognition as more than a 'pawn on a global chessboard' forced it to detonate a nuclear device in 1974. Pakistan's future policy is to remain closely tied to Indian actions. If India openly starts a weapons programme, the deep-rooted Pakistani fears of India, especially after its active role in the dismemberment of Pakistan in 1971, would put tremendous pressure on Pakistan to take appropriate measures to avoid a nuclear Munich at India's hands in the event of an actual conflict, which many Pakistanis think very real.

4.3 How to contain horizontal proliferation

I have already described the various incentives a nation might have for producing nuclear weapons. Below are some of the main points which can contribute towards containing horizontal proliferation:

(a) The super-Powers must make good their commitment to Article VI of the NPT. Unabated production and testing of nuclear weapons discredit this in the eyes of the non-nuclear States and accentuate the discriminatory nature of the NPT. A voluntary complete ban on the testing of nuclear weapons would be a good initial step. It would be a positive act and would save them from the hypocrisy of preaching one thing while practising something different.

(b) Super-Power guarantees to non-nuclear States against threat or use of nuclear weapons could make a positive contribution to the containment of nuclear weapons. It would take away the incentive to go nuclear at the huge cost of industrial development and the people's welfare.

(c) The industrialized countries must honour commitments made to the developing countries. The unilateral cancellation of all assistance and nuclear fuel to Pakistan by Canada after the Indian nuclear test (through no fault of Pakistan's) has directly led to the efforts by Pakistan to set up a complete nuclear fuel cycle and not to be subjected to such humiliation in future. The cancellation by France of the reprocessing plant (though it was approved by the IAEA) added fuel to the fire and forced Pakistan to work on an enrichment plant to ensure domestic nuclear fuel for all future nuclear power plants. India has recently been subjected to the same treatment by the United States with regard to the fuel for the Tarapur reactor, and though France has made good the American refusal, there are good reasons to believe that India will do all in its power to avoid this humiliation in the future.

(d) Regional co-operative and non-aggression or friendship agreements must be actively encouraged by the super-Powers with the support of the United Nations. A lot of regional conflicts or disagreements are creating security problems for many nations and they fear for their survival. United Nations resolutions and mutually-agreed pacts (as in the case of Kashmir by India) have been blatantly flouted creating a situation where there is an incentive to go nuclear. There are other regional conflicts and differences such as the Middle East, Turkey-Greece, Argentina-Brazil, etc., where super-Power persuasion and help could avoid a nuclear race and contribute to peace and stability.

(e) The super-Powers must behave as super-Powers and must not interfere in the internal affairs of other non-nuclear nations. Aggression or interference is bound to be counter-productive, and the non-nuclear nations will have great incentives, and good reasons, to go nuclear to safeguard their independence and sovereignty. With their backs to the wall, they will not hesitate to use these weapons, even against a formidable adversary.

(f) Developing countries should not be indiscriminately denied the benefits of nuclear power, but proper and adequate safeguards must be made to ensure proper functioning of their facilities and handling of nuclear materials. Denial or refusal of such facilities will be counter-productive and these countries will go all out to create domestic facilities with all the inherent dangers of misuse and proliferation.

(g) One of the best means of containing nuclear proliferation is agreement by regional regimes to mutual inspection of facilities. Pakistan has all along proposed to India to open nuclear facilities for mutual inspections. Both countries are claiming that their nuclear programmes are solely for peaceful purposes and they are not engaged in the manufacture of nuclear weapons. The main difference, however, lies in the fact that, irrespective of the discriminatory nature of the NPT, Pakistan has time and again offered to open nuclear facilities for mutual inspection, which India has always refused under one pretext or another, even to the extent of using arguments insulting the intelligentsia of the world. An agreement between the two countries would drastically change the emotional suspicion-ridden atmosphere between the two countries and could serve as an example for other nations to follow. The sub-continent could be free from the dangers of a mad nuclear race. In the absence of India signing the NPT or a bilateral agreement with Pakistan, Pakistan cannot sign the NPT and cannot allow itself to be subjected to nuclear blackmail. The Indian military intervention in East Pakistan in 1971, the inability of China and the unwillingness of the United States to assist Pakistan against an Indian attack and, above all, the Indo-Soviet defence agreement of 1971 that is aimed at Pakistan, has put Pakistan in a special perspective and unless and until watertight safeguards for its sovereignty and security are forthcoming, no government can take unilateral action and jeopardize the existence and security of the country.

India's unsafeguarded huge plutonium stock is enough to give nightmares to any neighbouring country.

(h) The establishment of a regional nuclear-weapon-free zone on the same lines as the Treaty for the Prohibition of Nuclear Weapons in Latin America of 1968, commonly known as the Tlatelolco Treaty, can contribute substantially to the non-proliferation of nuclear weapons. The Treaty can work as a model for all other regions, including the Indo-Pakistan sub-continent and South-East Asia. In the absence of NPT commitments, such zones can be a valuable source of reduction of horizontal proliferation. Both the United States and the USSR support this Treaty, and all the nuclear-weapon-possessing countries have pledged that the statute of the denuclearization of Latin America will be respected. Pakistan has also been the champion of a similar proposal to declare South-East Asia a nuclear-weapon-free zone. The proposal has been adopted by the United Nations a number of times, but unfortunately, as in the case of mutual inspection, India is the biggest opponent of this proposal. Pakistan sincerely believes that the signing of such an agreement would usher in an era of peace and trust in the sub-continent and would make practical and valuable contributions to containment of horizontal proliferation. As in the case of the Tlatelolco Treaty, the super-Powers and the other nuclear-weapon States can guarantee the sanctity of such a treaty. In this connection, the recent news that Brazil and Argentina have reportedly agreed in principle to develop a mutual inspection regime for their nuclear facilities is very heartwarming and can serve as an example for India and Pakistan.

5. *Risks of nuclear war by accident*

Irrespective of vertical or horizontal proliferation, there is a real danger of nuclear war by accident due to technical failure or malfunctioning, or to accidental detonation or launching of a nuclear weapon. Nuclear war can also be started by unauthorized action, human error or sheer madness. There is moreover a very great danger of a person, or a group of persons, responsible for launching nuclear weapons going insane and deciding to launch a nuclear attack on the enemy, eliciting immediate retaliation and causing a real holocaust. In the presence of these dangers, the ideal solution is not to minimize war, but to stop such a horrible and devastating war altogether by completely eliminating nuclear stockpiles.

6. *Militarization or development*

Any nation that decided to establish a weapon industry (especially nuclear weapons) must commit huge resources to the programme. The requirements depend on the sophistication and the quantity of the weapons, but a major weapon programme has a direct relation to nuclear proliferation as it provides a sound engineering basis for it.

Total world military expenditure has gone to about $500 billion. Weapons production is widespread and advances in military technology are being made at a very fast rate. Total world military expenditure is more than total world-wide government expenditure on education. Weapons development and production programmes in all countries show remarkable resilience to the economic difficulties of the people. $20–30 million is considered peanuts to buy a fighter aircraft, whereas a university is deprived of $20–30 thousand for valuable research equipment. In spite of poverty, hunger and lack of medical facilities, defence industries (and with them the threat of nuclear proliferation) continue to mature and spread. The arms race in conventional weapons and especially the capacity of more and more countries to develop and manufacture their own major weapons is creating a dangerous situation. The financial and technical resources devoted to the development and production of conventional weapons and nuclear weapons are awesome. The development programmes in all those countries which are directly or indirectly involved in conventional and/or nuclear weapons production are suffering badly. This is not limited to the developing countries. Conditions in the United States, the United Kingdom, the USSR and France, and more so in China and India, are far from satisfactory. Large numbers of people live in shameful conditions, cannot afford two proper meals and have no roof over their heads. The starvation in Ethiopia, Chad, Sudan and India should serve as a clear pointer and eye-opener for all. Unless good sense prevails and some positive steps are made towards universal disarmament, the horizontal and vertical proliferation of conventional (and ultimately nuclear) weapons will almost certainly continue. If the super-Powers can come to an agreement on mutual disarmament and can create an atmosphere of mutual trust, industrial and social development at a reasonable pace can be undertaken by non-nuclear-weapon States for the welfare of humanity.

7. Conclusion

Nuclear proliferation is running only in one direction. It is almost impossible that the world will ever see the end of proliferation. However, as time goes on, the severe shortcomings of nuclear deterrents are becoming widely understood and appreciated as inhuman, irrational and barbarous. The problem of nuclear weapon proliferation will not be solved until the incentives, discussed earlier, are removed and until nuclear weapons are outlawed by a universal international consensus as morally unacceptable. Fortunately for all of us, the awareness of the threat posed by nuclear and non-nuclear weapons today has been appreciated enough by all those who matter—scientists, writers, philosophers, theologians, politicans, civil servants, and even armed forces personnel—and they have realized that there is no choice but to halt this mad arms race and to do everything humanly possible for disarmament or face that ultimate absurdity, total annihilation. The consciousness of people all over the world has awoken and a consensus has emerged today that proliferation or accumulation of these tools of destruction must be banned, must be eliminated. The greatest shock and damage to the NPT was done by India's detonation of a nuclear device in May 1974. A country that was proclaiming all along that it was the champion of non-violence shattered a highly precarious and delicate balance of nuclear power. By one act India destroyed the faith that the NPT was working.

In short, it can be said that although the NPT has fallen far short of what is essential to ensure only the peaceful use of nuclear technology, it still represents a genuinely positive development in the efforts by the super-Powers and others to establish a peaceful international nuclear energy regime. The late President Lyndon Johnson had hoped of the NPT that 'It will be for all the world the brightest light at the end of the tunnel since 1945', and former United Nations Ambassador Arthur Goldberg said 'The NPT will assure that control over nuclear weapons, with their catastrophic power of destruction, shall spread no further among the nations of the earth'. The Soviet Deputy Foreign Minister Kuznetzov asked the United Nations General Assembly 'Who profits more from the Treaty—nuclear or non-nuclear nations; all States stand to gain from the Treaty on the Non-Proliferation of Nuclear Weapons?' More than 15 years have passed since the NPT was signed with such hopes and although all has not been as ideal as one would have liked, the situation is not so hopeless either. All forecasts of wide proliferation have failed and dates given repeatedly for impending Pakistani, Israeli, South African, Libyan and Iraqi nuclear bombs have not come true. There is still hope that good sense and intelligence will prevail over madness and that we will not devastate our beautiful world. The following acts strengthen this hope and optimism:

(a) The Tlatelolco Treaty (February 1967)
(b) The Treaty on the Non-Proliferation of Nuclear Weapons (1968)
(c) The Threshold Test Ban Treaty (July 1974)
(d) The Supplier's Agreement (London Club, 1976)
(e) The Nuclear Non-Proliferation Act (1978)
(f) Large anti-nuclear demonstration in Bonn
(g) Simultaneous European anti-nuclear-weapon rallies throughout European capitals (October 1981)
(h) Very large anti-nuclear-weapon demonstrations against President Reagan in Europe (June 1982)
(i) Call by Catholic Bishops for nuclear freeze (May 1983)
(j) United States House of Representatives approves resolution calling

on Administration to negotiate an immediate and verifiable mutual nuclear-weapon freeze

(k) Huge anti-nuclear demonstrations in European capitals

(l) United States film *The Day After* seen by record audience of 100 million, etc.

Furthermore, the Antarctic Treaty of 1959 declaring it a nuclear-weapon-free zone, the Treaty on the Prohibition of the Emplacement of Nuclear Weapons on the Sea-Bed and the Ocean Floor and in Sub-Soil Thereof of 1971, the Treaty to Ban Nuclear Weapons in Outer Space (1967), the Second Bilateral Agreement between the United States and the USSR to reduce the risk of nuclear war (1971), similar agreements between the USSR and France (1976), and between the USSR and the United Kingdom (1977), the agreement between the United States and the USSR on the Prevention of Incidents on the High Seas (1972), SALT I (1972), the ABM Treaty between the United States and the USSR (1972), the Standing Consultation Commission of 1972 between the United States and the USSR, the Prevention of Nuclear War Agreement of 1973 between the USSR and the United States, and the SALT II Agreement of 1979 (still to be ratified by the United States) are big concrete steps towards reducing the risk of nuclear war and making this world safer. The real possibility of an unintentional nuclear war has aroused great concern among large sections of the public. People from all walks of life are increasingly alarmed and conscious of the prospects of a sudden doomsday. As a result of this, sensible people all over the world are insisting on total disarmament and stringent measures on nuclear proliferation. They are carrying out demonstrations, holding conferences and publishing literature to force the super-Powers, and other nuclear and near-nuclear weapon countries, to face up to the fact that they are no longer the prime arbiter and others could also call the shots. In the light of the above-mentioned positive actions taken by the super-Powers and other nuclear-weapon States, we hope that the Third Review Conference will be more constructive, especially now that there is a universal international consensus on nuclear disarmament, and that concrete and positive steps will be taken towards reduction and eventual disarmament of nuclear weapons. I hope that this Colloquium will be able to make positive contributions towards that noble cause.

Before I conclude my observations, I would like to remind the distinguished audience of the statements made by three distinguished public figures:

(1) In present-day conditions there is no way out. Indeed, there are only two ways: either peaceful coexistence or the most destructive war in history. There is no third way.

(Mr. N. Khrushchev, 14 February 1956)

(2) It may be possible to have a just war, but there can be no such thing as just mutual obliteration. It is vital that we see modern weapons of war for what they are—evidence of madness.

(The Archbishop of Canterbury, 1981)

(3) Our fine great buildings, our homes will exist no more. The thousands of years it took to develop our civilization will have been in vain . . . there will be no help, there will be no hope.

(Earl Mountbatten)

In the end I would like to draw attention to the advice given by the great Danish physicist Professor Niels Bohr to President Roosevelt and Prime Minister Churchill in a memorandum dated 3 July 1944:

The fact of immediate preponderance is that a weapon of unparalleled power is being created which will completely change all future conditions of warfare. Quite apart from the question of how soon the weapon will be ready for use and what role it may play in the present war, this situation raises a number of problems which call for most urgent attention. Unless, indeed, some urgent agreement about the control of the use of the new active materials can be obtained in due time, any temporary advantage, however great, may be outweighed by a perpetual menace to human security.

Both Roosevelt and Churchill failed to understand the advice given by this genius and 40 years after it there is precious little evidence that the six nuclear power States are willing to give up the temporary advantage obtained through nuclear weapons. What Professor Bohr failed to grasp was the overwhelming importance and prestige the 'temporary advantage' gave to the politicians of many countries. Let us hope that the super-Powers do not forget this when they sit down in September 1985 to review Article VI of the NPT, and that they listen to all for the safety and betterment of our beautiful world.

Unanswered Questions

Session I Debate

Questions put to Dr. Hans Blix

David Lowry

Is it helpful to the nuclear safeguards inspectorate that electric utilities wipe clean the record of plutonium production by reactor from their computers, as is the current practice of the Central Electricity Generating Board in Great Britain?

Gwyn Prins

Once laser isotope separation is with us, do you believe that its spread can be controlled? How?

In what way should the problem of LIS be tackled in the NPT review?

Questions put to Professor José Goldemberg

Ibrahim Badran

How realistic is the assumption of energy requirements for developing countries as seen by the correlation between GNP growth and energy demand growth in developed countries? Historically, the demand for energy starts slowly then increases through industrialization, exceeding the rate of GNP growth. When sophisticated technology is locally achieved, a slow-down can take place. Moreover, in hot climates energy requirements may equal or exceed energy requirements for the same productivity of human beings.

Mary Davis

How small would a nuclear reactor have to be in order to meet the needs of a small developing country?

Question put to Dr. Frank von Hippel

Gwyn Prins

In your estimation, how long will it be before laser isotope separation technology becomes viable for extensive use?

What will be its effect upon the maintenance of the already problematic division between 'civil' and 'military' programmes?

Unanswered Questions

Session II Debate

Question put to Mr. Régis Debray

Jean-Pierre Stroot

Mr. Olof Palme told us that, although Sweden—a sovereign State—had the technical capacity to manufacture nuclear weapons, it had decided not to do so because it considered that there were only disadvantages in becoming a nuclear power. France has taken the opposite decision. What advantages, other than heuristic considerations or hypotheses that it lets Paris 'into the club', does France find in its policy?

Questions put to Professor Anatoly Gromyko

Simon Henderson

How does the Soviet Union's supply of an unsafeguarded uranium diffusion enrichment plant to China in the 1960s tie in with your country's stand on proliferation?

Konstantin Volkov

We do agree with you that nothing is more important—and more urgent—for mankind than peace; we know that without peace nothing positive and lasting can be achieved in the world. You mentioned briefly the relation between the arms race and development. United Nations economists, some of whom are members of our Peace and Disarmament Movement, in particular, those who are experts in African and Asian questions, are extremely worried by the short-term, medium-term and long-term repercussions of the increasing waste of financial resources on arms in general, both by industrialized and developing countries, and on nuclear weapons by nuclear Powers. Over the last few years, all international organizations in the United Nations system have been increasingly and alarmingly deprived of the financial means necessary for their programmes of aid to developing countries. This trend has led to a further deterioration in the economic and social situation of most of the newly politically independent countries. Could you make a comment on this situation?

Question put to Professor Anatoly Gromyko and Dr. Krishnaswami Subrahmanyam

Daniel Lack

Dr. Subrahmanyam has made some interesting observations about the United States chain of command with regard to the possible use of nuclear weapons. Does he, or Professor Gromyko, have any information to offer about the chain of command for such a decision by the other super-Power which might be helpful in assessing the relative risks and recommending common measures by the super-Powers to contain the risk of undue and uncontrollable delegation of the fateful decision on either side.?

Unanswered Questions

Session IV Debate

Questions put to Dr. Georgi Arbatov

Freimut Duve

Would you comment on the agreement (early June in Bonn) between the SPD and SED (German Democratic Republic and Federal Republic of Germany) on chemical weapons? Could such a bilateral regional agreement, in your opinion, be an example for other bilateral agreements under the great Powers? Could you name other examples?

Daniel Lack

Does Dr. Arbatov agree with the proposition that mutual confidence-building measures to improve trust and good faith in the disarmament negotiations between the USSR and the United States of America include such questions as concessions on human rights, as defined in the Helsinki Final Act, and improvement in the fields of economic and cultural co-operation? Does he see any linkage or interdependence between any of these confidence-building measures?

Angelo Miatello

It would appear that in France fast breeder reactors can also be used for military purposes. The exploiting company (see Super-Phénix) is composed *inter alia* of Italian multinationals. Does such joint activity (Italian and French companies) violate the 1947 Peace Treaty with Italy, in which Article 51 specifically prohibits Italy from manufacturing, testing or possessing nuclear weapons? In other words, has the 1947 Peace Treaty become null and void (for Italy)?

Abdul Tabibi

Today the main danger is conventional arms and not atomic weapons, which we hope will never be used except as a deterrent. During the last six years in Afghanistan, one million people have been killed or maimed and one-third of the population has been forced to leave their country. Wouldn't a political solution in Afghanistan help confidence-building?

Konstantin Volkov

You stressed the paradox 'more and more arms and less and less security'. The United Nations Secretary-General shares this view. As a result of the unprecedented and increasing waste of mankind's material and intellectual resources, the international organizations in the United Nations system, deprived of the necessary financial means, are increasingly prevented from carrying out their social, economic and technical programmes and aid to developing countries.

Many of us in the international organizations, especially in the United Nations, consider that there is no realistic prospect whatsoever for a lasting solution of some crucial international or regional issues, such as the Middle East conflict, apartheid, hunger, etc., as long as the disarmament process and the move towards a lasting peace have not started. What is your feeling on these two questions?

Questions put to Professor Kenneth Galbraith

Pierre Lehmann

No mentally sound person would devote time to constructing arms of any kind if left alone. Yet, as we have heard, a large number of people produce arms today. Why?

Probably because people are not left alone. They are made into civilians and soldiers to serve the interests of the nation State to which they happen to belong. Nation States do not seem able to function without war, or at least a latent state of war. You have implied as much in your talk. Shouldn't we then try to find ways of dismantling nation States progressively and devise other ways of organizing relations between people? Do you think this Utopian proposal has any chance? Is it less Utopian than the hope of surviving with nation States?

Laurent Rebéaud

What is your personal position regarding SDI?

Konstantin Volkov

If I am not mistaken, you said that in both major nuclear countries—the United States and the USSR—there are some quarters which do not favour any genuine nuclear arms control. Could you indicate which are, in your opinion, the quarters in the Soviet Union which are against any genuine nuclear arms control for economic, bureaucratic or other reasons?

Questions put to Mr. Richard Perle

David Albright

Last year the United States insisted on an unprecedented level of physical protection on a shipment of separated plutonium from France to Japan. With the amount of separated plutonium in international commerce increasing, what other steps will the United States take to ensure that terrorist groups will not steal or embezzle some of the plutonium and use it to extort concessions from governments?

Wolfgang Biermann

You commented that there was evidence indicating that the USSR had violated the 150 kt limit of the Threshold Test Ban Treaty. The experts on verification on the Pentagon's own scientific panels stated that they dispute this evidence very strongly. Who is right, the Pentagon's seismic experts or Richard Perle?

Damian Durrant

Would it not be more constructive to expend American financial and technical expertise with the Soviets on developing effective means of verification of arms control agreements, such as the comprehensive test ban, which would surely be more technically feasible and expedient than long-term highly expensive research into BMD and ASAT weapon systems? Would Mr. Perle please clarify his view that the comprehensive test ban would not lead to any reductions in nuclear arsenals?

Freimut Duve

You seem to imply that Western Europe's criticism of SDI is partly a consequence of Russian campaigning. Do you accept the genuine reasons for our scepticism and are you willing to take our arguments against a new gigantic leap of the defence trade seriously?

David Fischer

We have heard your defence of SDI and other United States defence policies as well as criticism of their Soviet counterparts. How would you propose to improve relations between the two super-Powers and avert the danger of nuclear catastrophe?

Jozef Goldblat

Assuming that SDI becomes a reality and that nuclear weapons become obsolete, as President Reagan has predicted in his famous speech, how will the United States defend Western Europe against a possible Soviet attack carried out with overwhelming conventional forces? In other words, what will be the fate of the present NATO doctrine of first use of nuclear weapons in defence of Europe?

Colin Hines

On several occasions at this Colloquium, the question of the imminent growth of the plutonium economy in Europe has arisen. What is the Department of

Defense's attitude to this development, particularly now the spectre of nuclear terrorism is so much in America's mind?

David Lowry

If the SDI programme is purely defensive and intended to increase global as well as Western security, why does the United States not ask the Soviet Union to share in the development stages, as has been done for the United States' allies in Western Europe, Israel and Japan? And why don't you ask them to share whatever SDI technological developments they have made thus far, in reciprocal arrangement?

Christopher Paine

Please describe the current Administration's policy toward the use of separated plutonium in world commerce.

Does the Department of Defense have a different view from the State Department and the Department of Energy regarding the security threat represented by weapons-usable nuclear materials in world commerce?

Is it fair to say that the Reagan Administration is 'hard' on Communism, but 'soft' on the prospect of nuclear terrorism?

Andy Sundberg

If the Soviet political system is inherently evil and mendacity is an integral strategic and tactical behavioural component of this system, how can you justify that holding negotiations between the United States and the USSR can give any positive result?

Gordon Thompson

Do you accept that trends in strategic posture under the Reagan Administration are leading to lower stability in times of crisis?

Marjorie Thompson

Mr. Perle refers to free and open discussion in the West and to the existence of a variety of views. He also refers to the Soviet occupation of Eastern Europe. He says there have been great reductions in the megatonnage of the United States arsenal, that the United States central command will not have neutron weapons. As far as free and open discussion goes, what does he say about changes in NATO strategy involving early use of nuclear weapons without parliamentary consultation and the lack of a parliamentary debate on SDI?

As far as occupation goes, how much does he think the British people know about 100 plus United States bases in the United Kingdom?

On reductions in megatonnage, would he not agree that the more accurate one's weapons are, the less megatonnage one needs?

He says that the United States will be sending the 155 mm enhanced radiation shell, which Richard Wagner from the Pentagon thinks Britain has agreed to but which ministers deny. Has the United States asked Britain to store it?

Finally, why are the peace movements of Europe vitriolically attacked as dupes of Communism if you welcome discussion?

Konstantin Volkov

Why has the United States Government not responded positively to the following Soviet proposals or statements:

1. an immediate freeze of nuclear arms
2. cessation of nuclear tests
3. no first use of nuclear arms?

Questions put to the Honorable Senator Theodore Stevens

Jozef Goldblat

Assuming that the SDI becomes a reality and that nuclear weapons become obsolete, how will the United States defend Western Europe against the feared Soviet attack? What will happen to the NATO concept to use nuclear weapons first in defence of Europe?

Mycle Schneider

The French Government doesn't exclude the militarization of the international fast breeder Super-Phénix. Do you think that such a step (by the French Government) would violate the spirit of the NPT? What would be the reaction of the American Government?

Jürgen Streich

Senator Stevens said that SDI would work without nuclear explosive weapons. But what about the Pentagon directive of 19 June 1985 stating that nuclear explosives will play a main role in SDI? What about the X-ray lasers and what about Teller's plans to destroy atomic warheads in the end-phase by nuclear explosions?

Marjorie Thompson

In his talk, Senator Stevens referred to 'both sides of the ideological dispute'. Is he aware that many Europeans don't see themselves as being involved in any ideological dispute, but believe in peaceful coexistence? As far as ideology goes, the presence of 100 plus United States bases in Britain, authorized without parliamentary consultation, and the lack of a debate on SDI, make such ringing phrases as freedom, alliance and democracy a joke. Could he comment?

Questions put to Dr. Georgi Arbatov and the Honorable Richard Perle

Peter Herby

Would your country agree to refrain from *verifiable* research on space weapons?

Manuel Tello

The research and development of SDI is quite a costly enterprise. President Reagan has said that the United States is willing to share with the Soviet Union the results of that research. Dr. Arbatov has just said that he does not believe in the offer. I wonder whether Dr. Arbatov or Mr. Perle would care to comment on the following idea: why not invite the Soviet Union to carry out the research with the United States and thereby divide the cost of the whole programme in half?

Question put to Dr. Georgi Arbatov and the Honorable Senator Theodore Stevens

Pierre Lehmann

The peaceful intentions of your respective countries are difficult to believe because:

—United States-Nicaragua: why do you try to strangle this country?
—USSR-Afghanistan: why don't you let these people solve their problems among themselves?

Question put to Professor Kenneth Galbraith and the Honorable Richard Perle

Alexander MacLeod

This Colloquium has underlined the connection, in terms of opportunity cost, between the arms race and world economic development. Would you care to justify the cost, in terms of lost economic development opportunities, of a 'Star Wars' research programme which, by your own admission, may fail in its objective?

Questions put to the Honorable Richard Perle and the Honorable Senator Theodore Stevens

Brian Fitzgerald

Vice-President Bush has sought support in Europe for SDI by offering 'full partnership' to allies participating in 'Star Wars' research. Does this mean that United States allies, such as Germany, which are non-nuclear-weapon States, will participate in research on the X-ray laser? Because that weapon utilizes a nuclear detonation, would that not represent a violation of Articles I and II of the NPT? Or does it mean that the term 'full partnership' is intended to exclude some areas of research?

Question put to all the speakers

Alix Lhote

SDI aims to set up a defensive network, a sort of defensive 'shield'. However:

1. could the possession of such a network not lead to a temptation to strike first?
2. one of the ways of overcoming such a defensive network would be to saturate the enemy target (a very costly solution that already appears to be technically possible). Doesn't this make the United States–USSR negotiations pointless? What do the speakers think?

Unanswered Questions

Session V Debate

Question put to the Honorable Senator Edward Kennedy

Mycle Schneider

The international fast breeder Super-Phénix (France) is to be started up within the next few months. The first core (at least) will contain plutonium of United States origin. In spite of that fact, the French Government refused to exclude the option of using Super-Phénix for military plutonium production purposes. How do you evaluate the significance and the consequences of this situation concerning American nuclear non-proliferation policy?

Question put to the Rt. Hon. Dr. David Owen, M.P.

You have referred to the role of scientists from nuclear weapons laboratories in Britain and the United States in lobbying to prevent a Comprehensive Test Ban Treaty. The same phenomenon is also reported in France. If this lobbying is improper, what should be done to stop it?

Question put to Ambassador Lewis Dunn and the Rt. Hon. Dr. David Owen, M.P.

Damian Durrant

Could Mr. Dunn elaborate on his view that a comprehensive test ban would delay missile reductions by undermining confidence in existing deterrence, and would Dr. Owen care to comment on this issue?

List of Speakers

AGA KHAN, Prince Sadruddin
International Civil Servant, President of the Groupe de Bellerive, Geneva

ARBATOV, Dr. Georgi
Director, Institute of the USA and Canada, Academy of Sciences of the USSR

BERGSTRÖM, Professor Sune
Nobel Prize Winner; Karolinska Institutet, Stockholm

BLIX, Dr. Hans
Director General, International Atomic Energy Agency (Vienna)

BOVEN, Professor Theo van
Professor of Law, Limburg University, Maastricht; Chairman, Commission of the Churches on International Affairs, World Council of Churches

BUSH, The Hon. George
Vice-President of the United States

DEBRAY, Mr. Régis
Maître des Requêtes au Conseil d'Etat, France

DHANAPALA, HE Jayantha
Permanent Representative of the Democratic Socialist Republic of Sri Lanka to the United Nations, Geneva

DUNN, Ambassador Lewis A.
Assistant Director, US Arms Control and Disarmament Agency

GALBRAITH, Professor John Kenneth
Harvard University

GOLDEMBERG, Professor José
President, Energy Company of the State of Sao Paulo, Former President of the Association of Scientists of Brazil

GROMYKO, Professor Anatoly A.
Director of the Institute of African Studies of the USSR Academy of Sciences, Corresponding Member of the USSR Academy of Sciences, Member of the Soviet Scientists' Committee for Peace against the Nuclear Threat

HASSAN BIN TALAL, HRH
Crown Prince of Jordan

HIPPEL, Dr. Frank von
Woodrow Wilson School of Public and International Affairs and Center for Energy and Environmental Studies, Princeton University

JORTNER, Professor Joshua
University of Tel Aviv

KENNEDY, The Hon. Senator Edward
Senator for Massachusetts (Democratic), Washington D.C.

KOKOSHIN, Dr. Andrey
Vice-Chairman, Committee of Soviet Scientists for Peace Against Nuclear Threat; Deputy Director, Institute of the USA and Canada, Academy of Sciences of the USSR

MAZRUI, Professor Ali A.
Department of Political Science, University of Michigan

OWEN, The Rt. Hon. Dr. David
Member of Parliament, United Kingdom, Leader of the Social Democratic Party

PALME, The Hon. Olof
Prime Minister of Sweden

PEREZ, HE Carlos Andres
Former President of Venezuela

PERLE, The Hon. Richard
Assistant Secretary, United States Department of Defense

DE PERROT, Mr. Michel
Physicist, Research Fellow, Geneva International Peace Research Institute

QIAN, HE Jiadong
Ambassador of the People's Republic of China to the Conference on Disarmament, Geneva

ROTBLAT, Professor Joseph
Professor Emeritus of Physics, London University

SAGAN, Dr. Carl
Center for Radiophysics and Space Research, Cornell University

SALAM, Professor Mohammed Abdus
Nobel Prize Winner; Director, International Centre for Theoretical Studies, Trieste

SHAKER, HE Mohamed I.
Ambassador, Permanent Mission of the Arab Republic of Egypt to the United Nations, New York

STEVENS, The Hon. Senator Theodore
Senator for Alaska (Republican), Washington D.C.

SUBRAHMANYAM, Dr. Krishnaswami
Director, the Institute for Defence Studies and Analyses, New Delhi

VELIKHOV, Dr. Yevgeny P.
Deputy Director, USSR Academy of Sciences

List of Participants

(excluding those from Permanent
Missions to the United Nations and the Media)

ABRAHAM, Mr. Thomas
Research Associate, United Nations Institute for Disarmament Research, Geneva

ADKINS, Mr. Bruce M.
Electrical Engineer and Energy Consultant, Power for Good, France

ADOR, Mr. Robert
Geneva

AGAEV, Mr. Ednan
Research Co-ordinator, United Nations Institute for Disarmament Research, Geneva

ALBRIGHT, Mr. David
Research Associate, Federation of American Scientists, Washington

AL-HAFEDH, Dr. Mehdi
Economic Expert, United Nations Industrial Development Organization, Vienna

ALTMANN, Mr. Cecil
President, Société Colbert, Geneva

AMATI, Mr. Daniele
Physicist, CERN, Geneva

ANET, Mr. Bernard
Scientific Adviser, NC Laboratory Spiez, Switzerland

ARBER, Mr. Didier Marc
Programmer, Neuchâtel

AUBERT, Mr. Maurice
Vice-President, International Committee of the Red Cross, Geneva

AYRTON, Mr. Stephen
Professor, Institute of Mineralogy, Lausanne University

BADRAN, Dr. Ibrahim
Under-Secretary, Ministry of Industry, Amman, Jordan

BALLANTYNE, Mrs. Edith
Secretary-General, Women's International League for Peace and Freedom, Geneva

BALLARD, Ms. Margaret
Clinical Psychologist, London

BAUD-DESHORTIES, Mrs. Georgette
Psychologist, Geneva

BAUER-LAGIER, Mrs. Monique
Deputy of the Republic and Canton of Geneva to the Council of State, Geneva

BEER, Dr. Henrik
Member ICIHI, Geneva

BELL, Mr. John Stewart
Physicist, CERN, Geneva

BENECKE, Mr. Jochen
Physicist, Max-Planck Institut, Munich

BERRASATEGUI, Mr. V.
Department for Disarmament Affairs, Geneva

BESSE, Mr. Antonin
Board of Directors, United World College, Paris

BESSE, Mrs. Antonin

BETCHOV, Mr. Robert
Researcher, Canadian Peace Research

BIERMANN, Dr. Wolfgang
Arms Control Group, SPD, German Coordinating Group of the Five Continents Peace Initiative, Bonn

BISHOP, Dr. Amasa S.
Former Director, UN Economic Commission for Europe, Genolier, Switzerland

BLANCHARD, Mr. Francis
Director General, International Labour Office, Geneva

BLUMENTHAL, Dr. Susan
Washington

BOAINAIN, Ms. Alice
Secretary, Institute for Planet Synthesis, Geneva

BOREL, Mr. Dominique
Delegate, International Committee of the Red Cross, Geneva

BORNER, Mr. Alain
Head of the Department of Economy, Geneva

BOURDET, Mr. Claude
President, Movement for Disarmament, Peace and Freedom, Paris

BRENNAN, Mr. Gerald
Legal Adviser, Department of Foreign Affairs, Canberra

BUDTZ, Mr. Lasse
Member of Danish Parliament, Frederiksberg, Denmark

BURGOS, Mrs. Elizabeth
Director, Maison de l'Amérique latine, Paris

CAMPICHE, Mr. Samuel
Ambassador, Gstaad, Switzerland

CANEL, Ms. Irene
IFSDA, Sweden

CANTINI, Dr. Giorgio
Geneva

CANTINI, Mrs. Vilma
Geneva

CARLSSON, HE Mr. Bernt
Ambassador, Sweden

CHAPMAN, Mr. Daniel
Geneva

CHAVANNE, Mr. André
Councillor of State, Geneva

CHAVANNE, Mrs. Renée
Geneva Representative of Socialist International Women, Geneva

CHILDERS, Mr. Barry
Coordinator, US–UK Freeze International, Geneva

COE, Mrs. Joanne
Secretary of the United States Senate

COPEL, General Etienne
General on detachment, St. Germain-en-Laye, France

CORDOVEZ, Mr. Diego
Under-Secretary-General for Special Political Affairs, United Nations, New York

CUENDET, Mr. Antoine
Professor, Medical Faculty, Geneva

CURRY, Mrs. Sally
Coordinator Peace Education, Peace Research Institute, Dundas, Canada

DAFFLON, Mr. Roger
Former Mayor of Geneva

DAHLITZ, Dr. Julie
Senior Researcher, United Nations Institute for Disarmament Research, Geneva

DAMASKINOS, Archbishop
Orthodox Centre of the Ecumenical Patriarchate, Geneva

DAVIES, Mr. Ben
Programme Assistant, Quaker United Nations Office, Geneva

DAVIS, Ms. Mary
Member of Nuclear Subcommittee of National Energy Committee, Lozanne, France

DEVAUD, Mr. Charles
Priest, Roman Catholic Church of Geneva

DHAMI, Mr. Sadhu Singh
Retired Official of the International Labour Office, Geneva

DIN, Mr. Allan
Physicist, Stockholm International Peace Research Institute, Solna, Sweden

DUCOMMUN, Ms. Rosalie
Women for Peace, Geneva

DUCRET, Mr. Bernard
Secretary General, Geneva University

DUNLOP, Mr. Nick
Secretary-General, Parliamentarians for World Order, New York

DUPRE, Mr. Guy
General Secretary, CILRECO, France

DURRANT, Mrs. Cornelia
Greenpeace International

DURRANT, Mr. Damian
Disarmament Coordinator, Greenpeace

DUVE, Mr. Freimut
Social Democratic Party, Member of the Bundestag, Bonn

DYE, Mr. Robert
Executive for Programmes and Services, World Alliance of YMCAs, Geneva

EDMONDS, Beverly C.
Head of the American Bureau, World Association for the School as an Instrument of Peace, Geneva

EHRENSTEIN, Mr. Dieter von
Professor of Physics, Bremen University

EHRENSTEIN, Dr. Iselin
Bremen

EISENBART, Dr. Constanze
Senior Research Fellow, Protestant Institute for Interdisciplinary Research, Heidelberg

EK, Mrs. Simone
Director, International Relations, Rädda Barnen International, Geneva

EMMENEGGER, Mr. René
Mayor of Geneva

ENTELL, Mr. Peter
Nyon, Switzerland

ERTAN, Mrs. Filiz
Department of Disarmament Affairs, United Nations, Geneva

ERCHOV, Dr. Iouri
Principal Officer, United Nations Conference on Trade and Development, Geneva

ESSAAFI, Mr. M'hamed
Under-Secretary-General, United Nations Disaster Relief Office, Geneva

ERCHOV, Dr. Iouri
Principal Officer, United Nations Conference on Trade and Development, Geneva

ESSAAFI, Mr. M'hamed
Under-Secretary-General, United Nations Disaster Relief Office, Geneva

FAESSLER, Mr. Marc
Director, Protestant Research Centre, Geneva

FAGEN, Mrs. Laura
Economist, Geneva

FAGEN, Mr. Melvin
Former Director, United Nations Economic Commission for Europe, Geneva

FARHI, Ms. Andrée
United Nations Representative, International Council of Jewish Women, Geneva

FERSHT, Mr. Eric
Disarmament Campaign Director, Greenpeace

FIGUEREDA-PLANCHART, HE Mr. Reinaldo
Former Ambassador, Venezuela

FINGER, Mr. Matthias
Geneva University

FISCHER, Mr. David
Retired, Former Assistant Director-General, International Atomic Energy Agency, Vienna

FITZGERALD, Mr. Brian
Greenpeace International

FORNEY, Mr. Jean-Jacques
Professor of Physics, Geneva

FRANCESCHETTI, Dr. Albert
Physician, Geneva

FRANCESCHETTI, Mrs. Clara
Author, Geneva

FRICAUD-CHAGNAUD, General Charles
President, Foundation for National Defence Studies, Paris

GALLINER, Mr. Peter
Director, International Press Institute, London

GASTEYGER, Mr. Curt
Professor, Graduate Institute of International Studies, Geneva

GAUDRY, Mr. Roger
Professor, former President of Montreal University, Montreal

GAUHAR, Mr. Bilquis
Adviser, Third World Foundation, London

DE GENDT, Mr. Robert
Secretary, Committee for European Security and Co-operation, Brussels

GIACONE, Mr. Franco
Professor, Geneva International Peace Research Institute

GIACOSA, Mr. Juan Carlos
Secretary-General, International Youth and Student Movement for the United Nations, Geneva

GIARINI, Mr. Orio
Economist, The Risk Institute, Geneva

GILLETT, Mr. Nicholas
Director, Nuclear Weapons Freeze Campaign, Bristol, United Kingdom

GIOVANNINI, Mr. Bernard
Professor, Physics Department, Geneva University

GLOVER, Ms. Margaret
Parliamentary Worker, Campaign against Arms Trade, Marlow, United Kingdom

GOBLE, Mr. Norman M.
Secretary General, World Confederation of Organizations of the Teaching Profession, Morges, Switzerland

GOKAL, Mr. Abbas K.
Chairman, Gulf International Group of Companies, Geneva

GOLDBLAT, Mr. Jozef
Senior member of the research staff, Stockholm International Peace Research Institute, Solna, Sweden

GORE, Senator Albert
United States Senate

GOSLING, Mr. David
Director of Church and Society, World Council of Churches, Geneva

GOTTSTEIN, Mr. Klaus
Director of Research Unit, Max-Planck Society, Munich

GRANGER, Ms. Jacqueline
Representative in Geneva, Society for International Development

GRIMSSON, Dr. Olafur Ragnar
President, Parliamentarians for World Order, New York

GRINEVALD, Mr. Jacques
Researcher, Geneva International Peace Research Institute, Geneva

GRUBER, Mr. Howard
Professor, Geneva University

GSPONER, Dr. André
Independent Scientific Research Institute, Geneva

GUICHERD, Miss Catherine
Student, Graduate Institute of International Studies, Geneva

GUNN, Dr S. William
Special Adviser to the Secretary General, League of Red Cross and Red Crescent Societies, Geneva

HACKETT, General Sir John
Author, Coberley Mill, United Kingdom

HAGEDORN, Dr. Rolf
Physicist, honorary staff member, CERN, Geneva

HALLE, Mr. Louis Joseph
Honorary Professor, Graduate Institute of International Studies, Geneva

HAMMARSKJOLD, Mr. Knut
Secretary General, International Air Transport Association, Geneva

HART, Senator Gary
United States Senate

HARTLAND, Ms. Jenny
Chairman, Northern Friends Peace Board, Leyburn, United Kingdom

HAWKINS, Mrs. Sebia
Greenpeace, USA

HAY, Mr. Alexandre
President, International Committee of the Red Cross, Geneva

HEGEDUS, Mrs. Zsuzsa
Researcher, National Centre for Scientific Research, Paris

HEINZMANN, Mr. Hildebert
Deputy Director, Federal Office of Civil Defence, Bern

HEMMERICH-BARTER, Mrs. Ursula
Soroptimist International, Geneva

HENTSCH, Mr. Léonard
Treasurer, International Union for Conservation of Nature and Natural Resources, Geneva

HEPTONSTALL, Mrs. Sonia
Representative to the United Nations, Soroptimist International, Geneva

HERBY, Mr. Peter
Associate Director, Quaker United Nations Office, Geneva

HERNDL, Mr. Kurt
Assistant Secretary-General for Human Rights, United Nations, Geneva

HINES, Mr. Colin
Director, Greenpeace Non-Proliferation Treaty '85 Campaign, London

HOCKE, Mr. Jean-Pierre
Director, International Committee of the Red Cross, Geneva

HOFSETH, Mr. Paul
Council for Environmental Studies, Oslo University

HOWARD, Dr. William
National Coordinator, Nuclear Weapons Freeze, United Kingdom

IISAKA, Mr. Yoshiaki
Adjunct Secretary General, World Conference on Religion and Peace, Geneva

JACOBS, Ms. Margaret
Disarmament Intern, Women's International League for Peace and Freedom, Geneva

JANKOW, Dr. Robert
President, Instrumatic SA, Geneva

JANSEN, Mr. Hans
Assistant Secretary-General, International Youth and Student Movement for the United Nations, Geneva

JOYCE, Mr. James Avery
International Lawyer, London

KELLENBERGER, Mr. Eduard
Professor of Microbiology, Basel University

KIENAST, Ms. Giselle
Secretary, Geneva University

KIENER, Mr. Eduard
Director, Federal Energy Office, Bern

KILJUNEN, Mr. Kimmo
Secretary-General, International Peace Bureau, Geneva

KOECHLIN, Mr. Jean-Claude
Deputy Director, Atomic Energy Commission, Paris

KOMATINA, Mr. Miljan
Secretary-General of the Conference on Disarmament, United Nations, Geneva

KOWARSKI, Mrs. Kate
Geneva

KOZLOWSKI, Mr. Anthony
Executive Director, International Council of Voluntary Agencies, Geneva

KRAUS, Mr. John
Director of External Relations, General Agreement on Tariffs and Trade, Geneva

KRAUS-GURNY, Dr. Liselotte
Jurist, Geneva

KUNTZEL, Mr. Matthias
Die Grünen im Bundestag, Bonn

KUNZ, Mr. Raymond
Diplomatic Counsellor, Federal Department of Foreign Affairs, Bern

KUPPERMAN, Mr. Robert
Senior Associate, Center for Strategic and International Studies, Washington

LACK, Mr. Daniel
Legal Adviser

LAMBERT, Mrs. Nilda
Soroptimist International, Geneva

LANNOYE, Dr. Paul
Researcher, Namur University, Belgium

LASSEN, Mr. Hans
Information Attaché, United Nations Economic Commission for Europe, Geneva

LAUKO, Dr. Karoly
Permanent Representative, World Peace Council

LAWRENCE, Ms. Elaine
Greenpeace International

LEHMANN, Mr. Pierre
Physicist, Société d'Etude de l'Environnement, Vevey, Switzerland

LEPRINCE-RINGUET, Mr. Louis
Honorary Professor, Collège de France, Paris

LHOTE, Mr. Alix
General Secretary, International Federation of Resistance Movements, Vienna

LIECHTENSTEIN, Prince Hans Adam von

LINDOP, Mrs. Patricia
Professor, London University

LINDT, Mr. August R.
Former Swiss Ambassador, Bern

LIOZNOVA, MRS. TATIANA
Producer, People's Artist of the USSR, Moscow

LOWRY, Mr. David
Research Associate, European Proliferation Information Centre, London

LUDLOW, Professor Peter
Director, Centre for European Policy Studies, Brussels

LUKIC, Mr. Reneo
Researcher, Interdisciplinary Centre for Research on Peace and Strategic Studies, Paris

MACBRIDE, Seàn, S. C.
President, International Peace Bureau, Geneva

MCCLELLAN, Mr. Joel
Director, Quaker United Nations Office, Geneva

MCLEAN, Ms. Scilla
Research Director, Oxford Research Group, Woodstock, United Kingdom

MCTAGGART, Mr. David
Chairman, Greenpeace International

MACE, Mr. Charles
Retired, Taninges, France

MALINVERNI, Mr. Giorgio
Professor, Geneva University

MANOS, Mr. Stephanos
Ekali, Athens

MARKEY, Congressman Edward
United States Congress

MAROIS, Mr. Maurice
Professor of Medicine, Institut de la Vie, Paris

MARTENSON, Mr. Ian
Under-Secretary for Disarmament Affairs, United Nations, New York

MARWAH, Mr. Onkar
Senior Research Fellow, Asian Centre, Graduate Institute of International Studies, Geneva

MATHIAS, Senator Charles
United States Senate

MERCER, Mr. Edgar Howard
Professor, Hawaii University

MERCIECA, Mr. Charles
Executive Vice-President, International Association of Educators for World Peace, Harvard University, USA

MIATELLO, Mr. Angelo
Researcher, Geneva School of Translation and Interpretation

MICHELI, Mr. Dominique
First Vice-President of the Grand Council, Geneva

MONTALUISA VIVAS, Mr. Juan
Student, Graduate Institute of International Studies, Geneva

MONTICONE, Ms. Regina
Executive Political Officer, Parliamentarians for World Order, New York

MOREL, Mr. Nicolas
Engineer-physicist, Federal Polytechnic, Lausanne

MORIN, Mr. Guy
Physicians for Social Responsibility, Basel

MOTTU, Mr. Daniel
President, Moral Rearmament Foundation, Geneva

MOYNIHAN, Senator Daniel
United States Senate

MROZ, Mr. John Edwin
President, Institute for East-West, New York

MUHLETHALER, Mr. Jacques
President, World Association for the School as an Instrument of Peace, Geneva

MÜLLER, Dr. Harald
Senior Research Fellow, Centre for European Policy Studies, Brussels

MULLER, Mrs. Marlyse
Political Scientist, Geneva

MYERS, Mr. Norman
Senior Associate, International Union for the Conservation of Nature and Natural Resources

MYSYROWICZ, Mr. Ladislas
Professor, Geneva University

NEIRYNCK, Mr. Jacques
Professor, Federal Polytechnic, Lausanne

NEWMAN-BLACK, Ms. Marjorie
Non-governmental Organizations Liaison Officer, United Nations Children's Fund, Geneva

NISSIM, Mr. Haim
Engineer, Comité contre Verbois nucléaire, Begnins, Switzerland

NUNN, Senator Sam
United States Senate

OAKES, Ms. Sheila
General Secretary, National Peace Council, London

OKER-BLOM, Mr. Nils
Professor, Chancellor of Helsinki University, Helsinki

OLTRAMARE, Mr. Yves
Lombard, Odier & Cie., Geneva

OPELZ, Mrs. Merle
Head, International Atomic Energy Agency Office, Geneva

OTTO-HALLENSLEBEN, Dr. Anna
Information Service, United Nations, Geneva

OUSSEIMI, Mr. Khaled
Managing Director, Groupe Gefinor, Geneva

PACHACHI, Mr. Adnan
Minister, Government of the United Arab Emirates, Geneva

PAINE, Mr. Christopher
Staff Consultant, Non-Proliferation Policy, House of Representatives, Washington

PARRA, Ms. Erica
Women's International League for Peace and Freedom, Geneva

PELL, Senator Claiborne
United States Senate

PERRET-GENTIL, Mr. Willy
President, Ecologie et Liberté Hauterive, Neuchâtel

DE PERROT, Mrs. Erica
Nyon, Switzerland

PERSSON, Dr. Lars
Ministry of Agriculture, Stockholm

PETIT, Mr. André
Deputy Director, Atomic Energy Commission, Paris

PETITPIERRE, Mrs. Anne
President, WWF Switzerland, Geneva

PETTITI, Mr. Louis
Judge at the European Court of Human Rights, Paris

POSTERNAK, Mr. Jean Marc
Professor emeritus, Geneva University

PRATT, Mr. David
Secretary for Democratic Minority

PREMONT, Mr. Daniel
President, Association of international consultants in human rights, Geneva

PRINS, Dr. Gwyn
Lecturer, Emmanuel College, Cambridge

RAJKUMAR, Mr. R. J.
Secretary General, Pax Romana, Geneva

EL RAWI, Mr. Najib
Representative of Muslim World League Organization, Geneva

REBEAUD, Mr. Laurent
President, Federation of Swiss Ecological Parties, Geneva

REINER, Mr. B. F.
Permanent Representative to the United Nations, International Federation for Housing and Planning, Geneva

RENAUD, Mr. Jean-Denis
Sociologist, Geneveys-sur-Coffrane, Switzerland

RENTCHNICK, Dr. Pierre
Professor, Faculty of Medicine, Geneva University

REVERDIN, Mr. Olivier

RHOADS, Ms. Anne
Programme Assistant, Women's International League for Peace and Freedom, Geneva

RINGGENBERG, Maître Cécile
Doctor of Law, Geneva

RITCHIE, Mr. Cyril
President, Federation of International Institutions, Geneva

RIZWI, Mr. Zia
Secretary, Independent Commission on International Humanitarian Issues

ROBERTSON, Mrs. Harry W.
Executive Committee, International Peace Bureau, Geneva/National Peace Council, United Kingdom

ROGNON, Mr. Jacques
Deputy Director, Forces motrices bernoises, Berne

DE ROUGEMENT, Mr. Jean-Luc
Publisher, Helios Publications, Paris

DE ROUGEMONT, Mrs. Nanik
President, ARCADIE (Association against Pollution), Geneva

ROWE, Dr. Dorothy
Consultant psychologist, Eagle, United Kingdom

SAGER, Mr. Fritz
Deputy Director, Federal Office of Civil Defence, Bern

SANDERS, Mr. Ben
Provisional Secretary-General of the Third NPT Review Conference, United Nations, Geneva

SANDOZ, Mr. Yves
Deputy Director, International Committee of the Red Cross, Geneva

SCHMIDT, Mr. Frank
Assistant Director General, World Wildlife Fund, Gland, Switzerland

SCHNEIDER, Mr. Mycle
Director of WISE-Bulletin International, World Information Service on Energy, Paris

SCHNEIDER, Mr. Rudolf
Secretary General, Institute for Planet Synthesis, Geneva

SCHWAB, Mr. Klaus
Professor, Geneva University

SCICLOUNOFF, Mr. Pierre
Lawyer, Geneva

SEGOND, Guy-Olivier
Councillor, City of Geneva, Geneva

SEIGEL, Mrs. Leila
President, International Council of Jewish Women, Geneva

DE SENGER, Mr. François
Administrator, Geneva

SIDJANSKI, Mr. Dusan
Professor, Geneva University

SLESSER, Mr. Malcolm
Professor, Resource Age Institute, Scotland

DE SMAELE, Dr. Albert
Former Minister, Brussels

SOTTAS, Mr. Eric
United Nations, Geneva

SPAULDING, Mr. Seth
Director, International Bureau of Education, Geneva

DE SPOELBERCH, Mr. Guillaume
Managing Director, Aga Khan Foundation, Geneva

SPRINGER, Mr. Jeffrey
Student, Webster University, Geneva

STEINBERGER, Mr. Jack
Physicist, CERN, Geneva

STREICH, Mr. Jurgen
Greenpeace, Federal Republic of Germany

STROOT, Mr. Jean-Pierre
Vice President, Geneva International Peace Research Institute

STRUB, Mr. François
Lawyer, Institut national genevois, Geneva

SUNDBERG, Mr. Andy
Member, Democratic National Committee, United States of America

SUY, Mr. Erik
Under-Secretary-General, United Nations Office at Geneva

SYMONIDES, Prof. Janusz
Director, Polish Institute of International Affairs, Polish Peace Committee, Warsaw

TABIBI, Mr. Abdul Hakim
Former Minister and Ambassador, World Muslim Congress, Geneva

TARZI, Mr. Wahid
Deputy Director-General, United Nations Office at Geneva

TERENZIO, Mr. Pio-Carlo
Secretary General, Inter-Parliamentary Union, Geneva

TERWISSCHA VAN SCHELTINGA, HE Mr. Frans J. A.
Ambassador for Non-Proliferation, Ministry of Foreign Affairs, The Hague

THIERRY, Mr. Hubert
Deputy Director, United Nations Institute for Disarmament Research, Geneva

THOMPSON, Mr. Gordon
Coordinator, Proliferation Reform Project Studies, Cambridge, Mass., United States of America

THOMPSON, Dr. James
Senior Lecture in Psychology, London University

THOMPSON, Ms. Marjorie
Parliamentary Officer, Campaign for Nuclear Disarmament, United Kingdom

TIBBETTS, Mr. Peter
Intern, World Council of Churches, Geneva

TOLHOEK, Mr. Hendrik A.
Professor, Groningen University, Netherlands

TOWSLEY, Ms. Lona
Information Officer, World Confederation of Organizations of the Teaching Profession, Morges Switzerland

TOWNSEND, Mr. Douglas
Assistant Secretary, Nuclear Policy Branch, Department of Foreign Affairs, Canberra, Australia

TREILLE, Mr. Daniel
Physicist, CERN, Geneva

TREMBLEY, Mr. Jacques
Senior Physicist, CERN, Geneva

TRIPP, Mr. Charles
Deputy Director, Programme for Strategic and Security Studies, Geneva

TSCHOPP, Mr. Peter
Professor, Geneva University

VAANANEN, Mr. Pentti
General Secretary, Socialist International, London

VALTICOS, Mr. Nicolas
Secretary General, Institute of International Law, Geneva

VEUTHEY, Dr. Michel
Head of the Division of International Organizations, International Committee of the Red Cross, Geneva

VIEUX, Mr. Robert
Chief of Protocol, Geneva

VINCINEAU, Mr. Michel
International Association of Democratic Lawyers

VITALE, Mr. Bruno
Professor, Naples University, Italy

VOLKOV, Mr. Konstantin
Vice-President, United Nations and Related Agencies Staff Movement for Peace and Disarmament, Geneva

VOLLERIN, Mr. Bernard
Marketing Director, Battelle Research Centres, Geneva

WEERAMANTRY, Mr. Christopher
Professor of Law, Monash University, Clayton, Vic., Australia

WEID, Mr. Denis von der
President, Antenna International, Fribourg, Switzerland

WEINGAERTNER, Mr. Erich
Executive Secretary, Commission of the Churches on International Affairs, World Council of Churches, Geneva

WEINGARTEN, Ms. Lee
Geneva Representative, War Resisters International, Geneva

WELLHAUSER, Mr. Pierre
State Councillor, Geneva

WHEELER, Mr. Joseph C.
Deputy Executive Director, United Nations Environment Programme, Nairobi

WINDASS, Mr. G. S.
Director, Defence Research Trust, Banbury, United Kingdom

WINKLER, Dr. Theodor
Political Adviser, Federal Military Department, Zollikofen, Switzerland

WIONCZEK, Mr. Miguel
El Colegio de Mexico, Mexico

WITSCHI, Ms. Lori
Swiss League against Vivisection, Geneva

WRIGHT, Mr. H. Dudley
President, Orbisphere Corporation, Geneva

WUTHRICK, Mr. Jean Pierre
Physicist, National Centre for Scientific Research, Palaiseau, France

YOSHIDA, Mr. Yasuhiko
Representative for Europe, Division of Economic and Social Information, United Nations, Geneva

YOUSSOUFI, Mr. Abderrahman
Deputy Secretary General for International relations, Union of Arab Lawyers, Cannes

ZANGGER, Mr. Claude
Deputy Director, Federal Energy Office, Bern

ZIEGLER, Mr. Jean
Professor, Geneva University and Paris University (Sorbonne)

ZOFKA, Dr. Zdenek
Historian, Krailling, Federal Republic of Germany

List of Participants from the Permanent Missions to the United Nations

ALGERIA
HE Mr. Bachir OULD-ROUIS
Permanent Representative

ARGENTINA
HE Mr. Julio CARASALES
Permanent Representative to the Conference on Disarmament
Mr. Roberto GARCIA-MORITAN
Minister Plenipotentiary

AUSTRALIA
HE Mr. Richard BUTLER
Permanent Representative for Disarmament Matters
Mr. Richard A. ROWE
Counsellor

AUSTRIA
Mr. Günter BIRBAUM
Minister

BANGLADESH
HE Mr. A. H. S. Ataul KARIM
Permanent Representative

BELGIUM
HE Mr. Marcel DEPASSE
Permanent Representative to the Conference on Disarmament

BOLIVIA
HE Mr. Crespo ALFONSO
Permanent Representative

BRAZIL
HE Mr. Paulo NOGUEIRA BATISTA
Permanent Representative
HE Mr. Celso de SOUZA E SILVA
Ambassador for Disarmament Affairs

BULGARIA, PEOPLE'S REPUBLIC OF
HE Mr. Konstantin TELLALOV
Permanent Representative

BURUNDI
HE Mr. Térence SANZE
Permanent Representative

BYELORUSSIAN SSR
Mr. Vladimir GREKOV
Permanent Representative

CANADA
Mr. J. Fernand TANGUAY
Chargé d'affaires, a.i.

CHINA, PEOPLE'S REPUBLIC OF
Mr. Lin ZHONGREN
Counsellor

CYPRUS
HE Mr. Andros NICOLAIDES
Permanent Representative

CZECHOSLOVAKIA
HE Mr. Milos VEJVODA
Permanent Representative
Mr. Andrej CIMA
Second Secretary

DEMOCRATIC KAMPUCHEA
HE Mr. Hac Team NGO
Permanent Representative

ECUADOR
HE Mr. Galo LEDRO
Permanent Representative

EGYPT
HE Mr. Saad ALFARARGI
Permanent Representative
Mr. Marawan BADR
Counsellor

FINLAND
HE Mr Paavo RANTANEN
Permanent Representative

FRANCE
HE Mr. Robert de SOUZA
Permanent Representative
HE Mr. Jacques JESSEL
Permanent Representative to the Conference on Disarmament
Mr. Gérard MONTASSIER
Deputy Permanent Representative to the Conference on Disarmament
Mr Aubert RENIE
Second Secretary Delegation to the Conference on Disarmament

GERMAN DEMOCRATIC REPUBLIC
HE Dr. Harald ROSE
Permanent Representative

GERMANY, FEDERAL REPUBLIC OF
HE Dr. Henning WEGENER
Permanent Representive to the Conference on Disarmament

GREECE
HE Mr Athanasios PETROPOULOS
Permanent Representative
Mr. Mercure CARAFOTIAS
First Secretary

HOLY SEE
Monsignor Giuseppe Bertello
Chargé d'affaires a.i.

HUNGARY
Mr. Ferenc GAJDA
Counsellor
Mr. Janos JELEN
Mr. Tibor TOTH
Third Secretary

INDIA
HE Mr. Muchkund DUBEY
Permanent Representative
Dr. S. SHARMA
Disarmament Relations

INDONESIA
HE Mr. Sularto SUTOWARDOYO
Permanent Representative

IRELAND
HE Mr. Francis Mahon HAYES
Permanent Representative

ITALY
HE Mr. Mario ALESSI
Permanent Representative to the Conference on Disarmament

JAMAICA
HE Mr. K. G. Anthony HILL
Permanent Representative

JAPAN
Mr. Masabumz SATO
First Secretary

LEBANON
HE Mr. Ibrahim KHARMA
Permanent Representative

Jordan

HE Mr. Ghaleb Z. Barakat
Permanent Representative

Mr Mazer El-Tal
Third Secretary

Mexico

HE Mr. Manuel Tello
Permanent Representative

HE Mr. Alfonso Garcia Robles
Permanent Representative to the Conference on Disarmament

Morocco

HE Mr. Ali Skalli
Permanent Representative

New Zealand

Mr. Allan Maxwell Bracegirdle
Second Secretary

Nigeria

HE Mr. Benson Owa Tonwe
Permanent Representative

Norway

Mr. Sten Lundbo
Counsellor (Disarmament)

Pakistan

HE Mr. Mansur Ahmad
Permanent Representative

Panama

Mrs. Ruth Decerega
Deputy Permanent Representative

Poland

HE Mr. Stanislaw Turbanski
Permanent Representative

Portugal

Mr. Antonio Maria Rego de Mello e Castro
Counsellor

Romania

HE Mr. Ion Datcu
Permanent Representative

Senegal

HE Mr. Alioune Sene
Permanent Representative

South Africa

HE Mr. Jeremy Brown Shearar
Permanent Representative

SPAIN
HE Mr. Alfonso de la SERNA
Permanent Representative
HE Mr. José Manuel LACLETA MUNOZ
Legal Affairs and Disarmament

SWEDEN
HE Mr. Rolf EKEUS
Disarmament Affairs

SWITZERLAND
HE Mr Anton HEGNER
Permanent Representative
Mr. Jean-Pierre VETTOVAGLIA
Minister

SYRIAN ARAB REPUBLIC
HE Mr. Adib DAOUDY
Permanent Representative

TANZANIA
HE Mr. Wilbert Kumalija CHAGULA
Permanent Representative

TUNISIA
HE Mr. Fouad MEBAZAA
Permanent Representative

TURKEY
Mr. Metin ORNEKOL
Counsellor

UKRAINIAN SSR
Mr. Andrei OZADOVSKI
Permanent Representative

USSR
HE Mr. Mikhail SYTENKO
Permanent Representative
HE Mr. Victor ISRAELYAN
Disarmament Affairs
HE Mr. Victor KARPOV
Space and Nuclear Weapons Talks
HE Mr. Youly KVITSINSKY
Space and Nuclear Weapons Talks
Mr. Valery LOCHTCHININE
Counsellor
Mr. T. BAGUIROV
Third Secretary
Mr. Alexei NIKOLAEV

UNITED KINGDOM
HE Mr. Ian CROMARTIE
PermamentRepresentative to the Conference on Disarmament
Mr. Richard EDIS
Counsellor

UNITED STATES OF AMERICA
HE Mr. Gerald CARMEN
Permanent Representative
HE Mr. Donald LOWITZ
Disarmament Affairs
HE Mr. Warren ZIMMERMANN
Delegation to US–USSR Nuclear and Space Arms Talks
HE Mr. Max Kampelman

URUGUAY
HE Mr. Julio A. LACARTE-MURO
Permanent Representative

VENEZUELA
Mr. Enrique TER HORST
Chargé d'affaires a.i.

YUGOSLAVIA
HE Mr. Kazimir VIDAS
Permanent Representative

List of Participants from the Media

ALDAG, Mr. Eric J.
Photo-reporter, E. J. Press, Geneva

AMDOUNI, Mr. Noureddine-H.
Correspondent, Radio suisse internationale, Geneva

BALLIN-DUFEY, Ms. Luisa
Correspondent, Noticiero Latino-americano, Geneva

BARTON, Mrs. Béatrice
Correspondent, TV romande, Téléjournal, Geneva

BERGER, Mr. Roman
Editor, Tagesanzeiger, Zurich

BLAGOJEVIC, Mr. Momcilo
Correspondent, Yugoslav Press Agency, Geneva

BOCCA, Ms. Eliana
Correspondent, Mexican News Agency

BOHLE-MOLL, Ms. Rose-Marie
Correspondent, Aerzte-Zeitung Tannay, Switzerland

BONAFIELD, Mr. Michael
Correspondent, The Washington Times, Washington

BOSSHARD, Mr. Antoine
Correspondent, Journal de Genève, Geneva

BRUGGMANN, Mr. Alexandre
Editorialist, Tribune de Genève, Geneva

BUFFLE, Mr. Jean-Claude
Correspondent, 24 heures, Bolligen, Switzerland

BURAAS, Mr. Anders v. Tangen
Geneva Correspondent, Verdens Gang (Oslo)

BURGER, Dr. Rudolf
Correspondent, Radio suisse alémanique

BURKART, Mr. Ernst
Correspondent, Deutsche Presse-Agentur, Geneva

BURKE, Mrs. Judith
Assistant Editor, UIT, Geneva

CATON, Mr. Scot
Assistant Executive for Programs, International Christian Youth Exchange, Berlin

COLCHESTER, Mr. Nicholas
Foreign Editor, Financial Times, London

CRAMER, Bénédikt P.
Correspondent, Le Matin, Paris

CRANE, Mr. Ralph
Photographer, Time-Life and Camera Press, Geneva

DANES, Mr. Johann-Georg
Correspondent, Austrian Press Agency and Austrian Broadcasting TV, Vienna

DAURE, Mr. David
Director for Switzerland, Agence France Presse

DE YOUNG, Ms. Karen
London Bureau Chief, The Washington Post, London

DICKSON, Mr. David
European Correspondent, Science, Gif-sur-Yvette, France

DRUCKMANN, Mr. L.-H.
Revue Juive, Geneva

SUBRAMANIAM-DUELLA, Mrs. Chittra
Correspondent, India Today/India Press, Neuchâtel

DUFEY, Mr. Alberto
Geneva Correspondent, Excelsior (Mexico)

DYLAWERSKI, Mr. Edward
Correspondent, Polish Press Agency, Geneva

ENGELSON, Ms. Suzanne
Correspondent, Les Services Publics, Geneva

EULER, Mr. Michel
Photographer, Associated Press

FILLET, Mr. Claude
Correspondent, Reuters, Geneva

FLAKS, Mr. Marco
Radio suisse internationale, Geneva

FRANCK, Ms. Nicolette
Geneva Correspondent, La Libre Belgique

FURSDON, Major-General Edward
Defence correspondent, The Daily Telegraph, London

GARBELY, Mr. Frank
Geneva Correspondent, Profil Vienna/Wochenzeitung, Zurich

GASTAUT, Ms. Thérèse
Director, United Nations Information Service, Geneva

GAUHAR, Mr. Altaf
Editor-in-Chief, South Magazine, London

GOBIUS, Mr. Otto W.
Geneva Correspondent, VOA and Radio, TV Netherlands

GRANDJEAN, Mr. Philippe
Correspondent, Radio suisse romande, Coppet, Switzerland

GRAZ, Ms. Liesl
Correspondent, The Economist, Epalinges, Switzerland

GUEST, Mr. Iain
Geneva correspondent, The Guardian, London

HEIMAR, Mr. Bjorn
Chief Foreign Director, Aftenposten, Oslo

HENDERSON, Mr. Simon
Correspondent, Financial Times, London

HIRANO, Mr. Jiro
Geneva Correspondent, NHK Japan Broadcasting Corporation

HIRSCH-LABREVEUX, Ms. Irene
Geneva Correspondent, El Sol de Mexico

HUDGINS, Ms. Christine
Reporter, Nucleonics Week

HUTCHISON, Mr. Robert A.
Journalist, Geneva

IBANEZ-MARTIN, Mr. Francisco
Correspondent, Radio Nacional de Espana, Geneva

KAREN, Mr. Lauri
Geneva Correspondent, Helsingin Sanomat, Finland

KISTER, Mr. Kurt
Defence Correspondent, Süddeutsche Zeitung, Munich

KLOPFENSTEIN, Mr. Freddy
Director, La Vie Protestante, Geneva

KOHLSCHÜTTER, Mr. Andreas
Diplomatic Correspondent, Die Zeit, Ronco, Switzerland

KORJEV, Mr. Evguéni
Head of Bureau, Agence TASS, Geneva

KROON, Mr. Robert
Correspondent, Time Magazine, Genolier, Switzerland

KRUITHOF, Mr. Rommert
Geneva Correspondent, Netherlands Radio

KUKLINKSKI, Mr. Mariusz
Polish Press Agency, Warsaw

LEE, Mr. Christopher
Defence and Foreign Affairs Correspondent, BBC, London

LEMARESQUIER, Ms. Mireille
Permanent Correspondent in Geneva, Radio-France

LEVINSON, Dr. Macha
Editor, Revue Internationale de Défense, Geneva

LEWIS, Ms. Flora
Foreign Affairs Columnist, The New York Times, Paris

LEWIS, Ms. Ginna
Producer-Interviewer, 'Freely Speaking', Radio 74

LIMAN, Mr. Adrian-Mac
Geneva Correspondent, Tiempo, Madrid

LIPSKY, Mr. Seth
Editorial Page Editor, The Wall Street Journal/Europe, Brussels

LORENZ, Ms. Marion
Correspondent, Norddeutscher Rundfunk

MACLEOD, Mr. Alexander
Diplomatic Editor, The Scotsman, London

MARTIN, Mr. Georges-Henri
Editorial Correspondent, Tribune de Genève, Geneva

McGREGOR, Mr. Alan
Correspondent, The Times/Swiss Radio International, Geneva

MAURICE, Mr. Antoine
Foreign Affairs Correspondent, Journal de Genève, Geneva

MEKHONTSEV, Mr. Vladimir
Correspondent, Agence Novosti

MILLER, Mr. Bill

MOSSU, Mr. Laurent
Correspondent, Le Figaro

MOSTOFI, Mr. A.
Correspondent, Tribune de Genève, Geneva

NAEF, Mr. André
Head of the International Service, Tribune de Genève, Geneva

NAKAMICHI, Mr. Masaki
General Correspondent, Yomiuri Shimbun, Tokyo

NETTER, Mr. Thomas
Geneva Correspondent, The New York Times

OOSTRA, Mr. Roel
Staff-editor, NCRV Television, Bussum, The Netherlands

PANDINI, Mr. Attilio
RAI, Geneva

PAUCHOD, Mr. Michel
Correspondent, Le Courrier, Geneva

PELLEGRINI, Mr. Rolf
Correspondent, Radio Suisse alémanique, Bern

PICK, Ms. Hella
International Affairs Correspondent, The Guardian, London

PIPER, Mr. Hal
Baltimore Sun, London

RAGHAVAN, Mr. Chakravarthi
Correspondent, Inter Press Service, Geneva

RAUBER, Mr. Sari
Correspondent, Maariv, Tel-Aviv

ROJO, Mr. Oscar
Managing Editor, World Paper, Boston

ROSSIGNEUX, Mrs. Brigitte
Correspondent, Dossiers du Canard Enchaîné, Paris

RUSSELL-WASSERMANN, Ursula
United Nations Correspondent, Journal of World Trade Law, London

SALOMONSON, Mrs. An
Editor Opinion Page, NRC Handelsblad, Rotterdam

SANDSTROM, Ms. Mari
Correspondent, Swedish media, Geneva

SAVIO, Mr. Roberto
Director General, Inter Press Service, Rome

SCHLEIN, Ms. Lisa
Geneva Correspondent, ABC News

SCHLOSSER, Mr. François
Correspondent, Nouvel Observateur, Paris

SCHORDERET, Mr. Jean-Marcel
Producer, Télévision Suisse Romande, Geneva

SCHUIN, Ms. Anik
Correspondent, Le Courrier, Geneva

SIMONITSCH, Mr. Pierre
United Nations Correspondent, Frankfurter Rundschau

SMADJA, Mr. Claude
Head of International News, Télévision Suisse Romande, Geneva

SONNENBERG, Mr. Joachim
Geneva Correspondent, Press Agency ADN

SPILKER, Mr. Reinhard
Freelance Correspondent, ARD Radio, Bonn

SPRECHER, Mr. Jean
Geneva Correspondent Radio/TV, RTL Paris–Luxembourg/Radio Canada Montreal

STAUB, Mr. Hans O.
Editor, Die Weltwoche, Zurich

STIERNLOF, Mr. Sture
Bonn Correspondent, The Arbetet, Malmö Sweden

SVARRE, Ms. Karin-Lis
Danish Broadcasting Company

SZYNDZIELORZ, Mr. Karol
Chief Political Commentator, Zycie Warsawy, Warsaw

VATERLAUS, Mr. Max
Photoreporter, Keystone Press, Geneva

VEDENIAPIN, Mr.
Soviet Television, Geneva

VICHNIAC, Mrs. Isabelle
Le Monde, Paris

VLACHOS, Ms. Helen
Editor, Kathimerini Daily Newspaper, Athens

WADLOW, Mr. René
Editor, Transnational Perspectives, Geneva

WAN, Mr. Xianghua
Geneva Correspondent, Guangming Ribao, China

WATSON, Ms. Brenda
Reporter, Associated Press News Agency, Geneva

WEEKS, Mr. Steve
Head of Bureau, Reuters, Geneva

WERMUS, Mr. Daniel
Correspondent, Tribune de Genève, Geneva

WILLIS, Mr. David
Third World Correspondent, The Christian Science Monitor, Boston, USA

WYENBERGH, Mr. van
Zurich Correspondent, Frankfurter Allgemeine, Frankfurt

XIAN HUA, Mr. Wang
Geneva Correspondent, Guangming Ribao, China

YANAGISAWA, Mr. Yasumasa
Geneva Correspondent, Asahi Shimbun, Japan

ZHENGDE, Mr. Ren
Geneva Correspondent, Agence Chine Nouvelle

Members of the Groupe de Bellerive

SADRUDDIN AGA KHAN.
International Civil Servant.

HENDRIK B. G. CASIMIR.
Physicist. Former Research Director of the Philips Company.

JACQUES FREYMOND.
Honorary Director of the Graduate Institute of International Studies, Geneva.

MARTIN M. KAPLAN.
Former Director of Medical Research, WHO. Director-General, Pugwash Conferences on Sciences and World Affairs, Geneva and London.

OLIVIER LONG.
Ambassador. Former Director-General of General Agreement on Tariffs and Trade (GATT), Geneva. President of the Foundation Board of the Institute of Higher Studies in Public Administration of the University of Lausanne.

NIALL MACDERMOT.
Jurist. Secretary-General, International Commission of Jurists. Former Minister of State for Planning and Land in the British Government.

OVE NATHAN.
Professor of Physics, Rector of the University of Copenhagen.

OLIVIER REVERDIN.
Professor of Greek, University of Geneva. Former President of the Parliamentary Assembly of the Council of Europe.

DENIS DE ROUGEMONT.
Philosopher and writer. President of the Centre Européen de la Culture, Geneva. Author of "L'Avenir est notre affair" and over 30 other books.

PAUL SIEGHART.
Barrister. Trustee, European Human Rights Foundation. Chairman, Executive Committee, British section of the International Commission of Jurists.

LUKAS VISCHER.
Director of the Protestant Office for Ecumenism in Switzerland. Professor of Ecumenical Theology, University of Berne.

WILLIAM A. VISSER'T HOOFT.
Pastor. Honorary President, World Council of Churches.

Text of the Treaty on the Non-Proliferation of Nuclear Weapons

The States concluding this Treaty, hereinafter referred to as the "Parties to the Treaty",

Considering the devastation that would be visited upon all mankind by a nuclear war and the consequent need to make every effort to avert the danger of such a war and to take measures to safeguard the security of peoples.

Believing that the proliferation of nuclear weapons would seriously enhance the danger of nuclear war,

In conformity with resolutions of the United Nations General Assembly calling for the conclusion of an agreement on the prevention of wider dissemination of nuclear weapons,

Undertaking to co-operate in facilitating the application of International Atomic Energy Agency safeguards on peaceful nuclear activities,

Expressing their support for research, development and other efforts to further the application, within the framework of the International Atomic Energy safeguards system, of the principle of safeguarding effectively the flow of source and special fissionable materials by use of instruments and other techniques at certain strategic points,

Affirming the principle that the benefits of peaceful applications of nuclear technology, including any technological by-products which may be derived by nuclear-weapon States from the development of nuclear explosive devices, should be available for peaceful purposes to all Parties to the Treaty, whether nuclear-weapon or non-nuclear-weapon States,

Convinced that, in furtherance of this principle, all Parties to the Treaty are entitled to participate in the fullest possible exchange of scientific information for, and to contribute alone or in co-operation with other States to, the further development of the applications of atomic energy for peaceful purposes,

Declaring their intention to achieve at the earliest possible date the cessation of the nuclear arms race and to undertake effective measures in the direction of nuclear disarmament,

Urging the co-operation of all States in the attainment of this objective,

Recalling the determination expressed by the Parties to the 1963 Treaty banning nuclear weapon tests in the atmosphere, in outer space and under water in its preamble to seek to achieve the discontinuance of all test explosions of nuclear weapons for all time and to continue negotiations to this end,

Desiring to further the easing of international tension and the strengthening of trust between States in order to facilitate the cessation of the manufacture of nuclear weapons, the liquidation of all their existing stockpiles, and the elimination from national arsenals of nuclear weapons and the means of their delivery pursuant to a Treaty on general and complete disarmament under strict and effective international control,

Recalling that, in accordance with the Charter of the United Nations, States must refrain in their international relations from the threat or use of force against the territorial integrity or political independence of any State, or in any other manner inconsistent with the purposes of the United Nations, and that the establishment and maintenance of international peace and security are to be promoted with the least diversion for armaments of the world's human and economic resources.

Have agreed as follows:

Article I

Each nuclear-weapon State Party to the Treaty undertakes not to transfer to any recipient whatsoever nuclear weapons or other nuclear explosive devices or control over such weapons or explosive devices directly, or indirectly; and not in any way to assist, encourage or induce any non-nuclear-weapon State to manufacture or otherwise acquire nuclear weapons or other nuclear explosive devices, or control over such weapons or explosive devices.

Article II

Each non-nuclear-weapon State Party to the Treaty undertakes not to receive the transfer from any transferor whatsoever of nuclear weapons or other nuclear explosive devices or of control over such weapons or explosive devices directly, or indirectly; not to manufacture or otherwise acquire nuclear weapons or other nuclear explosive devices; and not to seek or receive any assistance in the manufacture of nuclear weapons or other nuclear explosive devices.

Article III

1. Each non-nuclear-weapon State Party to the Treaty undertakes to accept safeguards, as set forth in an agreement to be negotiated and concluded with the International Atomic Energy Agency in accordance with the Statute of the International Atomic Energy Agency and the Agency's safeguards system, for the exclusive purpose of verification of the fulfilment of its obligations assumed under this Treaty with a view to preventing diversion of nuclear energy from peaceful uses to nuclear weapons or other nuclear explosive devices. Procedures for the safeguards required by this article shall be followed with respect to source or special fissionable material whether it is being produced, processed or used in any principal nuclear facility or is outside any such facility. The safeguards required by this article shall be applied on all source or special fissionable material in all peaceful nuclear activities within the territory of such State, under its jurisdiction, or carried out under its control anywhere.

2. Each State Party to the Treaty undertakes not to provide (*a*) source or special fissionable material, or (*b*) equipment or material especially designed or prepared for the processing, use or production of special fissionable material, to any non-nuclear-weapon State for peaceful purposes, unless the source or special fissionable material shall be subject to the safeguards required by this article.

3. The safeguards required by this article shall be implemented in a manner designed to comply with article IV of this Treaty, and to avoid hampering the

economic or technological development of the parties or international co-operation in the field of peaceful nuclear activities, including the international exchange of nuclear material and equipment for the processing, use or production of nuclear material for peaceful purposes in accordance with the provisions of this article and the principle of safeguarding set forth in the preamble.

4. Non-nuclear-weapon States Party to the Treaty shall conclude agreements with the International Atomic Energy Agency to meet the requirements of this article either individually or together with other States in accordance with the Statute of the International Atomic Energy Agency. Negotiations of such agreements shall commence within 180 days from the original entry into force of this Treaty. For States depositing their instruments of ratification or accession after the 180-day period, negotiation of such agreements shall commence not later than the date of such deposit. Such agreements shall enter into force not later than 18 months after the date of initiation of negotiations.

Article IV

1. Nothing in this Treaty shall be interpreted as affecting the inalienable right of all the Parties to the Treaty to develop research, production and the use of nuclear energy for peaceful purposes without discrimination and in conformity with articles I and II of this Treaty.

2. All the Parties to the Treaty undertake to facilitate, and have the right to participate in, the fullest possible exchange of equipment, materials and scientific and technological information for the peaceful uses of nuclear energy. Parties to the Treaty in a position to do so shall also co-operate in contributing alone or together with other States or international organizations to the further development of the applications of nuclear energy for peaceful purposes, especially in the territories of non-nuclear-weapon States Party to the Treaty, with due consideration for the needs of the developing areas of the world.

Article V

Each Party to this Treaty undertakes to take appropriate measures to ensure that, in accordance with this Treaty, under appropriate international observation and through appropriate international procedures, potential benefits from any peaceful applications of nuclear explosions will be made available to non-nuclear-weapon States Party to this Treaty on a non-discriminatory basis and that the charge to such Parties for the explosive devices used will be as low as possible and exclude any charge for research and development. Non-nuclear-weapon States Party to the Treaty shall be able to obtain such benefits, pursuant to a special international agreement or agreements, through an appropriate international body with adequate representation of non-nuclear-weapon States. Negotiations on this subject shall commence as soon as possible after the Treaty enters into force. Non-nuclear-weapon States Party to the Treaty so desiring may also obtain such benefits pursuant to bilateral agreements.

Article VI

Each of the Parties to the Treaty undertakes to pursue negotiations in good faith on effective measures relating to cessation of the nuclear arms race at an early date and to nuclear disarmament, and on a Treaty on general and complete disarmament under strict and effective international control.

Article VII

Nothing in this Treaty affects the right of any group of States to conclude regional treaties in order to assure the total absence of nuclear weapons in their respective territories.

Article VIII

1. Any Party to the Treaty may propose amendments to this Treaty. The text of any proposed amendment shall be submitted to the Depositary Governments which shall circulate it to all Parties to the Treaty. Thereupon, if requested to do so by one third or more of the Parties to the Treaty, the Depositary Governments shall convene a conference, to which they shall invite all the Parties to the Treaty, to consider such an amendment.

2. Any amendment to this Treaty must be approved by a majority of the votes of all the Parties to the Treaty, including the votes of all nuclear-weapon States Party to the Treaty and all other Parties which, on the date the amendment is circulated, are members of the Board of Governors of the International Atomic Energy Agency. The amendment shall enter into force for each Party that deposits its instrument of ratification of the amendment upon the deposit of such instruments of ratification by a majority of all the Parties, including the instruments of ratification of all non-nuclear-weapon States Party to the Treaty and all other Parties which, on the date the amendment is circulated, are members of the Board of Governors of the International Atomic Energy Agency. Thereafter, it shall enter into force for any other Party upon the deposit of its instrument of ratification of the amendment.

3. Five years after the entry into force of this Treaty, a conference of Parties to the Treaty shall be held in Geneva, Switzerland, in order to review the operation of this Treaty with a view to assuring that the purposes of the Preamble and the provisions of the Treaty are being realized. At intervals of five years thereafter, a majority of the Parties to the Treaty may obtain, by submitting a proposal to this effect to the Depositary Governments, the convening of further conferences with the same objective of reviewing the operation of the Treaty.

Article IX

1. This Treaty shall be open to all States for signature. Any State which does not sign the Treaty before its entry into force in accordance with paragraph 3 of this Article may accede to it at any time.

2. This Treaty shall be subject to ratification by signatory States. Instruments of ratification and instruments of accession shall be deposited with the Governments of the Union of Soviet Socialist Republics, the United Kingdom of Great Britain and Northern Ireland and the United States of America, which are hereby designated the Depositary Governments.

3. This Treaty shall enter into force after its ratification by the States, the Governments of which are designated Depositaries of the Treaty, and 40 other States signatory to this Treaty and the deposit of their instruments of ratification. For the

purposes of this Treaty, a nuclear-weapon State is one which has manufactured and exploded a nuclear weapon or other nuclear explosive device prior to 1 January 1967.

4. For States whose instruments of ratification or accession are deposited subsequent to the entry into force of this Treaty, it shall enter into force on the date of the deposit of their instruments of ratification or accession.

5. The Depositary Governments shall promptly inform all signatory and acceding States of the date of each signature, the date of deposit of each instrument of ratification or of accession, the date of the entry into force of this Treaty and the date of receipt of any requests for convening a conference or other notices.

6. This Treaty shall be registered by the Depositary Governments pursuant to Article 102 of the Charter of the United Nations.

Article X

1. Each party shall in exercising its national sovereignty have the right to withdraw from the Treaty if it decides that extraordinary events, related to the subject-matter of this Treaty, have jeopardized the supreme interest of its country. It shall give notice of such withdrawal to all other Parties to the Treaty and to the United Nations Security Council three months in advance. Such notice shall include a statement of the extraordinary events it regards as having jeopardized its supreme interests.

2. Twenty-five years after the entry into force of the Treaty, a Conference shall be convened to decide whether the Treaty shall continue in force indefinitely, or shall be extended for an additional fixed period or periods. This decision shall be taken by a majority of the Parties to the Treaty.

Article XI

This Treaty, the English, Russian, French, Spanish and Chinese texts of which are equally authentic, shall be deposited in the archives of the Depositary Governments. Duly certified copies of this Treaty shall be transmitted by the Depositary Governments to the Governments of the signatory and acceding States.

In witness whereof the undersigned, duly authorized, have signed this Treaty.

DONE in triplicate, at the cities of London, Moscow and Washington, the first day of July, one thousand nine hundred and sixty-eight.

Index